NAEYC PROGRAM ADMINISTRATOR DEFINITION AND COMPETENCIES

I. Program Administrator Definition

The program administrator is the individual responsible for planning, implementing, and evaluating a child care, preschool or kindergarten program. The role of the administrator covers both leadership and management functions. Leadership functions relate to the broad plan of helping an organization clarify and affirm values, set goals, articulate a vision, and chart a course of action to achieve that vision. Managerial functions relate to the actual orchestration of tasks and the setting up of systems to carry out the organization's mission.

Functions of the program administrator include the following:

- *Pedagogy*—Creating a learning community of children and adults that promotes optimal child development and healthy families
- *Organizational development and systems*—Establishing systems for smooth program functioning and managing staff to carry out the mission of the program; planning and budgeting the program's fiscal resources; managing organizational change and establishing systems to monitor and evaluate organizational performance
- *Human resources*—Recruiting, selecting, and orienting personnel; overseeing systems for the supervision, retention, and professional development of staff that affirm program values and promote a shared vision
- *Collaboration*—Establishing partnerships with program staff, family members, board members, community representatives, civic leaders, and other stakeholders to design and improve services for children and their families
- *Advocacy*—Taking action and encouraging others to work on behalf of high-quality services that meet the needs of children and their families

The administrator may have different role titles depending on the program type or sponsorship of the program. Common titles include director, site manager, administrator, program manager, early childhood coordinator, and principal.

II. Core Competencies: Relevant Information for Selecting Annual Professional Development
Options (adapted with permission from the Illinois Director Credential).

The core competencies needed for effective early childhood program administration fall into two broad categories: management knowledge and skills and early childhood knowledge and skills. These are not discrete categories; they overlap conceptually and practically.

A. Management Knowledge and Skills

Administrators need a solid foundation in the principles of organizational management, including how to establish systems for smooth program functioning and how to manage staff to carry out the mission of the program.

1. Personal and professional self awareness
   - Knowledge and application of adult and career development, personality typologies, dispositions, and learning styles
   - Knowledge of one's own beliefs, values, and philosophical stance
   - The ability to evaluate ethical and moral dilemmas based on a professional code of ethics
   - The ability to be a reflective practitioner and apply a repertoire of techniques to improve the level of personal fulfillment and professional job satisfaction
2. Legal and fiscal management
   - Knowledge and application of the advantages and disadvantages of different legal structures
   - Knowledge of different codes and regulations as they relate to the delivery of early childhood program services
   - Knowledge of child custody, child abuse, special education, confidentiality, antidiscrimination, insurance liability, and contract and labor laws pertaining to program management
   - Knowledge of various federal, state, and local revenue sources
   - Knowledge of bookkeeping methods and accounting terminology
   - Skill in budgeting, cash flow management, grant writing, and fund-raising
3. Staff management and human relations
   - Knowledge and application of group dynamics, communication styles, and techniques for conflict resolution
   - Knowledge of different supervisory and group facilitation styles
   - The ability to relate to staff and board members of diverse racial, cultural, and ethnic backgrounds
   - The ability to hire, supervise, and motivate staff to high levels of performance
   - Skill in consensus building, team development, and staff performance appraisal

4. Educational programming
- Knowledge and application of different curriculum models, standards for high-quality programming, and child assessment practices
- The ability to develop and implement a program to meet the needs of young children at different ages and developmental levels (infant-toddler, preschool, kindergarten)
- Knowledge of administrative practices that promote the inclusion of children with special needs

5. Program operations and facilities management
- Knowledge and application of policies and procedures that meet state and local regulations as well as professional standards pertaining to the health and safety of young children
- Knowledge of nutritional and health requirements for food service
- The ability to design and plan the effective use of space based on principles of environmental psychology and child development
- Knowledge of playground safety design and practice

6. Family support
- Knowledge and application of family systems and different parenting styles
- Knowledge of community resources to support family wellness
- The ability to implement program practices that support families of diverse cultural, ethnic, linguistic, and socioeconomic backgrounds
- The ability to support families as valued partners in the educational process

7. Marketing and public relations
- Knowledge of the fundamentals of effective marketing, public relations, and community outreach
- The ability to evaluate the cost benefit of different marketing and promotional strategies
- The ability to communicate the program's philosophy and promote a positive public image to families, business leaders, public officials, and prospective funders
- The ability to promote linkages with local schools
- Skill in developing a business plan and effective promotional literature, handbooks, newsletters, and press releases

8. Leadership and advocacy
- Knowledge of organizational theory and leadership styles as they relate to early childhood work environments
- Knowledge of the legislative processes, social issues, and public policy affecting young children and their families
- The ability to articulate a vision, clarify and affirm values, and create a culture built on norms of continuous improvement and ethical conduct
- The ability to evaluate program effectiveness
- The ability to define organizational problems, gather data to generate alternative solutions, and effectively apply analytical skills in its solution
- The ability to advocate on behalf of young children, their families, and the profession

9. Oral and written communication
- Knowledge of the mechanics of writing, including organizing ideas, grammar, punctuation, and spelling
- The ability to use written communication to effectively express one's thoughts
- Knowledge of oral communication techniques, including establishing rapport, preparing the environment, active listening, and voice control
- The ability to communicate ideas effectively in a formal presentation

10. Technology
- Knowledge of basic computer hardware and software applications
- The ability to use the computer for program administrative functions

B. Early Childhood Knowledge and Skills

Administrators need a strong foundation in the fundamentals of child development and early childhood education to guide the instructional practices of teachers and support staff.

1. Historical and philosophical foundations
- Knowledge of the historical roots and philosophical foundations of early childhood care and education
- Knowledge of different types of early childhood programs, roles, funding, and regulatory structures
- Knowledge of current trends and important influences impacting program quality
- Knowledge of research methodologies

2. Child growth and development
- Knowledge of different theoretical positions in child development
- Knowledge of the biological, environmental, cultural, and social influences affecting children's growth and development from prenatal through early adolescence
- Knowledge of developmental milestones in children's physical, cognitive, language, aesthetic, social, and emotional development
- Knowledge of current research in neuroscience and its application to the field of early childhood education

3. Child observation and assessment
- Knowledge and application of developmentally appropriate child observation and assessment methods
- Knowledge of the purposes, characteristics, and limitations of different assessment tools and techniques
- Ability to use different observation techniques, including formal and informal observation, behavior sampling, and developmental checklists
- Knowledge of ethical practice as it relates to the use of assessment information
- The ability to apply child observation and assessment data to planning and structuring developmentally appropriate instructional strategies

4. Curriculum and instructional methods
- Knowledge of different curriculum models; appropriate curriculum goals; and different instructional strategies for infants, toddlers, preschoolers, and kindergarten children
- Ability to plan and implement a curriculum based on knowledge of individual children's developmental patterns, family and community goals, institutional and cultural context, and state standards
- Ability to design integrated and meaningful curricular experiences in the content areas of language and literacy, mathematics, science, social studies, art, music, drama, movement, and technology
- Ability to implement antibias instructional strategies that take into account culturally valued content and children's home experiences
- Ability to evaluate outcomes of different curricular approaches

5. Children with special needs
- Knowledge of atypical development, including mild and severe disabilities in physical, health, cognitive, social-emotional, communication, and sensory functioning
- Knowledge of licensing standards as well as state and federal laws (e.g., ADA, IDEA) as they relate to services and accommodations for children with special needs
- Knowledge of the characteristics of giftedness and how educational environments can support children with exceptional capabilities
- The ability to work collaboratively as part of family-professional team in planning and implementing appropriate services for children with special needs
- Knowledge of special education resources and services

6. Family and community relationships
- Knowledge of the diversity of family systems; traditional, nontraditional, and alternative family structures as well as family life styles; and the dynamics of family life on the development of young children
- Knowledge of sociocultural factors influencing contemporary families, including the effect of language, religion, poverty, race, technology, and the media
- Knowledge of different community resources, assistance, and support available to children and families
- Knowledge of different strategies to promote reciprocal partnerships between home and center
- Ability to communicate effectively with parents through written and oral communication
- Ability to demonstrate awareness and appreciation of different cultural and familial practices and customs
- Knowledge of child rearing patterns in other countries

7. Health, safety, and nutrition
- Knowledge and application of practices that promote good nutrition, dental health, physical health, mental health, and safety of infants-toddlers, preschool, and kindergarten children
- Ability to implement practices indoors and outdoors that help prevent, prepare for, and respond to emergencies
- Ability to model healthful lifestyle choices

8. Individual and group guidance
- Knowledge of the rationale for and research supporting different models of child guidance and classroom management
- Ability to apply different techniques that promote positive and supportive relationships with children and among children
- Ability to reflect on teaching behavior and modify guidance techniques based on the developmental and special needs of children

9. Learning environments
- Knowledge of the effect of the physical environment on children's learning and development
- The ability to use space, color, sound, texture, light, and other design elements to create indoor and outdoor learning environments that are aesthetically pleasing, intellectually stimulating, psychologically safe, and nurturing
- The ability to select age-appropriate equipment and materials that achieve curricular goals and encourage positive social interaction

10. Professionalism
- Knowledge of laws, regulations, and policies that affect professional conduct with children and families
- Knowledge of different professional organizations, resources, and issues affecting the welfare of early childhood practitioners
- Knowledge of center accreditation criteria
- Ability to make professional judgments based on the NAEYC "Code of Ethical Conduct and Statement of Commitment"
- Ability to reflect on one's professional growth and development and make goals for personal improvement
- Ability to work as part of a professional team and supervise support staff or volunteers

Source: From NAEYC. 2007. *NAEYC Early Childhood Program Standards and Accreditation Criteria: The Mark of Quality in Early Childhood Education.* Washington, DC: Author. www.naeyc.org/files/academy/file/Program%20Admin%20Def%20 and%20Competencies.pdf. Reprinted with permission from the National Association for the Education of Young Children (NAEYC). www.naeyc.org

NAEYC EARLY CHILDHOOD PROGRAM STANDARDS, INCLUDING TOPIC AREAS

STANDARD 1: RELATIONSHIPS

Topic Areas

1.A.: Building Positive Relationships among Teachers and Families
1.B.: Building Positive Relationships between Teachers and Children
1.C.: Helping Children Make Friends
1.D.: Creating a Predictable, Consistent, and Harmonious Classroom
1.E.: Addressing Challenging Behaviors
1.F.: Promoting Self-Regulation

STANDARD 2: CURRICULUM

Topic Areas

2.A.: Curriculum: Essential Characteristics
2.B.: Areas of Development: Social-Emotional Development
2.C.: Areas of Development: Physical Development
2.D.: Areas of Development: Language Development
2.E.: Curriculum Content Area for Cognitive Development: Early Literacy
2.F.: Curriculum Content Area for Cognitive Development: Early Mathematics
2.G.: Curriculum Content Area for Cognitive Development: Science
2.H.: Curriculum Content Area for Cognitive Development: Technology

To avoid confusion in the numbering system, there are no criteria labeled 2.I.

2.J.: Curriculum Area for Cognitive Development: Creative Expression and Appreciation for the Arts
2.K.: Curriculum Content Area for Cognitive Development: Health and Safety
2.L.: Curriculum Content Area for Cognitive Development: Social

STANDARD 3: TEACHING

Topic Areas

3.A.: Designing Enriched Learning Environments
3.B.: Creating Caring Communities for Learning
3.C.: Supervising Children
3.D.: Using Time, Grouping, and Routines to Achieve Learning Goals
3.E.: Responding to Children's Interests and Needs
3.F.: Making Learning Meaningful for All Children
3.G.: Using Instruction to Deepen Children's Understanding and Build Their Skills and Knowledge

STANDARD 4: ASSESSMENT OF CHILD PROGRESS

Topic Areas

4.A.: Creating an Assessment Plan
4.B.: Using Appropriate Assessment Methods
4.C.: Identifying Children's Interests and Needs and Describing Children's Progress
4.D.: Adapting Curriculum, Individualizing Teaching, and Informing Program Development
4.E.: Communicating with Families and Involving Families in the Assessment Process

STANDARD 5: HEALTH

Topic Areas

5.A.: Promoting and Protecting Children's Health and Controlling Infectious Disease
5.B.: Ensuring Children's Nutritional Well-being
5.C.: Maintaining a Healthful Environment

STANDARD 6: TEACHERS

Topic Areas

6.A.: Preparation, Knowledge, and Skills of Teaching Staff
6.B.: Teachers' Dispositions and Professional Commitment

STANDARD 7: FAMILIES

Topic Areas

7.A.: Knowing and Understanding the Program's Families
7.B.: Sharing Information between Staff and Families
7.C.: Nurturing Families as Advocates for Their Children

STANDARD 8: COMMUNITY RELATIONSHIPS

Topic Areas

8.A.: Linking with the Community
8.B.: Accessing Community Resources
8.C.: Acting as a Citizen in the Neighborhood and the Early Childhood Community

STANDARD 9: PHYSICAL ENVIRONMENT

Topic Areas

9.A.: Indoor and Outdoor Equipment, Materials, and Furnishings
9.B.: Outdoor Environmental Design
9.C.: Building and Physical Design
9.D.: Environmental Health

STANDARD 10: LEADERSHIP AND MANAGEMENT

Topic Areas

10.A.: Leadership
10.B.: Management Policies and Procedures
10.C.: Fiscal Accountability Policies and Procedures
10.D.: Health, Nutrition, and Safety Policies and Procedures
10.E.: Personnel Policies
10.F.: Program Evaluation, Accountability, and Continuous Improvement

Source: NAEYC. 2007. *NAEYC Early Childhood Program Standards and Accreditation Criteria: The Mark of Quality in Early Childhood Education.* Washington, DC: Author. Reprinted with permission from the National Association for the Education of Young Children (NAEYC). www.naeyc.org

PLANNING
AND ADMINISTERING EARLY
CHILDHOOD PROGRAMS

Tenth Edition

Nancy K. Freeman
University of South Carolina, Columbia

Celia A. Decker
Northwestern State University

John R. Decker
Sabine Parish, Louisiana, School System

Boston   Columbus   Indianapolis   New York   San Francisco   Upper Saddle River
Amsterdam   Cape Town   Dubai   London   Madrid   Milan   Munich   Paris   Montreal   Toronto
Delhi   Mexico City   São Paulo   Sydney   Hong Kong   Seoul   Singapore   Taipei   Tokyo

Vice President and Editorial Director: Jeffery W. Johnston
Senior Acquisitions Editor: Julie Peters
Development Editor: Bryce Bell
Editorial Assistant: Andrea Hall
Vice President, Director of Marketing: Margaret Waples
Senior Marketing Manager: Christopher D. Barry
Senior Managing Editor: Pamela D. Bennett
Senior Project Manager: Linda Hillis Bayma
Senior Operations Supervisor: Matthew Ottenweller
Senior Art Director: Diane C. Lorenzo
Cover Designer: Bryan Huber
Cover Image: Mac H. Brown
Full-Service Project Management: Penny Walker, Aptara®, Inc.
Composition: Aptara®, Inc.
Printer/Binder: Edwards Brothers
Cover Printer: Lehigh Phoenix/Hagerstown
Text Font: ITC Garamond Std

Credits and acknowledgments for materials borrowed from other sources and reproduced, with permission, in this textbook appear on the appropriate page within the text, or below.

The selected core competencies that appear on the first page of each chapter are from NAEYC. 2007. *NAEYC Early Childhood Program Standards and Accreditation Criteria: The Mark of Quality in Early Childhood Education.* Washington, DC: Author. www.naeyc.org/files/academy/file/Program%20Admin%20Def%20and%20Competencies.pdf. Reprinted with permission from the National Association for the Education of Young Children (NAEYC). www.naeyc.org

Every effort has been made to provide accurate and current Internet information in this book. However, the Internet and information posted on it are constantly changing, so it is inevitable that some of the Internet addresses listed in this textbook will change.

Photo Credits: All photos by Mac H. Brown/Merrill.

Library of Congress Cataloging-in-Publication Data
Freeman, Nancy K.
  Planning and administering early childhood programs / Nancy K. Freeman, Celia A. Decker, John R. Decker.—10th ed.
    p. cm.
  Prev. ed. cataloged under title.
  ISBN 978-0-13-265692-4
  1. Early childhood education—United States.   2. Educational planning—United States.   3. Day care centers—United States—Administration.   4. Instructional systems—United States.   I. Decker, Celia Anita. II. Decker, John R. III. Title.

  LB1139.25.D43 2013
  372.210973—dc23   2011050494

10 9 8 7 6 5 4 3 2 1

PEARSON

ISBN-10:   0-13-265692-2
ISBN-13: 978-0-13-265692-4

About the Authors

Nancy K. Freeman is an associate professor of early childhood education and director of the Child Development and Research Center at the University of South Carolina. A former child care director and preschool teacher, she currently works closely with the campus child care center. Nancy has authored scholarly publications and made conference presentations on topics such as professional ethics, service learning, and the preparation of the child care workforce. She is chair of South Carolina's State Advisory Committee on the Regulation of Child Care Facilities, has served as president of the National Association of Early Childhood Teacher Educators (NAECTE), and is coauthor of a regular column on professional ethics published by NAEYC.

Celia A. Decker retired after 38 years of service in early childhood education. At the time of her retirement, she held the position of professor of early childhood education at Northwestern State University and served as the program coordinator of graduate studies in early childhood education. In addition to coauthoring this text, she is the author of *Children: The Early Years* and its supplements and coauthor of *Parents and Their Children,* both published by Goodheart-Willcox Company. She has presented papers at national, regional, and state annual meetings of many professional early childhood associations. She has served as a consultant for Head Start, Even Start, and local school systems.

During her years as a kindergarten teacher in an inner-city school system and as a college professor, she has received many honors. In 1994, she was selected as the Outstanding Professor at Northwestern State University.

John R. Decker retired after an elementary teaching and administrative career of 37 years. Before entering the field of education, he served as a district scout executive for Kaw Council, Boy Scouts of America, Kansas City, Kansas. His educational career included elementary teaching positions in inner-city schools, in an open education program, and in rural public schools. He also served as assistant professor of education and taught college courses in education and supervised preservice teachers in a federally supported college-based program. He has frequently given speeches and workshops for professional organizations. He has been recognized for his 30-year membership in Phi Delta Kappa.

Preface

P*lanning and Administering Early Childhood Programs,* Tenth Edition, continues the tradition of excellence begun by Celia and John Decker. Its purpose is to contribute to the professional preparation of prospective and in-service program administrators by providing specific guidance on how to plan for, implement, market, and evaluate programs serving children from birth through school age.

NEW TO THIS EDITION

The tenth edition represents a significant revision of the text. Refinements have focused on making the book practical, relevant, current, and readable. This revision was led by Nancy Freeman, Ph.D., with contributions from Tere Holmes and Kris Curtis. Tere is president/CEO of Early Care and Education Strategies Plus, LLC, based in Houston, Texas. She works with clients on strategic planning, training, and capacity development. Kris is an early childhood educator, administrator, and advocate. She is the former president of the Texas Association for the Education of Young Children (TAEYC) and former director of education for the Children's Courtyard.

This revision includes new features to enhance the applicability of the content to real program decision making, such as the following:

- New mini-cases at the beginning of each chapter that highlight the experiences of two directors and how they conduct themselves on the job and are challenged by and resolve tasks in "A Better Way" further along in the chapter.
- New Learning Outcomes at the beginning of each chapter provide students with concrete goals for each chapter and support their success in the course.
- New Check for Understanding application questions at the end of chapters, along with existing Reflection items, provide instructors with additional assessment items.

Each chapter is aligned with NAEYC's 2007 Program Administrator Competencies, and the text includes expanded discussions of:

- Updated nutritional recommendations including USDA's MyPlate guidelines
- Increased attention to reducing childhood obesity and supporting breastfeeding
- Additional information about enhancing energy efficiency, including LEED guidelines
- Expanded lists of equipment and materials with age-group-specific recommendations
- Budget development, including helpful formulas and guidelines

This edition reflects our ongoing commitment to children from birth through school age and their families. We are guided by our commitment to provide high-quality programs of early care and education that help all children and families reach their fullest potential. Administrators hold the key to quality programming. It is our goal to equip them with the expertise and skill they need to be effective instructional leaders while handling the responsibilities of running an efficient and fiscally sound operation. The extensive references and online and print resources listed in this edition can provide readers with in-depth understandings of many topics.

PEDAGOGICAL FEATURES

Readers will find the three subdivisions of the book helpful because they parallel the administrator's planning processes: developing the program's goals and vision; creating a framework for the program's successful operation; and implementing a quality program that supports children's learning, growth, and development. In addition, the following features help—engage students in becoming—effective directors by involving them in authentic situations and challenges.

- Realistic vignettes in each chapter highlight key points and demonstrate how an effective administrator might apply these principles to the center she directs.

> **Marie's Experience**
>
> *Marie has been successful over the years in keeping her center in compliance with all licensing regulations. She is proud of her teachers and is confident that the center consistently goes above and beyond licensing provisions designed simply to keep children healthy and safe. She knows that the center provides high-quality care to the children it serves, but it has never pursued accreditation or participated in her state's optional Quality Rating and [...] because of the time and effort involved [...] Her families have confidence in her prog[...] this additional assurance that it provide[...] and day out.*

> **A Better Way**
>
> *In spite of the fact that Marie is confident in the quality of her program and the center's enrollment has remained strong, she has begun to reconsider her decision not to participate in the state's QRIS. She has learned that the state has recently made grants to purchase classroom materials available to centers that participate at its higher levels, and that there are special benefits to becoming fully accredited. These benefits are particularly attractive during these difficult economic times. For those reasons, she has researched a number of accreditation systems that, if she were to earn accreditation, would automatically qualify her center for the state's highest ranking. She has decided that the time, money, and effort invested in pursuing accreditation would pay off in the long run, and she has sent for the accreditation self-study materials. Her decision was made easier by the fact that she has great confidence in her assistant director and hopes that she will take the lead in managing the accreditation process by leading staff development on the accreditation process, completing required paperwork, and collecting and organizing documentation.*

- The "Application Activities" in each chapter give readers opportunities to practice completing tasks that are the director's responsibility.

> ## Application Activity
>
> Assume you are working with a class of 3- to 5-year-olds. Select a learning center as the focus of this project. Propose a layout for this learning center. Begin by selecting furniture, equipment, and toys by consulting Appendix 4 for suggested materials as well as recommendations on vendors' websites (see Appendix 1 for suppliers) and other professional resources. Once you have selected the furniture, toys, and equipment, arrange that equipment in the classroom. It would be helpful to sketch your plan on graph paper. (Search for "free graph paper" on your online search engine.) Give the director an estimate for how much your recommendation will cost by referring back to the catalogs you used to create your plan.

- Photographs, tables, and figures are used throughout the text to (a) summarize research or show conflicting points of view, (b) visually present the organization of a concept, and (c) give practical examples.
- The Trends and Issues and Summary sections will also help readers focus on the main themes of the book.
- The end-of-chapter assessments are aligned with the Learning Outcomes and major sections of each chapter.

TO REFLECT

1. What is the public's perception of your program? Is the public perception aligned with the program's vision and mission? If not, what changes will you make to more closely align your program's operations with its vision and mission?
2. What is your program currently doing to actively cultivate a positive perception among clients whom you already serve and the community at large? Are there features of your facility or your provision of service that are likely to foster the development of a negative perception of your program? What can/should you do to change?

3. In your community, what type of marketing strategies do early childhood care and education programs typically use? Browse the Internet and try to locate child care programs in your area. What content is presented on the Web? How easy is it to find information that you might be interested in?
4. What are the needs and desires of the parents and families in your community? Are there needs that are presently not being addressed by programs in your area?

CHECK AND APPLY YOUR UNDERSTANDING

1. Describe why your program's facility is instrumental in its success.
2. Think about the importance of service delivery and list the top four reasons customer service is critical to the success of your program.

3. Discuss the various components of a thorough marketing plan.
4. Think about Purple Cows. List three other remarkable products and how marketing played a role in their success.

We have designed this text to be useful for all early childhood administrators. Although early childhood programs are operated under a wide variety of auspices, a great deal of overlap remains among the competencies needed by their leaders. We have attempted to provide a balance of research-based statements, implementation strategies, and resources to prompt further investigation.

Like the nine editions that have come before, this edition will aid in the initial planning of early childhood programs and be a source of helpful information after programs are underway. The purpose of this book will be realized when the reader makes wiser judgments about planning and administering early childhood programs.

TEXT ORGANIZATION

Chapter 1 provides an overview of early care and education and program administration. It defines the most common types of programs for young children; emphasizes the importance of quality programming; and considers how recent social, economic, and political developments have affected the field.

Part One, Constructing the Early Childhood Program's Framework, includes three chapters. **Chapter 2** identifies how the field's history and its prominent theorists provide the philosophical bedrock upon which programs of early care and education are based. It advises program administrators that the values of the community should shape the development of their program's vision and mission statements and considers the role these foundational documents should play in the program's operation. It includes guidance for the director as he takes steps to implement the program, including strategies to evaluate the program's success in reaching its goals. **Chapter 3** examines regulations related to many aspects of the program's operation and explores the interplay among regulations, accreditation criteria, and other standards of practice including the Quality Rating and Improvement

Systems (QRIS) in place in many states. **Chapter 4** guides administrators developing program policies and procedures as well as handbooks for staff, families, and administrators.

Part Two, Operationalizing the Early Childhood Program, includes four chapters addressing important administrative topics. **Chapter 5** provides an overview of issues related to staffing, such as factors that contribute to high turnover and low levels of compensation. It includes job descriptions and identifies roles and qualifications of various personnel. The chapter describes the director's leadership, collaborative, and management roles. It also provides specific strategies for interviewing, hiring, and evaluating personnel. **Chapter 6** identifies issues to consider when planning a program's facility. It addresses topics ranging from site selection, classroom floor plans, and playground design to equipping classrooms to support children's learning, growth, and development. **Chapter 7** explains how funding impacts the program quality and discusses innovative funding ideas. It identifies direct and indirect sources of revenue, including a summary of state and federal investments in early care and education. This chapter also provides specific guidelines for developing a budget and for preparing financial reports. **Chapter 8** addresses effective marketing. It stresses that marketing is much more than an advertising campaign; instead, it is the actual fulfillment of the program's vision and mission and how the program's services are perceived by the children and families it serves. The chapter concludes with a description of specific strategies that can help readers effectively market their program to potential families, including guidance about how to develop a quality website and the effective use of social media.

Part Three, Implementing the Children's Program, discusses the administrator's role in planning and overseeing the program's services. **Chapter 9** addresses the director's role in leading curriculum development, implementing the program, and providing needed supports. **Chapter 10** concerns the administrator's role in meeting children's nutritional needs, reducing childhood obesity, encouraging breast-feeding, controlling infectious diseases, and ensuring a safe environment while instilling lifelong nutrition, health, and safety habits. **Chapter 11** identifies approaches to assessing children's learning, growth, and development. It offers practical advice about how to record, assess, and report children's performance on assessment and screening tools. **Chapter 12** describes effective strategies for creating respectful collaborative relationships with diverse families and working with stakeholders in the community. **Chapter 13** identifies the characteristics that set professionals apart from other workers, examines the ethical dimensions of early childhood program administration, and identifies strategies for becoming an effective advocate for children and families.

NEW! COURSESMART eTEXTBOOK AVAILABLE

CourseSmart is an exciting new choice for students looking to save money. As an alternative to purchasing the printed textbook, students can purchase an electronic version of the same content. With a CourseSmart eTextbook, students can search the text, make notes online, print out reading assignments that incorporate lecture notes, and bookmark important passages for later review. For more information or to purchase access to the CourseSmart eTextbook, visit www.coursesmart.com.

INSTRUCTOR ANCILLARIES

The following materials are available to registered instructors in the Instructor Resources section of www.pearsonhighered.com.

Online Instructor's Manual

The Instructor's Manual includes chapter overviews; *To Reflect* pieces, which serve as class discussion starters; and *Instructional Activities*, activities for both in-class and out-of-class use that apply the material in the text.

Online Test Bank

Test items in multiple-choice, short answer, and essay format are available to instructors in the Online Test Bank.

Test Gen

This powerful assessment generation program helps instructors easily create and print quizzes and exams. Questions and tests are authored online, allowing ultimate flexibility and the ability to efficiently create and print assessments anytime, anywhere.

Test Bank Conversions for Various LMS Formats

The online Test Bank has been converted to a number of LMS formats.

Online PowerPoint Slides

PowerPoint slides of key concepts from the text are available to instructors. Easily accessed and organized by chapter, they are colorful, simple, and straightforward and may be customized to fit instructors' needs.

ACKNOWLEDGMENTS

We thank Sherry King, director of the Children's Center at the University of South Carolina for her feedback and guidance; Judy Reddekopp, Dana Hale, Francie Kneece, and Wenjia Wang of the University of South Carolina for their help with manuscript preparation, including research and logistical support, and Mac Brown for taking pictures to illustrate key points in the text.

Julie Peters, Bryce Bell, and Linda Bayma at Pearson and copyeditor Linda Benson have offered valuable feedback and patiently answered many questions along the way. They have made significant contributions to this project's success.

We thank the following reviewers of this edition for their helpful comments: Jerry Ann Harrel-Smith, California State University Northridge; Jennifer M. Johnson, Vance-Granville Community College; Karri Karns, Iowa State University; Beatrice Paul, Salem State College; and Carroll Tingle, University of Alabama.

Brief Contents

APPENDICES

Contents

APPENDICES

Overview of Early Care and Education and Program Administration

Learning Outcomes

After studying this chapter, you should be able to:

1. Describe why attending a quality child care program has long-lasting benefits for the children who are enrolled.
2. Discuss the types of early childhood programs.
3. Understand the special services that exist in child care.
4. Describe the differences between structural and process quality in early care and education programs.
5. Differentiate the various roles of the center director or administrator.
6. Distinguish among the characteristics of a variety of leadership styles.

NAEYC Administrator Competencies addressed in this chapter:

Early Childhood Knowledge and Skills

1. Historical and Philosophical Foundations
Knowledge of current trends and important influences impacting program quality. Knowledge of research methodologies.

8. Leadership and Advocacy
Knowledge of organizational theory and leadership styles as they relate to early childhood work environments.

Child care is a way of life for many of America's young children. About 53% of both parents, 60% of single mothers, and 76% of single fathers with children under age 6 are in the labor force (U.S. Department of Labor, Bureau of Labor Statistics, 2011), and nearly three out of four children with working mothers are cared for by persons who are not their parents (Urban Institute, 2004). This represents a major change in the American family since the 1970s. In 1976, when the women's movement had just begun, 31% of mothers of young children were in the labor force (Lerman & Schmidt, 1999). Today's figures indicate a twofold increase in maternal employment and child care participation in one generation.

Just as the demand for child care has changed over the years, so has our country's interest in, and support for, programs of early care and education. Consider the differences among the following:

- Family-focused programs of the 1940s that provided child care and other services for "Rosie the Riveter," American women who were building ships and other materials needed by the war effort.
- Comprehensive Head Start programs that were the centerpiece of the 1960's War on Poverty. Head Start was designed to provide care and education, medical screenings, and needed social services to bootstrap children and families out of poverty.
- Child care designed to meet the needs of "liberated women" who entered the workforce in record numbers in the 1970s.

• Programs focused on meeting the first benchmark of the Goals 2000 panel that challenged America to ensure that all children had the opportunities they needed to come to school "ready to learn."

The field's knowledge base has expanded as it has responded to current needs, interests, and the existing level of political support. Today, early childhood programs are likely to advocate for increased public support by relying on brain research and longitudinal studies showing that young children reap lifelong benefits from high-quality early childhood programming, particularly when it is coupled with intensive parent involvement and education (Center on the Developing Child at Harvard University, 2007; Schweinhart et al., 2005; Shonkoff & Phillips, 2000).

Early care and education programs can realize the promise of these strands of research while meeting the current needs of America's children and families:

1. We need available and affordable child care for working families (Olson, 2002).
2. We have a responsibility to minimize the effects of identified risk-producing conditions such as poverty, low birth weight, maternal depression, family violence, parents with low educational attainment and low levels of literacy, and chronic health conditions and disabilities. Each of these factors increases the likelihood that children will struggle in school, and the chances for success are greatly reduced when children face multiple risk factors in their early years (Center on the Developing Child at Harvard University, 2007; Shore & Shore, 2009).
3. We need a workforce that can compete in the worldwide knowledge economy (Carnegie Corporation of New York, 1994; Committee for Economic Development, Research, and Policy, 1987, 1991, 1993; Rolnick & Grunewald, 2003).

While it is true America does not yet have a robust infrastructure that provides all families with affordable, accessible high-quality programming for their young children, early childhood initiatives have attracted unprecedented attention in recent years. One example is that the federal No Child Left Behind legislation required states to develop *Good Start Grow Smart* standards describing what preschool children should know and be able to do. In recent years, there has been an emphasis on developing infant and toddler early learning guidelines that often align with these standards. These guidelines provide a common language to describe the developmental trajectory of typically developing infants and toddlers. It is noteworthy that this work has continued even in a difficult economic climate. In 2008, 22 states had Infant/Toddler Guidelines in place (Petersen, Jones, & McGinley, 2008); as of 2010, 31 states had implemented them for our youngest children (National Infant & Toddler Child Care Initiative and ZERO TO THREE Policy Center, 2010).

Another way to gauge the public's support for early childhood programs is to consider the number of states that support preschoolers, particularly 4-year-olds. In 2005–2006, 38 states had state-funded pre-K programs serving 20% of all 4-year-olds, up from 17% in 2004–2005 and just 14% in 2001–2002 (Barnett, Hustedt, Hawkinson, & Robin, 2006). In the 2009–2010 school year, 40 states, including Alaska and Rhode Island, supported pre-K, serving 27% of the country's 4-year-olds. But the hard fact is that funding for pre-K declined in 19 of the 40 states, a reduction of nearly $30 million. That reduction would have been much greater in the 2009–2010 school year if it had not been for $49.3 million in American Recovery and Reinvestment Act (ARRA) funding (Barnett et al., 2010). These trends point to difficult times ahead if funding streams are not replenished when ARRA funding ends. Even in this gloomy economy, however, 14 states increased the percentage of their 3- and 4-year-olds enrolled in these programs. One reality that has not changed with the fluctuations in public support is that preschool programs are consistently less well funded than are programs for primary-age children, and teacher qualifications and other characteristics of quality vary greatly (Barnett et al., 2006).

Challenges remain as the field strives to increase quality, affordability, and accessibility to meet the needs of increasingly diverse communities. It is our hope that this book equips current and future administrators to provide high-quality programming in their own centers. We also hope that it prepares you to advocate for the societal and governmental support needed to provide all young children with the opportunities they need to enhance their chances for success in school and beyond.

Application Activity

Visit the National Child Care Information and Technical Assistance Center website listed at the end of this chapter to review your state's requirements to serve as a program administrator. Are you qualified now? What would you need to do to be eligible to serve as a director? Are the qualifications the same or different in two neighboring states? What are these differences?

WHY ARE THE EARLY YEARS IMPORTANT?

Many young children attend child care for more than 2,000 hours per year. That is about twice the amount of time older children spend in public school classrooms. In fact, the cumulative total time young children spend in child care may equal the total time they spend in school from the beginning of kindergarten until they graduate from high school (Children's Defense Fund, 2006). These figures help us appreciate why young children's child care experience has a lasting impact on their learning, growth, and development. Potential benefits of high-quality care have been documented to include enhanced social, emotional, learning, language, and cognitive development that increases their chances for success in school and beyond (Barnett, 1995; Burchinal, Roberts, Nabors, & Bryant, 1996; National Institute of Child Health and Human Development [NICHD] Early Child Care Research Network, 1998; Ramey & Ramey, 1998). As a program administrator, you will have an opportunity to ensure program quality so that these potential benefits are realized.

Children comfortably engaged in independent reading is a signal that the environment is safe and secure for the children.

Putting Programs of Early Care and Education into Context

Effective program administration begins with an understanding of the history and traditions of early care and education. This overview will provide a starting point as you learn about program planning and implementation, effective management, and leadership.

Today's early childhood programs continue the field's rich traditions. They are an indication of society's commitment to its youngest and most vulnerable members. Recent efforts to invest in programs for young children, even in difficult economic times, point to a growing appreciation for the fact that a child's earliest experiences have lifelong implications and, to a large extent, set the stage for future success (Shonkoff & Phillips, 2000). This conviction is based, in large measure, on an appreciation for the vulnerability of very young children's developing brains and the windows of opportunity that are uniquely open during their first 3 years (Center on the Developing Child at Harvard University, 2007; Cranley Gallagher, 2005).

Even while science has provided mounting evidence of the importance of the early years, too many children begin school with disadvantages that are hard, and sometimes impossible, to overcome. As many as 39% of America's young children live in low-income homes (Shore & Shore, 2009). Minorities shoulder the biggest burden of poverty: 36% of African American, 35% of American Indian, 31% of Hispanic or Latino, 13% of Asian and Pacific Islander, and 12% of White (non-Hispanic) children live in households at or below federal poverty levels (Annie E. Casey Foundation, 2009). The effects of poverty during infancy and early childhood can have lifelong implications. Low-income families are less likely to seek prenatal care; are less able to provide pregnant women and young children with adequate nutrition; may not fully immunize their children against childhood illnesses; and are more likely to live in unsafe, stress-producing neighborhoods (Center on the Developing Child at Harvard University, 2007; Children's Defense Fund, 2006). Advocates who appreciate the potential benefits of experiences in quality programs need to focus, in particular, on those children most at risk for school failure as they map the course of early childhood in the years to come.

TYPES OF EARLY CHILDHOOD PROGRAMS

One of the first challenges encountered when studying programs of early care and education is the confusion about the meaning of *early childhood*. Professional organizations, state departments of education, researchers, and other stakeholders sometimes use vague synonyms or different chronological ages or developmental milestones when they refer to "young children." The National Association for the Education of Young Children (NAEYC) has defined *early childhood* as the period from birth through age 8 (NAEYC, 2009). That is the definition we will use throughout this book, with a particular emphasis on young children served in community child care settings.

One way to classify early childhood programs is by considering the program's sponsor. Early childhood programs are operated by

- state agencies (e.g., public prekindergarten, kindergarten, and primary-grade programs operated in public schools)
- federal agencies (e.g., Head Start and Early Head Start)
- private for-profit or nonprofit organizations (e.g., community preschools or parent cooperatives, employer-sponsored child care, faith-based programs, programs operated by service or philanthropic organizations)
- colleges and universities that use them as clinical settings and as research laboratories

Early childhood programs may also be described by referring to their historical roots, which include health care, social services, home economics or family and consumer science, and education (Meisels & Shonkoff, 2000). Today, as in the past, early childhood programs reflect the social interests, political trends, and community priorities of the day (Garbarino & Ganzel, 2000; Sameroff & Fiese, 2000).

Most Common Types of Child Care

State-operated public schools and federally funded Head Start programs serve particular populations of young children from birth through age 4. State-funded pre-K programs are sometimes located in public schools, but they can also be housed in community programs that are reimbursed for their services. These publically funded programs have specific operating procedures and are governed by mandated standards. You will want to learn more about these programs if you anticipate a career in a government-operated program of early care and education.

The two most commonly encountered types of child care that are the primary focus of this book are child care centers and family child care. A **child care center** is a non-residential facility serving 13 or more children and operating fewer than 24 hours a day (National Child Care Information and Technical Assistance Center, National Association for Regulatory Administration [NARA], 2010). Many programs serve children from birth through school age for 10 to 12 hours a day, adjusting their schedule to meet the needs of working families. Most serve the same children and families on a regular basis, but others accept children on a drop-in occasional basis. Child care centers are regulated by states' licensing agencies. While many for-profit centers are owned and operated by individuals or family corporations, some are operated as large chains or are franchises. Not-for-profit centers are typically sponsored by state and local governments, religious groups, service or philanthropic organizations, or parent cooperatives. About 60% of America's 3- to 5-year-olds participate in child care on a full-time or part-time basis (Annie E. Casey Foundation, 2009).

Family child care is nonresidential care provided in a private home other than the child's own. About 25% of America's children under age 6 attend family-based child care at least once a week (Annie E. Casey Foundation, 2009). In small family child care homes, the number of children is limited—approximately six, including the caregiver's own children. Many states differentiate between small home programs and those serving 7 to 12 children in **large family child care homes** or **group child care homes**. Family child care homes are most frequently operated as independent businesses, but they are occasionally part of a **system** (i.e., have a sponsoring organization that has been authorized by the state to approve and monitor their services), as is the case for home providers operating on military bases.

Wide variation exists among states' regulatory requirements for small and large family child care programs. In some states, operators must simply submit evidence that providers have undergone criminal background checks and have taken other essential steps to ensure children's safety and well-being. In others, home-based programs are held to standards similar to those applied to child care centers. You will want to become familiar with your state's requirements if you are considering opening a program for young children in your home.

Informal care includes a large network of unregulated "kith and kin" providers caring for children in their homes. They are usually relatives, friends, or neighbors of the children they serve. Some researchers estimate that nearly one-half of all young children,

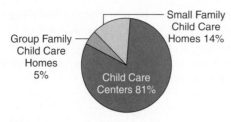

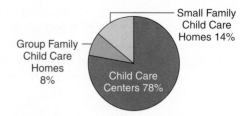

Figure 1.1
2005 Licensed Capacity reports the percentage of children served in child care centers, group family child care homes, and small family child care homes

Source: Data from *The 2005 Child Care Licensing Study: Final Report*, by the National Association for Regulatory Administration and National Child Care Information and Technical Assistance Center (NARA/NCCIC), 2006, Conyers, GA: National Association for Regulatory Administration.

Figure 1.2
2008 Licensed Capacity reports the percentage of children served in child care centers, group family child care homes, and small family child care homes

Source: Data from *The 2008 Child Care Licensing Study: Final Report*, by the National Child Care Information and Technical Assistance Center, National Association for Regulatory Administration (NARA), 2010, Lexington, KY: NARA.

particularly infants, in nonparental care are using informal, unregulated child care arrangements at least some of the time (Brown-Lyons, Robertson, & Layzer, 2001; Paulsell, Mekos, Del Grosso, Rowand, & Banghart, 2006).

As you study Figures 1.1, 1.2, and 1.3, note that the supply of spaces in center-based, group family child care homes, and small homes remained relatively stable between 2005 and 2008. Notable variations are small shifts away from center-based care and a slight increase in group family child care homes that typically serve 7 to 12 children. This shift may reflect the high levels of unemployment in many parts of the country during the most difficult periods of the recession of 2008–2009 when there was less demand for out-of-home care for young children. The increase in group home enrollment may also be an indication that outreach efforts aimed at home providers have resulted in increased numbers of registered or licensed providers joining the system to have access to quality enhancement initiatives such as the *Arizona Kith and Kin Project* (Association for Supportive Child Care, 2011).

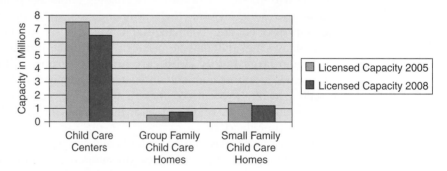

Figure 1.3
Comparing Licensed Capacity 2005 and 2008 illustrates changes in the licensed capacity of child care centers, group family child care homes, and small family child care homes in 2005 and 2008

Sources: Data from *The 2005 Child Care Licensing Study: Final Report*, by the National Association for Regulatory Administration and National Child Care Information and Technical Assistance Center (NARA/NCCIC), 2006, Conyers, GA: National Association for Regulatory Administration and *The 2008 Child Care Licensing Study: Final Report*, by the National Child Care Information and Technical Assistance Center, National Association for Regulatory Administration (NARA), 2010, Lexington, KY: NARA.

Special Services in Child Care

Infant and toddler child care serves children from birth to age 3. The demand for services for these young children is great: In 2005, 42% of 1-year-olds and 53% of 12- to 24-month-olds experienced nonparental care at least once a week (ZERO TO THREE, 2007). But, in spite of this high demand, the supply of infant/toddler care is inadequate, in large measure because of the high cost of maintaining the low ratios (one caregiver to three or four children) that are the hallmark of quality. It is also very difficult to provide consistently high-quality care for very young children. The now-classic Cost, Quality, and Outcomes study reported that 40% of infant/toddler programs were of poor quality, and only 8% were determined to provide quality care (Cost, Quality, and Child Outcomes Study Team, 1995). Federal initiatives, including portions of the Child Care and Development Fund (CCDF) earmarked for programs serving infants and toddlers set-aside, are designed to funnel increased funds to specialized training and technical assistance for caregivers (ZERO TO THREE, 2007). Some of these efforts designed to increase the availability of quality infant/toddler care are still in the early stages of implementation. Their effectiveness will be evidenced in the years to come.

Another trend affecting child care providers is an increase in the demand for and number of programs offering **school-age child care** (SACC), which is nonparental care for children from kindergarten through age 15. It includes services provided by child care centers; large and small family child care homes; parks and recreational departments; and youth groups such as YMCA/YWCA, Boy and Girl Scouts, and Boys & Girls Clubs of America. SACC operates when school is not in session—before and after school, on school holidays, and during the summer. Many states exempt programs for school-age children from child care regulations (NARA, 2010). As of 2010, 15 states had adopted separate school-age licensing standards addressing, most frequently, the physical environment, child-staff ratios and maximum group size, staff qualifications and background, health and hygiene, and program activities (NARA, 2010).

Children with **identified special needs** are served in increasing numbers by community child care programs. According to the U.S. Department of Education, Office of Special Education and Rehabilitative Services, Office of Special Education Programs (2007), 34% of all young children with disabilities are being served primarily in early childhood programs, and an additional 16.4% of children with disabilities are enrolled in early childhood programs part time. While federal legislation (the Americans with Disabilities Act [ADA]) requires that early childhood programs make reasonable accommodations to serve young children with disabilities, the inclusion of these children among their same-age peers is just as much a moral obligation. Inclusive early childhood programming benefits all children, not just children with disabilities. When used in this manner, the term **inclusion** refers to the complete integration of children with disabilities into the community in which they live. This complete integration is not simply a matter of placement (the child is in the physical proximity of typically developing peers) but rather all children (regardless of disability) becoming part of the community of children that is established within a classroom or program. In this way, effective inclusion will result in meaningful engagement of typically developing children with children who have disabilities and the establishment of durable social relationships. Effective inclusion, however, is not easily accomplished and will require collaboration among child care administrators, general education teachers, special education service providers, and local education agencies to ensure that the children and staff get the needed services and professional development necessary to be effective.

A final trend is the growing need for care for children who are **mildly ill** or who are recovering from surgery. These programs provide a valuable service to working family members who would otherwise have to miss work when their child is unable to participate in child care because of a minor noncontagious condition. Five types of care are available for children who are mildly ill: (a) centers that care only for sick children, (b) programs within hospitals, (c) "sick rooms" at regular child care centers, (d) specialized family child care homes, and (e) in-home care or visiting nurse services. Programs vary on which illnesses or conditions they will admit or exclude; for example, many programs are not able to serve children with infectious diarrhea or those with a high fever. Some states have separate regulations for programs serving children who are ill (NARA, 2010).

Application Activity

Review your state's child care regulations (go to nrckids.org and click on the link for State Licensing and Regulation Information) to identify the kinds of programs they address and to identify any programs that are exempt from regulation, such as those serving school-age children.

QUALITY: THE OVERRIDING CONCERN

The growing appreciation for the potential benefits of quality programs of early care and education has strengthened funding agencies' and policy makers' commitment to ensuring that all families have access to programming that can support and enhance young children's development, growth, and learning. These benefits can be realized, however, only in high-quality programs with characteristics linked to positive outcomes for children.

Characteristics of Quality

Researchers and policy makers assess a child care program's quality by evaluating its structural and process characteristics. Measures of **structural** quality include group size, child-adult ratio, and the extent of teachers' and administrators' specialized education and training. Many of these features are readily observable and are addressed in states' licensing regulations. Dimensions of **process** quality include some assessments that are straightforward

The caregiver is facilitating a group game with her children.

and easy to evaluate and others that are more nuanced and difficult to quantify. An example of an easy-to-observe dimension of process quality is an evaluation of the center's health and safety practices. Dimensions that are more difficult to assess include measures of caregivers' sensitivity and responsiveness, measures of cognitive and language stimulation, and characterizations of peer interactions as positive or negative. While an observer might develop an opinion about a program's quality by observing these kinds of teacher-child interactions, assessments of these dimensions of quality require trained assessors using standardized instruments that are generally not available to program administrators.

Parent Choice and Quality

Families may not consider quality differences in choosing programs. In fact, discrepancies often exist between parent and expert ratings (Helburn & Culkin, 1995a, 1995b). These reasons may explain the discrepancies:

1. Parents may not have good consumer information on choosing child care. Some parents choose programs without expert advice or knowledge of quality characteristics they should look for when selecting child care. Other parents may have information, but they may not read or understand it. Parents also make decisions based on convenience and the recommendations of family members and friends, rather than on data supporting the quality indicators of a particular program. Many parents have never seen good programs for comparison purposes. Child Care Resource and Referral agencies (CCR&Rs) are moving toward providing parents with more specific information on programs, such as the director's qualifications, the adult-child ratio, and regulatory compliance. Some states are rating centers, which can be one of the easiest ways to make parents good consumers.

2. Parents may have few choices in some geographical areas.

3. The values parents place on a specific aspect of a program may overshadow quality aspects. Parents may be looking at costs, hours of services, and convenience of location. Research findings suggest that parents also seem to look for a shared value system with providers. Several studies indicate that experts need to reevaluate the "fit" between program goals and what families perceive as their needs. For example, Zinzeleta and Little (1997) found that parents were seeking programs with a heavy academic emphasis and shared religious values or wanted to protect their children from certain values. Thus, family members must be involved in designing and implementing high-quality services for children.

A strategy many states have adopted to help families become more informed consumers of child care is the use of a Quality Rating System (QRS) or Quality Rating and Improvement System (QRIS). These systems use easy-to-understand symbols, like stars, to represent differing levels of quality. Like the diamonds AAA uses to rank restaurants and hotels (AAA, n.d.), they summarize a comprehensive evaluation of the program's structural and process characteristics, indicating a range of quality from adequate to exemplary. Quality rating systems can be either voluntary or mandatory. Either way, they are an effective way to help families make informed decisions when they select care for their young children.

HOW CAN DIRECTORS MOVE THEIR PROGRAMS TOWARD EXCELLENCE?

Now that we have discussed the importance of providing high-quality child care and education services to young children, we will turn to the description of the roles, responsibilities, and professional attributes of early childhood program administrators. As the "person in charge," the director of any center-based early childhood program will engage in different types of activities that ultimately influence the level of quality that will be attained and has a significant impact on a center's ability to be successful. Also refer to the first four pages of this text for NAEYC's definition of an administrator and competencies for program administration.

The Roles of a Director

An effective early childhood program administrator must be able to assume different roles within the organization and attend to different aspects of the program to ensure that the services provided to children and families are indeed those that are valued and/or warranted. In her position as a director, she will assume each of the following roles within the organization:

Leader: In this role, a director must maintain a future orientation, focusing on the continuous improvement of the services provided to children and their families. As the leader of the program, the director's role is to ensure that there is a vision for what the program aspires to become. This vision is created by considering the values and needs of relevant stakeholders, the professional knowledge borne from current theories and research, and the professional wisdom gained from experiences in the field of early childhood education. Once the vision is developed and agreed upon by staff and other stakeholders, she must develop a plan for how to facilitate continuous improvement efforts that will result in achievement (or an approximation) of the vision.

Manager: In this role, a director is primarily focused on the center's daily operations. The effective program administrator works to ensure that children and families are receiving the services that they need and want. As the program's manager, the director observes staff to ensure that they are fulfilling their responsibilities, while at the same time interacting with children and families to gauge their level of satisfaction. The effective administrator actively monitors the organization's financial health by monitoring its income and expenditures. Using his skills as an effective marketer, the director works to ensure that the center has sufficient enrollment through effectively marketing the program to the community.

Coach: In the role of the coach, the director focuses on providing professional development and technical assistance to all staff members as a means to increase their level of performance. While the knowledge and skills of the staff will be enhanced through many forms of professional development, the coach is keenly aware that to be effective, she must first acknowledge the strengths of individual staff members, then identify areas of needed improvement, and finally develop a plan to increase these skills and competencies. By coaching all staff to continually improve, the director acts as a bridge between the roles of manager and leader. The coach, aware of the vision for excellence, is continually monitoring daily performance and looking for opportunities to propel the entire team forward, closer to achieving the ultimate goal—excellent quality early care and education for all children.

Leadership Styles

The studies of effective leadership styles from the past were focused on identifying the characteristics and behaviors of effective leaders in the hope of being able to describe very specifically what one might learn and then do if she wanted to become an effective leader. Investigation in this area has resulted in the identification of areas of competence and personal characteristics exhibited by effective leaders (Dulewicz & Higgs, 2005):

Areas of Competence

- **Envision:**   the ability to identify a clear picture for the future and clearly articulate the vision in a way that inspires others toward action
- **Engage:**   communicating effectively with individuals so that they understand how they will contribute to the achievement of the vision
- **Enable:**   acting on a belief in the talent and potential of individuals, and creating the environment in which these can be realized
- **Inquire:**   being open to real dialogue with those involved in the organization and encouraging free and frank debate of all issues
- **Develop:**   working with people to build their capability and help them make the envisioned contribution

Personal Characteristics

- **Authenticity:**   being genuine and not attempting to "play a role," not acting in a manipulative way
- **Integrity:**   being consistent in what you say and do
- **Will:**   a drive to lead, and persistence in working toward a goal
- **Self-belief:**   a realistic evaluation of your capabilities and belief that you can achieve required goals
- **Self-awareness:**   a realistic understanding of who you are, how you feel, and how others see you

While an awareness of these competencies and traits is important, it is even more important that effective leaders employ strategies and select from a repertoire of behaviors that are uniquely suited to the context in which they are currently working. There are three distinct classifications of leadership styles (goal oriented, involving, engaging) and the organizational context (low change, moderate change, and high change) for which they are best suited. Table 1.1 provides an illustration of how different leadership behaviors match different organizational contexts.

As you can see from Table 1.1, an effective leader will at times take charge of a situation and at other times act more as a facilitator. When an organization is in a low-change mode of operating, it is often more appropriate for the leader to make decisions critical to continued operation and to provide specific guidance to staff to ensure that the organization continues providing high-quality services. When there is a high degree of change (e.g., beginning a new program or service), successful leaders facilitate high

Table 1.1
Match Between Leadership Styles and Organizational Context

Leadership Styles	Change Context		
	Low Change	Moderate Change	High Change
Goal Oriented: Leader sets direction and plays a significant role in specifically directing others to achieve key goals. Leader-centric.	Yes	Maybe	No
Involving: Less leader-centric than goal oriented. Focus is on providing strong sense of direction but encourages collaboration in identifying specific tasks and how goals will be achieved.	Maybe	Yes	Maybe
Engaging: Focus is on facilitating others in identifying the direction and the means for achieving necessary goals. The leader is more concerned with the development of others than on maintaining a specific direction of change.	No	Maybe	Yes

levels of collaboration among many relevant stakeholders to capitalize on the collective wisdom of the group and to ensure that all engaged parties agree that change is necessary. One of the most important tasks facing a program director in the context of significant change is encouraging stakeholder ownership of the process and the end result. An effective director facilitates this high level of buy-in through a collaborative process in which all key stakeholders believe that they have a voice.

The Journey Begins . . .

We hope that this book will be a guide on your journey toward becoming an effective program administrator. You will not be on this journey alone. We have woven the stories of two program directors into each chapter. They bring different experiences to their work and are working in very different settings. You will meet both of them in this chapter, and one will be featured in each of the following chapters. You will learn about their struggles to try new strategies and develop new skills. We hope you will identify with some of their struggles—and will celebrate their successes.

Meet Marie

Marie is in her early 40s and has been working in the early care and education field for 18 years. She went to college full time while working on a degree in business administration, and she worked part time for a licensed for-profit child care center near campus. Initially, Marie thought of this preschool teaching position as "just a job," but it didn't take long for her to develop a real passion for working with children and having the opportunity to make a difference in their lives.

As a result of this growing interest and focus, Marie soon made a change in her degree plan and began coursework in early childhood education. She worked for the same child care center for more than 5 years, moving from a preschool classroom to the school-age room, and eventually she became the assistant director. Marie was still the assistant director when the time came to graduate and make the decision about her career. Because the center director who Marie had worked with during college was still in that position, she made the choice to search for a management position in another licensed child care center.

Soon after graduation, Marie's career search ended when she accepted a position at a child care center licensed for 150 children. She was hired as the assistant director, reporting to the center director who had been there for nearly 5 years. Marie thrived in her role and was given many opportunities to use her past experience and knowledge to mentor the center's teachers. Marie's performance was rewarded on several occasions with words of praise, recognition at parent events, and a well-deserved salary increase. After a year, the director announced that she was expecting her first child and would not be returning to work. Marie was offered the director position, and she had every confidence in the world that she could excel in that role because she knew she had received the proper training and mentoring in her previous position.

Over the past 13 years, Marie has remained at the same center. She has enjoyed the challenges of managing the business and operations of this large center but recognizes that there is always more to know. She is committed to continuing to acquire the knowledge and skills she needs.

Meet Grace

Grace is in her early 30s and has worked in child care since she was in high school. She went to college part time and graduated several years ago from the local technical college with an associate's degree in early childhood education.

She became a full-time assistant teacher while still in school and then became a lead teacher after she graduated. She has worked with children from ages 2 to 5.

Over the years, Grace has worked in large and small for-profit and nonprofit programs. She had never considered becoming a director but was encouraged to apply for the position when the long-time director at the nonprofit center where she has worked for the past 3 years moved away. The center is licensed for 90 children. She was the most experienced teacher at the center, was very popular with children and parents, and seemed ready for a new challenge. Furthermore, the center's board of directors believed that the center had gotten into a rut—the facility was getting a bit run down, they were constantly dealing with teacher turnover, and enrollment had its ups and downs. In short, it was a "good enough" program— but not the quality the board of directors expected.

Grace wasn't too surprised when she got the job, but now, as she begins her first full year as director, she is overwhelmed with everything she needs to know and do to keep the center's license in good standing and to make sure everything is running smoothly, let alone improve the program's quality. She is getting used to thinking of herself as a leader and manager, but she doesn't feel qualified for many things she's now responsible for. She has no experience or training to help her make hiring, budgeting, marketing, or purchasing decisions. She has always been familiar with her state's licensing regulations, but there are so many issues they address that she never paid attention to as a classroom teacher. For example, now she's responsible not only for getting her own annual professional development, including the additional requirements for directors she had never had to worry about before, but also for ensuring that her staff gets the annual training they need to comply with licensing regulations. What's more, she knows she needs to lead some of that staff development herself, to become a mentor and coach for the entire staff, and to evaluate their performance. She's worried that these duties will be particularly difficult because she will be navigating the shift from being a teacher to being a director— she is now supervising teachers who were her peers just a few months ago.

Your Own Journey

You will not become an effective early care and education administrator simply by reading this book or any other book on early childhood programs. It takes years of experience in concert with a process of continual program evaluation and reflection. It is our hope that this text will help you on your journey to becoming an effective program administrator by describing the characteristics of quality program development and management. Throughout the text, you will find authentic examples from successful early care and education programs. In addition, we have developed worksheets and forms that might also be useful to you as you work to either develop or improve a program for young children. While we do not attempt to provide solutions to all situations you might encounter, we have endeavored to identify the essential knowledge and skills that will set you on the path toward success.

SUMMARY

Early childhood programs have experienced growth unlike any other U.S. enterprise except technology. The increased demand for child care and education in a society whose workforce involves and will continue to involve more women and greater ethnic and racial diversity has fostered this growth, as have the desire to help children in poverty get a better start in life and the expanding body of research demonstrating the benefits of high-quality programs.

Early childhood programs, taken collectively, constitute a diverse, rather uncoordinated system supported by various individuals and by public and private organizations with differing historical roots. The quality of early childhood programs has become an overriding concern following the release of data from national studies of child care. Besides the concern over quality, other trends and issues include (a) diverse program practices, (b) more emphasis on the child within the family setting and meeting the family's needs, (c) a belief in the need to build community partnerships that consider local needs and cultural values, (d) an emphasis on collaboration and linkages across various auspices funding early childhood programs, and (e) a comprehensive view (i.e., care and education) of high-quality programs for *all* children.

USEFUL WEBSITES

Caring for Our Children: National Health and Safety Performance Standards: Guidelines for Early Care and Education Programs, 3rd ed. (2011), developed by the National Resource Center for Health and Safety in Child Care and Early Education

nrckids.org/

This website's link to individual states' child care regulations can be found by clicking on "State Licensing and Regulation Information." It highlights recent changes to states' child care regulations, which can help you stay up-to-date.

Qualifications for Center Directors, compiled by the National Child Care Information and Technical Assistance Center

nccic.acf.hhs.gov/pubs/cclicensingreq/cclr-directors.html

This state-by-state summary of qualifications will help you stay up-to-date on requirements for becoming a center director.

Kids Count Data Book, sponsored by the Annie E. Casey Foundation

datacenter.kidscount.org/DataBook/2010

This comprehensive resource is revised annually. It reports data on many measures of child well-being. State-by-state, regional, and national data can be helpful as you learn about your community or prepare reports or funding proposals.

National Association for the Education of Young Children (NAEYC)

naeyc.org

This is the largest early childhood professional organization. Its home page has a large collection of resources for teachers and caregivers, administrators, and families.

National Association of Child Care Professionals (NACCP)

naccp.org

This organization serves the child care industry and the owners, directors, and administrators of child care programs.

TO REFLECT

1. As you embark on the process of becoming an effective program administrator of a high-quality early care and education program, think about the reasons or life circumstances that have led you to this point in your career. Why do you want to be an early childhood program administrator? What personal characteristics or skills do you possess that will help you?
2. As the director of a respected child care program, you have been asked to address an upcoming local school board meeting about the importance of early care and education. The board is planning to implement a new systemwide preschool program. What arguments for care would be effective to use when addressing this group, which is more likely to be concerned about educational benefits such as school readiness and academic skills?

CHECK AND APPLY YOUR UNDERSTANDING

1. List ways children can benefit from attending a quality child care program.
2. List the types of early childhood programs and describe the differences among them.
3. Consider the benefits of offering special services such as infant and toddler care in the child care setting.
4. Think about the differences between structural and process quality, and make a list of those differences.
5. Discuss with a peer the various roles of a center director and the relevance of each to the child care program.
6. Understand the characteristics of a variety of leadership styles.

CHAPTER 2

Developing a Vision, Mission, and Program Evaluation

Learning Outcomes

After studying this chapter, you should be able to:

1. Explain the importance of having a clearly articulated program philosophy.
2. Understand why it is important that the program reflect the diversity of the community.
3. Describe what should be considered when developing the vision for the program.
4. Discuss the importance of the mission statement.
5. Describe the importance of creating routines and systems to ensure the program's smooth operation.
6. Identify the specific evaluation tools that can be used in early childhood programs to ensure the delivery of quality programming.

Marie's Experience

Marie's center has been operating for a number of years without offering programs to assist families financially with their tuition. As a result of recent changes in the neighborhood and the current economic conditions, families that could benefit from a scholarship or subsidy programs have withdrawn. Marie realized through conversations with a diverse group of family members and community leaders that there might be ways to offer the quality early care and education programs that the families had come to know, but at a reduced tuition rate.

An effective early childhood administrator or director must be aware of all of the program influences and components that contribute to the development of a high-quality program for young children. With this awareness, the director begins planning for success by developing a **vision** for a high-quality program designed to support children's development and learning. The program's vision must align with the sponsor's **purpose**, based on an articulated **philosophy** of care and education; reflect the **cultures** and **values** of the children

NAEYC Administrator Competencies addressed in this chapter:

Management Knowledge and Skills

1. Personal and Professional Self-Awareness
Knowledge of one's own beliefs, values, and philosophical stance.

8. Leadership and Advocacy
The ability to articulate a vision, clarify and affirm values, and create a culture built on norms of continuous improvement and ethical conduct. The ability to evaluate program effectiveness. The ability to define organizational problems, gather data to generate alternative solutions, and effectively apply analytical skills in its solution. The ability to advocate on behalf of young children, their families, and the profession.

Figure 2.1
Process for Program Planning and Evaluation

and all of the families served; and meet the **community's needs**. After creating the program's vision, the next steps include sharing the vision with all stakeholders, making revisions when necessary; working collaboratively to develop a program **mission statement**; creating an implementation and **program assessment plan** and timeline; and, finally, implementing the program using these tools as roadmaps to success. Program planning is, in fact, a continuous cycle for the successful administrator.

The program director or administrator will use information from program assessment activities as a starting point for future planning. Of utmost importance is the congruence and alignment among all of these program components. Misalignment of any component is likely to impact the overall effectiveness of the program and will inhibit the program's ability to meet the needs of the children and families being served. Review Figure 2.1 to understand the relationships among the program's vision, mission statement, goals, and evaluation.

PROGRAM INFLUENCES

Whether you are managing an early childhood program currently operating or planning for one that is in development, you need to consider the stakeholders' values and those of the local community. It is important to understand that the community's demographics will impact these values. They need to be the foundation upon which the program's mission and vision are built. Also be certain to keep the program's philosophy in mind to ensure that the program meets the needs of its intended clientele.

Considering the Values of the Community

The values of all who have a stake in the outcomes of the child care and education program (director, staff, families, children, public school professionals, and the local community) should be carefully identified and thoughtfully incorporated into the center's vision. Each stakeholder group expects certain results from the early care and education services you provide. In fact, these values actually have a direct impact on the program's ultimate outcomes. Consider asking the following questions to identify the key values of the stakeholders you will be serving:

1. What do you expect your child to know or be able to do to be a successful adult? Why are these knowledge and skills important?
2. From your perspective, what value might an early childhood program add to your community?
3. What do you expect of the teachers and caregivers who interact with your child?
4. What are the most important services that our program might provide to the community?

While early childhood professionals might be interested in different outcomes than other stakeholder groups, it is the responsibility of the program administrator to mediate

conflicting interests when they arise. It is also the responsibility of the program administrator to seek input from the full constituent base.

A Better Way

*Based on the information that Marie gathered from neighborhood contacts, she
determined that resources were available to assist some of her families with the cost
of their children's early childhood experience. Marie contacted local resource
and referral agencies to gather information about the variety of subsidy programs,
and she became involved with those programs. Marie has now seen an increase
in her enrollment and knows that while participating in these programs had not
been done in the past, it was a much better way to attract new families and offer
alternatives to families that were faced with decisions regarding their continued
enrollment.*

Developing the Program Philosophy

The first considerations that come to mind when thinking of the program philosophy are
likely to be the **epistemological** (the nature of learning) and **pedagogical** (the nature of
teaching) beliefs that will guide its operations. Although these are important considerations for all early care and education programs, they are not the only aspects of the program that should be guided by the program philosophy. Here again it is worth mentioning
the importance of alignment between a program's philosophy and its vision and mission.
The program philosophy not only includes the beliefs that guide the selection of curriculum, but it also should be the guide for all interactions within the organization, including
those between administration and staff, staff and clients (children and families), members
of the staff, and program personnel and representatives from the sponsoring agency and
the larger community. For example, if an administrator values the work of John Dewey
(1897), then the importance of democratic values should pervade all interactions among
staff, children, and families, resulting in the cultivation of a truly democratic culture
throughout the program.

The philosophy of an early childhood care and education program should be heavily
influenced by the knowledge base of the field. Although educators are not in total agreement regarding the research and theories that most accurately describe the nature of
development and learning, the field is unified in the understanding that practice should
be informed and guided by a combination of child development theory (that is based on
direct observation of children) and philosophical beliefs regarding the purpose and function of educational programs.

Brief Review of Early Childhood Theory and Philosophy

The sources that will help you ground your program in the field's traditional knowledge
base are the teachings of its major theoretical and philosophical thinkers. The field's
prominent theoretical positions come from (a) psychological theories that help answer
questions related to what and how children can learn and (b) the ecological perspective
of the child (the sociocultural context) that examines the impact of socialization processes
on the child's development. The philosophical position comes from how we value children individually and collectively, both now and in the future. That means our philosophy determines what we think children ought to know and be able to do. In addition to
these commonly relied upon sources that have long guided curriculum development and
selection, there is an emerging belief that education programs should base curricular and
instructional decisions on scientific evidence. It is important that we do not limit our

instructional selection decisions by what has been done (Wolery & Odom, 2000). Instead we should base our decisions on evidence, in the form of research, professional wisdom, and family and professional values.

Psychological Theories: Three major views of children's development and learning have influenced early childhood education. The first school of thought, which permeated the literature from the 1930s through the 1950s, is the **maturational view**, in which development is seen as the result of the maturation of structures within the individual (Gesell, 1931). According to this view, genetics substantially determines development (Plomin, 1997). Maturationists contend that teachers should provide educative experiences when the child shows interest. Today's maturationists believe that genes guide the process of maturation, and teaching or nurturing determines the specific content an individual learns (e.g., naming colors or naming days of the week or months of the year) and influences, to some degree, the rate and extent of learning. Through the use of norms, maturationists have developed "expectations" for children at different ages that prevent a child from being hurried by poorly timed experiences. In the 1950s, the integration of assumptions from psychoanalytic theories with the maturational theory brought about the child development approach (Jersild, 1946).

The second school of thought is the **behavioral-environmental view** (Skinner, 1938). In this view, the environment, rather than genetic construction, has the dominant role in learning. Learning is viewed as environmental inputs and behavioral outputs. The focus is not on mental processes but on eliciting and reinforcing verbal, perceptual, and motor behaviors. Behaviorism provides a theoretical rationale for the traditional view of teaching as direct instruction with sequenced goals and objectives and corresponding materials. The teacher describes or models desired behaviors and reinforces the child for making appropriate responses through effective praise. Some psychologists see this approach as having two serious limitations: (a) learning is limited to the acquisition of specific items of information and (b) the child's motivation for learning may be different from what the teacher intended (e.g., the child may be motivated by individual attention from the teacher rather than by his or her own success).

The third school of thought is the **constructivist view**. Constructivism, as formulated by Jean Piaget in the 1920s, saw children as interacting with their environment and constructing their own intellect. Constructivists, who directly challenge the behaviorists, view genetic makeup and environment (nature and nurture) as more or less equal in shaping development. Unlike the behaviorists, both maturationists and constructivists describe the child as moving from one stage to another. Unlike maturationists, who see the progression of development at more or less predictable ages, constructivists see development as the result of experiences with objects and consultation with people, coupled with the way the individual interprets, recognizes, or modifies experience.

Lev Vygotsky was a contemporary of Piaget. His theory (Vygotsky, 1978) complements Piaget's by emphasizing socially constructed knowledge. Although Vygotsky agreed with Piaget about the role of personal experiences, he also believed that knowledge was constructed as a result of social experiences with peers and adults. To Vygotsky, initial learning begins on the social plane—that is, learners are guided by the instruction of others. Cognitive strategies are eventually transferred to the psychological plane (i.e., humans learn of their own volition), but these learnings are permanently imbued with their social origins. Because he theorized that cognitive development occurs in a social-cultural context, his theory can be classified as **social constructivism**.

Ecological Perspectives: Ecological perspectives are concerned with how learning and development are influenced by the uniqueness of a person's environment. Bronfenbrenner (1979, 1989) asserted that an ecological perspective should be applied to all behaviors.

He suggested that people live in multiple environments simultaneously (Bronfenbrenner, 1986) and described the ecological context that a child experiences and that affects development as four overlapping systems:

- Microsystems are immediate and powerful socializers of children and include their family, child care or school, and peers.
- Mesosystems are interactions between microsystems, such as parent-teacher interactions or employer-supported child care.
- Exosystems, such as parents' jobs and their circle of friends, are made up of relationships children are not a part of but can impact them. An example of the impact of an exosystem is a job that requires a child's mother to travel out of town frequently.
- The macrosystem is made up of the socioeconomic, racial or ethnic, geographic, ideological, religious, and political cultures in the child's environment. Culture has a profound effect on children's experiences.

Two theories with ecological perspectives are of interest to early childhood educators. Erik Erikson's (1950) **psychosocial theory** describes how children develop the foundation for personality and mental health. Erikson noted that the environment shapes personality through both limitations and freedoms; that is, it provides the range of behaviors and learning circumscribed by society as directed through significant relations, such as with parents, and provides freedom of choice for the individual throughout his life. He stated that his eight developmental crises (e.g., sense of trust versus mistrust) are universal, but that the central problem (e.g., weaning) faced in a given crisis period is culturally determined.

As previously mentioned, Vygotsky's theory, which he aptly described as "mind in society" (Vygotsky, 1978), has an ecological perspective. The learner engages in problem-solving activities in which an adult or more capable peer guides and models (called *scaffolding* by Wood, Bruner, & Ross, 1976) ways to solve the task that are between each child's independent problem-solving capability and what he or she can do with assistance, called the **zone of proximal development (ZPD)**. Through participation in authentic cultural activities with social interactions, children learn cultural "tools of the mind" (i.e., symbol systems, such as language) and eventually use these tools to engage in internal cognitive activity. This is how the child's social environment provides the needed support system that allows the child to develop new competencies; that is, learning in a social context leads to development.

Philosophical Positions: Schools are designed to meet social purposes. This fact has been recognized since the time of Plato, who described education in *The Republic* as preparation of children to do the state's bidding. Like Plato, Dewey believed that education is the fundamental lever of social progress (Dewey, 1897). Conversely, during the 1960s, the emphasis on psychological theories almost overshadowed philosophical positions. Some early childhood professionals expressed the opinion that psychological theory alone could not be the sole basis for determining program design (Egan, 1983; Hunt, 1961).

Several program designers suggested that a blend of the psychological and philosophical views was needed. Kohlberg and Mayer (1972) stated that philosophically desirable ends must be rooted in the "facts of development": "Philosophical principles cannot be stated as ends of education until they can be stated psychologically" (p. 485). They also saw psychological theories as having either implicit or explicit values and stated that when theories are used as the basis for program design, they become ideologies.

The need for a philosophical position as a foundation for program design seems clear. Whether the lack of a philosophical basis is the result of a vague ideology, dominance of psychological theories, or other causes, the dilemma posed by this gap in value base was pinpointed by Sommerville (1982), who stated, "Children are going to school for an ever-longer period, but we seem less and less sure about what they should be getting from it" (p. 16). That observation leads us to pose this critical question, "What kind of U.S. citizen do we need to meet the challenges and opportunities of the 21st century?" Like Dewey (1916), we must emphasize the importance of communicating the values we will share in our programs and schools.

Several ideas for values have been suggested, including the Golden Rule, which is seen as a common value taught in most major religions. Other values often suggested are "honesty, caring, fairness, respect, and perseverance" (Smith, 1997, p. 233). NAEYC and the National Association of Early Childhood Specialists in State Departments of Education (1991) have suggested that a free society "should reflect the ideals of a participatory democracy, such as personal autonomy, decision making, equality, and social justice" (p. 28).

Synthesis of Theories and Philosophies: When NAEYC first issued its position statement on developmentally appropriate practice (DAP) (Bredekamp, 1987), the statement seemed to lean heavily on psychological theories for age-appropriate and individually appropriate curricula. Some asserted that DAP did not address (or obscured) other aspects of program planning (Kostelnik, 1992; Spodek, 1991; Swadener & Kessler, 1991). In an attempt to address these concerns, NAEYC (1997) issued a revised statement acknowledging that curricular decisions must be based on knowledge of child development and learning, an understanding of individual children's characteristics and strengths, and the social and cultural contexts in which children live. The most recent position statement on developmentally appropriate practice (2009), which has been expanded into book length by Copple and Bredekamp (2009), retains its emphasis on the importance of culturally, individually, and age-appropriate programming, while calling on early childhood professionals to reduce the achievement gap by improving teaching and learning.

Spodek's (1991) dimensions for program planning and evaluation present a synthesis of psychological theories, ecological perspectives, and philosophical positions. Spodek called for the use of these three dimensions for judging educational programs:

1. Developmental (considers what children can learn and the methodology employed in teaching)
2. Cultural (acknowledges society's values—that is, what we want children to be and become)
3. Knowledge (addresses what children need to know today and in the future to function successfully)

Katz (1991) recommends asking these three interrelated questions to identify appropriate program development: (a) What should be learned? (this deals with goals), (b) When should it be learned? (this deals with child development) and (c) How is it best learned? (this considers program implementation of goals).

PROGRAM COMPONENTS

Countless interactions occur between early childhood professionals and the children and families they serve each day. The sum of these interactions establishes the program's ultimate level of quality. Effective program planning, attending to the essential components of high-quality care and education, will increase the effectiveness and consistency of everyday interactions throughout the early care and education setting. When a program has earned a reputation for consistently achieving a high level of quality, families will seek admission. For instructional purposes we have identified three aspects of programs for young children that must be planned, implemented, and evaluated:

- Curriculum (programming and services directly designed to meet the care and education needs of the children and their families)
- Daily operations management (staff management, systems development, and daily problem solving)
- Financial management

Decisions made about each of these components have an effect on all other programmatic components. For example, if Sara, the new director of a proprietary child care center, was interested in establishing a child care program that included children with significant special needs with typically developing children, the curriculum must take into consideration the wide variety of abilities that the children in each classroom are likely to have. She would also have to ensure that the staff working in these classrooms have the requisite training, experience, and professional support so that each child receives the instruction and services that he or she is entitled to in order to develop to his or her maximum potential. Financial considerations might involve collaboration with the local agency that oversees the Individuals with Disabilities Education Act (IDEA) Part C programming to procure classroom materials and equipment that would lend themselves to the specific abilities and needs of all children in the program.

Curriculum: The Program for Children and Families

Early childhood curriculum includes much more than the daily activities and learning centers that teachers plan for their children. Curriculum includes all aspects of the program that influence what and how the children might learn. Such components include not only the daily planned engagements and the learning centers, but also the incidental conversations between caregivers and the children; the physical layout of the facility; the provision of materials and supplies to which the children have access; the expectations for children's behavior; procedures for transitioning between activities; arrangements and routines for eating, sleeping, and toileting/diapering; and the age grouping of the children. While the specific process for designing the curriculum is described elsewhere, at this stage in the planning process, it is important to begin investigating and identifying how you will go about curriculum design and implementation. In the next section, we will provide information for you to consider as you embark on deciding if you will use an established curriculum model (and which one) or whether you will design your own.

Deciding on Curriculum

Curriculum models have had a major impact on program goals, administrative and pedagogical decisions, and program outcomes. However, the very nature of models raises many issues and uncertainties.

Theory as Program Informant: Program developers often wonder if it is important to select one curriculum approach to ensure program consistency or if a curriculum model should be one of several program sources. Some programs are based on several developmental theories, and some professionals call for other disciplines, such as philosophy, sociology, and anthropology, to be used as informants during curriculum development.

Many professionals believe that the cultural context of children's development and experiences must inform curriculum development. That is, one size does not fit all. This emphasis means that the universality of development has been challenged (Gardner,

1999); that is, the fact that children develop many valued skills and knowledge in many types of environments is gaining support (Goncu, 1999). Ever since the 1980s, when the works of Vygotsky and Bronfenbrenner were being popularized, early childhood curriculum specialists have stressed the importance of basing curriculum on children's culture (Rogoff & Chavajay, 1995). Many researchers are now calling for culturally congruent approaches that take familial and community cultural values into account in assessing needs for a program service, in planning and delivery services, and in measuring program outcomes (Ladson-Billings, 2009). This approach is in sharp contrast to the idea of "cultural deprivation" that was prominent in the 1960s.

Another problem of using developmental theory as an informant is that theory is continually changing. Stott and Bowman (1996) discussed how programs informed by developmental or learning theory promote practices based on concepts no longer supported by research.

Finally, some professionals believe that curriculum models should not be standardized. They see children, teachers, and even families as designers of an emergent curriculum. This is the approach of the schools developed in Reggio Emilia, Italy, introduced to U.S. educators by the publication of *The Hundred Languages of Children* (Edwards, Gandini, & Forman, 1998). Conversely, the demand for accountability has led to interest in curriculum models developed by experts and then transported to various sites for implementation. Within-model variation has led to questions as to whether "typical" programs can have the same effects as exemplary programs using the same model (Barnett, 1986; Haskins, 1989). Kagan (1991) believed that transporting models will not work and that program developers should launch site-specific models. Furthermore, even if a model has been adopted at another site, it is not known how far the program can deviate from its model (e.g., in expenditures per child) before the positive effects disappear. Weikart (1981, 1983) emphasized that the success of a program for young children was based on the quality of the program implementation rather than the model.

Program Quality and Effectiveness of Models: Some professionals believe that the best way to promote program quality is through the adoption of models (Pogrow, 1996). Frede (1998) found the following commonalities in models with long-term effectiveness:

1. Coherent programs with curriculum content based on needed school-related knowledge and skills
2. Qualified teachers who use reflective teaching practices aided by qualified supervisors
3. Low teacher-child ratios and small group sizes
4. Collaborative relationships with parents

Search for the "Best" Model: Even among high-quality programs, effectiveness must be interpreted with caution. Programs differ in their target populations, duration, and administrative and pedagogical components. The effects of high-quality programs also depend on their reception by children, teachers, and families. Researchers need to determine which aspects of a program (curriculum, other aspects, or both) are beneficial and for whom (Barnett, Frede, Mobasher, & Mohr, 1987; Hauser-Cram, 1990; Horowitz & O'Brien, 1989; Jacobs, 1988; Powell, 1987a, 1987b; Sigel, 1990). This problem is confounded by the association between the curriculum goals selected and the teaching techniques employed (Miller, Bugbee, & Hyberton, 1985). Thus, one question that needs to be answered is, "Under what conditions does the model work?" (Guralnick, 1988; Meisels, 1985). Other questions also need to be answered:

1. Can exposure to a high-quality program serve as a barrier to environmental risks, or are other efforts needed (e.g., housing) to maximize benefits (Horowitz & O'Brien, 1989)?

2. Can benefits of quality programs accrue to *all* children? (Target populations to receive interventions have been rather limited.)

The search for the "best" model is still an issue. While there are links between programs' goals and child outcomes, differences of opinion remain about which outcomes are most important.

Services Offered

While the services offered by an early childhood program are likely to be focused primarily on the care and education of the children, how a single program defines appropriate care and education will be determined by the program's vision, sponsorship, and the values of the families and community served by the program. Some centers provide comprehensive care and education services that might include access to onsite health care professionals (medical, dental, counseling), transportation to and from the center and the child's home, extended hours of care or overnight services, after-school programming for elementary school children, care for children who are mildly ill, family (adult) education programming, child care staff professional development training, academic tutoring, or developmental screening for children with special needs. Once a center administrator has evaluated the needs of the stakeholders who are served by the program and decided on the services that will be offered, a significant amount of planning will be required to ensure that the center has the resources and professional knowledge and skill to effectively deliver needed services. (See Table 2.1 for a *Service Delivery Planning Sheet.*)

Daily Operations Management

Operations management includes the program administrator's responsibility to see that both process and structural program characteristics are consistently maintained. Part of the planning process is establishing systems to ensure that the program's clientele consistently

Table 2.1
Service Delivery Planning Sheet

Family/Community Need	Service to Meet the Need	Necessary Resources (Human or Material)	Anticipated Cost	Will Service Be Provided? Y/N and Rationale for Decision
List the results of your family/community needs assessment in this column. Reserve each block for individual needs.	Describe or list service(s) that is/are likely to address this need for families.	List any and all resources that will be necessary to deliver this service.	Identify the real cost of providing this service by identifying labor costs, facility costs, and any equipment and supplies that would be necessary to provide the service.	Based on the impact that this service might have on the perceived quality of the program, and the determination that the costs associated with the service are reasonable and affordable. Regardless of the decision, include a rationale for the service for later reference.

The Facility Maintenance Checklist below identifies the areas of the classroom that are to be monitored for cleanliness, organization, and maintenance. Each staff member is expected to complete this checklist at the conclusion of his/her shift. If an item on the checklist is not clean or organized, take the appropriate action to make sure that it is as it should be prior to leaving the facility. If an item is in need of repair, please take the appropriate action to ensure the children's safety. This may require that the item be removed from the children's access. If an item is broken and is not repairable, discard the item and make a note indicating that a replacement is needed. Use the notes section of the checklist to document anything that you are not able to address immediately and that might need the attention of the building administrator.

CLASSROOM: TEACHER:					4-year-olds	SHIFT: AM / MIDDAY / PM (Please Circle)
M	T	W	TH	F	**AREA**	**Notes**
					Entry Way to the Classroom: Free of litter; cubby area is organized; all children's names are clearly legible.	
					Block Center: Blocks and other toys are appropriately stored, clean, and in good repair.	
					Dramatic Play: All materials are in appropriate bins, and clothes are hanging.	
					Table Manipulatives: All materials are in labeled bins, and all labels are facing out.	
					Book Center: All books are organized on the book shelf. All books are right side up, with front cover facing out.	
					Circle Time Rug: White board is clean; rug is free of litter; materials for the next group time are prepared and in the green tub.	
					Snack/Lunch Area: All tables are clean; chairs are tucked under the table; trash cans are empty.	
					Rest Mats: Stacked neatly in storage closet.	
					WEEKLY TASKS	
▉					Sanitize blocks	
	▉				Dramatic play materials laundered	
		▉			Table manipulatives sanitized	
			▉		Rest mats sanitized	

Figure 2.2
Facility Checklist

receives the expected level of service. Systems are simply a structured plan for service delivery that includes explicit descriptions of desired results, comprehensively articulates the process for delivering services, and describes the process for continually monitoring that the desired results are actually achieved. For example, in an attempt to ensure that the facility is clean, organized, and well maintained, a child care administrator might design a *facility checklist* (Figure 2.2) that creates a system for making sure that the center is clean, organized, and well maintained. The checklist indicates the expected frequency of inspections. It is important to use templates that can be found through a variety of sources both online and through various professional development programs. This will reduce the amount of time spent "inventing" systems that may already exist and work well to meet the program's objectives.

In addition to checklists, program directors create staff manuals that articulate program goals and staff performance expectations. These manuals should include all necessary procedures to establish the minimum level of performance for all job responsibilities and duties.

Financial Management

The financial health of the early care and education program must be planned for and actively overseen. This includes monitoring the flow of funding (income and expenses) and reporting the financial health of the program to sponsoring organizations. The child care administrator needs to include in the planning stage how she intends to monitor the program's financial standing. For example, will she use a financial software program to help with billing and payroll or a comprehensive child care management tool such as *Child Care Manager* or *ProCare?* A number of programs are available; the choice will depend on how many locations are involved and whether the financial data will be Web based or on the center's computer. The administrator will also need to determine if the software will be proprietary or nonprofit and identify any local agencies or programs that might be able to subsidize the costs of providing high-quality care and education data management services.

DEVELOPING A VISION: THE FOUNDATION FOR ALL OTHER PROGRAM COMPONENTS

All high-quality early childhood programs have some characteristics in common. All adhere to appropriate licensing regulations. All are situated in facilities designed or adapted for use by young children, provide appropriate equipment and supplies to support caregiving routines and active and quiet play, plan carefully for the curriculum they offer the children in their care, and develop a plan for assessing their success.

Beyond these basic features, high-quality programs vary enormously. Little consensus exists as to the goals that are the best for children; no universally accepted strategies are available to reach these goals, and many approaches to program evaluation exist. A successful program administrator knows what he wants to accomplish, has determined the niche he hopes his center will fill, and has a vision for the program. This vision is not a roadmap to program implementation; instead, it is a broad and ambitious view of what the administrator hopes the program can accomplish and more specifically what the program will look like in operation. For example, the center may want to serve the children of low-income mothers pursuing higher education to increase their chances of breaking the cycle of poverty, or it may, instead, envision a small faith-based program to provide socialization experiences for the children of working mothers in an upper-middle-class neighborhood. No matter what the purpose of the program, the chances of realizing its potential will depend, in large measure, on how clearly the administrator understands what is to be accomplished.

Program planning should be a collaborative process.

In small, privately owned programs, the director (who is often the owner as well) usually identifies this vision by taking into account his professional and financial goals. In nonprofit programs and large proprietary programs, this strategic planning might be carried out collaboratively. The director may present her vision of the contribution she hopes the program will make to the community and the children and families it serves to the board of directors for discussion and approval, or the director may work with a board of advisors (a group constituted by families, staff, and community members) to develop the program's vision collaboratively. A program's vision should be future oriented. It is an opportunity to "dream big" and should describe what the program hopes to accomplish for children, families and the community.

In developing the vision for a center, it might be wise to consult potential stakeholders to conduct a needs assessment for the community in which the center is presently located or will be located in the future. The needs assessment should include a survey of what child care and education services are offered, stakeholder satisfaction with these services, and an assessment of the demographic information for the population of the area.

In addition, the vision for a program should be influenced by professional knowledge of what constitutes high-quality programming. Such programming draws upon theoretical, philosophical, and empirical understandings of the aims of education and best practices that support children's physical, social, emotional, and academic development and learning.

The vision for the program should include absolutely every aspect of the program, as each has an impact on all others (as discussed previously). When visualizing the ultimate goal of the program, the director could contemplate the sights, sounds, emotions, and outcomes of all stakeholders. Imagine walking into this ideal center: how are you greeted, what do you hear, what do you see, what do you smell, who are the people in this setting and how are they interacting with each other? As you observe and walk around the facility: what color are the walls, what types of materials are present? Once you have engaged in this visualization, you must then articulate this vision in a way that other people can understand. This is important because the next step in drafting your vision is sharing it with others. If the center that you are directing is currently in operation, you will need to share this vision with its staff, the families being served, and other community members who might have a stake in the ultimate outcome (e.g., public or private schools that typically accept the children once they graduate from your program). If, on the other hand,

Developing Your Vision

Step 1:   Reflect on your personal values, hopes, and dreams. Close your eyes and visualize the ideal child care and education program on a typical day of operation. In this visualization, take a tour of the facility and answer the following questions:

- What do you see on the walls, floor, and ceiling?
- What sounds do you hear?
- What are the children, families, and teachers doing?
- If you were to interview a child, parent, and teacher, how would they describe their experience at the center?
- What services are provided?
- What are the ultimate outcomes you hope to achieve through provision of these services?

Step 2:   Articulate a complete narrative description of this visualization. Be sure to include every perceptible characteristic (sights, sounds, smells, touch). As you are putting this visualization into words, think not only of the physical characteristics, but also the feelings that you experienced while touring this ideal setting.

Step 3:   Share this narrative with a group of stakeholders. Elicit feedback by asking the following questions:

- What aspects of this visualization do you find appealing?
- Are there aspects of typical child care programs that are absent from this description?
- Are there characteristics of the visualization that are troubling?
- What suggestions do you have to strengthen this vision?
- If the center is in operation, how might it be improved?

Step 4:   Taking the feedback from the stakeholder group meeting, revise the vision statement, print it out, frame it, and hang it in a location where you will see it frequently.

Figure 2.3
Vision Development Worksheet

the center is not yet operating, you will need to get input from potential stakeholders or, if appropriate, a board of directors/advisors. To help you with this process, use the worksheet presented in Figure 2.3.

DEVELOPING THE PROGRAM'S MISSION STATEMENT

Once the program's vision has been identified and agreed upon, the next step is to create the organization's mission statement. This is a clear expression of the program's purpose. A program's mission statement should be a simple, short, easy to remember statement that all employees will be able to understand, memorize, and use in their day-to-day practice as a guide for their work with children and families (Meshanko, 1996). The mission statement should be applicable to all decisions made throughout the program, including major programmatic decisions, classroom-level curriculum decisions, and decisions that impact individual children and families. Because of the broad reach and importance of the mission statement, it is highly recommended that all stakeholders be included in its development or refinement. A clear and well-understood mission statement should be the foundation for everything that happens in the center. It can be used by the director when she is coaching a teacher in appropriate guidance strategies, answering a father's questions about his toddler's day, and helping the cook plan healthy but affordable meals.

IMPLEMENTING THE PROGRAM

After carefully considering all the factors that influence the program and after the vision and mission of the program have been articulated, the director or board must **operationalize the program**. The "ideal" program seems to be the one that best suits the needs of the particular children and families served. Personal beliefs, whether an articulated or implied set of values, influence decision making.

To operationalize the program, the director needs to develop and describe its pedagogical and operational components. Use the mission statement to determine its pedagogical components by asking the following questions:

1. What are the goals and objectives of my early childhood program?   To provide an environment conducive to the development of the whole child? To develop creativity? To build a healthy self-concept? To spur self-direction in learning? To teach young children academic skills? To provide intensive instruction in areas of academic deficits and thinking skills?

Creating a vision and mission involves actually visualizing the types of experiences you hope the children will engage in.

2. What provisions for children's individual differences are consistent with my program's goals?   How are individual differences accommodated in all academic areas, including all developmental areas (psychomotor, affective, cognitive)? How do classroom environments and activities reflect children's cultures? How are activities presented to support children's multiple intelligences?

3. What schedule format is needed to facilitate my program's objectives?   A full- or half-day schedule? The same session length for all children, or session length tailored to each child's and parent's needs? A predetermined or flexible daily schedule based on children's interests?

Administrators must also consider questions pertaining to the operational components of the program, such as the following:

1. What staff roles are necessary to implement the learning environment as described in my program philosophy?   How many teachers, assistant teachers, floaters, substitutes, and support personnel do I need? How will I screen applicants to be certain my staff is made up of teachers and caregivers who can develop learning environments that support child-directed and adult-led instructional activities; infant/toddler caregivers who understand how caregiving routines contribute to very young children's learning and development; office staff who can assume some of the center's bookkeeping and record-keeping tasks; and food service, bus driver, and custodial personnel who will support the program's instructional and administrative staff?

2. What staff positions (director, teachers, assistant teachers, floaters, cooks) are needed to execute my program?   What academic or experiential qualifications are required or desired for each position? What type of orientation or in-service training is needed? What child-staff ratio is required?

3. What equipment and materials are required?   What kinds of self-correcting materials and those that encourage creativity best fit the children's needs? What furniture will support independence, such as low tables for toddlers instead of high chairs, or serving dishes so that meals can be served family style? How do we provide children opportunities to choose from a variety of meaningful, hands-on activities?

4. What physical arrangement is compatible with the goals of my program?   How are classrooms arranged to ensure constant supervision; opportunities for individual, small, and large group activities; and providing children a sense of privacy? How does the playground support social and language development along with physical skills?

And then the crucial question must be answered: "Do the answers have a supportable rationale?" Make sure that you carefully consider your answers. Try to weed out irrelevant beliefs, inappropriate values, and outdated information. Is what you have written culturally relevant, supported by research, developmentally appropriate, and timely?

PROGRAM EVALUATION AND GOAL DEVELOPMENT

Once a new program's vision and mission statements have been developed and agreed upon and an implementation plan has been adopted by all appropriate stakeholders, the next step in the process of a new program's development is to assess its potential to fulfill its stated mission and vision.

Existing programs should evaluate their success meeting the program's agreed-upon vision and mission. This program evaluation should be comprehensive, identifying areas of strength and those needing improvement. Evaluation should include assessments of the administrator's and the staff's effectiveness; fidelity of curriculum implementation; and

Table 2.2
Assessing Local Needs Through Culturally Sensitive Questions

- What services do the families in this community want and need?
- What are the values of the families in this community (e.g., tradition versus innovation, competition versus cooperation, independence versus interdependence)?
- What communication skills are needed to work effectively with the families in this community?
- What leadership style is likely to work well in this community?
- What services are now available in this community? Are there children or families who do not have access to locally available services that they need? Are any cultural barriers preventing these children or families from accessing the services they need?
- What human resources are available in this community?
- What material resources (e.g., parks, health care providers, social service agencies) are available in this community?
- How are these resources perceived by the local population? Is there an institution such as a church or a community center that is the hub of the local service network?

measures of child, family, and employee satisfaction. Programs that incorporate a community's strengths and address local needs and interests effectively is often referred to as being **culturally competent** or **sensitive** (see Table 2.2).

EVALUATING THE PROGRAM

Administrators are held accountable for the programs under their leadership and direction. With an increased demand for excellence, evaluation has become one of an administrator's most significant responsibilities. One reason is that funding sources are likely to require evaluation reports. In addition, the staff and participating families make judgments about the program's quality on a day-to-day basis. Administrators need information to respond to each of these groups.

A discussion of evaluation leads to classification of the types of evaluation. Dopyera and Lay-Dopyera (1990) identified two types of evaluation: intuitive and formal.

Intuitive Evaluation

Intuitive evaluation might be called a personal construct or practical knowledge. It is a notion about what constitutes the right way to achieve a goal. Unlike planned formal evaluation, intuitive evaluation concerns how people perform on a minute-by-minute basis.

Early childhood teachers and administrators have notions about their professional practice. Although these notions guide their day-to-day practice, they are difficult to articulate. These notions come to light when a clash occurs between one's own ideas or actions and those of someone else or when the outcomes of what one expects and what happens differ.

Studies of intuitive evaluation (Clark & Peterson, 1986; Katz, 1984; Spodek, 1987) have established two points:

1. Early childhood educators take their book-learned knowledge and guided observations and integrate them with their values and practical knowledge. This knowledge is integrated by each individual teacher from his or her theory-based knowledge, accumulated experience, and understanding of milieu and self.

2. Intuitive evaluation is important because educators must often make judgment calls so quickly that they do not have time to reflect on theory and empirical findings; thus, intuitive evaluation guides practice.

Formal Evaluation

Formal (or planned) evaluation has its roots in funding agencies' demands for accountability. With an increasing number of mandates for evaluation, there has been an increase in the number of available measures of program quality, and activities involving formal evaluation have increased. Many educational endeavors require formal evaluation, such as needs assessment, program analysis, cost effectiveness (the effectiveness of a program as it relates to cost per child), and program impact (positive changes in the child or family that affect society).

Administrators must determine the appropriate type of formal evaluation to serve their needs (objectives-based evaluation, standards-based evaluation, and evaluation research). Both objectives-based and standards-based evaluation address accountability. Evaluation research is concerned with the interplay of various aspects of a given program related to outcomes.

Objectives-Based Evaluation: **Objectives-based evaluation** focuses on what children achieve as a result of participation in a specific program and is the most common form of formal evaluation. Thus, the criteria used for evaluation are program specific (developed by examining the program's goals and objectives). The analyses of evaluation data provide information on the degree to which a program's goals and objectives are met.

Evaluation may be conducted at two points in the program. **Formative evaluation** is used to determine the effectiveness of various aspects of the program (e.g., grouping practices) while program changes are still being made. **Summative evaluation** determines the effectiveness of the overall program at some ending point.

Standards-Based Evaluation: **Standards-based evaluation** is an appraisal of a program based on a set of standards (criteria) developed outside the specific program. These standards may be deemed worthwhile by a professional association (e.g., the NAEYC/National Academy of Early Childhood Program Accreditation or National Accreditation Commission for Early Care and Education Programs), the funding or monitoring agency (e.g., Head Start Performance Objectives), or a researcher (e.g., the Early Childhood Environment Rating Scale).

Following are several standards-based evaluations that focus on the overall environment of the classroom or program and are designed to measure the quality of the learning environment.

1. **High/Scope Program Quality Assessment (PQA).** The PQA was developed by the High/Scope Educational Research Foundation (1998). The PQA has 72 items that cover these attributes of quality: learning environment, daily routine, adult-child interaction, curriculum planning and assessment, parent involvement and family services, staff qualifications and staff development, and program management. Each item is scored on a 5-point rating scale.

2. **Early Childhood Environment Rating Scale–Revised (ECERS-R).** The ECERS was developed by Harms and Clifford in 1980 and revised most recently in 2005. They view an early childhood program as an ecological system with more parts than just the individuals within the program. The ECERS is used to examine 43 attributes that cover these areas of quality: space and furnishings, personal care routines, language and reasoning, activities, interactions, program structure, and parents and staff. Ratings are given

for each area, and a total rating can be calculated for each group. Scores on all the groups within a center may be compiled to get a total quality score.

3. Family Child Care Environment Rating Scale—Revised (FCCERS-R). The FCCERS was developed by Harms and Clifford in 1998 and revised most recently in 2007. It follows the same pattern as their ECERS. The FCCRS-R is used to examine 38 attributes that cover these areas of quality: space and furnishings for care and learning, basic care, language and reasoning, learning activities, social development, and adult needs. Each item is described in four levels of quality: inadequate, minimal, good, and excellent. Eight supplementary items are provided for homes enrolling children with special needs.

4. Infant/Toddler Environment Rating Scale—Revised (ITERS-R). The ITERS was developed by Harms, Cryer, and Clifford in 1990 and revised, most recently in 2006. It follows the same pattern as their ECERS and FCCERS. The ITERS-R consists of 39 items for the assessment of the quality of center-based child care for children up to age 30 months. Items are organized under these categories: space and furnishings, personal care routines, listening and talking, activities, interaction, program structure, and parents and staff. Each item is presented on a 7-point scale, with descriptors for 1 (inadequate), 3 (minimal), 5 (good), and 7 (excellent).

5. School-Age Care Environment Rating Scale (SACERS). The SACERS was developed by Harms, Jacobs, and White (1995) and follows the same pattern as the ECERS, FCCERS, and ITERS. The SACERS consists of 49 items for the assessment of the quality of child care programs serving children ages 5 to 12. Items are organized under these attributes: space and furnishings, health and safety, activities, interactions, program structure, staff development, and supplementary items (for children with special needs).

6. Assessment of Practices in Early Elementary Classrooms (APEEC). The APEEC was developed by Hemmeter, Maxwell, Ault, and Schuster (2001) and follows the same pattern as the ECERS, FCCERS, ITERS, and SACERS. The APEEC, designed for kindergarten through grade 3 classrooms, consists of 16 items in these domains of classroom practice: physical environment, instructional context, and social context.

Specific aspects of programs can be assessed as well. Some examples include (a) Child's Adjustment to the Program (Nilsen, 2000, p. 265), (b) Early Childhood Work Environment Survey (Bloom, 2010), (c) Parent Evaluation of Child Care Program (*Child Care Information Exchange,* June 1989, pp. 25–26), and (d) Safety Checklist (Frost, 1992, pp. 346–350).

Researchers are working on instruments needed for empirical studies of DAP. Hitz and Wright (1988) developed an instrument to note the degree of change in academic emphasis of early childhood programs (from developmentally inappropriate practices [DIP] to DAP). Bryant, Clifford, and Peisner (1991) developed an instrument to determine teachers' knowledge and attitudes about DAP. Similarly, Oakes and Caruso (1990) measured teachers' attitudes about authority in the classroom and developed observation instruments to confirm the "self-reports." Charlesworth, Hart, Burts, Thomasson, Mosley, and Fleege (1993) thought of DIP and DAP on a continuum. They developed the Teachers Belief Statements, the Instructional Activities Scale, and the Checklist for Rating Developmentally Appropriate Practice in Kindergarten Classrooms. There are additional standards-based assessments you may want to investigate.

An Important Consideration

Evaluation generates information that should be used for program enhancement. The most meaningful evaluations are often those stimulated by internal factors rather than those resulting from external mandates. Evaluations mandated by external sources are perceived as useful only when data are also used for local program purposes. Program quality needs to go beyond structural variables that researchers have associated with high-quality child and family outcomes (Katz, 1999) and also include process characteristics such as teacher-child interaction.

To overcome the concerns expressed about the uses of assessment data and the potential consequences to program personnel, staff must acknowledge the interdependent nature of all program components. Evaluation must include all components and all people involved in a program and be ongoing. Pressure for answers from within and without the program will not seem so unbearable, or the difficulties involved in overcoming content and methodological problems so insurmountable, if one keeps in mind the major purpose of program evaluation, which is to identify opportunities for improvement. If evaluation is seen as a means for program improvement, it becomes a continuous process, and its results become starting points for future planning.

SUMMARY

The administrator's main task is providing leadership in program planning, implementation, and evaluation. The administrator, as an early step, will identify and articulate the vision that she has for the program. The factors that should influence the program vision are a synthesis of community and stakeholder values, empirical evidence, psychological theories, ecological perspectives, and philosophical positions. Once the program vision has been developed, a succinct mission statement should be created that may effectively communicate to stakeholders what the program will do and can be used by all staff members as guidance in all interactions with children and families.

The administrator must then understand and choose a curriculum approach and implementation plan that addresses the needs of all stakeholders and, as supported by evidence, will likely result in desired outcomes for children and families. A curriculum model consists of the program philosophy, the administrative and pedagogical components, and the program evaluation. The development of the program's vision and mission are critical because programmatic research points to a consistent relationship between program focus and program outcomes. Every aspect of implementation of the program's administrative and pedagogical components should be in keeping with the program's vision, mission, and philosophy.

The administrator's final step is making program evaluation plans. Evaluation may be of two types: intuitive and formal. Unplanned, intuitive evaluation is constantly happening; thus, attempts should be made to understand the criteria used by those involved in the local program in their intuitive evaluations. Formal or planned evaluation may be objectives based, standards based, or outcomes based. The administrator and the staff should jointly determine the reasons for evaluation (e.g., needs assessment, program effectiveness), the appropriate type of evaluation, the specific instruments to be used, and the timing of the implementation for both formative and summative evaluations. Evaluation results should provide feedback for future program planning.

USEFUL WEBSITES

Child Care Evaluation Checklist, provided by the Marin Child Care Council

www.mc3.org/child_care_evaluation_checklist.php

This is a website with resources to provide parents with options and information about early care and education programs.

Tips and Tools on Child Care, developed by ZERO TO THREE

www.zerotothree.org/early-care-education/child-care/

ZERO TO THREE is a nonprofit that focuses on quality programming for children from birth to age 3. This resource has links to information on twins in child care, starting child care, and other topics of interest to families and directors alike.

TO REFLECT

1. A local corporation is interested in providing child care for its employees. The personnel manager has been asked to ascertain whether the corporation should plan for an onsite program or make a community investment in child care (through encouraging family satellite programs or using corporate reserve slots). What type of data should the personnel manager collect and analyze before making a decision?

2. A potential proprietor is considering child care as a small business. As the first step, a needs assessment instrument should be devised and implemented. What types of items should be included in the needs assessment instrument?

CHECK AND APPLY YOUR UNDERSTANDING

1. Consider the components of a program philosophy and write a sample philosophy that you might use in an early childhood program.

2. List several examples of characteristics that might be useful in determining the diversity of the community around a child care program that you are familiar with.

3. Evaluate the vision of a national company and consider whether or not, in your opinion, a vision is part of that company's culture.

4. Take a few minutes to select your favorite product or service. Go to its website and research the company's mission statement. Think through the experience that you have personally had with that product or service and make notes about how it measures up to what is stated in that mission statement. Would you make changes to the mission statement based upon your personal experience?

5. Discuss the components of the operational model that you believe are critical in an early care and education program.

6. Think about what the evaluation tool for your program would look like. Write down your thoughts and consider with whom you would share the results of the program evaluation. Why is it important to share the results of each evaluation?

Understanding Regulations, Accreditation Criteria, and Other Standards of Practice

Learning Outcomes

After studying this chapter, you should be able to:

1. Compare and contrast your state's child care licensing regulations and selected accreditation standards, identifying ways in which they are similar and different.

2. Develop a strategy to participate in your state's Quality Rating and Improvement System (QRIS) and, if appropriate, to move to a higher level.

3. Summarize applicable employment laws and other provisions that protect employees from discriminatory practices.

Marie's Experience

Marie has been successful over the years in keeping her center in compliance with all licensing regulations. She is proud of her teachers and is confident that the center consistently goes above and beyond licensing provisions designed simply to keep children healthy and safe. She knows that the center provides high-quality care to the children it serves, but it has never pursued accreditation or participated in her state's optional Quality Rating and Improvement System (QRIS) because of the time and effort involved in satisfying its requirements. Her families have confidence in her program and do not seem to need this additional assurance that it provides high-quality services day in and day out.

Large numbers of families rely on out-of-home care for their infants, toddlers, preschoolers, and school-age children during the workday. In 2009, there were 329,882 licensed child care facilities in the United States with a capacity to serve more than 9.8 million children. About 60% of the licensed facilities are child care homes; more than 75% of the children served in out-of-home settings are enrolled in child care centers (National Child Care Information Center and Technical Assistance Center [NCCIC]/National Association for Regulatory Administration [NARA], 2010).

Regulations and standards guide all aspects of the life of an early childhood care and education program—its children and their families, its staff, director, and board. They are designed to give

NAEYC Administrator Competencies addressed in this chapter:

Management Knowledge and Skills

2. Legal and Fiscal Management Knowledge and application of the advantages and disadvantages of different legal structures. Knowledge of different codes and regulations as they relate to the delivery of early childhood program services. Knowledge of child custody, child abuse, special education, confidentiality, anti-discrimination, insurance liability, contract, and labor laws pertaining to program management.

5. Program Operations and Facilities Management Knowledge and application of policies and procedures that meet state/local regulations and professional standards pertaining to the health and safety of young children.

Early Childhood Knowledge and Skills

5. Children with Special Needs Knowledge of licensing standards, state and federal laws (e.g., ADA, IDEA) as they relate to services and accommodations for children with special needs.

10. Professionalism Knowledge of laws, regulations, and policies that impact professional conduct with children and families. Knowledge of center accreditation criteria.

families that rely on child care peace of mind that the health and welfare of their children are safeguarded while they are away from home. Although regulations and standards may be defined in various ways, we use the following definitions in this book:

1. A *regulation* is a binding rule that has been created by a governing body outside of the early childhood program.
2. A **standard** is a statement of expectations for program characteristics and performance.

Regulations and standards are closely linked. Together they create benchmarks related to a program's facility, programming, staffing, and other dimensions of quality. Child care programs must comply, for example, with licensing regulations related to staff-child ratios, that is, the number of children one adult may legally be responsible for.

While state child care regulations set a minimum accepted standard of care, accreditation standards identify criteria that have been shown to improve the quality of children's experiences. Your state's regulations might allow one caregiver to care for up to five infants, but the NAEYC Accreditation Standards allow one caregiver to be responsible for no more than four infants at a time (NAEYC, 2011).

Regulations and standards play an important role as programs develop policies and procedures that guide its day-to-day implementation.

CONSIDERING REGULATIONS

Regulations are the rules, directives, statutes, and standards that prescribe, direct, limit, and govern early childhood programs. They set minimum standards to (a) protect young children's health and safety, (b) ensure equal access to care for eligible children and families, and (c) ensure compliance with zoning and other business-related aspects of the center's operation. These regulations are standards of practice no program is expected to fall below.

Some of the specific regulations that apply to a particular program depend on the auspices under which it operates. Is it a nonprofit organization that is part of a public elementary school or operated by a faith-based organization? Is the center a federally funded Head Start or a corporate-sponsored work-site program? Is it part of a for-profit chain or operated by an individual entrepreneur? Is it located in an urban, suburban, or rural setting? The next section identifies the kinds of regulations, rules, and statutes you must be aware of and, when applicable, abide by when you are a center director.

Specific Types of Regulations

If you are creating a new center, you are likely to be particularly attentive to regulations related to zoning and the required square footage of classrooms. These are two of many issues that must be addressed before you receive a Certificate of Occupancy, a statement from the appropriate local governmental agency indicating that a building is suitable for use. A new center must have a Certificate of Occupancy before applying for initial licensure and permission to legally operate as a child care program.

Other regulations, such as those governing staff-child ratio and group size, affect the center's day-to-day operations and require you to be constantly vigilant to be certain you are in compliance. Our discussion will begin with issues related to facilities and the business of child care. Most of these regulations apply to all programs (e.g., zoning, fire regulations, and laws governing services for children with special needs). Other regulations apply only to specific kinds of programs (e.g., public schools or Head Start).

Regulations to Address When Establishing a New Program

Zoning Regulations: Zoning regulations define how land may be used. State zoning laws allow each city and town to divide its land into districts. Within those districts, the municipality can enact zoning codes that regulate land use and can include specifications related to buildings' structure and their use. Generally, zoning regulations become more stringent as population density increases; that is, more rules about land use are likely in the center city than in the suburbs, and suburbs are likely to have more regulations than do rural areas.

Interestingly, child care is frequently treated as a "problem use." Child care centers are often prohibited from residential neighborhoods because of concerns about the noise and traffic they are likely to generate. They are also often not permitted in commercial areas because business districts are not considered good places for children. Some states are working to prevent localities from enacting restrictive policies related to the construction and operation of child care facilities.

Building Codes and Requirements Related to Fire Safety and Sanitation: Building codes and regulations related to fire safety and sanitation are parts of laws addressing public safety and health. A child care center in a particular locale may be covered under municipal ordinances or locally enforced state regulations. Building codes address the structure's wiring, plumbing, and building materials. Fire regulations describe allowable types of building construction and set standards related to regulating alarm systems and fire extinguishers. They specify how combustible materials are to be stored and require that building evacuation plans be posted. The *Life Safety Code Handbook* available for purchase from the National Fire Protection Association (NFPA) provides guidelines for appropriate fire codes for centers, group homes, and family child care.

Sanitation codes are mainly concerned with food service operations; diaper changing and bathroom facilities; and procedures for washing toys, equipment, and furniture. Sanitation standards specify, for example, where sinks are to be located (i.e., in the same area as the toilet and in the central diapering area) and require that washable toys be sanitized daily. These issues are often addressed in licensing standards established and enforced by state departments of social services but are sometimes the responsibility of local health departments. The American Academy of Pediatrics (AAP), American Public Health Association (APHA), and the National Resource Center for Health and Safety in Child Care (NRCHSCC) have jointly produced *Caring for Our Children: National Health and Safety Performance Standards: Guidelines for Out-of-Home Child Care,* 3rd edition (AAP/APHA/ NRCHSCC, 2011), a comprehensive discussion of recommended standards for child care, including the rational for suggested standards, references, and comprehensive appendices. This edition includes a number of new standards, including recommendations for increasing children's physical activity, limits to screen time, preventing children's exclusion from services, and mental health education. The website for this comprehensive resource is included in the list at the end of this chapter.

Regulations That Guide Program Development and Implementation

Licensing: Minimal Quality Regulations: **Licensing** is the procedure by which a person, association, or corporation obtains from its state licensing agency a permit to operate or continue operating a child care facility. The District of Columbia, the Department of Defense, and 49 states (all except Idaho) license child care facilities (NCCIC/NARA, 2010). The licensing agency (typically the state's department of human services, social services, or health) enforces the baseline requirements established by state governments and makes decisions to issue or deny license applications.

Child care licenses are valid for varied periods of time. Twelve states offer non-expiring licenses; in 31 states, a license is good for 1 or 2 years; and licenses are good for varied periods of time in the other 8 states (NCCIC/NARA, 2010).

Features of Child Care Licensing Laws.   A **child care center** is generally defined as a nonresidential facility providing child care services for less than 24 hours a day (NCCIC/NARA, 2010). Many states have specific standards for small family child care homes (usually up to 6 children); large family or group child care homes (typically 7 to 12 children cared for by the provider and a full-time assistant); and child care centers serving 13 or more children on a regular basis, usually more than 30 days per year (AAP/APHA/NRCH-SCC, 2011). In addition, some states have separate regulations for programs that serve school-age children, infants and toddlers, and mildly ill children or provide drop-in services (NCCIC/NARA, 2010). Each state defines these terms and explains the rules that govern program operations in their regulations.

Regulations are generally reviewed by an appointed child care advisory board which reviews regulations on a mandated cycle. States are encouraged to take care that this advisory board reflects the state's cultural and ethnic diversity and includes representatives from all stakeholder groups: for-profit and not-for-profit operators and caregivers, parents of children enrolled in child care, agency personnel, child development and health care professionals, citizens, and politicians (AAP/APHA/NRCHSCC, 2011). This board typically proposes changes to licensing regulations based on current beliefs about how to safeguard children's physical and emotional well-being.

The advisory board usually presents proposed regulations in a series of public hearings, giving interested citizens the opportunity to express their concerns and/or support for recommended changes to existing regulations. Changes to the proposed regulations may be necessary before revised regulations are submitted to the state legislature for adoption. Some states provide a gradual phase-in of new rules, particularly when the changes have economic ramifications as do those affecting group size or staff-child ratios.

Child Care Center Regulations

Regulatory laws governing child care centers differ widely from state to state.[1] Their purpose is to set minimum standards of care; that is, they are designed to prevent harm to children rather than to ensure the provision of exemplary care. They must balance the state's responsibility to protect children in out-of-home care with the pressures of the marketplace, that is, the ability of providers to meet the established minimum standards. The National Association of Child Care Resource and Referral Agencies (NACCRRA) regularly compares the regulations of all states and the Department of Defense (DOD), which regulates child care programs serving military personnel. The report released in 2011 identifies 15 benchmarks that consider the adequacy of regulations related to safety, health, and early learning, as well as provisions for regulatory oversight and enforcement. It also compares results with findings of the 2007 and 2009 reports. States' regulations are rated on a 150-point scale. The most recent report indicates that the adequacy of regulations ranges from 129 for the DOD to 17 for Idaho, which lacks state-level child care regulations. The authors conclude "state standards vary greatly and few really set policies to keep children safe and in a setting to promote their healthy development" (National Association of Child Care Resource & Referral Agencies [NACCRRA], 2011, p. 59). They recommend that the U.S. Congress raise the standards for programs eligible for federal child care block grant subsidies, a strategy they propose will motivate states to revise regulations to mandate higher levels of quality.

[1]In this discussion of child care regulations, the District of Columbia is considered to be a state.

It is important that all personnel attend training sessions to help them become thoroughly familiar with applicable licensing regulations.

All states' regulations are now online. You may want to compare your state's regulations with those of another nearby state to identify how they are alike and how they are different. To review regulations of a specific state, follow the links from the website of the National Resource Center for Health and Safety in Child Care and Early Education listed at the end of this chapter.

Areas addressed in most licensing codes include the following (AAP/APHA/NRCH-SCC, 2011):

1. Introduction to licensing laws and procedures. For purposes of licensing, states permit individuals to care for other people's children if they apply for and are given permission (a license) by the authorized agency of the government. The introductory section of licensing regulations defines terms such as *child care center* and *director*; identifies the programs that must be licensed and, when appropriate, those that are exempt; describes how applicants obtain and submit an application for a license; identifies required inspections and approvals; indicates the duration of the license and describes the renewal process; identifies situations that would result in license denial, revocation, or nonrenewal; stipulates how the license is to be posted on the premises; and provides other state-specific general information. (An overview of licensing procedures is provided in Figure 3.1.)

2. Organization and administration. State licensing laws require an applicant to identify the program's purposes and its sponsoring organization, to indicate whether the program is for-profit or not-for-profit, and to describe its administrative structure (e.g., director, board of directors). They often require programs to have policies describing the services they provide children (e.g., eligibility and admission criteria, termination policies, nondiscrimination provision, and fees) and may also require plans to ensure the center's financial solvency.

3. Staffing. This section of the regulations describes required staff-child ratios, educational prerequisites, mandated criminal background and abuse and neglect registry checks, and the minimum age requirements for center employees. Regulations might, for example, permit a 16-year-old with a high school diploma or GED (certificate given for completing tests of General Educational Development considered to be equivalent to a high school diploma) to serve as a director in one state but might require the director to be at least 21 and hold a bachelor's degree in another. Likewise, there are states in which

1. Obtain zoning approval.

2. Submit building plans to the fire marshal for approval.

3. Schedule fire, sanitation, and child care licensing inspections (to occur in that order).

4. Recruit employees to fill all staff positions. Become familiar with state licensing regulations, paying particular attention to:

- Background checks required of staff
- Age, education, and experience requirements for director and other staff
- Requirement that staff trained in first aid and CPR be onsite during operating hours

5. Post license and open for business.

Figure 3.1

An Overview of the Process of Opening a Licensed Child Care Center

an employee enrolled in high school or a GED program is qualified to be a lead teacher, and in other states lead teachers must hold, at a minimum, a CDA (Child Development Associate) credential (NCCIC/NARA, 2011). We will address issues related to staff requirements in more detail later in this chapter.

4. Facilities, supplies, equipment, and transportation. Licensing codes typically require applicants to satisfy health department and fire marshal requirements before applying for a license to operate a child care center. All states that regulate child care specify the amount of indoor space (square footage) available per child. Most states regulate the amount of outdoor space, require that indoor and outdoor equipment be safe and in good repair, and require outdoor fencing. The majority of states require centers to ensure children's security by keeping daily attendance records and establishing policies for accepting children in the morning and releasing them at the end of the day. Many require programs to create emergency preparedness plans and to conduct regular fire drills. Almost all states have regulations related to transporting children in vehicles. Most require the driver to have a valid driver's license, address the driver's minimum age, and require the vehicle be kept in good repair. Many require children to be secured in safety restraints (NCCIC/NARA, 2010).

5. Health and safety. All states that regulate child care require participating children to have either specified immunizations before they are allowed to participate or documentation indicating why they are exempt from this requirement. All also describe procedures for administering medications to children while they are in care. In addition, most require children and staff to have a physical exam. Other health and safety issues often addressed in regulations include descriptions of required health forms for children and staff, requirements for reporting injuries and infectious illnesses, hand-washing requirements for children and staff, diapering procedures, rules related to smoking and firearms, and guidelines for keeping animals (NCCIC/NARA, 2010).

6. Activities and equipment. Almost all states (49 of 51) have some regulations specifying the types of activities centers must make part of children's daily schedule. Regulations typically require active and quiet play indoors and out, nap or rest time, individual and group activities, and regular meals and snacks. Many states also require programs to explicitly address social, emotional, physical, cognitive, and language and literacy development. Specific regulations are likely to require, at a minimum, fine-motor toys and manipulatives, books and materials to support literacy, props to support dramatic play and make believe, and art supplies (NCCIC/NARA, 2010).

7. Discipline. All states that license child care centers have regulations related to behavior management, guidance, and discipline. Many states stipulate that programs use "no harsh discipline" and prohibit specific practices such as forced napping, locked time-out, or yelling at children. Two states allow corporal punishment under certain circumstances (NCCIC/NARA, 2010).

8. Parent involvement and communication. Most states require that parents be involved in, and informed about, the program their child attends. Strategies for involving families include providing them with written copies of the program's policies and procedures, logging children's daily activities, regularly scheduling parent/teacher conferences, and permitting families to visit the facility during hours of operation with and without prior notice (NCCIC/NARA, 2010).

9. Nutrition and food services. All states that regulate child care specify the required nutritional content of the meals and snacks served to children while in care. Most have specific rules related to feeding infants, indicate the number of snacks and meals for older children and the time intervals between them, and require the center to post a menu of the meals and snacks it serves (NCCIC/NARA, 2010).

Application Activity

Working in small groups, refer to your state's online child care regulations to become familiar with requirements related to required activities and equipment (go to nrckids.org and click on the link for State Licensing and Regulation Information). Assume you have the basic tables, chairs, resting cots, and bookshelves to equip a class-room for infants, toddlers, and 3- or 4-year-olds. What would you purchase if you had $1,000 to spend to enhance the collection of fine-motor toys, books and literacy materials, dramatic play, or art center? Use a catalog or the website of a school-supply company (see Appendix 1) to identify specifically what you would select.

Family Child Care Regulations

Regulation of small and large family child care remains inconsistent. Forty-four states (86%) regulate small family child care homes and 39 states (76%) regulate large group homes, but this oversight remains largely voluntary. Many states continue to struggle with the fact that the majority of child care homes remain outside the state's regulatory system (NCCIC/NARA, 2010).

Regulations that apply to family child care homes are typically similar to those for child care centers. The main differences in the family child care regulations concern

1. How the number of children will be counted (all children on the premises for supervision, including the caregiver's own children, are counted in the home's approved capacity)
2. How keeping infants and toddlers affects the count (most family child care homes have mixed-age groups)
3. How the inside and outside areas of the home, and the family's personal possessions, must be childproofed to ensure children's health and safety.

These accident-prevention regulations are likely to address how children are to be protected from dangerous features, such as stairs, and dangerous items, such as weapons, which are found in some homes.

Some professionals question whether center-based regulations should apply to family child care programs. Others are concerned, however, that regulations for home-based centers remain largely voluntary.

Registration is a process by which providers certify that they have complied with a state's licensing regulations. Eligible programs that complete registration are often qualified to participate in assistance programs such as the U.S. Department of Agriculture food program or are able to accept children who receive a child care subsidy.

Registered providers are usually required to certify that they have met identified health and fire standards. Some states also require registered child care homes to conduct criminal background checks on individuals who work with or are around children. In many instances, however, registration is simply a sign-up procedure.

Concerns About Regulatory Policies

In spite of advocates' efforts to enact child care licensing regulations that set high expectations, concerns about the quality of current licensing standards remain:

1. Some states' child care regulations exempt a large number of programs. The most frequent exemptions apply to part-day programs, those operated by faith-based organizations, public schools, and day camps, (NCCIC/NARA, 2010). After-school programs have, historically, been unregulated. This gap is closing, however. To date, 13 states have adopted abbreviated licensing standards for services for school-age children. These less comprehensive regulations most often create standards related to the physical environment, child-staff ratios and maximum group size, staff qualifications and background, health and hygiene, and program activities (U.S. Department of Health and Human Services, 2006).

2. Licensing codes often fall below standards recommended by the American Academy of Pediatrics or NAEYC in critical indicators of quality, such as child-staff ratios, group size, and the education and training of staff members (AAP/APHA/NRCHSCC, 2011; NACCRRA, 2011).

3. Many states' licensing agencies face challenges providing training to licensing staff, keeping caseloads at recommended levels, and having adequate resources to provide regular onsite monitoring to ensure effective enforcement and meaningful technical assistance (NCCIC/NARA, 2010).

Advocates calling for higher licensing standards recommend that states eliminate exemptions and create incentives for all programs caring for children to be licensed. They also recommend reduced licensing staff caseloads so that inspectors will be able to visit programs regularly and will be able to provide technical support as needed.

Additional issues that advocates in some states are working to change relate to staff qualifications, group size, and staff-child ratios. They call for licensing standards that reflect current research identifying characteristics of quality related to positive child outcomes and for streamlined licensure processes (Cost, Quality, Outcomes Study Team, 1995; NAEYC, 2011; NCCIC/NARA, 2010).

Public Agency Regulations: Publicly funded early childhood programs are typically not subject to state child care licensing regulations. Instead, programs operated by the public school system fall within the jurisdiction of the state's educational agency (SEA), and Head Start programs are regulated by federal guidelines.

Many states have an office of early childhood education within its department of education. That state office works with

- Districts, principals, and teachers providing oversight and technical assistance
- The public, sharing information about standards, regulations, and trends and issues in early childhood education

- Legislators and other policy makers who shape and influence legislation that affects early childhood programs

The National Association of Early Childhood Specialists in State Departments of Education (NAECS/SDE) is a national organization, founded in 1972, that provides resources and networking opportunities for state-level early childhood leaders. It also helps unify members' efforts to advocate for policies that support quality programming for young children.

Application Activity

Compare Head Start Program Performance Standards (follow the Head Start Performance Standards link) with your state's licensing standards (go to nrckids.org and click on the link for State Licensing and Regulation Information). Identify the ways this federal program for low-income families sets a higher standard of care than is required for many programs operated under different auspices.

Staff Credentials

Recognition of an administrator's and a teacher's expertise is called *credentialing, certification,* or *licensure.* High demand for early childhood program personnel, inadequate compensation, high staff turnover, and the lack of professional consensus regarding relevant qualifications have contributed to programs with minimally qualified teachers and caregivers.

Administrators' Qualifications.   Advocates for quality urge policy makers to require directors to satisfy the same requirements regardless of who is sponsoring the early childhood program they lead (Morgan, 2000). The fact remains, however, that states' child care regulations continue to set minimal educational, age, and experience requirements for directors working in licensed facilities.

Most directors are former classroom teachers. Their training and experience are likely to have made them familiar with young children and the fundamentals of developmentally appropriate instruction. These experiences, however, have not equipped them with the expertise in organization theory and leadership, management, staff development, legal issues, fiscal management, and marketing they need as a program administrator (Bloom, 1989; Mitchell, 2000). That means they most often learn on the job or by turning to their licensing or funding agency for assistance.

The CDA credential is the most frequently required form of specialized training an individual needs to become a center director. That means a director must have a high school diploma or GED and demonstrated competence meeting CDA's six goals shown in Figure 3.2. The CDA credential is considered equivalent to 9 to 12 credit hours of professional education. The popularity and usefulness of this credential have declined, however, because of the Head Start reauthorization and other initiatives to raise the bar of professionalism in child care (Freeman & Feeney, 2006).

A number of states offer a director's credential, most often in their community college or technical college system, but implementation of a required administrator's credential is in its infancy in most locales. Only four states currently require directors to hold this credential in administration (NCCIC/NARA, 2010). There are other ways to become qualified to direct a child care center, however. States offer directors a number of alternative routes that specify varying combinations of education and experience (NCCIC/NARA, 2010).

Administrators' qualifications are another area in which early childhood programs operated by state and federal governments are bound by different regulations than child

Goal I.   To establish and maintain a safe, healthy learning environment

Goal II.   To advance physical and intellectual competence

Goal III. To support social and emotional development and to provide positive guidance

Goal IV.   To establish positive and productive relationships with families

Goal V.   To ensure a well-run, purposeful program responsive to participant needs

Goal VI.   To maintain a commitment to professionalism

Figure 3.2
CDA Competency Standards

Source: Based on CDA Competency Standards published by the Council for Professional Recognition, n.d.

care programs operated by nongovernmental entities. Administrators of public schools offering early childhood programs including prekindergarten (or child development) classes, kindergarten, and primary grades must hold a state administrator's certificate. This means they are required to hold a valid teaching certificate, have had teaching experience, and have taken specified graduate courses in administration. Although public school administrators are well educated and experienced in "school matters," few states require specialized knowledge in early childhood education serving children from birth to age 8 and are ill equipped to provide supervision and instructional leadership to early childhood teachers.

Head Start does not require any specific training for directors. Just as in other child care settings, most directors come from the ranks of classroom teachers. Those who come from outside Head Start usually have extensive experience in programs serving children living in low-income communities. Head Start offers new directors' workshops, week-long regional training sessions, tailored administrative consultation, and the Head Start Management Fellows program to prepare new directors to meet performance standards and other regulations.

Evidence indicates that neither principals (Charlesworth, Hart, Burts, & DeWolf, 1993; Mead, 2011; National Association of Elementary School Principals [NAESP], 2005) nor child care directors (Caruso, 1991) have had thorough training in developmentally appropriate instructional strategies that create curriculum reflecting children's individual needs, interests, and strengths. While those who have had training in early childhood care and education tend to see the importance of this developmentally appropriate approach to instruction (Charlesworth et al., 1993), teachers continue to struggle with administrators who lack these understandings (Goldstein, 1997; NAESP Foundation Task Force on Early Learning, 2011; West, 2001).

NAEYC's Accreditation Standards (2007) identify directors' core competencies (see the first four pages of this book). These competencies and the management and leadership functions listed next are a helpful place to begin a consideration of what effective directors must need to know and be able to do. Program administrators have responsibilities related to

- **Pedagogy.**   Creating a learning community of children and adults that promotes optimal child development and healthy families.
- **The Center's Organization and Systems.**   Establishing systems for smooth program functioning and managing staff to carry out the program's mission, planning and budgeting the program's fiscal resources, managing organizational change, and establishing systems to monitor and evaluate organizational performance.

- **Human Resources.**   Recruiting, selecting, and orienting personnel. Overseeing systems for the supervision, retention, and professional development of staff that affirm program values and promote a shared vision.
- **Collaboration.**   Establishing partnerships with program staff, family members, board members, community representatives, civic leaders, and other stakeholders to provide quality services for children and their families.
- **Advocacy.**   Taking action and encouraging others to work on behalf of high-quality services that meet the needs of children and their families.

The director's knowledge and skill are increasingly recognized as essential components of quality (Mims, Scott-Little, Lower, Cassidy, & Hestenes, 2008; Vu, Jeon, & Howes, 2008). Bachelor's or master's degree programs in early childhood administration are being offered by an increasing number of colleges and universities. Online programs have proliferated in recent years, but it is important to investigate them before enrolling because not all degrees earned through online institutions are recognized as qualifying graduates for positions that require postsecondary degrees. Programs offered by highly respected institutions (e.g., Carnegie Mellon University's H. John Heinz III School of Public Policy and Management, National Louis University's Center for Early Childhood Leadership) do, however, provide their graduates with knowledge and skill and a respected degree that will qualify them for many leadership positions. These degree programs represent important steps toward increasing directors' knowledge, skill, and professionalism and should lead the way in efforts to document how the director's level of skill and expertise contribute to quality.

Teachers' Qualifications: Teachers' qualifications, including the extent and duration of their preservice field experiences and the characteristics of their ongoing professional development, have a significant impact on the program's quality. They are an important factor in determining the likelihood that the program will contribute to children's growth and development and their success in school and beyond (Early et al., 2006; Kontos, Howes, & Galinsky, 1997; Mims et al., 2008; Snider & Fu, 1990; Vu et al., 2008).

Teachers' Qualifications in Head Start and Child Care Programs.   Although child care is still seen by some as an unskilled occupation, there is a rising tide of commitment to increasing the professionalism of the child care workforce. The movement toward professionalism was fueled, in part, by Head Start's 2007 reauthorization, which mandated that by 2013 at least 50% of all Head Start teachers in center-based programs have at least an associate degree (Administration for Children and Families [ACF], 2007).

States' child care regulations also address teachers' qualifications. The most common minimum qualification for teachers is experience with or without a high school diploma or GED. A number of states require master teachers to hold at least a CDA credential.

Certification of Teachers in Public School Early Childhood Programs.   All states require teachers working with young children in public schools to hold at least a bachelor's degree and to be certified, but states' requirements vary greatly. Some states' early childhood certification qualifies teachers to work with children from birth to second, third, or fourth grade, or to age 8; others prepare them for work with children from birth to age 5 or when they are in kindergarten; some extend from pre-K into the primary grades, and still others address only pre-K and kindergarten age groups. Sometimes states combine early childhood with special education certification, and others offer only add-on certification that builds on preparation to teach elementary-age children (Jones, Martin, & Crandall, 2009). Some states require certified teachers to hold a master's degree for initial certification, and many require candidates to pass standardized tests such as Praxis. Suffice it to say that states' approaches to early childhood certification are varied and change so frequently that it is difficult to keep up-to-date on the latest regulations (Jones et al., 2009).

States also use different terms to describe the same kind of programming. It is not clear, for example, if *pre-K, nursery,* and programs for *3-year-olds* are the same kinds of programs (Fields & Mitchell, 2007). In addition, certification requirements vary from requiring an in-depth preparation in growth and development, instruction in appropriate strategies for teaching young children, and supervised student teaching to add-on and alternative certification programs that require just a few courses and little or no supervised practical experience.

Students graduating in good standing from a state-approved early childhood program can expect to be recommended for certification in the state where their college or university is located. They are also eligible for certification in states that have developed reciprocal certification agreements with the state of the institution granting their degree.

The National Board of Professional Teaching Standards (NBPTS) has been offering early childhood certification since 1987. The rigorous NBPTS certification process requires candidates to submit a portfolio documenting their teaching skills and to pass a comprehensive written exam. Many states supplement the salaries of NBPTS-certified teachers. NBPTS certification is a nationally recognized credential so teachers can maintain their certification if they move from one state to another.

In recent years, the importance of placing appropriately certified teachers in public school early childhood classrooms has become more important than ever. Federal No Child Left Behind (NCLB) legislation enacted in 2001 requires classroom teachers in public schools receiving federal funds to be "highly qualified," that is, working with the age group for which they are fully certified. This is one criterion included in mandated school report cards that evaluates public schools' ability to reach expected levels of excellence.

Specialized Teacher Qualifications.   Several additional certification programs may apply to teachers of young children. The instructional staff of Montessori schools that belong to the American Montessori Society (AMS) must, in addition to satisfying state licensing or certification requirements, meet AMS certification requirements for working with infants and toddlers and in early childhood (ages 2 1/2 to 6 years), elementary, or secondary programs.

The Program for Infant/Toddler Care (PITC) out of the WestEd Center for Child and Family Studies certifies trainers qualified to conduct trainings, coach, and provide technical assistance to caregivers working with children from birth to age 3. The High/Scope Foundation offers specialized training that qualifies teachers for High/Scope certification. In addition, the High/Scope Educational Research Foundation awards accreditation to qualified programs that demonstrate their ability to implement the High/Scope curriculum accurately.

ACCREDITATION

Accreditation is a voluntary system of evaluation that measures a program's success meeting the accrediting organization's established standards of practice. Review Table 3.1 for a comparison of licensure and program accreditation programs.

Accreditation represents a recognized standard of excellence. As publically funded prekindergarten (4K or pre-K) programs have grown in popularity, some states have enacted regulations requiring programs receiving state monies to be accredited or to be actively working toward accreditation (Education Commission of the States [ECS], 2002).

A study of directors' perceptions of the benefits of accreditation found that 55% of directors of accredited programs thought their programs were more visible, and 38% reported that accreditation made marketing easier. More than 90% of directors reported that they believed the quality of their programs increased because they pursued accreditation.

Table 3.1
A Comparison of Licensure and Program Accreditation

Licensure	Accreditation
Mandatory	Voluntary
Developed by governmental agencies and funding agencies.	Developed by professional organizations.
Minimal level of quality.	Higher-than-minimal standard of quality.
Requires full compliance.	Requires substantial compliance.
Enforced at state and local levels.	Nationally validated and enforced.
Failure to comply can result in revocation of the center's license; it cannot operate legally.	Failure to comply may mean the center loses accreditation, but it can continue to operate legally.

They identified improvements in areas of curriculum, administration, health and safety, and the physical environment. The directors also stated that children benefited from better staff morale, improved knowledge and understanding of developmentally appropriate practice (DAP), and parent understanding of the components and standards necessary for high-quality care (Herr, Johnson, & Zimmerman, 1993).

Accredited and nonaccredited early childhood programs have been shown to differ in the following areas: innovations and acceptance of change; goal consensus; opportunities for staff development; economic stability; and clarity about policies, procedures, and communication (Rohacek, Adams, & Kisker, 2010).

The NAEYC Academy for Early Childhood Program Accreditation was established in 1985 and is generally accepted as the "gold standard" of quality programming. It is the most well known and most widely respected accreditation in the field. Just a few hundred centers were accredited in 1988; by 2007, as the public became more informed about the importance of quality, more than 10,000 accredited programs were serving nearly 1 million children. In 1999, the NAEYC Academy for Early Childhood Program Accreditation began reinventing NAEYC's accreditation system. Revised Early Childhood Program Standards and Accreditation Criteria were approved in 2005 and took effect in September 2006. Revisions were designed to increase the reliability of program evaluation, improve the system's responsiveness and the timeliness of onsite validation visits, and raise the bar of quality. It is noteworthy that the number of accredited programs has declined. NAEYC reported about 7,000 accredited centers in 2011. One reason might be the increased rigor and cost of the NAEYC accreditation process or the proliferation of alternative accreditation systems that put some of the same benefits (i.e., enhanced payments in states' voucher systems or exemption from some taxes) within easier reach.

Specifics about NAEYC accreditation can be found by following links to *Accreditation of Programs for Young Children* from the NAEYC website (see the fifth page of this book for the NAEYC Accreditation Standards).

There are four steps to acquiring NAEYC accreditation. Centers must:

1. Enroll in a **self-study** that helps the program identify the strengths it brings to the accreditation process, identify areas in which it needs to concentrate improvement efforts, and make and implement specific program improvement plans to address all accreditation standards. Programs can take as long as they need to complete this self study.

2. Submit an **application for accreditation** in which the program indicates it will complete the formal self-assessment, document how it has met each standard,

and make progress toward meeting identified accreditation criteria within one year.

3. Become a **candidate** for accreditation by submitting the required self-assessment report and other documentation describing the program's structure and the qualifications of administrators and staff.

4. Host an **onsite visit** scheduled for within 6 months of the submission of its candidacy materials.

Once they have earned accreditation, centers must submit four annual reports over the 5-year term of accreditation. Fees are assessed at each step of the process. The initial cost of accreditation for small centers (10 to 60 children) totals $1,275, with an annual report fee of $300. Centers enrolling between 241 and 360 children pay $2,375 to become accredited and an annual renewal fee of $450. Larger centers are assessed $275 during the application process for every additional 120 children over the original 360, and an additional $100 per year for every additional 120 children. Accredited programs must reapply and successfully complete the entire process before the end of their 5-year accreditation term.

Many programs begin accreditation but stall during self-study either in the initial process or during reaccreditation. Talley (1997) found several reasons for abandoning the process. Almost two-fifths of the directors reported a lack of time, and almost one-third reported problems with staff turnover or program instability as the major reasons for failure to complete the accreditation process. Three other frequently mentioned barriers to success were new directors who felt ill equipped to successfully achieve accreditation, saw the application process as overwhelming, and viewed other program concerns as higher priorities. Although a few program directors with strong, stable staff and healthy environments believed accreditation was not important, most failed to complete the required self-study because they were unsure about the quality of their program and their chances for success.

In addition to NAEYC, the following organizations have developed accreditation criteria and procedures for early childhood programs: the Association of Christian Schools International (ACSI), the Council on Accreditation (COA), the National Accreditation Commission for Early Care and Education Programs (NAC), the National After School Association (NAA), the National Early Childhood Program Accreditation (NECPA), the National Lutheran School Accreditation (NLSA), and the National Association for Family Child Care (NAFCC).

Public schools are accredited by their state education agency and possibly by the Southern Association of Colleges and Schools (SACS). Among the six regional accrediting associations, only SACS has an arrangement for accrediting elementary schools. Accreditation from some of the organizations identified is also available to programs operated by public schools.

QUALITY RATING AND IMPROVEMENT SYSTEMS

Quality Rating Systems (QRS) and Quality Rating Improvement Systems (QRIS) are systematic statewide approaches "to assess, improve, and communicate the level of quality in early and school age care and education settings" (NCCIC, 2011). Quality Rating Systems are designed to inform parents and other interested citizens about the quality of participating child care programs and to increase the quality of local programming. Since the implementation of the first QRS in Oklahoma in 1998, they have attracted the attention of communities from coast to coast. By 2011, 25 states had a QRS or QRIS in place (NCCIC, 2011), and all remaining states were in the process of piloting, exploring, or designing a statewide improvement system (NCCIC, 2010).

A QRS provides a gradual process for bridging the gap between the minimum standards set by each state's child care licensing standards and the high standards that reflect research-based best practices. The number of steps between basic licensure and the highest level of quality varies from two steps beyond licensure to six (NCCIC, 2010). The majority of existing QRS identify four steps above licensing, and in most cases the highest level of quality includes national accreditation by an accepted national accreditation system (Mitchell, 2005).

All Quality Rating Systems include components of the following elements:

1. Standards identify two or more levels of quality above the floor created by mandatory licensing regulations.
2. Valid and reliable assessments of quality are used to assign ratings and monitor compliance with standards. Most statewide systems use an environmental rating scale, for example, the *Early Childhood Environment Rating Scale-Revised* (Harms, Clifford, & Cryer, 2005), as one measure of quality. Other instruments used to assess program quality include the Child and Caregiver Interaction Scale, the Arnett Caregiver Interaction Scale, the Early Learning and Literacy Classroom Observation (ELLCO), the Program Administration Scale (PAS), and the Classroom Assessment Scoring System (CLASS) (NCCIC, 2010).
3. Outreach and professional development support efforts promote participation in voluntary rating systems and provide technical assistance to programs striving to attain a higher-than-minimal rating.
4. Financial incentives motivate many programs to participate in their state's QRIS or QRS system. Incentives can include grants to improve learning environments, bonuses, eligibility for merit awards and loans, and higher tiers of reimbursement through the federal child care subsidy system (NCCIC, 2010).
5. Parent and community education is designed to help the public understand the system and how it benefits children, families, and the community's early care and education system. QRS and QRIS programs use easily understood symbols, most frequently an increasing number of stars, to identify each level of quality (Mitchell, 2005).

Twenty-five states have a statewide system with all five of these elements (NCCIC, 2011). States' approaches to creating a QRS vary. Some make their system a statewide venture, while others limit their implementation to particular counties or metropolitan areas, particularly during their pilot phase. In some systems, all centers are required to participate; in others, participation is voluntary. Follow links from the website of the U.S. Department of Health and Human Services Administration for Children & Families listed at the end of this chapter for information about each state's QRS, QRIS, or tiered reimbursement system.

A Better Way

In spite of the fact that Marie is confident in the quality of her program and the center's enrollment has remained strong, she has begun to reconsider her decision not to participate in the state's QRIS. She has learned that the state has recently made grants to purchase classroom materials available to centers that participate at its higher levels, and that there are special benefits to becoming fully accredited. These benefits are particularly attractive during these difficult economic times. For those reasons, she has researched a number of accreditation systems that, if she were to earn accreditation, would automatically qualify her center for the state's highest ranking. She has decided that the time, money, and effort invested in pursuing accreditation would pay off in the long run, and she has sent for the accreditation self-study materials. Her decision was made easier by the fact that she has great confidence in her assistant director and hopes that she will take the lead in managing the accreditation process by leading staff development on the accreditation process, completing required paperwork, and collecting and organizing documentation.

MEETING LEGAL REQUIREMENTS

Some standards do not directly involve the protection of children and their families. They concern the business aspects of early childhood programs, such as the legal existence of private programs, fiscal regulations, and regulations applying to hiring and terminating personnel. Owners and operators of child care programs must think carefully about the risks they assume when they and their employees are responsible for the safety and well-being of other people's children. They need to be well aware of the financial liabilities they may face, for example, if a child were to be seriously injured while under the supervision of their employees or their responsibility if an employee were to injure a child in care. Potential owners and operators of child care programs need to be informed as they make decisions about a number of legal aspects related to child care program operation.

Legal Existence of Private Programs

Proprietorship, partnership, limited liability company (sometimes called an "LLC"), and *corporation* are legal categories for four types of private ownership. Legal requirements for operating an early childhood program under any of these categories vary from state to state. This discussion focuses on common features of the laws. If you are planning to establish a private early childhood program, you should seek legal advice about laws and regulations that may apply. Various forms for business entities are summarized and compared in Table 3.2.

Proprietorship: Under a **proprietorship**, a program is owned by one person. Another name for this type of business entity is *sole proprietorship*. The owner has no partners or other co-owners, and there is no separate legal entity, that is, there is no LLC or incorporation. Sole proprietorships may consist purely of a single owner-operator or may have one or more additional persons (called "agents") doing work for the single owner. The legal requirements are simple. To create a proprietorship, the owner simply starts a business and complies with any business license, fictitious name, or other requirements imposed on small businesses by state or local law. Thus, if the owner is not going to name the center after himself or herself, a fictitious name registration, such as "Jack and Jill Center" may need to be filed.

In a sole proprietorship, the owner has full decision-making authority as long as decisions are consistent with governmental regulations (e.g., the owner must report business revenue and expenses on his or her personal tax return). The owner may sell or give away the business operation or go out of the business with no restrictions except the payment of outstanding debts and the completion of contractual obligations.

A major drawback relates to the potential for full personal liability on the part of the owner for the liabilities of the business. Because of the risks inherent in ownership of a child care program, the proprietorship form of doing business is not recommended, even assuming the owner carries liability insurance to protect against legal risks. The owner may be held personally liable for contractual or other liabilities beyond the owner's ability to control, and the liability may exceed the owner's personal funds or insurance coverage, leading to personal bankruptcy.

Partnership: In a **partnership**, two or more people join together for the purpose of running an enterprise as co-owners. A partnership may involve several individuals or entities as copartners. For example, other partnerships or corporations may serve as partners in a child care center's ownership and operation.

Table 3.2

Comparison of Business Entities

Entities	Sole Proprietorship	General Partnership	Limited Partnership	Limited Liability Corporation (LLC)	S Corporation	C Corporation
Liability protection	No	No	General partnership has unlimited liability; limited partners are like corporation shareholders.	Yes	Yes	Yes
Reduced entity taxation	Yes	Yes	Yes	Yes	Yes	No
Business debts separate from owners?	No	No	No for general partnership; yes for limited partnership.	Yes, unless guaranteed.	Yes, unless guaranteed.	
Easy to form?	Yes	Yes	No	No	No	No
Filing requirements other than business license	None	None	Yes	Yes	Yes	Yes
Management	Owner controls	Partners	General partner controls.	Either member managed, like a general partnership or manager-managed, like a corporation.	Both these entities are usually managed by board of directors, although special management agreements may be permitted; directors typically delegate to officers and other agents.	
Permanence	No	No	Harder to dissolve.	Harder to dissolve.	Yes	Yes
Transferability of interests	Can assign	Same as GP	Freely transferable; subject to agreement.	Freely transferable; may be subject to agreement.	Freely transferable; may be subject to share transfer agreement,	

Note: The two most important entity choice factors are *liability protection* and reduced *tax liability*. As the chart reflects, the most favored entities in these regards are the LLC and the S Corporation. Each entity offers different benefits and features different drawbacks. State laws vary. You should consult with your tax advisor before deciding which form of entity is best for you.

A partnership is a distinct legal entity, meaning it exists apart from the owners. Unless there is an agreement to the contrary, a partner may sell or give away his or her interest in the partnership only if all other partners consent. If one partner dies, the partnership is dissolved.

The law recognizes two types of partnerships:

1. General partnership—In this type of partnership, each partner is a legal co-equal. Subject to agreements to the contrary, each partner has a right to an equal share of the profits and losses from the business and an equal right to control the company. When it comes to decison making needed for carrying on the usual business of the partnership, each partner has full authority to make binding decisions independently of other partners. In other words, all the partners do not need to be consulted before normal business decisions are made by one of them. Each partner faces personal liability to creditors or tort claimants (a tort is a civil wrong). As with the sole proprietorship form of doing business, operating a child care program as a general partnership is risky (and hence not recommended) because the partnership can be held responsible for wrongs committed by the center's employees, and this may result in personal liability for each partner. As with a proprietorship, the partnership may have to obtain a business license and may have to file a true name certificate. As with the sole proprietorship, the general partnership is not taxed as a separate entity. It must, however, file an information return reporting its revenues and expenses to federal and state taxing authorities. As with the limited partnership discussed next, many general partnerships have written partnership agreements spelling out how the business is to be run and the partners' rights in relation to each other.

2. Limited partnership—Formation of a limited partnership requires a filing with the state government, typically with the secretary of state. The entity consists of one or more general partners and one or more limited partners. Each general partner faces risks identical to those of a general partnership. When it comes to personal liability, limited partners are different from general partners or proprietorship owners. They do not face unlimited personal liability for the losses of the company. Each limited partner is responsible for and may be held liable to the extent of his or her capital contribution to the partnership. In other words, if the business suffers a catastrophic loss, the general partners may be personally wiped out financially. The limited partners stand to lose only whatever financial investment they made in the limited partnership; their other personal assets are not at risk. In exchange for limited liability, limited partners are not allowed to participate in the day-to-day control of the partnership. Once operations begin, the tax and business filing requirements for the limited partnership mirror those for the general partnership.

Limited Liability Company (LLC):   An LLC, like a limited partnership and a corporation, is a separate legal entity in the eyes of the law. Thus, owners of an LLC must file with the state government, typically with the secretary of state, to establish their business. In many states, an LLC may consist of one or more members. In other words, if state law permits, a single owner can establish the business as an LLC.

An LLC has two key benefits. The first is shared with sole proprietorships and partnerships; the second is not. The shared benefit is flow-through taxation. An LLC owner has the ability to declare that the business will be taxed as if it were a partnership, meaning that there is no separate tax levied on the business entity itself. Alternatively, the owner may declare that the LLC will be taxed as if it were a corporation.

The second major benefit of LLC status separates the LLC from sole proprietorships and general partnerships and is very valuable. That benefit is *limited liability,* which frees the owner from personal liability for wrongs committed by others that lead to claims against the entity. Like the limited partner in the limited partnership, the owner of an LLC risks his or her personal investment in the business but does not face unlimited personal liability for the business's debts or for actions of employees or co-owners. On the other hand, functioning as an LLC (or, for that matter, as a corporation) will not permit the entity's owner to escape personal liability for wrongdoing he or she *personally* commits.

The LLC is a flexible entity when it comes to management structure. With multiple owners, the LLC can be operated with corporate-like formalities (through a board of directors, for example) or like a partnership, with each member playing a role in decision making. This latter type of management style, called *member managed*, is the standard way LLCs are run, but a more formal board of directors system can be agreed to by the members.

LLCs are typically more difficult to dissolve than partnerships. Depending on state law, an LLC may not dissolve when one of the members dies. As with partnerships, LLC members typically agree on a contract, called an *LLC operating agreement*, spelling out rules on how the business is to be operated and the members' rights.

Corporation: A corporation is a legal entity, just like the limited partnership and the LLC. It may be established on a for-profit or not-for-profit basis. Corporations typically exist forever unless dissolved by the board of directors or through court proceedings. Like LLCs, corporations offer the benefit of limited liability to their members.

Many private early childhood programs are legally organized as LLCs or corporations because of the protection from personal liability for the owners. Work-site child care programs may be organized as divisions of the parent company, subsidiary entities, or as independent not-for-profit corporations.

The corporation protects individuals from certain liabilities by creating a decision-making board of directors. The board typically delegates decision-making power to a manager or to a single director. Board members are typically protected for their good faith business decisions under the "business judgment rule," even when the decisions turn out poorly. It is advisable to buy "errors and omissions" or "directors and officers" liability insurance coverage in order to protect decision makers from personal liability for actions (or inactions) occurring on behalf of the entity that causes injury to others.

Individual board members can be held personally liable in certain circumstances, however, such as for their own personal wrongdoing (e.g., fraud) or for the failure of the corporation to pay withholding taxes on employees' salaries. However, the risk of personal financial liability is greatly diminished in a corporation, as compared with the proprietorship or partnership.

In addition to diminished personal financial liability, regulations governing taxation may provide incentives for a child care center to operate as a corporation. It is possible to limit corporate taxes on the entity by qualifying for "Subchapter S" status. Any program owner should seek professional tax advice before deciding on a proposed entity's form and final structure.

Because the corporation is a legal entity, several documents must be filed with appropriate state offices. The forms are usually somewhat different for for-profit and not-for-profit corporations. Three documents are required to complete the incorporation process:

1. Articles of incorporation or certificate of incorporation. The organization's legal creators, or incorporators, use this form to provide the public with information about the corporation, such as the name and address of the entity; its purposes; whether it is a for-profit or not-for-profit corporation; its powers, for example, to purchase property and make loans; membership, if the state requires members; names and addresses of the initial board of directors; initial officers; and the date of the annual meeting.

2. Bylaws. The IRS requires bylaws if the corporation is seeking tax-exempt status. Bylaws operate as internal rules of order. Most corporations have them. They explain how the corporation will conduct its business and what tasks are to be performed by the various officers and the board and describe voting and meeting requirements.

3. Minutes of the incorporators' meeting.   After the incorporators prepare the documents identified earlier, an incorporators' meeting is held. The name of the corporation is approved, and the articles of incorporation and bylaws are signed. The incorporators elect officers and the board of directors, who will serve until the first meeting of the members. Various business actions, such as authority to open a bank account, are approved. In for-profit corporations, the incorporators vote to authorize the issuance of stock. Minutes of the incorporators' meeting and subsequent board meetings are kept in a *Minutes Book*.

Once the state accepts the articles of incorporation for filing, the corporation's life begins. The incorporators no longer have power. Board members carry out the purposes of the organization, and the shareholders own the organization.

When corporations dissolve, they must follow state law if they are for-profit corporations and must follow federal regulations if they are not-for-profit corporations. Early childhood programs may operate as either for-profit or not-for-profit corporations. For-profit corporations are organized for the purpose of making a profit. Early childhood programs in this category, as well as proprietorships and partnerships, are businesses.

A for-profit corporation may be a *closed corporation*, in which members of a family or perhaps a few friends own stock, or a *public corporation*, in which stock is traded on exchanges.

If the for-profit corporation makes a profit, it may pay taxes on the profits; individual stockholders file personal income tax forms listing items such as salaries and dividends received from the corporation. From a taxation standpoint, a closed corporation with a Subchapter S status functions like a partnership for the most part; thus, its tax liability as an entity is limited.

Earnings retained in the business typically are not subjected to corporate tax. Money paid out by the corporation as a return to the owners, called dividends, generally are subject to taxes paid by each individual owner and reported on his or her personal tax return.

The main purpose of not-for-profit corporations is, as their name suggests, other than making a profit, but such corporations are permitted to have net income. Any surplus, or profit, however, must be kept in the business and used to promote the purposes of the organization as set forth in the articles of incorporation. In other words, the profit has to be used for the center's purposes.

Child care has two types of not-for-profit corporations: (a) those organized for charitable, educational, literary, religious, or scientific purposes under Section 501(c) (3) of the Internal Revenue Code and (b) those organized for social welfare purposes under Section 501(c) (4) of the Internal Revenue Code. Tax-exempt status is not automatic. The not-for-profit corporation must file for and be granted tax-exempt status at both the federal and state levels.

Some standard procedures guide the operational formalities for early childhood programs. The owner must recognize that the entity, whatever the type, is separate and distinct from himself or herself. Separate bank accounts should be obtained for any early childhood program. The failure of an LLC or corporation to maintain financial records separate from those of its owners will jeopardize limited liability protection. Creditors or tort claimants may seek to "pierce the corporate veil," stripping away limited liability protection and holding the owners personally liable for the company's obligations, even when limited liability protection might otherwise apply.

Careful record keeping for financial and management purposes is a standard requirement for proper management. Not-for-profit corporations with a certain income level and other programs receiving monies from certain funding sources are required to have an audit. In most states, not-for-profit corporations are required to file an annual financial report following the audit.

Franchises and chains may fall under any of the foregoing legal categories of private organizations but are most often corporations or LLCs. Franchises and chains are differentiated as follows:

1. A **franchise** is an organization that allows an individual or an entity to use its name, follow its standardized program and administrative procedures, and receive assistance (e.g., in selecting a site, building and equipping a facility, and training staff) for an agreed-upon sum of money, royalty, or both. Two popular child care franchises are Kiddie Academy and The Learning Experience.
2. A **chain** is ownership of several facilities by the same proprietorship, partnership, or corporation. These facilities are administered by a central organization. Kinder Care Learning Centers is an example of a chain.

Fiscal Regulations

Many fiscal regulations are specific to given programs. Contractual undertakings and Internal Revenue Service regulations, however, must be complied with by all early childhood programs. Fraud or failure to comply with fiscal regulations may result in serious consequences, including the risk of civil or criminal liability.

Contracts: **Contracts** are legally enforceable agreements that may be oral or written (e.g., insurance policies; employment contracts; contracts with parents for fees; contracts for food, supplies, and services; contracts with funding sources; and leases). A contract has three elements:

1. The **offer**—the buyer's proposal to the seller or the seller's invitation to the buyer to purchase a given object or service at a stated price (money or service)
2. **Acceptance**—the buyer's acceptance of an offer or the seller's acknowledgment of the buyer's willingness to accept an offer
3. **Consideration**—the legal term for the price or value of what each party exchanges (e.g., a subscription to a professional journal for $40 per year)

Breaking a contract is called a **breach**, and the potential penalty is referred to as **damages**.

IRS Regulations: Many Internal Revenue Service (IRS) regulations apply to all early childhood programs:

1. **Employer identification number**—Each organization employing people on a regular salaried basis is required to obtain a federal employer identification number. A program cannot file for a tax-exempt status without first having obtained this number using IRS Form SS-4.
2. **Tax returns**—Employers file quarterly tax returns, IRS Form 941. This form is filed with the regional IRS service center. A penalty is assessed for late filing. Salaried employers of public early childhood programs file the appropriate schedule on IRS Form 1040. All private programs must file tax returns. Sole proprietors and partnerships with other income file the appropriate schedule on Form 1040, partnerships without other income file IRS Form 1065, for-profit corporations file Form 1120, and not-for-profit corporations file Form 990.
3. **Withholding Exemption Certificates and IRS Form 1099**—A Withholding Exemption Certificate, IRS Form W-4, is required for each employee. The certificates are used for determining the amount to withhold for federal, state, and city income taxes.

The form indicates marital status and the number of dependents and must be completed before the first paycheck is issued. Employees must sign new forms if their marital status or the number of dependents changes or if they want more of their wages to be withheld. An annual statement of taxes withheld from an employee's earnings (Form W-2) is sent to each employee no later than January 31 of the year following the year in which the employee was paid. Occasionally, early childhood programs hire someone to do a temporary job, such as plumbing or electrical work. Because withholding taxes would not have been deducted from the wages, all centers paying $600 or more to any individual who is not a regular employee must file IRS Form 1099 reporting the transaction.

Laws That Protect the Staff and the Program

You need to be aware of regulations designed to protect the employee and the program. Laws that protect the staff include those that prevent discrimination, relate to minimum wages, ensure adherence to regulations created by the owner/operator or the board, determine eligibility of staff who meet identified qualifications to serve in particular positions, staff members' potential vulnerability to legal actions, and the civil rights of employees with disabilities.

Title VII of the Civil Rights Acts of 1964 and as Amended by the Equal Opportunity Act of 1972:   Fair employment practices are mandatory for organizations, companies, and people having contracts with the federal government. The practices are also mandatory for any company employing or composed of 15 or more people. Employers subject to this act and its amendment must not discriminate against any individual on the grounds of race, creed, color, gender, national origin, or age. Employment practices must be based on relevant measures of merit and competence. The employer must also base job qualifications on bona fide occupational qualifications (BFOQ); thus, job descriptions must clearly specify the tasks to be performed.

Americans with Disabilities Act: The Americans with Disabilities Act (ADA), P.L. 101–336, was signed into law on July 26, 1990. The ADA established civil rights for people with disabilities. The part of the law concerning employment states that employers with 15 or more employees must avoid job-related discrimination based on the employee's disability. To be protected under the law, the employee must satisfy BFOQ that are job related and be able to perform those tasks that are essential to the job with reasonable accommodations (e.g., making the facility accessible, modifying equipment, modifying work schedules, providing readers or interpreters), if necessary. Furthermore, the employer is legally liable if other employees discriminate or do not make adjustments to accommodate employees with disabilities (Surr, 1992).

Fair Labor Standards Act: The Fair Labor Standards Act of 1938 as amended applies equally to men and women. Employers subject to this act and its amendments must pay employees the current minimum wage; overtime (hours worked over the 40-hour week) at the rate of 1 1/2 times the employee's regular rate of pay; regular wages and overtime pay for attendance at training sessions, whether the sessions are conducted at the place of work or at another site; and equal wages for equal work. The act does not apply to members of one's immediate family.

Family and Medical Leave Act: The Family and Medical Leave Act (FMLA) of 1993 requires companies and organizations with 50 or more employees to grant those who have worked for them for at least 12 months up to a total of 12 workweeks of unpaid leave during any 12-month period for one or more of the following reasons:

- the birth and care of a newborn child of an employee
- to care for an adopted or foster child
- to care for an immediate family member (spouse, child, or parent) with a serious health condition
- to take medical leave when unable to work because of a serious health condition

Potential Vulnerability to Legal Actions: Three principles often apply in legal actions involving any business:

1. An employee is hired to perform certain types of duties, with certain expectations as to how these duties will be performed. When an employee's actions fall within the sphere of actions that would normally be expected of such an employee, the employee is said to be "acting within the scope of employment." The employer is liable for wrongs committed by the employee when acting within the scope of authority but is usually not liable when the employee is acting outside of the scope of employment.

2. In general, employers are responsible for all torts (civil wrongs) committed by employees when those employees act within the scope of employment. The legal phrase used for this principle is *respondent superior* ("the boss is responsible"). This principle does not apply to independent contractors (nonemployee workers, like electricians or plumbers), who usually are responsible for their own torts.

3. A supervisor or principal who is in charge of workers may be responsible for torts committed by the subordinate workers acting within the scope of employment and subject to the supervisor's or principal's control.

Laws in Addition to Licensing That Protect Children

In every state, child care providers are mandated reporters. Mandated reporters are professionals who have a legal responsibility to report suspected neglect or physical or sexual abuse to appropriate child protective service authorities such as the state's Department of Social Services or Department of Child & Family Services. Failure to report suspected abuse or neglect can result in criminal or civil penalties. That means that a mandated reporter who does not comply with this law can face fines and/or imprisonment and can lose her job or her license for not reporting. Early childhood professionals must be familiar with the indications of child maltreatment and state laws regarding reporting suspected cases.

In most cases, individuals are responsible for reporting suspected abuse or neglect. A director, principal, or other supervisor cannot prevent an employee who has reason to suspect that a child has been mistreated from making a report. Programs should include information about requirements related to reporting abuse and neglect in handbooks distributed to families and staff.

Legal Responsibilities and Vulnerabilities: Individuals' legal and financial vulnerability varies, as described earlier, depending on the program's ownership and the agreements that have been formalized between and among owners. Programs that are fully liable for compliance with laws and in cases of personal injury are sole proprietorships, partnerships, and for-profit corporations.

Liability is limited in some states by the charitable immunity doctrine for programs operated as not-for-profit corporations. Public agency programs, such as public school early childhood programs and Head Start, have generally been immune from full liability as provided by Section 1983 of the Civil Rights Act (Mancke, 1972). Under the Civil Rights Act, immunity was not extended to the following three types of suits:

1. Intentional injury (e.g., corporal punishment resulting in lasting injury to body or health; restraint of a person, such as physically enforcing time-out; and defamation, such as implying a student's lack of ability in nonprofessional communication)
2. Negligence (e.g., failure to give adequate instruction, failure to take into account a child's abilities, improper supervision, inadequate inspection of equipment)
3. Educational negligence (careless or incompetent teaching practices; Scott, 1983)

Several implications can be drawn concerning the potential vulnerability to legal action. First, all employees should have job descriptions spelling out their scope of authority. Second, adequate staffing, safe facilities and equipment, administrative diligence, staff awareness and training in care of children, and documentation will do much to reduce the risk of torts (acts that may result in legal suits brought against the center and/or its employees). Finally, everyone involved in programs should realize that situations leading to liability are ever-present concerns and that all employees are vulnerable to legal actions.

SUMMARY

Regulations are the rules, directives, statutes, and laws that prescribe, direct, limit, and govern early childhood programs. They are designed to create a safety net for young children and to identify a level of quality no program should fall below. Standards describe expectations for programs. Like regulations, they can apply to program facilities, teachers' qualifications, curriculum construction, and many other aspects of early care and education programming.

Some standards are optional, such as the high standards of NAEYC Program Accreditation, and others pertain to certain kinds of programs, such as the Head Start Performance Standards. Regulations and standards go hand-in-hand. They create a context for early childhood programs provided under a wide range of auspices and are an important part of your study of early childhood program planning and administration.

USEFUL WEBSITES

Individual States' Child Care Licensure Regulations, developed by the National Resource Center for Health and Safety in Child Care and Early Education

nrckids.org/STATES/states.htm

This interactive map connects with links to each state's child care regulations.

National Accreditation Organizations for Early Childhood Programs, developed by the National Child Care Information and Technical Assistance Center (NCCIC)

nccic.acf.hhs.gov/poptopics/nationalaccred.html

This table summarizes the setting, age level, components of the accreditation system, and contact information for a range of accreditation organizations.

Information about states and communities operating, piloting, exploring, or designing a Quality Rating and Improvement System (QRIS), developed by the U.S. Department of Health and Human Services Administration for Children & Families

nccic.acf.hhs.gov/qrisresourceguide/index.cfm?do =qrisstate

This interactive color-coded map indicates which states have a QRIS in place, and which states' systems are in development. Specific information is available by clicking on individual states.

Caring for Our Children: National Health and Safety Performance Standards: Guidelines for Early Care and Education Programs, 3rd ed. (2011), developed by the American Academy of Pediatrics, the American Public Health Association, and the National Resource Center for Health and Safety in Child Care and Early Education

nrckids.org/

This comprehensive guide is intended as a resource for administrators, policy makers, consultants, and others committed to ensuring children's health and safety in out-of-home settings.

Head Start Program Performance Standards (Regulations Part 1304)

eclkc.ohs.acf.hhs.gov/hslc

Performance Standards are updated annually in the spring. They can be found by following links for Head Start information from this website.

The 2008 Child Care Licensing Study (2010), prepared by the National Child Care Information and Technical Assistance Center and the National Association for Regulatory Administration

www.naralicensing.org/Licensing_Study

This in-depth report includes information about all states' regulations and includes useful data tables that compare states' regulation on varied criteria.

We Can Do Better Ranking of State Child Care Center Standards and Oversight, developed by the National Association of Child Care Resource and Referral Agency States' Rankings

www.naccrra.org/publications/naccrra-publications/we-can-do-better

These resources can be found by following links on the website.

Fire Safety in Day Care Centers: What Parents Need to Know, developed by the Fire Department of the City of New York, Office of Fire Prevention

www.nyc.gov/html/fdny/pdf/safety/fire_safety_education/2010_02/20_fire_safety_in_child_care_centers_english.pdf

This handout includes questions families should ask about a center's fire prevention practices and includes a fire safety checklist families can use to evaluate the center's efforts to ensure their children's safety while in care. It can also be found by searching for "fire safety in child care centers" on the NYC.gov website.

TO REFLECT

1. Serving as the director of a program caring for children is a tremendous responsibility. The existing system of laws, regulations, and voluntary standards provides guidance and protection to newcomers as well as experienced veterans. Which of these laws, regulations, or voluntary standards do you find most beneficial? Can you point to particular sections that you find most helpful? Why?
2. Review the process to become an NAEYC-accredited center. Identify the skills you now have and those you would need to develop to pursue NAEYC Program Accreditation.

CHECK AND APPLY YOUR UNDERSTANDING

1. Identify the agency that oversees child care licensure in your state and report important provisions such as adult-child ratio and group size.
2. Identify three national early care and education accreditation systems and select the one with the most rigorous standards.
3. Identify the measures of program quality included in your state's QRIS or QRS. If your state has not yet adopted a QRIS or QRS, investigate the system of a neighboring state.
4. List three federal laws that child care centers must follow.

CHAPTER 4

Establishing Policies and Procedures

NAEYC Administrator
Competencies addressed
in this chapter:

**Management Knowledge
and Skills**

4. Educational Programming
The ability to develop and implement
a program to meet the needs of
young children at different ages and
developmental levels (infant/toddler,
preschool, kindergarten). Knowledge
of administrative practices that
promote the inclusion of children
with special needs.

**5. Program Operations and
Facilities Management**
Knowledge and application of policies
and procedures that meet state/local
regulations and professional standards
pertaining to the health and safety of
young children.

6. Family Support
Knowledge and application of policies
and procedures that meet state/local
regulations and professional standards
pertaining to the health and safety of
young children.

**9. Oral and Written
Communication**
Knowledge of the mechanics of writing
including organizing ideas, grammar,
punctuation, and spelling. The ability
to use written communication to
effectively express one's thoughts.

Learning Outcomes

After studying this chapter, you should be able to:

1. Discuss the contributions a comprehensive staff manual, family handbook, and administrative manual make to your center's smooth operation.

2. Describe how you would begin the process of developing a family handbook for a new program.

3. Develop an outline for a staff manual, listing the major headings you would include.

Grace's Experience

When Grace stepped in to serve as her program's director, she discovered that she was not sure how to handle many of the routine tasks that were now her responsibility. Previous directors had led the program effectively, but she found that there was no guidance beyond her own history with the center and the institutional memory of some other long-time employees. No policies or procedures had been established about interviewing prospective employees, filling openings from the waiting list, and planning for staff vacations.

Regulations, policies, and procedures are linked in many ways. In this chapter, we discuss how policies and procedures guide a program's operations. They ensure compliance with applicable federal, state, and local laws, regulations, and standards, while helping the program achieve its particular mission and reach its goals.

CONSIDERING POLICIES AND PROCEDURES

Policies address issues that are critical to the center's operations and include rules employees must follow. *Procedures* are step-by-step instructions for following established policies.

Policies describe the program's specific plans for achieving particular goals. They can apply to employees as well as participating families. Policies often answer the question, "What is to be done and by whom?" A policy might state that the director is responsible for recruiting and retaining qualified staff. Other policies clarify expectations of employment. An example of this kind of policy is one that establishes the length of employees' annual paid vacation. A third group of policies describes rules participating families are expected to follow. An example of this kind of policy might state that children's birthday celebrations are not to include sugar-filled treats such as cupcakes and candy.

Policies should be written as comprehensive statements describing previously made decisions, identified guiding principles, or already agreed-upon courses of action that will help the program achieve its goals. Many policies will be included in a program's family handbook and/or staff manual, but other written policies might serve as a resource for program administrators to ensure consistency and fair treatment for employees and families alike.

Procedures describe specific strategies for complying with established policies. They may identify, step-by-step, how to reach agreed-upon goals and may include forms developed to accomplish these tasks. Like policies, most procedures will be included in appropriate staff manuals and family handbooks; others apply only to administrators and are less widely circulated.

Procedures that apply to all employees describe applying for vacation time. These procedures should indicate where the form for requesting a vacation is located, how far in advance and to whom requests are to be submitted, and when employees can expect a response to their vacation request.

Procedures that apply to families should be included in the family handbook. Examples include a request that families notify the center if their child is sick and will not be attending for several days or describe the procedure for identifying individuals authorized to pick up their child at the end of the day.

Some procedures apply only to administrators. When filling a staff vacancy, the director may be required to (a) post a notice in the staff break room, (b) advertise in the local paper, and (c) list the job opening on an online website such as CareerBuilder or Craigslist. It would not be appropriate to include this procedure in the widely circulated staff manual, but it would be important for it to be included in the program's administrative manual that ensures consistency in carrying out many administrative tasks.

Policies and Procedures Guide for Employees and Families

Policies and procedures describe each stakeholder's responsibilities and guide their interactions. In addition to addressing laws, regulations, and standards, policies and procedures that apply to program personnel should reflect reliance on the profession's *Code of Ethical Conduct* designed to "offer guidelines for responsible behavior" (NAEYC, 2011b). That is, they describe how "good early childhood professionals" are expected to behave and what they aspire to be like as they work with young children and their families, colleagues, employers, and the community.

The **staff manual** is an internal document that describes qualifications for employment; includes job descriptions; and spells out employees' rights and responsibilities, including the expectation that all employees are to comply with laws, regulations, and standards designed to safeguard the health, safety, and well-being of children, families, employees, employers, and the community. The staff manual should additionally create clear expectations related to employees' professionalism and reliance on ethical standards. It should contribute to the creation of the center's culture of caring; ensure the center's smooth day-to-day operation; and should guide employees' interactions with one another, the families they serve, and the community. In short, the staff manual helps the center stay on course for accomplishing its goals and achieving its vision. A comprehensive staff manual increases the likelihood that policies and procedures will be implemented consistently.

Families, like employees, play a critical role in ensuring that the program's operations comply with applicable laws, regulations, and standards. A program's **family handbook** is distributed to the parents and/or guardians of all participating children and may also be posted on the program's website. It should include information about the program's operations, policies, and procedures. Examples of regulations-based policies families are responsible for following include requiring children to submit proof of specific immunizations and requiring children with identified contagious conditions to be isolated or excluded until they are no longer contagious.

The family handbook also includes specifics about the program's day-to-day operations. It is likely to provide guidance about how children should dress, describe nap-time routines, and specify drop-off and pickup procedures. Many programs also have policies addressing holiday observances and create guidelines about bringing toys from home.

In addition, the family handbook should make it clear that this program's operations and interactions are guided by the *NAEYC Code of Ethical Conduct*. In fact, the Code requires that programs "shall inform families of program philosophy, policies, curriculum, assessment system, and personnel qualifications, and explain why we teach as we do" (Code of Ethics, Principle 2.2). The family handbook is an essential tool for systemically communicating with all families.

Finally, the **administrative manual** is a tool that guides the administrator's decision-making process. It is likely to include specific information about the employee salary scale; waiting list policies; and benefits, such as reduced tuition for an employee's child, that are at the director's discretion to use when trying to attract particularly desirable personnel.

Like the program's staff manual and family handbook, the administrative manual should reflect reliance on the *NAEYC Code of Ethical Conduct* and should additionally specify that administrators' interactions are guided by the Code's *Supplement for Early Childhood Program Administrators* (NAEYC, 2011c) in Appendix 3.

Unlike the staff manual and the family handbook, the administrative policies and procedures manual is not distributed. Only the program's director and the governing and/or advisory boards have access to this sensitive information. It is important, nonetheless, even in small proprietary programs, to write down administrative policies and procedures. This ensures fair and equitable treatment and simplifies the director's day-to-day decision making by addressing in advance the commonly occurring issues he is likely to face on a regular basis. It can also serve as a guide when facing infrequently occurring situations, such as orienting a new director. In this way, it serves as the program's institutional memory.

Consistent reliance on established manuals and handbooks is essential. All employees need to be familiar with and to be held accountable for consistently and reliably following both the family handbook, which guides their interactions with participating children and families, and the staff manual, which guides their relationships with their coworkers, administrator, clients, and employer. Together they create shared understandings about the program's operations. When the director follows the administrator's manual, established policies and procedures will be followed, even when there are changes in leadership.

DEVELOPING AND USING POLICIES AND PROCEDURES

Licensing Requirements

Many states' child care regulations require that licensed programs have written policies and procedures for staff and families covering particular aspects of their operation. Manuals for center personnel may be required to address the following issues:

- Job qualifications, including education, training, and experience
- Essential job functions

- Staff performance evaluation procedures
- Termination procedures

Licensing regulations in many states require that topics such as the following be addressed in handbooks for families:

- Ages of children served
- Hours and days of operation
- Procedures for releasing children at the end of the day
- Procedures for handling illness and injuries
- Procedures for notifying families of field trips
- Notification that child care providers are mandated reporters of suspected child abuse and neglect
- Accepted forms of discipline (NCCIC/NARA, 2010)

Advocates have recently urged states to require child care providers to develop written emergency plans that specific action steps in human-made or natural disasters (NACCRRA/Save the Children, 2010). The state board of education may also require school-based programs for young children, such as prekindergarten and after-school programs, to create policies and procedures addressing specific aspects of their operation.

Requirements Addressed by Voluntary Standards

The family handbook, employee manual, and the administrative manual of programs participating in voluntary accreditation or their state's Quality Rating Improvement System (QRIS) are required to meet additional standards above and beyond those imposed by licensing regulations. NAEYC Accreditation Standards, for example, require programs to provide families with information, including policies and procedures, *in a language the family can understand* (NAEYC, 2011a). This example shows how accreditation standards that exceed minimal state licensing requirements shape a program's operations.

NAEYC Accreditation Standards also address teachers' preparation, knowledge, and skills. While state regulations may allow lead teachers to be enrolled in high school or a GED program, NAEYC requires that lead teachers in accredited programs have at least an associate's degree or the equivalent. In addition, NAEYC requires that at least 75% of the lead teachers in an accredited program hold a bachelor's degree in early childhood or a related field (2011a). That means the staff manual in an accredited center must describe minimal requirements for lead teachers, and the administrative manual should specify that the director is responsible for ensuring that at least 75% of the program's lead teachers have at least a bachelor's degree. These policies will guide the director when making hiring and promotion decisions and will guarantee compliance with applicable accreditation standards.

NAEYC requires other written personnel policies that go substantially beyond licensing requirements. For example, they must describe

- Roles and responsibilities, qualifications, and specialized training required of staff and volunteers
- Salary scales and descriptions of benefits for full-time employees, including health insurance, leave, education, and retirement plans

Some of this information will be included in the widely circulated staff manual, but other specifics will, instead, be part of the administrative manual.

Centers that are part of a franchise or chain are also likely to be required to satisfy specific non-licensure-related requirements. For example, the operator may require all employees to wear shirts with the center's logo, or all classrooms might be required to include specific information in an "introducing the staff" flyer posted outside each classroom. Dress codes and other organization-specific rules would be included in the center's staff manual.

Application Activity

Working in small groups, review the *NAEYC Code of Ethical Conduct* in Appendix 2. Develop an item you think would make a good addition to a program's staff manual that is suggested by one of the Code's core values, ideals, or principles.

How Do Policies and Procedures Contribute to the Center's Smooth Operation?

When programs thoughtfully and carefully create comprehensive policies and procedures and include them in appropriate family handbooks and staff and administration manuals, they eliminate any number of potential problems that would otherwise require a great deal of the director's time and energy. Well-developed policies and procedures can, for example, help determine how you should prioritize families on your waiting list.

Suppose two families paid the registration fee and put their children's names on the waiting list for a space in your 3-year-old classroom just days apart. Now, after several months, you have a long-awaited opening. Do you offer the slot to the first child on the list whose stay-at-home mother wants him to have a wider circle of friends? Or do you offer it to the family that came to you a few days later and now needs full-time child care so the mother, who has been job hunting for months and needs money for unexpected medical expenses, can accept the position she was recently offered?

Clear-cut policies aligned with your program's mission, goals, and core values would help you consistently reach fair, equitable, and defensible decisions. If your family handbook and program policies indicate you will *always* fill vacancies on a first-come, first-served basis, you would be bound to offer enrollment to the first family to pay the application fee. If, on the other hand, your mission prioritizes supporting families' economic self-sufficiency, and your policies state that you are *guided by* the established waiting list, you may elect to offer the spot to the second family that needs reliable child care to support the mother's employment.

Well-conceived policies and procedures also make program administrators more efficient. Instead of ricocheting from one emergency to the next, the director can turn to established policies and procedures to guide day-to-day decision making.

And finally, carefully crafted policies and procedures ensure consistency. Instead of relying on memory about how sensitive situations have been handled in the past, a director can turn to established policies and procedures, confident that the course of action will be fair to children, families, employees, and the community. Time invested in writing a complete administrator's manual can save time and reduce stress in the long run.

Who Is Responsible for Developing Policies and Procedures?

In small family-operated centers, owners or operators often serve as hands-on directors working directly with children, families, and employees. The director in these centers is likely to develop, interpret, and implement policies and procedures and probably has the autonomy to make decisions as the need arises.

Centers operated by a local sponsor such as a church, community organization, college, or university may have a board of directors and/or an advisory committee that works with the director in policy and procedure development and implementation. In these programs, the board is responsible for guiding the development of policies and procedures that reflect the sponsor's priorities. They are likely to take the lead in developing policies and procedures related to the maintenance and use of space and utilities, the program's fiscal health, days and hours of operation, and other steps the program can take to achieve the sponsor's goals in operating the early childhood program.

While the board focuses on creating a context for the center's operations, the director should be relied upon as the expert on matters related to young children and early care and education. She will have appropriate expectations about employees' strengths and needs, should be able to contribute to policies and procedures that promote positive relationships with the children and families served, and can provide advice about how to establish and maintain a good reputation in the community that reflects well on the sponsoring agency.

Large chains and franchises, Head Start, and public school programs usually have a formal organizational structure with established lines of authority. In these programs, policy formulation, interpretation, and implementation are likely to be formally structured, with the responsibilities of the director and board clearly identified. In these large organizations, the director is likely to serve as an expert and spokesperson for the early childhood program, working within this formal structure to advocate for the children and staff.

For example, a superintendent in a public school works with the school board on policies and procedures and sees that the adopted policies and procedures are implemented. This work, however, is carried out by assistant superintendents, principals, early childhood coordinators, and classroom teachers who directly implement programs for young children at the local level.

Characteristics of Viable Policies and Procedures

Administrators and boards developing policies and procedures need to consider if proposed items are (a) aligned with laws, regulations, and standards; (b) reasonable and needed; (c) have the potential to contribute to the program's efforts to fulfill its mission and achieve its goals; and (d) help the program take a proactive stance rather than a reactive approach to operations and decision making.

They need to be committed to devoting the time and effort required for creating and evaluating policies and procedures during their development. The program's leadership should also be committed to participating in the regular review of policies and procedures to be certain they remain aligned with changing laws, regulations, and standards; understandings of best practice; and addressing identified gaps, oversights, or duplications. Here are some characteristics of viable policies and procedures:

1. They conform with state laws and regulations, accreditation standards (when applicable), and to the policies of the funding agency.
2. They address as many frequently occurring situations as possible.
3. The staff and administrative manuals and family handbook must be aligned with one another.
4. They should be relatively constant. Policies should not change every time there are new members on the board. Procedures should be changed only when better strategies for accomplishing particular goals have been identified.
5. The family handbook and staff manual should be readily available so they can be consulted easily.

6. Generally speaking, policies and procedures should be followed consistently. When there are situations that frequently require the director to make an exception to an existing policy or procedure, the fact that a stated policy or procedure is not always followed should be clearly indicated. For example, consider the scenario described earlier when the director had to decide to whom she would offer an opening in the 3-year-old classroom. The policy on filling openings from the waiting list might say, "Spaces will be offered to families on the waiting list on a first-come, first-served basis unless there are compelling extraordinary circumstances." If exceptions to a policy or procedure are frequently made, the policy or procedure probably needs to be revised.

7. They may include a stipulation that they be reviewed annually.

Application Activity

Develop a *policy* (a rule about a critical issue) and *procedures* (step-by-step instructions for following that policy) for a staff manual or family handbook. Make sure that the policy or procedures you develop address a complex topic likely to require the director to make a difficult decision. Topics to consider are responding to a family's request for a particular teacher or classroom, working with a teacher who is going through a difficult divorce and whose attendance has not met the program's expectations, or a family that has been regularly bringing a child to the center during his class's nap time.

Developing and Revising Your Center's Family Handbook and/or Staff Manual

Developing the Family Handbook and Staff Manual for a New Program: The center's family handbook and staff manual are its official vehicles for communicating how it will achieve its vision while accomplishing its goals. When you have the opportunity to create the staff manual and family handbook for a new center, you will be developing policies and procedures that will set the program's course for the foreseeable future. It is important that these documents create a culture that respects children, families, and colleagues; encourages and nurtures relationships based on trust and respect; and anticipates frequently asked questions and ordinarily occurring situations to ensure the program's smooth operation.

The place to begin the process of developing these materials is with appropriate licensing, accreditation, and/or QRIS standards. You want to be certain you address all required topics. The next step is to consider how the program will contribute to the mission and help the program achieve the goals of the investors, the education committee of the sponsoring church, the board of a publicly funded agency, or whoever is preparing to begin serving young children and families.

If you become a director in a small center, you might be expected to single-handedly create its family handbook and staff manual. If you are working with a board, its members may be a resource upon whom you can rely. In either case, as a director of a new program, you will probably have neither a staff nor families to review preliminary drafts, so it will be particularly important to rely on professional resources such as this book. It would be wise to seek feedback from successful directors of existing programs as you develop these foundational documents. It is also advisable to ask a lawyer to review particular sections before they are finalized to be certain the policies and procedures they describe keep the center in compliance with applicable laws related to hiring, termination, including individuals who have special needs, handling confidential information, and other issues that may have legal dimensions. A member of your governing or advisory board or an experienced director in your community may be able to help you locate a lawyer who can provide this service at a reasonable cost.

Developing a Family Handbook and Staff Manual for an Existing Center or Making Major Revisions to Existing Documents: If you become the director of a program that has a record of regulatory compliance and success but lacks a comprehensive and up-to-date family handbook and/or staff manual, your job will be to begin by making "the way we do things here" explicit. That is, you would work to describe how the center's "business as usual" approach has helped it comply with laws, regulations, and standards and achieve its goals in the service of young children and their families.

A director embarking on the creation of these materials for an existing program or a substantial revision of the programs' existing family handbook and/or staff manual will want to work with a small group of staff and the center's governing or advisory board if applicable to be certain she has accurately described current policies and procedures. It would also be wise to ask a few families to review a proposed family handbook to be certain they find it to be comprehensive, clear, and easy to understand.

Once you have a preliminary draft of a new or substantially revised family handbook or staff manual, it is time to give employees an opportunity to provide feedback. This effort will help you confirm that your descriptions of existing policies and procedures are accurate, reasonable, and fair and will increase the likelihood staff will take ownership of them. While all feedback on draft materials should be carefully considered, it is unlikely administrators and boards will incorporate every suggestion made by the center's employees. It is essential, however, that staff can see evidence that their feedback has been thoughtfully considered. Remember that they are the face of the center, both within the program and out in the community. They have a unique perspective that will add an important and much needed dimension to these materials.

Refining the Existing Family Handbook and/or Staff Manual: Because professionals are continually engaged in reflective practice, the director, with the board if appropriate, should lead the staff through a systematic review of all policies and procedures on a regular basis. This effort will ensure that they reflect not only where the center *is* on its journey toward excellence, but also *where it can make progress* in achieving its goals. The family handbook and staff manual should be updated at least annually, but the process of their revision should be an ongoing one that encourages all staff to continually consider how these guidelines are contributing to the center's smooth operation. Annual review of these materials may comply with a formal policy established by the program's governing board.

A Better Way

Grace was surprised by how much time and energy she found herself investing in routine tasks. She had to seek approval from the governing board every time she needed to fill a vacancy, when making anything but the most clear-cut decisions about offering admission to children on the waiting list, and when switching from one food service provider to another to save money. She felt she needed more autonomy and hoped that clear guidelines about how to make those kinds of decisions might make the board willing to trust her to make good decisions.

Grace realized that a contribution she should make to the center's ongoing long-term success would be to create an administrative manual. She knew it might take as long as a year to accomplish this goal, but she was confident it would be worth the time and effort. The first step she took was to review the NAEYC Code of Ethics and its Supplements. Then she contacted the directors of other high-quality centers in her community to ask if they would share their handbooks (which she realized they may not be willing to do) or, alternatively, if they would meet with her and help her develop a draft table of contents that would serve as an outline for the manual she was developing. She also networked with directors of leading programs similar to hers when she attended her state's early childhood conference. Once she had a good draft of a proposed administrative manual, she took it to her governing board for its approval. She was pleased when the board made some additions and then approved it promptly. It is now an indispensible tool that has streamlined the decision-making process and has made her more consistent and efficient.

Using Established Policies and Procedures

Whether implementing existing or newly established policies and procedures, employees' morale, the program's reputation, and its overall success will depend on each staff member's commitment to knowing and complying with both the spirit and the letter of agreed-upon policies and procedures.

It is the program administrator's responsibility either alone or with the center's corporate office or board of directors to interpret and ensure consistent compliance with these programmatic guidelines. That means not only that the director follows them without fail, but also that he holds each employee and all participating families accountable for abiding by them consistently.

We recommend that staff be required to "sign off" on the staff manual and family handbook annually to signify that they know and are committed to following the policies and procedures they describe, and that families be asked to commit to knowing and following policies and procedures described in the family handbook when they enroll and at the start of each year.

CATEGORIES OF POLICIES AND PROCEDURES

Policies and procedures should cover as many aspects of the early care and education program's operation as possible. There are, of course, wide variations across programs, but most programs of early care and education have policies and procedures in the following categories:

1. Program overview.   Any discussion of policies and procedures should begin by providing an overview of the program, its purpose, vision, goals, and objectives.

2. Program services.   These policies and procedures state the primary program services to be provided (e.g., care, education), along with other services (e.g., food, transportation, social services, parent education) offered by the program.

3. Administration.   Some specific areas included in administrative policies and procedures are the makeup of and procedures for selecting or electing members to the board of directors, board committees (e.g., executive, personnel, finance, building, program, nominating), advisory group, parent council, or other councils or committees; policies related to the appointment and functions of the director and supervisory personnel; and the administrative operations, such as the organizational chart and membership and functions of various administrative bodies.

4. Personnel policies.   All programs need to have the following documentation in place:
- Job descriptions and qualifications
- Recruitment, selection, and appointment procedures
- Staff training and professional development requirements

- Performance review timeline and procedures
- Salary schedules and fringe benefits
- Payroll schedule (e.g., the 15th and 30th of the month, every other Friday)
- Policies related to excused and unexcused absences
- Personal leave and vacation policies
- Termination policies

Personnel policies of publicly funded programs must include nondiscrimination, equal opportunity clauses and must be in compliance with the Americans with Disabilities Act. Employees may also be covered by the Pregnancy Discrimination Act of 1978 and the Family Leave Act of 1993. The websites of the U.S. Equal Employment Opportunity Commission and the U.S. Department of Justice, Americans with Disabilities Act (ADA) home pages listed at the end of this chapter include advice about how to avoid discriminatory practices and indicate information related to these issues that should be included in staff manuals (e.g., causes of termination, procedures for termination, appeal process for termination). You may want to review the website of the U.S. Equal Employment Opportunity Commission (see the address for this website at the end of this chapter) for additional specifics.

5. Services to children.   These policies and procedures describe who is eligible for the program's services. Sometimes eligibility is determined by governmental or agency mandates; sometimes families must document financial need; and in other instances, programs may give priority to particular populations, for example, the members of the sponsoring church or employees of a particular business. These policies also describe

- Maximum group (class) size
- Child-staff ratio for each age group
- Enrollment options (e.g., full time, part time, drop-in)
- Program services and provisions for child's safety and welfare (e.g., accident procedures, insurance coverage)
- Types of assessments used to document children's progress and procedures for sharing assessment information with families
- Termination of program services

6. Health and safety.   This category of policies and procedures may cover

- Physical exams required before employment or admission
- Procedures for screening children's health daily
- Care or exclusion of ill children
- Procedures for administering medications
- Health services offered by the program (e.g., screening, immunizations)
- Management of injuries and emergencies
- Nutrition and food-handling guidelines
- Provisions for rest or sleep
- Staff training in health and safety (e.g., Which staff members have CPR and first aid training?; Is there always a trained staff member onsite?)
- Surveillance of environmental problems

Rely on appropriate professional resources such as NAEYC's *Healthy Young Children* (Aronson, 2002), and *Caring for Our Children* (AAP/APHA/NRCHSCC, 2011) for specific guidelines created by health care professionals. Refer to the *Caring for Our Children* website listed at the end of this chapter for comprehensive information related to obesity prevention, including information for parents.

7. Business, budget, and financial issues.   Some areas included in policies related to the program's finances include

- The identification of person(s) responsible for the program's financial management, including the creation and monitoring of the budget
- The system of accounting

- Requirements for fiscal record keeping and routine reporting
- Audit requirements

Financial policies should describe the sources of funding (e.g., fees paid by families, grants, contracts) and guidelines and procedures for purchasing goods and services. Financial policies should additionally describe how the program will create and manage the contingency fund that should be established to pay for significant unplanned expenses, such as a new roof or furnace, or how to pay employees in case the program should have to close for a week, a month, or even longer because of illness, a natural or human-made disaster, or a facility problem.

8. Record keeping.   Policies and procedures should indicate
- What kinds of records are kept on each employee and on each child
- Where records are kept, including provisions for their security
- Identify who, under what circumstances, has access to these records

They should identify procedures for ensuring compliance with the Family Educational Rights and Privacy Act (FERPA) as it relates to children's and families' rights to privacy in educational settings. Refer to the website listed at the end of this chapter for a description of applicable provisions of FERPA.

9. Families.   These policies and procedures describe ways the program interacts with families and meets families' needs. Particular issues to address in this category of policies and procedures include
- Description of the program's philosophy
- Procedures and policies related to enrolling and withdrawing children, including notice to be given when withdrawing a child
- Days and hours of operation
- The calendar for the coming year, including scheduled holidays
- Policies related to families visiting their child's classroom (i.e., Is there an "open door" policy? Can family members visit at any time of the day? Is an appointment necessary before entering the classroom?)
- Descriptions of how program personnel will communicate with families, including daily or weekly logs, newsletters, email, teacher conferences

Policies related to families should also include information about opportunities for them to be engaged in the program by serving on advisory groups, accompanying children on field trips, and contributing as a classroom volunteer. And finally, it should include information about the structure and purpose of the parent-teacher organization, including information about planned family events and fund-raising.

10. Public relations and marketing.   These policies and procedures guide outreach into the community, including community representation on advisory committees or governing boards, relationships with allied agencies and associations, and the use of facilities by outside groups. There will also be expectations about how the administrator creates a presence in the community and how the program creates its unique identity. These policies may also indicate if the center advertises when enrollment applications are accepted or when registration opens to the public.

WHAT TOPICS NEED TO BE ADDRESSED IN THE STAFF MANUAL?

Your program's staff manual is the vehicle that communicates and formalizes many of the program's policies and procedures. It serves as a reference and roadmap for administrators and employees alike. The staff manual often overlaps with the family handbook, but it may address issues in more depth or with a different emphasis. It also builds on and expands state regulations. In addition to including a statement that all employees are required to know and adhere to applicable licensing regulations and to rely on the *NAEYC Code of Ethical Conduct,* major topics that you may want to address and elaborate on in the staff manual include the following:

1. **Program Overview**
   - States the program's purpose, philosophy, mission, vision, goals, and objectives.
   - Includes the program's address, phone and fax numbers, email address, website, and Federal Employer Identification Number (FEIN) number.
2. **Program Services**
   - Identifies ages served and hours of operation.
   - Identifies curriculum models (e.g., Creative Curriculum, High/Scope) or approaches to early care and education (e.g., Program for Infant/Toddler Care) teachers and caregivers are expected to implement.
   - Summarizes age-appropriate expectations, including the center's guidance and discipline policies; suggestions for creating an appropriate learning environment; and strategies for appropriately challenging, communicating with, and nurturing young children.
   - Identifies learning standards addressed at each age level (e.g., *Infant/Toddler Guidelines, Good Start Grow Smart* standards for 3- and 4-year-olds, state learning standards if appropriate for 4- and 5-year-olds).
   - Describes required documentation of curriculum planning. Are teachers required to submit lesson plans in advance? If so, what should they include?
   - Describes how caregivers and teaches are expected to provide parents with information about their child's growth, development, and learning using agreed-upon assessment strategies at regularly scheduled parent conferences.
3. **Administration**
   - Includes an organizational chart with a description of the makeup of advisory and/or governing boards.
   - Establishes a chain of command and indicates who will be contacted for help in the case of an emergency if the director is not available.
4. **Personnel Policies**
   - Gives notice that the program adheres to applicable nondiscriminatory, equal opportunity, American with Disabilities, and Family Leave laws.
   - Indicates, if applicable, that employment is "at will" and briefly describes this policy.
   - Includes job descriptions and qualifications for all positions.
   - Identifies all information and forms required for employment (i.e., background checks, physical exams, educational records, references, Federal Employment Eligibility Verification [I-9], and Internal Revenue Employee's Withholding Allowance Certificate [W-4] forms).
   - Summarizes required fringe benefits (e.g., workers' compensation, Social Security) and other benefits available to employees (e.g., health insurance, retirement) who wish to participate.
   - Describes indicators of possible abuse or neglect, puts teachers and caregivers on notice that they are *mandated reporters* of suspected child abuse or neglect, and identifies where they can find additional information about their community's child protective services.
   - Describes staffing patterns (e.g., lead teacher, assistant teacher, floater) and how teaching teams are expected to share instructional, caregiving, and housekeeping responsibilities.

- Identifies daily work hours, break and lunch time scheduling, and how work hours are to be recorded.
- Identifies schedule and frequency of pay days (e.g., every other Friday, the 1st and 15th of each month).
- Describes when the program will conduct an orientation for new employees and includes a general description of its content.
- Describes the probationary period, if any, for new employees. Indicates its length and how it affects terms of employment (e.g., eligibility for benefits, earned leave).
- Describes policies and procedures related to sick leave, personal leave, family leave (e.g., maternity, paternity, or family illness or death), jury duty, time off for medical or dental appointments, and vacation. Identifies forms used to request leave or vacation, where those forms can be found, and to whom they are to be submitted. Indicates how far in advance they should be submitted and when employees will know if leave or vacation has been granted.
- Identifies whom to call when sick and unable to work.
- Describes when substitutes are used and how they are contacted and scheduled.
- Identifies staff meetings employees are required to attend. Indicates how often required meetings are usually scheduled (e.g., monthly at lunch time) and indicates if employees are paid for this time.
- Stipulates the number of hours of in-service training required annually. Is in-service training offered onsite? Are employees paid during training? Are employees supported if they attend local, regional, or national conferences? Is support available for courses at local colleges or universities? Does the program participate in the Education and Compensation Helps (T.E.A.C.H.®) scholarship program offered by many states? (See the website listed at the end of this chapter for more information about the T.E.A.C.H.® program.)
- Describes procedures used to evaluate staff performance and either includes copies of observation and performance evaluation forms or indicates how they can be found.
- Describes policies related to raises and bonuses. Can employees expect annual cost-of-living raises? Are raises based on merit? Are bonuses regularly awarded? Do raises and bonuses depend on the program's financial status?
- Describes disciplinary or corrective action procedures, including procedures for filing an appeal.
- Describes where staff can locate supplies and how they can request needed supplies, materials, and equipment.
- Describes the program's policies related to the use of personal cell phones, the center's phones, computers and office equipment, and the Internet.
- Describes dress code for all staff.
- Identifies where staff are to park.
- Indicates that the center is a nonsmoking facility or identifies where smoking is permitted.
- Indicates if employees are allowed to bring their preschool or school-age children with them to work and if they are, under what circumstances.
- Describes resignation and termination procedures. Indicates if exit interviews are offered, and if so, with whom.

5. **Services to Children**
   - Describes admission criteria and identifies any populations (i.e., siblings of currently enrolled children, members of the sponsoring church) who are eligible for preferential admissions.

The director should review the staff manual with all employees when they are hired and regularly thereafter.

- Indicates if the program is inclusive, that is, if children with identified special needs are welcome to enroll. Describes the development and use of Individual Family Service Plan (IFSP) and Individual Educational Program (IEP), if appropriate.
- Includes annual calendar indicating dates the program is closed and dates of required staff work days.
- Identifies staff-child ratios for each age group served.
- Identifies group size for each age group served.
- Describes how transitions from one room to the next are planned (e.g., Are they based on children's age or on their developmental level?) and how they are implemented.
- Stipulates that teachers and caregivers are responsible for supervising the children in their care at all times, both indoors and out, when they are awake and asleep.
- Describes policies related to child guidance and discipline and summarizes recommended practices.
- Describes the program's assessment practices, identifies assessment instruments used (i.e., Ages and Stages Questionnaire, Work Sampling System) and includes a general description of expected documentation of learning and development, including the content of children's portfolios, anecdotal records, and so on.
- Describes suggested strategies to help children adjust to the program.
- Indicates expectations about lesson and unit plans. Are they to be turned in regularly? To whom? What are they to include?
- Describes the program's policies about classroom pets and animal visitors. Are they allowed or encouraged? Are they allowed to be out of a cage? What hand-washing practices are required?
- Describes expectations about outdoor play. Where are outdoor play areas? Do infants spend time outdoors? Do children regularly visit nearby parks? Are children expected to play outside every day except during extreme weather? When would they stay indoors?
- Describes appropriate activities for days when children must remain indoors.

- Describes the program's policy about field trips. How are field trips approved, scheduled, and supervised? How are children transported?
- Describes the program's policies related to holiday and birthday celebrations, being sensitive that some families' beliefs mean that they prohibit their children from participating in any celebrations.
- Describes any extra optional activities offered on a fee-for-services basis.
- Describes procedures to follow if a child has not been picked up at the end of the day.
- Describes how staff and families are notified in the event of severe weather or other natural disaster or environmental risk (e.g., chemical spill).

6. Health and Safety
- Summarizes ordinary and universal precautions that reduce the likelihood that infectious and contagious diseases, including blood-borne pathogens, will be spread.
- Describes hand-washing practices for children and adults.
- Describes practices specific to infant rooms:

  - Details diaper changing practices designed to protect children's health and safety.
  - Indicates that adults must remove their shoes upon entry.
  - Requires infants be placed on their backs to sleep to prevent sudden infant death syndrome (SIDS).
  - Indicates if families provide formula and baby food and where they are stored if provided by the center.
  - Indicates how bottles of formula or breast milk are heated (microwaves are NEVER used to heat breast milk or formula).
  - Describes how food and bottles brought from home are stored and labeled and when they must be discarded.
  - Describes provisions in place for nursing mothers who want to visit the classroom to nurse their babies and indicates if there is a lactation room where mothers can express breast milk for later use.
  - Indicates if families provide diapers, wipes, creams, and ointments and where they are stored if provided by the center.
  - Describes how infants are fed (e.g., Are bottle-fed babies always held? Are older infants placed in high chairs or do they sit in child-sized chairs?)

- Describes appropriate labeling and storage of children's cribs and rest cots.
- Details sanitizing and washing procedures for toys, cots and cribs, sheets, bibs, and so on. (Sanitizing solution is made by mixing 1 tablespoon of bleach to 1 quart of water or 1/4 cup of bleach to 1 gallon of water. This solution must be made daily.)
- Describes procedures for storing and giving children prescription and over-the-counter medications.
- Explains fire and emergency evacuation procedures, including where children would be taken if they could not return to their classrooms and how families would be notified in case of an emergency.
- Details sick child exclusion policies, identifying when children should not come to school and when they are ready to return.
- Describes plans to provide children needed first aid, including how minor injuries will be handled (e.g., What incident reports are to be filed?) and how parents will be notified if emergency medical care, including transport by ambulance, is needed.
- Describes procedures if a teacher becomes ill or is injured, how children's safety will be safeguarded, and how supervision will be assured.

- Describes how children will be released at the end of the day. Indicates how families notify the program if someone other than the usual parent or caregiver will take their child home, including what form of identification is required before a child will be released to someone other than the usual parent or caregiver.
- Sets expectations for toilet training and describes toileting routines. Indicates if children of particular ages are required to be potty trained. Describes how the program supports potty training. Indicates if children are always accompanied in the bathroom and if bathroom time is part of the daily routine.
- Indicates if the program provides breakfast, lunch, and/or snacks. Does the center follow U.S. Department of Agriculture (USDA) or other published dietary guidelines? If children bring food from home, does the program provide any guidelines about what should or should not be brought to school? Is it a peanut-free program? May children and staff bring fast food (e.g., McDonald's)?
- Describes steps to be taken when certain allergies or other dietary restrictions are observed.
- Describes mealtime routines. Are meals served family style? Are teachers and caregivers expected to eat with the children? Is conversation encouraged?
- Indicates teachers' housekeeping responsibilities (e.g., Do they take out the trash, sweep their floors, clean sinks and bathrooms at the end of the day?).
- Details, by whom, and how often the facility and playground are checked to note their condition and identify repairs that may be needed.

7. **Business and Financial Issues**
   - Details established fees and tuition.
   - Describes how fees and tuition are collected and teachers' responsibilities (if any) related to fee collection.
   - Indicates how payments are handled if enrichment activities are provided on a fee-for-services basis (e.g., dance, gymnastics, art).

8. **Records**
   - Describes content of employees' personnel files and identifies individuals who have access to these records.
   - Describes content of children's files and identifies individuals who have access to these records.
   - Summarizes teachers' and caregivers' responsibilities to comply with the Family Educational Rights and Privacy Act.

9. **Families**
   - Describes how teachers and caregivers are expected to communicate with families (e.g., daily logs, communication notebooks, regular emails, monthly newsletters).
   - Indicates if the center has an open-door policy that welcomes parents at any time. Are there any restrictions about when they can visit (e.g., not at nap time)? Are siblings welcome?
   - Describes how teachers and caregivers are expected to communicate concerns about a child's behavior. Indicates how confidentiality of all children and families is maintained.
   - Indicates how families notify the center if an individual unknown to the center staff will be picking up their child at the end of the day.
   - Describes frequency and content of parent-teacher conferences.
   - Indicates if the program offers parent education sessions. If so, when are they held? Who is eligible to participate?
   - Indicates if the program has a Parent-Teacher Organization or PTA. Describes its purpose and major activities. Indicates how teachers can become involved.

10. **Public Relations and Marketing**
    - Some teachers may be willing to speak to civic groups, or they might reach out to other child care programs or neighborhood religious communities in need of training or parent education classes. When it is seen as a community resource, the program reflects well on itself and the field of early care and education.
    - Employees should be reminded that they are the face and voice of the program in the community. Even when they are not working, their behavior reflects on the center.

Remember that employees are expected to know and consistently abide by all policies and procedures included in the employee manual as well as the family handbook. Some topics, such as job descriptions, are most appropriately addressed in the employee manual; others, such as guidelines for birthday celebrations, are described in the family handbook.

WHAT TOPICS NEED TO BE ADDRESSED IN THE FAMILY HANDBOOK?

The family manual should have a warm and friendly tone and be polished and professional. That means it is easy to read and understand, avoids professional jargon, and includes no errors in spelling or grammar. Illustrations should be respectful of children and families (avoid "cute") and should reflect the cultural and ethnic diversity of the families you serve. In addition, you should make every effort to have the manual translated into the home language of every family enrolled in your program. It does not communicate with your children's parents if they cannot read and understand its contents. Families are expected to agree to follow the policies and procedures described in the handbook. We recommend that you ask them to "sign off" to signify their commitment to do so.

Consider addressing the topics listed next as you prepare a family handbook. Some information, such as the program's overview and description of services, belongs in both the staff manual and the family handbook. Other information, such as specifics about when and how to pay fees, is appropriately covered in more depth in the family handbook than in the staff manual. Additional topics, such as staff qualifications, are addressed more briefly in the family handbook than in the staff manual. The emphasis you put on each topic in these program-specific materials will reflect the audience you are addressing, the program's purpose, and the population it serves.

1. **Program Overview**
   - States the program's purpose, philosophy, mission, vision, goals, and objectives and its general approach to instruction (e.g., Is this a play-based program?).
   - Indicates the program's licensure and, when applicable, accreditation or quality rating.
   - Affirms that the program is committed to the field's core values, ideals, and principles as stated in the *NAEYC Code of Ethical Conduct*.
2. **Program Services**
   - Identifies ages served and hours of operation.
   - Gives notice that the program adheres to applicable nondiscriminatory, equal opportunity, and Americans with Disabilities laws.
   - Identifies curriculum models (e.g., Creative Curriculum, High/Scope) or approaches to early care and education (e.g., Program for Infant/Toddler Care) implemented by the program and briefly describes their essential characteristics.
   - Describes services provided and routines for before and/or after school for school-age children (e.g., homework time, activity options).

- Indicates where parents are to park at drop-off and pickup times.
- Describes policies related to termination of services, including notice families are expected to give if they plan to withdraw their child from the center.

3. **Administration**
   - Includes organizational chart including a description and makeup of advisory and/or governing boards.
   - Lists current staff and their assignments.

4. **Services to Children**
   - Describes admission requirements, including birth-date cutoffs and identifies any populations (e.g., siblings of currently enrolled children, members of the sponsoring church) who are eligible for preferential admissions.
   - Includes the annual calendar, indicating dates the program is closed and any dates the center does not operate on its regular schedule (e.g., Are there half-day sessions to give teachers time for parent conferences or staff development?).
   - Indicates staff-child ratios and group size for each age group served.
   - Describes how transitions from one room to the next are planned (e.g., Are they based on children's age or on their developmental level?) and how they are implemented.
   - Describes the amount of interaction between children of different ages, particularly if the program serves school-age children.
   - Describes how children should dress (e.g., play clothes that may get dirty or wet, shoes that are safe for running and climbing) and reminds families that children will play outdoors in all but extreme weather.
   - Indicates the program's ability and willingness to meet the needs of children with identified special needs and any requirements (e.g., an extra employee in the classroom under certain circumstances) that may apply.
   - Describes the program's policies related to child guidance and discipline.
   - Describes morning drop-off and afternoon pickup routines, including advice on helping children transition into the program and adjust to its day-to-day routines.
   - Describes the program's policy about classroom pets and animal visitors.
   - Describes expectations about outdoor play. Where are outdoor play areas? Do children regularly visit nearby parks? Children are to dress to play outside every day except during extreme weather.
   - Describes the program's policy about field trips, including a description of how families will be notified of an upcoming trip, what kind of permission form will be required for children to participate, how children will be transported and, if appropriate, invites families to help with supervision.
   - Describes the program's policies related to holiday and birthday celebrations.
   - Lists supplies children are expected to bring from home (e.g., rest mats, toothbrush, blanket for nap time, change of clothes).
   - Describes procedures that will be followed if a child has not been picked up at the end of the day.
   - Describes any extra optional activities offered on a fee-for-services basis and the related responsibilities of regular center staff.
   - Describes how families are notified if the program will be closed, will open late, or will close early because of severe weather.

5. **Health and Safety**
   - Identifies required immunizations and health exams required for enrollment.
   - Describes hand-washing practices followed by children and adults.
   - Describes plans to provide children needed first aid, including how minor injuries will be handled and how parents will be notified if emergency medical care, including transport by ambulance, is needed.

- Describes procedures for giving children prescription and over-the-counter medications. Indicates if a form must be completed to give the program permission to administer medications and where that form can be found.
- Explains emergency evacuation procedures, including where children would be taken if they could not return to their classrooms and how families would be notified in case of an emergency.
- Describes practices specific to infant rooms:

  - Indicates that adults must remove their shoes upon entry.
  - Notifies families that infants will be placed on their backs to sleep to prevent sudden infant death syndrome (SIDS).
  - Indicates if formula and baby food are provided by the center or if they are brought by children's families.
  - Stipulates how bottles of formula or breast milk are heated (microwaves are NEVER used to heat breast milk or formula).
  - Describes how food and bottles brought from home are stored and labeled and when they must be discarded.
  - Describes provisions in place for nursing mothers who want to visit the classroom to nurse their babies or arrangements that support mothers wishing to pump breast milk for later use.
  - Indicates if the center provides diapers, wipes, creams, and ointments or if they are brought by children's families.
  - Describes how infants are fed (e.g., Are bottle-fed babies always held? Are older infants placed in high chairs or do they sit in child-sized chairs?)

- Sets expectations for toilet training and describes toileting routines. Indicates if children of particular ages are required to be potty trained. Describes how the program supports potty training. Indicates if children are always accompanied in the bathroom and if bathroom time is part of the daily routine.
- Details sick child exclusion policies, identifying when children should not come to school and when they will be permitted to return. See Figure 4.1 for an example of how your family handbook might describe when a child should stay home from school.
- Requests that children bring a complete change of clothes (including socks) to be left at the center.
- Describes how children will be released at the end of the day. Indicates how families notify the program if someone other than the usual parent or caregiver will take their child home, including what form of identification is required before a child will be released to someone other than the usual parent or caregiver.
- Indicates if the program provides breakfast, lunch, and snacks and follows U.S. Department of Agriculture (USDA) or other published dietary guidelines.
- Provides guidelines about what should or should not be brought to school if children bring food from home (e.g., Is it a peanut free program? Will food from home be refrigerated? Can it be heated? May children bring fast food, such as McDonald's?).
- Details what steps are taken to be certain food allergies and other dietary restrictions are respected (e.g., those based on religious practices or preferences for only organic foods).
- Describes mealtime routines. Are meals served family style? Do teachers and caregivers eat with the children? Is conversation encouraged?

6. **Business and Financial Issues**
   - Details established fees and tuition for each age group, including registration fees, materials fees, late fees, and returned check policy.

When Should Your Child Stay Home?

We hope your child will be able to come to the center regularly, but there are times when children should stay home for their own safety and well-being or to prevent the spread of a contagious condition.

Children should stay home when they are ill.

These are symptoms that mean your child should not come to school:

Blood in stools
Diarrhea (negative stool cultures required for some illnesses)
Difficult breathing
Fever accompanied by behavior changes or symptoms of an illness until the child receives a professional evaluation
Inexplicable irritability or persistent crying
Lethargy (more than usual tiredness)
Mouth sores with drooling
Persistent abdominal pain
Rash with fever or behavior change
Uncontrolled coughing
Unspecified respiratory tract illness
Vomiting (two or more times in 24 hours)
Wheezing

Your child should not come to school if he or she has:

Chicken pox (until lesions have dried)
Haemophilus influenza, type b (Hlb) infection
Head lice (until after first treatment)
Hepatitis A (until one week after onset)
Herpes simplex (sores and drooling)
Impetigo (until 24 hours after treatment begins)
Measles (until 6 days after rash appears)
Meningitis
Mumps (until 9 days after swelling)
Pertussis (until 14 days after laboratory-confirmed onset)
Purulent conjunctivitis (until 24 hours after treatment begins)
Rubella (until 6 days after rash appears)
Scabies (until treatment is completed)
Shingles (if sores have not crusted)
Streptococcal pharyngitis (until 24 hours after treatment begins) or other streptococcal infections
Tuberculosis

Family Emergency

Your child probably needs to be with you or other familiar family members in the case of the death or serious illness of a loved one. You know your child best, however, and we want to help if the familiar school routine would be a comfort. Please be in touch in these kinds of circumstances so that we can know how to help you and your child.

During Extreme Weather

The center will be closed when local schools close because of extreme weather. Listen to local radio and TV stations or check the Internet. We follow the decision made by the Richland School District in case of school closings. You will NOT hear an announcement specifically from our school.

Figure 4.1
Sample of a family handbook's description of when children should stay home from school and when they may return.

- Describes when fees and tuition are due and how they are collected (e.g., Are credit or debit cards accepted? Are checks mailed or dropped into a box on the director's desk?).
- Describes when late fees and returned check fees are assessed and how they are to be handled.

7. **Records**
   - Identifies birth, immunization, physical examination, residency, or other documentation requirement for admission.
   - Identifies materials families must submit before their child can participate in the program, such as emergency contact information, acknowledgement of having received the family handbook, and so on.

8. **Families**
   - Puts families on notice that teachers and caregivers are mandated by law to report suspected child abuse or neglect to the local child protective service agency.
   - Informs families that corporal punishment will never be permitted in the center.
   - Identifies how families can expect teachers and caregivers to communicate with them (e.g., daily logs, communication notebooks, regular emails, monthly newsletters).
   - Indicates if the center has an open-door policy that welcomes parents at any time. Are there any restrictions about when they can visit (e.g., not at nap time)? Are siblings welcome?
   - Describes how teachers and caregivers are expected to communicate concerns about a child's behavior. Indicates how confidentiality of all children and families is maintained.
   - Describes frequency and content of parent-teacher conferences.

Help Your Child Get Ready for School—Family Checklist

We are looking forward to a productive and fun school year. We want to be certain your child gets off to the very best start possible. Please read this handbook carefully and complete this checklist to be sure you and your child have everything ready for school to begin.

Have you read this handbook? _____

Have you completed and signed the emergency information form? _____

Have you asked your emergency contacts if they are willing to be "on call" if your child needs them? _____

Have you completed and signed the health history form? _____

Has your physician completed and signed the physical examination form? _____

Has your physician completed and signed the immunization record form? _____

Has your dentist signed the dental report form? _____

Does your child have comfortable play clothes and sturdy shoes to wear to school? _____

Do you have the needed supplies? (book bag, blanket for rest time, etc.) _____

Are all sweaters, jackets, hats, and mittens labeled? _____

Have you put an extra set of clothes (head to toe) in a labeled zip-lock bag? _____

Are you helping your child anticipate your family's school day routine? _____

Do you have any questions you'd like to discuss with center personnel?

Figure 4.2
This checklist helps ensure a smooth start to a new school year.

- Indicates if the program offers parenting classes. If so, when are they held? Who is eligible to participate?
- Indicates if the program has a Parent-Teacher Organization or PTA. Describes its purpose and major activities. Indicates how can families become involved.
- See Figure 4.2 for an example of a Family Member's Checklist to communicate beginning-of-school routines in a straightforward and easy-to-follow format.

9. **Public Relations and Marketing**
- Indicates that the director and selected teachers may be willing to speak to civic groups or may be available to work with other child care programs or neighborhood religious communities in need of training or parent education classes. When seen as a community resource, the program reflects well on itself and the field of early care and education.

WHAT INFORMATION SHOULD BE IN THE ADMINISTRATOR'S MANUAL?

This material will, in all likelihood, be available only to the director and her supervisor(s), which may be an advisory or governing board or the corporation's regional and/or national coordinator.

The issues addressed in an administrator's manual are likely to be more idiosyncratic than those addressed in either the family handbook or the staff manual. Examples of items that may be addressed in the administrative manual include the following:

- Details related to salary scales, raises, and bonuses (if applicable).
- Details of interview and hiring procedures. How are references checked? Is time in the classroom part of the interview process? Are potential employees approved by a board or its representatives?
- Details of termination procedures.
- Conditions for the availability of employee tuition discounts. Is this benefit available to all employees? Is it a discretionary benefit that may be offered to employees with specific credentials?
- Describes how the yearly calendar is developed. Does the director consult with local schools? Professional organizations whose conferences the staff attends?
- The director's responsibilities related to recruitment of both staff and families.
- The timelines related to licensure and accreditation. When is the program up for renewal? What reports are required to licensure and accrediting bodies?

If you become a program director, you will want to find out about existing guidelines you will be expected to follow. During your tenure, you will want to continue to develop this resource. It will make your life, and that of your successor, much easier if all this information can be found in a central, organized location.

SUMMARY

While regulations, statues, and standards and the program's mission statement, goals, and objectives create a framework for a program's operations, it is the program-specific materials—its family handbook, staff manual, and administrative manual—that apply these rules and regulations to a program's day-to-day operations. The formulation, implementation, and evaluation of these materials are the responsibilities of the board of directors and the program administrator.

When a program has thoughtfully developed policies and procedures that are clearly and consistently communicated to staff and families, many potential problems can be eliminated. Well-conceived policies and procedures also save the program director a great deal of time and energy. They give him or her the opportunity to focus on the important work of caring for and educating the young children entrusted to the program and its staff. You will find that time devoted to the creation of these materials is time well spent. They put your program on track for smooth operation. When staff morale is high, parents are the program's biggest boosters, and children's days are spent in an environment that enhances their learning, growth, and development.

USEFUL WEBSITES

Related Federal Laws and Regulations

Employment Law Guide: Laws, Regulation, and Technical Assistance Services, sponsored by the U.S. Department of Labor

www.dol.gov/compliance/guide/index.htm

This government resource provides an overview of employment laws that can help your program be in full compliance with all rules and regulations.

Family Educational Rights and Privacy Act (FERPA), sponsored by the U.S. Department of Education

www.ed.gov/policy/gen/guid/fpco/ferpa/index.html

This is a comprehensive description of practices mandated by FERPA and can help your program stay in full compliance.

U.S. Equal Employment Opportunity Commission, sponsored by the U.S. Equal Employment Opportunity Commission

www.eeoc.gov/

This government website provides information to help ensure that your program's practices are in full compliance with equal opportunity requirements.

The Pregnancy Discrimination Act of 1978, sponsored by the U.S. Employment Opportunity Commission

www.eeoc.gov/laws/statutes/pregnancy.cfm

This government website explains how the Civil Rights Act of 1964 protects pregnant women.

Family and Medical Leave Act (FMLA), sponsored by the U.S. Department of Labor

www.dol.gov/compliance/laws/comp-fmla.htm

This government website includes information about all aspects of the FMLA.

Family and Medical Leave Act Compliance Assistance Home Page, sponsored by the U.S. Department of Labor

www.dol.gov/whd/fmla/index.htm

This government website includes materials related to FMLW in a wide variety of languages including Spanish, Chinese, Korean, Thai, Vietnamese.

Americans with Disabilities Act (ADA), sponsored by the U.S. Department of Justice

www.usdoj.gov/crt/ada/adahom1.htm

This government website provides a complete description of the practices required by ADA and includes regular updates to help programs remain in compliance.

Commonly Asked Questions About Child Care Centers and the Americans with Disabilities Act, sponsored by the U.S. Department of Justice

www.ada.gov/childq&a.htm

This resource interprets the ADA specifically for programs of early care and education.

Materials to Guide the Development of Policies and Regulations

Caring for Our Children: National Health and Safety Performance Standards: Guidelines for Early Care and Education Programs, 3rd ed. (2011), developed by the National Resource Center for Health and Safety in Child Care and Early Education

nrckids.org/

This up-to-date and comprehensive resource, created in collaboration with the American Academy of Pediatrics, addresses a wide variety of topics and provides valuable information.

Protecting Children During Emergencies: Recommended Standards for Child Care During Emergencies, developed by National Association of Child Care Resource and Referral Agencies and Save the Children

www.doh.state.fl.us/demo/ems/emsc/ProtectChildrenInChildCareDuringEmergencies.pdf

This report provides guidance to help programs of early care to prepare for emergencies promptly and safely.

North Carolina Child Care Services Association: T.E.A.C.H.® Early Childhood Project

www.childcareservices.org/ps/teach.html

This resource describes the goals and objectives of the T.E.A.C.H.® project that supports early childhood teachers' professional development.

TO REFLECT

1. What might be some consequences if a director did not consistently apply policies and procedures described in the family handbook or staff manual? How would the program's operations be affected? What effect would this behavior have on morale? Who would be responsible for bringing these issues to her attention? Would the *NAEYC* *Code of Ethical Conduct* or the *Supplement for Early Childhood Program Administrators* guide your decisions?

2. We recommend that you ask a few trusted families to review your program's family handbook as it is being developed and finalized. What are the benefits and the risks of asking for feedback before the document has been finalized?

CHECK AND APPLY YOUR UNDERSTANDING

1. Describe how staff and administrative manuals are the same and how they are different.
2. List groups that need to know and follow your center's family handbook.
3. Identify federal laws and regulations that apply to programs of early care and education.

CHAPTER 5

Leading and Managing Personnel

NAEYC Administrator
Competencies addressed
in this chapter:

**Management Knowledge
and Skills**

3. **Staff Management and Human
   Relations**
Knowledge and application of group
dynamics, communication styles, and
techniques for conflict resolution.
Knowledge of different supervisory
and group facilitation styles. The
ability to relate to staff and board
members of diverse racial, cultural,
and ethnic backgrounds. The ability
to hire, supervise, and motivate staff
to high levels of performance. Skill in
consensus building, team development,
and staff performance appraisal.

8. **Leadership and Advocacy**
Knowledge of organizational theory
and leadership styles as they relate to
early childhood work environments.
Knowledge of the legislative process,
social issues, and public policy
affecting young children and their
families. The ability to articulate a
vision, clarify and affirm values, and
create a culture built on norms of
continuous improvement and ethical
conduct. The ability to evaluate
program effectiveness. The ability to
define organizational problems,
gather data to generate alternative
solutions, and effectively apply
analytical skills in its solution. The
ability to advocate on behalf of young
children, their families, and the
profession.

Learning Outcomes

After studying this chapter, you should be able to:

1. Describe the trends in staffing and the importance of recruiting qualified staff.

2. Understand the relationship of staff qualifications to the success of the program.

3. Identify opportunities for collaboration within the community.

4. Articulate the importance of professional development for staff members.

5. Describe the various personnel records used in the program.

Marie's Experience

Marie has been working with a diverse group of staff members for a number of years. Recently Marie has seen a shift in the qualifications for teachers in her state. This shift has made it necessary for Marie to be very diligent in her hiring practices. In past years, Marie was able to recruit her staff through word-of-mouth and referrals from both families and other staff members.

The staff is the single most important influence on the quality of early childhood programs. The best programs are likely to have highly qualified staff and low teacher turnover (National Research Council & Institute of Medicine [NRC & IOM], 2000). A disparity exists, however, among teachers' professional preparation, the program's ability to offer them compensation equivalent to similarly qualified individuals in other fields, and growing accountability and families' demands for quality programming. Furthermore, if staff members find the working conditions inadequate, children do not do well in the program. To ensure job satisfaction for staff as well as program quality, three criteria must be met in staffing: (a) The staff must meet at least minimal qualifications for their specific duties, although an employer hopes to select employees who have the most potential; (b) all employees must understand and agree with the program's vision and mission; and (c) all employees must accept personal ownership and responsibility for the program. The program director has the responsibility to ensure that these criteria are met. Through careful screening of applicants and effective hiring practices, you help set the stage for a high-quality program. Once the stage is set, however, you must actively work to retain staff by establishing and maintaining a positive organizational culture, providing appropriate training and professional development, ensuring that all of the staff members are adequately compensated for their work, and that staff have an overall sense of satisfaction as a result of their work in your program.

TRENDS IN STAFFING

Advocacy efforts have resulted in an increased recognition of the importance of early childhood education. In addition to the acceptance of kindergartens and primary programs as an integral part of the public education system, consensus is growing that communities should have sufficient high-quality infant, toddler, and preschool programs to meet the developmental needs of all children whose families want to enroll them. What's more, these community programs need to be offered at a cost that families and society can afford.

All the characteristics of high-quality programs depend on adequate numbers of well-trained staff members. Early childhood programs need increasingly larger staffs for several reasons. First, more early childhood programs are offering comprehensive, full-time care. Full staffing means a greater demand for well-qualified staff. Second, an adequate adult-child ratio based on the ages and needs of children served and a small group size are major factors in program quality. Adult-child ratios will vary based on individual states' regulatory mandates. In an effort to improve program quality, some centers choose to adhere to ratios that are lower than the state required ratio. Third, with the inclusion of children with special needs, demand increases for support staff to screen and identify these children and to engage children with special needs in general education classrooms (Hebbeler, 1995). According to the U.S. Census Bureau, there are 884,235 paid employees in child care establishments and 700,046 self-employed child care providers in the United States (U.S. Census Bureau, 2010). The child care workforce is large and diverse.

Staff Shortage: A Deep-Rooted Problem

The biggest quality issue facing early childhood care and education programs is the difficulty in recruiting and retaining qualified staff members. Retention of staff especially affects program quality by impacting the emotional security of children enrolled in the program, increasing stress among teachers and caregivers who remain employed at the center, and increasing operating costs (Carroll, Smith, & Oliver, 2008; Hale-Jinks, Knopf, & Kemple, 2006). All of these impacts can make fulfilling your program vision and mission increasingly difficult. Historically, the **turnover rate**, the number of teachers who leave a program during the year, has been extremely high. A now-classic study reports that the annual turnover rate is as high as 40% among early care and education personnel in the United States (Center for the Child Care Workforce, 2004). This trend continues to be a concern, citing low compensation, high job stress, inadequate training, and a lack of administrative support as causes of these high levels of staff turnover (Baumgartner, Carson, Apavaloaie, & Tsouloupas, 2009; Carrol, Smith & Oliver, 2008; Hale-Jinks et al., 2006; Machado, 2008).

Low Compensation: The Worthy Wage Campaign, initiated by the Center for the Child Care Workforce, sought to expose the association of low pay with the difficulty in recruiting qualified staff and the association of high turnover rates among child care workers with low-quality programs. The 2010 census reports that child care personnel earn, on average, $17,440 per year compared with kindergarten teachers' salaries of $28,170

(Bureau of Labor Statistics, U.S. Department of Labor, 2010). Child care teachers earn less than janitors, cooks, and chauffeurs (Barnett, 2003). Predictably, the highest turnover rates tend to occur in programs that pay the lowest salaries; conversely, the lowest turnover rates are typically in programs that pay the highest salaries (Carrol, Smith, & Oliver, 2008; Machado, 2008; Quality, Compensation, and Affordability, 1998; Whitebook, Sakai, Gerber, & Howes, 2001). Staff compensation and turnover rate are also associated with measures of program quality, such as accreditation. For example, studies have found that nationally accredited programs had the lowest center turnover rate, but the centers that did not maintain their accreditation did not differ in turnover rate from programs that had never sought accreditation (Quality, Compensation, and Affordability, 1998). Compensation, however, should not be limited to hourly wages or annual salary; child care professionals do not commonly have health insurance, sick leave, paid vacation, reimbursement for professional development, and performance bonuses as part of stand-ard compensation packages (Hale-Jinks et al., 2006). Whitebook et al. (2001) investigated changes in child care staffing from 1994 to 2000 and found that the key factors that led to lower turnover among teachers and directors were higher-than-average salary and compensation packages. With this in mind, the program director and/or governing board would be wise to contact an appropriate professional (insurance provider/accountant) to explore the feasibility of providing a compensation package that exceeds the market standard. While inadequate compensation is likely to have a significant impact on job satisfaction and staff turnover, there are other factors that you, as the center director, should be mindful of when endeavoring to reduce staff turnover.

High Job Stress: Job stress experienced by individuals working in early care and educa-tion settings has been linked by researchers to lower job satisfaction, teacher burnout, and ultimately job turnover (Baumgartner et al., 2009). Factors that early childhood caregivers have identified as contributing to high levels of stress include long hours; noisy and busy classrooms; the physical demands of the job; and being constantly overwhelmed by unpre-dictable stress-inducing situations, such as conflict among children and angry parents (Baumgartner et al., 2009; Curbow, Spratt, Ungaretti, McDonnell, & Breckler, 2001).

Inadequate Training: The work of early care and education professionals is difficult and complex. Teachers with limited specific preparation to work in early childhood set-tings are likely to find the work stressful and unsatisfying. They are likely to see this early care as a *job* rather than a *profession*. Thus, they are less likely to feel a personal commit-ment to the children in their care. While the research describing the need for a specific level of education has not clearly identified a link between specific educational qualifica-tions of teaching staff and early childhood outcomes (Early et al., 2006), there is consen-sus within the field regarding the need for increased professional development in order to raise the level of quality experiences for young children in center-based care and edu-cation programs (Marshall et al., 2001; National Early Childhood Accountability Task Force, 2007; Phillips, Mekos, Scarr, McCartney, & Abbott-Shim, 2000; Whitebook, 2001). We all appreciate how challenging it can be to provide quality care that keeps children safe and healthy, develop nurturing relationships with a diverse population of children and their families, and implement meaningful educational experiences. These teachers deserve systematic professional preparation and cohesive, ongoing professional develop-ment that supports their work. They need to be given opportunities to learn about evi-dence-based best practices, to be guided in strategies to reflect upon their daily teaching, and to have regular opportunities to evaluate their work. They need to be helped to see themselves as professionals with specialized knowledge and expertise.

We all appreciate how the staffing crisis and high turnover are detrimental to all involved. Children are affected by the change in rituals and by the loss of people associated with the rituals. Insecure children spend less time involved with peers and more time in "aimless wandering" and show declines in cognitive activities (Whitebook et al., 1990). Changes in staff are especially detrimental to infants and toddlers. Those who experience more staff turnover do not score as well on cognitive tests (Clarke-Stewart & Gruber, 1984) and develop less secure attachments (Carnegie Corporation of New York, 1994; Cryer et al., 2005), as compared with infants and toddlers experiencing no turnover in care. Families also find that it takes time to feel comfortable with new staff. Of course, staff are affected too. An unstable work environment caused by high levels of turnover tends to decrease predictability for children and staff, which has the effect of raising stress levels. This unstable work environment leads to even more turnover, which over time leads to lower quality care and education services (Whitebook & Sakai, 2003). There is, however, reason to hope. Program administrators, through their role as leaders and managers, influence the organizational climate and many of the factors that influence staff turnover. Throughout this chapter, we will present strategies that will help program administrators set the stage for success in attracting and retaining staff, the cornerstone of a high-quality program.

STAFFING AN EARLY CHILDHOOD PROGRAM

After developing a program vision and mission, an administrator is faced with the task of determining the staff needed and of matching job requirements with existing staff members. This task is a continual one; staffing patterns change as a program expands, as the needs of the center change, or as enrollment increases or declines.

Roles and Qualifications of Personnel

Although all staff members must be in good physical and psychological health and have the personal qualities necessary to work with young children, their specific qualifications will depend on their specific role. Even roles with the same title may vary from program to program and with the age of the children that the staff member will be responsible for.

Personnel may be classified as either primary program personnel or support program personnel. **Primary program personnel** have direct, continuous contact with children, and are often individuals with a higher level of qualifications and experience. **Support program personnel** provide services that support or facilitate caregiving and the instructional program. Although staff members are classified by the primary responsibilities they shoulder, they may occasionally contribute to the center's smooth operation by assuming different duties. For example, a teacher may occasionally clean the room or serve food, or a dietitian might discuss good eating habits with children or console a child who drops a carton of milk. In addition, a teacher may meet the requirements necessary to drive vehicles owned by the program and be asked to transport children to and from home or school.

Director: A **director** is the individual who is typically in charge of the total program. Directors of early childhood education programs in public schools are often supervisors or resource personnel. The title of *director* is frequently given to the person legally responsible for the total program and services. Caruso and Fawcett (1999) used the following terms to define the roles of directors: *executive director* (administers a large child care agency that may include several social services programs), *program director* (runs the day-to-day operations of a program), *educational coordinator* (is responsible for the educational component, including staff development and curriculum development, of an agency or a single program), *head teacher* (oversees one or more classrooms), and *supervisor* (oversees teachers and support personnel). Although this book's focus is primarily on the role of the program director, organizations differ and so do the roles of their directors.

Director's Role.   Regardless of the type of early childhood program or the title of the director, many responsibilities are similar but have been characterized in different ways. For example, Hayden (1996) described the following five administrative roles: technical responsibilities (e.g., regulations and policies, budgets), staff relations, educational planning, public relations (e.g., advocacy, networking, fund-raising, marketing), and symbolic (i.e., director as a symbol for the identity of the group). Carter and Curtis (1998) used the equilateral triangle to conceptualize the role of a director. The roles, which are of equal importance, are managing and overseeing, mentoring, and building and supporting community. Morgan (2000) listed eight roles of directors and competencies for each role. Bloom (2000b) interviewed directors regarding their perceptions of their roles and used linguistic metaphorical analysis of the data. Almost 29% of all directors talked about "leading and guiding"; 28% referred to their role as balancing multiple tasks; and 25% saw their role as "caring and nurturing" the entire community.

We consider directors' responsibilities to include both a **leadership component** (i.e., the people-oriented or human resources role) and a **management component** or the technical (i.e., organizational, program, business), nonperson aspects of administration. (For more specific examples of leadership and management roles, see Figure 5.1.) Bloom (1997) suggested that clear distinctions cannot be made between leadership and management functions in most early childhood programs; most directors have both responsibilities, and the functions themselves overlap. For example, the director may write the program's goals and then articulate the goals to others. The administrative role becomes more complex with the size of the program and the location (i.e., a program located at multiple sites is usually more complex than a program located at one site). The need to balance the leadership and management roles for program success has been studied on a historical basis by Hewes (2000). In stressing the need for a balance among tasks, Neugebauer (2000) likened a successful program director to an orchestra director; that is, he or she must "be able to blend all the talents of the individual performers" (p. 98). In sum, the director has the leadership role in managing quality in the program.

Professional Qualifications of Directors.   As discussed, the professional qualifications of directors vary, depending on the program's organizational pattern and applicable licensing, accreditation, or Quality Rating System (QRS) requirements. Several initiatives have examined the director's role and debated the possibility of requiring directors to have specialized credentials as part of the licensing and/or accreditation process for center-based sites. While some states have begun to require a specific director credential, it is not a universal requirement. Be sure to review your state's rules and regulations as you plan your own education and professional development. Even though the credentials required by individual states can vary, it is advisable to become knowledgeable about the acceptable credentials and how the specific approved credentials meet the needs of the program.

Essential directors' knowledge and competencies have been identified by the NAEYC through its program accreditation standards. (See the first four pages of this text for NAEYC Program Administrator Competencies.) The general consensus is that administrators should have early childhood professional knowledge and administrative competence. More specifically, Brown and Manning (2000) identified four areas of knowledge needed by directors, and Neugebauer (2000) and Morgan (2000) developed comprehensive lists of needed competencies. Many of these competencies have been described in depth. Some include visionary skills (Carter & Curtis, 1998), communication skills and team building (Jorde-Bloom, 1997), a sense of self-efficacy (Leithwood & Jantzi, 2008), human resource management (Ryan, Whitebook, Kipnis, & Sakai, 2011), financial management (Ryan et al., 2011), supervision (Caruso & Fawcett, 1999), and culturally relevant leadership and community partnership skills ("Taking the Lead Initiative," 1999).

Director's Responsibilities

Leadership

Articulates program vision, mission, and philosophy.

Works with staff to plan entire program component based on goals.

Communicates policies and procedures, needs, program objectives, and problems with all interested parties—board, staff, parents, and their agencies; motivates others to take their responsibilities; resolves conflicts.

Affirms values of program and serves in advocacy roles in concert with various community agencies through community-wide endeavors and through professional organizations.

Serves as a model in terms of the code of ethics (see Appendices 2 and 3).

Delegates leadership roles and certain responsibilities to others when appropriate. Continues his or her own professional development.

Management

Writes or adopts and implements all regulations, policies, and procedures.

Abides by all contracts and/or agreements.

Serves as personnel manager by doing the following:

- Conducting a needs assessment
- Recruiting and selecting staff
- Hiring both teaching and support staff
- Planning placement
- Filling staff roles with substitutes when needed
- Developing a communications system (e.g., meetings)
- Supervising staff and planning professional development
- Evaluating staff
- Maintaining personnel records

Enrolls and places children in appropriate programs and involves family members in their children's placements.

Plans and maintains records on children and family members.

Develops program calendar and overall daily scheduling (e.g., meal times).

Follows procedures and manages property by doing the following:

- Planning or locating adequate facilities and maintaining building and grounds
- Ordering and maintaining equipment, materials, and supplies
- Maintaining all property records (e.g., mortgage or lease payments, insurance, inventories)

Plans finances by doing the following:

- Mobilizing resources
- Developing the budget
- Planning marketing strategies
- Working with funding and regulatory agencies
- Writing proposals for grants and governmental assistance programs

Develops an efficient internal and external (PR) communications system.

Plans program evaluation as needed.

Figure 5.1
Program Director's Responsibilities: Leadership and Management

Stages Described by Anthony (1998)

Stage 1: Organizing and Surviving (first year)

Learn by trial and error

Learn much new information

Manage stress

Stage 2: Managing and Focusing (second year)

Develop expertise in specific program areas

Extend knowledge and support beyond local program

Develop time management skills

Stage 3: Leading and Balancing (third or fourth year)

Develop a vision for the program

Include others in achieving goals

Stage 4: Advocating and Mentoring (fifth or sixth year)

Share professional expertise

Expand current program

Avoid burnout

Stages Described by Bloom (1997)

Beginning directors (first year)

Eager to make a contribution and to be liked

Face reality (e.g., needed stamina, amount of paperwork, needs of others, lack of support)

Major problems are lack of management skills, seeing simple solutions to complex problems, and seeing events from personal perspective

Competent directors (between one and four years)

Have problems with time management

Know their strengths and weaknesses

Often overcome problems of beginning directors

Master directors

See themselves as change agents, mentors, role models, and advocates

Engage in reflective practice

Make role expectations clear to others and use a flexible style to meet needs of staff members

Seek consistency between espoused theory and reality

Stages Described by Caruso and Fawcett (1999)

Beginning

Try to conceptualize roles

Imitate models from past experiences

Use different approaches (trial and error)

Figure 5.2
Stages of Directors' Development

Avoid responsibilities by pretending not to have enough time

Gradually work out authority relationships

Extending

Somewhat ambivalent about role

Discuss problems and conflicts objectively

See differences in staff members

Understand program better

Maturing

Make conscious decisions

Are accountable for their actions

Are more sensitive to others

Assess themselves accurately

Not as burdened by problems

Figure 5.2 (Continued)

In reality, however, many administrators step into their roles without the needed competencies. Less than 20% of all directors have planned a career in administration. Most said they reached their current position because others saw their leadership potential. About 90% come from the ranks of teachers (Bloom, 1997), often they were in Katz's (1995) "Renewal Stage" of their career when teachers are looking for new challenges. Thus, competencies are learned through work experience, and work experience becomes a critical factor in program quality (Cost, Quality, and Child Outcomes Study Team, 1995). As new directors learn the needed competencies, they go through the stages shown in Figure 5.2.

Along with work experience, directors use other tools for developing competencies. Many engage in self-study. Besides professional reading materials, other frequently used means of self-study include professional conferences, workshops, a variety of online resources using the Internet, and interest groups. Often community groups conduct forums and other programs of benefit to early childhood program directors. Other directors learn through director mentors ("Taking the Lead Initiative," 2000). Directors also use published assessment tools (Freeman & Brown, 2000; Schiller & Dyke, 2001; Sciarra & Dorsey, 1998; Talan & Bloom, 2004) as a form of professional development.

Personal Qualifications of Directors.   Regardless of the program, personal characteristics of effective directors are similar. Because of the number and complexity of their responsibilities, successful directors are usually dedicated, focused, and organized. Effective directors must be able to see the program holistically and recognize interconnections. Other characteristics include physical and mental stamina, openness to new ideas, communication skills, flexibility of expression and thought, acceptance of their own capabilities and fallibilities, the ability to learn from mistakes, a willingness to share credit with others, cheerfulness, warmth and sensitivity to both children and adults, a personal sense of security, a desire to succeed, and honesty. Directors must remain open to input from their constituents—the parents, children, and the community that they serve. It is imperative that a director keeps an open mind and is willing to respond when a concern or suggestion is brought to his attention.

Primary Program Personnel: Just as there should be no distinctions between care and education, distinctions between child care workers and teachers are no longer useful. The following definitions for teaching staff are currently being used by NAEYC as part of its program accreditation criteria (NAEYC, 2005):

> ***Teachers*** are defined as the adult with *primary* responsibility for a group of children. For the purposes of NAEYC accreditation, a *group or classroom of children* is defined by the criteria for maximum group size for children of different ages/developmental levels. The teacher must spend the vast majority of time with one group of children who attend at the same time, rather than dividing time between classrooms or floating between groups. Primary responsibility for multiple groups of children, who attend at the same time, cannot be assigned to any one or single teacher.
>
> ***Assistant Teachers (or Teacher Aides)*** are defined as adults who may work under the direct supervision of a Teacher. Assistant Teachers/Teacher Aides can work independently in a teacher's absence, but for the vast majority of the time, the assistant teacher/teacher aide works directly with the teacher in the same space with the same group of children.

Role of Primary Personnel.   Except for tasks specific to the age group served, very few distinctions exist among the roles performed by teachers in early childhood programs. Teachers' responsibilities include the following:

- Assuming a leadership role in the program
- Articulating and implementing the program's vision, mission, and philosophy and working consistently to help the program attain its goals
- Communicating kindly and respectfully with all children
- Communicating effectively, respectfully, and consistently to the families of children in the classroom
- Observing strict confidentiality in issues related to the program and specific family information
- Responding effectively to children's behavior

Professional Qualifications of Primary Personnel.   The tasks performed by teachers of young children are essentially the same; as a result, entry-level qualifications are similar in most community-based programs. Regardless of whether professional development occurs as preservice or in-service training, or is primarily in the form of formal education, onsite coaching and mentoring, or a conference workshop, professional development should be knowledge based as opposed to conventional wisdom (Griffin, 1999). A good source for determining the core content of early childhood professionals' knowledge base are NAEYC's (2009) Standards for Early Childhood Professional Preparation Programs, which can be revisited at greater depth and breadth at higher levels of preparation.

Personal Qualifications of Primary Personnel.   Personal characteristics associated with an effective teacher are difficult to define. Opinion varies as to what constitutes a good teacher of young children. In addition, teaching styles (which reflect an individual's personality traits, attitudes, etc.) are interwoven with teaching techniques (methodology). Characteristics of effective teachers may be specific to the age of the children and vary with the cultural group served. Because teaching is so complex and multifaceted, more research needs to be conducted on personal characteristics as they impact teaching effectiveness (Early et al., 2006).

Characteristics and skills often associated with effective early childhood teachers include warmth, flexibility, integrity, sense of humor, physical and mental stamina, vitality, emotional stability and confidence, naturalness, and an ability to support development without being overprotective (Elicker & Fortner-Wood, 1995). Feeney, Moravcik, Nolte, and Christensen (2010) observed that the most important characteristic of a good teacher is the ability to be with young children rather than do for them. Balaban (1992) described 12 roles that teachers play with young children; among these are as anticipators and planners, listeners and watchers, protectors, providers of interesting environments, elicitors of language, and smoothers of jangled feelings. In addition to having these characteristics, teachers who work with infants should be able to develop close bonds with infants, "read" behavioral cues (e.g., distinguish among cries), and make long-term commitments to programs so that infants are provided continuity (Balaban, 1992; Honig, 1993).

Support Program Personnel: The major role of the program's support personnel is to furnish services that support or facilitate the program. Support personnel include dietitians and food service personnel, medical staff, psychologists, caseworkers, maintenance staff, general office staff, transportation staff, and substitutes. In small proprietorships, food service, maintenance, and office work are often done by the director, teachers, and in some cases volunteers.

A new category of support program personnel is **case manager**, a position created through the Individualized Family Service Plan (IFSP) requirements of Part C of P.L. 105-17 to provide services to children who have special needs and their families. Similar in role to caseworkers, case managers are child and family advocates who serve as a linking agent between families and needed service agencies. Unlike caseworkers, who are traditionally from the social work profession, IFSP case managers are chosen because of expertise in relation to a given child's primary disability and thus may be, for example, nutritionists, physical therapists, or speech pathologists.

Some categories of support personnel are found mainly in public school and government-funded early childhood programs. For example, **early intervention specialists** are teachers or consultants who specialize in the development and learning of children with special needs. Other special education consultants include occupational therapists, physical therapists, and speech-language pathologists (Wesley, 2002).

Support program personnel must meet the qualifications of their respective professions. They must also know child development and have age-appropriate expectations. Personal qualifications include the ability to communicate with children and to work with all adults involved in the program.

Substitute personnel should have the same professional qualifications and personal characteristics as the regularly employed personnel whom they replace. To ensure program continuity, careful plans should be made for substitute teachers (see Figure 5.3). Such plans are most essential when substitute personnel will be working alone (e.g., in a self-contained classroom), especially in kindergartens and the primary grades.

Assessing Needs and Recruiting Staff Members

The director and the board determine the specific characteristics of the personnel they are seeking and the minimum characteristics that will qualify an applicant for employment. The director may seek a diverse staff through an informal needs assessment or a rigorous affirmative action plan. Because the budget is usually limited, the director must also determine priorities. Other considerations include the availability of potential staff and the amount of training and supervision potential employees would need to work effectively in the program. The requirements and job responsibilities of each position must be formalized into job descriptions.

Possible steps when recruiting staff include developing and gathering recruitment materials, advertising, evaluating applicants' job applications, obtaining documentation of credentials, interviewing, and hiring for a probationary period. The director, the personnel

Prepare children for the possibility of a substitute; for example, have potential substitutes visit the room.

Write these procedures in detail and keep them in a notebook on the desk or in another obvious location:

- Routines for greeting children as they arrive
- Meals, snacks, and toileting routines
- Basic activities for each block of time in the schedule and frequently used transitions; alternate activities to be used might also be included based on the interests of the children in the group
- Routines for moving children outdoors and to other places in the building (e.g., library)
- Routines for emergencies
- Administrative duties (e.g., attendance count, meal count, collecting snack money, sending notes home)
- Routines for departure, including a listing of those who ride buses, travel in private cars, and so on

Write plans for 2 to 3 days that do not overburden the substitute; place materials needed for plans in a given drawer or on a given shelf noted in written plans.

Have an up-to-date list of children and note any children with special needs including dietary restrictions and how those needs are met (children's name tags can be helpful).

Leave note on desk with semi-regular activities such as "duty" responsibilities.

If the substitute did a good job, call and express your appreciation. Inform the director or the building principal of the quality of the substitute's work so that a decision can be made about possible rehiring of the substitute. (Also remember that many teachers begin their teaching careers by doing substitute work.)

Figure 5.3
Plans for Substitute Teachers

administrator, or a committee from the board is responsible for advertising available positions and leading the search process. NAEYC adopted a general but comprehensive antidiscrimination policy in 1988 stating that employment decisions must be based solely on the competence and qualifications of persons to perform "designated duties" ("NAEYC Business," 1988). These policies are aligned with **affirmative action**, which requires employers to take positive steps to recruit and provide an accepting working environment for minorities and women. The Americans with Disabilities Act (ADA) addresses another kind of diversity by protecting the rights of persons with disabilities. Information about ensuring that your program satisfies affirmative action and ADA requirements is readily available on the Internet.

Developing and Gathering Recruitment Materials: Recruitment materials must include job descriptions that list duties in terms of "essential functions" and how frequently each function must be performed, responsibilities, and authority and must list the qualifications and skills required. Documentation of the program's compliance with nondiscrimination laws should be included in recruitment materials including employment advertising and applications (National Association of Child Care Professionals [NACCP], 2009).

In addition, it is advisable to include physical requirements that may be necessary for the position, such as the ability to lift, sit, and stand. Public relations brochures, website information, Web-based orientation programs, and policy manuals are also good recruitment materials.

Child Development Teacher

Early childhood teachers wanted for a college-sponsored child development center. Responsibilities include planning and implementing developmentally appropriate activities for a group of twelve 3-year-old children. A.A./A.S. degree in child development/early childhood education or a CDA certificate required; teaching experience preferred. Essential functions include implementing a developmentally appropriate curriculum while supervising children to ensure their safety. Applicants must be able to lift, carry, and hold children. Write for an application to Ms. A. Jones, Director, Johnson County Community College Child Development Center, (*address*), email (*ajones@ourcenter.com*), or call (*telephone*) Monday through Thursday between 2:00 and 4:00 p.m. Deadline for applications, August 1. We are an Equal Opportunity Employer.

Center Director or Assistant Center Director Position

Qualifications include a bachelor's degree with 12 credit hours in ECE and four courses in child development, plus at least one year of management or supervisory experience in a licensed child care facility. –OR–

An associate's degree in ECE or related field with a plan of study to include a bachelor's degree plus two years management or supervisory experience in a licensed child care setting. –OR–

A CDA with a plan of study to a bachelor's degree plus 3 years of management or supervisory experience in a licensed child care center.

Candidate should be outgoing and possess strong marketing and public relations skills; have the ability to control costs while maintaining quality educational programs and services; ability to represent the company in a positive, professional manner. Competitive salary, benefits, and relocation cost incentives. (EOE)

Please respond by emailing (enter name and email address of hiring manager) by (enter date).

Figure 5.4
Sample Newspaper Advertisements

Advertising: The director should first notify persons already involved in the program of an opening and then make the advertisement public. The advertisement should summarize the job description and state all nonnegotiable items, such as required education and experience, so that unqualified applicants can be quickly eliminated. The advertisement should also describe the method of applying and the deadline for application. Figure 5.4 is an example of advertisements for a teacher and director.

Many programs are now using Internet-based recruiting tools such as Careerbuilder, Monster.com, and Craigslist to cast a broader net in hopes of reaching more of the intended population of potential recruits. Considering that many of the individuals in the recruitment pool today do not read printed newspapers or career publications, it is important that directors remain open to experimenting with the Internet world of recruiting.

A Better Way

As Marie has begun to use electronic media to recruit staff, she has had to refine the content of her position postings. By focusing more on the educational requirements and the specific position responsibilities listed in her current job descriptions, Marie has found that recruiting, hiring, and retaining qualified staff are easier and more manageable.

PERMISSION TO CHECK REFERENCES FORM
VALLEY VIEW CHILD DEVELOPMENT CENTER

Applicant Name: _____

Position applied for: _____

I authorize all past employers, schools, persons, and organizations having relevant information or knowledge (whether favorable or unfavorable) to provide it to _____. I specifically waive any other required written notification. I hereby release _____, its officers, employees, and agents and any employers, schools, persons, and organizations from all liability in responding to inquiries in connection with my application for employment with _____.

_____   _____
Applicant's Signature   Date
_____

Reference Check Information

Company Name _____   Telephone Number _____

Supervisor/Contact Name _____   Title _____

Dates of Employment _____   Position Title _____

Starting Salary _____   Ending Salary_____

Please Provide Information Regarding the Applicant's Performance in the Following Areas:

Attendance:_____

Work Habits: _____

Employee/supervisor relations: _____

Employee/peer relations: _____

Specific duties: _____

Are there any problems, concerns, or reasons you may know that would prohibit this applicant from caring for young children? If so, please explain.
_____

Do you have any concerns about this applicant working as the only adult in a classroom of young children? If so, please explain.
_____

Why did the applicant leave your company?
_____

Would you recommend this person for rehire?   Yes   No
Why or why not?
_____

Additional comments: _____

Reference check completed by

_____   _____
Name   Title

_____
Date

Figure 5.5
Sample Employee Application

Potential employees might apply for a position at your center in various ways. You might be willing to accept applications by telephone or applicants might complete an online application or email their materials to the center. Applicants might fill in a simple application form or submit a file with a résumé, transcripts, references, and evidence of other credentials. The method of applying and accepting applications will depend on the abilities and experiences of applicants and their access to the Internet, email, or Web-based application forms. The director's time is another factor to consider when planning how to conduct a search. For example, if written communication abilities are not a part of the job description, applicants could respond to the questions on the application form in person or over the telephone. Figure 5.5 is an example of a simple permission to check references form that applicants would complete as part of the application process.

When the deadline for applications has passed, the director or another staff member in charge of hiring will screen applications to eliminate unqualified applicants. The applications of those eliminated should be retained along with the reason for their rejection to adhere to the affirmative action requirement that requires the listing of reasons for rejection. It is always courteous to send a personal letter or email to applicants who have been eliminated from the potential pool.

Obtaining Documentation of Credentials and Interviewing: The director or person(s) interviewing should obtain the following documents:

1. References.   The director can legally contact all references given on the application and all former employers concerning work history and character. These references are aids in learning how the applicant performed in the eyes of others. It is important to contact both professional and personal references. Detailed information gathered in the reference process should be documented, signed, dated, and filed by the individual checking the reference. This is an important task and one that should not be abbreviated. It is advisable not to accept preprinted reference letters without first placing a personal call to the person whose signature appears on the letter to verify authenticity. A sample introductory letter and accompanying reference form are shown in Figure 5.6.

2. Employment Eligibility Verification.   Ask to see applicants' driver's license and passport or birth certificate. The U.S. Department of Justice, U.S. Immigration and Customs Enforcement (ICE) has a form with instructions for obtaining employment eligibility verification that is used to establish identity and employment eligibility for non-U.S. citizens.

3. Criminal History Records Checks.   Since 1985, many states have passed laws requiring national criminal history records checks for child care center employees. These laws were implemented to comply with federal legislation. Criminal history records checks are one of the only ways to defend against a claim of *negligent hire,* in which an employer is held responsible for injuries to a third party if the injury was foreseeable or if the employer did not investigate the employee's background before finalizing the appointment.

Following the screening of applicants and obtaining documentation, all promising applicants should be interviewed. Use the following steps in the interview process:

1. The director must follow established board policies concerning the nature, setting, and person(s) conducting the interview (e.g., board's personnel committee in large programs or the board member, director, or staff members who would be supervising the new employee) and determining who will make the final decision regarding selection.

2. The director must be careful to follow Title VII of the 1964 Civil Rights Act prohibiting discriminatory hiring practices. The rule of thumb is that all questions asked of the applicant must have a "business necessity." Some questions to avoid are date of birth or age, marital status, spouse's occupation, pregnancy issues and number of children, child care arrangements, religious affiliation (although inquiry may be made whether the

Johnson County Community College Child Development Center

TO: _____

FROM: _____

RE: _____
(Name of applicant)

This applicant has given your name as a person who can provide a reference on his or her qualifications. We want to select teachers whose professional preparation, experience, and personality can be expected to produce the best results at our Child Development Center. Please give your full and frank evaluation. Your reply will be kept in strict confidence. Please assist both us and the center.

Please call me if you would rather discuss this applicant with me personally.

Thank you for sharing your insights about the strengths and potential of this applicant.

Sincerely yours,

I. M. The Administrator
Program Director

How would you describe the applicant's ability in each of the following areas?

1. Knowledge of young children's development:
2. Ability to plan developmentally appropriate activities to enrich and extend children's development and learning:
3. Ability to implement planned activities to enrich and extend children's development and learning:
4. Ability to use positive guidance including disciplining techniques with children:
5. Ability to assess children's learning and development:
6. Ability to organize a physical setting:
7. Ability to work with family members:
8. Ability to work with other staff members as a team:
9. Capacity for professional and personal growth:

On the basis of your present knowledge, would you employ this applicant in a program for which you were responsible?_____

Please explain: _____

What opportunity have you had to form your judgment of this applicant?_____
_____

Additional remarks: _____
_____

| _____ | _____ | _____ |
| (Date) | (Signature) | (Title) |

Figure 5.6
Sample Introductory Letter and Reference Form

scheduled workdays are suitable), membership in organizations (except those pertaining to the position), race or national origin (except for affirmative action information), arrest record, type of discharge from the military, union memberships, and disabilities (ask only whether the person can perform job-specific functions).

3. For teaching positions, the beliefs and values of teachers need to be consistent with those of the program's vision, mission, and philosophy. The interview should reveal the applicant's ideas and attitudes toward children. To understand the values and beliefs that support an interviewee's teaching practices, the interviewer should ask "open-ended" questions about how the applicant sees his or her role in working with young children. It is also appropriate to ask applicants to discuss their experience and give details related to those experiences, rather than respond with simple yes or no answers. Interviewers who would find a written discussion guide helpful can use Bloom, Sheerer, and Britz's (1991) assessment tool "Beliefs and Values" (pp. 232–233), which is designed to encourage adults to reflect on their attitudes and beliefs about children, families, and the teacher's role. Some teachers bring professional teaching portfolios that can be used to document interview answers (Hurst, Wilson, & Cramer, 1998). It is important that interview questions match the type of candidate (e.g., with more mature candidates, focus on experiences rather than on career paths; Newman, Vander Ven, & Ward, 1992). This will give program personnel more insights into the applicant's skills, knowledge base, and experience level.

4. After ascertaining the applicant's beliefs and attitudes toward children, teaching, and learning, the interviewer should discuss and answer questions about the program, such as the program's vision, mission, and philosophy; the ages of enrolled children; guidance and discipline practices; how children are assessed; the degree of family involvement; a complete description of the job, including salary, the length of school day and year, opportunities for promotion, fringe benefits, sick leave and retirement plans, consulting and supervisory services, and the nature and use of assessment to determine job performance and advancement. This information might be covered again during the orientation process, and for future reference, a staff policy handbook containing such information should be made available to those hired. It is extremely important that expectations are reviewed and acknowledgement of understanding between the candidate and the interviewer is established. For example, if the current opening is for a teacher to work 30 hours per week, but the successful applicant needs to remain open to working additional hours, the interview is a good place to clarify this expectation.

Hiring: The applicants are informed about the decision of the search process at a given date and in a specified manner. See the sample offer letter in Figure 5.7 that you may want to adapt to send to successful applicants.

During the interview process, it is important to communicate expectations related to the anticipated timing of the hiring decision and then adhere to that timeline. This is a good opportunity to show the applicant that meeting commitments is important to the program administration. The successful candidate might be asked to sign an employment agreement and other required personnel papers when offered the position. If no applicant is hired, the recruitment process is repeated. Hiring the correct candidate who will meet the needs of the program is important. Managers often make hiring decisions based on convenience and neglect to find the right candidate for their program. Convenience hires can result in increased turnover, because such hiring decisions may not work out in the long term.

Many programs ask newly hired employees to complete a probationary period during which the director or hiring committee observes how compatible the person's teaching or administrative philosophy is with the program. The conditions of the probationary period must be clearly communicated to the new employee before hiring. The trial period should last six months or less, and pay might be slightly less than the agreed-upon full

Name of New Employee   May 19, 201X
1234 Street Name
City, State, Zip Code

Dear *Name of New Employee*,

On behalf of <u>*Center's name*</u>, I am pleased to offer you the position of center director for the <u>*name of center*</u>. You will be responsible for managing the early care and education facility located at <u>*enter the address of the center here*</u>. You will directly supervise the center staff at this center. I believe that you have many professional skills and experiences that will contribute to the success of our program. Find listed below the terms of your employment. If you have any questions, you may reach me at <u>[phone number]</u>. Please sign and return one copy of this agreement to me and retain the second copy for your files. Please send the agreement to

> *Center Name*
> *Attention: Appropriate Person's Name*
> *9876 Street Name*
> *City, State, Zip Code*

Terms of Employment

Date of Employment:	<u>*Enter Start Date*</u>, or sooner if you are released earlier by your current employer.
	<u>*Name of appropriate person*</u> will work with me to determine and schedule your training plan.
Salary:	<u>*Enter Amount as either hourly wage or annual salary*</u>. Employees are paid on <u>*enter appropriate payday schedule*</u>.
Bonus Potential:	<u>*List any applicable bonus plans*</u>.
Employee Benefits:	<u>*List any applicable benefits that the new employee is eligible for and the effective dates.*</u>

<u>*Name of new employee*</u>, we are looking forward to having you join the team at <u>*center name*</u>. I look forward to the contributions that you will make to our program. I hope that you will accept this offer of employment and the terms of your employment with <u>*center name*</u>.

Sincerely,

Signature of Supervisor or Hiring Manager

I accept these terms of employment.

_____   _____
          Signature   Date

Figure 5.7
Sample Offer Letter

salary during this time. If you plan to pay a reduced wage during this probationary period, it must be at or above the federal or state minimum wage.

Orientation of new teaching staff prior to starting in the classroom is critical to success and is sometimes required by state licensing regulations (NCCIC/NARA, 2010). A comprehensive written orientation plan should be consistently implemented with each new employee and completed documentation kept in the employee's file. This orientation gives you an opportunity to review key program documents with the employee. Documents should include program mission, philosophy, and history; job description; organizational chart; personnel policies; operating procedures; staff manual and family handbook; licensing/regulatory standards; accreditation requirements; and curriculum (NACCP, 2009). In addition to reviewing required documents, new employees should be introduced/welcomed to your program. A tour of the facility; introduction to key people including children, families, and coworkers; and time to observe the classroom to which they have been assigned will assist in a smooth transition.

INVOLVING THE CENTER IN THE COMMUNITY

An early childhood program is an organization that operates within the cultural and community contexts in which it is located. The human and financial resources of the local community affect programs. On the human side, directors interact with other community leaders (i.e., leaders serving various agencies and special interest groups and directors of other early childhood programs), select and hire staff members and recruit volunteers from within the community, and serve community clients (i.e., children and their families). On the financial side, the program is affected by the community's economic base and resources devoted to children and families.

Because each community has a culture that affects the early childhood program, directors must understand the local community. In building a knowledge base of the community culture, the director lays the foundation for a quality program (Brown & Manning, 2000) by doing the following:

1. Using the type of organizational structure (e.g., democratic) and the definition of leadership (e.g., collaborative) and characteristics (e.g., open communication style) that are most effective in this particular setting.
2. Developing program services based on a vision of community needs and values.
3. Being sensitive to the needs of staff members and volunteers.
4. Providing welcoming exterior and interior physical environments. Remember, the playground, parking lot and front door create the community's first impression of your program.
5. Promoting a sense of belonging and community through the involvement of families and members of the broader community.
6. Exploring other values, explaining why certain policies are needed, and resolving conflicts between professional and personal values.
7. Gaining the insights needed for resource development, marketing, advocacy, and networking within the local community for in-service training of staff members, connecting families to other community resources, and promoting community projects.
8. Staying connected with professional organizations that support early care and education initiatives and offer professional development opportunities. Organizations such as NAEYC, Association for Childhood Education International (ACEI), Southern Early Childhood Association (SECA), ZERO TO THREE, National Child Care Association (NCCA), and NACCP offer professional development and networking

opportunities at the local, state, and national levels. These organizations often combine national, state, and local memberships to keep you informed about national, regional, and local issues and provide professional development and networking opportunities.

BUILDING A POSITIVE AND PRODUCTIVE WORK CLIMATE

As previously discussed, administrators' responsibilities include both leadership and management components. Leadership is the ability to balance the organization's need for productivity and quality with the needs of the staff. It is the ability to set high and demanding expectations while maintaining positive relationships with employees. Leadership involves the process of making decisions that mold ever-changing goals and of securing the needed commitment to achieve the program's goals. Because leadership directly affects program quality, the term *leadership* seems to be replacing the term *administration.*

Even with great vision and commitment, all programs must function smoothly on a day-to-day basis. Thus, administrators are also responsible for the management component, which focuses on the specific tactics of getting and keeping the program running and provides continuity for program functioning.

Leadership in early childhood care and education is different from leadership in other organizations. Ideas about leadership in early childhood programs have not been based on traditional constructs. Kagan and Bowman (1997) suggested that traditional theories might not have been appropriate because these constructs represent a hierarchical model with a top-down view (i.e., vested right to use unilateral decision making) and a male-oriented (i.e., power-oriented) stance. This hierarchical model emphasizes results, not relationships. Since the 1970s, researchers have noted that the leadership styles in fields in which women predominate are more collaborative in nature (Hennig & Jardin, 1976; Lawler, Mohrman, & Ledford, 1992; Morrison, 1992). Collaborative models see leadership as authoritative rather than authoritarian (Rodd, 1998); leaders in these models are committed to the growth of those under their leadership and thus to closing the status gap. These leaders use their authority mainly in implementing ideas coming out of the group process and in handling emergencies. Followers of collaborative leaders are committed to the ideas of the leader because they feel involved and valued (Kelley, 1991). Thus, collaborative leadership emphasizes both results and relationships. The early childhood field has had a long history of "shared leadership" (Kagan, 1994) or "participatory management" (Jorde-Bloom, 1995). Parents and professionals shared leadership in parent cooperatives and Head Start. Today, the emerging effort is toward networking and collaboration.

People in an early childhood program are not only individuals but also part of a group—called the **faculty** or **staff**. Along with the personalities of these individuals, their roles and positions within the group shape their collective behavior or form the group's personality (Barker, Wahlers, Watson, & Kibler, 1987). In all organizations, including early childhood programs, responsibilities are carried out as a result of interpersonal relations more than of formal roles. Interpersonal relations include the way planning is conducted, decisions are made, and conflicts are resolved (Hoy & Miskel, 1987).

Staff members develop perceptions about their program. The collective perceptions comprise the *culture,* which can be described in terms of how (a) the group understands and supports the leader's vision for the program, (b) the staff is involved in the collaborative effort and maintains collegiality during the process, and (c) the staff believes the administrator can provide both the expertise and time to manage the program and the needed level of parent involvement and interaction with the staff. Staff members are often motivated by a culture that is less formal and encourages collaboration.

Creating and Communicating a Culturally Relevant Vision

Leaders can shape their organizational environment and transform the lives of those in their program and even the wider community. Carter and Curtis (1998) called for directors to have big dreams about the roles their programs can play in reshaping their communities. Many professionals admire the schools of Reggio Emilia Italy because they were created from a culturally relevant vision.

To have a culturally relevant vision, program directors must continually reexamine their programs in terms of the changing needs of clients, community, and trends in the field. Rapid social changes have occurred in the lives of young children and their families (Pew Research Center, 2010). Drucker (1990) speaks of leaders seeing the connection between the missions of organizations and marketing (Who are your clients? What do they need and value? Do you offer what they need and value?). In response to shifts in the demographic makeup of the community, increased numbers of single-parent families, women's increased presence in the workforce, and high unemployment levels, a new transdisciplinary knowledge base is forming in early childhood care and education (Stott & Bowman, 1996), and the need for family-centered services and collaboration with other community agencies is growing (Kagan, Rivera, Brigham, & Rosenblum, 1992). Effective leaders have adapted their programs to meet the needs of clients and to make use of "best practices" knowledge.

The continual adaptation of services has required leaders who can create and communicate a culturally relevant vision. Carter and Curtis (1998) provided these practical suggestions for creating such a vision:

- Recall the vision that brought you to this field.
- Share memories of positive childhood experiences.
- Discuss positive experiences portrayed in children's books and how those could be implemented in your program.
- Ask family members to share their hopes for their children who are entering your program.

The vision provides the direction for innovative decisions to bridge the gap between present services and projected needs. Without a vision, the leader will be caught too frequently in *crisis change* (i.e., response to an unexpected occurrence) or *transformational change* (i.e., radical alteration of the organization in order to survive; Rodd, 1998). Visions always involve changes. Unlike reacting to crisis and transformational changes, initiating innovative changes allows leaders to move their programs in the desirable direction for the following reasons:

1. Leaders can ponder the best- and worst-case scenarios and take only carefully calculated risks. Once they have foresight into the needed changes, they are willing to accept change and convince others to accept it; in short, they are mission driven (Collins & Porras, 1994).

2. Leaders can study the entire picture of change from a systems perspective. A systems perspective, according to Bloom and colleagues (1991), involves (a) changing people's knowledge, skills, or attitudes; (b) changing the process (e.g., goal setting, decision making); and (c) changing the structure (e.g., goals, policies, housing, budget). If all three are not changed, dysfunction occurs in the system. Looking at changes from a systems perspective allows the leader to measure costs (time, money, disruption) versus positive results (services wanted or needed by clients, effectiveness, efficiency).

3. Leaders can evaluate results. For example, results may be considered positive when they bring status to a program, are cost effective, or produce efficiency. Because change takes time and occurs in stages, Likert (1967) suggested that leaders need to wait a minimum of two years to see real change. As noted in longitudinal programmatic research, output can be delayed. Even when the change in programs seems simple, intervening variables often cause delay (e.g., How long would it take to change staff attitudes concerning the inclusion of children with developmental delays in general education classrooms?).

Leaders must communicate—literally sell—their visions to their staff. If innovative change is to be effective, the leader must begin with the vision, identify why any change is needed, set goals and objectives, delegate responsibilities, set standards of performance, and establish time frames. It is important to also provide sufficient feedback on the change that is taking place. Progress monitoring can involve the staff and encourage the staff to be a part of achieving the established vision. Change through collaborative endeavors takes longer than top-down change. Although a leader may mandate some changes, lack of trust in the vision or even in the leader often occurs in authoritarian situations. Many changes require collaboration to be effective because they are often implemented by the staff (e.g., curriculum changes). When such change is needed, include the staff in developing an action plan for delivering the desired results in a manner that will allow for achievement of the goal.

Collaborating

Program effectiveness is most efficiently achieved through collaboration. Directors may view their early childhood programs as having more effective collaboration than do staff members (Bloom, 1995). To establish a collaborative culture, staff members need to perceive the center administration as collaborative. Staff perceptions can be checked through individual interviews/conversations and other formal means (Bloom et al., 1991; Smylie, 1992). Programs might choose to conduct informal surveys of the staff to determine the level of contentment with the program. When the staff has input into the operation of the program, they tend to take more initiative and feel more connected to the management and program goals. Early childhood programs must go beyond a verbal commitment to collaboration to actually using the process.

The following four levels of decision making can foster the development of a collaborative work environment when they are appropriately used:

a. **Unilateral**—The director makes the decisions.
b. **Consultative**—The director seeks input from others before making the decisions.
c. **Collaborative**—The director and others analyze the problem, generate and evaluate possible solutions, and then decide on the action.
d. **Delegative**—The director provides information, and others make the decision (Bloom, 2000a).

In business, terms for shared decision making include *total quality management, site-based management, quality circles, management by consensus,* and *participatory management*. Leaders must determine whether a decision should be determined through collaboration. Collaborative decision making is more appropriate for novel situations that call for problem solving than for routine decisions. Bloom also stated that directors should consider the personal interests or stakes of others in the issue and others' degree of input-competence. Directors must be forthright about how input from others will be used.

Steps in Collaborating: The steps in collaborative decision making are much like those in any process of decision making. The first step is pinpointing the problem. Assessing needs allows others to understand that improvement is a shared responsibility. To pinpoint a problem, one has to realize that the symptoms are not necessarily the problem itself. Thus, one has to collect accurate data. Data can be collected through anonymous questionnaires or interviews (see Bloom et al., 1991) or through documents or staff's or children's records. Multiple stakeholders need to be engaged in the process of identifying the problem, so that the process is collaborative right from the start.

For collaboration to truly be effective, the program director must engage in meaningful, nonthreatening communication.

The second step involves considering different potential solutions and assessing each one. The main question is, "What do we need to do to achieve our goal?" Decisions should be based more on evidence than on personal opinion or tradition. The *NAEYC Code of Ethical Conduct* (see Appendix 2) and its *Supplement for Early Childhood Program Administrators* (see Appendix 3) should also guide the process when working to resolve ethical dilemmas.

Finally, the group must select the best alternative, develop a plan of action, and implement it. Once a course of action has been decided upon, more decisions must be made, such as who will do each aspect of the plan, what is needed to accomplish the plan (time and monetary resources), and how and when improvements will be measured.

Roles of the Leader During Collaboration: Collaborative teamwork occurs when individual needs are subordinated to achieve program goals. The director serves as the leader and facilitator of the team. During the process of collaborating, the leader keeps the task structure clear (i.e., helps the group determine the problem or issue, the goal to be achieved, the process to attain the goal or desired results, and the timeline required to meet the goal) and ensures constructive relationships. To be successful, a leader must assume several responsibilities.

Motivating Collaborative Efforts.   The leader must encourage the participation of the entire group involved in the proposed change. Rodd (1998) stated that individuals have "the right to be cautious about anything new but not the right to not grow and develop" (p. 132). Several suggestions for motivating participants are as follows:

1. The leader must convince others that the job itself is important. Because early childhood care and education are inherently important work, leaders find it relatively easy to convince others that their jobs are important. Still, leaders must build a sense of community and foster the "we" feeling of meeting the dynamic needs of children and their families. The leader needs to remain sensitive to the skill sets of those who become involved in the project. Select team participants with complementary skills that are needed to complete the job successfully.

2. The leader must know staff attitudes. Several instruments are available to help with this (see Bloom et al., 1991, pp. 42, 170–176, 253–255). Shoemaker (2000) developed an "Analysis of Staff Motivation" questionnaire (pp. 158–160).

Reflective Listening Skills

- Understanding content
- Comprehending body language, including eye contact, tone of voice

Response Skills

- Setting decision-making parameters
- Stating reflections of another's comments as part of the response
- Being sensitive to others' values and feelings
- Using appropriate self-assertion when needed

Figure 5.8
Needed Communication Skills

3. Leaders need to build employees' self-esteem. Bandura (1982) theorized that people must be convinced that they will be successful before they attempt to reach their goals. Thus, leaders need to (a) have a democratic organizational climate that provides appropriate autonomy, (b) coach for collaborative work, (c) provide staff needed training and time to learn new skills, and (d) reward individuals with recognition and greater responsibility along with external rewards (e.g., salary increases, job security, peer recognition).

Communicating with Others.   The success of your leadership will rest almost totally on your ability to communicate because that is how you can attain shared meanings. During collaboration, leaders must communicate their commitment to have an impact on the lives of young children and their families and to live their program's vision. Understanding differences in values and using culturally sensitive communication is important.

To be successful, leaders must recognize barriers to communication (e.g., differences in cultures, staff members working in separate rooms and/or with different age groups, interruptions and noise level). To move the collaborative process forward, they must listen, reflect, provide support and objective feedback, and consider the effects their words have on others. Figure 5.8 describes two communication skills you will need to be successful.

Overseeing Conflicts.   Collaborative decision making leads to fewer conflicts than does either an authoritarian approach, in which employees feel left out of the decision-making process, or a permissive approach, which gives employees little guidance about expectations. Conflicts that do arise in collaborative decision making are most likely caused by participants' subjective beliefs (Clyde & Rodd, 1989) and because collaboration is not majority rule but requires consensus building.

Leaders can manage conflicts in a constructive way by describing the conflict situation, communicating understandings of the various perspectives, brainstorming for alternatives, and trying and evaluating alternatives to find the best solution. Focusing on issue-based conflict—not on personal conflicts between individuals—is important because it can lead to the creation of the group's "collective wisdom" (Jones & Nimmo, 1999).

Managing

Management skills are necessary for program survival. Managing is the technical aspect of administration. The director is the technical expert who is responsible for the execution of the program. The specific tasks vary from program to program.

Excellent managers are good at time management (getting tasks done quickly without undue stress). Interruptions and not keeping interactions with others to the point are the main enemies of time management in early childhood programs. Effective time management requires organizing the office, setting goals and matching smaller tasks to goals, establishing priorities among activities, investing maximum time in productive activities, doing the necessary but undesirable tasks efficiently, and analyzing impediments to completing tasks. Directors should be aware that it is acceptable to take time for independent thought and reflection and time to work privately on projects that require focused attention. It is appropriate to find a quiet area to work on a project without interruption.

Delegating Responsibilities: Effective leaders distinguish between the tasks they must do and those others can do. Trusted employees can assume some tasks related to the center's management, but the director cannot delegate leadership responsibilities (Freeman & Brown, 2000). When delegating responsibilities, the leader must match the tasks to staff members' skills and interests. Employees can also volunteer for tasks, but the leader has to ensure a match between the individual's competence and the desired result. The leader should have knowledge of the interest level and abilities of the participating staff to provide positive input and follow through on the action steps needed to reach the goal.

As part of the delegating process, leaders need to be clear about what needs to be done, the deadlines for completion, and the staff members' levels of authority and accountability. Leaders must explain that they will not be supervising the tasks but are available to help gather needed tools, provide related information, and support the efforts of the team.

ENRICHING THE PROFESSIONAL LIFE OF THE STAFF

One of the most important roles of the director is to nurture conditions that lead to enriching the staff's professional life. Directors must assess both collective and individual needs and then plan ways to meet both. It is important to ask the staff what each personally needs to be motivated. Some may be motivated by additional responsibility, others by peer recognition.

Assessing Staff Professional Development Needs

Defining competence in terms of what teachers need to know and be able to do is difficult. Certain core knowledge and skills are needed and must be acquired by all early childhood professionals through training and experience because they are correlated with classroom quality and positive teacher behaviors. All personnel need to refresh their current skills and learn new ones that will help them keep up to date with current understandings of best practice. They are also likely to need help discarding inappropriate practices and replacing them with more appropriate ones.

Because early childhood personnel differ widely in their educational backgrounds and are at different stages in their careers, they bring unique individual needs to their work. Early childhood professionals serve in different roles, too. For example, family child care providers have different needs from personnel in child care centers (Trawick-Smith & Lambert, 1995). Similarly, differences exist within the child care center setting based on the size of the program and the ages of children served. Thus, effective leaders must assess both the collective and the individual needs of staff members to improve the quality of the program and provide appropriate opportunities for professional growth and development.

Professional development should continue throughout a staff member's tenure, as each staff member continually works to improve knowledge and skills in his or her work with young children. To be effective, professional development must be seen as an active process of growing and learning, and not as a product (e.g., a workshop presented by someone else). Thus, professional development plans should be based on a systematic review of staff knowledge and performance and include self-reflection as part of the process in determining specific topics for professional development. Directors need to set a schedule that allows for a one-on-one review of the professional development plan and the opportunity to update the plan during the staff member's employment. Abbott-Shim (1990) recommended the use of data from individual job performance assessments, needs assessment surveys, and program evaluations. Data can be collected in the following ways:

1. **Staff job performance assessments** show the strengths and weaknesses of individual staff members. A summary of strengths and weaknesses of staff members can be used to determine potential training areas.
2. **Needs assessment surveys** give staff the opportunity to indicate topics of perceived needs. The director summarizes the responses and identifies training needs. A simple needs assessment survey is presented in Figure 5.9.
3. **Program evaluation measures** provide comprehensive evaluation, including sections measuring staff competencies, family perceptions of program strengths and weaknesses, and child outcomes.

Application Activity

Think about the current staff evaluation system that you have in place. When was the most recent formal evaluation of staff performance and knowledge? What was the outcome of that evaluation? Based on the information presented earlier, how could you strengthen the staff evaluation process at your center, and how could you better use the results to lead your staff's professional development?

Identifying Individual Needs: Staff training has to be individualized because staff members are unique individuals at different stages of development, with individual learning styles, different abilities and teaching styles, and different roles in your program. For example, Katz (1995) identified four stages of development and the training needs of inservice teachers at each stage:

1. **Survival.**   The first year of teaching is filled with self-doubt. Teachers need onsite support and technical assistance. During this phase, teachers need to receive more support from their mentoring partner and the management team in the program. Paying attention to and responding to teachers' needs will help ensure success.
2. **Consolidation.**   During the second and perhaps third year, teachers consolidate the gains they have made and focus on specific skills. They need onsite assistance, access to specialists, and advice from colleagues. These teachers are eager to continue learning and implementing what they have learned in their classrooms. Encourage them to use their ideas and to bring their professional development experiences to their classrooms.
3. **Renewal.**   During their third and fourth years, teachers often find that participation in professional organizations energizes them and helps them reflect upon their practice. It is ideal for teachers in this phase of their professional career to mentor new staff members and to play a roll in providing training for team members that will allow them to showcase their talents in the classroom.
4. **Maturity.**   After their fifth year, teachers are likely to benefit from additional formal education, participating in professional conferences, and making contributions to the profession (e.g., writing for publication). These teachers are committed to the program and need to be recognized for their dedication. Their needs should be assessed and met so that they remain connected to the program.

Needs Assessment Survey of
Johnson County Community College Child Development Center

We need some information regarding your specific needs for training. After reading the entire list below, check 6 topics (from the 48 listed) that you would like to have covered in in-service training. After checking, rank the topics in order of importance, with "1" being the most important to you.

Child care

_____ Regulations/legal issues
_____ Evaluation of children
_____ Mainstreaming exceptional children
_____ Health and safety

Child development

_____ Physical development (general)
_____ Social development
_____ Cognitive development
_____ Emotional development
_____ Morals/values development
_____ Language development
_____ Motor skill development

Curriculum

_____ Art
_____ Oral language
_____ Writing
_____ Literature
_____ Prereading skills
_____ Mathematics
_____ Social studies
_____ Science
_____ Music
_____ Gross-motor play
_____ Fine-motor play
_____ Incorporating computers
_____ Incorporating multicultural/multilingual learnings
_____ Cooking experiences

_____ Sand/water/mud play
_____ Woodworking experiences
_____ Block-building experiences
_____ Dramatic play experiences
_____ Infant/toddler caregiving as curriculum

Organization and management

_____ Arranging physical environments
_____ Use of indoor equipment/materials
_____ Use of outdoor equipment/materials
_____ Effective scheduling
_____ Transitions
_____ Grouping
_____ Encouraging effective child–child interactions
_____ Encouraging effective child–adult interactions
_____ Encouraging effective child–material interactions
_____ Guiding children's behavior (discipline)

Staff needs

_____ Credentials/training requirements
_____ Communication skills
_____ Team teaching
_____ Evaluation
_____ Policy development

Families

_____ Family education
_____ Family involvement
_____ Family support
_____ Meeting needs of special families
     (e.g., single parents)

Figure 5.9
Staff Training Needs Assessment Survey

Providing Professional Development

As previously noted, early childhood care and education are part of a two-tiered system of teacher regulation. Unlike public school teachers, who have a preservice credential, many teachers in community-based programs come to their work with little formal preparation (Mitchell, 1996). This has important implications for professional development in typical child care centers. We are much more reliant on in-service training to ensure that all staff members are able to meet the care and educational needs of the children in their charge. Thus, the director often is responsible for planning and implementing **staff development activities** (all activities that aid staff in providing quality for the early childhood program). Staff development is designed to ensure that all staff members receive/construct needed knowledge, skills, and attitudes that will facilitate the provision of high-quality services to children and families. Most professionals see staff development as a major catalyst in the development of high-quality programs for young children.

Regrettably, planning and implementing staff development have not been easy tasks for directors. The Cost, Quality, and Child Outcomes Study Team (1995) found that centers scored low on opportunities for professional growth. Regardless of the difficulties involved, directors play critical roles in the quality of their programs through leadership in professional growth opportunities (Bredekamp, 1990; Jorde-Bloom & Sheerer, 1991). The number of organizations providing professional development opportunities for staff has increased. The director needs to remain connected to these professional groups and organizations that are providing high quality low-cost or no-cost professional development in her community. Improving the quality of personnel occurs through encouraging and supporting more formal education, mentoring and coaching for professional development, providing various group professional development activities, urging professional affiliations, and assessing job performance. Most states have increased the focus on the use of career lattice systems that provide opportunities to advance in the profession by successfully completing professional development activities that award credentials, certifications, and/or degrees focused on improving knowledge and skills (NCCIC, n.d.).

All staff development activities need to involve the following:

1. **Active learning.** Active learning involves activities such as collaborating on a project, debating issues, and participating in community programs. Active learning is a way to balance practical and theoretical knowledge, allow adults to learn in the same ways we want children to learn, and stimulate creativity (Cuffaro, 1995; Jones, 1986; Piscitelli, 2000).
2. **Reflective practice.** Reflective practice requires teachers to think about their experiences and interactions and allows them to adjust activities based on their reflections. Many resources are available to help teachers become more reflective (Rand, 2000; Tertell, Klein, & Jewett, 1998).
3. **Individualized activities.**   Staff training must move away from the cookie-cutter approach to an individualized one. Content is determined by assessing collective (i.e., local program) and individual needs. Staff members need to have input into the planning of their professional development options.

Encouraging Formal Education: From its beginning, the kindergarten movement required a course of study for prospective teachers. As kindergartens and other early childhood programs became part of the public schools, teachers were required to obtain degrees from postsecondary institutions and state-granted teaching certificates. Local boards of education also required refresher courses or work toward an advanced degree for renewal of a contract and pay raises. Katz (1995b) indicated that teachers in the stages of renewal and maturity (after 3 to 5 years of experience) are likely to seek out college-level work.

Unlike public school teachers, preschool teachers, especially those working in child care centers, more often pursue formal education after employment. To encourage staff members to pursue formal education as an in-service activity, directors must (a) coordinate training offered by institutions and staff members' needs and availability for training, (b) work out other problems associated with training (e.g., classroom coverage during work hours and baby-sitting and transportation services for after-hours training), (c) supervise field experiences, (d) provide options for assistance with the cost of the formal education (scholarship options can be researched and provided to the teachers), and (e) provide salary increments or career advancement as recognition for completed work. To encourage staff members to acquire more formal education, a growing number of states have launched scholarship initiatives, the best-known of which is T.E.A.C.H.® (Teacher Education and Compensation Helps) Early Childhood project. T.E.A.C.H.® began in North Carolina in 1990 and has spread to 21 other states and the District of Columbia (Child Care Services Association, n.d.). Teachers receive scholarships, funded in part by their employing center, to study early childhood education at a 2- or 4-year college or university. They are eligible for bonuses at benchmarks along the way and when they complete their program of study. They are expected, in turn, to commit to continue working in their sponsoring program for at least one more year (Olson, 2002).

Mentoring as a Form of Professional Development: **Mentoring** is the supporting and coaching of a *protégé* (novice staff member) by a *mentor* (educated, experienced, and dedicated staff member). In some cases, mentoring takes the form of *peer coaching* (which involves two or three teachers at about the same stage in their careers), which gives colleagues a chance observe one another's teaching and provide feedback and support. The overall purpose of mentoring is to serve as a bridge between preservice training and early practice or for experienced practitioners to learn new skills at any time in their careers.

Values of Mentoring.   As a result of the challenges beginning teachers often face and the high rates of teacher turnover and attrition, professional development in the form of mentoring is gaining support. Mentoring enhances the work of the mentor and the knowledge and skills of the protégé. More specifically, research on mentoring shows that mentoring builds leadership (Whitebook, Hnatiuk, & Bellm, 1994), helps counter high turnover rates (Kremer-Hazon & Ben-Peretz, 1996), increases feelings of professional growth (Rosenholtz, Bassler, & Hoover-Dempsey, 1986), and instills a sense of community (Newman, Rutter, & Smith, 1989). Mentoring seems especially appropriate in predominantly female careers because women appear to benefit from more mentor-initiated contact, more feedback, and more modeling than do men (Schneider, 1991). Because of its success, mentoring is now seen in public schools and in many states' early childhood care and education career lattices.

Mentoring Models and Processes.   Mentoring models can work in various ways. For example, some mentors work with one type of program (e.g., family child care), whereas others work with more than one type. Some serve as mentors in specific areas (e.g., the use of assistive technologies or developing literacy skills), whereas others work with their protégés on all aspects of their tasks (e.g., obtaining a CDA credential). Variations in the setting (e.g., the protégé's classroom) and approaches (e.g., one-on-one mentoring, one mentor to several protégés, and peer mentoring) are also common (Bellm, Whitebook, & Hnatiuk, 1997; Center for Career Development in Early Care and Education at Wheelock College, 2000; "Taking the Lead Initiative," 2000).

The mentor and the protégé's mentoring process usually work this way:

1. The mentor is assigned a protégé and gets to know the responsibilities and program settings of the protégé.
2. With the protégé, the mentor helps establish expectations for the process.
3. The protégé discusses perceived needs (e.g., the protégé might want to use Bellm et al.'s [1997] "Self-Evaluation Checklist" [pp. 91–93]).
4. The protégé and mentor agree on specific goals.
5. The mentor and protégé develop a plan of action (i.e., meeting times and how the mentoring will work).

6. The mentor and protégé prepare a plan of action; the protégé tries out the plan; the mentor observes and gathers data; the mentor and protégé take some time to reflect on outcomes before discussing the results; the protégé reflects on his or her teaching with the mentor's help (e.g., What do you think happened? How did _____ affect the outcome?). The protégé draws inferences.

7. Together the protégé and mentor decide whether goals and strategies should be incorporated into the teaching repertoire or whether they need to be refined or alternative ideas selected.

Requirements for Effective Mentoring.   Following are some requirements of effective mentoring:

1. Select the best mentors possible. Although some mentor qualities may vary by culture, generally mentors should
    a. be committed to keeping information shared within the coaching partnership confidential
    b. have training and experience in child development and early childhood education, adult learning, reflective practice, and leadership
    c. be adept at focusing on the practical, not the abstract (Bearwald, 2011)
    d. have the ability to be supportive of protégés and build a collaborative approach (Knight, 2011)
    e. use different mentoring methods to match protégés' abilities and learning styles and the goals to be achieved, and be creative problem solvers
    f. have good communication, observation, and recording skills to identify mentee's competencies as well as to target skills and competencies to improve (Bearwald, 2011)
    g. be able to clarify differences in opinions, knowledge-based "best practices," and mandates
    h. be good role models
    i. be willing to provide honest feedback
    j. be willing to continue the relationship long term for additional support
2. Match the mentor with the protégé based on the protégé's needs, abilities, and learning style. Mentoring and coaching partnerships are most effective when they are voluntary (Bearwald, 2011).
3. Find release time for the mentor, the protégé, or both.
4. Provide necessary coverage of the mentor's and protégé's responsibilities during the process. The mentor and protégé should have adequate time without interruptions.
5. Collect resources on mentoring.
6. Budget stipends and wage increases for both mentors and protégés when/where applicable.

Providing Group Professional Development Activities: Staff development can also be presented in a group setting. As with mentoring, the content presented in professional development sessions should be accurate and timely and should address issues the staff has identified as being of interest. Presentation techniques should fit staff members' prior knowledge, skills, comfort levels, and interests. We have found, for example, that some staff members are not comfortable with role-playing activities. They should not be forced to participate, as doing so can reduce the amount of information they retain and later implement in their classroom. It is important that trainings include a variety of instructional techniques to highlight the content and hold participants' interest. Alexander (2000) describes many practical and effective training techniques.

Finding time for group training sessions can be difficult. Staff development needs to occur on a regular basis, with staff receiving release time or appropriate compensation. Nap time is usually not an appropriate time for staff development. The following are several ways of scheduling staff development:

1. The center may close on specified days for staff development. Families should be given these dates on the center's calendar, which they receive when they enroll. Many programs are using holidays such as President's Day, Columbus Day, or Veteran's Day for training. These holidays are typically easier for families to schedule alternate child care when they are given adequate advanced notice; they will also better understand and support the reason for the closure.

2. The center may close for a week during periods of low enrollment, for example, during the week between Christmas and New Year's. These are also excellent times for hiring substitute help or getting volunteers.

3. Evening sessions can work. It helps if you are able to provide dinner and have child care for staff, but these accommodations should not take the place of required compensation.

Discussions.   Staff can learn a great deal by discussing and solving their own problems. That is why staff meetings should sometimes be used for discussions (see Figure 5.10 for tips on prompting discussion at staff meetings). In these meetings, the director needs to take care not to monopolize the conversation. This should be an opportunity for staff members to *share* ideas with one another. It can also be a valuable opportunity for teachers to reflect on their own work.

Staff members can also gain self-confidence when encouraged to lead a discussion on a topic that focuses on an area of their personal expertise. For example, if a teacher is particularly adept at vehicle safety procedures, he might present information during discussions prior to the start of the academic school year or during the summer season when transportation arrangements may change and new staff members might be joining the team.

Staff can also gain from the sharing of personal narratives—sharing the story of their own professional journey. Change in teaching often occurs through the process of listening and responding (Cinnamond & Zimpher, 1990). The use of narratives is not new in early childhood education (Ashton-Warner, 1963; Pratt, 1948).

Discussions can occur on any aspect of the program. Open-ended discussions are good ways to honor the diversity of beliefs and values about program goals and policies staff

- Divide discussion content into categories (e.g., children's program, parents, administration). Decide which category is covered at a given time (e.g., children's program—first Tuesday of each month; parents—second Tuesday of every other month). Routine announcements may be distributed at the end of each meeting or handled in other ways.
- Make meetings relevant to those in attendance. Thus, in some cases, assistant teachers may not need to meet with lead teachers.
- Prepare an agenda a few days before a scheduled meeting. Make any needed materials available at this time. The agenda should indicate the amount of time for presentation and for discussion.
- Start and stop the meeting on time.
- Distribute minutes of the meeting to staff.

Figure 5.10
Tips on Leading Staff Meeting Discussions

might bring to their work (Carter, 1992). Exchanges of ideas and feelings about issues and role clarification (see Bloom et al., 1991, pp. 233–252) are most helpful. Open discussions when new policies or changes to existing policies are proposed are also important. The staff should understand the importance of the new or changed policy and, when possible, should play a role in its development. Staff discussions might also work through ethical dilemmas staff members are facing. This kind of collaborative problem solving can contribute to the professionalism of the entire teaching team (Feeney & Freeman, 1999/2005/2011). Consider the ideas in Figure 5.10 to encourage discussion at staff meetings.

Workshops and Consultations.   Workshops are the most common form of in-service training (Kisker, Hofferth, Phillips, & Farquhar, 1991). They may be provided through outside sources (e.g., professional organizations) or developed by staff members. The term *workshop* implies that the session will be activity oriented, as opposed to a presentation only, and workshops often center on one topic. Teachers need to have options about training topics. (See Abbott-Shim, 1990; Alexander, 2000; Bloom, 2000; and Carter, 1993, for some ideas.)

If consultants are to yield lasting results, they must be viewed as resource people and not as "experts" hired to solve problems. They need to be aware of the real-life concerns of staff (Trawick-Smith & Lambert, 1995) and facilitate staff members in resolving their own problems. When a director decides to bring a consultant into her center, she must identify potential resource people, describe (in writing) the center's training needs, and ask that the potential consultant present a proposal describing the services he can provide.

Figure 5.11 contains information that should be included in a workshop or consultation proposal. Figure 5.12 is an example of a form to evaluate a workshop or consultation.

Self-Study in Accreditation and Program Evaluation.   The accreditation process is a major avenue for staff development because it involves self-study. Certain items from other program evaluations are appropriate for staff development, too. All programs can benefit from the use of professional journals, books, audiovisual materials, and online resources. Professional organizations publish many useful materials in many formats, and numerous resources are available through educational websites.

Workshop or Consultation Proposal

The following information must be submitted for consideration as a resource person for the Johnson County Community College Child Development Center:

>   Name, address, day and evening phone numbers of individuals submitting request
>
>   Main presenter résumé (title, academic and professional background)
>
>   Names, addresses, and résumés of other presenters
>
>   Objectives of presentation
>
>   Outline of presentation
>
>   Concept:
>
>   Delivery strategy:
>
>   Time required:
>
>   Method to be used to evaluate workshop effectiveness
>
>   Resource materials provided by consultant
>
>   Special requests (e.g., observation in center before presentation, audiovisual equipment)

Figure 5.11
Example of a Workshop or Consultation Proposal

Evaluation of_____
Johnson County Community College Child Development Center

Rate each item on a 3-point scale: 1 (Excellent), 2 (Satisfactory), and 3 (Poor).

	Rating	*Comments*
Objectives related to training needs	_____	_____
Content related to training needs	_____	_____
Content was accurate	_____	_____
Content applicable to work with young children	_____	_____
Content was clearly organized	_____	_____
Content clearly presented	_____	_____
Delivery strategies were engaging	_____	_____
Delivery strategies encouraged give-and-take among staff members and between staff and presenter(s)	_____	_____
Resource materials are practical	_____	_____

Comments: _____

_____

_____

_____

Figure 5.12
Form to Evaluate a Workshop or Consultation

Encouraging Professional Affiliations: Professional organizations publish journals, position papers, and other materials to contribute to members' professional growth and competence. Their websites often have a great deal of information on just about any topic of interest that you can imagine. Regrettably, however, many staff members do not belong to any professional organization (Feeney, et al., 2010; Galinsky, Howes, Kontos, & Shinn, 1994).

These organizations can make significant contributions to staff members' knowledge and expertise. They are likely to have local, state, and national meetings that provide opportunities for participants to network and to learn about recent developments in the field. These meetings can also provide opportunities to learn about new products that have been developed specifically for early care and education programs. Professional organizations also advocate at local, state, and national levels for issues related to young children and families. Some organizations offer opportunities for travel and study, research assistance, and consultation. Others provide personal services to members, such as insurance policies and loans. Finally, membership in a professional organization says to families and the community in general, "I am joining with others in an effort to provide the best for our children." See Appendix 8 for a list and websites of many professional organizations concerned with early care and education.

Assessing Job Performance: Directors have the overall responsibility for staff assessment. Sometimes a board member is also involved. Some large corporate systems use regional staff administrators to assist with the assessment process. In public schools, principals and central office supervisors assess staff.

Purposes.   Assessing job performance provides a mirror for what is happening in the program; that is, assessing job performance can aid in determining the effectiveness of the program in attaining its vision and diagnosing some of its problems. Caruso and Fawcett (1999) stated that "probably no other supervisory process has the *potential* to affect the quality of learning experiences for children as what staff members learn about themselves" (p. 151). The process of assessing job performance aids staff members in realizing that they are professionals (Duff, Brown, & Van Scoy, 1995).

Assessment may be formative or summative. **Formative assessment** is diagnostic (reflects the strengths and weaknesses of a staff member) and is used to promote growth. Formative assessment usually focuses on one issue or a group of related issues at a time (e.g., planning or arranging the physical facility). When teachers view the assessment process as one that helps them learn and improve, self-assessment is a valuable form of formative assessment. **Summative assessment** lets people know how they perform against certain predetermined criteria. Summative assessment "sums up" performance in that it looks at overall performance. Thus, summative assessment is used to guide decisions such as continuing employment, offering tenure, recommending individuals for promotions, and awarding merit pay. For the present purposes, only formative assessment is considered because all other purposes of assessment, such as tenure and merit pay, should be based on performance.

Criteria for Assessment.   Criteria for assessment should reflect the staff member's specific responsibilities and be appropriate for that person's professional level. Some assessment items, such as how seriously staff take their responsibility to honor confidentiality, apply to all employees. Other criteria will vary depending on the employee's role and responsibilities. Generally, personnel who provide similar services should be assessed according to the same criteria. Personnel serving in dissimilar roles will, in many cases, be assessed according to different criteria.

Assessments should be based on observations of performance and the observer's perceptions of the staff member's intentions. Several assessment tools are available and can be adapted to fit local needs. Some sources of criteria include the following:

1. The common elements that "define what all early childhood professionals must know and be able to do" (p. 13) based on a position statement of NAEYC (Willer, 1994)
2. The CDA competency standards (Council for Early Childhood Professional Recognition, 1996)
3. "Criteria for High-Quality Early Childhood Programs" given in the guide to accreditation by the National Academy of Early Childhood Programs (NAEYC, 2005)

Besides having the director observe their performance, staff members need to be reflective of their own performance through self-assessment. Although few self-assessment scales are available, some examples ask teachers to reflect on their performance, their satisfaction with their career choice, the health of their collaborative relationships, and their long-term career goals (Duff et al., 1995).

Methods of Observing and Recording.   After criteria for assessing personnel performance have been determined, they must be incorporated into an assessment instrument. Program-specific assessment procedures may include the following:

1. **Narratives** based on observations. These observations may be open ended or may focus on specific areas, such as guidance of children or planning. During observations, the director observes the staff member and notes specific strengths and weaknesses of the performance on the basis of the criteria selected for that particular job category. A staff member is sometimes asked to make a self-assessment based on personal recollections. Videotapes

are also becoming a popular means of affirming the director's observations, the staff member's self-assessment, or both. Videotapes do not seem as judgmental as verbal or written critiques. Observations can be done periodically throughout the year and should not be seen as an annual event. Teachers will thrive on consistent observation and feedback throughout the year.

2. Portfolios are also being used in some programs. A portfolio is a collection of materials (e.g., written work, audio or video recordings, photographs) that teachers collect and assemble to represent their performance. Thus, portfolios are an extension of narratives.

3. Interview procedures may be developed as assessment instruments. On the one hand, an interview may take the form of an open-ended discussion concerning strengths, performance areas needing improvement, and discussions on how to make needed improvements. On the other hand, some interview forms may, in actuality, be verbal rating scales.

4. Checklists and **rating scales** usually list assessment criteria in categories. Many checklists and rating scales also include an overall assessment for each category of characteristics, for total performance, or for both. Although checklists and rating scales are written assessment instruments, each instrument has a distinctive style. The checklist can be used to indicate those behaviors satisfactorily completed by a staff member. The administrator may check "yes," "no," or "not applicable" (see Figure 5.13). A rating scale, a qualitative assessment of performance, represents successive levels of quality along an inferior-superior continuum. The levels of quality may be described in different ways. (See Figures 5.14, 5.15, 5.16, and 5.17.)

	Yes	No	Not Applicable
Children have continuous adult supervision	———	———	———
Children were helped with negative emotions	———	———	———

Figure 5.13
Checklist to Assess Teachers' Performance

A balance between child-initiated and adult-initiated activities was noted

| Excellent | Good | Fair | Poor |

Figure 5.14
Example 1: Rating Scale with Quality Described in Words

a   Excellent
b   Above average
c   Average
d   Below average

Creative in teaching   a b c d

Figure 5.15
Example 2: Rating Scale with Quality Described in Words

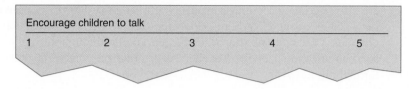

Figure 5.16
Rating Scale with Quality Described in Numerals

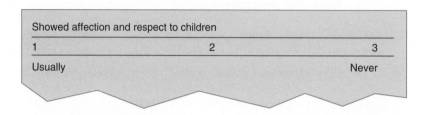

Figure 5.17
Rating Scale with Quality Described in Words and Numerals

Steps in Assessing: Directors should observe staff members many times before doing a formal observation. Caruso and Fawcett (1999) suggested these steps:

1. Schedule pre-observation conference to review the purposes of the observation, discuss concerns, seek input from the teacher, and plan procedures.
2. Conduct the formal observation.
3. Conduct the supervisory conference by setting the agenda, reviewing goals, and providing detailed feedback during which you discuss strengths and weaknesses and make future plans.
4. Complete a post-conference analysis.

Frequency of Assessment.   Informal assessment, especially self-assessment, should be conducted continually; however, the policy-making body should plan, determine the frequency of, and schedule formal assessment. Formative assessment should be conducted several times per year. Inexperienced teachers often need more assessments than do experienced teachers. Summative assessments are most often conducted annually.

Concerns.   Directors need training and experience in assessing job performance. They must realize that observations are not totally objective but are affected by beliefs and values, stress, and program constraints beyond their control. Directors can avoid some bias by getting a second opinion (i.e., asking another administrator to review the completed forms) before conferencing with teachers. Directors should ask themselves, "Can I provide evidence to support this statement?" When talking about both strengths and weaknesses, directors should be careful about using superlatives, which can be misleading. Directors should take the time to document examples of both positive contributions that have been exhibited in the review period and specific examples of areas in need of improvement. It is also important that teachers receive ongoing feedback, particularly if there are concerns, to avoid any unforeseen surprises during the conference. Directors should take the time to provide "on the spot" feedback when they observe less-than-expected levels of performance and also when they observe staff making extraordinary contributions to the program.

Regardless of the criteria chosen and the instruments selected, several basic principles need to be followed out of respect for each teacher and because annual assessment records are legal documents. Staff must (a) know they will be assessed, (b) understand that their assessment is based on program goals and their job description, (c) be informed of the process, (d) know they will receive verbal and written results, (e) be informed about how the results will be used, and (f) be assured that their assessment results are confidential and accessible only to those entitled to the information.

PERSONNEL SERVICES AND RECORDS

State boards of education and licensing agencies require that certain personnel services be provided and records kept by early childhood programs under their respective jurisdictions. In addition to providing those mandated personnel services and records, local boards of education or boards of directors may provide additional services and require other records permitted by state law. The director must be aware of such requirements and comply fully with them.

Contract and Terms of Employment

A **contract** is an agreement between two or more parties. In early childhood programs, a contract is an agreement between each staff member and the director or board specifying the services the staff member must provide and the specific sum of money to be paid for services rendered. Contracts may differ, depending on the job description (e.g., teacher, assistant teacher). All contracts/agreements should conform to the following guidelines:

- Written agreement as opposed to an oral one
- Specific designation of the parties to the contract
- Statement of the legal capacity of the parties represented
- Provision for signatures by the authorized agent(s) and by the teacher
- Clear stipulation of the salary to be paid
- Designation of the date and duration of the contract/agreement and the date when service is to begin
- Definition of the assignment

In signing a contract/agreement, an employee indirectly consents to obey all rules and regulations in force at the time of employment or adopted during the period of employment. Policies that most directly affect employees may include hours per day and days per week they are expected to work; the number of paid vacation days they are entitled to; specific requirements, such as dress code or driver's license; sick, emergency, and maternity/family leave policies; procedures for arranging for substitutes; the insurance coverage they will have; policies related to salary increases and fringe benefits; and available retirement plans. Each employee should have a written copy or access to an electronic version of all current policies.

The employee may receive a contract/agreement for a specified period of time, perhaps an annual or a continuing contract/agreement. Contracts or agreements for a specified period of time must be renewed at the end of that time period. The two most common types of continuing contracts or agreements are **notification** and **tenure**. An individual having a notification continuing contract/agreement must be notified on or before a given date if the contract/agreement is not to be renewed. A tenure contract/agreement guarantees that an employee cannot be dismissed except for certain specific conditions, such as lack of funds to pay salaries, neglect of duty, incompetency, failure to observe regulations, and immorality. Furthermore, a dismissed tenured employee has the right to a hearing in which the board must prove just cause for the dismissal. Programs offering tenure require that an employee serve a probationary period of a given number of years (usually three or five) before receiving a tenure contract/agreement. Directors need to review the specific employment guidelines in their state to determine acceptable employment agreements.

Special service contracts or agreements may also be written when a limited service is to be performed by a temporary employee (e.g., consultant). This type of contract/agreement must clearly specify the services to be rendered; the date(s) services are to be performed, including any follow-up services; any special arrangements, such as materials to be supplied by a temporary employee (or by the employer); and the fee. The signatures of the temporary employee and the requester should be affixed to the contract/agreement, and the transaction should be dated.

Job Descriptions

A written, up-to-date job description is needed for each personnel category. Job descriptions should include the following: (a) job title, (b) minimum qualifications, (c) primary duties and responsibilities, (d) working conditions, (e) additional duties, (f) reporting relationships and limits of authority, (g) physical requirements, and (h) benefits. The Economic Employment Opportunity Commission (EEOC) examines job descriptions for a section called *essential functions* (a part of the primary duties and responsibilities). If someone is not employed because of a disability, the director or board must be prepared to show that the function is essential to the job and cannot reasonably be performed by the person with the disability or by another staff member. (Essential functions must be in each job description prior to advertising.) Job descriptions should be specific to the particular early childhood program and position rather than adopted from another program. A potential employee should review the job description before signing a contract/agreement; all employees should keep their job descriptions in their files so that they can review them at any time.

Application Activity

Do you have a job description for each hired position at your center? If not, create one that addresses all eight of the items identified earlier. If you currently have a job description for each hired position at your center, review them to make sure that they contain all of the recommended information, and that the job description is up to date. A sample director's job description is shown in Figure 5.18 and a sample job description for a lead teacher is shown in Figure 5.19.

Insurance and Retirement Plans

Various kinds of insurance and retirement plans protect employees and organizations. Adequate coverage is expensive but essential. Some types of insurance and retirement plans may be mandated by state or federal laws, whereas other types may be voluntary. It is important to become familiar with the types of insurance and retirement plans that are required for individual programs.

CENTER DIRECTOR

Job Description

REPORTING RELATIONSHIPS

- The director reports to the board or others.
- The assistant director, receptionist, kitchen manager, lead teachers, assistant teachers, van drivers, and substitutes report to the director.

QUALIFICATIONS

The center director's qualifications must meet or exceed state licensing requirements for age, education, and experience. A bachelor's or an associate's degree in early childhood education is preferred.

JOB SUMMARY

The center director has overall responsibility for the operation of the center. Ensures that the center is operated in accordance with company and state licensing standards. Follows operating procedures to provide an educational, caring, and safe environment for children and families. Maintains highest standards by being visible and involved daily in the classrooms. Promotes the positive image of the program in the community. Keeps accurate financial records, manages the center's finances effectively, and maintains the center's sound financial position.

ESSENTIAL RESPONSIBILITIES AND STANDARDS OF PERFORMANCE

General

- Manages the center in compliance with state and local regulations and established policies and procedures.
- Effectively resolves problems related to the management of the center. Seeks assistance when appropriate.
- Maintains administrative records for the center.
- Ensures implementation of a developmentally appropriate program in each classroom.
- Maintains appropriate, required records on staff and children.
- Plans work schedules and supervises staff.
- Assists in lesson planning.
- Evaluates staff performance.
- Keeps fully apprised of all activities in the center.
- Prepares and forwards reports and forms as required.
- Represents the interests of the center in the community.

Fiscal Responsibilities

- Maintains an accurate financial accounting of the center's operation and protects the center's monetary assets.
- Ensures that classroom equipment is inventoried and maintained in good repair. Secures replacements or repairs following established procedures.
- Prepares and submits all required reports.
- Prepares accurate payroll, accounting, and operations reports by deadline.
- Takes responsibility for the center's assets and cash, makes daily deposits, and manages classroom supplies.
- Ensures accuracy and timely collection of tuition in accordance with established policies and procedures.
- Makes purchases necessary to center operation while maximizing operational profit.
- Maintains good working relationships with the licensing board representative and the local health department.

(Continued)

Figure 5.18
Sample Director's Job Description

Center Staff

- Maintains proper child-staff ratios and encourages high-quality teacher-child interactions.
- Ensures that each staff member receives and understands his/her job description, policies and procedures, and orientation materials.
- Maintains personnel records and ensures confidentiality.
- Maintains a training file on each employee.
- Maintains a current substitute list.
- Maintains up-to-date records for each child in care.
- Coaches and counsels staff.
- Conducts performance reviews as outlined in the staff manual.

Enrollment

- Works to fully enroll all classrooms to ensure budgeted income.
- Interviews parents and children before enrolling.
- Ensures that parents complete forms required by the company including those required by the appropriate regulatory agencies.
- Conducts orientation for newly enrolled families.
- Is available to parents at their convenience—listens attentively to their concerns and takes appropriate action.
- Informs parents of their child's progress.
- Keeps parents apprised of center activities.
- Develops and implements a marketing plan that includes community events.
- Tracks all inquiries, converts inquiries into parent tours, and converts tours into enrollments.
- Participates in the preparation of Individual Education Plans (IEPs) on all children with special needs.

Relationships with Families

- Maintains effective communications with families.
- Conducts parent meetings and other conferences as appropriate.
- Ensures that a developmental checklist is completed for each child and that the child's progress is communicated to the parents regularly.
- Regularly solicits feedback from parents in order to improve the center.

Health and Safety Requirements

- Understands and implements emergency procedures in cases of fire, tornado, chemical leak, or other emergencies. When necessary, can administer CPR/first aid, including lifting and carrying injured children.
- Trains staff in all center safety policies and procedures.
- Requires staff to enforce all safety policies and procedures in compliance with all regulatory agency requirements.
- Maintains up-to-date health records for all children and all staff members.
- Implements all standards necessary to ensure a clean, safe, and healthy environment, including universal precautions.
- Maintains a clean, safe, healthy environment through scheduled cleaning and frequent visual checks.
- Informs parents if their child has been exposed to a communicable disease.
- Ensures that a staff member certified in CPR *and* first aid is always present at the center, per state requirements.
- Establishes and maintains an emergency plan and emergency telephone numbers.

Figure 5.18 (Continued)

> - Conducts emergency drills in accordance with licensing requirements.
> - Maintains building, equipment, and grounds to ensure a safe environment that meets licensing safety standards.
> - Understands and implements policies related to inclusion or ill or injured children.
>
> ### Physical and Mental Requirements
>
> Child care demands physical fitness and mental acuity as staff care for children who cannot care for themselves. The center director:
>
> - Must be able to react quickly with sound judgment and problem-solving skills in complex and critical situations, such as injuries and accidents.
> - Must be qualified and able to perform the duties of any staff member—from teacher to kitchen manager to van driver.
> - Must use excellent verbal and written communication skills with parents, children, and staff.
> - Must be capable of lifting, carrying, and holding children weighing up to 60 pounds.

Figure 5.18 (Continued)

Federal Insurance Contributions Act (FICA):   Most centers are required to pay FICA, or Social Security, tax. FICA tax is generally used for retirement purposes. Tax rates are set at a percentage of the employee's salary. The employer deposits the amount of the employee's contributions collected as payroll deductions plus an equal amount from the employer quarterly. This money needs to be deposited in a separate account because commingling of federal funds is prohibited by law. Employers are required to submit a quarterly report on FICA taxes. All organizations, including tax-exempt programs, are responsible for keeping up with current tax laws.

Workers' Compensation Insurance: Workers' compensation is liability insurance compensating an employee injured by an accident in the course of and arising out of employment. (Independent contractors are not covered. Directors should insist that any contractors doing work for a program certify that they are adequately insured so that they cannot later claim to have been acting as an employee. Documentation of this coverage should be kept on file with the contract/agreement covering the particular project.) Workers' compensation is required in most states, but many states have exceptions for certain classes of employers, such as organizations with few employees or those wishing to self-insure. The insurance company pays 100% of all workers' compensation benefits required by state law. Injured employees and, in the case of death, their dependents are eligible for one-half to two-thirds of their weekly wages, plus hospital and medical benefits. In most states, employees, in turn, give up their right to sue employers for damages covered by the law.

State Unemployment Insurance: State unemployment insurance is required in most states and varies considerably from state to state. A questionnaire must be completed about the employees' activities and the tax status of the early childhood program. The insurance rates are figured as a percentage of total wages and are different for for-profit and not-for-profit corporations.

Liability Insurance: Liability insurance protects the organization or employees from loss when persons have been injured or property has been damaged as a result of negligence (rather than accident) on the part of the institution or its employees. However, almost any "accident" that occurs is usually considered the result of negligence. The extent to which

LEAD TEACHER

Job Description

REPORTING RELATIONSHIPS

- The lead teacher reports to the director and may also take direction from the assistant director.
- The lead teacher may supervise assistant teachers.

QUALIFICATIONS

The lead teacher's qualifications must meet or exceed state licensing requirements for age, education, and experience. A bachelor's or an associate's degree in early childhood education is preferred. Previous work experience in child care is also preferred.

JOB SUMMARY

The lead teacher plans and implements the daily curriculum for children in his or her classroom. Curriculum activities will be designed to promote the children's social, emotional, physical, and cognitive development. Oversees and coordinates the children's personal care, hygiene, learning activities, specialized programs, and positive guidance. Maintains classroom records and developmental checklists. Ensures that classroom is consistently clean and safe. Informs parents of their children's progress on a daily basis and offers both formal and informal parent-teacher conferences regularly.

ESSENTIAL RESPONSIBILITIES AND STANDARDS OF PERFORMANCE

- Recognizes and considers the background, special needs, interests, learning style, and temperament of each child.
- Helps children learn to think creatively, to solve problems independently, and to respect themselves and others.
- Treats each child with dignity and respect. Uses positive guidance techniques consistent with center policies and procedures.
- Plans and implements curriculum activities that promote the children's social, emotional, physical, and cognitive development.
- Keeps accurate, current records of each child's developmental milestones.
- Creates a developmentally appropriate environment consistent with the program's philosophy and goals.
- Establishes developmentally appropriate room arrangement, décor, and learning environment in the classroom.
- Implements and participates in family-style meals and snacks; models good table manners.
- Establishes and maintains a safe, healthy, nurturing learning environment. Strives to prevent injuries. Handles emergencies, accidents, and injuries appropriately if they occur.
- Establishes and maintains primary caregiving relationships.
- Understands and implements emergency procedures in case of fire, tornado, chemical leak, or other emergency. When necessary, can administer CPR/first aid, including lifting and carrying injured children. Uses proper lifting procedures and seeks assistance if necessary.
- Must be physically and mentally able to react appropriately and immediately to unexpected circumstances.
- Must be able to bend and stoop to interact on child's level. Must be able to interact and communicate with children in the classroom and on the playground (run, jump, demonstrate physical exercises).
- Must be able to stand approximately 95% of the workday.
- Maintains educational materials and equipment. Keeps classroom safe, neat, and clean.
- Immediately notifies director of needed repairs to equipment and toys in the classroom, in the building, and on the playground.

Figure 5.19
Sample Lead Teacher's Job Description

- Interacts profesionally with parents, staff, and visitors.
- Plans formal parent conferences with director's approval. Provides daily written communication to parents of infants, toddlers, and 2-year-olds. Maintains a professional relationship with parents.
- Maintains strict confidentiality regarding children and families.
- Promotes and maintains good rapport and working relationships with other staff members.
- Participates in staff training sessions, meetings, and programs as requested by the director and sponsored by the center. Willing to lead session if requested to do so by the director.
- Supervises assistant teachers to ensure the physical and emotional well-being of each child in the classroom. Mentors assistant teachers in the required skills and expertise needed to ensure a nurturing classroom environment.
- Observes, records, and reports to the director any significant individual or group behavior that might affect the well-being of children enrolled at the center.
- Prepares and forwards forms requested by the director.
- Willing to perform other duties, if required and qualified, to ensure a safe, healthy, nurturing environment for children and families, including cleaning, cooking, driving, or managing the center in the temporary absence of the director.
- Meets or exceeds state training requirements.
- Understands and implements inclusion policies (where applicable).
- Understands all current state and local regulations.

Figure 5.19 (Continued)

an institution or its employees can be held liable varies from state to state, and a liability policy should cover everything for which an institution is liable. In most states, programs providing transportation services are required to have vehicle insurance, including liability insurance.

Health Insurance and Hospital-Medical Insurance: Health insurance, whether fully or partially paid for by the employer or taken on a voluntary basis and paid for by the employee, may take one of three forms: (a) medical reimbursement insurance, (b) medical service or prepaid medical care, and (c) disability income benefits. Hospital-medical plans fall into three groups: (a) basic hospitalization and medical coverage, (b) major medical insurance, and (c) closed-panel operation (service available from a limited number of physicians, clinics, or hospitals).

Crime Coverage: There are several ways to protect the program against loss resulting from the dishonesty of employees or others. See a reputable insurance agent for coverage availability in your area and relative costs.

Retirement Programs: The Social Security (FICA) tax is usually mandatory and is used as a federal retirement program. Most public school program personnel are also covered under state retirement programs, paid on a matching fund basis by employer and employee. Other programs may also have retirement plans in addition to Social Security coverage.

Personnel Records

Personnel administration involves keeping records and making reports in accordance with state laws, licensing regulations, the program's governing body requirements, and federal legislation concerning privacy of personal information. Public and private schools must keep personnel records for all employees—both instructional staff and support personnel. In most cases, local programs keep personnel records, and reports are submitted to their respective state governing boards (licensing agency or state board of education). However, the governing board may inspect locally kept records.

Personnel records is a collective term for all records containing information about employees. Although these records vary from program to program, they usually address the following specifics:

1. *Personal information records* are kept by all early childhood programs. Programs need to keep files for all employees that include the employee's legal name, address, telephone number(s); evidence of U.S. citizenship or a *Work Authorization for Non-U.S. Citizens* form issued by the U.S. Department of Labor; and Social Security number. Employees need to inform the center's administration when there are changes to this personal information (e.g., if they are to move or change their phone number) so that these records can be kept current. Program administrators should determine what information is required by regulatory agencies, their board, or others responsible for the program to be certain they have satisfied all requirements.

2. *Personal health records* signed by an appropriate health care professional are often required. These records may be detailed, requiring medical results from a physical examination or specified laboratory tests, or may be a general statement that the employee is free from any mental or physical illness or has limitations that might adversely affect the health of children or other adults or their ability to perform required tasks (NARA/NCCIC, 2010). When medical records are required, it is important to implement systems to keep the information confidential so that compliance to the 1996 HIPAA (Health Insurance Portability and Accountability Act) is maintained. HIPAA protects individually identifiable health information; operating in full compliance with HIPAA as it pertains to both employee and student information is necessary.

3. Evidence of having completed required *criminal background checks*, which may include a check of the state's criminal history record, federal fingerprint records, and state child abuse and neglect registries (NCCIC/NARA, 2010).

4. *Emergency information* is required by many programs. This information includes the names, addresses, and telephone numbers of one or more persons to be contacted in an emergency; the name of a physician and hospital; and any medical information, such as allergies to drugs or other conditions, deemed necessary in an emergency.

5. *Records of education, training, and other qualifications* are required by many states' licensing regulations, accreditation, or QRS systems. They must include the names of schools attended, diplomas or degrees earned, transcripts of academic work, and the registration number and type of teacher's or administrator's certificate or any other credential the employee has earned (e.g., a bus driver's license, food service certification, and child care permit). They also record employees' participation in annual in-service trainings required by many states' licensing regulations (NCCIC/NARA, 2010).

6. *Professional or occupational information records,* including the places and dates of previous employment, names of employers, and job responsibilities.

7. *Professional or occupational skill and character references* are included in the personnel records. In most cases, these references are for confidential use by the employer. These records should be obtained by the administrator or her designee and signed to indicate authenticity. When possible, written and verified employment references should be obtained. Many states require that two to four written references or notes from references given orally be included in the employee's file.

8. *Service records* are kept by some programs. These records contain information concerning the date of current employment, level or age of children cared for or taught or program directed, extended absences or leaves taken, in-service education received and conferences attended, committees served on, salary received, and date and reason for termination of service.

9. *Insurance records* are kept by all programs involved in any group insurance.

10. *Job performance assessment records* are placed on file in many programs. Certain forms must be treated as legal documents, but observer's informal notes should be shredded after they have fulfilled their purposes and required retention time has been met.

Personnel of many early childhood programs, especially Head Start and others receiving federal funding, are covered under the Privacy Act of 1974 (P.L. 93-579). Because a person's legal right to privacy must be guarded, administrators must keep abreast of the laws pertaining to record keeping and record security. For example, the Privacy Act of 1974 requires federal agencies to take certain steps to safeguard the accuracy, currentness, and security of records concerning individuals and to limit record keeping to necessary and lawful purposes. Individuals also have a right to examine federal records containing such information and to challenge the accuracy of data with which they disagree (Title 5, Section 552a, 2011).

SUMMARY

The factors that influence the effectiveness of early childhood programs are incredibly multifaceted and complex. All research studies support the fact that the behavior of adults in early childhood programs has an important impact on children and their ability to thrive in these programs.

The qualities of teachers of young children have been studied extensively. The question of what professional qualifications (knowledge and skills) and personal characteristics (personality traits and values) people need to work effectively with young children has no simple, definitive answer. A great deal of consensus does exist, however. Directors are responsible for overseeing the creation of a positive and productive work climate for staff, enriching the professional life of staff members, keeping accurate records, and providing other personnel services. Positive job conditions support job satisfaction and act to reduce staff turnover, which, in turn, leads to improved quality of services to children and families.

USEFUL WEBSITES

Career Path Example, provided by Bright Horizons Family Solutions

   www.brighthorizons.com/resources/pdf/careerpath.pdf

This chart outlines possible career options and gives a clear depiction of how a career lattice can work within an organization.

Early Care and Education Career Path, South Carolina Center for Child Care Career Development

   abcqualitycare.org/ECECareerPath.pdf

This page describes one representative state's career path from the GED through to the terminal degrees of Ph.D. and Ed.D. It can be a helpful tool for educators developing their professional development plan from beginning to end.

TO REFLECT

1. Preschool and kindergarten teachers in public school settings are often at the bottom of a pecking order. Sometimes the discrimination is subtle (e.g., their opinions on schoolwide matters are not acknowledged), and sometimes the discrimination is very open (e.g., they are teased about "playing all day" or majoring in "Sandbox 101").

How can early childhood teachers in public schools gain the respect of their colleagues and administrators?

2. Director X is frustrated because she knows her staff does not particularly respect her as their administrator. She was picked for her position from the ranks of the teachers, although she knew she wasn't the best teacher. She had

not actively sought the position and was surprised but pleased when it was offered to her. She has tried three approaches to leadership, and all have failed. First, she tried praise (and sparse criticism) as a way to please everyone. Next, she tried putting less emphasis on her position (and the authority that goes with it) by taking the smallest office and answering her own phone, and so forth. Finally, she tried to show her staff that she "earned her salary" by becoming a workaholic and working as much as she could—early, late, and on weekends. Why did each approach fail? What should Director X do to gain respect?

3. Director Y has four candidates for a teaching position with preschool children. From interviews, he notes the following: Candidate 1 sees herself in a mothering role. Candidate 2 sees himself aiding children's development, especially their academic development. Candidate 3 wants to build a "little democratic community" in which children's decision making is most important. Candidate 4, who has read some of Montessori's writings, believes in order and organization. What would the classroom be like under each of these four candidates? What criteria should the director use in selecting one of the four candidates?

4. Before taking her position as director of a large corporate early childhood program, Director Z has been sent to a weeklong seminar for directors. She is disappointed because she believes that many of the skills she is learning are not applicable to early childhood program leadership. How is leadership in early childhood programs different from leadership in other organizations? What are the implications?

CHECK AND APPLY YOUR UNDERSTANDING

1. Select five individuals currently working in early care and education and ask each one of them two questions related to career recruitment:
   a. What resource do you think of first when starting a job search to assist you in sourcing job openings?
   b. How likely would you be to use an Internet-based career search tool to locate job postings?

2. Describe in detail the staff qualifications that you believe are most important to the success of an early care and education program.

3. Take a moment to write down the various members of the community who you believe could assist in recruiting qualified staff members for your program. List how you would approach those community partners and how you would use them to assist you in your recruiting efforts.

4. Develop a three-month, six-month, and annual professional development plan for a new preschool teacher.

5. Describe the importance of obtaining detailed references on employees prior to hiring them to work in an early childhood program.

CHAPTER 6

Creating Quality Learning Environments

Learning Outcomes

After studying this chapter, you should be able to:

1. Develop a step-by-step plan for building a new facility or renovating an existing structure.

2. Design an entry/exit area that is inviting to children and families as they come for the day, fits into the neighborhood, and has a workable traffic pattern.

3. Select lighting fixtures, floor coverings, wall treatments, and a color scheme that would combine to create a comfortable and aesthetically pleasing setting for children, caregivers, and families.

4. Identify the features you would include in a playground for preschoolers ages 3 to 5.

5. Identify characteristics that make classroom books and other instructional materials free from bias.

Marie's Experience

After 13 successful years as the center director, Marie now has the opportunity to oversee the construction of a new wing that will include five new classrooms, a teachers' workroom, and a family resource room. She has always felt well prepared to manage the center's finances and to serve as its instructional leader, but she had no experience to prepare her for this endeavor. Now that it's almost time to break ground, she realizes she has learned a great deal about zoning regulations and building codes by working with the architect and contractor. She still thinks she has a lot to learn, however, about designing the new wing's interior spaces and is looking for resources to help her avoid making costly mistakes. She has turned to this chapter for guidance on issues such as selecting floor coverings and color schemes and for figuring out what she will need to equip the classrooms and support areas.

NAEYC Administrator Competencies addressed in this chapter:

Management Knowledge and Skills

5. Program Operations and Facilities Management

Knowledge and application of policies and procedures that meet state/local regulations and professional standards pertaining to:
- the health and safety of young children.
- the ability to design and plan the effective use of space based on principles of environmental psychology and child development.
- knowledge of playground safety design and practice.

Early Childhood Knowledge and Skills

1. Historical and Philosophical Foundations

Knowledge of current trends and important influences impacting program quality.

9. Learning Environments

Knowledge of the impact of the physical environment on children's learning and development.
- The ability to use space, color, sound, texture, light, and other design elements to create indoor and outdoor learning environments that are aesthetically pleasing, intellectually stimulating, psychologically safe, and nurturing.
- The ability to select age-appropriate equipment and materials that achieve curricular goals and encourage positive social interaction.

Learning environments speak to both children and adults in powerful ways. Wide open spaces invite children to "run like the wind," whereas small intimate areas suggest quiet play and can provide a private moment in the midst of a busy classroom. Materials also suggest ways to behave and feel. Some say, "Play with me, I'm sturdy. I'm here for you to manipulate and explore; you can figure me out and be successful when you work with me." Others say, "Touch carefully because I'm fragile. I might break" or "I'm hard to figure out. I'm not meant for you."

The learning environment also communicates the program's vision, values, and goals to adults. Visitors to the Reggio Emilia schools in Italy are, invariably impressed by the attention invested in aesthetics: classrooms are inviting and light filled, areas for active play are separate from spaces for quiet concentration, there are safe places to keep works in progress, and the lunch room has furniture and furnishings that reflect the local culture and create a relaxed and homey atmosphere.

An intentionally created environment demonstrates an understanding of how children develop and learn while providing opportunities for child-child, child-material, and child-adult interactions. It supports adults in their work, giving them ready access to the resources they need and a place to relax for a while in the middle of a busy day, and it welcomes families, creating a home away from home.

In this chapter, we discuss how the center's environment can be either inviting, relaxed, and comfortable, letting children know they are free to explore or intimidating, formal, and stiff, making them feel reluctant to enter, stressed, and on guard. We provide guidelines for making indoor and outdoor spaces engaging, attractive, and safe places that bring out the best in young children, the adults who work with them each day, and the families that entrust their children to the center's care.

PLANNING A NEW OR RENOVATED FACILITY

Some early childhood programs have brand-new buildings designed and built to their specifications, others are housed in existing structures renovated for their use, and still others share their space and may need to adapt it to fit their needs. Each of these arrangements can successfully meet the particular needs of the children for whom it is planned.

If you have the opportunity to design a new center or modify an existing one, your first task is to consider the following issues:

1. Determine how much area you need to accommodate the building, the outdoor play space, paths and parking spaces, and landscaping so that the facility fits into the neighborhood. Experts recommend that the site provide 325 sq ft to 574 sq ft per child (Olds, 2001). You will also want to consider whether or not to include enough area for future growth.

2. Research applicable building and zoning regulations or hire a lawyer and/or contractor who can help you navigate these requirements.

3. The safety of the children and staff is your primary concern. Consider hazards, such as nearby water or busy streets, when selecting a potential property. Take them into account when locating doorways, driveways, and parking areas, and design safeguards to protect children and adults from danger.

4. Zoning laws in many areas and federal laws that apply to programs receiving direct or indirect federal assistance require that buildings be fully accessible to students and employees with physical, vision, hearing, and other disabilities. Their needs should be taken into account in all stages of facility planning.

5. Most of the building's occupants will be young children who may spend as many as 10,000 hours per year there. The facility should be child oriented and also comfortable for adults.

6. Flexibility is essential. Both indoor and outdoor spaces should be planned to accommodate children's changing interests.

7. Plan spaces for children intentionally. Provide large areas that invite children to run and climb, and small spaces that encourage them to fit themselves into hardly big-enough nooks and crannies. Include areas for boisterous play as well as for being quiet; offer children spaces where they can be together with their entire class, where they can interact with one or two peers, and also places to be alone. Consider how you can add interesting architectural features such as inviting alcoves, skylights, or porches, and how mindfully selected furnishings such as nonpoisonous plants and flowers; artwork; and curtains, wall hangings, and tablecloths made of beautiful fabrics can soften the environment. All these features add to the center's livability and to its aesthetics (Olds, 2001).

8. The Americans with Disabilities Act (ADA) requires early childhood programs to accommodate children and adults with special needs in the "least restrictive environment." It provides a foundation for efforts to provide inclusive programs that benefit all participants—individuals who have disabilities and their able-bodied peers. As you plan your facility, remember that ADA mandates that indoor and outdoor facilities be accessible for all children and adults so that those with and without disabilities can safely take part in activities and can choose from the range of activities it offers. Accessibility is a priority because it is the first step toward welcoming children with disabilities into an inclusive setting. Descriptions of specific features of integrated settings are beyond the scope of this book. Review the websites listed at the end of this chapter for detailed information to guide your efforts to create a fully inclusive setting.

9. If you are establishing a new center, you will need to select all the furniture, equipment, and materials. These are complex decisions that will take a significant amount of time and effort.

10. Cost is always a consideration. Building the facility and equipping its classrooms will require a large initial investment. The program's sponsor will recoup these costs over many years if high-quality materials are purchased from the very beginning.

Planning for a large center or a multisite program often begins with the appointment of a committee charged with developing preliminary or conceptual plans that are then turned over to a drafter or architect who will develop a specific proposal. In small programs, the director is likely to single-handedly plan facility construction or renovation. Corporate chains and franchises usually have employees who manage the construction and renovation of their centers based on a prototypical design. Facilities for public school prekindergartens and kindergartens are planned by the local board with input from the principal and/or the early childhood coordinator and sometimes classroom teachers.

Regardless of whether the structure is old or new or whether it is operated by a public, private, or nonprofit entity, facility planners should take the following steps to progress from facility planning, to building and equipping the center, to finally opening the doors to children and families:

1. Program planners should identify the program's specific needs. Consider its maximum enrollment, the ages of children served, anticipated special needs of children served, expected group sizes, and the hours of operation.
2. Planners should familiarize themselves with construction issues they need to address by reading about facility planning in this book and other professional resources, meeting with experts in the field, and visiting programs similar to the one they are planning.
3. Program planners will want to explore energy-saving features such as solar heat, high-efficiency heating and cooling systems, and energy-saving appliances. You may even want to pursue Leadership in Energy and Environmental Design (LEED) Certification. See Table 6.1 for more specific information on LEED Certification criteria.

Table 6.1
LEED Certification Criteria Summary

Schools that are LEED certified undergo a comprehensive review that considers their site, construction materials, and the efficiency of appliances and fixtures. Some components of LEED certification are likely to apply to an early care and education facility. LEED certification criteria also consider whether issues of sustainability are included in the curriculum as appropriate.

Location and Site Plan

- Urban sites are located near community resources such as the post office, supermarket, restaurants, and fire station, etc.
- Trees and vegetation are protected, and the center includes ample open spaces.
- Fixtures reduce light pollution.
- Water-efficient landscaping captures rainwater or uses non-potable water for irrigation.

Transportation

- The center has access to public transportation.
- The center is within walking distance of students' homes.
- The center has convenient racks for bicycles.

Construction

- Wood used in construction is certified in accordance with the Forest Stewardship Council's principles and criteria.
- Ceilings and other surfaces have appropriate sound-absorbent materials.
- Natural light is provided through windows and skylights.
- Humidity is controlled to prevent mold.

Building Components

- Materials used throughout emit minimal odors and irritating/harmful fumes. Special attention is paid to
  - Adhesives and sealants
  - Paints and coatings
  - Flooring systems
  - Composite wood
  - Furniture and furnishings
- The center uses renewable energy, including solar, wind, and geothermal power.
- The center provides easily accessible area for recycling of paper, corrugated cardboard, glass, plastics, and metals.
- Appliances and plumbing fixtures are efficient.
  - Toilets use no more than 1.6 gallons/flush.
  - Restroom faucets use no more than 2.2 gallons/minute.
  - Clothes washers use no more than 7.5 gallons/ft^3/cycle.

Complete information on LEED certification can be found at *LEED 2009 for Schools: New Construction and Major Renovations* by U.S. Green Building Council, Washington, DC. http://www.usgbc.org/DisplayPage.aspx?CMSPageID=1586

4. Planners need to work closely with all appropriate agencies to be certain their plans are in compliance with building; fire prevention; licensing; and, when appropriate, accreditation regulations.

5. Planners should identify construction benchmarks along the way to document progress toward project completion.

6. Programs operated by a board of directors will probably be required to submit their plans to the board for approval before construction begins.

7. The director or another representative of the program needs to work closely with the architect or drafter and the contractor, and perhaps with a banker, accountant, and attorney, to be certain planning and construction go smoothly.

Early childhood programs sometimes share facilities with other groups. In some communities, weekday preschool and Sunday school programs use the same classrooms, activity rooms, and kitchens on different days of the week. In other locales, programs for early care and education are housed in community centers where classes and meetings are held in the evenings and weekends when the children are not there. Programs that share space successfully create clear expectations about the following issues:

- Cleaning (i.e., Who will clean the rooms and buildings and how often will they be cleaned?)
- Equipment storage (i.e., Where will materials be stored and who will have access to them?)
- Classroom setup (i.e., May the weekday program use the bulletin boards? May they label children's cubbies? May decorations and materials for religious holidays used by the Sunday school be left up during the week?)

Clear channels of communication are needed for these arrangements to be successful, but it is worth the effort when well-designed community resources are used to benefit many children and families.

In other instances, early childhood programs lease their facilities. Program personnel should seek a long-term lease, determine in advance if the lease is renewable, clarify who is responsible for which kinds of repairs, and have a clear understanding as to how the building and the grounds can be altered (i.e., May the center build ramps, paint walls, or erect fences and playgrounds?).

Each of these arrangements can work, but it takes time and effort to create a well-planned environment that will support the program's vision, goals, and objectives and help it realize its mission to serve young children and their families.

Program planners need to address many issues related to the building's exterior and interior design. Even small details can communicate the program's values, goals, and purpose. They create a first and often lasting impression on the community, families, and children.

THE FACILITY'S ENTRY/EXIT AREA

Children and families see the entry/exit area when they arrive every morning and when they leave every afternoon. It has the potential to be warm and inviting or intimidating, cold, and institutional, creating barriers for children and their families. The entry/exit area is also the view most often seen by the public, and the public's opinion of a program may be based, in large measure, on what can be seen from the street.

The area should be a comfortable scale, rather than large, imposing, and institutional. It should use landscaping, lighting, ramps, and natural materials that invite children and parents to enter (Read, 2007). Windows are an important feature because they help children and parents feel comfortable as they prepare to transition into child care in the morning. Some entryways provide views of indoor and outdoor activity areas from a foyer, porch, or courtyard. Displays of children's work; photos of families, children, and staff members; and information about upcoming events are all welcome additions that can create a sense of belonging for children and families. They also communicate the center's purpose and goals to visitors (Curtis & Carter, 2003).

Convenient parking should be available near the center's front door so parents will be able to linger at drop-off and pickup times (Greenman, 2005). It is important to incorporate a curb cut and ramp near the parking lot to accommodate individuals with disabilities. The ramp should be at least 36 in. wide; the slope should be gradual, at least 12 ft long for each 1 ft of incline, and should include handrails. In addition, thresholds to entrances should be no more than 3 in. high and doors should open easily and have at least 32-in. clearings.

For security reasons, the center's entrance should be designed to control access. A receptionist should be stationed near the entrance area when family members are arriving in the morning and leaving in the afternoon. Many programs now require parents to ring a doorbell or enter a personal code to unlock the front door, and some have installed observation cameras near all entries and in the parking lot to add an extra measure of security.

INDOOR SPACE

Each group of children has its own classroom with space for active, quiet, and messy play; cubbies for children to store personal belongings; and areas for caregiving routines such as diapering and toileting, snack preparation, and storage. The facility must also have adult restrooms, administrative and storage areas, and a custodial closet with access to water and safe storage of cleaning supplies. Many programs also have a kitchen, a lunchroom, an activity area, a reception area, a family room, and a staff break room.

Lighting, Acoustics, Ventilation, Heating, and Cooling

Lighting: Maximizing your use of natural light is important because it is inviting and homelike. Natural light from large windows, balconies, and porches improves children's and adults' moods, reduces fatigue and eyestrain, helps the body maintain circadian rhythms, destroys bacteria and mold, and is a source of vitamin D (Edwards & Torcellini, 2002; Olds, 2001). What's more, children learn about the weather by observing frost, fog, rain, and snow; they learn about the passage of time by noticing patterns of light and shade; and they learn about the natural and human-made world when they can see it from their classroom. They can see best from windowsills 18 to 24 in. high.

How you use natural light will depend to a great extent on your climate and site-specific considerations. Determine how much sun is ideal as you plan each classroom's directional orientation. Is your weather cold and snowy, where warming sun would be welcome? Do you have many months that are hot and steamy, making it important that you avoid direct sun as much as possible? The answers to those questions will help you decide if it is better for classrooms to face east toward the morning sun, west so they are bathed in afternoon light, or if a southern or northern exposure without direct sun is best. Do not forget to take into account the impact of large buildings or nearby trees that block the light.

After you have planned to maximize natural light in such a way that you have avoided excessive heat or glare, you will need to plan how you will supplement sunlight with artificial lighting. Optimum lighting plans use light purposefully, making decisions based on how each space will be used. Some lighting will be direct and some will be indirect, fixtures will be mounted at various heights, and task lighting will illuminate workspaces where children and adults need to see details well, such as when they are reading and writing. Illumination is measured in foot-candles (or lumens, the metric measure). Experts recommend these levels of illumination for children's classrooms: 50–100 foot-candles on work surfaces children use for reading, painting, and similar activities; 30–50 foot-candles for active play; at least 20 foot-candles on stairs, landings, driveways, and entrances; and no more than 5 foot-candles in sleeping areas. (American Academy of Pediatrics [AAP]/American Public Health Association [APHA]/National Resource Center for Health and Safety in Child Care [NRCHSCCEE], 2011). Your licensing specialist may measure the illumination in specific areas of the building with a light meter. Because lighting should be tailored to meet children's specific needs, different banks of lights controlled separately or dimmers are good additions to the lighting plan.

Federal legislation passed in 2007 mandates the gradual phase-out of incandescent bulbs beginning with 100-watt bulbs on January 1, 2012. In January 2013, 75-watt bulbs will be discontinued, and 60-watt and 40-watt bulbs will follow in 2014 (Energy Independence and Security Act, 20007; O'Donnell & Koch, 2011). It would be wise to plan lighting that uses compact fluorescent bulbs (CFLs), which can last 9 to 10 years and are 75% more efficient than incandescent bulbs that give off the same light; light-emitting diode (LED) bulbs, which can last 20 years and are seen as the wave of the future; or halogen bulbs, which are also energy efficient. You will want to be certain that fluorescent bulbs are warm, with the full spectrum of light, rather than traditional fluorescent bulbs that produce light that is harsh and apt to leave children and adults tired at the end of the day (Edwards & Torcellini, 2002; Olds, 2001).

Of course, each classroom in most buildings will have a different directional orientation and a different exposure to natural light, so it will be important to plan window coverings, appropriate color schemes, and artificial lighting techniques based on its particular needs.

Acoustics: We are bombarded all day long with noises from highways, airplanes, telephones, vacuum cleaners, dishwashers, lawn mowers, and leaf blowers. When working in child care, the sounds surrounding us are likely to also include crying children, noises from play such as those created by hammering toys and falling towers of blocks, and the voices of children and adults. As adults, we have learned to tune out many of the sounds in our environment, but children are acutely aware of them. Overexposure to high noise levels can create chronic stress, including persistent startle or "fight-or-flight" reactions. Other physical responses can include headaches, hyperactivity, tense muscles, indigestion, the inability to concentrate, irritability, and poor sleep habits (Olds, 2001). In short, high noise levels are harmful to children and adults alike.

The first strategy to keep sound at a healthy level is to keep group sizes small and to have rooms large enough that you can separate areas for noisy active play from those for quiet pursuits. You can take additional steps to make sure that the sounds children hear most are human voices directed personally to them, noises that characterize the productive hum of children at play, live and recorded music, and the sounds of nature.

Building construction and furnishings can also help reduce noise by (a) limiting the amount of noise from the outdoors that comes into the classroom, (b) minimizing the noise from the building's heating and air conditioning system, and (c) providing plenty of materials that absorb sound such as carpets, stuffed furniture, curtains, and acoustical ceiling tiles. You can also take steps to cushion the sounds of noisy play; for example, consider an area rug in the block center (Gonzalez-Mena & Eyer, 2009; Stewart, 2009).

Ventilation, Heating, and Cooling: Child care regulations are likely to stipulate that all indoor areas must have good ventilation designed to minimize odors, extreme temperatures, and humidity, which can be achieved by opening the windows (with screens), using safely installed fans, or using window units or central air conditioning. They typically specify that rooms should be draft free between 65°F and 75°F in the winter and between 68°F and 82°F in the summer.

Floors, Ceilings, Walls, and Colors

Floors, ceilings, and walls should be coordinated so they are aesthetically pleasing but also both functional and durable. The colors you select will influence the children and adults who come to the center every day.

Floors: Young children need flooring that is comfortable to play on, will tolerate getting wet during messy play, will not stain if there are spills at mealtimes, and can be cleaned easily when bathroom accidents happen. Flooring materials should also be able to withstand hard wear, should not become slippery when wet, and should not give off toxic fumes.

Carpet and resilient flooring such as vinyl and linoleum are the most frequently used flooring materials in child care settings. Resilient floorings with a matte finish that are not slippery when wet are best for areas designed for water play, painting, sand play, and eating and toileting areas. Vinyl and linoleum generally come as 12-in. squares or 6-ft-, 9-ft-, or 12-ft-wide sheets. They are both good choices.

Most programs create zones for active and quiet play by combining resilient flooring with wall-to-wall carpet or area and throw rugs. Carpet is softer, helps minimize injuries, reduces glare, is more comfortable, and more effectively absorbs noise than resilient flooring. All child care settings are enhanced by carpeted areas, but it is particularly important to include carpet in infant rooms because very young children spend so much time on the floor. When choosing carpet, consider the fiber (nylon and natural fibers such as wool are the most durable), the pile (cut pile or cut and loop pile are more desirable than loop pile because they are softer and feel more like home), and construction (woven and tufted carpets usually wear better). Consider the carpet's backing, padding, and glue. Even though they are not visible, they have the potential to add allergens and toxins to the environment. When possible, select natural materials that are free of pesticide residues and latex-based products that are not apt to emit toxic fumes (Hurd, 2009; Olds, 2001). Area rugs can provide a different, interesting texture, and bamboo mats, oriental rugs, and braided and hooked rugs can reflect the community's culture (Bullard, 2010). Be sure to secure area rugs with double-sided tape to prevent trip-and-fall accidents and repair them promptly if they begin to ravel or fray.

A final issue to consider is how you will keep floors warm and free from drafts. Radiant heating is one possibility, particularly in cold climates, but this kind of heat does not eliminate drafts. Baseboard heating provides floor warmth and freedom from drafts.

Ceilings: When possible, ceiling heights and finishes should be varied to create intimate spaces and visual interest and to accommodate furnishings of various heights. These variations can reduce noise and are aesthetically pleasing. Even when ceilings are all the same height, mobiles, banners, canopies, and hanging fabrics can create intimate spaces and expand play opportunities. One way to create ceiling interest is to mount a beam across the room from which you can hang basket chairs, plants, toys, or fabric. It is essential to be certain nothing hung from the ceiling creates a fire hazard and satisfies regulations of the fire marshal (Olds, 2001).

Walls: Walls play important roles in every child care facility. They define spaces, provide acoustical separation, and are used for storage and display and as communication centers. Try to vary wall surfaces with carpet, fabric, mirrors, brick, wood, tile, stone, or stucco in addition to traditional drywall (Olds, 2001).

Paint and vinyl coverings are the most popular wall finishes for spaces with children. Paint is an economical choice, comes in a virtually endless variety of colors, and semi-gloss and gloss finishes are able to withstand frequent washing. It is easy to repaint and freshen up painted surfaces. Vinyl wall coverings come in a variety of grades and price ranges and are stain resistant and durable. They can be difficult to apply, however, and can be difficult and expensive to remove. Hard plastic surfacing can be practical in areas such as bathrooms that receive heavy use. This material is not appropriate for general use, however. It creates a sterile and institutional feel rather than one that is warm and inviting (Olds, 2001). Corner moldings and wall bumpers may be needed in high-traffic areas. When possible, choose natural materials to retain a homelike rather than an institutional feel.

Consider adding visual interest by using mirrors, fabric, display areas, and murals on walls, particularly in hallways and common areas. They can create a sense of place, define areas for a variety of purposes, and be attractive and welcoming.

Colors: Much of the color in a room comes from its walls. Color choice depends on several criteria: Bright colors and busy patterns are apt to be overstimulating, while neutral colors are relaxing and help children focus their attention on classroom materials and events (Lally & Stewart, 1990).

When selecting colors for classrooms and other areas in the center, take these factors into consideration:

1. The amount of light in the room.   Soft pastels may be best for a southern or western exposure, but a northern exposure may need a strong, light-reflecting color such as yellow.

2. The size and shape of the room.   Mirrors, light wall colors, and cool colors such as blue and green make rooms look larger. If slightly different shades of the same color are used on opposite walls, narrow rooms appear wider. Bright colors make walls look closer and are more appropriate in large rooms (Olds, 2001). Bright colors should be used with extreme caution, however. Brightly colored rooms often appear cluttered and may make it difficult for children and adults to be at their best.

3. The perception of clutter.   The environment of many early childhood programs is full of bright colors, commercial classroom materials, and decorations that look fine when the classroom is empty, but become overstimulating when children and adults use the space (Tarr, 2004). Overstimulating environments can create stress and make it difficult for children and adults to focus.

4. The influence of color on school performance.   Neutral colors such as beige can reduce tension and the affects of anxiety and can increase children's sense of well-being (Johnson & Maki, 2009). The use of various colors may be most important in infant and toddler programs because children perceive color over form (shape) until age 4. In rooms with young infants, yellow may be a good choice because it is the first color babies can perceive (Olds, 2001).

5. Preschool-age children, ages 3 to 5, have distinct preferences for the color of their school environment.   They prefer cool colors such as blue, green, and light purple over warm colors such as orange, red, and yellow (Reed & Upington, 2009).

6. The psychological impact of colors.   Bright reds have been shown to create excitement. Yellows, deep purples, and greens are restful. "Ethnic" color pallets may help create a sense of belonging (Caples, 1996).

Storage and Display

Storage and display areas are essential elements of a well-designed facility. They are too important to be left to chance and should be addressed in the earliest stages of planning.

Storage: Child care programs never seem to have enough storage! Planners should anticipate the need to store equipment, furnishings, kitchen and cleaning supplies, and consumables, such as the following:

- Rest mats or cots
- Children's belongings
- Indoor large-motor equipment
- Supplies purchased in bulk, like paint and paper
- Administrative materials, supplies, and archived records
- Shared curriculum and audiovisual materials, including those used on a rotating basis
- Seasonal materials, such as holiday decorations
- Extra furniture and equipment
- Food and kitchen supplies
- Outdoor toys and equipment
- Custodial and maintenance equipment
- Cleaning supplies (Olds, 2001)

Adequate storage contributes to a rich curriculum because teachers are able to accumulate and use a variety of resources to respond to children's interests. Well-designed storage in classrooms and adult areas also enhances efficiency, creates predictability, reduces clutter, extends children's play, enhances children's developing classification and sorting skills, and contributes to the creation of a community of learners in which children share responsibility for the learning environment.

A general rule-of-thumb is that 10% of the center's square footage should be devoted to storage areas that are not accessible to children (Olds, 2001). This will include teachers' professional libraries, rotating instructional materials and toys, and adults' personal belongings. They should be stored where they will be accessible to teachers as needed. It is often effective to mount storage for adults' materials on classroom walls, where they are readily available but do not take up valuable floor space (Torelli & Durrett, n.d.). Other materials, such as cleaning and cooking supplies, medicines, personal records of children and staff, and financial records need to be in closed, locked storage (Bullard, 2010).

Classrooms should have cubbies for children and storage for adults' personal belongings as well as low open shelves arranged with labeled baskets and open bins to give children opportunities to make choices. The design and materials from which storage units are made should be compatible with their purpose. Large, low open shelves provide room to store blocks in an orderly fashion. Resting-cot closets with louvered doors allow air circulation. Waterproof containers are needed in water play centers.

Well-designed storage helps children and staff find what they need and keep materials and equipment in good condition; they can also be aesthetically pleasing. Large toy boxes are inappropriate storage except for moving heavy materials (e.g., hollow blocks) because they do not allow easy access and children are likely to "dump" toys in at cleanup time rather than arranging them so they can easily be found later.

Display: Display areas create opportunities to communicate the program's activities, history, and values while shaping its identity on a day-to-day basis. Displays can also be useful in creating connections between the center and children's home life. They contribute to the creation of a sense of belonging for all who enter its doors (Curtis & Carter, 2003).

Displays can also enhance and document children's learning by making learning visible to themselves, their families, and visitors (Katz & Chard, 2000). That means they are mounted on the wall at children's eye level or on low shelves where children can study them in depth. Infant/toddler caregivers can mount documentation on the floor or on walls near the floor.

When displays become documentation of children's learning, as they do in programs based on the Reggio Emilia approach, they move beyond describing what children did to include the teacher's interpretation and explanation. They provide insights into what children were thinking and coming to understand.

Classroom Configuration, Furniture and Furnishings, and Room Arrangement

Classrooms are the most important areas of the building because they are where children spend most of their time. Classroom configuration refers to classrooms' size and shape. Teachers and caregivers arrange the furniture and furnishings at their disposal to create comfortable and productive environments for the children in their care.

Room Size: Room size is one of the most important features to consider when planning a facility. Classrooms should be large enough to accommodate a variety of appropriate activities and small enough to be intimate. Children are happier, interact more, and dramatize fantasy themes more often in smaller rooms than they do in larger ones (Howes, 1983). They are also likely to be more talkative and to be less reluctant to come to school (Howes & Rubenstein, 1985 as cited in Trawick-Smith, 1992) when they are coming to a smaller classroom.

Many states' licensing regulations require at least 35 sq ft per child. For young infants, 35 sq ft per child in the primary activity area is adequate (Lally, Provence, Szanton, & Weissbourd, 1986), but an additional 30 sq ft per child is needed for each crib and the 2- to 3-ft clearance required between adjacent cribs (Olds, 2001).

It is easy to appreciate that older children need more room for active play. Their classrooms also need zones for different activities. Experts recommend 50 to 75 sq ft per child (Bergen, Reid, & Torelli, 2001; Lally et al., 1995; Olds, 2001). Rooms of this size provide space for children to become actively involved with one another and the materials, make it possible to provide spaces for one or two children to work quietly together, create opportunities for adults to work with individual children or small groups, and are likely to be more accommodating for children who have physical disabilities.

When floor space is limited and ceilings are high, space can often be stretched vertically with lofts and climbing structures. To protect children from injury if they should fall, indoor climbing structures should be surrounded by the same safe mats or surfacing they would have if they were outdoors or secured 4-in.-thick mats (Thompson & Hudson, 2003).

In warm climates, centers with minimal indoor space can compensate by using sheltered outdoor play spaces, like a covered porch or patio, for much of the year.

Room Shape: Long, narrow classrooms encourage running and sliding. Square rooms often have dead space in the center because activity areas are apt to be placed along walls instead of toward the center of the room. A classroom that is slightly longer than it is wide is the easiest to arrange and is likely to be inviting to children and their families.

Furniture and Furnishings: Once the scene has been set for quality care by selecting the building's color scheme, planning for natural and artificial light, installing floor coverings that support active and quiet play, and other details related to the center's structure and design have been addressed, it is time to select furniture and furnishings that will make the program come alive. All furniture selected for programs of early care and education should be **comfortable**. That means much of the furniture is **child sized**. Children's chairs should be sturdy and should allow children's feet to rest comfortably on the floor without bending their legs more than 90°. Refer to Table 6.2 for a chart indicating the size of tables and chairs that are typically appropriate for children of different ages. Note that the distance between the seat of the chair and the table surface should be approximately 8 in., so tables

Table 6.2
Recommended Table and Chair Heights for Young Children

Recommended Table Heights (inches)	12"	14"	16"	18"	20"	22"	24"	26"	28"–30"
Recommended Seat Heights (inches)	5"	6.5"	8"	10"	12"	14"	16"	Adult	
1-year-olds	50%	50%							
2-year-olds			60%	40%					
3-year-olds				100%					
4-year-olds				40%	60%				
5-year-olds					100%				
6-year-olds					50%	50%			
7-year-olds					20%	80%			
8-year-olds						80%	20%		
9-year-olds						40%	60%		
10-year-olds							100%		
11-year-olds							80%	20%	
12-year-olds							20%	80%	
13-year-olds and up								20%	80%

Based on international averages. Young children grow rapidly. If at all possible, have chairs of various heights on hand so you can provide each child a comfortable table and chair.

Source: Adapted from Community Playthings (n.d.). Used by permission.

must be sized to fit with the chairs. Vendors of school supplies such as Community Playthings and Environments provide guidelines to help you fit tables and chairs for each age group you serve. (See Appendix 1 for the websites of these vendors and other suppliers of furniture, equipment, and supplies.) Remember that children can grow very quickly. You need to have extra chairs and tables on hand so that all children can always be accommodated for meals, snacks, and other table activities. Children should also be able to easily reach toys on open shelves, and lofts and other equipment should be appropriately scaled.

Also provide comfortable furniture for adults. Ideas to consider include cozy rocking chairs or gliders (which are safer for little fingers), hammocks, and appropriately sized cubes or risers designed for adults to sit on. It is also important that your program be inviting to breast-feeding mothers who want to visit their babies during the workday. Arrange a comfortable place where mothers and their babies can concentrate on nursing and being together. This can be in the classroom or in another comfortable and cozy place nearby.

Furniture and equipment should also be **flexible** and **open ended**. It should be easy to rearrange the room to respond to children's needs and interests. We recommend rectangular tables that can accommodate four to six children. Such tables can be inviting and intimate during snacks and meals, are large enough for many arts and crafts projects, and can easily be combined to make larger workspaces when needed. Movable platforms, risers, large hollow blocks, movable tables, boxes, large pieces of fabric, clothespins, and other open-ended materials give children opportunities to arrange spaces to suit their needs. They enhance children's imaginative play and provide opportunities for problem solving, cooperation, and collaboration (Curtis & Carter, 2003).

Teachers and caregivers also benefit from flexible furnishings. At rest time, cots should be easy to arrange so that children can rest comfortably and undisturbed. On rainy days,

Risers are versatile because they provide storage while creating play spaces and play surfaces.

pushing the tables aside and laying down tumbling mats should not require a great deal of effort. What's more, teachers should be able to create a cozy corner to read a book or just talk with a child needing special one-on-one attention on the spur of the moment.

Furnishings should be **practical**. Tables and shelves need to be durable and lightweight; rounded corners can help prevent injuries. If space is at a premium, stacking chairs and storage systems are attractive options. All furnishings should be easy to keep clean. Their finish should be able to withstand frequent washing and disinfecting. Upholstered platforms, couches, and chairs should be covered with durable washable coverings.

And finally, all classrooms should be designed with an eye toward **aesthetics**. When classrooms are furnished in bright primary colors, tables, chairs, and shelves compete with classroom equipment, creating a busy and cluttered appearance. Natural wood shelving and furnishings give classrooms a warm, homey feel. As an added bonus, wood is sturdy and will age well. Plastics, on the other hand, feel more institutional, are less likely to be durable, and get dingy with age. Also consider natural materials such as wooden boxes, wicker containers, or small fabric bins when selecting containers for toys. They add texture and warmth, while bright plastic containers can contribute to visual clutter (Greenman, 2005). Other classroom furnishings and finishes should also be selected with an eye toward classroom aesthetics. Combining shelving and other pieces designed for child care with garage sale or thrift store finds can add character and interest to the classroom (Bullard, 2010).

While the furniture and furnishings needed by infants and toddlers are, in most respects, no different from those needed by older children, caregiving routines do create the need for some special equipment. Toddlers and preschoolers usually use cots for naptime; infants need cribs to sleep safely. Classrooms for both infants and toddlers need an area dedicated to preparing bottles and food as well as a diaper-changing area apart from all food preparation.

We advise against high chairs and other restraining equipment such as baby swings or standing toys. In their place, we recommend comfortable rockers so caregivers can hold children while feeding bottles and beginning them on solid food and small, low chairs that children can sit in when they are ready to begin to feed themselves. If you decide to use high chairs, be certain they have restraining straps that go around children's waists and between their legs. They should be folded and put out of the way when not in use because children are apt to climb on them if they are stored in the room.

Refer to Appendix 4 for a comprehensive list of suggested basic furniture and equipment for infant/toddler, preschool, and school-age classrooms. It will be a good guide as you plan purchases or updates to equipment and materials.

Other furnishings include clocks, wastebaskets, and nonpoisonous plants. Remember to plan for window treatments, including curtains that can add softness, color, and texture, and blinds that can help control light and heat. Securing the cords from blinds well out of children's reach is essential. They can be a strangulation hazard.

A Better Way

Marie has made a point of keeping all the classrooms in her center well equipped. She has created an efficient process for teachers to alert her when furniture and toys become worn or broken and need to be replaced—and over the years she has made many replacements. As she thinks about how to furnish the areas now under construction, she carefully studies her current classrooms to see what has gone well and what she might want to change. She realizes that the existing classrooms do not look much different today than they did when she first came to the center 14 years ago. The tables have red laminated tops, chairs are red molded plastic, storage bins are rigid plastic in primary colors, cushions in the reading centers are covered with sturdy red and blue vinyl, and the kitchen set in the housekeeping center has primary-color accents. She always thought the classrooms were bright and cheerful, happy places for children to spend their days.

Marie visited some centers in her community to get ideas for her new classrooms. One of the features she noticed in particular was the kind of furniture and furnishings most often used in quality centers. She saw several classrooms with natural wood furniture; a neutral color scheme; and homey touches like baskets, plants, and soft and homey cushions in the book center. Now when she looked carefully at her existing classrooms, she realized that while she thought they were bright and cheerful, to children they might be distracting and overstimulating. She studied the recommendations in this book and on the websites of vendors listed at the end of this chapter. She created a new way to equip her classrooms and felt that she really had learned a better approach to selecting classroom furniture and furnishings.

Principles of Arranging Classrooms: The arrangement of each classroom affects the quality of children's and adults' daily experiences. Every classroom should provide safety and security; should be predictable and promote autonomy; should meet the learning needs of children with varied abilities, temperaments, and learning styles; and should be convenient for children and adults.

The *Infant/Toddler Environment Rating Scale* (Harms, Cryer, & Clifford, 2006), the *Early Childhood Environment Rating Scale* (Harms, Clifford, & Cryer, 2005), and the *School-Age Care Environment Rating Scale* (Harms, Jacobs, & White, 1995) are widely used and readily available environment assessment tools that we believe can be valuable in helping programs arrange rooms; select, store, and use materials; and develop daily schedules that are associated with positive outcomes for children. These rating scales have a strong research base and are used by many states as a part of their licensing and/ or quality rating systems. They are excellent tools to guide you as you furnish and equip classrooms for children from birth through school age.

These guidelines will help you plan effective classroom environments:

1. The room arrangement should help the program meet its goals. Children should have opportunities to move freely and to choose which activities they want to pursue. Learning centers should communicate their purpose clearly. The block center looks different from the area for dramatic play, and areas to work with puzzles and other small manipulatives are set apart from the cozy area to enjoy books. Open areas and small tables allow adults to work with children individually or in small groups. An open floor plan also makes it possible for adults to supervise children from many locations throughout the room. See Figures 6.1 through 6.10 in later sections of this chapter for model floor plans designed for active learning.

2. The room should feel open and inviting while providing children with opportunities to concentrate and become engaged in their activities. The size, scale, and arrangement of toys, shelves, and partitions contribute to whether or not children find the classroom inviting or intimidating. Open rooms with clearly defined zones welcome children, let them clearly see the available play options, promote active learning and collaboration, provide needed privacy, can prevent negative behaviors such as aggression or withdrawal, and

Comfortable tables and chairs invite children to become engaged with interesting table-top activities.

reduce children's tendency to wander about the room (Maxwell, 2007; Trawick-Smith, 1992). Classrooms with high partitions and learning centers that are almost completely surrounded by room dividers and where toys are not clearly in sight are uninviting and intimidating. They do not invite young children to enter or to become actively involved.

3. The room arrangement should provide children with spaces that feel private. Chaotic and frantic behaviors are associated with classrooms that do not have private spaces for children to escape the busyness of classroom activities. Children benefit from areas that offer privacy to construct a sense of self and to "cocoon" when noise and other stimuli overwhelm them (Greenman, 2005; Hyson, 1994; NAEYC, 1998), to be cuddled (Hyson, 1994), and to focus on their special endeavors (Meltz, 1990) before gradually moving into the group (Olds, 2001).

Window seats, cozy corners, cabinets with the doors removed, a private corner of the room, and learning centers or workstations for one child all help meet indoor privacy needs (Greenman, 2005; Olds, 2001). They can give children a place to rest, observe, and recharge emotionally (Torelli & Durrett, n.d.).

4. The needs of children with disabilities should be considered when a room is being arranged. Room arrangements must permit *all* children **accessibility**, the ability to enter all parts of the environment including bathrooms and to access equipment and materials (Cryer, Harms, & Riley, 2003; Winter, Bell, & Dempsey, 1994), and **availability**, the ability to participate in all experiences (Cavallaro, Haney, & Cabello, 1993). A child who uses an assistive device is likely to require more space for movement. Wheelchairs require an aisle of 36 in. and corners of at least 42 in. Lofts, play pits, and other popular features included in many classrooms can limit access to children who use assistive devices.

Creating Learning/Activity Centers

Learning/activity centers are "carefully designed areas that contain planned learning activities and materials" (Kostelnik, Soderman, & Whiren, 2007, p. 112). They support hands-on learning; contribute to children's learning as they work on particular projects or themes; and accommodate children of various developmental levels, interests, and abilities. Classrooms with learning centers also provide teachers with opportunities to evaluate children's progress across developmental domains by observing their purposeful interactions with peers and carefully selected materials.

Each learning center should be arranged so that children can see what it has to offer and can understand how it is used. Learning centers should

1. Be located in a specific place well suited for the activity
2. Have clearly marked boundaries
3. Provide areas for play and for observing
4. Provide for storage and display of materials related to the specific center
5. Create a mood that sets them apart from other areas in the classroom (Olds, 2001)

Plan for both active and quiet zones that offer these five kinds of experiences every day:

1. *Quiet activities* such as listening to books, reading, and cuddling
2. *Structured activities* such as puzzles, construction toys, and manipulatives
3. *Craft and discovery activities* such as paint, play dough, water, sand, and woodworking
4. *Dramatic play activities* such as puppets, dress-up, and dramatic play
5. *Large motor activities* such as slides, climbing equipment, balls, and large blocks (Olds, 2001)

The *Environment Rating Scales* identified earlier can be helpful as you identify activity centers that are appropriate for infants and toddlers, preschoolers, and school-age children. These resources also describe how each center should be equipped.

Lofts create variety and can accommodate many different learning centers.

Defining Space: Boundaries between learning centers should be clearly defined but flexible so that they can be expanded or made smaller to respond to children's interests. Consider the classroom traffic patterns and make certain there are clear paths between centers.

Space can be defined by the placement of shelves, partitions, low walls, or furniture such as sofas and chairs. Boundaries can be created by varying the floor level through the use of platforms or lofts, by differences in colors or shades of wall paint or carpet, and by the use of targeted task lighting. Teachers must be able to visually supervise every area of the classroom. Spaces can be made to feel private, safe, and secure for children by creating partitions children are not able to see over, but adults can (Olds, 2001).

Before deciding how to define space for a learning/activity center, you will want to determine whether the space will be permanently used in this way. The colors of walls and carpet and the levels of floors are somewhat permanent, but movable partitions and storage units are not. Being able to add, eliminate, or change centers makes the room more flexible and responsive to children's interests and needs.

Allowing Sufficient Space: Each center needs to be large enough to accommodate the activities for which it is intended. More space is needed in centers designed for several children to play together as they do during dramatic play, and those where children need room to spread out as they do when they use unit blocks. Centers should be planned to provide both room to play and room for storage of related materials.

Providing Acoustic Isolation: Noise can easily become a problem, particularly in a small classroom. Sounds from one learning center should not interfere with activities in another. That means the block center that typically involves several children and materials that can be noisy should not adjoin the reading center where children come to quietly enjoy books. Noise-absorbing floor and wall coverings and acoustical ceiling tiles can help reduce the classroom's noise level. Other strategies to reduce noise include providing earphones in the listening center and low-pile carpet in the block center and by locating particularly noisy activities such as woodworking outdoors.

Arranging Equipment and Materials: Equipment and materials should be arranged and displayed in the center where they will be used. Open shelves encourage children to select materials independently and to return them when they are finished. It is helpful to label shelves, bins, and baskets with a picture or silhouette of items stored there to help children return them correctly. Accessibility is increased when needed materials are on lower shelves that can be reached from a wheelchair.

Children's safety should be your guide when arranging the classroom and organizing its storage. Heavy but portable items like large trucks should be placed on the lower shelves of cabinets. The CD player should be near an electric outlet so you don't need to use a long extension cord. Equipment that is not used every day should be stored to prevent damage but should be readily available. Everything in storage should be clearly labeled. Loose parts should be kept in a box with a lid or in a bag to keep them together. Store food, paper, paint, and other consumables so that you use the oldest materials first.

Learning/Activity Centers for Infants and Toddlers

Quality infant and toddler care is not simply a scaled-down version of a quality preschool program: "A well designed environment . . . supports infants' and toddlers' emotional well-being, stimulates their senses, and challenges their motor skills" (Torelli cited in Gonzalez-Mena & Eyer, 2009, p. 264).

But even as they are unique, classroom environments for infants and toddlers share many characteristics with classrooms serving older children. They should be safe, comfortable, convenient, and child sized. They need areas where children can be active, places to enjoy the company of their peers, and opportunities for one-on-one time with their primary caregiver. Their classrooms also need to be designed so that caregiving routines such as feeding, diaper changing, and sleeping are comfortable and convenient for caregivers. Caregivers must be alert and ready to adapt classrooms to match infants' and toddlers' rapidly changing developmental levels, interests, and abilities (Lally & Stewart, 1990).

Areas for infants and toddlers need to be interesting places full of beautiful sights, sounds, and textures that capture these babies' attention and lead them to explore and problem solve in their sensory and motor world. The following principles should guide your creation of infant/toddler environments:

1. Infants and toddlers need an environment that will keep them safe and healthy. Very young children explore toys with their mouths as well as their fingers. They pull up and climb on furniture and can be counted on to explore the environment in ways you never expected. Their health and safety must always be your number one concern. Frequent and proper hand washing is the single most important precaution you can take to keep children and caretakers healthy. Classrooms should have convenient sinks so that children and adults can wash their hands after every diaper change or trip to the bathroom, before every meal and snack, whenever their hands have been used to cover a cough or wipe a nose, and after being outside or touching pets.

Keep all dangerous materials locked and out of reach. Window blinds can be strangulation hazards; they need to be secured well out of the way of curious fingers. There should also be a routine for washing sheets, blankets, pillows, dress-up clothes, and other soft furnishings and for sanitizing toys that have gone in children's mouths.

2. Infants and toddlers need an aesthetically pleasing environment with beautiful colors, sounds, forms, and textures. You need to consider the color scheme, room arrangement, and furnishings of infant/toddler facilities to create a welcoming, homelike setting for your youngest children. They need to hear the sounds of live human voices, to enjoy natural sunlight and the outdoors, and to be fascinated by the beautiful colors and interesting textures that surround them.

3. Infant and toddler rooms should be designed to be "baby scale" and also "adult scale." An infant's perspective is very different from that of adults. We recommend that you get down on the floor to consider how the world looks from a baby's perspective. Take care to avoid harsh lights that shine in their eyes. Offer interesting objects to look at, to feel, and to hear. Adults who care for babies need comfortable adult-size furniture such as gliders, hammocks, sofas, and easy chairs that let them nurture and care for infants and toddlers in a relaxed, comfortable, and convenient environment.

4. Activity centers should have simple toys such as chunky crayons and papers of different colors; balls of different sizes and textures; tray puzzles with three or four pieces; board books; soft dolls; and simple props for make-believe, particularly blankets and bottles so they can care for their "babies." They also enjoy household items like pots and pans.

Infants and toddlers are egocentric. They are able to see the world from only their own perspective. They do not yet realize, for example, that their classmate wants a turn with the ball they find fascinating. They like to play side-by-side, but it is not appropriate to expect them to be able to share or to wait their turn. Thus, it is important to have duplicates of the same toy—several identical red trucks, blue balls, and baby dolls in pink dresses. That gives each child the opportunity to play with attractive and appropriate toys without having to wait or give up popular selections before they are ready.

5. Infants and toddlers need opportunities to be alone. Young infants are exploring their own bodies. They are fascinated by their fingers, are amazed when they find their toes, and are busy making sense of the sights and sounds that surround them. They need protected spaces where they can concentrate on learning about themselves and the world around them.

Mobile infants and toddlers need private areas for a different reason. They are active explorers, crawling into, climbing over, and running around everything in sight. It sometimes seems as if they never slow down. Quiet places to be alone or to spend time with a special caretaker help them relax and can prevent their becoming overstimulated.

6. Small activity centers for one or two children are more appropriate than the larger centers typical of programs for older children. A center for a young infant can be as small as a throw rug; mat; or window to look out of onto a birdfeeder, flowering tree, or a city street (Greenman & Stonehouse, 1996). For mobile infants and toddlers, an activity center might accommodate two children playing side-by-side. The important consideration is to provide young children with interesting vantage points, a variety of materials to examine, and freedom to explore their environments with their entire bodies.

7. Infants and toddlers need predictability and familiarity as well as novelty. Predictable routines and familiar environments comfort infants and toddlers. They are able to relax when caregiving routines and surroundings stay the same day after day, week after week. That is not to say that they do not enjoy novelty, but it does mean that classrooms for infants and toddlers should not be rearranged overnight, nor should all familiar toys be suddenly exchanged for new ones. Thoughtful caregivers add new materials to familiar centers;

for example, they add scarves to the dress-up corner to provide children with the chance to experiment with their shimmering colors and silky feel, but the dress-up corner has not moved and favorite items are still there. Another example of how you can add novelty while maintaining familiarity is by putting new books in the book corner, but keeping the book center where it is and keeping some favorite books along with the new ones.

Consider including these centers for infants and toddlers:

- Cozy, quiet area
- Book center
- Manipulatives such as shape sorters, puzzles with knobs, lacing toys
- Dramatic play/housekeeping center
- Building area (for older infants 18–36 months)
- Art area (for older infants 18–36 months)
- Sensory/Science area (for older infants 18–36 months)
- Music area (Knopf & Welsh, 2010)

See Figure 6.1 for an example of a floor plan of an infant room and Figure 6.2 for a floor plan of a toddler room. They illustrate some of the principles discussed here. Napping, feeding, and changing and toileting areas are discussed later in this chapter.

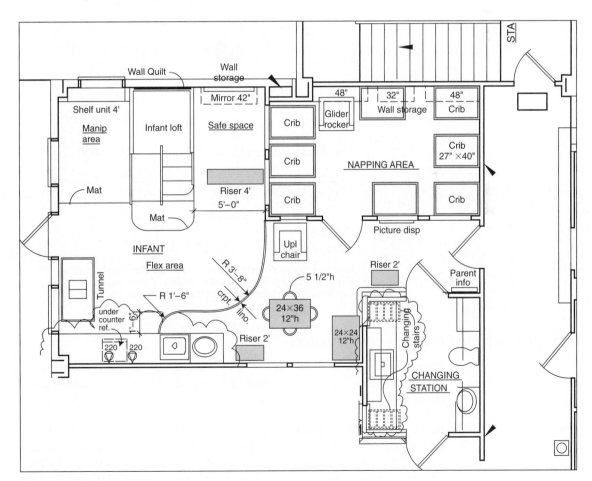

Figure 6.1
Infant Floor Plan

Source: Floor plan developed by Louis Torelli for the Children's Center at the University of South Carolina, Columbia, South Carolina. Used by permission of the University of South Carolina.

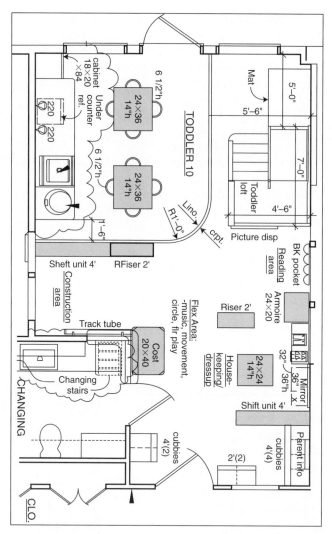

Figure 6.2
Toddler Floor Plan

Source: Floor plan developed by Louis Torelli for the Children's
Center at the University of South Carolina, Columbia, South
Carolina. Used by permission of the University of South Carolina.

Learning/Activity Centers for Preschoolers

Preschoolers have interests, needs, and abilities that set them apart from younger children. The following activity centers are recommended for preschool and kindergarten children.

Block Center: The **block center** is devoted to building with unit blocks and props such as people, animals, cars, and trucks. The block center might also have paper and pencils; Post-it® notes of various sizes, shapes, and colors to label structures or zoo-animal enclosures or to post opening and closing times of stores; or books with photographs of buildings, bridges, or other architectural features. Block centers are noisy and are best located on dense carpet, out of the flow of traffic. Various group sizes may be accommodated in the block center, but as a rule of thumb 3-year-olds need

586 blocks, 4-year-olds need 748 blocks, and children 5 and older need 980 blocks (Hirsch, 1996).

1. A small block center, about 75 sq ft, is appropriate for one or two children. Small block centers, if protected by storage units or defined by a pit or low platform, may be placed near the room entrance. Experienced teachers have noticed that playing with blocks can smooth some children's transition to school in the morning. Usually, about 100 to 150 blocks and a few accessories are shelved in a small block center.

2. A large block center, about 260 sq ft, can accommodate up to seven children. From 700 to 1,000 unit blocks or 80 or more hollow blocks are recommended for a large block area. A large block area should be located out of the flow of traffic where structures can be left up for more than one day.

3. A small set of hollow blocks (e.g., 10 long, 10 square, 10 boards), used in conjunction with dramatic play, are often stored in or near dramatic play centers, especially those that change themes throughout the year (e.g., store, post office, veterinarian's office, beauty shop, or farm).

4. Large outside block areas, for building with a full set of hollow blocks or unit blocks, are usually temporary arrangements. Because wooden blocks must stay dry, they will have to be transported in block carts or wagons to and from the outdoor block-building area.

Storage units found in the catalogs and on the websites of popular vendors are well suited for unit blocks. Blocks and accessories should be carefully stored so that block builders can find what they want. We recommend that you

   a. Store blocks lengthwise for quick identification (blocks cannot be identified by their shorter ends)
   b. Label each section of the shelves with tracings of the blocks so they can be returned after use
   c. Draw children's attention to the size of various blocks by shelving them seriated by length, with larger blocks on the bottom shelf
   d. Do not pack shelves too tightly
   e. Vary accessories from time to time to reflect children's current interests and units of study

Consider displaying pictures of buildings, bridges, and other structures near the block center. They can be photographs of neighborhood structures, pictures taken during class trips, or cut from magazines. Figure 6.3 is an example of a floor plan for an indoor block center.

Dramatic Play Center: Dramatic play centers are like a stage. They invite children to play make-believe as they reenact family life; role-play various occupations such as teacher, doctor, or barber; and act out familiar stories (Beaty, 1996). Props are usually displayed in the area that is designed specifically for children's spontaneous pretend play, but the truth is that dramatic play can occur almost anywhere in the room.

The most common theme for dramatic play, particularly for children age 3 and younger, is housekeeping. Older preschoolers and primary-age children often continue to play "house" but can enjoy a variety of play themes, particularly when their play is based on a field trip or other shared experience. Prop boxes are a good way to organize and store materials to support a particular theme such as grocery store, beauty shop, veterinary hospital, or flower shop (Boutte, Van Scoy, & Hendley, 1996; Myhre, 1993). Families often enjoy getting involved in dramatic play by sharing appropriate artifacts and expertise. This is a particularly good way to reflect the diverse cultures of the children enrolled in your program.

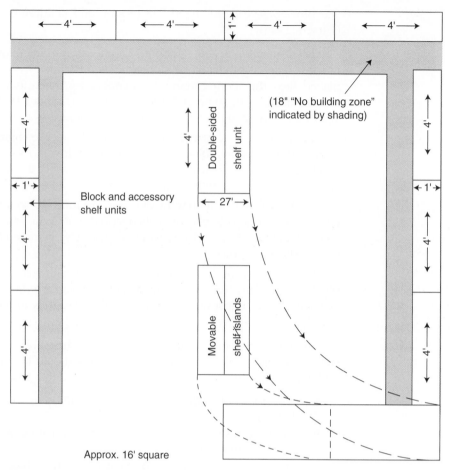

Figure 6.3
Large Indoor Block Center/Area

Many early childhood programs also have a puppet theater near the dramatic play or language arts center. Usually storage and display shelves and a freestanding puppet theater are all children need to use puppets as part of their make-believe play.

Art Center: This section of the room is devoted to the creation and display of children's artistic representations. These activities are important because they help young children develop their sensory and perceptual concepts of color, form, size, texture, and light and dark. They use artists' tools to awaken their aesthetic sensitivities, represent their ideas, display their creativity, express their emotions, and refine their small-motor skills.

The art center can be considered a small studio. It should offer a comfortable place to work without unrealistic constraints (e.g., "Don't drip paint on the floor because it will stain the carpet!"). It should provide shelves, racks, and cupboards for children to store supplies and works in progress and to display completed projects for others to admire.

Reggio Emilia schools provide a model for honoring the arts. The Reggio preschools have a separate art studio called an *atelier*. Their *atelieristas,* art teachers with a special-ized background in visual art, music, dance, theater, or design, scaffold children's explo-rations of a wide variety of artistic media.

Whether you have just a corner of the classroom or a separate room devoted to chil-dren's artistic expressions, the goal is to provide children multiple opportunities, over time, to use art materials in satisfying ways. Consider these guidelines for creating a well-designed art center:

1. It should look like a joy-filled studio. Ideally, it will be bathed in natural glare-free light, but you may need to rely on artificial light to give children plenty of illumination for their work. An art center near the playground might allow art activities to expand to outdoor areas. A sense of productive activity is enhanced when children's work is displayed in or near the art center.

2. The art center should have places for individual and group work. Work surfaces include the wall (porcelain boards and murals), tilted surfaces (easels), and flat surfaces (tables). The art center needs many storage shelves for supplies. Storage shelves for paper should have doors, although other storage shelves may be open. Drying art products will require lines or racks for paintings and mobiles and shelves for three-dimensional products.

3. Tables, wall coverings, and floors of the art center should be durable and easy to clean. Pretest surfaces to be certain they will not be stained by red paint. Floors should not be slippery when wet, and all surfaces should be made of quick-drying materials.

4. Access to a sink with plenty of counter space on both sides is essential for mixing paints, plaster of Paris, modeling compounds, and the like, as well as for cleanup. The sink should have appropriate strainers to catch clay, paste, and other materials and should have an accessible U-trap. The sink counter and the wall behind the sink should be covered with a durable, easy-to-clean wall covering.

5. The art center must be roomy enough to accommodate tables, easels, and children moving about with wet paintings. It is wise to plan for 100 to 150 sq ft.

Music Center: The music center is devoted to children's explorations of melody, pitch, rhythm, and harmony. It also exposes them to a wide range of musical genres, such as jazz, folk, classical, and reggae, and other musical traditions. Some musical activities such as listening to music, watching videos of music or dance performances, and looking at books and pictures associated with music and dance are receptive. Others are active, involving children in singing, playing instruments, and creating dances. Music is often part of circle time or other whole-group activities, so it may be convenient to locate the music center near the area used for whole-group meetings.

The music center may need only a corner of the room, especially if its activities can easily expand into the whole-group area. Because singing, playing instruments, and dancing are noisy, the center should be located where the music will not disturb others. Sound-absorbing materials should, if possible, be used on the floor.

The music center should be arranged with listening stations; displays of CDs and books related to music, dance, and the performing arts (stored so children can see the front of the book or CD); counters for xylophones, autoharps, CD players, and other "sound makers"; shelving or baskets for other rhythm and percussion instruments; and scarves, capes, and other dress-up clothes for dancing or marching.

Water and Sand Center: This is where children explore two of nature's most intriguing raw materials—water and sand. Because of concerns about allergies, sand is sometimes replaced with flax seed or other nonallergenic material, but the lessons remain the same. Sand and water tables help children learn many basic math and science concepts such as empty and full, heavy and light, more and less, shallow and deep, and measurement. Sand and water tables can be also used for other sensory explorations and messy activities (West & Cox, 2001).

The sand and water area can be relatively small; approximately 60 sq ft is sufficient. Sand and water tables need to be located near a sink and drain. They should be placed on a waterproof floor that does not get slippery when wet.

Shelving for water and sand toys must be waterproof. Many sand and water play toys are small so tote boxes usually work well. They can be labeled with pictures or words (e.g., *floating, measuring*) so they can be rotated as desired.

Carpentry or Woodworking Center: Older preschoolers and primary-age children enjoy carpentry and woodworking. Handling natural materials and real tools, hearing the sounds of cutting and hammering, and smelling sawdust are valuable sensory experiences. The woodworking center also provides children with opportunities to refine fine-motor skills and eye-hand coordination, helps develop logico-mathematical understandings, and gives them opportunities to represent the real world through their constructions.

Woodworking is a noisy center that requires about 60 sq ft. It must be located out of the flow of traffic in an easy-to-supervise area. Children need plenty of light and should be able to concentrate without distraction. The area must be equipped with a sturdy workbench and high-quality tools (Sosna, 2000), and children should be required to wear goggles. A storage rack with tracings of tools simplifies storage. The workbench and tools should be portable so they can be stored when not in use. Keep wood scraps nearby in boxes, baskets, and wooden bins.

Science and Mathematics Center: This area invites children to wonder, reflect, and problem solve about the scientific and mathematical world. Here they can see how science and mathematics are part of their everyday lives, learn to respect and appreciate the world of nature, and develop physical and logico-mathematical concepts related to math and science. All too often, the science and mathematics center consists simply of a window ledge with a plant and a small "discovery table." This approach misses many opportunities—science and math are fascinating to children and should be central to the curriculum.

That is why plants, an aquarium, and a cage for a small animal should be welcome in any corner of the room. Science and mathematical concepts are also taught outdoors and in the cooking, block, water and sand, and manipulative centers.

Generally speaking, science and mathematics centers should be at least 60 sq ft. That is large enough for the center to be the home base for caring for animals and plants and for other messy activities. The center should be near a sink, electrical outlets are needed for aquariums and incubators, and it should have flooring that is easily cleaned. Be careful to comply with state licensing regulations concerning food preparation areas and their proximity to animals in cages.

Some science and mathematics materials are left out throughout the year, but others are changed regularly. Consider the following criteria when planning a science and math center:

1. There should be plenty of display and work space. A counter at children's sitting or standing height can hold an aquarium, terrarium, plants, or animal cages. Tables or counter space can also hold materials that are not out all the time—magnets, prisms, seeds, rocks, sound makers, models of spaceships, dinosaurs, mathematics manipulatives, and so on. A centrally located table draws children's attention to the current activity (e.g., getting seeds from a pumpkin). A book display rack with a small area rug or floor cushions makes a cozy reading area. Plenty of display area is needed to document children's work and to display science pictures and posters.

2. Closed storage space such as a built-in closet can have open shelves at the top and built-in drawers to store science and mathematics items at the bottom. Tote bins are ideal for storage of math and science materials.

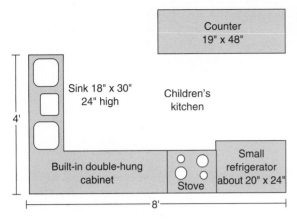

Figure 6.4
Cooking Center

Cooking Center: Cooking is a real activity. It is not pretend! Cooking activities are not designed to teach children how to cook. They are designed to promote good nutrition and healthy habits; to teach safety concepts; to enhance language, mathematics, and science learning; and to provide multicultural experiences. Cooking also promotes social interactions, fine-motor skills, decision making, and problem solving through enjoyable firsthand experiences.

Many early childhood programs do not have space for a separate cooking center, so it is often combined with the art and/or science/math center. An ideal cooking center, whether a separate or shared area, requires approximately 30 sq ft and looks like a small kitchen (see Figure 6.4).

The center needs a stove with a see-through glass oven door, a refrigerator, a sink, and storage cabinets. A microwave oven would be a good addition. Storage cabinets that hold dangerous items such as knives, electrical appliances, and cleaning supplies need to be locked. Pantry items need to be stored carefully to keep them fresh and pest free.

Manipulatives and Small Construction Toy Center: This area gives children opportunities to work with small objects that help them develop fine-motor skills and eye-hand coordination, solve problems, and develop spatial concepts. Many manipulatives invite children to play together, so they also support language and social competencies.

The center is usually located in a quiet part of the room with resilient flooring or low-pile carpet. It does not need to be large; approximately 100 sq ft should suffice. Children generally sit or stand at tables while building with Lego® pieces and sets like Magna-Tiles®, Magnet Builders, or Bristle Blocks; threading beads and using pattern cards; working on puzzles; and using other fine-motor toys. They need some open floor space for activities such as building with Lincoln Logs, playing with a marble chute, and working on floor puzzles. Storage cabinets with open shelves and baskets, totes, or trays or boxes

School-age children enjoy cooking and other activities they would do if they went directly home after school.

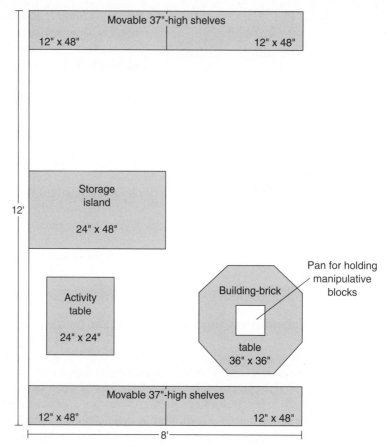

Figure 6.5
Manipulative and Small Constructive Toy Center

labeled with pictures and words keep materials in view and give children opportunities to independently choose what they want to work with. See Figure 6.5 for a sample floor plan for a manipulative and small construction toy center.

Language, Literacy, Writing, and Book Center: You will want to have books and writing materials throughout the room, but this is the area designed specifically to give children opportunities for looking and listening activities. It also offers children hands-on experiences with the written and spoken word. The ideal center would be large (approximately 150 sq ft) but subdivided into cozy sections for reading, writing, and listening. The center should be located in a quiet section of the room. Figure 6.6 provides a sample plan for a language, literacy, writing, and book center.

Consider the following criteria when planning a language and literacy center:

1. A loft can provide space for two book nooks. The loft itself could be equipped with a small book rack or book pockets that show the front covers of books (not their spines), a small puppet theater, and puppets. Beneath the loft, cozy floor pillows and task lighting could serve as a book nook for one or two children.

2. Adjacent to the loft can be an area equipped as a communications center, with computers and listening stations; a writing center with a variety of pencils, pens, and markers; and several kinds of lined and unlined paper, envelopes, shopping lists, Post-it® notes, and so on.

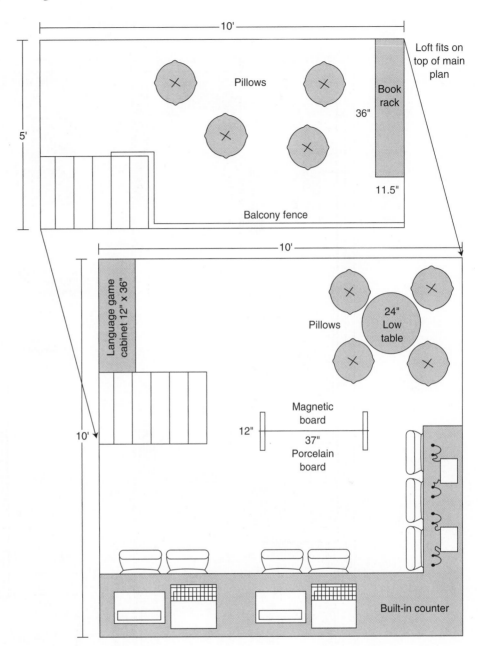

Figure 6.6
Emerging Literacy and Book Center

3. The third area could be equipped as a reading and storytelling area with book storage and display space, flannel and magnetic boards, and a wall pocket chart. It needs places to sit at a table, on a couch, or on the floor. The back of the reading center can serve as a language game area, with storage cabinets, a low table with floor cushions, a whiteboard room divider, and a magnetic board.

Other Areas: Many centers overlook the importance of providing private cozy spaces in all classrooms. This is important, particularly for children who spend long days in child care (Maxwell, 2007; Torelli & Durrett, n.d.). Private areas serve as places to tune out, to enjoy being by oneself for a few minutes, or to reduce excitement. A loft, a window seat,

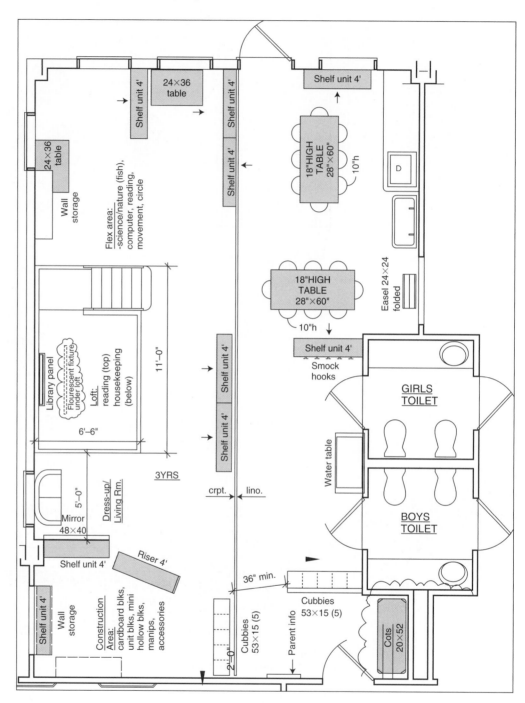

Figure 6.7
Floor Plan for 3-Year-Olds

Source: Floor plan developed by Louis Torelli for the Children's Center at the University of South Carolina, Columbia, South Carolina. Used by permission of the University of South Carolina.

or cozy chair also give children places to watch from before entering play. These areas may be particularly critical to the development of children with disabilities (Prescott, 1987).

Children also enjoy special-interest areas, such as an aquarium or terrarium; a rock, insect, or shell collection; a garden or bird feeder to observe from a window; a flowering hanging basket; and displays related to specific curriculum themes. Special-interest areas

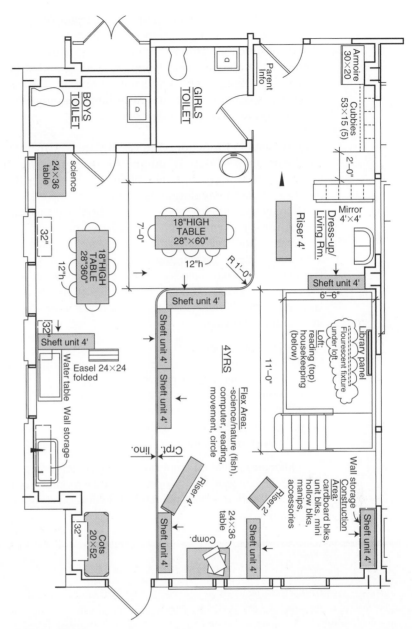

Figure 6.8
Floor Plan for 4-Year-Olds

Source: Floor plan developed by Louis Torelli for the Children's Center at the University of South Carolina, Columbia, South Carolina. Used by permission of the University of South Carolina.

can also be used to display "treasures" from home, with the understanding that preschool is not the best place for valuable or fragile items that cannot be replaced.

See the suggested floor plans for classrooms for 3-year-olds (Figure 6.7) and 4-year-olds (Figure 6.8).

Learning/Activity Centers for Primary-Grade Children

Learning centers for primary-grade children (ages 6 through 8) do not have to be as clearly defined as do centers for younger children. Related activities and content areas can be combined for older children. For example, a primary program might have these learning centers: cooking/science/art, dramatic play/music, reading, and mathematics/block construction. This is another way to cluster centers: art/cooking, construction, mathematics/computer, and language/reading and writing. Similar to preschool/kindergarten room design, messy and noisy areas are separated from less messy and quieter areas. The space, furniture, and furnishings requirements for each center are the same as those for centers previously described.

Activity Centers for School-Age Child Care: Activity centers for children who come to child care after school are unique for three reasons. First, school-age programs must accommodate a wide age range, often ages 5 through 10 or 12. Second, programs operate just 2 to 3 hours a day during the school year and typically all day during school holidays and summer vacation periods. Third, school-age programs often share their space with a school, preschool child care, or faith-based program.

Since school-age programs seldom have a space that is solely theirs, activity centers are often created by arranging mobile storage units or room dividers to fit their needs. It is also helpful to have access to a large storage closet or storage workroom to supplement the classroom storage units. The activities offered to school-age children should be similar to those they would do if they went home after school. School-age care centers should include the following:

a.   Cooking or snack areas
b.   Quiet areas for reading, doing homework, listening to music with headphones, creative writing, or just resting
c.   Workspaces for arts and crafts, including woodworking if possible
d.   Table games and manipulative areas
e.   A computer center with Internet access (with appropriate parental controls in place) and a printer

Other areas children enjoy are science centers and games such as ping-pong or foosball.

See the suggested floor plans for a classroom for school-age children who come after school and during school holidays and vacations (Figure 6.9).

Application Activity

Assume you are working with a class of 3- to 5-year-olds. Select a learning center as the focus of this project. Propose a layout for this learning center. Begin by selecting furniture, equipment, and toys by consulting Appendix 4 for suggested materials as well as recommendations on vendors' websites (see Appendix 1 for suppliers) and other professional resources. Once you have selected the furniture, toys, and equipment, arrange that equipment in the classroom. It would be helpful to sketch your plan on graph paper. (Search for "free graph paper" on your online search engine.) Give the director an estimate for how much your recommendation will cost by referring back to the catalogs you used to create your plan.

Additional Areas in Classrooms

Young children are learning all the time, not just in learning centers, but also as they are being cared for, and as they care for themselves. Facility planners need to consider areas for personal belongings and for caregiving routines, in addition to the activity areas described earlier, as they plan a child care facility.

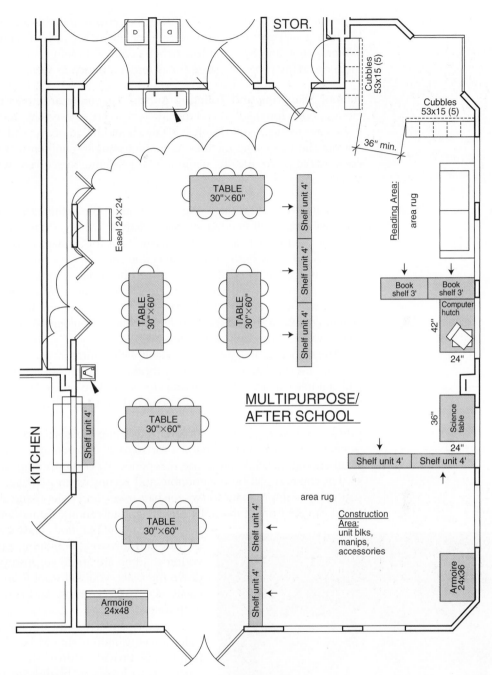

Figure 6.9
Floor Plan for School-Age Care

Source: Floor plan developed by Louis Torelli for the Children's Center at the University of South Carolina, Columbia, South Carolina. Used by permission of the University of South Carolina.

Children's Cubbies: Children should have their own individual cubbies for storing book bags, lunch boxes, coats, hats, special toys, and other items from home. Cubbies create a personal space for each child, help children learn to care for their possessions and respect those of others, and reduce the spread of contagious diseases. The area for cubbies should be close to the door and should have enough room for parents and teachers to help children settle in for the day. The floor covering in this area should be easily cleaned because it will get quite dirty during inclement weather. If children wear boots in the winter, you will want to locate a bench nearby for them to sit on to take them off and put them on. Many programs store boots under a bench as well.

Infants' Diapering and Toileting Areas: Diapering and toileting areas should be spacious enough for children and the adults who are supervising and helping them and need to be easy to clean and disinfect. They should be attractive and cheerful, decorated with mirrors and interesting pictures, communicating to children that this is an important and comfortable place. Ideally, diapering and toileting areas have windows for sunlight and ventilation.

Diapering Area.   The diapering area should be carefully arranged so that the caregiver can easily reach all needed supplies: diapers, wipes, creams or lotions, latex gloves, a foot-operated wastebasket with a plastic liner for sanitary disposal of soiled diapers and wipes, and a spray bottle with disinfecting solution (1/4 cup of household liquid chlorine bleach in one gallon of tap water, mixed fresh daily) for cleaning the diapering surface. Changing tables for older children are often designed with steps so that they can climb up, saving the caregiver's back from the strain of frequent lifting. If paper is used on the changing table, it should reach from the child's shoulders to beyond his feet (AAP/APHA/NRCHSCCEE, 2011; Lally & Stewart, 1990).

The diapering area must have a sink with warm running water, liquid soap, and paper towels. This sink cannot be used for food preparation or for washing dishes or caregivers' and children's hands. The diapering area should be situated so that the caregiver can keep an eye on other children while meeting individual children's caregiving needs.

Children's Toileting Areas.   Children's toileting areas should be conveniently located in or near classrooms. Plan one toilet for 10 to 20 children age 2 or older. Toilets should be small enough for children to use independently or sturdy step stools should be available so that children will be comfortable and secure when toileting. The height of the toilet seat must be appropriate for wheelchair users, and toilet tissue should be not more than 6 in. from the front of the toilet bowl. Handrails should be mounted on the wall for additional safety. Low partitions between, and in front of, toilets provide privacy while permitting easy supervision. Because young children are apt to surprise you with what they flush down the toilet, you will want to install multiple clean-outs, easily accessible U-traps, and separate shutoff valves for each toilet.

Lavatory sinks should be adjacent to but outside the toilet areas. Children should be able to reach sinks independently. Provide sturdy step stools if needed. Water faucets with levers or blades are easier to use than ones with knobs. They help children become independent. Water heaters should be set to 100°F to 120°F to prevent scalding. Dishwashing requires hotter water, so you will need a separate water heater for the kitchen. Children need access to liquid soap, paper towels, and a trash receptacle for towel disposal.

If you plan to install a drinking fountain, it should be located near the rest rooms, out of the flow of traffic, and should be low enough for children to use independently or by standing on a sturdy step stool. Select a fountain that will

Conveniently located child-size sinks contribute to children's autonomy and help develop healthy habits.

accommodate children with disabilities. You will want to have paper cups available for children not yet able to get enough water to quench their thirst directly from a fountain.

Food Preparation, Feeding, and Dining Areas

Infants' bottles and food are usually prepared in their classrooms. Classrooms need to be equipped with a sink specifically for food preparation, a small refrigerator, and a bottle warmer. Infants' milk and food should never be heated in a microwave oven. Microwaves create hot spots that can be dangerous. Infants should be held when they are bottle-fed and as they start solid foods. When they are able to sit on their own, they are ready to sit at a small table and to enjoy family-style meals with their classmates.

Older children are likely to eat snacks in their classrooms and lunch either in their classrooms or in a central lunchroom. Mealtimes should be opportunities for relaxed conversation. Tables and chairs should be child size and comfortable. Dishes and cutlery should be sized for small hands. All surfaces should be able to withstand frequent sanitizing.

All-day programs that serve breakfast and lunch need either a commercial kitchen or to make arrangements to have catered food brought in from outside. Another option is to have children bring their meals from home. Programs that serve only snacks do not need a separate kitchen—snacks; serving utensils; and disposable cups, plates, and napkins can be kept in classrooms.

Napping Areas

Napping areas should be cozy and relaxing. Each infant needs to follow his or her individual napping schedule and must have an individual crib that is in the same location every day. Licensing regulations are likely to specify spacing between cribs and may have other rules addressing sleeping rooms for infants. Infants must always be placed on their backs to sleep to reduce the risk of sudden infant death syndrome (SIDS).

Toddlers and preschoolers usually nap after lunch and can be expected to adjust to a regular napping schedule. Most programs plan for toddlers and preschoolers to rest in their classrooms. You will need room-darkening shades and an individual cot for each child. Children's cots should be placed in the same location every day. A calm atmosphere, books to look at, soft music, a favorite blanket or "lovey" from home, and a back rub often help children sleep restfully (Gonzalez-Mena & Eyer, 2009).

Developing Classroom Floor Plans

Once you have identified which of the activity/ learning centers described earlier best fit the program's goals, you will need to systematically develop floor plans to create an environment that will help you meet those goals. We recommend that you take the following steps as you design classroom layouts:

1. Determine how each classroom will be used. Identify the specific caregiving, educational, and developmental activities it is meant to support.

2. Consider which activities create a lot of traffic or are likely to be messy and wet (like entryways, painting, and eating), and which activities require quiet, cozy environments. When designing infant rooms, you also need to plan an area for cribs. They should be placed in a location that can be made dark and comfortable for sleeping. Select areas in each classroom for these wet and active activities, as well as spaces for quiet and cozy ones.

3. You will want to have at least five activity/learning centers in each classroom (Harms et al., 2005). Calculate the number of places needed for center play by multiplying the number of children by 1.5; for example, 20 children require 30 activity places. Having more choices than children lessens waiting time and offers a reasonable number of options.

Table 6.3
Determining the Anticipated Capacity of Each Learning Center

Center	Maximum Activity Places
Water table	4
Book	3
Easel	2
Manipulatives	4
Dramatic play	4
Blocks	3
	30 places

List the centers you plan to incorporate and note the maximum number of children you expect to be in each center at one time, as shown in Table 6.3.

This process will create a framework for the center you are creating and will generate priorities to guide your work.

Areas for Adults

Working in an early childhood program is physically and emotionally demanding. The quality of the work environment directly affects an adult's abilities to perform well. The center is also a home-away-from-home for the families it serves. It is important that areas designed for staff and families are comfortable and demonstrate that their contributions to the center are appreciated and valued.

Family Reception Area: The family reception area should be comfortable and well defined. It should invite adults to gather and provide a place for family members and staff to work together (Olds, 2001). It should provide information about the program, can be used to announce parent organization activities such as social events and fund-raisers or to show pictures after these special events, and can be a clearinghouse for information about the community. The reception area is an ideal place for displays that put the spotlight on children's learning. This area might also include materials designed to answer families' questions about child development, parenting, or other particular needs.

Adult Lounge/Rest Room: A comfortable lounge should be provided for all staff so that they have a place to relax during breaks. The lounge should have a sink, refrigerator, microwave, and a coffee machine so staff can prepare and eat snacks. This is also an appropriate place to display professional magazines and journals. If possible, provide a computer with Internet access so that teachers can email parents or search for professional information. For greater privacy, adult rest rooms should not be part of the lounge but should be located nearby.

Staff Workroom: Sometimes the adult lounge and workroom are combined, but ideally they are separate. The workroom is likely to be shared by teachers from several classrooms, and perhaps by all teachers in the facility. It needs desks or tables and chairs, shelves and cabinets for professional materials and supplies, office machines (e.g., paper cutter, laminator, photocopier, computer, and printer), and a sink. This is a good place for staff members' personal belongings. If it is used this way, each individual needs a spacious locker with a lock.

Professional Library: An early childhood program should have a professional library to keep staff informed and to help them in planning. The library is usually a storage and display area located in, or adjacent to, the director's office or the workroom. The library should include professional books; curriculum materials; journals and other publications of professional associations; advocacy materials; catalogs from suppliers of equipment and materials; and professional development software, tapes, or DVDs.

Office: The program director needs a place for private conversations with parents and staff and a secure place to store confidential financial, personnel, and child records. She needs a secure computer, a printer, telephone with answering machine, and a comfortable and convenient workspace with shelves for professional books and chairs for two or three visitors. It is wise to locate the director's office near the reception area located by the front door.

Isolation Area: One last indoor space you need to plan for is an isolation area to care for ill or hurt children until a family member arrives to take them home. It may be most practical to put the "boo-boo room" near the director's office or the reception area. It is good to have a bed or cot available and to have a few toys and books nearby. A small bathroom adjacent to the isolation area can be helpful.

OUTDOOR SPACE

Theorists such as Piaget and Vygotsky recognized the important contributions play can make to all developmental domains, and we recognize that outdoor play gives children opportunities to pursue vigorous, boisterous, self-directed pursuits. In fact, researchers have shown that outdoor play uniquely enhances motor development (Poest, Williams, Witt, & Atwood, 1990), provides sensory stimulation (Olds, 2001), presents opportunities to use language and solve problems (Rivkin, 1995), contributes to cognitive development (Bodrova & Leong, 2003; Perry, 2003), and provides children with opportunities to practice and develop social skills (Frost, Wortham, & Reifel, 2012; Klein, Wirth, & Linas, 2003).

Facility planners should devote at least as much time, care, and creativity designing outdoor areas as they do planning classrooms. A playground is not a frill—it is an absolutely essential part of a quality program of early care and education. In fact, when adults were asked about their favorite kinds of play as children, more than 70% described outdoor play experiences (Henniger, 1994). We are making memories for the children in our care!

General Criteria and Specifications for Child Care Playgrounds

Playgrounds have the potential to enhance every developmental domain, foster children's sense of wonder, appeal to all the senses, create a sense of place, preserve and enhance the site's natural features, and be aesthetically pleasing (Koralek, 2002; Olds, 2001; Talbot & Frost, 1989). They can contribute to the program's success in meeting its goals while meeting every child's needs for active play.

Planners should consider the playground's location, size, terrain, and surface. They must be certain the playground meets all safety standards and is accessible or has the potential to be made accessible to children with disabilities. These issues are discussed later in this chapter.

Location: If your facility has one playground, it should not surround the building because that arrangement would make supervision almost impossible. If each age group has its own playground, they can ring the facility, giving each group access to its specially designed play area.

If the facility will have just one playground, the south side of the building, which will have sun throughout the day, is generally the most desirable. To minimize the chance of accidents as children go in and out, plan for

- Door thresholds flush with the indoor/outdoor surfaces or a ramp if an abrupt change in surface levels is unavoidable
- Floor treatments that provide maximum traction as children transition from the playground to the classroom
- Doors with windows to prevent collisions

There should be a bathroom directly accessible from the playground or just inside the door to ensure constant supervision. A drinking fountain should also be easily accessible to children during outdoor play.

Size: Most states' licensing regulations require outdoor activity areas to have at least 75 sq ft per child. The amount of space required sometimes varies according to the age of the children, with infants and toddlers requiring less space than older children. NAEYC accreditation criteria require at least 75 sq ft per child "for each child playing outside at any one time. The total amount of required play space is based on a maximum of one-third of the total center enrollment being outside at one time" (NAEYC, 2005). Other experts recommend 100 to 200 sq ft per child and advise, when possible, that the playground be large enough to accommodate all children at the same time so that every child will be able to spend a significant amount of time outdoors every day (Olds, 2001).

The Fence: Most states and NAEYC Accreditation Standards (2005) require that playgrounds be surrounded by a fence or a natural barrier and gates that children cannot open. We recommend non-climbable barriers 4 to 6 ft high, with a gap at the bottom of no more than 3 1/2 in. A fence is essential when the playground is bordered by a dangerous area such as a parking lot, street, swimming pool, or a natural body of water (Frost, 1992). Many states also require fences as boundaries between areas for infant/toddlers and older children (Olds, 2001). These interior fences do not have to be as tall as those around the playground's perimeter.

When selecting fencing material, consider what children will hear and see on the other side of the fence. If the view is interesting, select chain link, lattice, or other materials that permit visibility. When the view is not desirable, the site is noisy, or there are concerns about vandalism, fences made of wood or concrete are better choices. Solid fences can incorporate different textures and colors or plantings to soften the view and create visual interest. Remember to consider how the fence looks from the inside of the playground and also how it fits into the neighborhood and whether it makes the center inviting or intimidating from the street (Olds, 2001).

In addition to having an entry from the building, the outdoor area should have a locking 12-ft gate large enough for large lawn maintenance equipment and trucks delivering sand. Be careful not to install permanent structures in such a way that they block sand delivery trucks from the sand play area.

Terrain: Outdoor play spaces with varied terrain are more interesting and more challenging than flat ones. When possible, retain the natural vegetation and incorporate existing slopes, trees, rock outcroppings, and other interesting features. If the play space is flat and barren, however, it is not difficult to create small hills that give children opportunities to climb, roll, and slide. It is also possible to add vegetation by planting a mix of shrubs, trees, and flowers. These features create private areas that invite exploration and make-believe (Olds, 2001).

Hills do not have to be large to be challenging. A hill that rises just 3 ft and has a gentle slope of no more than 10° is perfect for preschoolers. These hills and mounds

Well-designed outdoor environments enhance children's quality of life.

easily become part of the playscape; for example, a slide can be mounted on the slope of a small mound. Interesting paths for wheeled toys can also be created in rolling terrain.

Surface: Surfaces for infants and toddlers should be mainly grass, wood, sand, and dirt. Outdoor activity areas for older children should also have a variety of surfaces. All playgrounds need to be well drained, with the fastest drying areas nearest the building. Approximately one-half to two-thirds of the total square footage of the outdoor playground should be covered with grass, and about 1,000 sq ft should be covered in hard surfaces for activities such as wheeled-toy riding and block building. Some areas should be left as dirt for gardening and for realizing "a satisfaction common to every child—digging a big hole!" (Baker, 1968, p. 61). Areas underneath equipment need special resilient materials that are described later in the "Safety" and other "Other Considerations" discussions.

Shade and Shelter: Every playground should provide shelter and shade to protect children from wind and exposure to the sun. The amount of shelter you need to add will depend, in part, on your climate and the shade and shelter provided by trees, terrain, and nearby buildings. No matter what your climate, a covered play area, such as a verandah that gets plenty of air circulation, can serve as an extension of children's classrooms. It will be an inviting place for quiet play during warm weather and for active play when it is cold or inclement.

Storage: Storage is needed for loose parts such as wheeled toys, sand and water play accessories, balls, trucks, big blocks, and gardening tools. Since these toys are more likely to be used if they are stored near where they will be used, their storage area should either be attached to the main building in an area adjoining the playground, in an area children pass on their way to the playground, or in a free-standing outdoor shed located on the playground. If detached from the building, the outdoor shed should fit in and not detract from the main building and should, if possible, be positioned to break the wind. A single storage unit 12 ft long, 10 ft wide, and 7 to 8 ft high is sufficient for most early childhood programs.

Create a place for everything by equipping the storage area with hooks and shelves mounted within children's reach and bins children can manage on their own. This way, children are able to get the equipment out and help put it away. A high shelf to store seasonal items or materials for staff use is also useful.

Smaller lockable storage cabinets located near particular centers, such as sand, block building, and dramatic play, are ideal for some materials. These cabinets, like storage sheds, must be made of durable materials that can withstand moisture.

All outdoor storage areas should have slightly raised flooring to prevent flooding after heavy rains. A ramp makes it easier to move equipment into and out of the storage shed and minimizes tripping.

Outdoor Space Arrangement

The indoor space should be extended outdoors, and the outdoor space should be extended indoors. Together they enhance children's growth and development and support the program's goals.

Before planning an outdoor space, talk with staff, family members, and older children to learn what they would like to do outside. Visit other playgrounds and analyze the current site. In planning or redesigning outside play areas, evaluation tools can help identify what is missing and point you toward elements you would most like to include (DeBord, Hestenes, Moore, Cosco, & McGinnis, 2002; Frost et al., 2011).

Outdoor Areas for Infants and Toddlers: Many people think of playgrounds as spaces designed for vigorous rough-and-tumble play. They often assume there is no reason to create outdoor areas for very young children. But infants and toddlers are no different from older children. They too need fresh air and sunlight, delight in exploring nature, and benefit from time outdoors. But it is true that infants' and toddlers' outside environment is different from spaces for older children.

Four specific criteria are extremely important to consider when planning an outdoor area for infants and toddlers. First, it must be safe; that is, it should provide a gentle terrain for crawling, walking, running, and stepping up and down; it must be free of materials that would be harmful if eaten such as gravel, mushrooms, and plants with potentially dangerous leaves, flowers, or stems; and it must not have sand areas that could be used as a litter box by neighborhood cats—they must be covered securely when not in use. See Appendix 5 for a list of poisonous and nonpoisonous plants that might be in your environment.

Second, the area must be scaled to be comfortable and accessible for the very young. Young infants enjoy blankets put on soft grass in shady, protected areas. Lawns also encourage early crawlers to explore and toddlers to roll, tumble, and relax. Cruisers enjoy surfaces such as low benches or logs to support their explorations and for them to crawl over or around. Crawlers and beginning walkers also enjoy paths with interesting textures such as patterned rocks, colored bricks, and half logs buried along the way. Raised (15-in. maximum) walkways with railings also create appropriate challenges. Beginning walkers also need smooth surfaces to enjoy push and pull and ride-on toys (Gonzalez-Mena & Eyer, 2009; Lally & Stewart, 1990).

Third, outdoor areas should invite the sensory motor explorations of the very young. Differences in hardness, texture, color, temperature, and areas in the sun and shade are interesting places to crawl and walk and to use pull, push, or riding toys.

Fourth, infants and toddlers need loose materials for play. Many of the rattles, stacking toys, soft blocks, board books, and other materials they enjoy indoors can come outside with them. If teachers are going to be able to manage getting children and toys outdoors, the playground must be close and convenient to the classroom.

Spaces Specifically for Young Infants.   Nonmobile infants enjoy an enclosed area with a surface that encourages reaching, grasping, and kicking. The area should stimulate visual and auditory senses with colorful streamers, soft wind chimes, prisms and mirrors, and natural sounds such as breezes rustling in the trees and birdsongs. A stroller path adds an additional opportunity for exploration and might make it possible for babies to visit older siblings playing in other areas of the playground.

Spaces Specifically for Mobile Infants and Toddlers.   Five design principles can guide your efforts to create an appropriate play environment for mobile infants and toddlers:

1. Allow for a wide range of child-initiated movements via pathways, hills, ramps, and tunnels.
2. Stimulate their senses.
3. Provide for novelty, variety, and challenge.
4. Provide equipment that supports development, for example, cars where they can sit side-by-side and props that support their beginning pretend play
5. Make the area safe and comfortable (Frost, 1992)

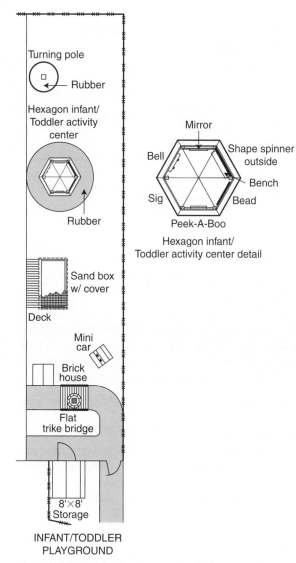

**INFANT/TODDLER
PLAYGROUND**

Figure 6.10
Infant/Toddler Playground

Source: Playground developed by Grounds for Play for
the Children's Center at the University of South Carolina,
Columbia, South Carolina. Used by permission of the
University of South Carolina.

The safe, natural environment—trees, shrubs, flowers, pinecones, and tree stumps—should be left undisturbed. As much as possible, play areas for mobile infants and toddlers need to integrate sensory, exploratory, and action-oriented devices. For example, a structure can have panels to look at and feel; objects like pulleys, drums, and steering wheels to manipulate; and climbers and slides that promote large muscle play.

Figure 6.10 is a plan for an infant and toddler playground. It illustrates some of the principles described earlier.

You might have the opportunity to create an area designed specifically for 2-year-olds. This would be a good investment because we expect children between 24 and 36 months of age to be able to run and climb, to be learning to peddle trikes, and to begin to engage in sustained make-believe play with their peers, but they are not yet ready for the complex play structures that are appealing to preschoolers. A 2-year-olds' playground should incorporate those materials that invite children to practice new skills and pursue their developing interest in social play. The playground plan for 2-year-olds in Figure 6.11 also includes an outdoor art studio with a picnic table, a easel for painting, storage and a water table that can be enjoyed by 2-year-olds and shared with older children.

Outdoor Areas for Older Children: Older children need playgrounds that enhance their developing motor skills, their advancing cognitive skills, and their growing peer interactions. Playgrounds for preschoolers should build on and extend the experiences they had when they were younger. For example, preschoolers still need structures that integrate sensory, exploratory, and action-oriented activities, but the structures should be more complex than those seen on toddler playgrounds. Like toddlers and 2-year-olds, preschoolers need dramatic play materials, but their props need to encourage more advanced symbolism and more cooperative play than do props for toddlers. Likewise, a smooth transition in playground design must occur in programs serving preschool and primary-age children. Primary-age children need more open grassy areas, more gymnastic types of apparatuses, and more pretend toys than do preschool children (Frost, 1992).

Play Experiences and Zones.   Like play indoors, outdoor play needs to meet the developmental needs of the whole child. Four types of play enhance preschoolers' and primary-age children's development:

1. Functional or exercise play that involves practice and repetition of gross-motor activities
2. Constructive play during which children use materials such as paint or sand to create
3. Dramatic or pretend play that often occurs in small, private spaces
4. Cooperative social play such as games with rules and sustained dramatic play (Johnson, Christie, & Yawkey, 1999)

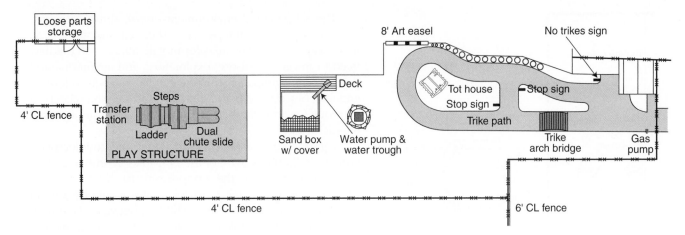

Figure 6.11
Playground for 2-Year-Olds

Source: Playground developed by Grounds for Play for the Children's Center at the University of South Carolina, Columbia, South Carolina. Used by permission of the University of South Carolina.

Like indoor classrooms, playgrounds have activity centers or zones (Perry, 2003). Some experts suggest that outdoor centers should duplicate the play experiences found indoors (Henniger, 1993), but others believe outdoor centers should be unique (Jensen & Bullard, 2002). Playgrounds with the following five play zones bridge these contrasting views:

1. A nature zone with plants, animals, and rocks that can be located in either an active or quiet area.
2. An adventure zone for construction and digging.
3. An active zone for play on play structures, for sand/water play, and for chase and ball games. Preschoolers need open grassy areas; primary-level children can handle chase and ball games on grassy or hard-surface areas.
4. A quiet area with easels, water/sand tables, a book nook, and a snack area.
5. A quiet play zone for dramatic play (Guddemi & Eriksen, 1992).

General Criteria for Arranging Zones.   Outdoor play is different from indoor play in several important ways. First, there are fewer restrictions. Children can be boisterous, rambunctious, and energetic; and there are less likely to be rules governing how materials are to be used and how many children can play in each center. Children usually have more freedom to do as they please when they are outdoors (Perry, 2003), and you are more likely to see children combine several kinds of activities into one theme outdoors than inside. For example, playing "car wash" is likely to involve children combining water play, dramatic play, and vigorous physical activity as they push, pull, and ride on wheeled toys. Multiple opportunities for particular kinds of play are more likely outdoors; for example, the playhouse under the play structure, tents under the trees, or the garden may all support cooperative dramatic play.

Outdoor playscapes should be designed to provide opportunities for quiet play as well as the vigorous activities we often think of as being typical on the playground. Children playing quietly need protection from their peers' rambunctious play as well as from wind or heat. Boulders, logs, park benches, and picnic tables can provide attractive seating for those engaged in quiet play. Smooth surfaces that are good for jumping rope, playing jacks, and board or card games can also be good for quiet play. Quiet play areas can be situated near shrubbery or large stones, in nooks created by changes in terrain, or on a veranda or other playground shelter.

Both active and quiet players need pathways to guide their transitions from one part of the playground to another. Clear paths can minimize conflict and prevent accidents (e.g., getting too close to swings). Pathways should lead to places of interest, like a garden; connect equipment within a zone; and connect play zones with each other. They can be made interesting by using curves and intersections; by including bridges; by having gates to open and close; by varying the path's texture and composition by using materials such as stepping stones, mosaics made of pavers, pretty rocks, or timber rounds; and by including special attractions like flowers, a butterfly or ladybug house, a wind chime, or a weather station along the path; and by including places to sit.

Specific Zones and Equipment.   Plan for your playground to have five play spaces per child. That way every child will have several play options from which to choose. Consider the following guidelines when planning for playground zones:

1. Open area.   The open area needs to be large for playing with balls, Frisbees®, and hula hoops, as well as for just running.

2. Road for wheeled toys.   A hard-surfaced area can form a tricycle, wagon, or doll stroller road extending through the outdoor space and returning to its starting point. The road should be wide enough to permit passing. A curving road is more interesting than a straight one. Avoid right-angle turns because they cause accidents. Like pathways, the road should have some challenges (e.g., a slight rise). Roads are more interesting if there are attractions like store fronts or gas stations along the way or archways to ride through. They should be made aesthetically pleasing by including flowers and shrubs.

3. Sandpit or sandbox.   Sand play is preschool children's most popular outside activity (Berry, 1993). Sand play can be provided by creating a sandpit or a sandbox. A sandpit can be a large mound or a narrow, winding river of sand. Children should have flat working surfaces, such as wooden boards or flat boulders, beside or in the sand. An outdoor sandpit should have a boundary element that "provides a 'sense' of enclosure for the playing children, keeps out unwanted traffic, protects the area against water draining from adjacent areas, and helps keep the sand within the sand play areas" (Osmon, 1971, p. 77). Boundaries can be built or created by the landscape.

A sandbox provides many of the same play opportunities as a sand pit but is smaller and more clearly defined. Whether you provide sand play in a sandpit or a sand box, the work area should sometimes be exposure to the sanitizing and drying rays of the sun but should also have shade available to protect children from the sun. Water should be available to enhance sand play.

All sand areas must be covered when not in use to prevent neighborhood cats from using them as a litter box. Sandbox covers are available from playground equipment vendors or can be made by securing shade cloth with heavy objects.

4. Water areas.   Water play is likely to be more energetic outdoors than it is inside. Playgrounds can feature birdbaths, fountains, elevated streams, water tables, sprinklers, and splash and wading pools. Water temperature should be between 60°F and 80°F (16°C and 27°C). Water play equipment need not be expensive. Children enjoy an inflatable or plastic pool and a spray nozzle or sprinkler on a garden hose as much as more expensive water play equipment. Be certain to follow licensing regulations, particularly as to required ratios, and health department regulations whenever children are near water.

5. Gardens.   Children enjoy gardens with any kind of plant life—flowers, vegetables, herbs, vines, shrubs, trees, and even weeds! An outdoor garden should be fenced to protect it from animals or from being accidentally trampled. Raised garden beds allow children in wheelchairs to participate.

6. Play structures.   Complex play structures are popular additions to many playgrounds. They are likely to include ladders, chains, ropes, and/or tire nets, making it possible for children with varied skill levels and abilities to get up to, and down from, any number of play platforms. Preschoolers usually find climbing up easier than climbing down, so multiple ways to navigate these structures are needed. Additional features of many complex play structures include swings, spiral and tube slides, horizontal ladders, and climbing walls. (Avoid tunnels because they cannot be adequately supervised.) Play structures accommodate vigorous play, often as part of cooperative social play that is so popular with this age group.

Figure 6.12 is a plan for a playground for preschool children. It illustrates some of the principles just discussed.

Regulations: Few, if any, regulations ensure the safety of outdoor play areas (Cradock, O'Donnell, Benjamin, Walker, & Slining, 2010). In fact, many states' child care regulations say little or nothing about playground safety, and even public school outdoor play areas are largely unregulated (Cradock et al., 2010; Wallach & Edelstein, 1991). Even though mandatory regulations are scarce, a growing body of research has documented the hazards commonly found on playgrounds (Frost, 2001), and widely accepted guidelines are now available to help ensure the safety of your center's outdoor play areas.

The U.S. Consumer Product Safety Commission's *Handbook for Public Playground Safety* is the definitive resource addressing safety issues on which those responsible for playgrounds in parks, schools, child care facilities, and other public places can rely. The handbook is frequently updated and is available online (see the Web address at the end of the chapter). It is a must-have reference that describes the characteristics of safe play spaces, identifies common risks, and describes how to avoid them.

Supervision: The single most important precaution you can take to ensure children's safety on the playground is to provide consistent supervision. Teachers must be aware of the location of every child and what every child is doing. Even though it may be tempting to view outside playtime as a break from classroom responsibilities, teachers need to be particularly vigilant to protect children from harm when they are outdoors. It may help teachers realize how important supervision is when they learn that almost 206,000 preschool- and elementary-age children receive emergency care from injuries that occurred on playground equipment every year. About 10% of those accidents occurred in child care settings. About three-fourths of all injuries on public playgrounds resulted from falls, primarily onto the surface under the equipment. For children age 5 and younger, 60% of all serious injuries involved the head and face. Children age 5 and older most frequently suffered sprains and fractures to their wrists, lower arms, and elbows (Josse, MacKay, Osmond, & MacPherson, 2009; Tinsworth & McDonald, 2001).

Ropes, shoestrings, cords, leashes, strings on clothing, and items tied to equipment can entrap children. More than half of all playground fatalities are caused by strangulation. *No ropes of any kind should ever be attached to playground equipment.* Teachers should also be particularly watchful around climbing equipment, specifically monkey bars and horizontal ladders, on which more than half of all injuries that result in hospital visits occurred. Other injuries were caused by swings, collisions with stationary equipment, protruding nails and screws, pinch points, sharp edges, hot surfaces, and playground debris (United States Consumer Product Safety Commission [USCPSC], 2008).

Adequate supervision requires the following:

1. Teachers need training in playground safety. Materials have been developed in recent years that help teachers become better at ensuring children's safety on the playground. See the addresses for Web-based resources from the National Program for Playground Safety and others at the end of this chapter.

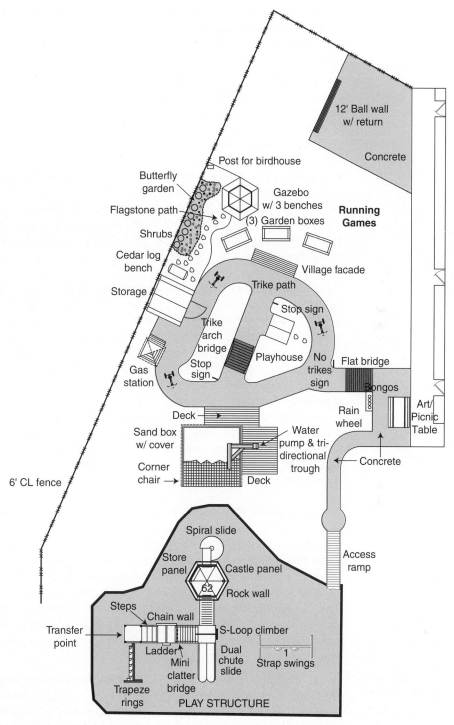

Figure 6.12
Preschool, Kindergarten, and Primary-Level Playground

Source: Playground developed by Grounds for Play for the Children's Center at the University of South Carolina, Columbia, South Carolina. Used by permission of the University of South Carolina.

2. Teachers need to be able to see the entire play area. Playgrounds should be designed with the importance of adequate supervision in mind, and teachers need to learn how to station themselves in different areas of the play yard so that, together, they can cover all areas used by the children.

3. Teachers should be actively involved with children while they are on the playground. Young children are learning all the time, indoors and out; the effective teacher is alert for opportunities to teach children new skills, to challenge them to reach their goals, to support their social and emotional development, to ask questions that prompt cognitive development, and to help them have fun.

Separating Play Areas: The *Handbook for Public Playground Safety* identifies "use zones" (formally called "fall zones"), which are the surfaces under and around specific pieces of playground equipment into which a child exiting or falling from that equipment is likely to land. These use zones must have protective surfacing and are to be kept clear. Toys must not be left in use zones, and children's paths from one part of the playground to another must not pass through them.

Equipment Hazards: Safe playgrounds are designed to meet the needs of a particular age group. Playgrounds for preschoolers include appropriate equipment, are scaled to fit typical 2- to 5-year-olds, and are laid out to create appropriate challenges for this age group. Playgrounds for preschoolers should be different in significant ways from areas planned for infants and toddlers and should also be distinct from playgrounds designed for 5- through 12-year-olds (Olsen, Hudson, & Thompson, 2010).

Safe playgrounds are also constructed from high-grade nontoxic materials that are appropriate for climate conditions, are correctly installed, and are well maintained.

A complete discussion of playground safety is beyond the scope of this book, but Table 6.4 summarizes safety specifications for some of the most popular equipment most likely to be on your playground. We recommend that you consult the USCPSC handbook for specific guidelines related to climbing structures, seesaws, spring rockers, and other equipment you are considering for your program.

Surfacing Under Playground Equipment: Hard-packed surfaces are to blame for many playground injuries (Olsen et al., 2010). Dirt and grass are not enough to protect children from injury. Protective surfacing is needed under any equipment from which a child might fall; when a child falls, either the surface gives to absorb the impact or the child gives with a resulting bruise, broken bone, spinal injury, head injury, or even death.

The following are three types of commonly used surfaces. We consulted the *Handbook for Public Playground Safety* to describe some pros and cons for each. You will want to consult with a playground safety expert when making decisions about which surface is best for your climate, your budget, and the playground equipment you plan to install.

1. Organic loose material (wood chips, bark mulch, engineered wood fibers, etc.). These are the least expensive options. They are readily available, are easy to install, drain well, are less abrasive, and are less likely to attract animals than is sand. It is difficult to maintain the recommended depth of 6 to 12 in. of organic material, however. These materials' cushioning potential is reduced when they are wet or frozen, they decompose and become compacted over time, are subject to microbacterial growth when wet, and must be frequently refurbished.

2. Inorganic loose material (sand, gravel, pea gravel, shredded tires). These are also low-cost options. They are readily available, easy to install, and do not encourage the growth of undesirable microbes. Maintaining a depth of 6 to 12 in. can be a challenge,

Table 6.4
Safety Specifications for Selected Playground Equipment

Swings: Single-Axis Swings That Go Back and Forth

- Surround swings with a low barrier such as a fence or a hedge to prevent children from running into the use zone.
- No more than two swings should be hung from one support.
- Swing seats should be lightweight. Rubber and plastic are recommended.
- Provide at least 24 in. between swings; 30 in. between swings and support posts.
- Provide full bucket seats for children age 4 and younger.
- Animal figure swings are *not* recommended.
- S-hooks holding swing seats and those connected to the supporting structure must be completely closed (the gap should not admit a dime).
- Cushioning material must cover 6 ft on either side of the swing and be 2 times the height of the supporting structure in the front and back.

Slides: Straight Chute Slide

- The platform at the top of the slide should be at least 22 ft long and should be at least as wide as the slide.
- Guardrails or protective barriers should surround the slide platform.
- There should be *no gaps* between the platform and the start of the chute.
- The slide's average incline should be no more than 30°.
- Sides should be at least 4 in. along the entire length of the slide.
- Metal slides should be placed out of the sun to prevent burning.
- The exit area should include at least 11 in. of horizontal surface and should be a designated distance from protective surfacing (this distance depends on the height of the slide).

Source: U.S. Consumer Product Safety Commission. (2008). *Handbook for Public Playground Safety* available at http://www.cpsc.gov/cpscpub/pubs/325.pdf.

however, because children's activities tend to scatter them. The cushioning potential of sand, gravel, and pea gravel are reduced when they are wet or frozen or when the humidity is high, but shredded tires retain their resiliency and are less likely to compact than other loose-fill materials. Each of these options has drawbacks. Sand blows away, gets on children's clothes and in their pockets and cuffs, is abrasive and damages interior floors and surfaces, and attracts cats that use it as a litter box. Pea gravel is unsuitable for children age 5 and younger and dangerous for those age 3 and younger because it can get into small children's eyes, ears, and noses. Gravel is hard to walk on. Shredded tires can stain clothing, may contain steel wires from steel belted tires, and may be swallowed.

3. Unitary materials (rubber mats poured into place onsite). These materials require virtually no maintenance, are easy to clean, have consistent shock absorbency, and are accessible to the handicapped. They require professional installation, are appropriate only for level surfaces, and their initial cost is relatively high. Some types are susceptible to frost damage.

Application Activity

Evaluate a particular piece of playground equipment at your facility's playground or a playground at a park nearby. Is it appropriate for the age group that uses it? Is it safely constructed? Does it have appropriate cushioning material? Report your findings to the class. If possible, use photos to illustrate your conclusions about the appropriateness and safety of this piece of equipment.

PURCHASING AND MAINTAINING EQUIPMENT AND MATERIALS

Some of the most important decisions a director makes when planning a facility are those related to the purchase of furniture, furnishings, equipment, and materials. Such decisions will impact the center's operations from its first day forward. It takes forethought and planning to have the needed equipment and materials on hand to support the program's basic operations and children's day-to-day activities. If purchasing decisions are not thoughtfully made, caregivers will not have what they need to keep children safe; will not be able to create smooth routines for arrivals, departures, mealtimes, and naptimes; will not have materials to engage children in meaningful activities; and will be stressed by classrooms that seem to be always chaotic and disorganized. Furthermore, if the wear and tear of daily use is not taken into account when purchasing tables, chairs, toys, and furnishings, there will undoubtedly be disappointments when they break and will soon have to be replaced, creating unanticipated expense.

Systematic planning for purchases of furniture, furnishings, equipment, and supplies makes it possible to compare similar products' materials, construction, and cost. Comparison shopping is quite painless now that suppliers' catalogs are posted online. Careful shopping will make it more likely that you will get what you need, the items you select will meet your expectations, and you will be able to avoid disappointments and costly mistakes and restocking fees that are often charged for returns.

Fortunately, even in new centers, many purchases can be made over time. You will want to make major purchases with start-up monies and at the beginning of each budget year. Consumables such as arts and crafts materials, seasonal supplies, and toys and books can be refreshed as needed throughout the year. It is always wise to set monies aside to purchase big-ticket items that may need to be replaced unexpectedly; to be able to offer teachers discretionary funds to refresh books, toys, and other materials that get hard wear; and to be able to purchase innovative products that you think are a good fit to help the program achieve its goals.

Purchasing Guidelines

Many factors need to be considered when making purchasing decisions. These suggestions may help you think systematically about purchases:

1. Select only safe, durable, relatively maintenance free, and aesthetically pleasing furniture, furnishings, equipment, materials, and supplies. To do otherwise is to risk being penny wise and pound foolish.

2. Be certain to purchase equipment and materials that are aligned with the program's theoretical foundation and will help achieve its goals. Look for materials that encourage creativity, experimentation, and peer social interactions. They can be used in child-directed ways and can accommodate children with varying degrees of competence and differing interests. Programs that implement different approaches to curriculum, such as Montessori or direct instruction, will use materials that are task directed, autotelic (self-rewarding), and self-correcting.

Regardless of the program's theoretical foundation, all materials must meet the needs of children with disabilities and must convey multicultural, inclusive, and nonsexist values. Look for multiethnic dolls and hand puppets as well as dolls with disabilities that come with assistive devices such as wheelchairs, walkers, braces, glasses, and hearing aids. Similarly, books, puzzles, and pictures selected for classroom use should depict various ethnic and racial groups, nontraditional sex-role behaviors, and a variety of family structures. Consider equipment and materials that can be used in a variety of situations and that embrace individual differences. As much as possible, teachers' input should guide the selection of classroom materials and supplies.

3. The director or business manager should keep an ongoing **inventory**, a record of the quantity of materials already purchased and the location of these items, and a "wish list" identifying items the center plans to purchase in the future. The inventory is an essential tool when planning purchases. It helps avoid duplication, determines what equipment and materials need to be replaced, determines insurance needs, can help calculate losses from theft, and contributes to the annual budget-planning process. The inventory should be kept electronically in a spreadsheet (such as Excel) or database (such as FileMaker Pro) format. It should be backed up regularly to a secure electronic location.

The inventory should list and identify all equipment and materials that have been purchased and delivered with the date of acquisition. For nonconsumable items, the inventory record should indicate any maintenance performed and estimate of the current cost of replacement (often more than the initial cost). Inventoried equipment should be marked with the name of the program, the classroom (when appropriate), and an inventory number.

4. The director or business manager should attempt to save money by negotiating prices whenever possible. When comparing costs, be sure taxes (when appropriate), shipping, and handling charges are included.

5. Be alert for sales and specials on consumable items, but take care not to overbuy.

6. Purchase only from reputable and well-established vendors of furniture, supplies, and equipment. (See Appendix 1.)

Purchasing Instructional Materials

A wide variety of instructional materials are available for caregivers and teachers of infants, toddlers, preschoolers, and primary-age children. Some require a significant investment to purchase a package designed to deliver specific content, such as literacy skills or themed monthly activities. Most emphasize teacher-directed activities to be used in particular ways.

Other materials, like books and computer software, are less substantial investments and offer teachers and caregivers opportunities to pick and choose the ones they think best suited for the particular children in their care.

Purchasing Kits and Sets: We advise you to carefully evaluate any kits or sets before investing in them by answering the following questions:

1. Do *all* the materials align with the program's theoretical foundation? Are their content and format developmentally and culturally appropriate?
2. How does having the kit benefit teachers? Does it save them time collecting or making materials? Do teachers need the kit or set as a guide in presenting concepts or skills?
3. How does the kit benefit children? Does it reflect the children in this community? Does it convey respect for diversity and inclusion? Are its activities authentic, and is it likely they will be meaningful for these children?
4. What is the total cost of this package, including shipping and taxes? Can several teachers use the same kit or set with their groups of children? Are special services such as training, installation, and maintenance needed? Are these extras included in the cost? What is the cost of replacement or consumable parts? Is other equipment, such as audiovisual equipment, needed for using the kit or set?
5. Are the materials and storage case durable, easily maintained, and safe?
6. How much space is needed to use and store these materials?

Purchasing Children's Books: Children's books should be a cornerstone in every early childhood program. It is important that children have access every day to quality children's literature. Children should have access to books representing various genres, including fiction, nonfiction, poetry, wordless picture books, books for emerging readers, and chapter books to be read aloud or independently for older children. Classrooms are enriched by board books that infants and toddlers can handle themselves, big books that entire classes can enjoy together, and quality hardcover and paperback books children can enjoy alone or with peers.

It is important to give children free access to a wide selection of quality books. They should not be kept nice and clean on the shelf but should be in children's hands where they can be enjoyed time and again, even if that means they sometimes get torn, stepped on, even written on in the process. Use the following criteria when selecting books for the classroom:

1. Does the book "promote the development of knowledge and understanding, processes and skills, as well as dispositions to use and apply skills and to go on learning?" (Bredekamp & Copple, 1997, p. 20). For example,
   a. Is the book's theme likely to be interesting to most young children (e.g., nature, machines, pets, babies)?
   b. Does the book have the potential to meet children's social and emotional needs? Does it explore issues such as welcoming a new baby, making friends, overcoming fears, resolving conflicts peacefully, or other issues faced at home or at school?
   c. Does the book contribute to a project or thematic study? Books to extend and enrich almost every concept are available.
   d. Does the book have a predictable outcome, rhyming words, alliteration? It could be a good opportunity to teach related skills to early readers.
   e. Would it be possible to "stretch" the book with follow-up activities like dramatic play, a cooking activity, artwork, or story writing?
2. Is the book considered high-quality literature (i.e., received an award such as the Caldecott)? Are the author and illustrator known for their quality work? Early childhood educators can use several sources such as those listed in Appendix 1 to identify quality literature that would make a valuable contribution to their classroom.

When thinking about books for the classroom, do not forget the local library. You have a limited book-buying budget, but a large collection of quality children's literature is as close as your neighborhood library or bookmobile. This is a resource that is too valuable to overlook.

Purchasing Computers, Cameras, and Related Hardware and Software: Center directors need to consider two issues when purchasing computers, cameras, printers, fax machines, data storage, peripherals, and related software. Administrators and teachers need to use technology in their work, and children age 3 and older benefit when they have access to developmentally appropriate computer programs, cameras, and printers in their classrooms.

Both hardware and software change so rapidly that it is impossible to make specific recommendations here, but suffice it to say that you should stay abreast of technological advances and bring them into the center to benefit administrators, teachers, and children.

To illustrate recent technology changes, consider how, in 10 to 15 years, online access has progressed from slow and unreliable dial-up service, to faster cable/DSL access, to virtually instantaneous wireless connectivity. Or think about how we take pictures today compared with 10, 15, or 20 years ago. Instamatic pocket cameras were cutting edge technology when first-year teachers entered the classroom in the mid-1960s. They would mail film to be processed, and if they were lucky, their pictures (3 in. × 3 in. snapshots) were returned in less than 2 weeks. What's more, a teacher's salary made it possible to take pictures only two or three times a year. Now digital cameras and video recorders come in every price range. The photos and videos they take can be fine-tuned with the click of a mouse. They can then be emailed immediately to families so they can see a picture of their toddler's first trip down the slide or hear their kindergartener read the story he wrote that morning. Technology is a tool with tremendous potential to enhance documentation of classroom events and teacher-family communication.

When purchasing hardware or software, research cutting edge technology, tap into the expertise of a parent or friend of the center, and purchase equipment that meets your needs and is aligned with the program's goals.

When purchasing computers for children's use, be sure to investigate products designed to meet their particular needs. In addition to desktop and laptop computers, consider products such as inexpensive, portable, lightweight, easy-to-use AlphaSmart word processing machines that do not connect to the Internet but give children the opportunity to compose journals, stories, and reports. Assistive technology can help children with and without disabilities be more successful navigating a computer. Adaptations range from a smaller mouse or a larger track ball to computerized interactive language systems.

Many software programs and websites are appropriate for young children. When selecting computer activities for the classroom, you will want to evaluate the contribution they can make to children's learning, growth, and development and their alignment with the program's goals and theoretical base. That is, you will apply the same kinds of criteria that you apply to any classroom equipment or activity.

Particular issues to consider when evaluating a computer-based activity follow:

1. Does it make effective use of the computer's capacity? Is it more than computerized flashcards?
2. Is it easy to use? Can children understand how it works and navigate through it independently?
3. What happens when you make a mistake? Is there violence, like an explosion, or simply a signal to try again?
4. Is it accurate and free from gender, racial, or other stereotypes?
5. Can it be played at various levels of difficulty to provide for differences in children's interests and abilities?

Shade (1996) summed up these criteria by asking this question about software for children: "Can the child make decisions about what he wants to do and operate the software to accomplish that task, with minor help from the adult?" (p. 18). You need to be certain that computers with Internet access are equipped with filters that control where children can go on the Internet. Websites with recommendations for keeping children safe online are listed at the end of the chapter.

Adults at the center also need to use computer technology. Many administrators purchase a *database management system*—software that allows them to create, maintain, and access a database for administrative functions. Common applications manage children's records; accounts receivable/payable; payroll; meal planning (U.S. Department of Agriculture); personnel management; general ledger; scheduling children and staff; online check-in and check-out; and report, letter, and label writing. Many software packages are now available. Small early childhood programs often use word processing programs, spreadsheet programs, or both to do their administrative record keeping.

Teachers and caregivers also need, more than ever, technology tools to help them with planning and implementation, to keep assessment records, and to communicate with families. The computers located in the teachers' lounge and/or workroom should have access to the Internet and email, should be connected to printers, and teachers should be able to use word processing to make them more efficient. Teachers also need access to quality digital cameras to document the growth, development, and learning of the children in their care.

Caring for Equipment and Materials

Caring for equipment and materials teaches children good habits and helps prevent expensive repairs and replacements. The following routines will help create and maintain an orderly and safe center environment:

1. Equipment and materials should be stored close to where they will be used. Storage areas should be arranged to minimize accidents and to maximize efficiency.
2. Teachers and caregivers should set a good example by using equipment and materials with care and returning them to their storage place when they are finished.
3. Children should be expected to help care for toys, equipment, and materials and to help keep the classroom, playground, and other areas of the center clean and tidy.
4. Spills should be cleaned up immediately. Children should be involved with the cleanup if it is safe, for example, if there is no glass that might hurt them.
5. An employee should be assigned to periodically check toys, equipment, and materials to make sure they are clean, make needed repairs, and discard items that are broken or have missing parts.

TRENDS AND ISSUES

The current issue most likely to have an impact on child care facilities relates to accountability, testing, and the troubling trend to replace time for free play with direct instruction and preparation for high-stakes tests. Child care administrators who are leaders in their communities need to be advocates for children and childhood. They must be prepared to stand their ground if this movement threatens programs that have traditionally been committed to a childhood with time for play—both indoors and out. Trends to eliminate free play threaten to undermine early childhood educators' efforts to keep child care a place for play and exploration.

SUMMARY

Environments, more than what anyone says or does, teach young children about the world and help them find their place in it. Environments create routines and predictability, signal children how they are expected to behave, and either instill children with hope or bury them in despair. Successful early childhood facilities require careful planning. The program's theoretical orientation, goals, and objectives should be reflected in every aspect of the facility's design.

If the child care facility is thought of as the stage upon which child-child, child-adult, and child-material interactions take place, then we can see the director's hand evident at the front door—where the curtain rises and expectations are set. The facility's public areas and each classroom are where the action is. They are the first act, where the actors are engaged in teaching and learning; working and playing; eating and sleeping; reading, writing, singing, and laughing every day.

The outdoor playground is the second act. It is very different from the first, but no less important for the learning and living that go on there. Adults working together are the stagehands. Families and teachers, behind the scenes, are working together to make sure the performance goes well. They are there to smooth small concerns before they become big ones, to cheer successes, and to resolve difficulties before the curtain comes down.

The materials and equipment teachers and caregivers use in their work with children are the set. It is safe and beautiful, full of interesting and sometimes unexpected details that delight. Everything has been thoughtfully and intentionally selected to help the players reach their goal. The set, along with the players, director, and first and second acts, are what make this play unique, unlike any performance that has ever been presented before, anywhere else, any time in history.

USEFUL WEBSITES

Healthy School Environment Resources, U.S. Green Building Council

cfpub.epa.gov/schools/

This site has links to resources for school administrators, architects, families and staff

New York's Green Cleaning Program, sponsored by the City of New York

greencleaning.ny.gov/Product/Default.aspx

This searchable website has information about a wide variety of environmentally friendly cleaning products from hand soaps and glass cleaners to carpet and floor cleaners.

Handbook for Public Playground Safety, published by the Consumer Product Safety Commission

www.cpsc.gov/cpscpub/pubs/325.pdf

This is the definitive resource on topics such as playground safety, covering construction, layout, and surfacing.

National Program for Playground Safety

www.uni.edu/playground/

This nonprofit organization is dedicated to helping the public create safe and developmentally appropriate play environments for children.

Commonly Asked Questions About Child Care Centers and the Americans with Disabilities Act, published by the U.S. Department of Justice Civil Rights Division

www.ada.gov/childq&a.htm

This website addresses child care directors' frequently asked questions about the application of ADA to programs serving young children.

Summary of Accessibility Guidelines for Play Areas, published by the United States Access Board

www.access-board.gov/play/guide/intro.htm

This website has links addressing issues of accessibility that can guide playground planners so that they will be in compliance with the Americans with Disabilities Act (ADA).

Boundless Playgrounds, sponsored by the nonprofit developer of inclusive playgrounds

www.boundlessplaygrounds.org

This website includes advice for planners of inclusive playgrounds and includes a virtual tour of an accessible playground and a searchable directory of fully assessable playgrounds throughout the United States.

Safekids, a privately sponsored project

www.safekids.com/

Safekids is designed to provide adults with information about keeping children safe online. It includes links to advice about children from early readers through teens.

A Parent's Guide to Internet Safety, sponsored by the U.S. Department of Justice and the FBI

www.fbi.gov/stats-services/publications/parent-guide/parent-guide

This letter to parents alerts readers to techniques used by predators to involve children in unsavory and unsafe online activities.

TO REFLECT

1. A carefully planned physical environment can help a program achieve its goals. Identify three or more goals you have for children in your care. How could each goal be promoted through a carefully created environment? For example, if your goal is to help children become good decision makers, a classroom with learning centers would give children opportunities to make meaningful decisions about what they will do each day.

2. Planning often involves compromises. For example, how can a director plan (a) for physical challenges on the preschool playground without creating undue risks for the young children and (b) for a hygienic yet soft environment for infants?

CHECK AND APPLY YOUR UNDERSTANDING

1. Identify issues you should address in advance if you are directing a program that shares space with a Sunday school or another community program.
2. Explain why children are more comfortable with entry areas that have windows.
3. Identify five activity/learning centers you believe are essential in a preschool classroom and prepare talking points describing how children benefit from each center to a family taking a tour of your center.
4. Identify the surfacing under playground equipment you think is most appropriate for your climate and your budget and justify your choice by summarizing its characteristics.
5. Develop a classroom checklist that teachers would use to alert the director to supplies that are running low or furniture or furnishings that need to be repaired or replaced.

CHAPTER 7

Financing and Budgeting

Learning Outcomes

After studying this chapter, you should be able to:

1. Describe the importance of continuous monitoring of revenue and expenses.
2. Describe the differences between start up, fixed, variable, and marginal costs.
3. Identify the components of an operating budget.
4. Describe the process of developing a proposal requesting external funding.

Marie's Experience

Marie's center has been running smoothly for two years and now the downturn in the economy has begun to affect her families. Many of the families enrolled in Marie's program have had to make changes to their enrollment schedules as a result of loss of employment, reduction in working hours, and a need to reduce their personal expenses. As a result they have had to make other arrangements for the care of their children, and Marie must now determine how best to control expenses and continue to operate the center in the black.

Early childhood programs are expensive. In 2010, the average annual cost of full-time center-based care for an infant ranged from $4,650 in Mississippi to $18,200 in the District of Columbia, while the average annual cost for full-time center-based care for a 4-year-old ranged from $3,900 in Mississippi to $14,050 in the District of Columbia. Child care costs represent more than 10% of the state's median income in 40 states. Many families pay more each month for child care than they do for housing. Center-based care for infants can be more expensive than attending a 4-year public college in 36 states, but these costs are borne almost exclusively by families because the same kinds of loans and grants that are available to defray the cost of post-secondary education are not available to cover child care costs (National Association of Child Care Resource and Referral Agencies [NACCRRA], 2011).

The cost of child care is stretching many families to the limit, but quality services are expensive. Many centers, particularly those serving low-income families, find it difficult to cover the full costs of providing

NAEYC Administrator Competencies addressed in this chapter:

Management Knowledge and Skills

2. Legal and Fiscal Management
Knowledge of various federal, state, and local revenue sources.
Knowledge of bookkeeping methods and accounting terminology.
Skill in budgeting, cash flow management, grantwriting, and fundraising.

quality services with the proceeds from the tuition their families are able to pay. The federal Child Care and Development Fund (CCDF) block grant program helps bridge the gap between what famiies can pay and the true cost of quality care by subsidizing child care for qualifying low-income families; even with these subsidies, the quality of care in many communities is mediocre (NACCRRA, 2011). These financial realities mean that program administrators are constantly faced with hard choices, for example, choosing between cutting costs or generating additional income if their programs are going to avoid a deficit and operate in the black. This difficult balance requires knowledge of basic budgeting and financial management and the ability to make informed decisions to ensure the fiscal health of the organization.

It is important to appreciate that both the scope and the quality of services are related to the financial status of a program. To maintain quality experiences for children and their families, a program must generate at least as much income as it expends; otherwise, the program cannot survive. Directors must manage local programs' resources and need financial management skills to do so. Directors must also become aware of market trends and demographics of their early care program. Few early childhood administrators receive adequate training in fiscal management. Such training is important for two reasons. First, fiscal tasks can take up to 50% of a director's time. Second, families, funding agencies, and taxpayers who believe that their early childhood programs are properly managed are more likely to support the program. As is true of all other aspects of planning and administration, fiscal planning begins with the goals of the local program. Unless the proposed services and the requirements for providing those services (in the way of staff, facilities, materials, and equipment) are taken into account, a budget cannot be adequately planned. Although program objectives should be considered first, probably no early childhood program is entirely free of financial limitations.

Fiscal planning affects all aspects of a program and should involve input from all those involved with it (e.g., the board of directors or advisory board, the director, and staff members). By considering everyone's ideas, a director can gain a more accurate picture of budgeting priorities, expenditure levels, and revenue sources. Planning and administering the fiscal aspects of an early childhood program must be a continuous process. Successful financing and budgeting will come only from evaluating current revenue sources and expenditures and from advance planning for existing and future priorities. Weekly and even daily monitoring of income and expenses will provide important information that can be used to strategically plan for fiscal success.

Not-for-profit programs are responsible to their funding agencies, for-profit programs are accountable to their owners and stockholders, and all programs are accountable to the Internal Revenue Service. Even if the average citizen does not understand the problems of financial management, any hint of misuse of funds will cause criticism. Administrators must budget, secure revenue, manage, account for, and provide a rationale for expenditures in keeping with the policies of the early childhood program in a professional and businesslike manner.

COSTS OF EARLY CHILDHOOD PROGRAMS

High-quality early childhood care and education programs are labor intensive and expensive. Most programs, except those funded with public monies, operate in a price-sensitive market. They are financed primarily by working parents and are only supplemented by public and private contributions.

Estimates of Program Costs

Reported costs of early childhood programs show extensive variation by the type of program, the level of training and size of the staff, sponsorship (whether it is a federal program, a public school, or a parent cooperative), the delivery system (center based, faith based, registered or licensed home), and the needs of the children enrolled (their ages and whether or not they have disabilities). Another factor contributing to variations in cost is whether the program is new or is offering additional services, thus incurring start-up costs. An ongoing program has only continuing, ordinary recurring costs. Geographic location, the amount of competition, development costs, and the general economy also contribute to the varying streams of revenue.

Varied Costs of Different Programs: The operating costs of different types of programs vary. Baseline tuition fees can be calculated by using an average rate, typically that of the full-time 3-year-old tuition. Many programs then increase the tuition for younger children and, in many cases, decrease weekly tuition for older children. State licensing regulations determine the number of children each employee can be responsible for. This is the staff-child ratio. It determines, to a large degree, the tuition that needs to be charged in order to meet budget obligations and for the program to achieve its goals. For full-time care, the fees for toddlers are typically from 12% to 18% higher than the costs for 3-year-olds, and the fees for infants can be expected to be 19% to 30% higher than the average full-time 3-year-old tuition rate. These percentages tend to be consistent from center to center and from state to state. Fees for before- and after-school programs for school-age children (SACC, school-age child care) are likely to be from 45% to 60% lower than the baseline 3-year-old rates. SACC fees, however, tend to vary dramatically from center to center; thus, the percentages are less helpful yardsticks. One reason for these differences is the addition of low-cost SACC on public school campuses and the attempts of child care providers to remain competitive in their pricing in order to protect the enrollment in their programs.

Directors should review their center's tuition rates annually to compare anticipated income with projected expenses. They may find they need to increase tuition between 2% and 8%. There is no escaping the fact that the cost of care is increasing and, in most cases, those increases have to be passed along to the families that have children enrolled in the program. Facilities in continuous use (e.g., preschool child care) are cost effective in comparison with facilities with downtime (e.g., half-day nursery schools, SACC programs). Many programs are able to schedule revenue-generating offerings, such as Mother's Morning Out, in the school-age space during school hours. Fully utilizing all available space in this way allows the facility to generate additional revenue in an otherwise empty space during that portion of the day.

Meeting the needs of children with disabilities is also expensive. Costs are a function of the type and degree of the individual child's needs and of the services being provided (e.g., transportation for children with physical disabilities is often more expensive than tutors for children identified as having learning disabilities). On the average, costs for centers that enroll children with disabilities are about 15% higher than those for centers that do not enroll these children (Powell, Eisenberg, Moy, & Vogel, 1994). However, the total costs per service hour is about 8% less for inclusive programs than for traditional special education programs (Odom, Wolery, Lieber, & Horn, 2002).

Program Quality and Costs: Researchers have also investigated the cost differential between high-quality versus minimal-quality programing. The definitive report of the Cost, Quality, and Child Outcomes Study Team (1995) estimated that the difference in market price for child care and the costs of going from minimal to quality services were

10% and from $4,940 to $5,434 per child year, respectively. This percentage assumes that 10% is spent on items related to quality enhancement.

The price that the child care market will bear, however, seems to remain low at the expense of program quality. Some of the reasons for the market's resistance to supporting quality programming include the following:

1. The government contributes to low-quality care when its agencies impose payments at *market rate* (i.e., subsidies are capped at levels determined by what families with average incomes are willing and able to pay) for child care services or fail to provide higher reimbursement for higher quality care. Generally speaking, government agencies use estimated costs to determine what they will pay for services and thus, to some degree, circularity results. In other words, because agencies pay a certain number of dollars, program designers plan their programs on the basis of expected amounts of money. If funded the first year, program designers write a similar program the next year in hopes of being re-funded. The agency pays approximately the same amount again, and the cycle continues. The program is thus designed around a specific dollar value whether or not it makes for the "best" program. What's more, it is difficult for owners or stockholders to approve budgets based on anticipated cash flow rather than historical financial information.

2. Personnel costs are the most expensive aspect of operating an early childhood program. Payroll expenses (employees' salaries and benefits) can be expected to range from 49% to 77% of the center's budget (SELF-HELP North Carolina Community Facilities Fund, 2002). It is important to remember that the auspices under which a program operates will influence how much of its resources will be devoted to personnel. A faith-based program housed in a church, for example, will have lower occupancy costs, freeing more resources to be devoted to payroll; a for-profit center will have higher occupancy costs and, therefore, limited funds available to support salaries and benefits.

Although the easiest way to make a program more affordable and to ensure profit/surplus is to decrease wages and increase the number of children per staff member, low wages and high staff-child ratios are associated with poor quality. Poorly paid employees are likely to be less qualified when they are hired and to have little incentive to increase their skills because there is likely to be no monetary rewards for doing so, and centers with low wages are likely to have higher rates of employee turnover. The converse is true, however. There is a positive relationship between program quality and budget allocations for teacher salaries and benefits; that is, programs that spent approximately two-thirds of their budgets on salaries and staff benefits tended to be of high quality, and quality diminished considerably in programs spending less than one-half of their budgets on salaries and staff benefits (Olenick, 1986). More recent research has supported the link between staff salary and program quality. In a comparison of nonprofit versus profit-generating child care programs, Sosinsky, Lord, and Zigler (2007) found that centers that paid higher wages tended to provide higher levels of quality care and education services.

The real earnings of child care teachers and family child care providers have decreased by nearly one-fourth since the mid-1970s (Bellm, Breuning, Lombardi, & Whitebook, 1992; Willer, 1992). The U.S. Bureau of Labor Statistics (2009) reported that in 2008 the median average hourly wage of child care workers, who bring varied educational backgrounds to their work, was $9.12. Hourly rates ranged from $7.75 to $11.30, typically with minimal benefits such as health insurance. Compare this to salaries earned by elementary school teachers with college degrees, who usually have generous benefits packages and a median hourly wage of $10.53. Salaries of center teachers in NAEYC-accredited programs are one-half those of public elementary school teachers. The gap widens as the years of experience increase (Powell et al., 1994).

3. Inadequate consumer knowledge on the part of families reduces incentives for centers to provide high-quality programs. Families should be helped to seek quality programs through additional education and informational publications. They also need to understand the full costs of quality programs and become advocates for subsidies that move program incomes closer to full costs. Programs need to offer information to their families on the benefits of high-quality programs, which can be shared at a family open-house or in a brochure that can be distributed during the enrollment interview process.

4. Directors also rely on volunteer help and in-kind donations of food, equipment, and supplies to help offset some of the costs of high-quality programs. Volunteer services and in-kind donations have been valued at about 3% of the full cost of operating the center. Donated occupancy (e.g., programs using facilities of religious organizations) reduces the full costs of center operations by about 6% (Cost, Quality, and Child Outcomes Study Team, 1995). As decisions are made to include volunteers in the program, it is critically important to verify what the state regulations require in order for volunteers to work directly with children and be counted in staff-children ratios (e.g., what are the requirements related to fingerprints, background checks, references).

Costs to Families

Programs primarily supported through user fees are expensive for families. Statistics cited at the beginning of this chapter describe the burden child care fees can be for many families, who are responsible for about 60% of all expenditures for child care. Federal, state, or local governments pay most of the remaining expenses (Stoney & Greenberg, 1996).

Because families living in poverty can sometimes have a portion or all their child care fees subsidized, their children are often as likely to be enrolled in high-quality early childhood programs as those children coming from high-socioeconomic families. Struggling families whose incomes are just above the poverty level are often priced out of quality programs, find themselves with few alternatives for the care of their children, and seek care in unlicensed and unregulated care. Subsidies that lower the price of child care often allow low-income parents to work. However, as their incomes rise, assistance with child care is decreased or cut off. Even if some assistance is available, the recent economic crisis has reduced states' investment in child care services. Not enough programs are available to serve families eligible for assistance. Furthermore, some child care programs are deciding not to participate in subsidy programs because of the lower-than-market reimbursement rates they pay or the cumbersome administrative processes that are required by many agencies. Besides income, other factors also preclude low-income families from higher quality programs, such as nonday shifts (41% of low-income mothers work these shifts) and residence in rural or low-income neighborhoods that do not have high-quality programs (Queralt & Witte, 1998; U.S. Bureau of the Census, 1997).

Costs to families differ for the following reasons:

1. Programs differ in costs because of the quality of services, geographic location, age of the children served, and the ability of the program to take advantage of economies of scale (i.e., serve more children or provide more hours of service than competing programs).

2. Even in programs that charge similar fees per child hour, the costs per family may vary because of different types of subsidies, including the following:

    a. Multi-child discounts.   About half of for-profit centers offer multi-child discounts; however, the fee discount varies greatly (Neugebauer, 1993).

    b. Fees subsidized by public funds.   Some programs provide care for children whose fees are subsidized through public funds. These government-funded subsidies are provided for children of low-income working families through the Child Care and Development Fund (CCDF) and Temporary Assistance to Needy Families (TANF). Rohacek and Russell (1998) found that the child care subsidy (a) can keep families from ever needing welfare, (b) can move families from welfare to work, (c) pays for itself in real dollars, and (d) helps develop the regulated child care system. They found that the best subsidy system gives more help to families with the lowest incomes—those with the greatest risk of returning to welfare.

c. **Tax credits and deductions**.   At both the state and federal levels, *tax credits* (taken against taxes owed) and *tax deductions* (amounts subtracted from income before computing taxes owed) reduce child care costs for eligible families who claim them. Families should determine their eligibility to claim the Dependent Care Tax Credit, Child Tax Credit, Earned Income Tax Credit, and the Dependent Care Assistance Program (DCAP). Because few eligible families claimed their tax credits, the National Women's Law Center (NWLC) launched the Child Care Tax Credits Outreach Campaign (NWLC, 2009). Both the National Women's Law Center and the National Center for Children in Poverty provide excellent information on taxes and child care; see Appendix 8 for their websites.

d. **Corporate/employer discounts**.   These subsidies can be substantial depending upon the contributions made by the employer toward child care tuition for its employees.

Although child care is expensive, not working can also be expensive because of a family's forgone income. The amount of forgone income when a family member provides child care services rather than obtaining outside employment is another expense that varies from family to family. The income is considered forgone when a family member provides child care services without payment. The amount of forgone income depends on the caregiver's employable skills and the availability of employment or on the caregiver's potential income. (Calculating forgone income also requires considering the cost of outside employment, such as transportation, clothing, organization or union dues, and higher taxes.)

Costs of Local Programs

Local program administrators often think of costs in terms of budget items, which are usually the operational program items used in cost-efficiency analysis. The following distinctions must be made in an analysis:

1. Start-up costs.   Start-up costs are the monies that must be available before a program is underway. These costs include monies for the building, equipment, and supplies; 3 months of planning; and, because most new programs under enroll during the first 6 months of operation and monies promised by external funding sources are often delayed, should also cover the first 6 months or longer of operation. Start-up costs will also include the labor costs prior to opening the program.

2. Fixed and variable costs.   Fixed costs (e.g., building rent and/or depreciation and property taxes) do not vary with the number of children served, but variable costs (e.g., building maintenance, food, teacher salaries, equipment, and materials costs) may.

3. Marginal costs.   Marginal costs are the increased cost "per unit" (total program costs divided by the number of recipients) of expanding a program beyond a given enrollment. Marginal costs may decrease to a given point and then increase when additional staff or facilities are required. By monitoring enrollment closely, decisions can be made quickly that allow a program to adjust its operating efficiencies to closely match the enrollment. This can be useful if the enrollment is either higher or lower than anticipated budgeted levels.

4. Capital versus operating costs.   Capital costs (e.g., building and in some instances furniture and equipment) are basically one-time costs, whereas operating costs (e.g., salaries, consumable materials) are recurrent. Building costs can also become monthly expenses depending on whether or not there is a mortgage or other financial obligation associated with the building.

5. Hidden costs.   Hidden costs are costs free to a program but paid by someone else (e.g., the donor of a facility). **Joint costs** are somewhat "hidden" too because they are shared costs (e.g., two separately funded programs that share a staff workroom or audio-visual equipment).

FINANCING EARLY CHILDHOOD PROGRAMS

The specific ways early childhood programs are paid for by families, the government, and corporations are referred to as **financing mechanisms**. The way the financing mechanism is administered (e.g., grants, contracts, loans, vouchers) is called an **administrative mechanism**. An administrative mechanism is governed by policy concerning the eligibility for and use of any funds (Brandon, Kagan, & Joesch, 2000). Although the majority of early childhood programs receive funds from families (e.g., fees, tuition, fund-raising, and donated goods and services), some programs are subsidized with funding from the government, philanthropic organizations, and corporations. These subsidies can be *direct* (i.e., paid directly to a given program, such as a grant) or *portable* (i.e., paid by users who had choices among programs enrolling children whose fees are subsidized—a child care voucher, for example).

Various regulations govern (a) a program's eligibility to receive revenue from a source such as the federal government, (b) procedures for obtaining revenue, (c) the use made of the revenue, and (d) which personnel are accountable for the expenditure. Because of the many types of programs and the intricacies and variations involved in funding, only a brief description of the sources of financing is given here.

Government Financing

Those who support public investments in quality programs of early care and education base their arguments on the current emphasis on school readiness, the popularization of brain development research, as well as efforts to ensure the success of economic development initiatives, and welfare-to-work reforms. These efforts have resulted in increased public support for early childhood programs. Federal, state, and local governments are earmarking monies from tax sources—sales, income, and other taxes—for government investments for child care. Although most states subsidize early childhood programs through general revenue dollars, some are funding them through "sin tax" revenues, such as taxes on alcohol sales and the gambling industry, or from tobacco settlement revenue. These taxes have been valuable in funding a variety of programs in a number of states. The problem is that revenue from many of these taxes have declined in recent years, and the funds child care providers receive have also decreased.

Government funding brings with it several ongoing concerns. Funds are not stable and fluctuate with changes in federal, state, and local governments' priorities. Lawmakers are forced to make difficult choices balancing many needs. Another concern is the bewildering array of funding agencies and assistance programs. No federal child care program exists, so the extent of federal involvement in early childhood programs is not easily determined. Along with the problem of dealing with the number of federal sources, a jumble of rulings from agencies results in different standards, programs are frequently deleted or added, and appropriations may fall below congressional authorizations. These changes can become confusing, and at times overwhelming, to child care administrators who find it difficult to stay informed.

A final concern has to do with the regulations that accompany funding, especially federal funding. Federal funds can be **categorical grants** (grants used for specified, narrowly defined purposes) or **general revenue sharing** (funds provided on a formula basis to state and local governments, with few or perhaps no restrictions on how the money is spent). The trend has been toward federal "deregulation." This middle ground is achieved through **block grants**, which provide federal aid to states for broadly defined activities. State or local groups can have greater discretion in designating programs to meet local needs. Recipients must comply with some federal regulations (e.g., fiscal reporting and nondiscrimination requirements). Monitoring changes in federal and state budgets is important so that as an operator of a program receiving funding from these sources you are aware of possible budget cuts and changes to funding levels. These changes can affect the ability of a program to adequately maintain its service level if there is no opportunity to revise budgets and modify the program's offerings.

Public School Financing of Kindergartens and Primary Programs: Public school programs are supported by local, state, and federal monies. Taxation is the major source of these monies; consequently, revenues for public school programs are closely tied to the general economy of the local area, the state, and the nation.

Local Support.   Tax funds, usually from real and personal property taxes, are used to maintain and operate schools; the sale of bonds is used for capital improvements and new construction expenses. According to the National Center for Education Statistics (1997), the richest districts spend 56% more per student than do the poorest. These low income neighborhoods often have less qualified teachers, fewer resources, and more distressed housing. In some cases, local school districts are making decisions that affect the class-size, quality of teachers, and program quality to meet budgetary mandates. The local school board's authority to set tax rates and to issue bonds for school revenue purposes is granted by the state; that is, it is established by statutes and regulations. When granted the power to tax, the local school board must follow state laws concerning tax rates and procedural matters in an exacting manner. In this way, the state protects the public from the misuse and mismanagement of public monies.

State Support.   The amount of state support for public schools varies widely from state to state. Almost every state takes steps to equalize the tax burden and educational opportunities among school districts. Generally, programs to equalize school funding begin with a definition of minimum standards of educational services that must be offered throughout the state. The cost of maintaining the standards is calculated and the rate of taxation prescribed. The tax rate may be uniform or based on an economic index reflecting the ability of a local school district to pay. If local taxes do not cover the cost of maintaining minimum standards, the balance of the costs is provided via state monies. States vary considerably in the machinery they use for channeling state monies to local school districts, with the most common plans being flat and equalization grants. Beginning in about 2000, the issue of equalizing funding among school districts within a state has resulted in a rash of school finance litigation. In a number of states, legislators have taken steps to effectively equalize the funding among school districts. The results are varied, but many legislators continue to make recommendations in this direction.

Many public and private schools have also found that entering into the after-school program market is a way to generate additional revenue for a particular school district. These programs often compete with local licensed programs for school-age children offered by child care providers. Programs in the public schools are not always required to meet the same health and safety licensing standards required of licensed child care providers, which causes concern among licensed providers in the community.

Federal Support.   Since the 1940s, the federal government has become the country's chief tax collector. Until recently, the trend had been toward unprecedented expenditures for education. Consequently, public schools (as well as other institutions, agencies, and organizations) relied more and more on federal assistance programs to supplement their local and state resources. Federal funding of public schools is used for two purposes: (a) to improve the quality of education (e.g., research, experimentation, training, housing, and equipment) and (b) to encourage greater effort by state and local districts to improve the quality of education by providing initial or matching funds for a program. Federal expenditures in education declined because of reductions in the types of programs funded or the amount of funds available in retained programs. However, the No Child Left Behind Act of 2001 (NCLB), signed into law on January 8, 2002, is a major reform of the Elementary and Secondary Education Act (ESEA) and redefines the federal role in K–12 education. Changes to the accountability measures built into NCLB have been proposed, but as of this writing, amendments to this bill have not been finalized.

State Financing of Prekindergarten Programs: Beyond their commitment to financing kindergarten and primary-grade programs in public schools, many states have committed to support additional early childhood programs, particularly those serving 3- and 4-year-olds. One explanation for states' increased involvement in early education, beginning in the late 1990s, is the passage of welfare reform legislation, the Personal Responsibility and Work Opportunity Act of 1996, which encouraged mothers to work or to pursue training or additional education.

Forty states now support services for 4-year-olds, but "relatively few states make significant efforts to serve children at age 3" (Barnett et al., 2010, p. 7). The National Institute for Early Education Research (NIEER) has been tracking enrollment, state spending, and quality of programs for 3- and 4-year-olds since 2002. NIEER's 2010 report showed that the number of 3- and 4-year-olds in state-supported pre-K has increased every year since it has been keeping records. From 2002 to 2010, the number of 3-year-olds served inched up from 3% to 4%, while the percentage of 4-year-olds climbed from 14% to 27%. Even with these increased numbers of children served, efforts to serve all children in quality programming suffered setbacks as a result of the economic downturn of 2008. In the 2009–2010 school year, 19 of the 40 states with pre-K programs reduced state funding. Even with an infusion of funds from the American Recovery and Reinvestment Act of 2009 (ARRA; sometimes called the *Stimulus Bill*), spending per child decreased by $114 (Barnett et al., 2010).

NIEER used 10 criteria to evaluate the quality of state programs serving 3- and 4-year-olds: (a) teacher has a bachelor's degree; (b) teacher has specialized training in early childhood education; (c) assistant has a CDA or higher; (d) teachers participate in at least 15 hours of in-service training each year; (e) programs address their state's early learning standards; (f) classes have 20 or fewer children; (g) staff-child ratio is 1:10 or better; (h) the program offers systematic screening and referral for hearing, vision, and so on; (i) the program serves at least one meal during the school day; and (j) regulators make regular site visits to monitor quality. Using that metric, quality has gradually increased from 2002 to 2010, with 25 states meeting seven or more benchmarks in the 2009–2010 program year, and most states meeting at least five (Barnett et al., 2010).

Although many states have made a commitment to support early childhood programs, the support is far from adequate. The amount of commitment varies widely across the nation and even between neighboring states, many states with high rates of poverty do not draw down all available federal funds, a state's wealth is not associated with its commitment to early childhood education, and early childhood programs are not high on the list of priorities to receive state funds (Adams & Poersch, 1997). The cost per child in state-sponsored early childhood programs varies considerably, too. Sandham (2002) reported that the variables that determine the cost are (a) the maximum income level at which a family is eligible, (b) the age at which a child is eligible, (c) the relationship between the family's income and the level of the subsidy, and (d) teacher salaries and qualifications.

States are attempting to tie financing with the quality of programs. For example, 4% of a state's allocation under the CCDF block grant and 25% of all new Head Start dollars must be spent on initiatives to enhance quality (Child Care and Development Fund Report of State and Territory Plans FY 2010–2011). All 50 states currently regulate the qualifications for teachers in child care settings, and 17 states require a higher level of qualifications for a lead/master teacher role. All 50 states also regulate the qualifications for center administrators or directors (NCCIC/NARA, 2010).

Federal Financing: In addition to providing some federal fiscal support to certain programs, such as the public schools, the federal government remains the primary source of support for some comprehensive early childhood programs. The federal government pays for early childhood services in two ways:

1. **Contracts and grants.**   Monies from contracts and grants flow directly to the programs. The funds are awarded based on a specific service to be provided and a given number of recipients or a targeted level of enrollment. Government agencies typically negotiate contract rates with a specific provider or group of providers. Rates are based on the amount of money that is available to purchase care and an assessment of the cost of providing the service (i.e., cash costs incurred in running the program).

2. **Vouchers.**   A voucher is a payment mechanism whereby funds are given to the family rather than the program and follow the child to the family-selected program. Vouchers include both purchase-of-service systems and cash payments. Voucher systems base reimbursement on the market rate.

The modern era of federal support for early childhood care and education began with Head Start in 1965. Other programs soon followed. Federal funding, targeted primarily to low-income families and including programs for young children, continued to grow until 1977. Although overall federal support declined from 1977 to 1988, support for early childhood programs (e.g., Head Start) remained rather constant in dollar amounts until recently; in actuality, however, federal support declined because the number of children living in poverty increased (Einbinder & Bond, 1992) and inflation took its toll on the value of the dollar.

Federal Assistance Programs.   Throughout the modern era of federal financing, the purpose of most federal assistance programs has been to accomplish particular educational objectives or to meet the needs of specific groups. Most federal assistance programs (a) require early childhood programs to meet specified standards; (b) give priority or restrict services to certain client groups; (c) require state or local support in varying amounts; and (d) specify funds to be used for certain purposes (e.g., food, program supplies), which in turn curtails programs' flexibility. Some of the major federal assistance programs, whose total funds dwarf state financing, include Head Start and Early Head Start, CCDF, TANF, Early Learning Opportunities Act, Children's Day Care Health and Improvement Act, Individuals with Disabilities Education Act (IDEA), and various food programs. The NCLB Act of 2001 is a $19 billion investment. Seven of the 10 title programs under the NCLB are described as follows:

1. **Title I—Improving the Academic Achievement of the Disadvantaged.**   The stated purpose of Title I is to ensure that all children have fair, equal, and significant opportunity to obtain a high-quality education and reach a minimum proficiency level on challenging state academic standards and assessments.

2. **Title II—Preparing, Training, and Recruiting High-Quality Teachers and Principals.**   The purpose of Title II is to fund professional development designed to impact students' achievement.

3. **Title III—Language Instruction for Limited English Proficient and Immigrant Students.**   The purpose of Title III is to help students attain English language proficiency to meet the challenges of Title I.

4. **Title IV—21st Century Schools.**   Title IV funds programs to prevent school violence and to foster drug-free environments. Title IV also funds the creation of Community Learning Centers (before- and after-school opportunities) to complement the school academic program.

5. **Title V—Promoting Informed Parental Choice and Innovative Programs.**   Title V includes educational block grants, charter schools, magnet schools, and funds for the improvement of education in local areas.

6. **Title VI—Flexibility and Accountability.**   Title VI funds are designed to enhance state and local assessment systems and to improve the dissemination of information on student achievement and school performance to families and community members.

7. **Title VII—Indian, Native Hawaiian, and Alaska Native Education.**   Title VII authorizes expenditures to meet the unique educational needs (e.g., language) of these groups.

Obtaining Federal Assistance.   Federal funding sources are constantly changing. The latest edition of the *Catalog of Federal Domestic Assistance* describes the federal agencies administering various assistance programs and the projects and services funded under these agencies. (See the Useful Websites section at the end of this chapter to help you begin the search for federal funding.)

Securing Federal Funds

Most federal funds are obtained by writing and submitting a grant proposal and having the proposal approved and funded. If your program decides to pursue federal funding opportunities, it is best if one person on the staff oversees the entire writing of the proposal, although input should be obtained from all those involved in the program. In fact, early childhood programs that plan to seek regular federal assistance may find it advantageous to hire a staff member with expertise in the area of obtaining federal as well as other funds, such as foundation grants, that require proposal writing. Proposal writing can vary according to an assistance program's particular requirements, but most use a similar format.

Certain terminology is used in obtaining federal funds and must be understood by those involved in locating appropriate grants and writing proposals. The following terms are frequently used:

1. **Assets.**   The amount of money, stocks, bonds, real estate, or other holdings of an individual or organization.

2. **Endowment.**   Funds intended to be kept permanently and invested to provide income to support a program.

3. **Financial report.**   A report detailing how funds were used (e.g., a listing of income and expenses, also referred to as a profit and loss statement or P&L).

4. **Grant.**   A monetary award given a program. Grants are of several types:

   a. **Bricks and mortar act**.   An informal term for grants for building or construction projects.

   b. **Capital support**.   Funds for buildings (construction or renovation) and equipment.

   c. **Declining grant**.   A multiyear grant that grows smaller each year with the expectation that the recipient can raise other funds to make up the difference.

    d. General-purpose grant. A grant made to further all of the work of the program, as opposed to assisting a specific purpose.

    e. Matching grant. A grant with matching funds provided by another donor.

    f. Operating-support grant. A grant to cover day-to-day expenses (e.g., salaries).

    g. Seed grant or **seed money.** A grant or contribution used to start a new project.

5. **Grassroots fund-raising.** An effort to raise money on a local basis (e.g., raffles, bake sales, auctions).

6. **In-kind contribution.** A contribution of time, space, equipment, or materials in lieu of a monetary contribution.

7. **Proposal.** A written application for a grant.

Proposal Planning

Proposal planning is, in essence, research. As is the case with any research, the first step is to identify the problem you want to solve. What is needed? If the assistance program you are pursuing sends out a request for proposals (RFP), the need is already defined in broad or general terms. When you identify the funding source you plan to pursue, it is important to understand the proposed project before you begin developing the proposal.

The second step in developing a proposal is describing the population, or potential population, served. You also need to demonstrate how critical or extensive the need is and present evidence that the proposed program would not duplicate existing services. Most proposals require that the needs be described in terms of the racial and ethnic makeup; geographic distribution; adults' educational attainment; and socioeconomic status, including levels of unemployment, school children's eligibility for free or reduced-price lunch; and a description of similar services available in your community.

Because proposals often have to be written quickly, often in as little as 2 to 4 weeks, we advise that you keep a notebook or computer file with current data or where to find it. These are some sources for data that will help you develop a comprehensive needs statement:

- Local community action associations and United Way agencies
- State or local Child Care Resource and Referral (CCR&R) agencies
- Department of Health and Human Services (local and state) and federal publications (found in the *Monthly Catalog of U.S. Government Publications*)
- U.S. Department of Commerce, Bureau of the Census
- U.S. Department of Labor, Bureau of Labor Statistics
- U.S. Department of Labor, Employment and Training Administration
- Kids Count published by the Annie E. Casey Foundation

Proposals also require a review of the literature that shows how others have addressed the problems you have identified and must demonstrate that the proposed project will not duplicate services in a local area.

The final step in writing the proposal is preparing a two- or three-page proposal prospectus. The prospectus should contain a statement of the problem, how you intend to address the problem, the target group to be served, the number of people to be served, and why the proposed early childhood program is needed. Developing the prospectus will help you clarify your thinking. It will also give you the opportunity to get feedback on your work, including the funding agency's reviewers. Some federal agencies require that a prospectus be submitted before they will accept a complete proposal.

Writing the Proposal

Federal agencies have their own guidelines for writing a proposal; they differ from agency to agency, and the guidelines should be followed exactly. Take the time to read each RFP carefully several times to become familiar with any particular nuances of the proposal that need to be addressed during the writing phase. Most agencies require proposals to follow this outline:

1. **Title page.** Title of project; name of agency submitting application; name of funding agency; dates of project; and names, addresses, and signatures of the project director and others involved in the fiscal management of the project.

2. **Statement of problem.** General and specific objectives, documentation of the needs and degree of each need, review of literature of programs that have tried to meet the specified needs, and description of any local programs currently involved in meeting specified needs. It is advisable to include as much information as possible, so that no questions are left unanswered.

3. **Program goals and objectives.** Description of broad program goals and specific, measurable outcomes expected as a result of the program.

4. **Population to be served.** What qualifications will children and families need for inclusion in the program? Will all who qualify be accepted? If not, how will the participants be chosen from those who qualify? The response needs to be inclusive and offer access to a diverse group of participants.

5. **Plan or procedure.** Were several alternative approaches available for solving the problem? If so, why was a particular alternative selected? How will each objective be accomplished?

6. **Administration of project.** What staffing requirements are being proposed? How will the program be managed? What is the program's capability to conduct the proposed project? Does the program have community support? Show a timeline of activities describing which activities will occur from the day of funding until project termination. A timeline can be developed using a project management software program. These elements of the proposal give the program officer a clear understanding of the timeline and commitments that have been established by the program's administration.

7. **Program evaluation.** What assessment tools will be used? Who will conduct the assessment? How and in what format will the evaluation be submitted? How frequently will program assessment be done, and how will the results be distributed?

8. **Future funding.** How will the operation of the program be sustained at the conclusion of federal assistance?

9. **Budget.** The budget must show sound fiscal management and evidence of decision-making authority that accurately and soundly meets the goals and objectives of the program's fiscal plan.

10. **Appendices.** These include job descriptions, director's résumé, organizational structure of the early childhood program, and other materials that provide needed details.

Some agencies also require completion of an application form that usually asks for information about the general subject; to whom the proposal is being submitted; the project title; the name of the person submitting the proposal; the program director's name, address, telephone number, and email address; the projected budget; the amount of funds requested; and the date the application is transmitted. Some agencies have a form for a 200-word proposal abstract. There are also forms assuring protection of human subjects and nondiscrimination.

Foundation Support

Many fields, including education, have benefited from philanthropic organizations such as foundations, trusts, and endowments. They are nongovernmental, not-for-profit organizations that promote public welfare, including initiatives targeting young children, through the use of private wealth. They are typically operated under a federal or state charter and administered by trustees. Foundations typically fund research, but they sometimes provide other kinds of support. The recent economic downturn has reduced funds available to some foundations, but others continue to prosper and to support worthy proposals. Foundations are required by their individual mission statements to offer funding to programs that address their specific goals. Large foundations often have many goals that are apt to change periodically. Smaller foundations are often limited to specific goals or specific geographic areas. A local philanthropic organization may be a good source of support to investigate as a potential provider of funds.

Similar to federal funds, foundation funds are obtained through the submission and approval of a proposal. The foundation's board of directors determines the guidelines for submitting proposals, sets a deadline for applications, reviews proposals, and selects recipients.

Employer Assistance

Employers sometimes provide their employees with child care assistance. Employer assistance can take some of the following forms:

1. Employers may contract with individual vendors to create a discount rate for specific programs.
2. Employers may subsidize child care costs by providing vouchers to employees.
3. Employees may receive assistance through a Dependent Care Assistance Plan (DCAP). DCAPs enable employees to use pretax dollars to purchase dependent care services if they are offered through a flexible benefit program (i.e., employers offer a choice of benefits from which employees choose). The federal Internal Revenue Code allows employers who have established a DCAP to exclude up to $5,000 of child care benefits per employee from federal and often state income taxes, FICA, and unemployment taxes. Benefits may come as cash, a voucher, or free or subsidized care in a child care facility. Usually the DCAP is a salary reduction that is returned to the employees as a reimbursement for child care expenses. (Any money *not* used for child care is *not* returned to the employee.) In short, a DCAP makes child care a nontaxable benefit. As such, salary reduction under a DCAP is more beneficial to higher income employees. For DCAPs to be beneficial for lower income employees, employers need to match the amount subtracted from the employee's salary or provide child care vouchers. Administrative costs of DCAPs are paid by employers.

Fees, Tuition, and Miscellaneous Sources of Funds

For-profit programs operate almost exclusively on tuition and fees. They are usually the most expensive child care option. Families that must pay more than 10% of their gross income for one or more children may need and qualify for subsidies. Directors should be prepared with a list of agencies that provide subsidies and provide the list to families that inquire about assistance in paying their child care expenses. Directors should also inform families about how to apply for tax credits.

Although child care is costly, for-profit independent centers do not make substantial profits. Financial problems are often the result of overestimating income from fees and tuition during the budgeting process prior to the beginning of a new fiscal year. Optimal fees and tuition for early childhood programs may be determined in several ways. One method is to determine costs and the amount of profit (or surplus) needed. The cost is then distributed among the children on a fixed fee, a sliding scale fee, or two fixed fees for different income brackets. Because the budget is often developed based on the program's capacity, and programs are not usually fully enrolled for the entire fiscal year, the tendency is to

Collecting tuition fee payments from families is essential for program survival.

overestimate income from fees. Budgets should allow for a 5% to 10% vacancy rate. The administrator may also compensate by using Morgan's (1999) method of calculating the previous year's **utilization rate** (i.e., divide the previous year's actual income by the maximum potential income from fees). A well-run center operates at a 95% or greater utilization rate; thus, the utilization rate is a good estimate even if fees are increased. A more accurate **break-even analysis** (a managerial tool that identifies the point at which a program generates enough revenue to cover expenses) is also explained in detail by Morgan (1999). Essentially, this is done by accounting for all of a program's annual expenditures, then identifying what level of income is necessary to meet these expenses. A director should use the break-even point to evaluate the impact of various changes, such as enrollment trends and the need to either raise or lower tuition. During this process it is important that the program administrator carefully consider any and all changes to the demographics of the community, competitive tuition rates from other programs within a 3- to 5-mile radius, and economic conditions on the state and federal fronts.

Application Activity

1. Based on your current enrollment and staffing patterns, how much would you have to raise individual children's tuition to provide all staff members with a 3% wage increase?

2. Using the same staffing and enrollment figures, how much would you have to increase tuition to compensate teachers with a salary comparable to early chidlhood public school teachers in your area? Be sure to use salaries for teachers with similar education and experience. Local school districts' websites may give specific data on wages and qualifications to use as a reference.

Use the following method to calculate the tuition increase needed to cover a proposed increase in employees' hourly pay:

1. Count the number of staff members who are eligible to receive an increase to their hourly wage.

2. Calculate the average hourly wage for these employees and apply the 3% increase to that total.

3. Calculate the total number of hours worked by all employees in a week. Multiply that number by 52 weeks in the year. That is the total annual cost of the proposed 3% increase in wages.

(Continued)

4. Divide the total cost of the wage increase (from item 3) by the number of children enrolled in the center to figure out how much more each child needs to pay each year to cover this wage increase. Divide that annual cost per child by 52 to determine how much you need to increase weekly tuition to cover this wage increase.

For example:

1. Let's say you have 20 staff members, 15 of whom work full time (40 hours per week) and 5 work part time (25 hours per week).

2. Determine the average hourly wage by totaling all employees' hourly wages and dividing that number by 20 (the total number of staff). *In this example, the average hourly rate is $12.00.* Multiply that average hourly rate by 0.03 (3%) to determine the amount of the proposed raise. *In this example, $12.00 × 0.03 = $0.36.* Add the amount of the proposed raise to the current average hourly wage to determine the proposed new average hourly wage. *In this example, $12.00 + 0.36 = $12.36.*

3. Multiply the total hours worked by all employees per week by the proposed $0.36 per hour increase in workers' hourly wages. *In this example, that is (15 × 40) + (5 × 25) = 600 + 125 = 725 hours/week × $0.36 wage increase = $261.00 wage increase per week.* Multiply that weekly cost by 52 weeks in a year to determine the annual cost of this wage increase. *In this example, $261.00 × 52 weeks = $13,572 annual cost of this wage increase.*

4. Assume that 150 children are enrolled in the center. Divide the annual cost of the wage increase by the number of children enrolled. *In this example, dividing the annual cost of the wage increase ($13,572) by 150 children = $90.48 additional tuition per year per child to cover this wage increase.* Divide that annual cost per child by 52 to determine how much you need to increase weekly tuition to cover this wage increase. *In this example, dividing $90.48 by 52 weeks = $1.74. That means you would need to increase tuition almost $2.00 per week to cover this $0.36 per hour wage increase.*

In addition to carefully calculating fees and tuition, an early childhood program must have definite policies that address the payment of fees. The center may lose income because of absenteeism or when children withdraw. Consider these suggestions as you establish payment policies:

1. Set an administrative fee that is charged when each child is enrolled and annually thereafter. This fee should be budgeted for and charged the same week each year so that families can plan ahead.

2. Families planning to withdraw a child should be required to give several weeks' (often 2 weeks) notice. The family should be billed for 2 or 3 weeks of care if notice to withdraw is not given in advance. Programs sometimes require that 2 weeks' tuition be paid in advance, to be credited when children age-out of the program. This deposit can be tapped to pay this withdrawal fee if advanced notice is not given.

3. Children on the waiting list must be enrolled within a stated period of time (1 or 2 weeks) after being notified that there is a place for them or their space will be forfeited. Contact all families on the waiting list regularly to determine if they are still interested in enrolling in your program. Many administrators forget to plan for vacations, part-time schedules, and flexible work schedules when enrolling children and inadvertently create waiting lists when spaces are actually available to enroll new families.

4. Payments must be made on time. A policy that assesses fees for late payments should be in place and must be administered equitably. Many programs allow families to pay weekly fees one day late, with late payment fees charged on the second day past due. It can be tempting to waive the late payment fees, but this practice reduces revenue that has been budgeted for in the fiscal plan.

5. When a child is absent for an extended period of time due to illness or vacation, it is in the best interest of the program to charge tuition for that enrollment slot. If the family wishes to withdraw the child during an extended absence, the administrator must explain that the slot may be given to a family on the waiting list, and that an additional registration fee may be necessary to re-enroll the child when returning to the program.

Although many programs are fully supported by tuition and fees, operating funds can come from other sources, including the following:

1. Public support via a community campaign can help make up the difference between the program's anticipated income and its expenses. For example, some programs qualify for United Way funds (which may be called by another name in your community). Specific eligibility requirements must be met to qualify for such local funds.

2. In-kind contributions are often available through community resources, such as a charitable organization.

3. Donations may be given in someone's memory, in honor of a special event, or scholarships may be awarded to families with a particular need (loss of employment, illness in the family, etc).

4. The early childhood program may engage in fund-raising projects, such as a community bake sale, or may contract with a vendor (such as a photographer) to sell goods or services to families with a portion of the profits coming back to the program. You should conduct a cost-benefit analysis before launching a fund-raiser. Yields of $10 to $25 per hour after expenses are of marginal value, but yields of more than $25 per hour are probably worthwhile. It is also important to review the state licensing and municipal regulatory requirements that might have specific requirements for fund-raising activities. These regulations might stipulate fingerprinting, background checks, and permitting of ancillary staff who help with the fundraising activity or volunteers who may also be assisting with the event. These clearances are especially important if there is an outside vendor who will be in close proximity to any of the children. Remember, it is essential that you ensure that children are supervised by an employee of the program at all times. Children should not be left alone with volunteers, vendors, or others not directly employed by the program.

It is also important to weigh fund-raising choices against the policies and philosophy of the program to ensure compatibility with nutrition and diversity objectives. For example, it would not be appropriate to sell cookie dough in a program that promotes healthy nutrition habits and does not include cookies as part of its meal plan.

BUDGETING

A **budget** is a list of all goods and services that the program must pay for. The budget is an annual plan for the financial success of the child care program. The budget must properly allocate both income and expenses to ensure desired results for all stakeholders. Budgets are important because no matter how good a program is, it cannot continue to operate if it is not on a sound fiscal foundation. Limited funds require administrators to make decisions about priorities, and most funding and regulatory agencies require information about monetary functions.

Regulations Governing Budget Making and Adoption

Budgets of small, privately owned programs are developed by their owners/directors and are not subject to regulations unless the program receives some subsidies from public funds. Budgets of larger private, franchised, and publicly funded programs are usually developed by local program directors, with the assistance of the senior management team or the superintendent of schools for public school programs. Efforts are usually made to include the opinions of various personnel in the first draft of the proposed budget. However, in some of these large programs, such as a corporate chain or community action association, the budget may be created at the level of the larger organization, and the director only monitors expenditures and submits financial reports. Budgets of larger private and publicly funded programs are subject to many budgetary regulations. Once created, the budgets are presented to the respective boards of directors or advisors for approval. In addition to requiring the board's approval, regulations may require that the budget be presented to licensing or funding agency personnel before approval. In publicly funded programs, funds and thus fiscal control may come from several governmental agencies that will be involved before the adoption process ends.

Developing a Budget

The budget serves as a financial plan for a given period of time. The budget is typically planned to coincide with the fiscal year that has already been determined by the board of directors or senior management. A fiscal year can follow a traditional calendar year, beginning on January 1, and ending on December 31, but it can begin at another time. Budgets are typically divided into 12 accounting periods. Budgets itemize income (revenues) and expenses (expenditures). Directors often prepare several types of budgets and can also expect to prepare several versions of the budget as the process proceeds to completion.

Types of Budgets: Directors of early childhood programs often work with two types of budgets. A budget projection and start-up budget are used in the beginning of the budgeting process. Operating budgets are used after a program is underway.

Budget Projections and Start-Up Budgets.   A **budget projection** (also called a *pro forma budget*) projects how the operation of a business will turn out based on certain assumptions. Loans from banks or start-up grants often require the submission of a financial plan. Although a *financial plan* includes a description of the program, a management summary, and many supporting documents (e.g., licensing status, insurance coverage, tax status, contracts, revenue projections), the major aspect is the financial data. Financial data will include a projected start-up budget, funding requests and repayment plans if applicable, a break-even analysis, a projected monthly cash flow for a year, and a projected timetable for self-sufficiency.

A **start-up budget** includes all the income and expenses incurred in starting a program. Morgan (1999) listed these categories of items in a start-up budget: (a) the capital cost of land, building, and equipment; (b) personnel costs for planning and implementing the program; and (c) *lag costs* (costs between the time one provides the service and gets paid). Other start-up expenditures may include training, meetings, publicity, and loan repayments. Start-up budgets vary depending on whether one initiates a completely new program or buys a currently operating program. Morgan put dollar amounts to categories of start-up expenses.

Operating Budget.   An **operating budget** includes items on which money will be spent once a program is operating near its planned capacity. The operating budget includes all the income and expenses for one calendar year (January 1 through December 31) or for one fiscal year. Operating budgets usually have three components: (a) a synopsis of the program; (b) specifically itemized expenditures for operating the program, including direct costs (items attributed to a particular aspect of the program, such as personnel salaries) and indirect costs (overhead items not attributed to a particular aspect of the program, such as interest on bank loans, utility costs, and advertising); and (c) anticipated revenues and their sources, including in-kind contributions. A program director commonly hears the terms *controllable expenses* and *fixed costs*. The controllable expenses are those that can be controlled directly or indirectly by the program director, for example, food costs, janitorial and maintenance costs, and office supplies. The fixed costs are typically established for a longer period of time and include rent, loan depreciation, and insurance costs. Before writing the budget, the administrator should list the program's objectives and needs, which are related and reflected in the written budget.

Budget Formats: Proposed revenues and expenditures must be presented in an effective way. Budgets are organized by headings, determined either by the funding agency or the local program. The headings are referred to as the **budget format**. There are two types of formats:

1. Functional classification.   This format assembles data in terms of categories for which money will be used, such as administration, services to children, family education, food and health services, and transportation. The advantage of the functional classification format is that one can readily link expenditure categories to program purposes. One disadvantage to this approach is that functional categories tend to be somewhat broad and thus raise questions regarding the expenditures within them. Another disadvantage is the lack of distinct classifications for some items; for example, subscriptions to professional journals may be listed under professional development or instructional supplies.

2. Line-item classification.   This format lists the sums allocated to specific aspects of the program (e.g., salaries of designated personnel, fuel for the vehicles, utilities including both electricity and water, telephone, postage). The major advantage of this approach is that it shows specific accountability for expenditures. This approach can be disadvantageous if the categories are narrow because the director has little power to make changes in expenditures.

Many computer-assisted finance programs are available for use in preparing budgets and in performing and recording financial transactions. These may have to be adapted to fit specific programs' needs.

Writing the Budget: The first step in writing a budget is to create an estimate of income or receipts. This section should clearly indicate expected monies from specified services, such as tuition, fees, contributions, and fund-raising projects. Morgan (1999) offered excellent examples of how to maximize a program's income by balancing children who attend full time and part time, monitoring enrollment and attendance, having waiting lists, and determining fees and collecting them. For purposes of income calculations, in-kind donations should be included only when the goods or services would have had to be purchased if they were not donated. (Some programs, such as Head Start, however, must recognize nonessential donations.)

The next step is to estimate costs. Estimated costs given as percentages of the total operating budget are as follows:

- Payroll—49% to 77%
- Occupancy costs (rent, mortgage, taxes, etc.)—6% to 23%

- Food—5% to 16%
- Educational equipment and materials—3%
- Insurance—2%
- Telephone, utilities, office supplies, maintenance and repairs, and health and social services—14%
- Supplementary services (screening/referral for children; family education and support)—3% (Powell et al., 1994; SELF-HELP North Carolina Community Facilities Fund, 2002)

Of the total operating budget for salaries, which may vary from 49% to 77% of the total budget in child care programs, 74% is for instructional staff, 13% is for noninstructional staff, and 13% is for benefits for all employees (Hayes, Palmer, & Zaslow, 1990). As shown, salaries account for the major part of the budget. In reality, for-profit centers making the most profits spend a lower percentage of their revenues on salaries (53.7%) than do centers making the least profits (62.4%; Stephens, 1991). Yet, as previously discussed, the quality of programs and salaries are highly correlated. Income must increase dramatically to provide the recommended level of compensation for early childhood professionals. For a quick estimate of operating costs, begin by considering salaries at least equal to 50% of the budget. The full cost per child is then calculated by this formula:

$$\text{Full cost per child} = \frac{\text{Teacher's annual salary}}{\text{\# of children in the group}} \times 2$$

After completing the expenditure section, the administrators should furnish actual figures for the current fiscal year. Any significant difference between current services and expenditures and those proposed should be explained. In planning the expenditure section, directors should keep the following points in mind:

1. Wages or salaries must be paid on time.
2. A desirable financial reserve is one that will carry a program through 3 months of operation.
3. A program may have cash flow problems. Federal funds do not pay ahead of time for expenses; receipts and proof of money spent are required for reimbursement, and even reimbursement checks may come irregularly.

To prevent cash flow problems, the director should observe the following practices:

1. Initial enrollment should not be overestimated.
2. Equipment estimates should be calculated on cost per use rather than on the purchase price. For example, it is more expensive to spend $100 on equipment and then not use it than it is to spend $500 on equipment that will be in constant use.
3. The number of staff hired should correspond to initial enrollment projections.
4. Enrollment variations—for example, a summer or spring-break dip in enrollment—should be expected and bugeted for.
5. The director should check with the governmental agency for its reimbursement schedule, which may be 6 months or longer, and then determine whether the local bank will give credit or a short-term loan to state or federally funded centers that receive governmental reimbursements.
6. Income should be credited when it is earned and expenses should be debited when they are incurred. This system, called *accrual accounting*, provides the most accurate picture of a center's financial standing.

A budget may be written in many ways, with only one absolute rule of budget formulation: Planned expenditures cannot exceed projected income. An example of a monthly budget is given in Figure 7.1.

Tuition (all age groups)	58,000
Hourly or Drop-in Care	900
Registration Fees	1,500
Absent Discounts (–)	2,200
Employee Discounts (–)	1,000
Promotional Discounts (–)	500
Subsidy Discounts (–)	4,000
Other Discounts (–)	700
NET REVENUE	52,000
Ancillary Income	500
Ancillary Expense (–)	210
NET ANCILLARY	290
Salaries & Wages	19,720
Bonus	350
Paid Time Off	2,000
Other Personnel Costs	400
TOTAL PERSONNEL COST	22,470
Food & Kitchen Supplies	2,040
Kitchen Supplies (Nonfood)	800
Educational Supplies	400
Parent Communications/Marketing	150
Miscellaneous	75
Office Supplies	200
Maintenance Consumables	150
Vehicle	750
Telephone & Utilities	700
TOTAL OTHER CENTER COSTS	5,265
CONTRIBUTION TO FIXED	24,555
Building Rent	8,000
Capital Charge	0
Property & Other Taxes	1,500
Depreciation & Amortization	0
Vehicle Lease	500
Maintenance Contracts (lawn care, etc.)	700
Insurance	2,000
TOTAL FIXED EXPENSE	12,700
CENTER OPERATING PROFIT	11,855
Center Overhead	0
Marketing	1,000
Other Overhead	750
TOTAL OVERHEAD	1,750
Debit	10,105

Figure 7.1
Budget Example—One Month

Reporting the Budget

Directors are required to give budget reports, which can take various forms: (a) a *budget comparison report,* in which one compares the previous month to the current month in each category; (b) an *annual report,* which lists the amount budgeted and the amount spent during the calendar or fiscal year; and (c) a *statement of financial position,* which reflects revenues earned and expenses incurred for a calendar or fiscal year.

To prepare reports accurately, all financial transactions should be recorded immediately. A checking account is the safest way to handle financial transactions and provides an audit trail. Directors in nonprofit programs need to be aware of the financial accounting standards required for their organizations; they can usually be found in the IRS Form 1023 related to the 501(c)(3) status of the program.

The director also needs to react to financial trends in a timely manner. Each week, the director should have the ability to review revenue that was generated and the expenses that were incurred during that week. Comparisons to the budget should be made and adjustments to expenditures, such as staff salaries, food costs, and so on, should follow. A noticeable reduction in the tuition charged should be reflected in the actual expenditures.

It is also necessary for the director to "flex" the budgeted expenses to the actual enrollment during these financial reviews. If an unplanned reduction in revenue occurs, expenses must then be reduced to follow that trend (e.g., if the program is running at 80% of its budgeted revenue and the food costs are budgeted at $5,000 for the month, the director needs to reduce the budgeted food costs by 20% to match the current enrollment). This is an example of flexing the expenses to meet the revenue trends. On the other hand, if the program is seeing higher than expected revenue and the occupancy of the center exceeds data included in the budget, some of the expenses can increase to adequately serve the children in care (e.g., if the revenue is 110% of the budgeted amount, the $5,000 budgeted food costs may not be enough to purchase adequate food products to serve the children in care; an increase to the food costs of 10% would be in line if approved by the appropriate stakeholders).

A Better Way

Marie knows that it is important to closely manage the expenses in her child care center. Stakeholders request reports related to any variances in the budget. She determines that her weekly tuition is budgeted to be $12,000, and the current weekly tuition billed is only $9,000. Marie must make some changes to her staffing plan and to her weekly expenditures to flex to this reduction in tuition. Since Marie is operating at only 75% of her budget, she must make some quick reductions in her controllable expenses. Her food budget each week is $720; Marie must reduce the weekly food expenditure by 25% to $648. This adjustment needs to be communicated to the team member who places the food orders for the center so that this adjustment can be made promptly. Marie will go through her budget and reduce each line item in much the same manner to ensure that her return is more favorable given the lower than anticipated revenue.

Planning for Large Expense Items

A director must pay particular attention to a number of large expense items when preparing and following a fiscal budget, including insurance, vehicle leases or purchases, and large appliances. Insurance is one expense that can fluctuate from year to year. Premiums can escalate with very little notice due to a number of economic factors.

Purchasing Insurance

Child care programs run as a small business in their own facility must carry adequate insurance on the building, its equipment, and materials. This coverage is required for mortgaged buildings. It is recommended for all programs that own their buildings and for the contents of rented buildings. General liability insurance is another necessity and in many states is a requirement for licensure and for receiving subsidies.

While states' laws differ, and this is one area where one size definitely does not fit all, we recommend that you discuss the coverages listed here with your personal insurance provider. If your provider does not offer child care insurance, he or she can probably put you in touch with someone who does. Explore the cost of purchasing these protections:

- Building and related structures. This insurance covers materials, equipment, supplies, additions, and new construction on the premises damaged by fire and lightning. Most policies can also cover losses from wind, hail, explosion (except from steam boilers), civil commotion, aircraft, vehicles, smoke, vandalism, and malicious mischief.
- Business income and extra expense. This coverage protects you if you are not able to continue the business because of a loss of property.
- Glass breakage. A nondeductible option may be available with this coverage.
- Sign coverage.
- Fences and walls within and surrounding the property.
- Sewer and drain backup.
- School bus insurance.

The director may be required to provide documentation of the building's value and the value of the equipment and supplies therein.

You will want to explore insurance on other types of property such as vehicles. Van or bus insurance will protect against losses from damage or destruction of the vehicle and its contents. Accident liability insurance is usually required by law. Theft insurance may also be desirable.

A program that is part of a chain or franchise, is operated by Head Start or a public school, or is a nonprofit organization run by a religious entity or community organization may have different insurance needs. You will want to inquire about existing insurance and consider if additional coverage is desirable.

When discussing the various insurance options with a representative of an insurance firm or brokerage, it is always a good idea to ask about deductible amounts and premium discounts that might be applicable.

TRENDS AND ISSUES

Although most people agree that high-quality programs of early care and education yield direct benefits to young children and their families while bringing long-term benefits to society, a disparity exists between what the public is willing to pay versus the real cost of high-quality care and education. The problem is simply defined: If quality goes up in terms of wages, child-staff ratios, and program services, programs become less affordable, and vice versa. All professionals agree that no trade-off should exist between quality and affordability; however, the reality is that trade-offs are occurring and that quality is, more often than not, the loser. The Carnegie Institute (Carnegie Corporation of New York, 1996) reported that the United States provides some of the worst services for children in Western society. As more and more programs fail to meet even minimum standards, a new question arises: "Will the money not spent today, along with major interest, be used to pay the piper in a not-so-distant future?"

Impact of the Economic Downturn on Children and Families

Fallout from the 2008 recession continues to impact services available to children and families. One result of the downturn has been high levels of unemployment or underemployment: Many parents have lost their jobs or their work hours have been reduced. These families are likely to have a particularly difficult time finding affordable child care, and without access to quality child care, their ability to secure better, full-time employment or to upgrade their skills by returning to school is limited, making unemployment and underemployment a vicious cycle. One solution would be to expand funding for child care to increase the number of jobs for those who care for children and to provide quality care for children whose parents are looking for new jobs or upgrading their skills (NACCRA, 2010).

Tight economies have also forced states to scale back their support for pre-K programs. Reducing the availability and quality of these programs means that fewer high-risk children will benefit from programs that have been shown to increase their chances for success in school and beyond. In addition, CCDF block grants and Head Start, the federal program designed to increase at-risk children's chances for school success, are not able to fund all eligible children (Watson, 2011). In sum, economic pressures have created new barriers for children already at risk for school failure.

Compensating a Skilled and Stable Workforce

Because early childhood care and education are essentially a service, high-quality programs depend on a skilled and stable workforce (Howes, Smith, & Galinsky, 1998; Vandell & Wolfe, 2000). Stagnant, low wages result in a nonstable supply of workers with inadequate skills and education. Funds to support professional training are limited. Most funds provide entry-level training only. Some potential sources of support for workforce development include the following:

- Child and Adult Care Food Program (CACFP)
- Child Care Development Block Grant (CCDBG)
- Child Care Development Fund (CCDF)
- Child Care Improvement Grants (Family Support Act)
- Job Training Partnership Act (JTP)
- Title II (NCLB)
- Local or state workforce agencies

Although investments in education have a positive effect on program quality, they have not had the same effect on compensation. The low wages that typify early care and education mean that teachers subsidize early childhood programs with forgone wages. Now that the link between the staffing crisis and teacher compensation is understood, *compensation initiatives* (initiatives that result in dependable and ongoing wage increases) continue their advocacy efforts (Whitebook, 2002). Initiatives vary with respect to the emphasis on the link between compensation and education/training (Whitebook & Eichberg, 2002). Some initiatives focus on wage increases or benefits tied to individual education/training, others focus on program eligibility to participate, and a few are system-based initiatives (e.g., U.S. Military's Personnel Pay Plan, Head Start Quality Improvement Act). (See the last section of this chapter for sources of summaries of some of those initiatives.)

Financing a System of Early Childhood Education

Without a coordinated system of services supported by financing strategies that provide needed resources, the goal of accessible, affordable, and high-quality programs for all children will not be fulfilled. The NAEYC (NAEYC Policy Brief, 2001) called for financing a system of early childhood education that includes (a) providing direct services to children in families with low incomes, (b) compensation for staff as a reward for additional education and a commitment to remain in a program for a longer period of time, and (c) funding the *infrastructure* (functions that support direct services).

Today, a major problem is the lack of financing coherence, which begins at the federal level, where the government cannot decide on one funding mechanism (e.g., tax credit or expansion of direct funding to early childhood programs) and thus has compromised by doing a little bit of everything. This lack of coherence in funding is perpetuated by the large numbers of federal agencies that administer federal funds and by the two major federal and state divisions (Department of Health and Human Resources and the Department of Education) that administer some of the federal funds and handle state supplementary revenues. By the time funds reach the local level, there is often no longer a good match between local needs and the goals of programs and no connection (transition) among programs. In all likelihood, many program services are duplicated, families will find either too many program options or no viable program for their children, and children will be placed in programs with inappropriate practices. A tripartnership among the federal, state, and local levels is needed to create a coherent funding policy that can make the most out of these bits and pieces. Kagan (2000) stated that financing an early childhood education system begins with obtaining concrete data on how much it will cost; how revenues should be generated and disbursed; and the appropriate balance of contributions from public, private, and family sectors.

SUMMARY

Programs for young children are expensive. A quality program is likely to cost $8,000 or more per child per year, depending on the age of the child and the locale of the program. Early childhood programs can be a large portion of the family budget, especially for middle- and low-income families. For many families, high-quality early childhood programs are simply not affordable, and the trend is to move those children to unlicensed and unregulated child care providers, such as family members or friends. It is important for early childhood professionals to get involved in advocacy efforts that support high-quality and licensed programs.

Public early childhood programs are financed through local, state, and federal funding sources. For-profit early childhood programs are supported primarily through tuition and fees.

Budgets must be carefully developed to ensure that they reflect the program's goals. Fiscal planning is one of the most important responsibilites of the program administrator. Without a healthy balance between program income and expenditures, the program will be forced to close.

Decisions about funding are decisions about program quality. Any trade-off between affordability and quality will result in a loss of benefits to young children, their families, and all segments of society. Without adequate staff compensation linked to training and experience, early childhood programs will continue to be of mediocre quality and experience high staff turnover rates. Without a coherent system for funding early childhood education, the chance that high quality programs will be available for all young children are diminished. Children, families and society will all suffer in the long run.

USEFUL WEBSITES

CLASP: Policy Solutions That Work for Low-Income People
www.clasp.org/

This comprehensive website has resources on many aspects of public policy in the early care and education arena.

Children's Defense Fund: A Strong, Effective, Independent Voice for *All* the Children of America
www.childrensdefense.org

This nonprofit is devoted to ensuring that all children have a healthy, fair, safe, and moral start toward their passage into adulthood. Its website has resources for action at the local level.

Grants from Lego
www.legochildrensfund.org/Guidelines.html

This is an example of the kind of grants available to child care programs. Programs considering applying for this support need to read the application criteria carefully.

U.S. Grant and Funding Sources
www.childcare.net/grantsusa.shtml

This website includes "Everything You Ever Wanted to Know About Starting a Daycare!"

NOZA Search Inc.
www.nozasearch.com/

This is a searchable database of philanthropic individuals and organizations.

Pre[K]Now
www.preknow.org/

This nonprofit organization advocates for increased funding to support prekindergarten services for young children and tracks states' efforts in this arena.

TO REFLECT

1. Parent X has had her child enrolled in your program for 3 years. Her child's tuition has always been paid on time. Recently, the parent lost her job when a local plant closed. Although you have a fee policy, she asks that you make an exception for her child until she can find another job. You also note that you have a waiting list of three other families that have steady employment. What should you do—keep the child whose parent cannot pay or follow your fee policy and enroll a child whose parents can pay?

2. Teachers subsidize early childhood programs with forgone wages. For example, the Cost, Quality, and Child Outcomes Study Team (1995) found that center-based teachers' forgone income was $5,200 a year, and a national report (Education Week, 2000) stated that public school teachers' forgone income was $7,894 per year. What would this amount to in a lifetime of earnings?

Many teachers work (e.g., planning, assessing, recording, attending meetings) beyond paid hours and spend out-of-pocket money on equipment and materials for their classrooms. As a professional advocate, how would you face the perverse equation of care costing too little to achieve worthy staff compensation and too much to be affordable for many families? Do you think capable teachers who like teaching are justified in leaving the profession for better pay? In striking for better pay?

3. With many government budget crunches, funding sources for early childhood programs are limited. Under these circumstances, should more affordable (and hence minimal quality) programs be offered to more children and families or should high-quality (and hence more costly) programs be offered to fewer children and families?

CHECK AND APPLY YOUR UNDERSTANDING

1. Describe the ways that detailed and complete financial information can benefit the governing body/board of an early childhood program.

2. List the steps involved in the funding process and the importance of each.

3. Develop a spreadsheet with the necessary line items to begin the budgeting process for an early care and education program.

4. Consider the staff in an established program and list the benefits to tenure and reduced turnover.

CHAPTER 8

Marketing Your Child Care and Education Program

Learning Outcomes

After studying this chapter, you should be able to:

1. Communicate the importance of facility design and environment when marketing the program.
2. Discuss service delivery and the important role customer service plays in a successful program.
3. Understand the necessary components of a marketing plan.
4. Describe the difference between internal and external marketing.
5. Describe the ways social media can be used to market the program.

Marie's Experience

Marie has been working with her staff to convey the importance of following through on promises that are made to families when they enroll. Three families recently made arrangements to remove their children from the program because of concerns with the toddler program. Marie took the time to personally talk with each parent about these concerns and found that the three families had discussing the toddler program at a recent birthday party. Apparently there had been a lack of attention on the part of the teacher to filling out anecdotal notes regarding the child's day and sending them home. On several occasions, none of the three families had received any feedback regarding their child's day and had gotten misinformation related to diaper changes and meal-time routines. As part of the enrollment process, the families had all been told that they would receive a daily note regarding their child's day. The families indicated that they had asked for the notes and were still not receiving consistent communication from the classroom teacher. As a group, these three families made arrangements to move the children to another area program.

NAEYC Administrator Competencies addressed in this chapter:

Management Knowledge and Skills

7. Marketing and Public Relations
Knowledge of the fundamentals of effective marketing, public relations, and community outreach. The ability to evaluate the cost-benefit of different marketing and promotional strategies. The ability to communicate the program's philosophy and promote a positive public image to families, business leaders, public officials, and prospective funders.

Marketing is about much more than simply advertising or publicizing your program. Marketing includes the type of services that you provide and to whom, the extent to which your customers are satisfied with your service, and the public image of your program. While making coffee and providing an enriching experience for young children are vastly different occupations, we can learn a lot from companies like Starbucks. Companies that effectively identify to whom they wish to provide services and how they intend to serve them and then use various strategies to publicize the features and benefits of their services. In this chapter, we will discuss ways that you can make your clients' experiences more rewarding than a simple stop at a coffee shop.

Application Activity

Think about your favorite experience as a consumer. What business do you thoroughly enjoy visiting? What is it about this business that continually brings you back? How does your interaction with this business make you feel? If the product or service that you purchase from this business were to increase in price, would you still purchase it?

Your favorite experience as a consumer might be at Starbucks Coffee.

Starbucks Coffee:

If you are a regular at Starbucks Coffee your attraction might be based not only on the fact that you enjoy the taste of the coffee that it makes, but also because you enjoy the experience of buying coffee at the particular location that you frequent. Some of the things you might particularly like about your preferred location might be (1) fast, reliable service (are you usually in a hurry when you stop in for a cup of coffee?), (2) consistently good flavor, and (3) the feeling that you are part of a "cultured" group (you know the lingo). It is likely that when you first walked into a Starbucks Coffee store you felt a bit awkward because the folks in line in front of you did not need a menu

and seemed to order their coffee using a language that you didn't fully comprehend. The woman who ordered immediately before you might have requested a "venti light mocha Frap, half-caf, no whip, with room." After learning the coffee lingo, you probably now feel as if you are part of a special group of coffee drinkers, a feeling that you get only when purchasing coffee at Starbucks, since other coffee places don't recognize the same lingo.

This description of ordering coffee at Starbucks illustrates how this company, through a well-thought-through marketing plan, has effectively communicated what goods and services it will provide, established a unique culture that is attractive to its intended customer base, and developed systems to effectively deliver exactly what the customer expects. In recent years, Starbucks has made changes to its marketing strategy to keep pace with the changing economy. It has expanded its product lines and incorporated a different level of training for its baristas. How can *you* translate your experience at Starbucks to operating an early care and education program?

MARKETING IS CRITICAL

Up to this point in the text, we have discussed the importance of defining your vision and mission for providing care and education services to young children and their families. We have also presented management strategies, aspects of facility planning, and finance and budget planning that are important considerations for the successful operation of an organization focused on the care and education of young children. While these topics are important to consider, arguably one of the most important aspects of your operation is your **marketing plan**.

Through this chapter, we will bring together the topics discussed in previous chapters and tie them back to the importance of your program's vision and mission. In doing so, we will help you think about your program and identify ways that you can make the experience of your clients fulfilling. Although many books define marketing for the general business world, few resources have been designed to explicitly apply basic marketing concepts to the practice of early care and education. Through this chapter, we will present the best thinking from the business world and apply it to the context of early care and education. The ideas and strategies will apply to a center in development and to a center that is currently in operation. It is essential however, that prior to engaging with the content in this chapter, you *have an established vision and mission for your early care and education program*. You will be encouraged to review this mission to identify the extent to which all aspects of your program and marketing plan align. You will also want to consider how the mission and vision of the program are consistently communicated to all constituents.

WHAT IS MARKETING?

According to a definition approved by the American Marketing Association "**Marketing** is the activity, set of institutions, and processes for creating, communicating, delivering, and exchanging offerings that have value for customers, clients, partners, and society at large" (AMA, 2007). In other words, contrary to popular perceptions, marketing encompasses much more than advertising. It includes deciding on the type of product you will offer, deciding what consumer (client) you will target **(market segmentation strategies)**, identifying that client's needs and wishes, then designing/refining your product to meet your client's needs, while giving consideration to all of the demographics that will potentially be impacted by the program. Following this line of thinking, the service that you provide to your clients (families and children) is marketing. The feeling that your customers derive from the service that you provide is marketing. The appearance and functionality of the physical facility that you have designed or are operating in is marketing. All of the materials that bear your organizational logo or bring your organization to the mind of clients or potential clients comprise marketing. Vehicles that the program might use to provide transportation to and from the center or a child's home are marketing. In this way, almost everything that your organization does or is perceived as doing might be considered part of your program's marketing strategy. Before we get into presenting the specific programmatic features that you focus on in developing your marketing plan, there is a principle of marketing that you must first fully understand.

This principle is best summarized through a common axiom within the marketing field: **Perception Is Reality**. This statement communicates the importance of almost everything that occurs in relation to your organization. What this saying really means, as it applies to the practice of working with young children and their families, is that whatever your clients perceive to occur is what they react to and results in the truth as they see it; this experience becomes the client's reality. For example, if you were to work with the owners and operators of a child care program to refine their marketing plan you would first meet with them to learn about their priorities and what they believe sets their program apart from others in their community. It could be that they are most proud of their program's robust curriculum that nurtures children and prepares them for school success, but they have discovered that many families view the service that they receive as primarily custodial. This perception has led to child and family attrition when children turn 4 years old; parents withdraw their children from the center and enroll them in "preschool" to prepare them for kindergarten. This is a common perception in the field of early care and education: that there are two distinct types of service providers—those who are considered primarily education service providers (preschools) and those that primarily provide custodial services to children (child care centers). The same can be said of the perception of Montessori-based programs and "child care" programs that clients do not see as structured enough. While many child care centers view their role as a combination of care and education, families that use these services and the general public might not recognize the educative value of these organizations based on their perception of what is occurring during the day. This perception is in all likelihood fostered by the fact that child care centers tend to prioritize meeting the needs of working families (i.e., they are open

Table 8.1
Child Care versus Preschool: Possible Influences on Perception

Program Characteristic	Child Care	Preschool
Days of Programming	Monday through Friday	M, W, F or T, TH Possibly Monday through Friday
Daily Hours of Operation	*6:00 A.M.–7:00 P.M.*	*9:00 A.M.–2:00 P.M.*
Annual Closings	Closed only on days of typical low enrollment; Thanksgiving, Christmas, New Years, July 4, Memorial Day, Labor Day	All nationally recognized holidays; closed several weeks during winter holidays; follow public school closings; also closed for teacher professional development days and for parent-teacher conferences
Daily Schedule	Large amounts of time for play in centers and outside; may have craft activity daily	Daily schedule, while it may include significant time for play, is labeled specifically to include typical curriculum subject areas (math, reading, science, social studies).
Curriculum	Described as eclectic or play based, with teachers emphasizing the importance of socialization, bodily functions, and self-help skills	Again, while many of the same values may be in place, the center clearly articulates a specific curriculum and is able to describe how the planned engagements support children's learning in traditional subject areas
Teacher Credentials/ Experience	Teachers/caregivers have a variety of professional education experiences; in some cases, limited experience in the field prior to joining the faculty or being placed in charge of a group of children	Teachers have some formal training in early childhood education, hold a CDA, AA, BA, or higher or hold a teaching certificate; have been working in the field for an extended period of time.
Cost	Economical, affordable for most families	Higher cost for fewer hours of service

for extended hours and closed only a few days of the year). Centers that are perceived by families as schools rather than child care centers offer limited hours of operation and follow the local schools' schedule. Even though the most effectively operated centers, preschool or child care, are likely to offer similar educative benefits to the children they serve, parents and the general public do not always recognize this to be true. With these insights in mind, you might identify some potential strategies that the program's owners could employ to actively change the public perception of their program as primarily custodial (see Table 8.1 for further elaboration).

It is in the best interest of your organization to learn to anticipate how your clients might perceive the types of services and interactions that they have with your center and then behave in ways that are likely to foster favorable perceptions. Thus, the essence of marketing your program is actively working to cultivate a positive perception of the service(s) that you provide to potential and current clients. This will be done most effectively by living up to the promises that you make to your clients through your mission and your articulation of the types of services that you provide. Through thoughtful planning of the environment and skillful program management, you can work to set the stage for the formation of a positive perception. With this in mind, we will now turn to the impact that facility design and service delivery have on the perception that clients may form about your program.

Facility Design and Environment

The physical appearance of your facility creates a first impression, sets the program's tone, and communicates volumes to your current clients and potential clients regarding your organization's culture, its quality, and the services you may provide. A center that has a large entryway equipped with comfortable chairs, decorative plants, magazines that might be of interest to families, and brochures highlighting community resources available to families with young children is likely to send the message to parents that they are welcome at the center. This setting might even foster a perception of the center as a warm and homelike place. While a detailed description of facility design has already been presented, take time now to consider the messages your current or planned facility is sending your clients and potential clients.

To help illustrate the many messages that may be sent through the physical environment of your center, look at Table 8.2, which identifies messages that might be associated with common child care physical environmental features.

A word of caution: For illustrative purposes through the following sections, we will present examples that are on different ends of a continuum. We describe some settings as institutional and some as homelike to help make our point concerning the connection between the environment of a center and the messages that might be interpreted by families; we are not attempting to endorse a stark institutional environment.

Table 8.2
Potential Messages from Typical Child Care Facilities

Positive Messages		*Negative Messages*	
Electronic keypad at the front door; code or visitor button must be entered for access to be granted	"This is a secure facility"	Soiled diaper or used fast-food wrappers in the parking lot	"This place is dirty"
Brief biography or letter of introduction for each staff member prominently posted	"The staff are (depending on the content) highly qualified, friendly, stable"	Biographies are not maintained and updated with staff changes	"This center must have a lot of turnover"
Posted daily schedules that detail the activities and engagements planned for that day	"The teachers have a planned curriculum" or "Children are learning here"	Generic daily schedule posted that includes bland titles such as Morning Circle, Center time, Lunch	"They are organized but it is not clear that careful thought has gone into the day's activities"
Recently completed children's artwork adorning the walls	"The children are valued"	It is now January and Halloween artwork is posted on the wall	This once positive message has now become negative: "The teachers' aren't attentive"
Facility smells of finger paint, crayons, etc.	"This is a school"	Classroom smells of a freshly soiled diaper (immediately following a diaper change)	"This is an unclean environment"
Certificate of Accreditation	"This is a quality program"	Certificate of GED, or high school diplomas of staff	"Teachers are not well educated"
From the classroom entryway, contents of bookshelves may be seen	"This is a fun and engaging place"	Toys and equipment are not placed on shelves in an organized fashion	"This place is chaotic"
Outdoor equipment is freshly painted and grounds are free of debris	"This is a fun and safe environment"	Paint on outdoor equipment is faded (sun bleached); some debris is present on the grounds	"This is not a safe place to play"

The wall adornments in your center send a powerful message to families regarding the nature of your program. The staff information posted on the wall of this center might effectively communicate to families that the teaching staff are qualified and highly valued.

When designing the physical facility or if you are currently operating a program, think about the message that you want to send to your clients regarding the type of place you are. Clients tend to form opinions of early care and education programs by using their senses. The smell, the sounds, and the sights are all important factors. If they affect the client in a positive way, this will translate into a lasting relationship with the program. If, for example, you are focusing on attracting and maintaining a clientele base that needs a professional/institutional feel, consider hard surfaces for flooring, limited wall decorations, and open and uncluttered classroom storage of materials. If, on the other hand, part of your organizational mission is to create a homelike setting, you should have softer flooring and wall colors, ample comfortable seating, fresh flowers, children's artwork, and a family message board. While a soft and comfortable environment is conducive to projecting a positive message to families, it should not get so comfortable that the facility appears disorganized or unclean. This would then project a very negative image to families regarding your ability to meet children's basic health and safety needs.

Service Delivery

Actually providing the services that you promise to your clients is the most important part of your marketing strategy. It is better to under promise and over deliver than vice versa. Your clients will absolutely remember all of the promises that were made during their initial program interview; this is especially true when clients have concerns or feel that they are not receiving the level of service that was described to them during the enrollment process. While the specific services that are offered to clients will vary from program to program, all centers have one feature in common: they primarily provide services to young children for which parents or other family members pay. The care and education services that we provide children include tending to their basic health and safety needs, providing opportunities to foster growth and development, and enhancing achievement of some academic gains. For some parents, the primary outcomes that they seek are safe, happy, and healthy children, while others are primarily interested in their children's academic preparation for school. It is our responsibility as service providers to determine what we will aspire to deliver, work to ensure that families understand the outcomes we are attempting to achieve, and then provide consistent evidence to families that we are indeed achieving these outcomes. The client is a good source of information and is likely to provide helpful feedback related to how well the services are being delivered. Be sure to ask the families in the program for this input. Encourage them to share concerns and compliments on a regular basis, so that they do not wait until a small incident becomes a bigger event because they have not shared their feelings about the program with the management team. The ways in which we do that may take many forms and will vary depending on the desired outcomes; surveys and or face-to-face conversations tend to work best in most programs.

The most important message that we can communicate to families that are primarily interested in custodial care is that their children are safe, cared for, and healthy in our care. We actively communicate this message by maintaining an environment where children are rarely injured; the facility is clean and organized; and the children are clean, nourished, and happy to attend. In our written communication to families, we might focus on describing the frequency and quantity of food consumed, the frequency and consistency of diaper changes, and a description of any special attention that a child was given to support emotional security. Spelling and grammar need to be correct and, most important, the name of the child must be spelled correctly. When family members arrive to either drop the children off or pick them up at the end of the day, they expect to see the children safely engaged in activity and the teacher interacting in a nurturing way with the children.

A Better Way

Marie was concerned and did her best to retain the three families by offering each of them a credit on their tuition and promising that the notes would be sent home regularly. Marie also provided additional training to her staff on the importance of effective family communication and following through on service delivery. The three families decided to stay in Marie's program and have since referred other families to the program. Marie understands the importance of delivering on her promises and having her team engaged in the service delivery process. Word-of-mouth can be extremely important to any program, impacting enrollment both positively and negatively. Keeping promises will almost always ensure positive word-of-mouth marketing.

When working with families whose primary goal is academic preparation, we should focus on sharing information with families that provides evidence that their children are "getting ready for school." We are not advocating having the children engage in activities that are inappropriate for young learners, such as worksheets; we are encouraging teachers to actively describe the educational benefits of their children's experiences while at school. For example, if a particular child spent a significant amount of time drawing a picture illustrating a recent trip to the park, the teacher can share with the parents how this use of symbols is related to early writing development. Through written communication to families, the teacher may highlight the specific skills the children have been working to acquire, describe upcoming content, and may even suggest activities that parents can engage in with their children at home to support the learning that has been occurring in the classroom. During classroom observations (drop off and pick up), parents interested in the academic development of their children will be looking to see the teacher engaged with the children in ways that appear to support learning. For example, asking a child to elaborate on her description of the difference between cats and dogs or seeing the children independently engaged in activities that can be described as educative.

For all families, regardless of their specific reason for seeking a center-based experience for their children, we must acknowledge that they want their children to be safe and successful. It would be wise to ensure that you send frequent messages to parents that communicate that the children are safe and meaningfully engaged in learning. Above all, we need to work to communicate to the families that bring their children to us that we care about and know their children as individuals. We can set the stage for fostering this perception by sharing simple child specific anecdotes (that address individual parent-desired outcomes) with families when they arrive at the end of the day to retrieve their child. An example of such an anecdote follows:

> Joey's family is primarily interested in his ability to make friends and develop social skills. When they come to pick up Joey this afternoon, you share the following story that chronicles a brief interaction between Joey and Stephen, a child new to the class. "Mrs. Johnson, I must share with you the wonderful thing that Joey did today while on the playground with the other children. Today was another little boy's first day in our classroom. During recess, he was having a difficult time adjusting to time away from his parents and was sitting by himself crying by the sandbox. Well, you know how much Joey loves that little red dump truck. He pushed the truck over to the new child, sat next to him, and gave him the truck saying, 'I know you're sad right now. Would this dump truck help you feel better? It is my favorite.' After that, the new little boy wiped the tears from his eyes and began playing with Joey. Your boy really is a special friend to the children here at school. Make sure that you tell him what a good friend he is."

This story did something very special for Joey's family. Not only did it communicate that their son is indeed learning the social skills that they value, but it also communicated to them that their son's teacher really pays attention to Joey. She cares enough about his family to share this precious story with them and helps the parents become engaged in the educational process by providing them the opportunity to praise their child for exhibiting a specific desired behavior.

The Marketing Plan

The process of developing a marketing plan is essential to maximize program potential. Through the identification of your program's mission, the articulation of specific objectives, an analysis of internal strengths and weaknesses and external threats and opportunities, and development of strategies designed to meet the objectives, you increase the likelihood that the message that you send to clients is consistent and portrays the desired image of your program. According to McNamara (2007), the process of developing a marketing plan begins with **market research** to find out

1. What specific groups of potential clients might have which specific needs
2. How those needs might be met for each group (or target market), which suggests how a program might be designed to meet the need
3. How each of the target markets might choose to access the service
4. How much the customers/clients might be willing to pay
5. Who the competitors are
6. How to design and describe the product such that clients will buy from the organization, rather than from its competitors (its unique value proposition)
7. How the product should be identified—its personality—to be most identifiable (its naming and branding)

Once you have done this research and evaluation, you must next turn to the important task of identifying goals and a marketing strategy that will support the accomplishment of these goals. A professional marketing firm will be helpful in conducting a market survey and providing insight regarding specific media and other strategies to advertise and publicize your program to potential clients. It is your responsibility to help the firm understand your program's vision, mission, and the specific services that you provide. Your organization should sketch out a marketing plan prior to contracting professional advertising firms. Different organizations use different formats to articulate their marketing plan, but almost all contain the same basic elements: mission statement, objectives, situation analysis, target market strategy, marketing mix, and implementation and evaluation plan (Lamb, Hair, & McDaniel, 2006). To help your program begin developing a marketing plan, use the outline provided in Figure 8.1 as a guide.

Strategies to Publicize Your Program: Internal and External Marketing

As part of your marketing plan, you will need to identify specific media outlets and other means of making potential clients aware of your program and the benefits they might gain if they were to enroll their children. In order to be effective and to maximize the financial resources that you dedicate to marketing, include both **internal** and **external marketing strategies**.

Internal marketing strategies are what you do to satisfy and retain current clients, which will likely result in positive word-of-mouth recommendations. External marketing strategies include the use of TV and radio advertisements, signs, brochures, and other printed or Internet-based materials to inform potential clients about the services that you provide. Although these forms of advertisements can be useful, research conducted by the Wisconsin Child Care Improvement Project (WCCIP, 2007) revealed that more than 90% of parents rely on recommendations from friends and family to inform their selection of child care. This finding is consistent with the common business claim that it is much more expensive to attract a new customer than it is to keep a current customer satisfied (Hiam, 2004).

As you decide on your final marketing plan, attend to both your internal and external marketing strategies, but be wise in how you allocate both human and financial resources. It is typically the internal marketing strategies that you use that will have the most impact on maintaining a program will full enrollment. The Wisconsin Child Care Improvement Project identified three groups of strategies that might be used by child care providers to attract and retain clients: internal strategies, external strategies, and initial point-of-contact strategies. See Figure 8.2 for a tip sheet outlining these strategies.

Guidelines for Print Media

One important way that you will communicate with the families that you serve and families that you might be able to attract to your center is with print media. Print media most commonly used by child care centers include letters, flyers, brochures, postcards, business cards, and signs. Consulting a visual artist or graphic designer to create a logo and format for print materials can be helpful, but it is not always affordable. Fortunately, with the application of a few basic principles and thoughtful consideration of the following questions, you can create documents that will effectively communicate with potential clients.

General Rules for Readable Print Media

- Use a font (no more than three per document) that is easy to read (avoid scripted or elaborate fonts and anything smaller than 11 points)
- Include your logo on everything you distribute to families
- Carefully edit for content and grammar before distributing
- Use headings that attract the reader's attention and convey a meaningful message

1. Program Mission Statement: A statement of the program's ultimate goal based on the provision of identified services and careful analysis of benefits sought by present and potential clients.
   a. Refer to Chapter 2 for further discussion on the development of a program mission statement.
2. Marketing Objective: A statement of what is to be accomplished through marketing activities.
   a. To be effective, the objectives should be realistic, measurable, and time specific. Objectives must help move the organization toward achievement of the program vision.
   b. Example: Our objective is to retain 85% of our current families during the transition from summer to fall enrollment and begin the upcoming session at 95% of our full capacity for enrollment.
3. Situation Analysis: Evaluating the context that your program will be marketed in.
   a. Internal Features: Determining the relative strength of organizational resources such as costs of service provision, marketing skills, financial resources, company image, employee capabilities, and available technology.
      i. Strengths:
      ii. Weaknesses:
   b. External Features: Analysis of the aspects of the marketing environment that include market forces, events, and relationships in the external environment that may affect the future of the organization or the implementation of the marketing plan.
      i. Opportunities:
      ii. Threats:
4. Target Market Selection: Selection of the specific clientele that you intend to attract through your market strategy.
5. Should be based on a recently conducted market opportunity analysis, which is a description and estimation of the size and sales potential of market segments that are of interest to the program and an assessment of key competitors in these market segments. Marketing Mix: The composition of program features that are selected to create a mutually satisfying exchange between the program and clientele.
   a. Product: Description of the services that you are providing
   b. Place: Location of the facility, making the services available in the place the clientele wants them
   c. Promotion: The strategies that you will use to educate and/or remind your clients of the benefits that your services provide
   d. Price: What the client must pay to receive the service; this must be affordable, yet high enough to ensure financial health of the organization
6. Implementation: A description that identifies the who, what, where, and when of the actualization of this marketing plan. Two essential elements that must be included are
   a. Task Description: An articulation of the specific tasks that must be accomplished to achieve the objective identified through the marketing plan
   b. Evaluation: Formal assessment of the effectiveness of these activities and progress monitoring of the achievement of the marketing goal

Figure 8.1
Marketing Plan Outline

Source: Based on *Marketing* (8th ed.), by C. W. Lamb, J. F. Hair, and C. McDaniel, 2006, Mason, OH: Thompson.

Internal Strategies

- Welcome parents at all times
- Invite feedback
- Respond positively to suggestions
- Include parents in activities and field trips
- Display photos of children at play
- Have evening family events
- Hold parent conferences regularly
- Be sensitive to diverse family structures

External Marketing Strategies

Advertising will be a significant part of your marketing plan and budget.
Advertising costs can range from free to very expensive.

Child Care Resource and Referral (CCR&Rs)

- Serve all areas of the state; maintain databases on *all* regulated child care in their region.
- At no cost to child care providers, parents contacting CCR&Rs receive a list of all regulated child care programs that meet their needs.

Printed Materials

- Business cards
- Outdoor signs
- Newspaper advertising
- Imprinted, t-shirts, caps, totes, etc.
- Brochures
- Posters/flyers

News Media

- Radio
- Television
- News releases
  - Hiring of a new director or teacher
  - Staff attendance at a national conference
  - Announcement of a new site or service
  - Special activities such as an unusual field trip or service project
  - Free health screening offered at center

Electronic Media

- Create an informative, easy-to-navigate website with information about the services you provide
- Create a Facebook page for your center
- Consider offering a reduction in your registration fee through Groupon, LivingSocial, or similar services

Special Events

- Participate in local parades
- Maintain a booth at a community fair
- Volunteer for a local fund-raising marathon

Other Marketing Ideas

- Invite elected officials to visit
- Invite news media
- Display children's art in the community, such as in the local library
- Partner with technical colleges and other training programs

Figure 8.2
Internal and External Marketing Strategies

Source: This tip sheet is based on one developed by the Wisconsin Child Care Improvement Project, March 1998, with funding from the WI Dept. of WFD, Office of Child Care, and DHFS.

General Questions to Consider

- What image of your program do you want to convey?
- What will draw potential clients' attention, hold their interest to read the entire brochure, and then call you?

Content to Include in a Brochure

- Website address, location, contact information including phone number and email address, and the name of the individual who will be talking with first-time visitors
- Program mission and philosophy
- Specific hours and days of operation
- Benefits of your program
- Special services offered to children and families
- Staff qualifications and other professional affiliations
- Staff and management team tenure

Website Design

In the current age of technology, having a "Web presence" has become an essential part of any marketing plan. Website design can be somewhat tricky and requires a fair amount of skill in creating a website that not only functions properly but also has a high "click through rate" when folks use a search engine such as Bing, Ask, Google, or Yahoo! to locate your center on the Web. We strongly recommend that you seek the assistance of an individual who is knowledgeable in this area—a poorly constructed or malfunctioning website can do more harm than good. At the end of the chapter, we have included a free website that might help get you started. The content on a website could include the same material in your brochure (possibly in expanded format) and added content that will encourage individuals to return to your website. This "hook" might be descriptions of appropriate activities that parents/family members might participate in with their child, a weekly blog describing

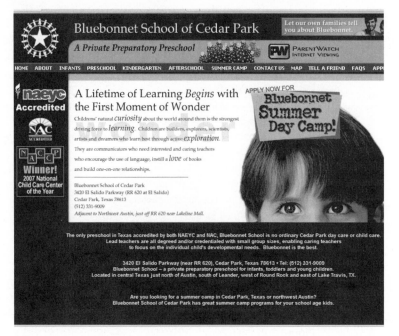

Figure 8.3
A successful program's website.

Source: Courtesy of Bluebonnet Schools, Inc.

what the children in your program are doing or learning about, or announcements of community events. Figure 8.3 is an example of a successful program's website.

Social Media

In this age of technology and Internet-savvy consumers, you should consider the use of social media in your marketing plan. Facebook, Twitter, LinkedIn, and other sites can add an additional layer of targeted marketing to any program. Engage someone who is knowledgeable in the use of social media to post, update, and possibly blog for the program. Using Hootsuite, Tweetdeck, or another tool to consolidate the posts for the program can prove beneficial in organizing the messaging that is used. Social media can be an extremely powerful tool in marketing when applied with thought and planning. Some economical ways to use social media sites for targeted advertising are available. Facebook and Google offer advertising opportunities and provide analytics to assist in tracking the effectiveness of individual ads.

Strategies for a Positive Initial Contact

As the old adage goes, you get only one chance to make a first impression, and a negative first impression will quickly help potential clients choose to enroll their child elsewhere. While a consistently high-quality and well-operated program will speak for itself, you should identify a plan for how you will handle a potential family's initial point of contact with you to ensure that a positive perception follows. Figure 8.4 provides some strategies that we have employed.

The Power of the Purple Cow

Seth Godin, a highly esteemed marketing and business consultant and author of *Permission Marketing* and *Purple Cow* (2002), eloquently defines the recent changes in the field of marketing. He has accurately portrayed conventional marketing strategies that rely primarily on external marketing strategies to be expensive and ineffective. One of the main points that he makes is that with advancing technology and the constant bombardment of advertisements that potential clients receive in the marketplace, they have learned to effectively ignore this type of advertisement. As a result of our ability to tune out marketing messages, successful businesses and organizations focus more of their external marketing resources (human and financial) on internal marketing strategies. Godin stresses, therefore, the importance of offering a truly remarkable product or service, what he calls the *Purple Cow*. An example of a Purple Cow is the iPod produced by Apple. Prior to its release, a relatively small group of individuals were downloading music from the Internet and listening to it via MP3 players. Once Steve Jobs and his creative crew at Apple created not only a unique and attractive MP3 player that was easy to use, but also a Web-based store to legally purchase music, an electronic music revolution was born. The first iPods were sold in 2001. Now they are everywhere, and the use of a lowercase "i" has become synonymous with innovative products, like the iPad, even if Apple does not release the device.

As you begin to develop your marketing plan and consider any revisions to the care and education services that you provide to children and their families, you must also think about how your program might become truly remarkable. Is there a service that families would value that you do not currently provide? Are there benefits that children gain from your program that you have not effectively communicated to others?

Initial Phone Contact

- Have phone located in an area with a minimum of noise.
- Answer promptly, three rings or fewer.
- Use an answering machine with a friendly message.
- Check for messages regularly.
- Return calls promptly.
- Maintain a phone log of inquirers.
- Follow up inquiries.

Initial Visit

- The visit begins outside; pay attention to the building's exterior and the entryway.
- Are outdoor play areas clean and appropriately staffed?
- Locate office where you can see visitors entering.
- What do parents hear when they enter?
- What do parents smell?
- What do parents see?

Greeting Parents and Children

- Greeting begins with your appearance.
- Welcome the child by bending down to eye level.
- Use visitors' names several times during the conversation.
- Listen to visitors' questions.
- On a tour, describe typical activities and point out signs of quality:
  - High level of staff training
  - Accreditation certificate
  - Absence of serious noncompliance notice beside license
- Sell your program:
  - A photo album of past events
  - Collection of past newsletters
  - Letters of testimonial from other parents
- Get information from the visitors.
  - Name
  - Address
  - Phone number
  - Child's birth date
  - Schedule needed
- Follow up with a thank you note immediately, and a phone call later.

Figure 8.4
Strategies for a Positive Initial Contact

Source: This tip sheet is based on one developed by the Wisconsin Child Care Improvement Project, March 1998, with funding from the WI Dept. of WFD, Office of Child Care, and DHFS.

SUMMARY

Throughout this chapter, we have presented some key points to consider regarding the marketing of your early care and education program. In bringing the service of child care and education to market, it is your job to make sure that you identify your intended market, understand the needs of the selected market, and monitor your provision of service to ensure that your clientele are completely satisfied. Through this process, you will need to design a plan that effectively communicates to your current clients (internal marketing) and to potential clients (external marketing) exactly what service(s) you provide and the benefits that might be derived from enrollment in your program.

USEFUL WEBSITES

The Market for Child Care, posted by the National Bureau of Economic Research

www.nber.org/reporter/spring02/mocan.html

This paper, developed by a member of the Cost, Quality, and Outcomes Study Team, examines market factors that impact the success of child care programs.

Child Care Market Rate Survey at the University of Texas at Austin

www.utexas.edu

Search "Child Care Market Rate Survey." This center conducts annual surveys of child care market rates in Texas. This information is interesting as an example from one state. You might want to search for similar studies conducted in your state.

All About Marketing, the Free Management Library

www.managementhelp.org

This website is a valuable introduction to the basics of marketing. Click on topics such as "Advertising and Promotions" and "Competitive Analysis" for specific information.

How Do I Create My Own Website?, Wise Geek—a site that gives "clear answers for common questions"

www.wisegeek.com/how-do-i-create-my-own-website.htm

This website answers beginners' questions about website creation and can get you started.

TO REFLECT

1. What is the public's perception of your program? Is the public perception aligned with the program's vision and mission? If not, what changes will you make to more closely align your program's operations with its vision and mission?
2. What is your program currently doing to actively cultivate a positive perception among clients whom you already serve and the community at large? Are there features of your facility or your provision of service that are likely to foster the development of a negative perception of your program? What can/should you do to change?
3. In your community, what type of marketing strategies do early childhood care and education programs typically use? Browse the Internet and try to locate child care programs in your area. What content is presented on the Web? How easy is it to find information that you might be interested in?
4. What are the needs and desires of the parents and families in your community? Are there needs that are presently not being addressed by programs in your area?

CHECK AND APPLY YOUR UNDERSTANDING

1. Describe why your program's facility is instrumental in its success.
2. Think about the importance of service delivery and list the top four reasons customer service is critical to the success of your program.
3. Discuss the various components of a thorough marketing plan.
4. Think about Purple Cows. List three other remarkable products and how marketing played a role in their success.

CHAPTER 9

Planning the Children's Program

NAEYC Administrator
Competencies addressed
in this chapter:

**Early Childhood Knowledge
and Skills**

4. **Curriculum and Instructional
   Methods**
Knowledge of different curriculum
models, appropriate curriculum goals,
and different instructional strategies
for infants, toddlers, preschoolers,
and kindergarten children. Ability to
plan and implement a curriculum
based on knowledge of individual
children's developmental patterns,
family and community goals,
institutional and cultural context, and
state standards. Ability to design
integrated and meaningful curricular
experiences in the content areas of
language and literacy, mathematics,
science, social studies, art, music,
drama, movement, and technology.
Ability to implement anti-bias
instructional strategies that take into
account culturally valued content and
children's home experiences. Ability
to evaluate outcomes of different
curricular approaches.

5. **Children with Special Needs**
Knowledge of atypical development
including mild and severe disabilities
in physical, health, cognitive, social/
emotional, communication, and
sensory functioning. Knowledge of
licensing standards, state and federal
laws (e.g., ADA, IDEA) as they relate
to services and accommodations
for children with special needs.
Knowledge of the characteristics of
giftedness and how educational
environments can support children
with exceptional capabilities. The
ability to work collaboratively as part
of family-professional team in
planning and implementing
appropriate services for children with
special needs. Knowledge of special
education resources and services.

Learning Outcomes
After studying this chapter, you should be able to:

1. Describe the three main dimensions of developmentally appropriate practice and why they are important to consider in planning the program.

2. Describe why the standards movement in early education has gained momentum and how early learning standards can be successfully incorporated into an early childhood program.

3. Describe three program supports that are important in managing an early childhood program.

4. Explain why child-initiated activities and scaffolding are important in implementing a developmentally appropriate curriculum.

5. Discuss what is meant by an *achievement gap* and what steps early childhood educators are taking to reduce this gap.

Marie's Experience

Marie has worked as director in her current program for more than 13 years and has had consistent enrollment of children and low staff turnover. Some of her teachers have been with the school longer than she has, and the program has a great reputation in the community. In the past year, Marie has become involved in state-level early childhood advocacy work, and she attended a meeting about efforts to develop a statewide, early childhood system that includes new early learning standards. In a recent meeting with her lead teachers, Marie gave out the early learning standards and suggested that the teachers think of ways in which they could incorporate the guidelines into the curriculum and schedule. She hoped that once the teachers had a chance to explore implementation of the new guidelines, she would then hold parent curriculum nights to help parents understand that the standards could be implemented in a developmentally appropriate manner.

As Marie walked down the hall one morning, she overheard a teacher of 2- and 3-year-olds rote counting out loud as a group, while she held up flash cards of numbers. Marie now knows she must also help her teachers implement the standards in a more developmentally appropriate way. Marie is hoping this chapter will help her inform teachers and parents about developmentally appropriate practices and how young children learn.

The focus of planning and administering an early childhood program is on children's activities. All other administrative tasks—meeting regulations, establishing policies, leading personnel, planning the physical facilities, and financing—are performed in the context of the work you do planning and implementing the children's program. The role of the director is to serve as the local program leader to fulfill the program's vision and mission by considering the knowledge and interests of children, the physical and social environments including the concerns of families and staff members, and standards for curriculum content. The director ensures that the program pedagogy is aligned with the vision and mission while being knowledgeable about and sensitive to program implementation.

In addition, the director serves as the program representative to the larger community and initiates collaboration with community agencies that provide support services (e.g., health care, family support, social services). The director oversees teachers responsible for program implementation at the classroom level. In order to ensure that the program remains in line with its mission and values, the director must spend dedicated time in the early childhood classrooms observing the actual implementation of the program. The importance of observation in early childhood curriculum and assessment is paramount in ensuring a high-quality program (Jablon, Dombro, & Dichtelmiller, 2007).

PROGRAM PLANNING

Curriculum, when thought of in its broadest sense, is an all-encompassing plan for learning. When clearly articulated, the planned curriculum serves as a way of helping teachers think about children and organize children's experiences in the program setting. Young children learn from every experience. They learn from being involved in individual and group activities, participating in physical care routines, interacting with peers and supportive adults, and from everything that they see and do while they are in out-of-home care. In short, everything in the program that children experience has the potential to impact children's learning. A joint position statement from the Division for Early Childhood (DEC)

Through the process of collaborative planning, teachers are more effective at identifying plans that are relevant and appropriate for the children they are working with.

and NAEYC (2007) suggested that a curriculum framework provides a set of recommended practices for (a) promoting active engagement and learning, (b) individualizing and adapting practices for each child based on ongoing data, (c) providing opportunities for children's learning within regular routines, and (d) working collaboratively and sharing responsibilities among families and professionals.

With this in mind, we turn to the process of deciding how you structure the curriculum to meet the needs of children and their families.

Starting with the Program Vision and Mission

It is important to intentionally and thoughtfully align curriculum with a program's vision, mission, and goals. Through this process, you will consider the needs of the children you hope to serve, consider family and community stakeholders' needs, and examine the theoretical and philosophical foundations of child development and learning. As a result, you will identify the goals you hope your program will achieve. As you now move ahead to establishing or revising the program curriculum, keep in mind the decisions that you made in developing your program mission. All aspects of your curriculum (e.g., planned engagements, available equipment and materials, daily routines, the role of the teacher) should help you accomplish the goals set forth in your program mission.

Developmentally Appropriate Practices: The Foundation of Excellence

While many early childhood programs select a specific curriculum model or approach to guide the program that they implement, most experts in the field agree that the single most influential document guiding the practice of high-quality early childhood programs is NAEYC's Developmentally Appropriate Practice (DAP) (NAEYC, 2009). The DAP position statement is not a program-based prescription; rather, it is an assertion that programs for young children should consider (a) present knowledge about child development and learning; (b) what we know about the strengths, needs, and interests of enrolled children; and (c) knowledge about the social and cultural contexts of the local community (Copple & Bredekamp, 2009). The dynamic nature of these three dimensions of knowledge will require changes in the stated program's theoretical foundation as knowledge changes.

Besides resources from program models and position statements such as DAP, accountability policies and state standards are a growing influence on preschool program planning. Nationally about 35% of all 4-year-olds are in publicly supported prekindergarten programs, including private early childhood programs that may qualify for state funding (Copple & Bredekamp, 2009). These publically funded programs are most likely to be accountable for developing programs aligned with learning standards and to be accountable for what children who participate in their programs know and are able to do.

Knowledge About Child Development and Learning: Knowledge about child development and learning should inform program curriculum planning (NAEYC, 2003). Best practice in early childhood education is based on knowledge of how children grow and learn rather than on assumptions (Copple & Bredekamp, 2009). In the 2009 position statement on DAP, NAEYC identified 12 principles of child development and learning that inform practice (NAEYC, 2009). Proponents of DAP assert that they can make general and reliable predictions about achievable and challenging curricula for most young children in a given age/stage range (Katz, 1995b). Research must be current and conducted in different cultures to be relevant (Lynch & Hanson, 1998). For example, the recent explosion of knowledge in the area of brain research from neuroscience, biology, and psychology has provided scientific support for what educators have long known: that the foundation for school and life success is rooted in the experiences of the earliest years (Espinosa, 2010). In addition, brain research has provided support for the principles of developmentally appropriate practices (Copple & Bredekamp, 2009) and is confirming what early childhood practitioners have asserted are the best ways to teach young children (Phipps, 1999; Schiller, 2010). Program administrators should keep abreast of new research by joining early childhood organizations and listservs and regularly visiting websites of organizations such as the National Association for the Education of Young Children, the National Association of Child Care Professionals, the National Center for Education Research, the National Institute on Early Education Research, Pre[K]Now, and ZERO TO THREE. See Appendix 8 for a listing of professional organizations that meet the needs of early childhood professionals.

Strengths, Needs, and Interests of Children: All educators realize that children have different needs and interests, and that these differences must be considered in planning. Teachers in traditional early childhood programs use continual observations and anecdotal record keeping on each child to determine challenging content and encourage child-initiated activities to implement much of the curriculum. Limited direct instruction is implemented, for the most part, with individuals or small groups rather than with the whole class. NAEYC recognizes that a balance of child-initiated and adult-guided experiences is important in developmentally appropriate programs (Copple & Bredekamp, 2009). Ultimately, whether an experience is child guided or adult guided, the teacher in the classroom is responsible for supporting children's learning. Through careful observation of children's needs and interests, the early childhood teacher ensures meaningful, experiential learning experiences that include activities in all developmental and curriculum areas.

Considering Children with Special Needs.   More than half of all preschool children with identified developmental delays are now included in some form of child care that serves typically developing children. The roots for the practice of inclusion began with the 1975 PL. 94-142 legislation that eventually became the Individuals with Disabilities Education Act or IDEA. IDEA governs how states and public agencies provide early intervention, special education, and related services to more than 6.5 million eligible children nationwide. IDEA, which was reauthorized in 2004, (Baumel, 2011) consists of two main parts: Part C ensures services to families and children birth to age 2, and Part B ensures services to families and children ages 3 to 21 (U.S. Department of Education, 2011).

Children with special needs are a diverse group and early educators are in a unique position to help identify and support these children. Early identification and intervention are important for children with special needs, including those with potential learning disabilities (Lyons, 2011) and those with emotional and behavioral differences (Gilliam, 2005; Nores & Barnett, 2009).

The early childhood program administrator serves as a liaison between the local program and the larger community in connecting children and families with available services. Administrators need to become familiar with special education law (IDEA) and recognize their role in identifying children with special needs. If a child qualifies for early intervention or special education services, a team of interdisciplinary professionals, including teachers, physical therapists, and occupational therapists, work together to develop the best educational plan and goals (Gartin & Murdick, 2005). The Individual Family Services Plan (IFSP) or Individual Education Plan (IEP) identifies tailor-made goals and required supports that will help a child with disabilities benefit from the early childhood program. The IFSP differs slightly from the IEP in that it is developed for children under age 3 and the services generally take place in the home or child care setting. Furthermore, the IFSP focuses on the needs of the child as well as the family. The IEP is developed for children ages 3 through 21, and services generally take place in the school setting (Ray, Pewitt-Kinder, & George, 2009). The 2004 amendments to IDEA require that all children, regardless of ability, have the opportunity to participate and make progress in the general curriculum (NAEYC & DEC, 2007). Services focusing on measurable, specified outcomes, required for an IEP, can also be beneficial for all young children. Children with disabilities benefit from developmentally appropriate, self-motivating activities that fit within pre-scribed IEP goals (Diener, 2009). Several early childhood special educators have designed strategies that combine DAP with the more teacher-determined environment typical in special education classroom (Hemmeter & Grisham-Brown, 1997; Horn, Lieber, Li, Sandall, & Schwartz, 2000; Mallory, 1998; Russell-Fox, 1997).

Considering Inclusion.   Federal legislation (IDEA) mandates that young children with special needs receive special education services in the **least restrictive environment** (LRE). This, for the vast majority of young children with special needs, will be a general education or preschool classroom. Placement decisions should be made based on the individual needs of the child, not on categories of eligibility or diagnosis. **Inclusion** has many meanings and can be described on a continuum. **Full inclusion** has come to mean that *all* children are served in a general education classroom setting with both general and special educators working collaboratively. **Partial inclusion** means that children with spe-cial needs may be included in general education settings for part of the day. **Self-contained special education** means that children with special needs are in self-contained classrooms with little or no interactions with typically developing peers. Shonkoff and Phillips (2000) indicated that the individualization of service delivery and making the intervention a coordinated family-centered one are essential features of intervention.

Full inclusion seems to be easier to implement at the preschool level than at any other level because (a) the educational goals recommended for early childhood and spe-cial education are similar (NAEYC, 1996), (b) early childhood and special education teachers often have experience with team teaching (Bergen, 1994), and (c) some states offer dual certificates in early childhood and special education. At the kindergarten and primary levels, partial inclusion may work best for all concerned because of (a) budgetary constraints that make it impossible for schools to provide personnel with specialized training and expertise to work alongside general education classroom teachers all day, (b) general education classroom can operate effectively with higher adult-child ratios—children who need special services can access them when they are taken out of the gen-eral education classroom, and (c) children with identified special needs are usually exempted from state-mandated curriculum standards that do not conform with DAP and are particularly inappropriate for young children with disabilities.

Implications of the IDEA amendments of 2004 and best practice create the expecta-tion that early childhood program administrators will work to provide an inclusive early childhood setting in which all children can be as involved and independent as possible (Watson & McCathren, 2009; Winter, 1999). As a result, not only do these children bene-fit, but all children in the larger group start to develop an understanding of similarities and differences (Copple & Bredekamp, 2009).

The Community's Social and Cultural Contexts: The child has to be seen as an indi-vidual in the context of his or her immediate and extended family (the *microsystem*) and as a benefactor of the connections among the child's family, neighborhood, school, and community (*mesosystems*) (Bronfenbrenner, 1989). These systems are embedded within cultural belief systems that shape children's and adults' experiences; influence children's development and learning; and are reflected by teachers' beliefs, values, and behaviors (Ray, Bowman, & Brownell, 2006). The program administrator needs to appreciate how the program of early care and education she leads represents the local community. She should take the community's attributes into account when making program decisions by showing that she appreciates how important it is that curriculum mirrors *all* participating children (King, Chipman, & Cruz-Jansen, 1994). This is how diversity is valued in early childhood programs and points to how important it is that program staff use a variety of strategies to learn about children's family and home culture.

Physical Environment.   Young children's experiences are tied to their immediate physical environment. Successful curricular activities are based on prior experiences and are more likely to be successful when they involve many firsthand, direct experiences and real objects to manipulate. Selection of curriculum content should relate to the real-life objects, experiences, and environment in children's lives. For example, it might not be appropriate to study the desert or the beach in all communities. Themes should be relevant to the children's real-life environment. The High/Scope Active Learning Framework addresses this issue in particular, by stressing the importance of providing children real-life examples of items when at all possible. For example, instead of a picture of an apple, children will learn more from handling an actual apple. They will learn how it smells, tastes, and feels (Hohmann & Weikart, 2002). Furthermore, visits to nearby fire stations, libraries, pet stores, and the like are essential for helping children apply learning to the larger world, such as when conducting investigations in the project approach to curriculum that will be discussed later in this chapter.

In quality programs, the social and cultural environment is closely tied to the program's physical environment. The general decor of the space should promote a warm homelike feel and reflect the cultures of the local community. The visuals displayed, music listened to, literature read, and dramatic play props should reflect the social and cultural composition of the families, staff, and community of the local program.

Social Environment.   Directors must also analyze the strengths and needs of families in local programs. Manifestations of the various community cultures include differences in

a. language (verbal and nonverbal) and conventions about its use
b. intellectual modes, such as learning and communication styles
c. social values, such as approaches to child rearing, skills nurtured in children, guidance ("discipline") practices, and attitudes about delays and exceptionalities

Creating an Anti-Bias Curriculum

The emphasis on infusing children's home cultures into educational settings began with the multicultural education movement of the 1970s. Those first efforts focused on including in the curriculum relevant cultural knowledge to help children learn more about themselves and others. Early childhood educators now work to develop an understanding of cultural diversity with the goal of supporting children's learning and development by understanding how culture affects learning (Day, 2006). Two documents were especially influential in creating a greater sensitivity to the social environment of early childhood programs:

1. Bias was brought into the spotlight through the publication *The Anti-bias Curriculum: Tools for Empowering Young Children* (Derman-Sparks and the ABC Task Force, 1989). A recent revision, *Anti-bias Education for Young Children and Ourselves,* expands principles of anti-bias teaching based on the authors' additional 20 years of experience (Derman-Sparks & Edwards, 2010).
2. NAEYC's (1995) recommendation that "the nation's children all deserve an early childhood education that is responsive to their families; communities; and racial, ethnic, and cultural backgrounds" (p. 1) has also been expanded upon in the revised DAP position statement (2009), which emphasizes the importance of basing program practices on what is culturally appropriate in addition to what is

developmentally and individually appropriate. It additionally addresses current concerns about lagging student achievement and calls for reducing the achievement gaps between various groups (specifically, low-income, African American, and Hispanic students and their peers from middle and upper class white homes) and increasing the achievement of all children in our country (NAEYC, 2009).

The local program's philosophy and practices should reflect the needs and strengths of families and the views of the staff. For example, Chipman (1997) called for

- Honoring various cultural learning styles (e.g., cooperative as well as competitive instructional strategies)
- Assessment that focuses on potential as well as performance and relies on multiple measures
- Awareness of multiple intelligences
- Greater cultural sensitivity when guiding and disciplining children
- Acceptance and inclusion of children with special needs
- Acknowledging and correcting subtle stereotypical messages

Some culturally embedded practices might never be considered DAP (Wardle, 1999), and others that might be developmentally inappropriate in some cultures could be appropriate in others. Nonetheless, program administrators have a responsibility to work to understand culturally embedded practices of the social environment in early childhood settings and to provide high-quality elements that include

- Positive relationships
- A comprehensive and coherent curriculum
- Rich, responsive language interactions
- Opportunities for meaningful parent involvement (Espinosa, 2010)

Many experts realize that merely adding multicultural content to a traditional curriculum is not enough. They remind us that what is needed is content approached from many cultural perspectives. The Quality 2000 Initiative (Kagan & Neuman, 1997) called for programs that promote cultural sensitivity and pluralism (Phillips, 1994b; Phillips & Crowell, 1994).

The following four core goals guide anti-bias education (ABE) for young children:

1. Each child will demonstrate self-awareness, confidence, family pride, and positive social identities.
2. Each child will express comfort and joy with human diversity; accurate language for human differences; and deep, caring human connections.
3. Each child will increasingly recognize unfairness, have language to describe unfairness, and understand that unfairness hurts.
4. Each child will demonstrate empowerment and the skills to act, with others or alone, against prejudice and/or discriminatory actions (Derman-Sparks & Edwards, 2010).

Program administrators actively support anti-bias and multicultural environments in several ways. Phillips (1994a) described three distinct ways to plan: (a) Programs can focus on changing negative responses to cultural diversity, (b) programs can begin with the culture of the home and build transitions to mainstream lifestyles, and (c) programs can embrace biculturalism by asking for families to help them maintain children's home cultural values and lifestyles.

Swick, VanScoy, and Boutte (1994) suggested several appropriate opportunities for promoting multicultural sensitivity:

- Educating families about building children's self-esteem
- Helping children explore their own culture through family and school activities

- Training families and teachers to assess their multicultural competence
- Supporting the development of skills needed to promote multicultural understandings
- Promoting intense teacher education concerning multicultural education

Program administrators recognize that actively including children's families in the program is a critical component of supporting cultural diversity and children's transitions between home and school. Consider these four principles of supporting family involvement:

1. Knowing yourself and your family's roots, beliefs, and attitudes
2. Learning from children and families about their particular styles and traditions
3. Creating positive relationships with others
4. Anticipating excellence from each child (Hohmann & Weikart, 2002)

The program administrator has the responsibility to consciously set the tone for family engagement and home-school partnerships. In doing so, he provides leadership in the development of a truly inclusive multicultural and anti-bias environment.

Application Activity

Review your program vision, mission, and goals. Based on your review, to what extent does your program align with the DAP guidelines presented by NAEYC?

The Standards Movement

An abundance of research supports the fact that high-quality early childhood programs result in improved outcomes for young children (Barnett, 2008; Belfield, Nores, Barnett, & Schweinhart, 2006; Dogget & Wat, 2010). In addition, every dollar invested in high-quality early childhood yields a positive economic return in improved child outcomes and social functioning. These findings have led to greater investments in early childhood programs, especially at the state level (Doggett & Wat, 2010; Espinosa, 2010). With increased political interest and public investment comes accountability. Current trends toward statewide Quality Rating Improvement Systems (QRIS) typically include standards for programs and for early learning. In general, *standards* have been defined as expectations for learning and development, but now the term may refer to any of the following:

- **Program standards.** Expectations for the quality of a program
- **Content standards.** What a child should know and be able to do within an academic area, such as mathematics
- **Benchmarks.** The knowledge and skills a child should have by a given time in school, such as the first semester of kindergarten
- **Performance standards.** Quality levels of performance with respect to the knowledge or skill described in a benchmark

Program standards have been part of early childhood care and education for many years. Program standards were written for nursery education as early as 1929. More recently, program standards were written for Head Start (called "Head Start Performance Standards"). Several professional early childhood associations have published accreditation standards that include a comprehensive quality improvement, self-study process for early childhood programs. Most accreditation self-study programs involve the use of classroom observations, parent and staff surveys, and ongoing professional development. Instruments designed to rate the quality of a learning environment are used in statewide quality rating and improvement systems. Examples include the Environmental Rating Scales (ERS) developed by Harms, Clifford, and Cryer and the Classroom Assessment Scoring System (CLASS) by Pianta, La Paro, and Hamre. Program standards are a critical component of the standards movement and help provide accountability in state-funded programs.

Early Learning Standards/Guidelines: NAEYC refers to content standards for young children as *early learning standards,* but the term *early learning guidelines* (ELGs) is commonly used in the literature to refer to content standards at the early childhood level. The standards movement, in which student outcomes on performance standards are linked to placement and retention decisions and to program accountability, began in elementary and secondary education in the 1980s. The development of the National Education Goals of 1989 led to a standards movement affecting all levels of education (Bredekamp & Rosegrant, 1995). In 2001, Head Start developed new standards, called the "Head Start Child Outcomes Framework," intended to guide the assessment of 3- to 5-year-old children enrolled in Head Start. In 2007, the Head Start Reauthorization Act required state governors to form an Early Learning Council charged with developing a high-quality early childhood system that includes a focus on early learning guidelines (Head Start Reauthorization Act, 2007).

The federal No Child Left Behind Act of 2001 continued to fan the flames of the standards-based movement in early education. The standards movement gained additional momentum with the Bush administration's *Good Start, Grow Smart* initiative. This program directed states to develop voluntary learning guidelines for children ages 3 to 5 as part of their use of the Child Care Development Block Grant (CCDBG) funds, which is the primary federal program related to child care services and quality.

The development of ELGs for infant and toddlers has been investigated by Scott-Little, Kagan, Frelow and Reid (2008), who stressed that the content of these guidelines must be appropriate to the development of infants and toddlers. In the 2009 DAP position statement, NAEYC clearly articulated that one policy area critical for developing high-quality systems of early childhood education includes developmentally appropriate practices, early learning standards, and related curricula and assessment (NAEYC, 2009).

The National Education Goals of 2010 also highlight that standards are clearly part of national educational reform law (National Education Reform Code, 2010). Furthermore, under the Obama administration, the American Reinvestment and Recovery Act (ARRA) of 2009 infused additional federal money into states to assist in their work to develop high-quality early childhood systems, including an emphasis on the implementation of early learning guidelines. As a result of this movement, all states and the District of Columbia have some form of early learning guidelines for children ages 3 to 5, and more than half are developing or have developed early learning guidelines for infants and toddlers (Daily, Burkhauser, & Halle, 2010). Several factors have contributed to the movement for early learning standards, including the following:

- Many states want their kindergartens and prekindergartens to have standards in alignment with state standards for older children as part of an effort to improve school readiness.
- Studies of brain development have increased the understanding of young children's capacity for learning (Bergen & Coscia, 2001; Espinosa, 2010; Schiller & Willis, 2008).
- An influential longitudinal study showed that many children had learned traditional kindergarten subject matter in literacy and mathematics in preschool programs (National Center for Education Statistics, 2000) and were thus prepared for more challenging content in kindergarten.

- The Committee on Early Childhood Pedagogy recommended that federal and state departments of education develop, field test, and evaluate curricula and companion assessment tools based on what is known about children's development. They recommended that content standards for the early years address these often omitted areas: phonological awareness, number concepts, methods of science investigations, and cultural knowledge and language (National Research Council [NRC], 2001).

Consider these characteristics of early learning guidelines, created with an eye toward preparing children to be successful in school:

- ELGs are created by states, usually with input from a variety of key stakeholders in the early childhood community.
- State ELGs are typically organized by developmental stages (e.g., birth to 18 months or 48 to 60 months) and articulate a range of skills and abilities in areas such as literacy, numeracy, and social-emotional and physical development that children should begin to demonstrate during these stages of development.
- Most early care and education providers are not required to use ELGs, with the exception of some state-funded preschool programs (Daily et al., 2010).

Application Activity

Locate your state's early learning guidelines for the ages of children that your program serves. In order to find them, do a Web search that includes your state name and either *early learning guidelines* or *early learning standards*. This ought to bring up a link to your state's education agency, which is most likely to house these guidelines. (Remember to search *early learning guidelines* or *early learning standards* or you will likely get your state's K–12 standards.) Review them and determine the extent to which your program's mission and goals align with the state curriculum expectations.

Literacy and Mathematics Standards: The early childhood years are the most important period for literacy development. The NRC (1999) stated that *functional literacy* is now defined as reading for information and interpreting ideas. This definition has increased literacy expectations. The International Reading Association (IRA) and NAEYC adopted a joint position statement in 1998 on literacy development in young children. This statement included

- A call for developmentally appropriate goals and expectations
- A developmental continuum for reading and writing development to be used for identifying literacy goals
- A cautionary reminder for program designers to take into account developmental variation.

Despite general agreement that children need support in learning to read, viewpoints differ about how best to support emerging literacy and early readers.

The emphasis on early learning standards for literacy development has resulted in state involvement in literacy initiatives not only for kindergartens and primary grades, but also for younger children. Some of these initiatives, such as the Every Child Ready to Read Projects (2011) that are often operated out of public libraries, focus on families, and others, such as the Minnesota Early Literacy Project (2011), and the Idaho Early Literacy Project (2010), focus on the training of preschool and child care teachers (Jacobson, 2002). These projects were developed by combining federal, state, and private monies.

Federal funding of many of these programs decreased in 2011. Some have survived, but others have been victims of the recent economic downturn (Pre[K]Now, 2011).

The National Council of Teachers of Mathematics (NCTM) and NAEYC adopted a joint position statement in 2002 and updated it in 2010. The associations affirmed that high-quality and challenging mathematics instruction for 3- to 6-year-old children is a vital foundation for later learning (NAEYC, 2010). Although the statement has many recommendations, it does not include a continuum of learning goals. However, NCTM (2000) had developed standards for prekindergarten through second-grade children prior to the development of this position statement. Experts advise that an early childhood mathematics curriculum for children ages 3 to 6 should include the major content areas of the NCTM standards in mathematics (NCTM, 2006) and should emphasize the three most important areas for preschoolers: (a) number and operations, (b) geometry/spatial relationships, and (c) measurement (Copple & Bredekamp, 2009). Following a research-based progression of topics in mathematics is particularly important because newly introduced concepts are built upon previous learning. Children who enter school with a strong foundation in mathematics are more likely to achieve academic success during their early school career (Brenneman, Stevenson-Boyd, & Freed, 2010).

In addition to these guidelines developed for literacy and mathematics instruction, efforts in recent years have focused on developing quality resources for curriculum planning in all content areas.

Stating Goals

Goals for a local program are typically broad and general statements about what the program hopes to achieve. Katz (1995a) stated that curricula at every level should address the acquisition and strengthening of these dimensions of growth:

1. **Knowledge.**   Children should have the knowledge the culture deems important. Knowledge includes representational knowledge (ideas, concepts, constructs) and behavioral knowledge (how to perform certain skills or enact certain procedures).
2. **Skills.**   Children should develop general intellectual skills (observing, gathering information, problem solving), more specific academic skills (decoding words, writing letters), and social skills (communicating, negotiating).
3. **Dispositions.**   Children should acquire positive dispositions or enduring habits of the mind (a desire to understand, a striving for accuracy, persistence, open-mindedness).
4. **Feelings.**   Children should develop positive feelings, which are subjective emotional or affective states (feel competent, feel accepted).

Translating Goals into Child Outcomes

Goals are a critical aspect of any curriculum. An effective curriculum helps children achieve goals that are developmentally appropriate and logically sequenced, so that children build knowledge on previously acquired skills (Copple & Bredekamp, 2009). High-quality programs ensure that the written curriculum addresses goals across all developmental and content areas, is aligned with state standards as applicable, and is clearly articulated to families (NAEYC, 2009). Program administrators need to hold the expectation that teachers use not only the planned curriculum, but also their knowledge and observations of each child to meet individual needs and goals.

Local programs further delineate goal statements by identifying *child outcomes* (competencies children need to acquire or strengthen) that will result from program completion.

Table 9.1

Sample Plan to Address Concept Development for a Prescriptive Curriculum Approach, Age Group: Preschoolers

Needed Competencies	*Sample Curriculum for Preschoolers*
Preschoolers need to	*For preschoolers, adults need to*
Identify eight basic colors (red, orange, yellow, green, blue, purple, black, and brown) by	
(1) matching	Provide materials for matching like colors.
(2) pointing to (3) naming	(a) Name colors (using colored paper) and ask child to point to color and (b) point to colors and ask child to name them.
(4) making secondary colors	Ask child to name primary colors and then secondary colors. Provide paints, color paddles, or crayons and paper and ask child to make secondary colors.
(5) coloring/painting with colors as directed	Provide a color sheet with directions for child to follow (e.g., color the ball "red").
(6) sorting color "families"	Provide materials showing various shades/tints of each of the eight basic colors. Ask child to group these into color families or to seriate shades/tints into color families.

Curricular competency lists may also include actions teachers take to assist children. The competencies most often identified by highly prescriptive approaches to curriculum are usually limited to addressing academic content knowledge and skills. Such competencies may include physical knowledge concepts, visual and auditory skills, language development, number concepts, and small-motor coordination skills. Competencies may also concern attitudes, such as persistence and delay of gratification. Broad competencies are often further defined as narrower concepts and skills that are then sequenced for implementation. Table 9.1 is an example of a plan to address preschool concept development written in a competency format. In this example, "identify eight basic colors" is the broad concept, and the six narrower concepts are numbered and listed in sequential order of difficulty.

Competencies cover all domains (i.e., physical, cognitive, language, social, and emotional) and may also cover Katz's (1995a) dimensions of development. Broad competencies permit the offering of a wide range of activities. Varying levels of skills and interests are accommodated through a range of performance criteria. Tables 9.2, 9.3, and 9.4 show examples of some of the competencies that might be addressed in these programs. Another example of competencies is the "Head Start Child Outcomes Framework" (Head Start Office, 2010).

Organizing the Curriculum

Curriculum activities must be organized. Children want to make sense of their physical and social worlds and to do so must build on their prior knowledge and skills. Thus, children cannot profit from a "grab bag" of experiences. An effective curriculum has been carefully thought through, takes place in the context of a predictable daily routine, and should be organized in a written format so that teachers are clear on the activities, the goals, and the child outcomes they hope to achieve. A written curriculum is recommended by NAEYC, so as to provide organization and intentionality to daily activities (NAEYC, 2009). However, this recommendation should not be interpreted to mean that an appropriate curriculum

Table 9.2

Sample Plan for Developing Competencies in a Traditional Early Childhood Program, Age Group: Infants and Toddlers

Needed Competencies	Sample Curriculum for Infants and Toddlers	
Infants and toddlers need to	For infants, adults need to	For toddlers, adults need to
Develop a sense of trust and a loving relationship	Read infant cues and meet infants' physical and psychological needs quickly and warmly.	Support attempts to accomplish tasks, comfort when tasks are frustrating, and express joy at successes.
		Respect security objects, such as a favorite toy.
Develop a sense of self	Call infant by name.	Name body parts.
	Place mirrors at eye level, including near the floor.	Respect children's preferences (e.g., toys and food).
		Support attempts at self-care.
Have social contact	Engage in face-to-face contacts, use physical contact, and have vocal interactions.	Help children control negative impulses and comfort when they fail.
		Help children become aware of others' feelings.
		Model interactions for children to imitate.
Explore their world	Provide opportunities for children to explore both indoor and outdoor environments, and ensure indoor environments are accessible and equipped with many objects to explore or bring objects and activities to them.	Provide support for active exploration (be near but refrain from too many adult suggestions for play).
Sample sensory experiences	Provide pictures and objects to touch, taste, and smell. Provide toys that make sound and action-reaction toys.	Place books and objects on shelves. Decorate room with pictures and real-life objects.
Undertake motor experiences	Provide safe places for movement. Encourage movement (e.g., place objects slightly beyond reach).	Provide safe places and equipment and materials that aid large muscle development (e.g., stairs, ramps, large balls, push/pull toys).
	Express joy at successes.	Express joy at successes.

must follow a commercial product. It may be developed from multiple sources, such as age-appropriate children's books, videos, and electronic media; teacher's observations; assessment data; early learning guidelines; and children's interests and inquiries. Curriculum may be organized as a listing of activities addressing separate concepts and skills designed to achieve a specific goal and may be primarily adult determined, or curriculum planning can take an integrated approach with a varying continuum of adult-initiated and child-initiated learning. Because the advantages of one form of organization become the disadvantages of the other, only the advantages of each will be discussed next.

Separate Concepts and Skills: To organize a curriculum by **separate concepts and skills**, key concepts are identified and carefully sequenced. The sequenced key concepts, along with teaching suggestions, are often provided in curriculum manuals. Teachers help develop the concepts in the prescribed sequence using the children's acquired competencies as the bridge to the next concept. For example, teaching number concepts

Table 9.3

Sample Plan for Developing Competencies in a Traditional Early Childhood Program, Age Group: Preschoolers and Kindergartners

Needed Competencies	*Sample Curriculum for Preschoolers and Kindergartners*
Preschoolers and kindergartners need to	*For preschoolers and kindergartners, adults need to*
Feel reassured when fearful or frustrated	Use positive statements.
	Provide comfort when frustrated and provide the rationale for rules as needed.
Become more independent	Provide opportunities for practicing self-help skills, such as dressing dolls and providing time and just the needed assistance in toileting and eating.
Make friends	Permit children to form their own play groups.
	Encourage onlookers to join a play group by helping them enter play situations, asking open-ended questions, and being of assistance in suggesting involvement in activities.
	Model positive social interactions for them to imitate.
Explore their world	Provide many materials that children can manipulate (e.g., water, sand, blocks, latches) in order to discover relationships.
	Provide dramatic play props for children to use in trying on roles.
	Allow substantial time for children to involve themselves in sustained play activity without interruption.
Exercise their large muscles and control their small muscles	Provide equipment to climb on, "vehicles" to ride on, and balls to throw and catch.
	Provide materials to manipulate (e.g., art tools, puzzles, pegs and pegboards, beads to string).
Engage in language experiences	Talk to, read to, sing to, tell and dramatize stories, and play singing games (e.g., Farmer in the Dell).
	Write children's dictated stories.
	Have classroom charts and other printed materials in view.
	Provide materials (e.g., paper and writing tools) for children to draw, scribble, write, copy signs, etc.
	Use descriptive language and open-ended questions to facilitate divergent thought, and expose to new vocabulary.
Express themselves creatively	Provide a variety of art media and various forms of music for creative expression.
Develop concepts of themselves and the world around them	Provide opportunities to learn skills (e.g., mathematics) and content areas (e.g., social studies, science) in integrated ways (while working on projects instead of times set aside to concentrate on each area).
	Encourage children to bring in pictures of their families and items from their home culture. Invite children to share about their unique culture. Offer experiences that relate to other cultures and customs through family involvement, shared reading, cooking, and projects across content areas.
Become familiar with symbol	Provide props for dramatic play.
	Provide books for "reading."
	Write children's dictated stories.
	Provide art and writing materials.
	Ensure the child's name is evident in multiple places in the classroom.
	Have children graph surveys of the class, favorite pets, foods, etc.
	Bring in or show children environmental print reflective of their community such as logos and common signs.
Make choices and implement their ideas	Permit children to select many of their own activities.
	Provide a physical setting that encourages individual or small, informal groups most of the time.

Table 9.4

Sample Plan for Developing Competencies in a Traditional Early Childhood Program, Age Group: Primary Grades/Levels

Needed Competencies	Sample Curriculum for Children in Primary Grades (Levels)
Children in primary grades (levels) need to	For children in primary grades (levels), adults need to
Show more self-control	Prevent overstimulation when possible and help children deal with fears and excitements (e.g., talking about them).
	Set clear limits in a positive way and involve children in rule making. Lead children in discussion of the rationale of rules and gather input from children on why a rule may be important. Children are more likely to follow rules they help develop.
	Ensure children have a balanced schedule with active indoor and outdoor activity and quiet and independent time. Examine the schedule to minimize waiting and long transitions; avoid long whole-group activities.
	Use problem solving to manage discipline problems.
Gain more independence	Permit children to identify areas needing improvement.
	Support children in their work toward mutually established goals.
Work with other children	Provide opportunities through small groups for children to cooperate with and help other children.
Explore their world	Provide materials that are concrete and related to ongoing projects.
	Plan for field trips and resource people to enhance classroom projects.
Use large and small muscles	Provide appropriate materials.
Use language as a way of both communicating and thinking	Provide materials for both reading and writing that will enhance ongoing projects.
	Provide quality literature.
	Read aloud stories and poems each day and ask child readers to share in the oral reading.
	Plan projects, such as preparing a class newspaper or making books.
Express themselves creatively	Plan ways to integrate art, music, dance, and drama throughout the day.
Develop concepts	Integrate curriculum (skill and content areas) in such a way that learning occurs through activities such as projects rather than in an isolated format. Provide a balance of child-initiated and teacher-facilitated involvement as needed to clarify concepts. Teacher is available to scaffold the child's learning by asking open-ended questions and stimulating inquiry, as well as introducing more advanced concepts and materials to support these concepts.
Use symbol systems	Provide manipulatives.
	Assist children in developing skills in reading, writing, and mathematics when these are needed to explore or solve meaningful problems. Offer opportunities to graph information and or collect relevant data (favorite foods, favorite toys, etc). Allow children to actively explore materials and document experiments and experiences through drawing, writing, or oral and written dictation.
Make choices	Provide opportunities to work individually and in small groups with self-selected projects and materials for a greater part of the time.
	Involve children in their own self-management (e.g., setting their own goals, budgeting their time, evaluating their own efforts, and cooperating with others).

may begin with rote counting followed by activities involving one-to-one correspondence, rational counting, recognition of written numerals, and number combinations (adding by using objects only, objects and symbols, and symbols only).

Curriculum organized by content-area concepts and skills has long been used with older children who are often taught separate academic content sometimes by different teachers during the school day. Early childhood program designers of direct instruction approaches and curriculum guides focused on a single academic area often organize the curriculum this way. As standards and skill-based curriculum guides have become more common in the early childhood, teachers may find themselves looking at multiple sources of discrete skills and concepts that are to be included in the curriculum and may benefit from integrating all these concepts into a master list (Helm, 2008).

Organizing the curriculum by separate concepts and skills has its advantages, including the following:

1. For some subjects, such as mathematics, researchers have identified a sequence of how particular concepts and skills build on others (Clements, Sarama, & DiBiase, 2003; Copple & Bredekamp, 2009).
2. Children develop concepts in a coherent manner.
3. In this age of standards and accountability, this method of organizing the curriculum ensures engagement with and, it is hoped, mastery of important ideas. This method is often seen as an efficient way to master standards that are important for program accountability.

Integrated Curriculum Approaches: An **integrated curriculum approach** involves choosing a topic or concept for extended investigation for which activities can be drawn from one or more academic disciplines (e.g., literacy, mathematics, science). Integrated curriculum has been more or less *the* approach used in early childhood programs with only a few exceptions. As such, the integrated curriculum has a rich history in early childhood education and is closely aligned with the guidelines provided by NAEYC through the position statement on developmentally appropriate practices (NAEYC, 1997, 2009). Several strategies can be used to plan an integrated curriculum: (a) choosing topics that permit the exploration of content across subject matter disciplines, (b) identifying concepts that are meaningful across the disciplines (e.g., literacy, patterns), and (c) identifying processes that are applicable to many disciplines (e.g., representation, scientific method). Many resources are available on the integrated curriculum (Dodge, Jablon, & Bickart, 1994; Hart, Burts, & Charlesworth, 1997; Helm, 2008; Hohmann & Weikart, 1995; Mitchell & David, 1992; Schickedanz, 2008).

Integrated curriculum approaches have many advantages, including the following:

1. Young children are active, self-motivated learners who learn best through self-initiated experiences rather than decontextualized teaching (Fromberg, 2002; Isenberg & Quisenberry, 2002).
2. Integrated approaches to learning foster the construction of knowledge and skills (Chaille & Britain, 1997), promote social interactions (DeVries, Reese-Learned, & Morgan, 1991), and encourage children to take responsibility for their own work (Jones, Valdez, Norakowski, & Rasmussen, 1994).
3. Children learning through integrated curriculum approaches showed high-level mastery of basic reading, language, and mathematics skills (Marcon, 1992). This finding was particularly significant for boys (Marcon, 1992) and for children from low-income families (Knapp, 1995).
4. High-involvement and low-stress activities promote the best learning (Rushton & Larkin, 2001; Santrock, 2011; Wolfe & Brandt, 1998).

5. In integrated approaches, children can use different combinations and degrees of each of the eight intelligences (i.e., logical-mathematical, spatial, linguistic, bodily-kinesthetic) (Gardner, 2011).

6. Children develop social competence best through cooperative efforts (Katz & McClellan, 1997) and feel successful when they engage in meaningful learning in an environment that encourages risk taking (Epstein, 2009; Fromberg, 2002; Isenberg & Jalongo, 2000; Schiller & Willis, 2008).

7. Integrated approaches permit the curriculum to be based on the needs and interests of children in the group and thus would not look the same from year to year or from one classroom to another. Rather than being preplanned, curriculum emerges from children's needs and interests, teachers' interests, objects and people in the environment, unexpected events, and values of the culture (Jones & Nimmo, 1994; Williams, 1997).

8. Integrated approaches to curriculum allow teachers to meet multiple learning standards while allowing children to be actively engaged in learning (Helm, 2008).

9. An integrated approach to curriculum takes advantage of the relationships between developmental domains and content areas as children's development and learning are connected (Koralek, 2008).

10. Increasing integration of learning within multiple content areas and across the daily schedule helps educators better manage their time and makes instruction and learning more meaningful for children (Schickedanz, 2008).

Providing Authentic Learning Opportunities

When it comes to integrated curriculum in settings for young children, there are a variety of ways to organize the learning engagements planned for young children; however, if careful thought is not given to the individual and collective experiences and interests of the children, what results is little more than a collection of cute yet ineffective learning opportunities.

Thematic Units and Projects: Two popular approaches to integrating the curriculum are *thematic units* and *projects*. A thematic unit usually has a narrower or more focused topic with more specific learning objectives than does a project, which is likely to follow children's interests and lines of inquiry.

Thematic units often last 1 to 2 weeks. Teachers choose the topics, plan the activities, and prepare the materials for various learning centers and other activities to correspond with the unit's topic. Ideally, teachers incorporate children's ideas about the theme into the curriculum and are responsive to the children's interests. During implementation, a lesson about the topic is presented by the teacher to the whole group, usually during circle time. Art, music, cooking, literature, and other activities reflect the unit's theme. When thematic planning is implemented superficially, teachers create competency-based activities to fit the current theme. For example, during a "Fall" unit, children may match upper- and lowercase letters written on laminated paper pumpkins and pumpkin stems. The child is expected to place the correct stem on each pumpkin. In this kind of activity children are not learning about pumpkins, nor is this decontextualized exercise likely to teach them much about matching upper- and lowercase letters, but this kind of activity might be repeated to go with the next topic, whether it be apples, mittens, or spring flowers. Another concern with thematic units is that teachers may be tempted to repeat them year after year. In some schools, all the teachers working with a particular age group (e.g., kindergarten) teach the same unit at the same time using many of the same materials.

When learning engagements are relevant and authentic, children are likely to be fully engrossed in the activity.

Teachers could make thematic units more DAP by carefully considering children's cultures and background knowledge, observing their needs and interests, allowing children's ideas to shape the curriculum, and by helping children see the connections between activities. For example, when implementing a unit on "Foods," children might share their favorite foods from home or parents might volunteer to bring in a favorite snack or lead a cooking activity that relates to their particular family's culture. Although the topics of thematic units may be teacher derived or predetermined from published curriculum resources, teachers have the opportunity to make themes relevant by paying close attention to the developmental level, interests, and cultures of the children. Experts tell us that all learners acquire facts and ideas by connecting and organizing them around unifying concepts (Bransford, Brown, & Cocking, 1999). Integrated curriculum approaches work toward this goal.

Projects: The *project approach,* an integrated curriculum approach, involves choosing an area of interest or a problem and incorporating curriculum areas into it (Katz & Chard, 2000). The project approach had its roots in progressive education (Dewey, 1916; Kilpatrick, 1918).

Ideally, project ideas emerge as opposed to being preplanned. Project ideas can result from children's natural encounters with the real environment, the mutual interests of the children and teacher, or the teacher's response to a need she identifies by observing children (Helm & Katz, 2010; Jones & Nimmo, 1994). The topic of the project is written as a narrative line used to convey the direction of children's investigation. Instead of using the broad thematic unit topic of "Water," a project topic might be "How We Use Water" or "The River in Our Town" (Katz & Chard, 2000). Criteria used for determining project topics include the following:

1. Topics must be related to children's own everyday experiences.
2. The study must involve real objects.
3. Opportunities must exist for collaboration, problem solving, and representation (e.g., artwork, block building, dramatic play).
4. It presents opportunities to develop competencies in all domains.

According to Helm and Katz (2010), projects go through three phases. In Phase 1, teachers begin thinking about a project topic and may even create a "web" to see the possibilities. A **web** is a visual representation (a diagram resembling a spider web) of curriculum possibilities. An *anticipatory web* is one to which children add their own ideas. If the program follows early learning standards, expected child outcomes may be added to the web or just listed (see Figures 9.1 and 9.2). The teacher checks for children's knowledge and interests by

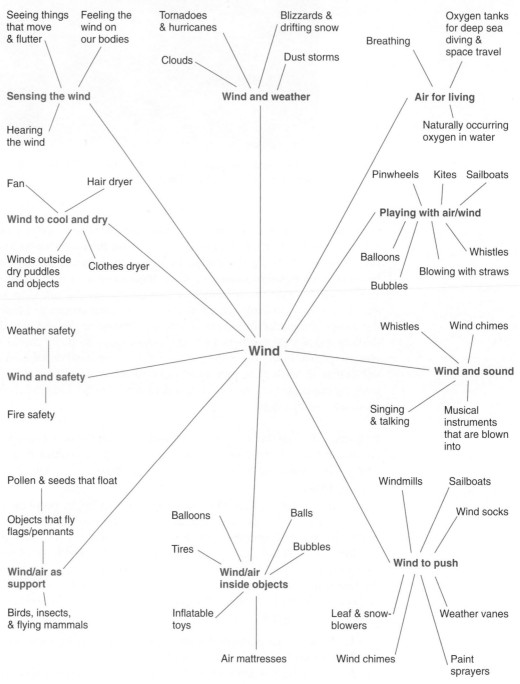

Figure 9.1
Anticipatory Concept Web

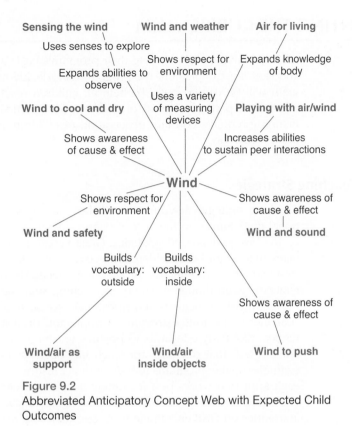

Figure 9.2
Abbreviated Anticipatory Concept Web with Expected Child Outcomes

having the children share their experiences about a topic and express them through representation (e.g., drawing, building, role-playing). Phase 1 lasts about 1 week and forms the basis for modifying plans. During the 2nd and 3rd weeks, Phase 2, children gain new information. They get firsthand, real-world experiences and are led to recall and represent details. Children have many opportunities to reflect on their expanding and refining knowledge through multiple representations. A project grows from the input of children, teachers, and families and through the introduction of materials. Phase 3 allows children time to further assimilate their ideas through play or share their understandings through documentation. Phase 3 often leads to new ideas and new projects. (For more information on the project approach, see the *Useful Websites* section at the end of this chapter for a link to the project approach website.)

Reggio Emilia–Inspired Emergent Curriculum: Another approach based on the principle of providing authentic learning is the *emergent curriculum approach* inspired by the schools of Reggio Emilia, Italy. These schools were established after World War II and have now attracted early educators from across the world who are seeking to understand this unique philosophy on teaching and learning (Wurm, 2005). Loris Malaguzzi, who is known as the founding father of the Reggio approach, explains that the Reggio philosophy of teaching children from birth to age 6 is based on the work of Dewey, Piaget, Vygotsky, and others (Desouza & Staley, 2002). A cornerstone of the philosophy is the belief that young children are competent learners who act like scientists in observing their world: asking questions, inquiring, structuring investigations, and documenting their understandings (Chaille & Britain, 1991). Learning grows out of children's inquiries and investigations and is supported by teachers who participate as co-learners, scaffolding and assisting with discoveries, (Desouza & Staley, 2002; Wien, 2008). The Reggio approach is not a curriculum program, but a philosophy of teaching and learning (Wurm, 2005).

IMPLEMENTING THE CURRICULUM

After identifying and planning their program's basic approach to curriculum, the director and staff must implement the program (i.e., decide how the specific features of the program will be carried out). To help all children reach their potential, planning must be done for a particular group of children, in a particular place, and at a particular time. Planning requires constant observation of children and a willingness to adjust program implementation.

Designing Teaching Strategies

Teaching strategies have to do with how teachers interact with children during instructional time. Similar to the lack of consensus on content, there is also a lack of consensus on the best pedagogical strategies. Great variation exists in the structure of teaching strategies that might be considered effective; continued research will help teachers identify strategies that are effective in attaining specific learning outcomes in specific learning contexts. Even though a variety of teaching strategies have been found to be effective, most curriculum theorists and researchers advocate a balance among the wide variety of strategies and learning structures. Copple and Bredekamp (2009) specifically address the tendency of early educators to polarize teaching strategies in early childhood education and suggest that our past approach has been characterized by *either/or* thinking. For example, quality programs use *either* direct instruction *or* child-guided activity: "In reality, each approach works best for different kinds of learning, and elements of both can be combined effectively" (Copple & Bredekamp, 2009, p. 49). Furthermore, these leading authorities on DAP encourage us to consider *both/and* thinking such as "children benefit *both* from engaging in self-initiated, spontaneous play, *and* from teacher planned and structured activities, projects and experience" (Copple & Bredekamp, 2009, p. 49).

Although a balance of teaching strategies is appropriate in most programs, early childhood programs and curricula that have been most effective tend to be child centered and responsive to individual needs and interests. Helm (2008) advised early childhood teachers to use many approaches to teaching knowledge and skills and suggested that they can be visualized along a continuum involving the degree of child initiation. For example, direct instruction, on one side of the continuum, would have less child initiation and choice, and the project approach on the opposite side of the continuum allows for the most child initiation and choice. Varying teaching strategies are appropriate at different times, but a developmentally appropriate classroom will be infused with child-initiated active learning whereby children are allowed to explore their environment and construct knowledge based on their interests.

Direct Instruction: Teacher-directed activities take a variety of forms and are commonly used in early childhood programs and kindergartens. Direct instruction is an effective method to convey content and information that is specific and is not likely to result simply from a child-initiated activity. For example, providing a 3-year-old with the opportunity to explore and manipulate a pair of scissors without any instruction in its appropriate use might result in injury. To learn the appropriate use and safety precautions, the child must be directly taught.

For more complex content, the instructional plan, often written as a lesson plan, usually includes clearly stated performance objectives, a procedure, and an assessment of the children's performance. Objectives and corresponding materials are based on sequenced concepts. Practice and drill may be part of the procedure a teacher uses to reinforce concepts.

A Better Way

Marie was concerned about how the teacher had the whole group participate in rote counting. She decided to hold a staff development meeting at which she went over the guidelines for developmentally appropriate practice in math. The teachers all brainstormed ways in which they could expose children to number concepts in a more hands-on and meaningful way. First they decided to develop a list of manipulatives and equipment that would be stored in the math and manipulative center. They also decided that they would make available numerous books on numbers that introduced counting. The teachers talked about ways to interact with the children throughout the day that would promote understanding of number concepts, such as counting the baby dolls while playing in the home center, or encouraging problem solving throughout the day, such as how many napkins to put out for snack or counting the blocks as they are put away.

The teachers began to understand that there really is a way to incorporate the standard of "understanding number concepts such as quantity" in a developmentally appropriate way and that direct instruction is not always the way to incorporate standards into the curriculum. Marie felt encouraged as teachers began to understand developmentally appropriate ways of incorporating standards into the curriculum. She now hoped that she could help parents, who wanted to be sure their children were developing academic skills, grow in their understanding during the curriculum nights she hoped to plan.

Child-Initiated Activities and Scaffolding: Child-initiated activities allow for active and experiential learning to take place, which allows children to construct meaning through their experiences with the environment. Many theorists and bodies of research view cognitive development from the constructivist interactive perspective. That is, "young children construct their knowledge and understanding of the world in the course of their own experiences, as well as from teachers, family members, peers and older children" (Copple & Bredekamp, 2009, p. 14).

In active learning environments, teachers support child-initiated activity by setting up meaningful and appropriate experiences in learning centers that allow for active exploration.

Effective early childhood curricula maintain a balance between teacher-initiated and child-initiated activities.

Teachers are available to help children enter play and support their learning. For example, in the High/Scope Active Learning Framework, children articulate their plan for activity to the teacher and then carry out that plan during center-based learning time. The High/Scope approach of Plan-Do-Review adds an element of intentionality to child-initiated activity (Hohmann & Weikart, 1995). Another type of assistance applies Vygotsky's theory of cognitive development. Children are aided in their pursuits by scaffolding, a direct support system provided to a child to perform in his or her *zone of proximal development* (ZPD), the distance between where the child is functioning independently and where he or she can profit from assistance by an adult or more advanced peer. Teachers play an important role in child-initiated activity by setting up the learning environment, making themselves available to children in order to provide scaffolding, asking open-ended questions to stimulate children's thoughts and inquiries, and providing support as needed. A developmentally appropriate program recognizes the important role of the teacher as a facilitator of learning in child-initiated approaches to teaching.

Program planners who implement child-initiated activities cite these reasons for their preference:

- Current brain research supports the value of child-initiated activity. In a 2008 policy brief published by the National Institute for Early Education Research (NIEER), "Brain Development and Its Implications," one policy recommendation states that preschools should embrace educational approaches that encourage child-oriented discovery over adult-directed instruction (Thompson, 2008).
- Teacher-directed activities on a large- or whole-group basis make it almost impossible to provide for various developmental levels, interests, or learning styles.
- Child-initiated activities enhance all areas of development (Frost, Wortham, & Reifel, 2012).
- Teachers can provide the needed structure for children's learning by (a) structuring materials, space, and time; (b) engaging in co-planning with children; and (c) providing scaffolding or short periods of direct instruction.
- Child-initiated strategies allow for children's active involvement and play: "Children talk more, integrate new knowledge, and are most engrossed and enthusiastic about learning while engaged in richly layered play" (Heidemann & Hewitt, 2010, p. 11).

Using Computers and Other Technologies

Computers have been in early childhood programs for more than two decades, and many young children have computers in their homes. Technology is rapidly advancing and is a part of our everyday lives. In the early childhood classroom, computers and other technology are tools for learning, just like blocks, paints, and storybooks, and are not to be set apart (Fox, 2003; Haugen, 1998). If used appropriately, technology will impact children's learning by extending and enriching many concepts offered in the classroom.

Connecting Technology to Young Children's Development: It is important to note that the term *technology* refers to much more than computers. Technological tools are rapidly expanding to include interactive media, digital cameras, audio and video recorders, smart boards, and other tools that may be used in the early childhood classroom (Carter, 2010). Because development occurs rapidly during the early childhood years, DAP with technology also changes to meet children's changing needs.

The position statement developed jointly by NAEYC and the Fred Rogers Center for Early Learning and Children's Media expands recommendations for technology and interactive media to include children from birth through age 8 (NAEYC, 2011a). Computers do not match the way infants and toddlers learn, so their use has not been recommended for this age group (Elkind, 1998; Haugland, 1999). For preschool children, DAP suggests that teachers make thoughtful use of computers and other technology in the classroom, not to replace children's learning with hands-on objects and materials, but rather to expand learning, to foster shared learning and interaction with computers and media, and to provide enough equipment for equal access and sustained involvement (Copple & Bredekamp, 2009). For this age group, important skills include learning how to seek out information and gathering and integrating knowledge from various sources, including appropriate use of the Internet (Haugland, 1999; Haugland & Wright, 1997). Researchers have found, for example, that children preferred working with a digital tablet than with paper and markers, indicating that tablets are an appropriate technology to use with preschool children (Couse & Chen, 2010).

Noting the Benefits: Research indicates that computer and interactive media activities can supplement other activities and also provide unique avenues for learning. Program designers must understand the connection between the types of computer/media activities and their benefits.

General Benefits.   Computers and other technologies have the potential to provide several benefits. First, children will learn about technology (e.g., people control technology by making up rules that control how technology works; different programs and equipment work by using different rules; technology is part of the everyday world). Second, new hardware and software features are permitting children with disabilities to use these technologies to enhance their ability to interact with peers and others in their environment (Behrmann & Lahm, 1994; Freeman & Somerindyke, 2001; Haugen, 1998). Third, some objects (e.g., shapes, pictures) can be manipulated more easily on the computer and allow for understanding concepts more easily than their concrete counterparts (e.g., actual blocks) in a child's hand (Copple & Bredekamp, 2009; Thompson, 1992). Fourth, technologies allow teachers to meet the diverse needs of children (Haugland & Wright, 1997). Finally, computers can aid social competence, such as communication, cooperation, and leadership; help develop positive attitudes about learning; and lead to feelings of self-efficacy (Cardelle-Elawar & Wetzel, 1995; Denning & Smith, 1997; Freeman & Somerindyke, 2001; Haugland & Wright, 1997; Nastasi & Clements, 1994). Additional studies have shown that when children use computers, they prefer to work with others rather than alone and prefer to seek help from peers rather than adults (Haugen, 1998).

Benefits of Selected Software and Integration.   Since computers can also be misused, educators must take responsibility for using them to the advantage of children. The joint NAEYC–Fred Rogers Center position statement on technology and young children calls for teachers to carefully evaluate software, integrate technology into the regular learning environment as only one tool of learning, and provide equitable access to technology (NAEYC, 2011a). The curricular values of these technologies are dependent on the selected software and the degree of technology integration into the curriculum. This is another reminder that the program's approach to teaching and learning must be considered when making all curricular decisions.

These guidelines are likely to lead you to consider **open-ended software**, with which children are free to do many activities (e.g., drawing rather than coloring in predrawn pictures, word processing). Research has shown that the use of open-ended software results in gains in intelligence quotients, nonverbal skills, structural knowledge, long-term memory, manual dexterity, and self-esteem (Haugland, 1992). Haugland also found that the gains were greater when children used supplemental activities

(activities beyond the computer). For example, when compared with a drill-and-practice group of children, the children who used open-ended programs showed gains of more than 50% over the drill-and-practice group in verbal, problem-solving, and conceptual skills, although the drill-and-practice group had worked on the computer three times longer. This finding supports principles of DAP and technology with the recommendation that children continue to have active hands-on learning experiences with real objects that support concepts learned with computers and interactive media. Research has also shown that open-ended software aids critical thinking (Clements & Nastasi, 1992; Kromhout & Butzin, 1993; Nastasi & Clements, 1994) and allows for the connection of ideas from different content areas (Bontá & Silverman, 1993). Fox (2003) suggests several considerations when choosing software for the early childhood classroom:

1. Learning features: How does the program support children's learning? Is it culturally appropriate?
2. Interactions: Does the program encourage child participation and problem solving, or does it make the child a passive recipient of knowledge?
3. Design: Does the program change and does it allow the child to set the pace? Does it support the child in initiating her own learning or does she need to rely on the teacher to manage it?
4. Play: Play is a vital medium for children's learning. Is the program inviting, inspiring, and interesting—that is, is it playful?

Several researchers in the arena of technology and DAP believe that early educators must more fully embrace technology and that early childhood teacher preparation programs should improve upon this area of professional development (Parette, Quesenberry, & Blum, 2009). Technology will clearly continue to expand and early childhood program administrators will need to continually consider the appropriate use of technology in the early childhood classroom.

Facilitating Effective Classroom Transitions

Transitions occur with changes of activity, location, or caregiver (e.g., when a parent leaves or picks up a child). The way transitions are handled either makes the day go smoothly and positively for children or causes chaos and negative reactions. Well-executed transitions incorporate the teachers' knowledge of individual and group needs (Taylor, 1999). Some general suggestions follow:

1. Begin the day on a calm and happy note. Early morning greetings and sharing are important. Consider using humor as brain research suggests that feeling content and happy enhances memory skills (Schiller & Willis, 2008).
2. Have a consistent daily routine and reduce the number of "between activity" transitions with large blocks of time. When transitions do occur, use both predictable transition activities that children have learned and novel transition activities to sustain attention.
3. When making a transition, do the following: (a) Prepare children by announcing the upcoming transition, (b) keep signals low-key (e.g., soft bell or quiet voice) and make the transition activity interesting but not too stimulating, (c) position yourself appropriately to offer assistance, and (d) begin new activities right away. Minimizing the amount of time children are made to wait will result in fewer behavioral issues.
4. Keep realistic expectations for children's behavior, and provide a limited number of choices to help children feel in control.

5. Prepare children in advance of moving them to a new location (e.g., "In five minutes we are going to start cleanup and move to the circle rug."). Advanced notice of transitions will help prevent children from becoming upset when they have to stop the play activity in which they are engrossed.

6. End the day pleasantly and calmly. Plan easy and quick ways to distribute notes or items to be sent home. Warmly acknowledge the departure of the group or each child. Research suggests that learning is enhanced when children have time to make sense and meaning out of new information (Sousa, 2006). Provide time for children to reflect on the day's activities. An end-of-the-day large-group time for reflection can help meet this goal.

Providing for Physical Care Routines

In traditional early childhood programs, physical care activities are used for socialization (e.g., table manners are emphasized during eating) and for cognitive enrichment (e.g., children discuss nutrition and the properties of foods—color, size, texture, and shape). Depending on the age of the children, physical care routines may take a large portion of the day in both half-day and full-day programs. Care routines provide valuable time for responsive caregiving and one-on-one discussion between teachers and children.

Planning for Special Times

Special plans must be suitable to children's needs and be as carefully developed as daily plans, although they require even more flexibility. Certain routines—especially eating, toileting, and resting—should always be followed as closely as possible.

First Days: Whether the first days represent children's first experience in an early childhood program or mark their entry into a different stage of the program, they are likely to view the first days with mixed feelings of anticipation and anxiety. The first days should be happy ones because they may determine children's feelings of security and their attitudes toward the program.

An infant or a toddler is likely to need a week to make a gradual transition to a program (Miller & Albrecht, 2000). Initiation of preschool and even kindergarten children is best done gradually, too. This time allows for the preliminary orientation of children to the program. If all children enter on the same day, additional adult assistance should be secured for the first days.

Planning for first days requires that more time and individual attention be given to greeting children and their families, establishing regular routines, and familiarizing children with teachers and the physical environment. For the first days, use equipment and materials and plan activities that most children of the age group are familiar with and enjoy and that require minimal preparation and cleanup time. Teachers need to enjoy this time of becoming acquainted with the children as well, as it sets the tone for developing a community of learners who will grow and learn together.

Field Studies: A field study or field trip is a planned journey to somewhere outside the school building or grounds. Early childhood programs have long used community resources to enhance children's learning and to broaden children's understanding of the local community. Field trips and resource people are used extensively in projects. Thoughtful planning of field trips and for resource people is important both because of benefits to children's learning and because of the added dangers of taking children beyond the building and grounds. When planning field studies, the teacher must do the following:

1. Help children achieve the goals of the program.

2. Make arrangements with those in charge at the destination. Directors should take the lead in developing an updated inventory of local places to visit and resource people suitable to their program's needs. This inventory should

- List the name of the place, its address, telephone number, website, and the person at the location in charge of scheduling visits and hosting visitors.
- Indicate how far in advance you need to make a reservation.
- Determine any age limitations. Is this an appropriate trip for 3-year-olds, or is it better suited for 4- and 5-year-olds?
- Indicate the time of day and days of the week visitors are welcome.
- Indicate the number of children that can be accommodated and the recommended adult-child ratio. Will you need parents to accompany the children?
- Indicate how long a tour and visit take.
- Should children dress in a particular way?
- Include additional comments such as notes from past visits.

Teachers should refer to this inventory in making plans. Make arrangements for the visit, and if the host is to talk with the children, make sure he or she can communicate with this age group. Make arrangements for the physical needs of children, staff, and other adults assisting with the field trip, such as locations of places to eat and rest rooms. One staff member should visit the destination before plans are finalized, particularly if your center has not visited this location in the past.

3. Obtain permission from the director or building administrator for the children to participate in the field trip. Policies of early childhood programs often require teachers to complete forms giving the specifics of the field trip. Follow local licensing standards/regulations with regard to advance notice of field trips; notice of field trips off school grounds may need to be posted 24 to 48 hours in advance.

4. Provide enough qualified volunteers to supervise the children safely. Good judgment and experience in working with young children are qualities to look for in volunteers. Volunteers should have a list of the names of the children under their care; when they do not know the children, name tags should be worn for easier identification. Name tags with your program's contact information are important when going to public attractions such as the zoo in case children become separated from your group. Program administrators must know licensing or regulatory requirements for volunteers, as some states require volunteers to have background checks before interacting with children. Volunteers should have an orientation that describes your expectations as to how they are to supervise children, the use of cell phones, appropriate language, etc.

5. Obtain written parental consent for each field trip and keep the signed statement on file. Note the example of a field trip permission form in Figure 9.3. The signed form is essential because the parent's signature serves as evidence that the parent has considered the potential dangers of his or her child's participating in the field trip. No statement on the form should relieve the teacher and director of any possible liability for accidents. Such a statement is worthless because a parent cannot legally sign away the right to sue (in the child's name) for damages, nor can staff escape the penalty for their own negligence, as shown in judicial decisions (*Fedor v. Mauwehu Council of Boy Scouts,* 1958; *Wagenblast v. Odessa School Dist.,* 1988).

6. Become familiar with the procedures to follow in case of accident or illness. Take children's medical and emergency information records in case emergency treatment is required during the field trip.

Dear Mom and Dad,

   Our class will be making a field trip to the Tasty Treats Bakery on May 13. A baker will take us on a tour of the bakery. We hope to learn how bread and rolls are made. We will be leaving school at 9:00 a.m. and will be returning in time for lunch. We will ride on a bus to the bakery and back to our school. We all think it will be fun to ride on the bus with our teacher, Mrs. Smith, and three mothers. Please sign the form below to give your permission for me to take the trip.

                                                                        Jody

---

I, _____ , give my permission for
                (Name of parent)

_____ to attend a field trip to
                (Name of child)

_____ .
                (Destination)

My child has permission to travel on the bus.

I understand that all safety precautions will be observed.

Date _____ Signature _____

Figure 9.3
Field Trip Permission Form

7. Make all necessary arrangements for transportation and determine whether all regulations concerning vehicles and operators are met. Highlight not only the location address on the field trip notification, but the route to be taken. Make sure that someone on the bus has a working cell phone to use in case of emergency or concern.

8. Prepare children by helping them understand the purposes of the field trip and the safety rules to be observed.

9. Evaluate all aspects of planning the field trip and the field trip itself.

Class Celebrations: Class celebrations are traditional in early childhood programs and require special planning. Directors need to consider the beliefs and preferences of families and staff members and local community customs concerning various celebrations. Celebrations should be inclusive of all the cultures in the school. Family and staff surveys are often helpful in determining which celebrations are to be included in the program. If celebrations are to be observed, specific policies should be written and provided to families.

Developing Supportive Relationships

Although many directors are aware of the importance of early brain development, fewer realize the importance of social and emotional competence. Recent research has confirmed that social and emotional competence is critical for a child's early school success and for later accomplishments in the workplace. Lack of social and emotional competence is linked to behavioral, social, and emotional problems. For example, preschool children, ages 3 through 5, have been shown to have the highest expulsion rates in the United States, three times that of school-age children, and these expulsions were primarily related to behavioral issues (Gilliam, 2005; Office of Special Education and Rehabilitative Services, 2007). As a result, early childhood practitioners have turned to early intervention with a focus on social competence and positive behavior support (PBS) principles. Ten years of research suggest that these principles offer guidance for practitioners and families in helping children with the early social competence they will need to succeed in both school and life (O'Dell et al., 2011). In addition, the Devereux Early Childhood Assessment (DECA) assesses children's resilience, initiative, self-control and attachment as an approach to early behavioral intervention (Devereux, 2011).

School involves social relationships with adults and peers. Children who are successful in school are confident, use friendly approaches with peers, can communicate emotions, are able to concentrate on and persist in tasks, can follow directions, and are attentive. Yet survey data showed that up to 46% of kindergarten teachers reported that at least half their class had specific problems in a number of areas in making the transition to school (Peth-Pierce, 2001). Several authors have suggested that building relationships with families before the kindergarten year begins can proactively support the transition to school (Jacobs & Crowley, 2010). Because infancy and the early childhood years are critical to the development of social and emotional competence, directors must give a great deal of attention to this aspect of children's development. The quality of the adult-child relationship is the most important aspect of the children's program. Most learning depends on the development of nurturing relationships, and children are more apt to explore and try new activities when they feel safe (Riley, San Juan, Klinkner, & Ramminger, 2008). Children whose teachers are sensitive and responsive and who give them attention and support are more advanced in all areas of development compared with children who do not have these positive experiences (Lamb, 1998; NICHD Early Child Care Research Network, 1998, 2000; NIEER, 2008).

Research suggests that unresponsive caregivers do not stimulate brain connections in children and can cause emotional stress, which releases stress hormones that actually impair brain function and learning (Stephens, 1999). The importance of warm responsive adult-child interactions in the early childhood environment is paramount, and program administrators who are responsible for recruiting teachers must always keep this in mind.

Caring as Infant/Toddler Curriculum: Close and caring relationships between very young children and significant adults provide the context for all aspects of very young children's growth, development, and learning (Gallagher & Mayer, 2008; Gonzalez-Mena & Eyer, 2011; Riley et al., 2008). Programs should assign primary caregivers and strive for continuity of care (Essa, Favre, Thweatt, & Waugh, 1999; Gonzalez-Mena & Eyer, 2011; Theilheimer, 2006). Primary care is accomplished by assigning each child to a primary and secondary caregiver, and continuity of care means these caregivers stay with a group of infants and toddlers until the preschool years.

Caregivers must also build supportive relationships with families. These relationships are particularly important when working with infants and toddlers because child-rearing practices related to children's eating, sleeping and toileting are culturally determined. Caregivers need to understand how families care for their children to make their practices as culturally congruent as possible (Gonzalez-Mena, 2008; Lally, 1995). Teachers of young children must open up dialogue and create positive environments in order to understand the differing cultural expectations parents may have (Gonzalez-Mena, 2008; Meece & Soderman, 2010).

For infants, the development of a secure attachment with their mother, father, and/or other primary caregiver is a critical social and emotional milestone (Raikes, 1996; Riley et al., 2010). Secure attachments in early childhood help set children up for later social-emotional and intellectual success (Dozier, Stovall, & Albus, 1999). One study found that 4-year-olds who were securely attached to their current teacher engaged in more complex play, were friendlier, and were less aggressive with peers in the child care setting (Howes, Hamilton, & Matheson, 1994). To facilitate this attachment, caregivers must be able to show empathy and develop rapport with babies. Babies share their emotions, and adults must be able to read the cues, engage in mutual gazes, and communicate with gurgles and coos and language, including happy and lulling songs (Honig, 1995). Reciprocal responsiveness between the adult and the baby has been likened to a dance (Gonzalez-Mena & Eyer, 2011; Honig, 2002; Raikes & Edwards, 2009).

By age 2, toddlers become more self-aware and want to gain some independence and self-control. As young children grow, they broaden their sense of competence as their capabilities expand (Epstein, 2009). Toddlers need enriched but safe environments that allow for active exploration. Good teachers show an attitude of total presence ("I am interested in you; I am here for you."). Teaching and caring for emotionally fragile toddlers require calmness and a sense of knowing when to do "more" and when to do "less" (Rofrano, 2002).

Nurturing Emotional Literacy: Peth-Pierce (2001) noted that young children, especially boys, enter school with emotional illiteracy. These children often misinterpret their own emotions and those of others. They often lack the ability to manage their emotions properly. Emotional literacy (intelligence) is based on three skill levels—perception, understanding, and managing (Salovey & Sluyter, 1997). Epstein (2009) suggested that emotional learning is the knowledge and skills needed to recognize and self-regulate feelings and that dealing with one's emotions is a prerequisite to socializing effectively with others.

Although a universality of emotions exists, culture affects the expression of emotions and the contexts in which they are expressed (Small, 1998). Thus, families and teachers often see "problem" behaviors and temperaments in different ways (National Center for Education Statistics, 2000). To be effective, emotional literacy skills must be interwoven into the daily curriculum. Some ideas include the following:

1. Empower children by helping them feel successful. Teachers can begin empowering by
   a. using both child-initiated and teacher-determined activities
   b. encouraging both interdependent and independent activities
   c. recognizing the uniqueness and contributions of each child
   d. focusing on achievements in all domains
   e. working individually with children
   f. saving and displaying products of achievement
   g. encouraging peers to say positive things about class members
2. Read stories that discuss emotions. Follow up with reflective questions (e.g., "How did _____ feel when _____?"). Relate the stories to children's lives (Birckmayer, Kennedy, & Stonehouse, 2008; Sullivan & Strang, 2002/03).
3. Extend children's vocabulary of "feeling" words.
4. Help children make inferences about expressions, body language, and tone of voice.
5. Create a "comfort corner" in which children can express feelings by writing, drawing, using puppets, and dictating into a tape recorder (Novick, 1998).

Encouraging Social Competence: **Social competence** is the ability to initiate and maintain good relationships with peers (Katz & McClellan, 1997). Epstein (2009) suggests that social-emotional learning or social competence has generally been thought to have four components:

1. Emotional self-regulation and awareness, responding to experiences with an appropriate range of emotions

2. Social knowledge and understanding, knowledge of social norms and becoming a member of the community
3. Social skills, strategies for interacting with others
4. Social dispositions, valuable character traits such as curiosity and humor or unpopular traits such as selfishness or argumentativeness

Children who are not competent are often labeled as aggressive or loners. Competent participation in a group is developmental and can be encouraged in the preschool years. Emotional literacy is tied to social competence. Understanding one's emotions and those of others and the ability to regulate one's emotions allow for the development of social competence. Beyond nurturing emotional literacy, teachers can aid social competence by reducing external controls and building a sense of community.

Reducing External Controls.   *Discipline* and *punishment* are terms that focus on external control by adults. Child development specialists and early childhood professionals have warned of the harmful effects of punishment, especially corporal punishment (Hyman, 1997). Any form of shame reinforces a negative self-label and leads to a self-fulfilling prophecy (Gartrell, 1995). In addition, we now know from brain research that threatening and negative environments actually retard the learning process (Sousa, 2006). Regrettably, external control is still used by many teachers.

As an alternative, "time-out" has become the major means of dealing with class problems. The use of time-out originated from the behaviorist theory of psychology, which suggested that the intent of time-out was to remove the child from the stimuli that were reinforcing the undesirable behavior. This original intent evolved into the concept that children need to be separated from peers to regain emotional control and to think about the effects of their behaviors. Time-out is a technique that punishes rather than teaches strategies for handling impulsive behaviors (Gartrell, 1998). Using time-out diminishes the child's feelings of self-worth and deprives the child of group membership (Marion, 1999). If our goal is to promote social-emotional development then excluding children from the group robs us of an excellent opportunity to teach needed skills (Kirkwood, 2011). In fact, the threat of time-out makes the class apprehensive and leads to a feeling of conditional acceptance (Clewett, 1988).

Another form of external control is the use of tangible rewards. Although tangible rewards are widely used with children with special needs in public school and therapeutic settings, there is much controversy over the use of tangible rewards (stickers, goodie jars) in preschool settings. Research suggests that overdependence on external rewards reduces intrinsic motivation (Kohn, 1991). Other research suggests while it may result in immediate measurable learning gains in some areas, these gains are countered by lower levels of motivation for continued learning (Shiller & O'Flynn, 2008).

Although praise is not punishment, it is a form of external control. Teachers praise when children "jump through their hoops" (Kohn, 2001). Praise is ineffective and harmful for these reasons:

1. Children may stop positive activities once attention is withdrawn.
2. Praise creates stress because children must continue their good behavior to retain their teacher's love.
3. Praise occurs only for observed actions (some actions are missed).
4. Praise makes children dependent on an adult's judgment of their efforts, as opposed to self-evaluation.
5. Praise may be used to control others (e.g., "I like the way _____ is sitting" means that others are not doing what the adult wants).

Nevertheless, effective praise or encouragement can be used to promote self-confidence. Effective praise is delivered privately (Marshall, 1995) and focuses exactly on what the child did as opposed to a generalization of "goodness" (e.g., "Thank you for picking up your books" rather than "You are a good helper" [Hitz & Driscoll, 1988]). Effective praise relies on describing children's actions as opposed to using judgmental language such as "good job." Encouraging statements allow children to feel proud of their own accomplishments and build their sense of self-worth.

Building a Sense of Community.   Teachers need to build a sense of community instead of using practices that single out individual children or small groups of children for punishment or praise. Building a sense of community involves facilitating the learning of democratic life skills such as seeing oneself as a worthy individual, working cooperatively as a member of the group, expressing emotions in non-hurtful ways, seeing the viewpoints and feelings of others, and solving problems in ethical ways (Gartrell, 1998). Some suggestions for building a sense of community are as follows:

1. Form teacher–child attachments to build trust (Betz, 1994).
2. Model and encourage the use of respectful language (Dunn, 2009).
3. Have a plan for welcoming new children to the group, which includes building a sense of cohesion among all children, for example, being the new child's buddy, playing getting-to-know-you games (Levine, 2008).
4. Model openness and empathy. Champion all children as equal participants, including those who may be stigmatized.
5. Work on projects and other small-group activities in which all children plan together, share responsibilities, and acknowledge one another's contributions.
6. Use class meetings to (a) make agreements that ensure an atmosphere free from exclusionary practices and ridicule, (b) work on biases, and (c) problem solve (Vance & Weaver, 2002). For younger children, use circle time (group time) as a time to build community by allowing children to participate, share, and recognize each child's contribution as valuable (Levine, 2008). Gathering in informal circles facilitates social interaction and belonging (Jones, 2008).
7. Be a facilitative coach for conflict resolution. This five-step approach to resolving conflicts often works: (a) Cool down, (b) help children state the problem, (c) brainstorm ways to resolve the issue, (d) try one alternative, and (e) follow up to see how things are going (Gartrell, 2000).
8. Use guidance talks with individual children. Discuss how their behaviors affect others, how positive approaches should work better for all concerned, and ways to make amends (Marion, 1999).

For children who have exceptionally challenging emotional or behavioral difficulties, special interventions may be needed. Program administrators should keep a resource file with contact information on appropriate professionals or agencies that may be of assistance to children and families experiencing these challenges.

Supporting Children Who Experience Stressful Events: Young children experience *stressors* (situations and events that cause stress) in their lives. Some stressors involve illnesses; others involve loss, such as parental separation or the death of a loved one; and others involve violence. Even school activities, especially program transitions and assessment, can be stressful. Brain research shows that all information is sent not only to the functionally appropriate place in the brain (e.g., the speech center) but also to the lower brain, which sorts its emotional significance. If the information is threatening, the normal thinking abilities are blocked (Wolfe & Brandt, 1998).

Teachers can work to create low-stress activities in the classrooms and to support children during stressful events in their lives. Some suggestions are as follows:

1. Acknowledge children's feelings and accept reactions that may seem "wrong." (A child's developmental stage affects reactions.)
2. Provide caring words to defuse upsetting events (Rushton & Larkin, 2001) and physical contact to help assure the child that he or she is safe ("Helping Young Children in Frightening Times," 2001).
3. Emphasize familiar routines at home and at school.
4. Avoid letting children see stressful events replayed many times. For example, turn off the television or get children involved in activities away from the television to prevent them from seeing replays of upsetting violence.
5. Express your own fears and sadness while remaining calm when talking to children and assure them that people are there to help those in need (Gonzalez-Mena & Eyer, 2011; Greenman, 2001).
6. Engage in classroom activities that release stress (discussions; physical activities; storytelling and dramatic play; sand, water, and block play; play with clay; and reading books that deal with these stressors).
7. Communicate with families about any changes noted in a child's behavior and provide suggestions concerning what families may do.
8. Use children's literature to help children cope with stressful events, including those in the news and changes in their families, such as the arrival of a new baby, a move, or divorce (Roberts & Crawford, 2008).

Considering Other Aspects of Implementing the Curriculum

Regardless of the program goals, several other points need to be considered before implementing the curriculum. Be sure you have adequate staff, space (that is arranged appropriately), materials and equipment, and time to implement each planned activity successfully. Plans must consider the needs of all children. Some children may need a different learning modality or challenge level. Planning also requires considering alternative activities to forestall problems that result from a lack of interest, inclement weather, unforeseen scheduling changes, or breakage of materials or equipment.

CREATING APPROPRIATE PROGRAM SUPPORTS

Decisions about grouping, scheduling, and staff responsibilities are the backbone or support of planning and implementing the local program. These decisions involve how you will manage children within a group and thus directly affect how care and education services are delivered.

Grouping

U.S. society acknowledges the importance of the individual; yet, a chaos-free society must have some conformity—some group mindedness. From birth until a child enters an early childhood program, the child's individuality is fostered, tempered only to some extent by the "group needs" of the child's family. In contrast, because of the number of children involved and the time limits imposed, early childhood programs are forced to put some emphasis on group needs except in infant and toddler programs. (Infants and toddlers function totally as individuals in quality programs.) Although the individual is most important throughout the early childhood years, group needs become more important as children get older.

NAEYC (2005) defines a **group** as the number of children assigned to a staff member or to a team of staff members occupying an individual classroom or a well-defined physical space within a larger room. In a quality program, all grouping decisions are made to facilitate adult-child and child-child interactions in the program.

Size of Group: Regardless of the program philosophy, the literature is replete with the benefits of small group sizes. Small classes are associated with more adult-child interaction, more individual attention, more social interactions, more complex play, and more teacher time given to fostering children's language and problem-solving skills (Howes, 1997; Kontos, Howes, & Galinsky, 1997). Small class size increases school-age children's achievement in reading, mathematics, and science; decreases grade repetitions; and increases graduation rates (Krueger, 1999). Small group size is critical to children needing more individual attention—infants and toddlers, children with special needs, and children who are experiencing a lack of continuity in their lives. Sadly, in spite of these recognized benefits, the fact remains that economic constraints sometimes stand in the way of maintaining the small groups research recommends (Wasik, 2008).

The National Academy of Early Childhood Programs recommends a maximum group size of 8 for infants birth to 15 months; 12 for toddlers up to 36 months; 18 for 3-year-olds; 20 for 4- and 5-year-olds, and a maximum group size of 24 for kindergarten-age children (NAEYC, 2011b). To determine the size of the group, the director must also consider the needs of the children, the skills of the staff, and the center's facilities.

Adult-Child Ratios: The **adult-child ratio** is the number of children cared for by each adult. Data from Howes, Phillips, and Whitebook (1992) showed that programs that met the NAEYC-recommended adult-child ratios were engaged in more DAP than were programs not meeting the NAEYC recommendations. NAEYC (2005) concluded that smaller group sizes and lower adult-child ratios are strong predictors of program compliance with indicators of quality, especially appropriate curriculum and positive adult-child interactions. Improving the ratio without reducing group size yields less positive results (Mosteller, 1995). To achieve program quality, the adult-child ratio is more important than the educational level of staff in infant and toddler programs; conversely, the educational level of the staff is more important than the adult-child ratio in programs for preschool and school-age children (NICHD Early Child Care Research Network, 1996). While all states have *required* ratios as a criterion for licensing, most high-quality programs work to provide lower than required ratios. In 2008, NAEYC revised its accreditation system and recommendations on adult-child ratios within group size. These NAEYC ratios have traditionally been considered the highest quality standard in early childhood programming and can be found at the NAEYC Torch Website or in the *Guide to Accreditation* published by NAEYC. Other early childhood program accrediting entities such as the National Association of Child Care Professionals (NACCP) and its associated National Accreditation Commission (NAC) and the National Early Childhood Program Accreditation (NECPA) offer criteria on adult-child ratios. In addition, many states are implementing quality rating and improvement systems that may include recommended adult-child ratios within group sizes. Program administrators must become familiar with state quality initiatives that may influence program decisions pertaining to ratios and group sizes. Given the importance of adult-child ratios within group size as a predictor of program quality, early childhood administrators need to carefully consider ratio and group size as a critical support to appropriate curriculum implementation.

Grouping Patterns: **Grouping**, or organizing children for learning, is an attempt to aid individual development in a group setting, that is, to make caring for and teaching children more manageable and effective. Once curricular plans are formulated and the basic delivery system is chosen, decisions about grouping patterns follow. Most early childhood programs group children by similar ages, such as infants birth to 12 months, toddlers 12 to 24 months, older toddlers 24 to 36 months, preschool ages 3 to 4, and prekindergarten ages 4 and 5. However, each program will determine the exact grouping that meets its program's goals. Some programs utilize mixed-age grouping wherein children of different ages learn and play together. This is common in family child care homes and in some Montessori programs.

Transitions between classrooms are handled differently depending on the program's goals; however, most programs transition children to older age groups on an annual basis so that they need to adjust to new teachers less frequently. Given the importance of warm reciprocal relationships, many programs work to keep teachers and children together over 2 or more years. This approach to grouping is called *continuity of care* or *looping*.

Noting that both Piaget (1959) and Vygotsky (1978) recognized that interactions with mixed-age peers support learning, some programs adopt a multiage grouping pattern, for example, serving 3- to 5-year-olds together in the same class. This approach is supported by DAP, which advises that curriculum is matched not only to the child's stage of development, but also to his or her individual needs. Similarly, Katz (1991) advised that early childhood programs must be responsive to a wide range of developmental levels and to the individual backgrounds and experiences of children. Programs that adopt this grouping pattern do so based on their conviction that individual needs can be met more readily in mixed-age groups.

Scheduling

Scheduling involves planning the length of the session and the timing and arrangement of activities during the daily session. Decisions about scheduling greatly influence children's feelings of security, the accomplishment of program goals, and the staff's effectiveness.

Length of Session: Programs of early care and education have traditionally included both full-day and half-day programs. The length of the school day is likely to reflect the needs of the families served and the auspices under which the program operates. Societal changes, such as increased levels of maternal employment and the growing emphasis on early learning standards, have resulted in an increase in the number of full-day programs, however, the quantity of time spent in school is not as significant as the quality of the experience.

Timing and Arranging Activities: Regardless of the length of the session, good schedules for early childhood programs have the following characteristics:

1. A good session begins with a friendly, informal greeting of the children. Staff should make an effort to speak to each child individually during the first few minutes of each session. A group activity, such as a greeting song, also helps children feel welcome. This is also a good time to help children learn to plan their activities.
2. The schedule should fit the goals of the program and the needs of the children as individuals and as a group. A balance should be maintained between physical activity and rest, indoor and outdoor activities, group and individual times, and teacher-determined and child-initiated activities.

3. The schedule must be flexible and able to respond to unexpected circumstances, such as inclement weather, children's interests that had not been anticipated (e.g., an unexpected and dramatic snowfall), and emergencies.

4. A good schedule should be readily understandable to the children so that they will have a feeling of security and will not waste time trying to figure out what to do next.

5. A good session ends with a time for reflection and a general evaluation of activities, straightening of indoor and outdoor areas, a hint about the next session, and a farewell. Children need to end a session with the feeling of achievement and with a desire to return. These feelings are important to staff, too!

Schedules must fit the length of the program day, week, and year. However, *scheduling* usually refers to the timing of daily activities. Local programs should devise their own schedules. Programs that serve children of different age groups must prepare more than one schedule to meet each group's needs. Even though each schedule will be different depending on the age group, the schedule should follow a predictable daily routine.

Schedules are often referred to as fixed or flexible. Programs place more emphasis on group conformity when they use a **fixed schedule**; that is, they expect children to work and play with others at specified times and take care of even the most basic physical needs—appetites and bodily functions—at prescribed times except for "emergencies." Often, programs for kindergarten and primary-grade children have fixed schedules. State departments of education/instruction often specify the total length of a school day and the number of minutes of instruction in each of the basic subjects.

Conversely, **flexible schedules** allow for individual children to make some choices as to how to spend their time and require children to conform to the group for only a few routine procedures (e.g., the morning greeting and planning session) and for short periods of group "instruction" (e.g., music, listening to stories). Infant programs have perhaps the most flexible schedules of all early childhood programs because infants stay on their own schedules. Child care programs often have flexible schedules because of their longer hours of operation, children's staggered arrivals and departures, and the varying ages of children the center serves. Flexibility is a must for children with special needs, too. McCormick and Feeney (1995) provided excellent suggestions for helping these children prepare for program transitions and follow transition directions. Furthermore, the health care services provided for children with special needs (e.g., ventilating, breathing treatments, tube feeding) should be planned to meet the individual needs of these children and when it causes least disruption to peers. Flexible schedules are more appropriate with emergent and integrated curricula (Jones & Nimmo, 1994; Rosegrant & Bredekamp, 1992). Rigid schedules undermine children's decision making and play (Wien, 1996). Of course, children need guidance in programs with flexible schedules. Because almost all programs use schedules, a few examples for different age groups follow. Examples are not given for infants, who follow their own schedules, or for public school kindergarten and primary programs because they adhere to state and local regulations regarding scheduling. Feeding, toileting, and resting were included in schedules for these groups; however, children should be free to use the bathroom or get a drink of water whenever they need to. The schedules are only suggestions; they are not prescriptive.

1. Toddler schedules—Toddler schedules usually revolve around the children's feeding and sleeping periods but should include lots of time for play activities both indoors and out. An example of a schedule for a full-day session is shown in Figure 9.4.

2. Preschool schedules—Preschoolers have the most flexible schedules of all early childhood programs. An example of a preschool center schedule is shown in Figure 9.5.

Daily Schedule

7:00–8:30 a.m.	Arrival, changing or toileting, dressing babies who are awake, and individual activities
8:30–9:00 a.m.	Breakfast snack, songs, stories, and finger plays
9:00–10:00 a.m.	Manipulative toy activities conducted by staff and changing or toileting
10:00–11:00 a.m.	Naps for those who take morning naps and outside play for others. (Children go outside as they awake.)
11:00–11:45 a.m.	Lunch and changing or toileting
11:45–1:00 p.m.	Naps
1:00–2:00 p.m.	Changing or toileting as children awaken and manipulative toy activities
2:00–2:30 p.m.	Snack, songs, stories, and finger plays
2:30 p.m. until departure	Individual activities

Figure 9.4
Toddler Schedule

Daily Schedule

7:00–9:00 a.m.	Arrival, breakfast for children who have not eaten or who want additional food, sleep for children who want more rest, and child-initiated play (which should be relatively quiet) in the activity centers)
9:00–9:30 a.m.	Toileting and morning snack
9:30–11:45 a.m.	Active work and play period, both indoor and outdoor. Field trips and class celebrations may be conducted in this time block
11:45–12:00 noon	Preparation for lunch, such as toileting, washing, and moving to dining area
12:00 noon–1:00 p.m.	Lunch and quiet play activities
1:00–3:00 p.m.	Story, rest, and quiet play activities or short excursions with assistants or volunteers as children awaken from naps
3:00–3:30 p.m.	Toileting and afternoon snack
3:30 p.m. until departure	Active work and play periods, both indoor and outdoor, and farewells as children depart with parents

Figure 9.5
Preschool Schedule

Daily Schedule	
6:30–7:00 a.m.	Arrival and activities such as quiet games or reading
7:00 a.m. until departure for school	Breakfast, grooming, and activities such as quiet games or reading
3:00–3:15 p.m.	Arrival from school
3:15 p.m. until departure	Snack and activities such as homework, tutorials, outdoor play, craft projects, table games, and reading

Figure 9.6
School-Age Schedule

3. School-age child care program schedules—School-age child care (SACC) programs usually follow very flexible schedules. An outline of an SACC program is shown in Figure 9.6.

TRENDS AND ISSUES

Four major trends and issues influence planning children's programs. One concern is creating a quality curriculum within today's standards-based environment. A second concern, closely tied to the first, is how to implement the curriculum using intentionality in teaching. The third concern is the growing achievement gap, and the fourth is meeting the needs of an increasingly diverse population that includes dual-language learners.

Defining Quality Curriculum: The Standards Movement

Concerns about program quality, including the quality of the curriculum, have been growing and fueled by the release of data from several national studies that showed the poor to mediocre quality of early childhood programs (Friedman & Haywood, 1994; Helburn, 1995; Kontos, Howes, Shinn, & Galinsky, 1995). The importance of curriculum quality as a foundation for lifelong academic and social competence was confirmed by two reports: *From Neurons to Neighborhoods: The Science of Early Childhood Development* (Shonkoff & Phillips, 2000) and *Eager to Learn: Educating Our Preschoolers* (NRC, 2001). In addition, a call for early learning standards became part of an effort to improve school readiness by improving content and pedagogy in the early years.

Seeing the Benefits: Early learning standards can be part of a high-quality system of program services to children. Curriculum standards can help identify important educational outcomes and can help build a coherent system of learning opportunities for children, even resolving some of the barriers to program transitions (Caldwell, 1991). Developing local curriculum standards can also be a means of building consensus between schools and families. Standards have become part of the early childhood landscape and continue to be a focus with the growing QRIS movement across states. Although there are concerns over standards in early childhood education, the early childhood literature is full of examples of how standards can be addressed in meaningful ways in developmentally appropriate learning environments through integrated curriculum approaches (Drew, Christie, Johnson, Meckley, & Nell, 2008; Helm, 2008).

Noting the Risks: Although every professional agrees on the need for "quality," curricular issues are far from resolved. Adopting standards can be beneficial, but doing so can be risky because standards reflect preferences. Several professional associations see the risks of early learning standards as being basically the same as the risks expressed about the trend toward "academic" programs that led to position statements addressing DAP. Following are some of the concerns about early learning standards:

1. Standards may focus on children's achievements rather than content and pedagogical improvements (Hatch, 2002).
2. They can result in inappropriate testing and assessment, and test scores can be used to penalize children (Gronlund, 2008; Shepard, Kagan, & Wurtz, 1998).
3. Because of developmental variability and heightened risks for some children, benchmarks are an added risk (Neuman, Copple, & Bredekamp, 2000).
4. Standards themselves can be too narrow if they are part of a fact- and skill-driven approach. Nonacademic strengths, such as emotional literacy, social competence, and positive approaches to learning, also predict success in school and in later life (Peth-Pierce, 2001; Raver, 2002).
5. Standards are not beneficial without highly qualified teachers and comprehensive school resources.
6. Direct instruction is assumed to be the only way to guarantee that standards are addressed; child-centered learning and exploratory learning are not trusted (Gronlund, 2008).

Issuing Standards on Standards: Because of the risks of early learning standards, NAEYC and the National Association of Early Childhood Specialists in State Departments of Education (2002) developed their joint position statement, "Early Learning Standards: Creating the Conditions for Success." These associations recommended that early learning standards be (a) significant, developmentally appropriate content and outcomes; (b) informed by research and developed and reviewed by all stakeholders; (c) implemented and assessed by ethical and appropriate means; and (d) supported by adequate program resources, professional development, and a partnership with families and other community members.

Intentionality in Teaching

Another current trend addresses the importance of intentionality in teaching (Copple & Bredekamp, 2009). These experts pointed out that although curriculum is important, it is the teacher who is of primary importance. DAP suggests that teachers should be intentional in all aspects of their teaching. Schiller (2009) discussed the importance of intentionality in teaching and states that it includes thinking carefully before doing. She suggested that intentional teachers are knowledgeable about best practice, and they give careful thought to setting up the learning environment, choosing curriculum, delivering information, and interacting with children. Intentionality in teaching will continue to be a growing component of high-quality programming as early educators work to meet the needs of an increasing diverse population.

The Growing Achievement Gap and Diverse Learners

Current early childhood literature points out that we continue to see a growing achievement gap in the United States with particular concerns about the performance of children living in poverty and those of African American and Hispanic descent (Copple & Bredekamp, 2009; Espinosa, 2010). Recent research shows that African American and Hispanic students continue to fail state tests in higher numbers than other groups (Rinde, 2011). NAEYC's DAP position statement calls for a reduction in the achievement gap by recognizing that behind these disparities in achievement lie differences in children's early experiences and access to high-quality early childhood schools. The achievement gap with children entering kindergarten is well documented and linked to poverty, but there is also much evidence to show that high-quality early childhood programs can have a positive impact on the achievement of low-income children (Espinosa, 2010).

The Growing Diversity of the United States and Dual-Language Learners

As discussed earlier in this chapter, the United States continues to become more diverse. Demographers estimate that by 2030, dual-language learners are expected to comprise 40% of the school-age population (Thomas & Collier, 2002). The terms *dual-language learners* (DLLs) and *English language learners* (ELLs) are used interchangeably in early childhood literature. Dual-language learners in the United States are most often of Hispanic descent and are more likely than other preschool children to live in poverty (Espinosa, 2010). Poverty compounds the challenge of closing the achievement gap. Dual-language learners of all backgrounds continue to grow in numbers in early childhood programs. These strategies have been suggested to help administrators meet the needs of dual-language learners:

- Clearly state your vision for what you want the program to become.
- Advocate for the possibilities and benefits of bilingualism in the classroom and supporting the home language of dual-language learners.
- Do your research. Do you know the trends in teaching and supporting second language acquisition?
- Organize professional development to help staff understand the stages of second language learning (Macrina, Hoover, & Becker, 2009).

Nemeth (2009) also discuss the home language mandate, which calls for early childhood programs to support children's home language as a necessity to providing high-quality programming.

SUMMARY

A curriculum is a way of helping teachers think about children and organize children's experiences in the program setting. The first step in program planning is to establish the program vision and mission. The director must then make statements concerning the local program's curriculum, which is often called the "program philosophy." The philosophy should be based on knowledge of children, the interests and needs of children, and the physical and social environment of the local program. Early learning standards may have to be considered as well. From these sources, goal statements must be generated and then translated into written program competencies that further refine them. The basic organization of the curriculum must be determined.

Plans must be made for implementing the curriculum. Deciding on the basic teaching strategies is most important. Other aspects of implementation include decisions about how computers will be used, classroom transitions, physical care routines, and special times. Plans for developing supportive relationships, both adult-child and child-child, are necessary to aid children in reaching program goals.

Directors and teachers must make decisions about group size and adult-child ratios, grouping children, and scheduling activities. These plans must conform to regulations and should be compatible with program goals. Four trends and issues seem to be occurring in program planning: (a) defining program quality in light of the standards movement, (b) intentionality in teaching, (c) the growing achievement gap, and (d) the increase in the diversity of learners in early childhood programs. Attempts are being made to resolve all of these issues, but many barriers remain.

USEFUL WEBSITES

The National Association for the Education for Young Children (NAEYC)

www.naeyc.org

This website has a collection of resources for parents and practitioners that includes links to position papers and resources in early childhood education, including membership information and descriptions of advocacy efforts at the national level.

The National Association for the Education of Young Children Torch Library

www.naeyc.org/academy/primary/torch

This website links to a resource database of the NAEYC accreditation criteria and related resources to support NAEYC accreditation. It requires visitors to log in, but membership in NAEYC is not required.

The National Center on Early Education Research (NIEER)

nieer.org/

The NIEER website provides the most current research in early education topics, including assessment and curriculum, as well as links to other relevant early childhood topics.

The National Association of Child Care Professionals (NACCP)

www.naccp.org

The NACCP website provides current information on early education topics for practitioners and information on membership, conferences, and advocacy. The NACCP also sponsors NAC accreditation, and links can be found on this website to accreditation information.

High/Scope Educational Research Foundation

www.highscope.org

This website provides information related to the High/Scope Active Learning Approach, including an online catalog with many resources to support active learning in early childhood education.

The Project Approach

www.projectapproach.org

The official website of the project approach as described by Sylvia Chard. The site provides detailed information and professional development opportunities on the project approach, including documentation of successful projects conducted with many age groups.

The Creative Curriculum

www.creativecurriculum.net

This website provides information on the Creative Curriculum and resources to support the implementation of this program.

Association Montessori Internationale

www.montessori-ami.org

This website outlines the philosophy and principles of the Montessori approach to early childhood education as traditionally proposed by Dr. Maria Montessori.

American Montessori Society

www.amshq.org

This website provides information about the Montessori curriculum as it has been modified for American society.

TO REFLECT

1. An early childhood director is faced with many families wanting a limited academic program for their children. What can the director say to explain the risks and lack of benefits of such a program? If the director's explanation is not accepted, what should he or she do? Should the director do as the families wish as a way of possibly ensuring the enrollment for the program? Should the director follow what he or she believes is "best practices" and hope that most families will stay with the program?

2. The director of a preschool center has called a meeting of the lead teachers for each of the five classrooms. According to their job description, lead teachers must take responsibility for the development of curriculum plans that will be implemented in their own classrooms. The director wants the group to develop a list of criteria that they can use in deciding on the appropriateness of themes or projects and the corresponding activities. What criteria could be used? (Be specific enough to be helpful.)

CHECK AND APPLY YOUR UNDERSTANDING

1. Identify resources that you as a director can rely on in helping your teachers understand age-related characteristics of each age group that your program serves.

2. Describe three methods that you will use to help teachers get to know the children and families in your program. Why is this an important part of program planning?

3. Explain why the standards movement has gained momentum in early childhood education and discuss how you would incorporate the standards in a developmentally appropriate manner.

4. Describe the benefits of child-initiated activity and why it is important in early childhood programs.

5. Why is continuity of care important for young children in group settings?

6. Describe the difference between fixed and flexible schedules. Why are flexible schedules more appropriate in the early childhood program?

CHAPTER 10

Providing Nutrition, Health, and Safety Services

Learning Outcomes

After studying this chapter, you should be able to:

1. Develop plans for healthy meals and snacks that meet young children's nutritional needs.

2. Evaluate a center's enrollment forms and policies to determine if they adhere to recommended practices designed to keep children healthy while they are in out-of-home care.

3. Design a safety checklist for an infant, toddler, or preschool classroom.

Grace's Experience

Grace's center has been running smoothly since the fall. Enrollment has been consistent, and turnover among lead teachers has not been a concern for several months. Now that it's winter, however, she's noticing more illness than before. It seems several teachers and a number of children are absent every day. She wonders if they are doing all they can to keep children and staff safe and healthy. And as she thinks about health and safety, she cannot help but also consider the nutritional value of the foods they've been serving. Could it be that their menus and food choices and even food preparation practices and hand washing in the classroom are contributing to some of the colds and stomach upsets that seem so frequent now? She begins to work more closely with the center's cook; to review health, safety, and nutrition guidelines; and to make these a focus of the staff development she's planning for later in the month. The information in this chapter helps her identify important issues to consider and guides her efforts to make improvements to make the center safer and healthier for both children and adults.

Recent years have brought an increased emphasis on ensuring that young children receive the best possible nutrition and protection of their health and safety while at home and in out-of-home settings. You are probably sensitive to the fact that health, safety, and nutrition are interrelated. Think, for example, how inadequate nutrition during infancy and early childhood can have a lifelong impact on children's health. When children are poorly nourished, even for a short period of time, they are apt to be less alert and prone to accidents and injury.

NAEYC Administrator Competencies addressed in this chapter:

Management Knowledge and Skills

5. Program Operations and Facilities Management
Knowledge of nutritional and health requirements for food service.

6. Family Support
Knowledge of community resources to support family wellness.

Early Childhood Knowledge and Skills

5. Children with Special Needs
The ability to work collaboratively as part of family-professional team in planning and implementing appropriate services for children with special needs.

6. Family and Community Relationships
Knowledge of different community resources, assistance, and support available to children and families.

7. Health, Safety, and Nutrition
Knowledge and application of practices that promote good nutrition, dental health, physical health, mental health, and safety of infants/toddlers, preschool, and kindergarten children. Ability to implement practices indoors and outdoors that help prevent, prepare for, and respond to emergencies. Ability to model healthful lifestyle choices.

A comprehensive approach to nutrition, health, and safety services in early childhood programs requires you to

- Provide nutritious meals and snacks.
- Make sure the environment for children's care and education is healthy and safe.
- Educate children, staff, and families on the importance of health, safety, and nutrition. This includes emphasizing the importance of prenatal care and nutrition as appropriate.

This comprehensive approach is supported by the third objective of Goal 1 of *America 2000* (U.S. Department of Education, 2001), which states, "Children will receive nutrition and health care needed to arrive at school with healthy minds and bodies, and the number of low birth weight babies will be significantly reduced through enhanced prenatal health systems" (p. 61). It is also addressed by NAEYC's Accreditation Standard #5 (NAEYC, 2007).

PROMOTING GOOD NUTRITION

Adequate nutrition is essential for physical growth and development. A healthy diet also supports children's immune systems so they stay healthy and have energy to play and explore. As part of society's current heightened interest in nutrition, early childhood programs are becoming more focused than ever on ensuring that children are offered a variety of appealing foods with high nutritional value. In addition, many children now spend the majority of their waking hours away from home. As a result child care has become a first line of defense for preventing childhood obesity (Kaphingst & Story, 2009). Thus, programs need to make sure that children have many opportunities throughout the day for gross motor activity.

Children are especially vulnerable to harm from malnutrition during periods of rapid growth. These effects can be particularly devastating during the prenatal period when inadequate nutrition can interfere with the development of the brain and central nervous system as well as the liver, kidneys, and pancreas. Maternal malnutrition can also cause babies to be born prematurely with low birth weights (Berk, 2008; Morgan & Gibson, 1991; Strupp & Levitsky, 1995).

Good nutrition remains critically important during infancy when, pound for pound, children need twice the calories as adults because 25% of their total caloric intake is devoted to growth (Berk, 2008). Children's appetites tend to become unpredictable during the preschool years when they are growing more slowly. During this period, caregivers should offer a variety of healthful choices and need not worry if they pick at their food and eat little at one meal because they are likely to make up for it by eating more later.

As a director of a program of early care and education, you will want to be sensitive to the fact that you will likely work with families that do not always have access to enough affordable and nutritious food to meet their basic needs. It is a sobering reality that reliable access to food is an issue for about 18% of all households with children under age 6 (or 36.2 million Americans, including 12.4 million children; Nord, Andrews, & Carlson, 2008).

Hunger is one of the greatest concerns among families living in poverty, particularly so in African American and Hispanic communities. The U.S. Department of Agriculture reports that 22.2% of African Americans and 20.1% of Hispanic families experience hunger and are not assured access to enough food for an active lifestyle (Nord et al., 2008). Low-income communities, particularly those with a diverse population, families headed by single women, or without reliable access to a vehicle to get to the grocery store, will benefit from information about community resources, such as food pantries, food banks, weekend backpacks programs, soup kitchens, or emergency kitchens operated by churches and other community organizations (Nord et al., 2008; U.S. Department of Agriculture, 2009). You might also be able to help families apply for the federal Supplemental Nutrition Assistance Program (SNAP, formally the Food Stamp Program). When you are familiar with these resources, you can help ensure that all the children you serve have reliable access to the high-quality nutrition they need for optimal growth and development.

Even while hunger and reliable access to nutritional food remain daily concerns for many families, increasing numbers of American children suffer from *misnourishment*—under-consuming important nutrients and over-consuming calories through high-fat and sugary foods (Bhattacharya & Currie, 2001). It is shocking that 73% of 2- through 5-year-old children and 87% of 6- through 9-year-old children have poor diets (Federal Interagency Forum on Child and Family Statistics, 2002). Critics blame much of this misnourishment on commercials for foods high in fat, sugar, and sodium and fast-food restaurants' menus that are full of high-fat and high-calorie offerings (Coleman, Wallinga, & Bales, 2010; Harris, Pomeranz, Lobstein, & Brownell, 2009; Kalich, Bauer, & McPartlin, 2009; Linn, 2004; Powell, Szczypka, Chaloupka, & Braunschweig, 2007).

Whether caused by the inability to access enough food or poor eating habits, the results of poor nutrition are the same. Children with poor diets are likely to be diagnosed as having *iron deficiency,* which has been associated with poor performance on measures of cognitive development including assessments of their mathematical and spatial abilities, disruptions in sleep patterns, and infrequent active play (Kordas, 2010). Children with iron deficiency have also been shown to be fearful, anxious, and depressed. These cognitive and behavioral problems tended to persist even with treatment (Lozoff, Jimenez, Hagen, Mollen, & Wolf, 2000). Those who work with young children have an important role to play in preventing iron deficiency both in the food they serve and in the guidance they provide to the families they serve.

Misnourishment and overconsumption of large portions of calorie-rich snacks high in fat and sugar and a sedentary lifestyle are major contributing factors to childhood obesity (Ambinder, 2010; Anderson & Butcher, 2006; Bar-Or, 2000; Coleman et al., 2010; Rideout & Hamel, 2006). Long-term risks are associated with letting children spend more than 2 hours each day watching TV or using computers and allowing them to eat in front of the TV; on the other hand, long-term benefits come from promoting an active lifestyle, for example, one that gives children opportunities to walk or ride their bikes to school (Coleman et al., 2010).

The definitions of *obesity* and *overweight* rely on the body mass index (BMI), which is a measure of weight in relation to height. *Overweight* is usually defined as being at or above the 85th percentile of the weight-to-height ratio, and *obesity* as being at or above the 95th percentile. The public was warned about the looming obesity epidemic more than 20 years ago (Javernick, 1988), and now rates of childhood obesity have reached alarming levels (Senate Committee on Health, Education & Pensions, 2008). Almost 32% of children in the United States are considered to be overweight and 11% are obese. Most disturbingly of all, those numbers are growing (Dehghan, Akhtar-Danesh, & Merchant, 2005; Senate Committee on Health, Education & Pensions, 2008). What's more, young children, particularly low-income African Americans, who are overweight during their preschool years are more likely to be overweight as they enter adulthood (Lee, Zoellner, Sandretto, & Ismail, 2010; Whitaker, Wright, Pepe, Seidel, & Dietz, 1997). Obesity and low levels of physical activity have lifelong implications, including an increased risk of early hypertension and diabetes (Perry, 2001; Stoneham, 2001); increased incidence of cardiovascular and digestive diseases (Dehghan et al., 2005); and an increased risk for asthma, sleep apnea (brief cessation of breathing during sleep); gallbladder disease; joint and skeletal abnormalities; and other health problems (Huettig, Sanborn, DiMarco, Popejoy, & Rich, 2004; Kaphingst & Story, 2009).

Obesity also affects children's quality of life. It brings psychological, emotional, and social risks, including an increased prevalence of childhood depression (Dehghan et al., 2005), social rejection, and withdrawal (Coleman et al., 2010; Huettig et al., 2004; Shoup, Gattshall, Dandamundi, & Estabrooks, 2008).

Consensus is growing that "interventions may need to focus on preschool-aged children to effectively address the childhood obesity epidemic in the United States" (Lee et al., 2010, p. 468). With more children than ever before in child care, programs of early care and education have a unique role to play in reducing childhood obesity. They can help children develop healthy attitudes about food and good eating habits by providing healthy choices during the day, and frequently offering children opportunities to prepare and eat new foods. Programs serving young children also have a unique opportunity to educate families about the importance of exposing their children to healthy choices such as fresh fruits and vegetables and whole grains (Kalich et al., 2009; Kaphingst & Story, 2009; Sweitzer et al., 2010).

A noteworthy effort to put the spotlight on childhood obesity has been launched by First Lady Michelle Obama. She highlights the *Let's Move: America's Move to Raise a Healthier Generation of Kids* initiative frequently during her public appearances and promotes the comprehensive interactive website listed at the end of this chapter. These resources could support your efforts to promote healthy eating and exercise in your center and in your outreach to families.

Application Activity

The website for the Centers for Disease Control and Prevention (CDC) BMI Calculator for Children and Teens is listed at the end of this chapter. Carefully weigh and measure a child older than age 2 and enter those data in this website. Bring the report to class with, if possible, a picture of the child. Consider whether the description on the CDC website—"underweight, healthy weight, at risk of overweight, or overweight"—seems accurate.

Providing and Serving Nutritious Meals and Snacks

Programs of early care and education have a responsibility to provide the children they serve nutritious and appealing meals and snacks to promote their general health, contribute to the development of healthy attitudes about food, and prevent obesity. They also have an opportunity to educate families about the importance of high-quality nutrition in the early years and to serve as a resource to ensure that all children have access to appropriate quantities of nutritious foods.

Meals and snacks served in early childhood programs often provide the majority of children's daily nutrition. The specific proportion provided by the program will, of course, depend on the amount of time the child spends at the center, but a good rule of thumb is that children younger than age 6 should be offered food every 2 to 3 hours (AAP/APHA/NRCHSCC, 2011). It is not uncommon for full-day programs to serve children up to four-fifths, and possibly more, of the food they eat each day.

Menu planning must consider dietary guidelines such as those described in USDA's MyPlate materials (which have replaced USDA's MyPryamid; Figure 10.1) and children's particular dietary needs, including food allergies or sensitivities and families' religious or culturally determined preferences such as a vegetarian diet or the avoidance of certain foods, such as pork (Holland, 2004). Programs should provide menus to families in advance to keep them informed about what their children will be offered while in care and to guide them in making food selections for the remainder of the child's day.

Figure 10.1
MyPlate Graphic
Source: U.S. Department
of Agriculture.

Remember that mealtimes feed the spirit as well as the body (Murray, 2000; Satter, 2000). While meeting children's nutritional needs, the center's food program has an opportunity to help children learn about new foods (Birch, Johnson, & Fisher, 1995) and experience new ways of serving foods. When meals are served family style, with serving platters, bowls, and pitchers on the table, they provide an opportunity to enjoy mealtime in a social setting where children can engage in relaxed conversations. These kinds of experiences promote children's social, emotional, and gross- and fine-motor skills and provide teachers and caregivers with opportunities to model polite conversation, encourage appropriate mealtime behavior, and teach children about good nutrition (AAP/APHA/NRCHSCC, 2010).

Regulations and standards related to ensuring children's nutritional well-being while in out-of-home care come from several sources. All are based on the Recommended Dietary Allowances (RDA) published by the Food and Nutrition Board of the National Academy of Sciences. The interactive website listed at the end of this chapter shows how much of each nutrient typically developing children need for optimum health, growth, and development.

Many states' licensing regulations and NAEYC's Accreditation Standards (2007) require that food be prepared, served, and stored in accordance with the U.S. Department of Agriculture's (USDA) Child and Adult Care Food Program (CACFP) guidelines. These guidelines for meals and snacks are the basis for examples presented in this text. The meal and snack patterns are based on the USDA's MyPyramid food guidance system for children 2 to 6 years old (U.S. Department of Agriculture, 2005). MyPlate dietary guidelines have recently been published. Choosemyplate.gov includes links to information on health and nutrition for pregnant and breastfeeding women, preschoolers, and children over 5. Go to MyPlate.gov to access these resources.

Food is likely to be a substantial part of an early childhood program's budget. Programs serving children eligible for free or reduced-price lunch can decrease these costs by participating in the USDA's National School Lunch Program and Child Nutrition Programs. Most not-for-profit programs and for-profit programs that serve a significant number of low-income children are eligible. Specific information about whom to contact in your state for information can be found at the end of this chapter.

All programs participating in the school lunch program must send representatives to mandated training sessions and must follow strict documentation requirements. It is imperative to check all regulations to avoid costly mistakes and delayed implementation and reimbursement. The guidelines below provide an overview of food program standards.

Guidelines for Feeding Infants

Because infants have such important nutritional needs, program directors and infant caregivers should work closely with families to create feeding routines that are relaxed, free from distractions, and focused on meeting the infant's physical and emotional needs. It is well established that breast milk provides the nutrition infants need for optimum growth and development. In fact, breast-feeding "offers lifelong health advantages [for babies] . . . contributes to the health of mothers and enhances the economic well-being of society" (U.S. Breastfeeding Committee, 2002, p. 1). What's more, breast-feeding, particularly when babies are exclusively breast-fed for at least 3 months, protects children from childhood obesity (Twells & Newhook, 2010). A growing number of states have laws supporting breast-feeding both in the workplace and in public (National Conference of State Legislatures, 2011). Child care programs need to take advantage of these legislated changes and their unique opportunity to encourage and support mothers to continue breast-feeding their babies after they return to work or school.

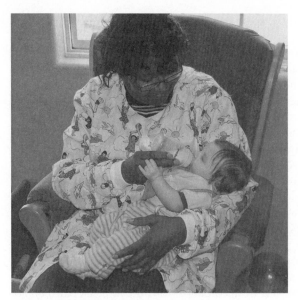

Mealtimes for infants should be time for intimate one-on-one interactions with their caregivers.

Child care programs can support mothers' efforts to continue breast-feeding when their babies enter care in several ways. The first is to design a comfortable place (not a bathroom) for mothers to nurse their babies or to pump milk to be fed to their babies later. The location should be equipped with an electrical outlet for electric breast pumps. This area should have a place for the mother to wash her hands and should offer a pillow to support her baby in her lap, a stepstool for her feet so she doesn't strain her back, and a convenient place to put a glass of water or juice to help her stay hydrated (AAP/APHA/NRCHSCC, 2011). The second way program directors can help is by being a cheerleader for breast-feeding mothers (AAP/APHA/NRCHSCC, 2011). You can encourage nursing mothers and connect them with support they may need, such as the services of a lactation consultant or information about where to rent an electric breast pump. And finally, you can help by increasing caregivers' knowledge about breast-feeding and its importance to mothers and their babies and by teaching staff how to properly store, handle, and feed breast milk (U.S. Breastfeeding Committee, 2002).

Directors can also support mothers' efforts to continue breast-feeding when their children come into care by recommending that they discuss their infant's usual eating patterns and their preferences with their child's caregivers. Caregivers need to know, for example, when the baby last nursed before coming in the morning, and if it will help the mother to have her baby hungry when she arrives at the end of the day or if she would rather feed him when she gets home. If mothers are coming to the center to nurse their babies during the workday, caregivers need to know if she will miss or be late for a scheduled feeding and must have a supply of expressed milk or formula on hand to feed the baby in her absence (AAP/APHA/NRCHSCC, 2011).

The USDA Infant Meal Pattern in Table 10.1 describes accepted feeding practices for infants up to 11 months old. Babies are usually ready for finger foods at about 8 months of age when they can pick up small items using the pincer grasp. Be careful to avoid anything that could be a choking hazard, such as raisins, nuts, popcorn, or small or hard foods such as sliced raw carrots (Hassink, 2006; National Food Service Management Institute, 2009). Note that fruit juice is now not recommended for babies younger than 12 months (AAP/APHA/NRCHSCC, 2011).

Directors should coach infant caregivers to follow these procedures when feeding infants:

1. Every effort should be made to have continuity of care during feeding. That means the same caregiver should plan to consistently feed each child.
2. Unless there are specific instructions to the contrary, young infants should be fed when the caregiver sees that the infant is signaling that she is hungry.
3. Keep breast milk or prepared formula in the refrigerator until just before feeding. Be certain to label each baby's bottle. It is important to give babies breast milk *only* from their mother, and that breast-fed infants are not fed formula without their mother's written permission.
4. Wash your hands before getting formula, food, or items used in feeding.
5. Milk and infant foods can be served cold. If the caregiver chooses to heat milk, bottles can be warmed by running them under hot water or by placing them in hot (not boiling) water for up to 5 minutes. Some centers use a crock-pot to keep hot water ready for warming bottles. Take care that the crock-pot is on a sturdy

Table 10.1
Child Care Infant Meal Pattern—CACFP

Birth through 3 Months	4 through 7 Months	8 through 11 Months
Breakfast		
4–6 fluid ounces of formula[a] or breast milk[b,c]	4–8 fluid ounces of formula[a] or breast milk[b,c]	6–8 fluid ounces of formula[a] or breast milk[b,c]; and
	0–3 tablespoons of infant cereal[a,d]	2–4 tablespoons of infant cereal[a]; and
		1–4 tablespoons of fruit or vegetable or both
Lunch or Supper		
4–6 fluid ounces of formula[a] or breast milk[b,c]	4–8 fluid ounces of formula[a] or breast milk[b,c]	6–8 fluid ounces of formula[a] or breast milk[b,c]
	0–3 tablespoons of infant cereal[a,d]; and	2–4 tablespoons of infant cereal[a,d]; and/or
	0–3 tablespoons of fruit or vegetable or both[d]	1–4 tablespoons of meat, fish, poultry, egg yolk, cooked dry beans or peas; or
		1/2–2 ounces of cheese; or
		1–4 ounces (volume) of cottage cheese; or
		1–4 ounces (weight) of cheese food or cheese spread; and
		1–4 tablespoons of fruit or vegetable or both
Supplement (Midmorning or Midafternoon Snack)		
4–6 fluid ounces of formula[a] or breast milk[b,c]	4–6 fluid ounces of formula[a] or breast milk[b,c]	2–4 fluid ounces of formula[a] or breast milk[b,c], or fruit juice[e]; and
		0–1/2 bread[d,f] or
		0–2 crackers[d,f]

[a]Infant formula and dry infant cereal must be iron fortified.

[b]Breast milk or formula, or portions of both, may be served; however, it is recommended that breast milk be served in place of formula from birth through 11 months.

[c]For some breast-fed infants who regularly consume less than the minimum amount of breast milk per feeding, a serving of less than the minimum amount of breast milk may be offered, with additional breast milk offered if the infant is still hungry.

[d]A serving of this component is required when the infant is developmentally ready to accept it.

[e]Fruit juice must be full strength.

[f]A serving of this component must be made from whole-grain or enriched meal or flour.

Source: Child & Adult Care Food Program Meal Patterns, United States Department of Agriculture, 2009, Washington, DC: Author. Available online at http://www.fns.usda.gov/cnd/care/programbasics/meals/meal_patterns.htm#Infant

counter and is out of children's reach. The water in the crock-pot should be heated to no more than 120°F and must be emptied, sanitized, and refilled each day. Shake warmed bottles and stir warmed food well and test the temperature before giving it to the baby. ***Never microwave bottles or baby food to heat them.*** Microwaving destroys nutrients in breast milk and creates hot spots that can burn babies' mouths and throats.

6. Feedings should be relaxed and enjoyable. Hold young infants comfortably in a semi-sitting position to reduce the risk of choking and to prevent milk or formula from entering the inner ear where it can cause ear infections. Hold the bottle so that liquid fills the nipple to prevent the baby from swallowing air as he sucks. Burp the baby over your shoulder or on your knees several times during the

feeding. Eye contact, talking with babies, and cuddling them are essential to support children's social and emotional development. And to create positive attitudes about eating, ***never prop bottles or permit infants to carry bottles while standing, walking, or running around.***

7. Most children are ready to begin mashed or pureed foods at about 6 months. Never put baby food into a bottle or feeding device unless specifically recommended by the baby's physician.

8. Pediatricians typically advise that caregivers introduce babies to single-grain iron-enriched cereals first, beginning with rice or barley, which are less likely to cause allergic reactions, followed by strained fruits and vegetables, and finally strained meats. It is particularly important to work closely with infants' families so that caregivers can coordinate the introduction of new foods. Begin solid food by offering one or two small spoonfuls of one new food at a time and continue it for 2 or 3 days before introducing the next new food. Introducing new foods slowly and one-at-a-time will help identify any food allergies or sensitivities the child may have.

9. Wash jars or containers of commercially prepared baby food before opening because they could be contaminated by disease-causing bacteria during shipping and storage.

10. Discard any food left in containers or dishes from which children have been fed. Once a spoon with saliva has been in any food, it must not be put back into its original container. Unused portions of baby food should be stored in the refrigerator in their original containers and discarded after 24 hours.

11. Encourage older infants to feed themselves using their fingers and appropriate utensils and to begin to drink from a cup (AAP/APHA/NRCHSCC, 2011).

Infants' and toddlers' mealtime experiences should be relaxed and enjoyable, and they need to be exposed to a variety of healthy foods presented in an appealing way. These young children are beginning to develop lifelong attitudes about healthy foods.

Guidelines for Feeding Young Children

A qualified cook will create menus and prepare foods children enjoy.

When you are the program director, you have a responsibility to create the expectation that staff will model the same mealtime behaviors that they expect from the children. They are to join in relaxed mealtime conversations, make nutritious choices, enjoy a wide variety of healthy foods, and welcome the opportunity to sample new and unfamiliar dishes when they are offered. Young children should be encouraged to enjoy a variety of nutritious foods. Table 10.2 is a meal and snack plan developed by the USDA.

These are some practices that will help your program provide safe, enjoyable meals and snacks:

1. Avoid foods that can be choking hazards to children younger than age 4. Do not serve whole grapes or olives; nuts; popcorn; chunks of raw carrots, pears, or apples; spoonfuls of peanut butter or bread that becomes gummy; chunks of hotdogs; stringy foods; or cherries with pits. Cut food into pieces no larger than 1/4-in. square for infants and 1/2-in. square for toddlers to 2-year-olds. Children's ability to chew and swallow should guide feeding practices (NAEYC, 2007).

Table 10.2
Meal Pattern for Children—CACFP

Breakfast Meal Pattern

Select All Three Components for a Reimbursable Meal

Food Components	Children Age 1–2	Children Age 3–5	Children Age 6–12[a]
1 milk fluid milk	1/2 cup	3/4 cup	1 cup
1 fruit/vegetable juice[b]; fruit and/or vegetable	1/4 cup	1/2 cup	1/2 cup
1 grains/bread[c] bread or	1/2 slice	1/2 slice	1/2 slice
cornbread or biscuit or roll or muffin or	1/2 serving	1/2 serving	1 serving
cold dry cereal or	1/4 cup	1/3 cup	3/4 cup
hot cooked cereal or	1/4 cup	1/4 cup	1/2 cup
pasta or noodles or grains	1/4 cup	1/4 cup	1/2 cup

Lunch or Supper Meal Pattern

Select All Four Components for a Reimbursable Meal

Food Components	Children Ages 1–2	Children Ages 3–5	Children Ages 6–12[a]
1 milk fluid milk	1/2 cup	3/4 cup	1 cup
2 fruits/vegetables juice,[b] fruit and/or vegetable	1/4 cup	1/2 cup	3/4 cup
1 grains/bread[c] bread or	1/2 slice	1/2 slice	1 slice
cornbread or biscuit or roll or muffin or	1/2 serving	1/2 serving	1 serving
cold dry cereal or	1/4 cup	1/3 cup	3/4 cup
hot cooked cereal or	1/4 cup	1/4 cup	1/2 cup
pasta or noodles or grains	1/4 cup	1/4 cup	1/2 cup
1 meat/meat alternate meat or poultry or fish[d] or	1 oz	1–1/2 oz	2 oz
alternate protein product or	1 oz	1–1/2 oz	2 oz
cheese or	1 oz	1–1/2 oz	2 oz
egg or	1/2	3/4	1
cooked dry beans or peas or	1/4 cup	3/8 cup	1/2 cup
peanut or other nut or seed butters or	2 tbsp	3 tbsp	4 tbsp
nuts and/or seeds[e] or	1/2 oz	3/4 oz	1 oz
yogurt[f]	4 oz	6 oz	8 oz

(Continued)

Table 10.2 (*Continued*)

Snack

Select Two of the Four Components for a Reimbursable Snack

Food Components	Children Ages 1–2	Children Ages 3–5	Children Ages 6–12[a]
1 milk			
fluid milk	1/2 cup	1/2 cup	1 cup
1 fruit/vegetable			
juice[b]; fruit and/or vegetable	1/2 cup	1/2 cup	3/4 cup
1 grains/bread[c]			
bread or	1/2 slice	1/2 slice	1 slice
cornbread or biscuit or roll or muffin or	1/2 serving	1/2 serving	1 serving
cold dry cereal or	1/4 cup	1/3 cup	3/4 cup
hot cooked cereal or	1/4 cup	1/4 cup	1/2 cup
pasta or noodles or grains	1/4 cup	1/4 cup	1/2 cup
1 meat/meat alternate			
meat or poultry or fish[d] or	1/2 oz	1/2 oz	1 oz
alternate protein product or	1/2 oz	1/2 oz	1 oz
cheese or	1/2 oz	1/2 oz	1 oz
egg[e] or	1/2	1/2	1/2
cooked dry beans or peas or	1/8 cup	1/8 cup	1/4 cup
peanut or other nut or seed butters or	1 tbsp	1 tbsp	2 tbsp
nuts and/or seeds or	1/2 oz	1/2 oz	1 oz
yogurt[f]	2 oz	2 oz	4 oz

[a]Children age 12 and older may be served larger portions based on their greater food needs. They may not be served less than the minimum quantities listed in this column.

[b]Fruit or vegetable juice must be full strength. Juice cannot be served when milk is the only other snack component.

[c]Breads and grains must be made from whole-grain or enriched meal or flour. Cereal must be whole grain or enriched or fortified.

[d]A serving consists of the edible portion of cooked lean meat or poultry or fish.

[e]One-half egg meets the required minimum amount (one ounce or less) of meat alternate.

[f]Yogurt may be plain or flavored, unsweetened or sweetened.

Source: Child & Adult Care Food Program Meal Patterns, United States Department of Agriculture, 2009, Washington, DC: Author. Available on-line at http://www.fns.usda.gov/cnd/care/programbasics/meals/meal_patterns.htm#Child_Breakfast

    2. Follow guidelines about the appropriate kind of milk for children of different ages. Whole milk is usually recommended for children 12–24 months old. Children age 3 and older are usually served 1% milk.

    3. Offer children small servings, with second helpings available if they are still hungry.

    4. When serving a new or unpopular food, try this approach:
       a. Serve a tiny portion with a more generous portion of a popular food.
       b. Introduce only one new food at a time.
       c. Introduce a new food to children when they are hungry.

d. Eat the food yourself.

e. Have children help prepare the food.

f. Keep offering the food because the more often children are offered a food, the more likely they are to try it.

g. You may want to introduce new foods as snacks before putting them on the menu.

5. Children are likely to enjoy special foods for holidays and birthdays, but holidays do not mean children are taking a break from nutrition. Festive foods can still be healthy choices (Wardle, 1990).

6. Do not serve the same food, or virtually the same food, such as meatballs and hamburgers, on consecutive days.

7. Make an effort to serve children the same kinds of foods they eat at home. This may require you to learn more about the foods families eat, including their cultural and religious preferences, and can be a good way to strengthen home-school relationships.

8. Take children's likes and dislikes into account when preparing and serving foods. Young children generally like a variety of foods (different sizes, shapes, colors, textures, and temperatures), foods prepared in different ways, foods served in bite-sized pieces or as finger foods, vegetables with mild flavors, fruit (but not vegetable) combinations, pleasing textures (fluffy, not gooey, mashed potatoes), and foods that are not too hot or cold.

9. Provide a pleasant physical environment and positive emotional climate for meals and snacks. The lunchroom or the section of the room used for eating should be quiet enough for children and adults to easily talk with each other. It should be attractive, with furniture, dishes, silverware, and serving utensils that are easy for the children to handle. Adults should join children at meals rather than hover over them while they eat. They should give children opportunities to make choices and recognize that it is not unusual for preschoolers to go through phases when they are picky eaters or even go on **binges** where they will want to eat only a certain food for a week or two. Children should not be "forced" or coerced to eat all the food on their plate, instead they should be encouraged to eat until they are satisfied (Coleman et al., 2010).

Review Figure 10.2, which is an example of a weekly menu for children 3 to 5 years old.

Children with Special Needs: Programs serving children who have special needs have a responsibility to make the accommodations necessary to ensure their access to nutritious meals and snacks. For example, some children may need special help feeding themselves, and children with metabolic disorders will need a carefully planned and monitored diet. Ask families and the child's health care provider to provide specific dietary information in writing when children's special needs require accommodations at mealtimes.

Application Activity

Use the menu ideas discussed earlier to plan a week of lunches for a group of toddlers or preschoolers. Prepare a shopping list that indicates how much of each item you would need to serve a class and two teachers for a week. Use NAEYC group sizes to determine how many children you will need to plan for.

Hillview Center

Date	Monday	Tuesday	Wednesday	Thursday	Friday
Breakfast					
Fluid Milk	¾ cup 1% milk[1]	¾ cup 1% milk	¾ cup 1% milk	¾ cup 1% milk	¾ cup 1% milk
Fruit, Vegetable or Full-Strength Juice	½ cup cantaloupe	½ cup apricots[2]		½ cup bananas	½ cup pears
Bread or Bread Alternate(s)	1/3 cup Cheerios	½ English muffin	½ slice whole wheat bread	¼ cup cooked oatmeal	1 blueberry pancake
Additional Food (Optional)			Boiled Eggs		1 tbsp reduced-calorie pancake syrup
Lunch					
Main Dish	Spaghetti	Chicken tacos	Hamburger	Oven-baked Chicken-D-29[3]	Turkey sandwiches
Fluid Milk	¾ cup 1% milk	¾ cup 1% milk	¾ cup 1% milk	¾ cup 1% milk	¾ cup 1% milk
Meat or Meat Alternative	1 ½ oz ground beef	1 ½ oz ground chicken	1 ½ oz lean hamburger patty	2 oz chicken	1 ½ oz roasted turkey breast
Vegetable or Fruit	¼ cup peaches	¼ cup lightly steamed carrots	¼ cup pear halves	¼ cup applesauce	¼ cup apricot halves
Vegetable or Fruit	¼ cup green salad, 1 tbsp shredded carrots	2 tbsp shredded lettuce, 2 tbsp diced tomato	¼ cup lettuce & tomato salad	¼ cup steamed broccoli	¼ cup orange-glazed sweet potatoes-I-12[4]
Bread or Bread Alternative	¾ cup pasta	1 tortilla	½ whole wheat bun	½ slice bread	½ whole wheat roll
Additional Food (Optional)	1 tbsp low-fat salad dressing	1 tbsp grated cheese, 1 tbsp salsa	Ketchup	1 tbsp butter	1 tsp light mayonnaise
PM Snack					
Choose 2 of These 4: Fluid Milk / Fruit, Vegetable or Full-Strength Juice / Bread or Bread Alternative / Meat or Meat Alternative	Fruit kabobs (⅛ cup fresh cantaloupe, ⅛ cup fresh banana, ¼ cup pineapple, ½ oz reduced fat cheddar cheese Water[4]	2 oz lowfat vanilla yogurt ½ cup diced peaches Water	½ oz reduced fat cheddar cheese and ½ oz wheat crackers (about 4 crackers) Water	½ cup fresh carrot sticks[5] with 1 tbsp low-fat ranch dressing ½ oz wheat crackers (about 4 crackers) Water	2 oz lowfat yogurt ½ oz graham cracker sticks (about 2 crackers) Water

[1]Nutritionists recommend serving whole milk for ages 1 and 2 and reduced fat milk for ages 3–5.
[2]Fruit is canned in juice, drained unless otherwise specified. Fresh fruits and vegetables are preferred.
[3]USDA Recipes for Child Care. Available online at www.nfsmi.org.
[4]Water is suggested as a beverage for all snacks even when other beverages are offered to encourage children to drink water.
[5]Lightly steaming carrots may make them easier to eat.

Figure 10.2
Sample Weekly Menu for Preschoolers

Hiring Staff and Meeting Requirements for the Food Service Program

Directors must consider more than the nutritional needs of children when planning the program's food services. They must also consider how food will be ordered, stored, prepared, and served and how the food service area will be kept clean and sanitary. That means they need to determine their staffing needs as well as the availability of storage for food and supplies and space and equipment for food preparation and cleanup. They must also ensure compliance with applicable sections of licensing, health department, and accreditation regulations and standards. All these decisions have financial implications. Consider these food service options:

1. Catered meal services are often an expensive option but may be desirable if the program does not have a kitchen.
2. Prepackaged convenience foods may be nutritionally inferior, are expensive, and require large freezers for storage and large ovens or microwaves for preparation.
3. Onsite meal and snack preparation requires a qualified staff and adequate storage space and food service equipment.

Hiring Staff: Having the help you need to prepare and serve meals and snacks in a reasonable length of time is important. Consider the recommended food service staffing patterns for different child care arrangements described in Table 10.3.

Your state's licensing standards or applicable federal regulations may identify the qualifications of food service personnel. Even with those regulations in place, however, some studies show that the employees responsible for planning menus and preparing meals in child care settings are likely to have had no specialized training in meal preparation (Drake, 1992; Romaine, Mann, Kienapple, & Conrad, 2007). If that is the case in the center you direct, you will want to explore the resources for professional development, menu planning, and food preparation provided at the end of this chapter. They can help your staff plan healthy, balanced meals. Licensing guidelines often require that menus documenting the nutritional value of meals and snacks served during the school day be prepared in advance. These menus may need to be made available during financial audits. Futhermore, if you are not able to hire a cook with specialized training in food planning, you may want to arrange for one to serve as a consultant.

Table 10.3
Food Service Staffing Patterns for Child Care Homes and Centers

Setting	Food Service Staff
Small and large family child care homes	Caregiver
Centers serving up to 30 children	Full-time child care Food Service Worker (cook)
Centers serving up to 50 children	Full-time child care Food Service Worker (cook) and part-time child care Food Service Aide
Centers serving up to 125 children	Full-time child care Food Service Manager or full-time child care Food Service Worker (cook) and full-time child care Food Service Aide
Centers serving up to 200 children	Full-time child care Food Service Manager and full-time child care Food Service Worker (cook) and one full-time plus one part-time child care Food Service Aide
Vendor food service	One assigned staff member or one part-time staff member, depending on amount of food service preparation needed after delivery

Source: Information from *Caring for Our Children: National Health and Safety Performance Standards: Guidelines for out-of-home child care programs* (3rd ed., p. 176), by the American Academy of Pediatrics, the American Public Health Association, and the National Resource Center for Health and Safety in Child Care, 2011, Elk Grove Village, IL and Washington, DC.

Snacks and mealtimes should be relaxed opportunities for social interactions.

Providing Facilities and Equipment: A local child care nutrition specialist or food service expert should work with the architect on the design of the food service areas of the facility. Food service equipment must be purchased, installed, and operated according to the standards of the National Sanitation Foundation (NSF), applicable public health regulations, or the USDA.

Purchasing Food: Planning food purchases helps control costs and reduces waste. Consider these suggestions:

1. Check several food companies or stores in the area for quality food at reasonable prices and for services you need, such as a line of credit and regular delivery.
2. Look for high-quality products. Your state's licensing regulations are likely to specify that you purchase only government-inspected meats, fish, and poultry; pasteurized grade-A milk and milk products; frozen foods that are kept hard frozen; and perishable and nonperishable foods that are wholesome, unspoiled, free from contamination, properly labeled, and safe for human consumption.
3. Fresh fruits and vegetables and minimally processed prepared foods are likely to have higher nutritional value; will help you avoid serving children foods high in transfats, sugars, and salt; and are apt to be appealing to children and adults alike.
4. Carefully calculate the quantities of food needed. Use standardized recipes that can be adjusted to provide the appropriate number of servings. See the resources at the end of the chapter for sources for recipes and menus.
5. Carefully consider the types of food (perishable or nonperishable) and the amount of storage space when deciding when and how much food to purchase.
6. Keep accurate records about the food purchased, when and how it was used, its cost, and any other notes that will help you make future purchases.

Meeting Sanitation Requirements: You can help prevent disease by carefully following all sanitation guidelines. Cleanliness must be considered in all aspects of food service. These are some recommended food service practices:

1. All food service employees must meet state and local health requirements, must wash hands thoroughly, wear clean clothes, take measures to keep their hair out of the food, be free from skin infections, and must not have a contagious disease when they prepare or serve food.

2. Preparation and serving utensils and dishes must be thoroughly washed, sanitized, and properly handled. Most state's licensing regulations describe specific procedures. They might say, for example, that the dishwasher should be set for a water temperature of 160–165°F (66–74°C), using 0.25% detergent concentration or 1 oz of detergent per 3 gal of water. These are typical instructions for washing dishes and food preparation equipment by hand:

    a. Wash with soap or detergent in hot water (110–120°F or 43–49°C).

    b. Rinse in warm water.

    c. Sanitize by immersing for at least 1 minute in clean, hot water (at least 170°F or 76°C) or by immersing for at least 3 minutes in a sanitizing solution of 1 tbsp household bleach per 2 gal of water.

    d. Air dry; do not wipe.

3. Foods should be checked on delivery to be certain they meet your specifications, protected in storage, used within the specified time.

4. Wash raw foods carefully and cook prepared foods properly.

5. Foods must be kept at appropriate temperatures before serving. Hot foods should be held at 140°F (60°C) or above and cold foods at 45°F (7°C) or below.

6. Dispose of all foods served and not eaten.

7. Help children learn how to wash their hands thoroughly and get them into the habit of washing their hands before eating.

Planning Nutrition Education

Programs of early care and education have an important opportunity to educate children and families about the importance of good nutrition. They can also help children develop healthy lifelong habits and attitudes about food.

Integrating Nutrition Education into the Curriculum: Early childhood programs should plan how they will teach young children about the importance of good nutrition and help them learn to identify the foods that will help keep them strong and healthy. These activities can easily be integrated across content areas in classrooms that actively engage children in meaningful activities. Consider these strategies to integrate nutrition education into the curriculum.

1. Teach children how foods support health, growth, and development, and help them develop positive attitudes about food and healthy diets.

2. Give children opportunities to learn about where food comes from and how it is prepared. This means children might participate in planting, caring for, and eating vegetables from an onsite garden or visit a farm, farmer's market, greengrocer, or supermarket to purchase foods to prepare in the classroom.

3. Plan, prepare, and serve nutritious snacks. Cooking experiences give children opportunities to follow directions and sometimes to read a recipe; count and measure ingredients; take turns and cooperate with others; refine their eye-hand coordination; and talk with peers and adults to learn new skills, solve problems, and ask questions. When children prepare food together, they also have opportunities to appreciate differences in food preferences and to eat foods prepared in different ways (Colker, 2005; Kalich et al., 2009; Ostrosky & Meadan, 2010). Many cookbooks and websites contain recipes to use with young children.

4. Provide opportunities for children to socialize during meals and snacks to develop good manners. This will help them enjoy meals in a variety of settings—home, child care, and restaurants or when visiting friends and family.

Serving Families' Needs:　We know that child care programs have the opportunity to influence children's attitudes about food, but the fact remains that families have a lifelong impact on children's eating habits and food preferences (Coleman et al., 2010; Sweitzer et al., 2010). Although children decide how much (or even whether) to eat, adults are responsible for the foods they are offered. Family members can help their children learn about nutrition and develop positive attitudes about healthy foods (Coleman et al., 2010; Satter, 2000; Sweitzer et al., 2010; Twells & Newhook, 2010). They need to be informed about a number of nutrition-related topics including the following:

1. Foods children need for optimum health, growth, and development
2. The important benefits of breast-feeding, particularly in early infancy
3. Strategies for helping children develop healthy attitudes about eating
4. Strategies for helping children enjoy a wide variety of fresh fruits and vegetables
5. The importance of helping children understand the intent of advertisements for foods high in fats, sugars, salt, and preservatives

Staff should make efforts to become acquainted with families' lifestyles: Do they frequently eat in restaurants? Do they cook at home, preparing foods "from scratch," or do they rely on prepared foods to make food preparation easier? Do they make it a priority to provide children organic foods or grow much of their family's foods themselves?

Consider adapting the Food Preferences form in Figure 10.3 to let families know that enjoying a variety of foods is part of your curriculum. This form also invites families to share foods that are favorites in their home with their child's classmates.

Child care personnel should also make an effort to stay informed if, for example, parents should become unemployed or face particular challenges providing for their family's

---

Child's name _____

Our center provides children with many opportunities to experience a wide variety of healthy foods. We hope you'll join us in encouraging your child to enjoy tasting unfamiliar fruits, vegetables, and other healthy offerings.

Perhaps you would like to send a snack, fruit, or vegetable that you enjoy at your home for your child to share with his/her classmates. This can be a good way to share your family's special traditions with your child's classmates.

Does your child have any identified food allergies? *Please let us know if they are so severe that we need to restrict foods (such as nuts) that come into the classroom.*

What are some of your child's favorite foods for breakfast, lunch, and healthy snacks?

Please let me know if you would like to share something that is a favorite at your home with our class.

Figure 10.3
Sample Favorite Foods Form

basic needs. Put families that may need assistance gaining access to adequate food in touch with appropriate social service agencies. Follow up to be certain their needs were met. Programs can reach out to all families by offering information about children's nutritional needs and how to meet them in demonstration classes, meetings, home visits and through newsletters. Consider the following suggestions:

1. Staff can help families plan nutritious meals by providing them with copies of the MyPlate food guidance system and by conducting workshops to help them apply these guidelines when planning family meals. The MyPlate website listed at the end of the chapter has helpful information to plan presentations.
2. Newsletters can include ideas for healthy kid-friendly meals, recipes that can help nurture young children's interest in healthy foods and snacks, and nutritional information for offerings at local fast-food restaurants to help families make healthy choices when eating out.
3. Printed program menus should be sent home so families can plan meals that supplement rather than duplicate school offerings.
4. Ask family members to participate in cooking activities.

A Better Way

As a beginning director, Grace was focused on feeding the children efficiently with food they would enjoy. She found a supplier who had a good selection of frozen waffles and toaster pastries for breakfast and pizzas, chicken nuggets, fish sticks, and the like for lunch. She knew the children would eat these familiar foods, so she made them the mainstays of the center's menu. She liked that these dishes would be quick and easy to prepare, and she believed the extra cost of prepared main dishes would be offset by lower personnel costs since there would be little preparation needed.

Grace was pleased when the local NAEYC affiliate sponsored a Directors' Forum meeting focused on managing food services. There she learned about the recommendation that her center, licensed for 90 children, should have a full-time cook or food service manager and a full-time food service aide. The trainers shared alarming statistics about the growing crisis of childhood obesity and shared resources to help center directors serve healthier meals and snacks. She also gave directors ideas about how to share this information with their families.

Grace left that training determined to spend more on food service personnel and less on prepared foods. She was convinced that she could save money by buying fresh fruits and vegetables from the local farmers' market, and that a good cook could find recipes for foods children would enjoy that were high in nutrition and low in salt, sugar, and fat. It did not take long for children to be enjoying homemade yogurt parfaits, chicken casseroles, and bean burritos.

Even though it took a bit more time to prepare fresh fruits and vegetables for snacks, it was rewarding to see children enjoying fresh local produce much of the year. An unexpected benefit was that Grace became acquainted with a local farmer who delivered peaches, watermelons, apples, and other foods directly to the center. The suburban children who attended her center learned more about their rural surroundings, the teachers found many teachable moments as the children got to know the farmer and to look forward to his deliveries, and families began to look for local farmers' markets to serve more fresh, local foods at their own tables.

Grace got on the road to serving the children at her center healthier foods as a result of just one hour of professional development. She really did learn a better approach to menu planning and food preparation!

PROMOTING GOOD HEALTH

Programs for young children began focusing on children's health in the mid-1940s (Child Welfare League of America, 1945). Although this interest has fluctuated over the years, efforts to enhance children's health status were brought front and center by the Goals 2000 legislation enacted in 1994. The first of these goals challenges the United States to guarantee that "all children in America will start school ready to learn [and will] receive the nutrition, physical activity experiences, and health care needed to arrive at school with healthy minds and bodies, and to maintain the mental alertness necessary to be prepared to learn" (Goals 2000, 1994). Progress toward that goal continues to motivate advocates and policy makers focused on children's issues.

Today, the definition of *health* has shifted from the absence of disease to a state of total physical, mental, and social and emotional well-being. Each of the three aspects of health contributes equally to a person's overall health. For example, physical health problems often cause young children to be listless, which results in less exploration and play. This decreases interaction in one's physical and social worlds and adversely affects cognitive and social and emotional development.

Conversely, a stressful cognitive, social, or emotional environment can lead to physical health problems. As a result of our increased understanding of this interactive relationship, early childhood professionals are giving increased attention to children's health and physical well-being.

Program directors must be concerned about the health of all those involved in their early childhood programs. They must develop health policies for children and staff in keeping with current information and must plan and oversee the implementation of the policies.

Assessing Health Status

Assessment of health is an appraisal of an individual's health status. Because health status is changing and dynamic, this appraisal should include a periodic in-depth assessment by a specially trained health care professional and continuous day-to-day observations.

Staff: Working in an early care and education program is physically demanding, exposes employees to infectious illnesses, can put individuals at risk for back injuries from frequent lifting, and can be emotionally stressful. The health of adults is a key element in the quality of an early childhood program. A staff member's illness can have serious personal consequences, can become a health hazard to children and other staff members; can interfere with the program's efforts to provide continuity of care; and can be costly if substitutes are frequently needed.

Planning to assess each staff member's health begins with the wording of the program's job descriptions. Each needs to be explicit about the physical demands required to successfully complete required tasks. Without this level of specificity, hiring or dismissal decisions may appear to be discriminatory. Although all employees must meet some requirements (e.g., being free from contagious diseases), others are more job specific (e.g., the ability to lift or visually supervise the children in their care).

It is wise to establish policies addressing the following:

1. The extent of the health history and medical examination required for employment, including specific requirements for employees in particular positions
2. Who can conduct the required physical examination and who can sign the required form (i.e., Is it acceptable for the form to be signed by a nurse practitioner or physician's assistant?)
3. Who pays for the pre-employment physical exam?

4. Who at the local program receives the information?
5. When must the report be received for the applicant to be considered for a specific position?

The medical assessment should be completed and reviewed before the job offer is made final and before the new hire comes into contact with children. Samples of staff health assessments can be found by following links to online resources at the end of this chapter.

Children: Children's health status must be documented before they can participate in a program of early care and education and should be assessed continuously while they are participating in the program. Most states' licensing regulations require that children have a medical examination and that they submit a health care professional's report that includes documentation that they have received the required vaccinations.

Samples of child health assessments can be found by following links to online resources at the end of this chapter. These sample forms ask for information about the child's health history, allergies, results of screening tests, documentation of the children's immunization record, and results of a recent examination. They may also ask for the date of the child's last dental examination. The medical professional is also asked to indicate any health problems or special needs and to describe accommodations the program may need to make.

Children sometimes become ill while in care. A systematic way to record symptoms and report them to the child's family is needed. See Figure 10.4 for an example of a symptom/incident notice.

Advocating for Preventive Health Care

Early childhood programs can have a significant impact on participating children's health. First, directors should be prepared to help families access health care their children may need, including dental services. Second, at the programmatic level, directors should have a plan in place to educate children, families, and caregivers about preventative health and safety, including recommendations for protecting children from the sun and steps they can take to reduce the spread of infection in the center.

Accessing Health Services: Health care professionals advise that all children should have a medical home providing "primary care that is accessible, continuous, comprehensive, family-centered, coordinated, compassionate, and culturally effective" (American Academy of Family Physicians, American Academy of Pediatrics, American College of Physicians, & American Osteopathic Association, 2007). Early childhood programs are often in a position to help families establish a medical or dental home for their children. Connecting families with quality primary care should be a focus of the outreach and advocacy efforts for programs enrolling children in need of these primary health care services.

Program directors should familiarize themselves with resources available in their communities so they can assist families that may need their help. Directors might begin gathering this information by checking with their local health department to inquire about community services such as clinics operated by hospitals and medical schools; voluntary groups such as the United Way, the American Red Cross, civic clubs, religious groups, and family service associations; medical assistance under Medicaid (Title XIX); armed forces medical services; and insurance and other prepayment plans so they can knowledgeably guide families toward services they may need.

Preventing Infections in Programs: Protection from infectious diseases is a daily concern of early childhood staff, families, and health care professionals. Although it is impossible to prevent the spread of all infectious diseases in any group (including a family), you can do a lot to reduce the risk of transmission.

We Wanted You To Have Some Special Information About Today ~

Child's Name _____ Today's Date _____

WE NOTED THESE SYMPTOMS OF POSSIBLE ILLNESS or INJURY

Major Symptoms

    Respiratory: runny nose; sore throat; difficulty in breathing; cough; other

        (Please describe)_____

        _____

    Skin: itch; rash; oozing; lesion; other

        (Please describe)_____

        _____

    Gastrointestinal: nausea; vomiting; diarrhea; trouble urinating; frequent urinating with
    pain; other

        (Please describe)_____

        _____

    Body movement: stiff neck; limp; other

        (Please describe) _____

    Nontypical food/fluid intake

        (Please describe) _____

        _____

    Concern about urination, bowel movement, and/or vomiting

        (Please describe) _____

        _____

    Nontypical crying, sleeping, other behavior

        (Please describe) _____

        _____

    When symptoms began _____

Your child ingested or came in contact with this potentially harmful substance (e.g., art
materials, cleaning materials, room paint, plants, animals)

_____

WE PROVIDED THIS FIRST AID OR EMERGENCY CARE

_____

_____

WE RECOMMEND THIS FOLLOW UP:

_____

_____

_____

_____

_____   _____
Signature of person completing form   Time form completed

Figure 10.4
Sample Symptom/Incident Notice

Vulnerability of Children: Infections are transmitted through direct contact (touching) blood, mucus, or other fluids from the respiratory tract and stool. Children are highly vulnerable for many reasons:

1. Child care routines create opportunities for close physical contacts among children and adults, such as those that naturally occur during feeding; diapering and toileting; sharing toys, art materials, and water tables; and the expressions of affection that bring children into close contact with peers and adults.

2. Children's immune systems are immature. They are typically very vulnerable to infection.

3. The scrapes children often have on their skin make it possible for germs to enter their bodies.

4. Children often do not know how to protect themselves from exposure to risks of infection.

Health concerns are greatest for infants and toddlers cared for in group settings. These very young children show an increased incidence of respiratory illness and diarrhea as compared with infants and toddlers not in group settings (Harms, 1992). It is important to take extra precautions to keep them healthy.

Strategies to Keep the Environment Healthy: When accepted practices are carefully followed, child care environments will be safe and healthy for both children and adults. Researchers have found that caregivers in many infant and toddler programs do not follow recommended practices when diapering, toileting, washing hands, or grooming children (Alkon et al., 2009; Cost, Quality, and Child Outcomes Study Team, 1995). Those findings highlight how important it is to help caregivers become informed about practices that support children's health and reliably follow these recommended practices. These practices help keep children and adults healthy:

1. Food service must strictly follow all recommended practices. The food supply must be safe and all foods and beverages must be stored, prepared, and served properly. Rely on appropriate agencies as well as licensing and accreditation standards to help you create routines that will keep children and adults healthy, and be certain those routines are followed consistently.

2. Dangerous microorganisms can thrive in the diapering area. The following practices will help reduce the risks associated with diapering. Refer to licensing and accreditation standards for specifics.

   a. Change children on a table with a plastic-covered pad that has no cracks. The table should have an edge to help prevent falls.

   b. Clean away any soil and then disinfect the diapering surface after every diaper change by spraying with a solution of 1 tbsp chlorine bleach to 1 qt water. The sanitizing solution must be made fresh daily. Leave the solution on the surface for 2 minutes to air dry or wipe down with a dry paper towel. Many centers line the changing table with paper that is removed after each diaper change.

   c. You may use disposable gloves to change diapers (a fresh pair for each diaper change), but gloves are not required for routine diaper changes that do not expose the caregiver to blood-borne pathogens (i.e., bloody diarrhea or diaper rash that has open sores). Gloves do not eliminate the need for careful hand washing.

   d. Dispose of used diapers, wipes, and changing table paper in a hands-free covered trash can, such as one with a foot pedal to control the lid.

   e. Post procedures for diapering in the diapering area.

3. Proper hand washing is the best way to stop the spread of germs. Children and adults should wash their hands

- When arriving for the day or moving from one group of children to another
- Before and after eating, serving food, or feeding a child; giving medication; playing in water used by more than one person
- After diapering, using the toilet, or helping a child use the toilet
- After blowing or wiping a nose or touching mucus, blood, or vomit
- After handling raw food that needs to be cooked (i.e., meat, eggs)
- After handling animals or any surfaces such as dirt or sand that might have been contaminated by animals
- After playing in a sandbox
- After handling garbage or cleaning supplies (AAP/APHA/NRCHSCC, 2011)

Proper hand-washing procedures require the use of liquid soap and warm running water. When you wash your hands properly, you rub your hands together vigorously for at least 10 seconds. That is about how long it takes to sing the alphabet song or "Row, Row, Row Your Boat." When you wash your hands properly, you include the backs of your hands, your wrists, between your fingers, and under your fingernails. After washing, rinse well, and then dry your hands with a fresh paper towel or a blow dryer. Avoid touching the faucet with just-washed hands by using a paper towel to turn off the water (Cryer, Harms & Riley, 2003; NAEYC, 2007).

Alcohol-based hand-sanitizing gels do not replace routine hand washing but can be helpful when soap and water are not readily available. Not all hand-sanitizer products are created equal, however. Be certain to select a product with at least 60% alcohol. Apply about 1/2 tsp directly to the palm of your hand, rub hands together to cover all surfaces, and keep rubbing until your hands are dry (Mayo Clinic, 2007). Hand-washing gels are toxic and flammable so they should be used with care. Children should not put their hands in their mouths until the alcohol evaporates (in about 15 seconds).

4. Even though the risk of exposure to blood-borne pathogens in child care settings is small, most states' child care licensing regulations require teachers and caregivers to have regular Occupational Safety & Health Administration (OSHA) approved training on universal precautions to prevent transmission of blood-borne diseases (e.g., HIV/AIDS and hepatitis B).

These are some of the basic principles of universal precautions:

a. Avoid touching blood and bodily fluids that might contain blood.

b. Wear disposable latex gloves when you encounter blood or bodily fluids that might contain blood; remove and dispose of the gloves carefully to avoid contaminating clean hands and surfaces; and wash your hands well when you remove the gloves.

c. Use disposable absorbent materials (e.g., facial tissue, paper towels) to stop bleeding. Discard blood-stained materials in a sealed plastic bag and place in a lined, covered garbage container.

d. Put blood-stained laundry in sealed plastic bags. Machine wash separately in cold soapy water and then wash separately in hot water.

e. Clean blood-soiled areas and disinfect with a solution of 1 part chlorine bleach and 9 parts water.

5. A clean facility will help children and adults stay healthy. Table 10.4 summarizes guidelines for cleaning and sanitizing floors, furnishings, and toys. The recommended sanitizing solution is made by mixing 1 tbsp chlorine bleach with 1 qt of water and must be mixed fresh daily.

You will want to create a cleaning and sanitation schedule and a checklist that makes employees responsible for keeping up-to-date with needed cleaning. Establish a regular day to perform weekly tasks, such as washing all linens on Friday, and a regular time to

Table 10.4
Cleaning and Sanitizing Frequency Table

Area	Clean[a]	Sanitize[b]	Frequency
Classrooms/child care/food areas			
Countertops/tables	X	X	Daily and when soiled
Food preparation and service surfaces	X	X	Before and after contact with food activity; between preparation of raw and cooked foods
Floors	X	X	Daily and when soiled
Door and cabinet handles	X	X	Daily and when soiled
Carpets and large area rugs	X		Vacuum daily when children are not present. Clean with a carpet cleaning method approved by the local health authority. Clean carpets only when children will not be present until the carpet is dry. Clean carpets at least monthly in infant areas, at least every 3 months in other areas and when soiled.
Small rugs	X		Shake outdoors or vacuum daily. Launder weekly.
Utensils, surfaces, and toys that go into the mouth or have been in contact with saliva or other body fluids	X	X	After each child's use; or use disposable, one-time use utensils or toys.
Toys	X		Weekly and when soiled
Dress-up clothes not worn on the head	X		Weekly
Sheets and pillowcases, individual cloth towels (if used), combs and hairbrushes, washcloths, and machine-washable cloth toys	X		Weekly and when visibly soiled (used only by one child)
Blankets, sleeping bags, and cubbies	X		Monthly and when soiled
Hats	X		After each child's use (or use disposable hats that only one child wears)
Cribs and mattresses	X		Weekly or before use by a different child
Mops and cleaning rags	X	X	Before and after a day of use; wash, rinse, and sanitize mops and cleaning rags.
Toilet and diapering areas			
Hand-washing sinks, faucets, surrounding counters	X	X	Daily and when soiled
Soap dispensers	X	X	Daily and when soiled
Toilet seats, toilet handles, cubicle handles, and other touchable surfaces; floors	X	X	Daily or immediately if visibly soiled
Toilet bowls	X	X	Daily
Doorknobs	X	X	Daily
Changing tables	X	X	After each child's use
Potty chairs	X	X	After each child's use. (Use of potty chairs in child care is discouraged because of high risk of contamination.)
Any surface contaminated with body fluids: saliva, mucus, vomit, urine, stool, or blood	X	X	IMMEDIATELY

[a]Cleaning is removing dirt and soil with soap (or detergent) and water.

[b]Sanitizing is removing dirt and certain bacteria so that the number of germs is reduced to such a level that the spread of disease is unlikely.

Source: NAEYC. (2007). *Standard 5: Health. A guide to the NAEYC Early Childhood Program Standard and Related Accreditation Criteria,* Table 2, p. 31. Washington, DC. Reprinted with permission from the National Association for the Education of Young Children (NAEYC). www.naeyc.org

Exclusion Because of Illness Policy

To protect the health of all children, the center follows the guidelines of the American Academy of Pediatrics for exclusion.

Children with the following illnesses are not to come to the center and may be sent home if these symptoms develop during the day:

- **Fever** of 100°F or higher as measured under the arm. Child must be fever free for 24 hours without fever-reducing medication. This includes fevers caused by ear infections.
- **Diarrhea.** Uncontrolled diarrhea, increased number of stools, increased water and/or decreased form that is not contained by the diaper or toilet use. The child may return to the center 24 hours after the symptoms stop.
- **Vomiting.** Two or more episodes of vomiting in the previous 24 hours. The child should remain home until vomiting resolves or a physician determines the condition to be noncommunicable and the child is not in danger of dehydration.
- **Chicken pox.** Until 6 days after onset of rash or until all sores have scabbed over.
- **Hand Foot Mouth disease (Coxsackievirus).** The child may return when he has no open, draining sores; no sores in the mouth; and is not drooling.
- **Head lice.** The child may stay until the end of the school day and may return after the first treatment with an approved lice-removal product.
- **Impetigo** or **Staphylococcus (Staph).** The child is excluded immediately and may return 24 hours after treatment is begun IF lesions are showing signs of healing AND oozing has stopped.
- **Pink eye (purulent conjunctivitis).** The child may return after the condition has been evaluated and treated.
- **Rash with fever or behavior change.** The child may return after a physician determines that it is not a communicable disease.
- **Ringworm or pinworm.** The child may stay until the end of the school day and may return after treatment is begun.
- **Roseola.** The child may return after rash and fever are gone.
- **Rotavirus.** The child may return after the diarrhea stops for 24 hours, which can be up to 9 days but no less than 2 to 3 days.
- **Scabies.** The child may return 24 hours after one treatment with prescription cream.
- **Streptococcal pharyngitis (strep throat).** Child may return to the center 24 hours after initial treatment and after 24 hours of being fever free.
- **Viral or bacterial infections.** Until treated and released by physician.
- **Symptoms of possible severe illness, such as unusual lethargy, irritability, persistent crying, difficulty breathing, or other unusual signs.** Until medical evaluation indicates it is appropriate to return to care.

The director, in consultation with the child's teaching team, will determine if a child is exhibiting any of these illnesses or symptoms. If it is decided that your child should be sent home, parents will be asked to pick up their child promptly. If your child is sent home with an *Exclusion for Illness Form,* its terms are strictly enforced.

Figure 10.5
Sample Exclusion Policy

Source: Based on the Exclusion Policy of the Children's Center at the University of South Carolina.

perform monthly tasks, such as the first Monday of the month. Table 10.4 indicates how often different areas of the center and classroom need to be cleaned and/or sanitized; refer to it to create a cleaning schedule.

NAEYC accreditation criteria and regulations in many locales also require early childhood programs to work with consultants with expertise in pediatric health and nutrition to provide feedback about the program's health and nutrition-related policies (Dooling & Ulione, 2000; NAEYC, 2007). These experts can help directors refine their policies and can help their staff implement appropriate policies effectively.

Communicating with Families: Centers should communicate with families regularly about issues related to children's health and well-being. These are some of the topics that should be addressed in communications with families:

1. Describe the program's exclusion policies, identifying symptoms of frequently occurring childhood illnesses and other symptoms such as fever or vomiting that indicate that children should not come to school. When appropriate, share information about community programs providing care for mildly ill children. See Figure 10.5 for a sample exclusion policy. You may find the sample Exclusion Form (Figure 10.6) useful but probably will not need to use it every time you send a child who has become ill home.

2. Provide strategies for caregivers and families to share information as children come to the center in the morning and when children rejoin their families in the afternoon. The program should provide forms for daily written communication between families and infant and toddler caregivers. There should also be a plan for teachers and caregivers of preschoolers and young school-age children to communicate with families if symptoms of illness appear.

Exclusion for Illness Form

Child's Name _____   Date _____

Classroom _____   Teacher(s) _____

Symptoms Observed _____

_____

Temperature _____   **Taken by:** ear   under the arm   by mouth   **Time** _____
                                                          (circle which)

Parent notified by _____ at _____ **AM or PM**

We are not able to care for sick children. Please refer to the Exclusion Policies in the *Parent Handbook* for clarification. Your child may return to the center when:

_____ S/he has been fever free for 24 hours without fever suppressants.

_____ Diarrhea has stopped for at least 24 hours.

_____ Vomiting has stopped for at least 24 hours.

_____ Other _____

We appreciate your cooperation.

Teacher's Signature _____

Director's Signature _____

Parent's Signature _____

Figure 10.6
Exclusion for Illness Form

Source: Based on the Exclusion for Illness Form of the Children's Center at the University of South Carolina.

CONTAGIOUS ILLNESS EXPOSURE NOTICE

ATTENTION PARENTS:

A child who was last in our center on <u>DATE</u> was diagnosed with Hand, Foot, and Mouth disease on <u>DATE</u>.

DESCRIPTION of SYMPTOMS:

- Small painful ulcers in the mouth
- Small water blisters or red spots located on the palms and soles, sometimes small blisters or red spots on the buttocks
- A low-grade fever between 100° and 102°
- General listlessness, malaise ("feeling sick")
- Symptoms appear 3–7 days after exposure

Children with Hand, Foot, and Mouth disease may not come to school if they have any open, draining sores; have sores in their mouth; or are drooling.

They may return to school when they are no longer drooling, when sores are no longer draining and can be covered, and when their temperature has been normal for 24 hours.

If your child develops any of these symptoms, you may wish to check with your doctor.

Please keep us informed!

Thank you

Figure 10.7
Sample Contagious Illness Exposure Notice

3. Inform families when their children have been exposed to a communicable disease. Describe the symptoms of the disease, how it is spread, how it is prevented or controlled, what the program is doing to prevent its spread, and what the family can do to stay healthy. A note on the door (see Figure 10.7) is sufficient for minor illnesses, but you need to send home a letter (or email families) if you should have an outbreak of a more serious contagious disease.

Some communicable diseases must also be reported to your licensing agency or the local health department, which in turn will make recommendations for informing families of children who may have been exposed. Figure 10.7 is a sample notice you might use when children have been exposed to a contagious illness.

Providing Care for Children Who Are Ill

Most child care programs will not be able to serve children who are ill. If you are interested in learning about recommended policies and procedures for serving children who are mildly ill or children with chronic health conditions that make it inadvisable for them to participate in programs for typically developing children, you will want to consult specialized resources and your state's child care regulations that apply to these special circumstances.

Caring for Children with Noncontagious Chronic Conditions and Disabilities

It is often appropriate and desirable for children who have a chronic noncontagious condition or an identified disability to participate in programs with their typically developing peers. These children may be eligible for support services under Part C or Part B of the

Individuals with Disabilities Education Act (IDEA). You will want to coordinate with the Individual Family Service Plan (IFSP) or Individual Education Plan (IEP) case manager to plan for how you will accommodate these children's special needs before they begin to attend your program. These are some issues to consider:

1. Will you need to adapt your program or routine activities to accommodate children with identified special needs?
2. Will you need to adapt the facility or acquire special equipment?
3. Do you need to anticipate the child's special dietary needs? Will she need to be fed or need other special help?
4. Do you have a plan in place to coordinate the administration of medicine with the child's family?
5. Do staff members need training in providing specialized care and emergency procedures (e.g., replacement equipment should failure occur, backup power source, supplemental oxygen, resuscitator bag, and suctioning catheter)?

Although some children require intensive services beyond those typically provided by an early childhood program, most children with a chronic illness or a disability will require only minor adaptations and will make a significant contribution to your program, children, and teachers.

Administrating Medication: Your program needs to establish policies describing how you will administer over-the-counter and prescribed medicines to children in your care. These procedures are likely to be part of your state's child care licensing regulations. They will address which medicines can be administered (i.e., prescription medications labeled for the specific child enrolled, over-the-counter medicines when ordered by a physician). Regulations will also describe appropriate storage, record keeping, and procedures if there is a medication error such as a missed dose. See Figure 10.8 for an example of a medication administration log that satisfies most states' requirements.

Promoting Children's Mental Health: Concerns about children's behavior and evidence of social and emotional delays or disorders are among the mental health issues childcare providers are likely to face. Troubling behaviors can include eating disorders and "inconsolable irritability, disrupted sleep, excessive hitting, and shyness" (Grabert, 2009, p. 14).

Medication Administration Log

Child's name _____

Date _____

Time	Medicine and Dose	Notes	Staff Member's Initials

(Give copy to parent when child is picked up.)

Figure 10.8
Sample Medication Administration Log

While some of children's challenging behaviors are the result of biological factors, such as prenatal stress, birth trauma, or congenital defects (Brennan, Mednick, & Kandal, 1991; Shore, 1997), they can also have environmental causes, such as the stresses created by living in poverty, exposure to violence, and even the impact of low-quality child care that fails to create a caring environment (Kaplan, 1998; Simmons, Stalsworth, & Wentzel, 1999; Slaby, Roedell, Arezzo, & Hendrix, 1995; Stanford & Yamamoto, 2001). Some children are also stressed and feel lonely when they are away from their families and are "one among many" for long hours each day (Vermeer & IJzendoorn, 2006).

Teachers often feel ill prepared to work successfully with children who have unmet emotional needs or acute behavioral problems. When children bring emotional problems or challenging behaviors into child care, they are often expelled (Gilliam, 2005) and are apt to increase teacher burnout and turnover (Upshr, Wenz-Gross, & Reed, 2009). These patterns point to the importance of accessing the services of mental health consultants who can model appropriate interactions for teachers, develop short-term home and classroom-based interventions, provide training to help teachers cope with these challenging behaviors, help centers develop targeted parenting education to address the particular issues they are facing, and link families with long-term services if necessary (Upshur et al., 2009).

Promoting children's mental health both at home and in out-of-home programs must be a top priority as you work with young children. Directors and staff may find these strategies helpful:

1. Provide staff in-service education about stressors that adults may confront in early childhood programs. For example, family members are likely to feel anxious when their child enrolls in child care for the first time, and they are frequently stressed by their efforts to balance the sometimes conflicting demands of the home and the workplace. Staff often feel stressed when trying to meet the needs of distressed infants, demanding toddlers, and aggressive or withdrawn preschoolers; when negotiating differences with family members; and with the challenges of the workplace. Finally, some children and adults are also experiencing difficult and possibly even abusive home lives; these "from home" stressors will be played out on the stage of the group setting.

2. Address children's exposure to violence. Directors and staff should work with families, civic leaders, and social agency professionals to promote activities aimed at reducing the risks of violence within the community and children's exposure to violent media.

3. Become familiar with descriptions and risk factors for child abuse and neglect (see Figure 10.9) and learn to recognize abuse and neglect (see Figure 10.10). Know how to respond if a child describes instances of what seem to be possible neglect or abuse (Austin, 2000) and have written policies on reporting suspected child neglect or abuse that are in line with your state's laws related to mandated reporters and the NAEYC *Code of Ethical Conduct*.

4. Develop strict program policies describing appropriate discipline and guidance within the center. Directors must be vigilant in the implementation of these policies and in protecting children from abuse or neglect while they are in out-of-home settings (Mikkelsen, 1997; NAEYC, 1996).

5. Work with families to create partnerships designed to maintain consistent expectations for children's behaviors.

6. Provide families with strategies for resolving conflicts and reducing violence in the home, including information about professional and emergency assistance.

7. Equip families with a rationale and strategies for limiting children's "screen time," that is, their use of electronic media including television, videos, and online and software games (Levin, 2003).

Physical Abuse	Physical abuse is non-accidental physical injury of a child inflicted by a parent or caretaker that ranges from superficial bruises and welts to broken bones, burns, serious internal injuries, and in some cases death. The definition of physical abuse includes actions that create a substantial risk of physical injury to the child.
Physical Neglect	Physical neglect is withholding, or failing to provide, adequate food, shelter, clothing, hygiene, medical care, education, and/or supervision, such that the child's physical, mental, or emotional condition is impaired or at imminent risk of being impaired.
Sexual Abuse	Sexual abuse occurs when a parent or caretaker commits a sexual offense against a child or allows a sexual offense to be committed, such as rape, sodomy, engaging a child in sexual activity, engaging a child in—or promoting a child's—sexual performance.
Emotional Abuse	Emotional abuse includes parents' or caretakers' acts or omissions that cause or could cause serious conduct, cognitive, affective, or other mental disorders. For example, torture, close confinement, or the constant use of verbally abusive language to harshly criticize and denigrate a child. It also includes emotional neglect—withholding physical and emotional contact to the detriment of the child's normal emotional development, and in extreme cases physical development.
Risk Factors	A combination of individual, relational, community, and societal factors contributes to the risk of child maltreatment. Although children are not responsible for the harm inflicted upon them, certain individual characteristics have been found to increase their risk of being maltreated. Risk factors are contributing factors—not direct causes. Examples of risk factors include

- Social isolation in families
- Parents' lack of understanding of children's needs and development
- Physical or mental disabilities in children that may increase caregiver burden
- Parents' history of domestic abuse and/or domestic violence
- Poverty and other socioeconomic disadvantages, such as unemployment
- Lack of family cohesion
- Substance abuse
- Young, single, nonbiological parents
- Poor parent-child relationships and negative interactions
- Parental thoughts and emotions supporting maltreatment behaviors
- Parental stress and distress, including depression or other mental health conditions
- Community violence

Figure 10.9
Defining Child Abuse and Neglect

Source: 2008 Child Abuse and Neglect Fact Sheet. Prevent Child Abuse New York Accessed from http://www.preventchildabuseny.org/resources/about-child-abuse/. Used by permission of Parent Child Abuse New York.

8. Equip staff with constructive coping strategies for dealing with children's challenging behaviors by
    a. Using positive guidance that teaches children what is expected rather than punishing them for "mistaken behavior"
    b. Implementing strategies for dealing with persistent and challenging behaviors (see the resource list at the end of the chapter)
    c. Recognizing children's behaviors that indicate the child may need to be screened by a health professional (Division of Early Childhood of the Council for Exceptional Children, 2007)

The Child

- Shows sudden changes in behavior or school performance
- Has not received help for physical or medical problems brought to the parents' attention
- Has learning problems (or difficulty concentrating) that cannot be attributed to specific physical or psychological causes
- Is always watchful, as though preparing for something bad to happen
- Is wary of physical contact with adults
- Is overly compliant, passive, or withdrawn
- Comes to school or other activities early, stays late, and does not want to go home
- Wears long sleeves or other clothing that hides injuries
- Explanation of how injuries occurred is not believable

The Parent

- Shows little concern for the child
- Denies the existence of, or blames the child for, the child's problems in school or at home
- Asks teachers or other caregivers to use harsh physical discipline if the child misbehaves
- Sees the child as entirely bad, worthless, or burdensome and does not recognize good qualities
- Demands a level of physical or academic performance the child cannot achieve
- Looks primarily to the child for care, attention, and satisfaction of emotional needs
- Has a history of being abused as a child

The Parent and Child

- Rarely touch or look at each other
- Consider their relationship entirely negative
- State that they do not like each other

Figure 10.10
Recognizing Child Abuse and Neglect

Source: Child Welfare Information Gateway of the U.S. Department of Health and Human Services Administration for Children (2007).

Protecting the Health of Children and Staff: Most states' child care regulations require staff to have training in pediatric first aid that includes rescue breathing and CPR and to participate annually in an OSHA-approved session on universal precautions that prevent the spread of blood-borne pathogens. This training protects children and adults alike.

Employees also need to know how to protect themselves from injuries and illnesses they might encounter at their work. Child care workers are constantly lifting, bending, and carrying children and equipment. It is not surprising that back injuries are the most commonly occurring occupational injury among child care personnel (Brown & Gerberich, 1993). One way to reduce these injuries is to train employees in proper lifting techniques. Another is to provide ergonomically designed changing tables that include steps so children can climb up to be changed, cribs that employees of all heights can reach, and adult-sized furniture so employees do not have to routinely use child-sized chairs or sit on the floor (AAP/APHA/NRCHSCC, 2011; Brown & Gerberich, 1993). Child care personnel are also frequently exposed to colds, coughs, and intestinal upsets that children bring to school. Proper hand washing and sanitization practices are essential, but even with these precautions, it can be hard to stay healthy when feeding, changing, and caring for children.

Adequate paid sick leave protects the health of both children and adults. When staff have a reasonable number of paid sick leave days, they are more likely to stay out of work when they are ill and to stay home until they are able to resume their duties without putting themselves, children, or other adults at risk of exposure to communicable diseases (AAP/APHA/NRCHSCC, 2011). Fully paid health insurance in child care programs is rare, however, and remains a focus of advocacy efforts in the field (Austin et al., 2009; Whitebook, Howes, & Phillips, 1998).

BEING SAFE

Protecting children's safety involves eliminating risks in the environment, preparing for emergencies, and being alert to unanticipated and yet-to-be-identified dangers. That means safety is a day-to-day concern for those who educate and care for children.

Addressing Environmental Safety

Ensuring children's safety in the environment includes setting appropriate limits; keeping the facility free from structural, chemical, electrical, and other potential hazards; protecting children when they travel to and from the center; and keeping them from dangers created by nearby vehicular traffic.

Setting Limits for Children: Children learn about themselves and the world around them by taking *risks*, but it is our responsibility to protect them from *hazards* that put them into potentially harmful situations. It takes maturity for children to be able to identify the difference between a manageable risk and a dangerous hazard. Adults are responsible for protecting children from danger.

The facility must, for example, have sturdy and reliable gates and fences that keep children away from traffic. There should be a system for monitoring the condition of these structural elements of the facility and for the safety of classrooms and playgrounds.

It is best to have a limited number of thoughtfully developed rules to protect the children you serve from hazards that may be present in your environment. Your environment should say "yes" to children's explorations, but you will inevitably need to set some limits to keep children safe. Rules should always be stated positively, emphasizing the desired behaviors rather than the prohibited ones. Say, for example, "Fences are to keep us safe. Climbing is fun. If you want to climb, play on the climbing wall."

Keeping Your Facility Safe: Each program needs to establish safety policies and procedures to address its particular circumstances. A safety checklist based on the facility's individual characteristics is needed, as is a system of accountability so that individual staff members are responsible for checking particular parts of the building. For example, who is responsible every day for making certain all doors are secured so children cannot wander off and unauthorized individuals do not have access to your center? Checklists and systems of accountability are essential so you can be certain these tasks are done regularly.

We recommend that teachers be expected to check their classrooms at least weekly for hazards such as loose carpets that could trip children or adults, broken furniture or toys, chipped paint, and missing outlet covers. Some repairs need to be made immediately; others can be corrected as part of the facility's routine maintenance.

The important point is to have a system in place to be certain that issues needing attention are identified and addressed. Developing and using a checklist will allow staff to be accountable for keeping their rooms safe and identifying repairs that need to be made. Staff should also be expected to be continually alert to safety hazards and notify administrators of repairs that must be made immediately or actions that should be taken to prevent children's contact with the hazard.

As the administrator, you should also monitor the U.S. Consumer Product Safety Commission (CPSC) website listed at the end of this chapter. You also need to be alert to recalls publicized in the media. The CPSC recalls toys and equipment found to have defects that could harm or even kill consumers. For example, millions of drop-side cribs have recently been recalled because of defects that entrapped children, putting them at risk for suffocation or strangulation. A few years ago, millions of toys were recalled because they contained excessive levels of lead. Lead poisoning, which lowers intelligence, creates behavioral problems, and diminishes school performance has been reported in 1 of every 30 children in the United States (Lanphear, 2001).

By following the advice of the CPSC, you will be able to remove toys found to put children at risk. You should not only remove toys and materials identified as being defective or harmful, but you should also notify families when recalls might involve toys, furniture, and materials they are likely to have in their homes.

Vehicular Safety

If your program transports children, you must take a number of precautions to keep children safe from harm. Staff eligible to drive children must

- Have a valid driver's license for the vehicle they will be driving
- Provide evidence of a safe driving record
- Have no record of substance abuse, violent crimes, or child abuse or neglect
- Not have recently used alcohol or drugs (including prescribed and over-the-counter medications) that could impair their ability to drive safely

You should keep a record of "the driver's license number, vehicle insurance information and verification of current state vehicle inspection on file in the facility" (AAP/APHA/NRCH-SCC, 2011, p. 289). All but four states address transportation in their child care licensing regulations (NCCIC/NARA, 2010). Standards typically address child-staff ratio, describe required supervision, and may require the vehicle be equipped with age-appropriate car seats.

Plan carefully for field trips that take children away from your facility. Decide in advance where and how children will be loaded into vehicles and where they will be unloaded. At least two adults must be with each group of children, but some trips will require closer supervision. Teachers should work with their director to determine how many extra adults are needed to safely take the children away from the center. Whenever children leave the school premises, teachers should take along children's emergency information, blank injury report forms, a first aid kit (see Figure 10.11), and a cell phone.

Preparing for Emergencies

Emergencies occur even when early childhood programs take every possible precaution to protect children's health and safety. You should develop emergency procedures in advance and train all staff so they are familiar with the plans. Consider the following issues when developing emergency plans for your program:

1. Plan how you will evacuate the building in the event of a fire or explosion. Post exit routes and emergency procedures near or on exit doors. Have completed emergency information forms and class lists on a shelf by each exit door.

First Aid Kit

Your first aid kit should be kept in a closed container and should be out of reach of children but accessible to child care staff at all times. If your center has a bus or uses one regularly, you will need one first aid kit for the center and another for the bus.

Be certain to restock your first aid kit after using it, and conduct an inventory regularly to be certain everything is there and in good condition. The first aid kit should contain at least the following items:

a) Adhesive tape

b) Antibiotic ointment

c) Bandages, including elastic wrap (e.g., Ace) and bandage strips (e.g., Band-Aid, Curad)

d) Disposable, latex-free, or nonpowdered latex gloves—at least two pairs (latex free recommended)

e) Eye patch or dressing

f) Flashlight

g) Gauze pads and roller gauze (sterile)

h) Liquid soap to wash injury and hand sanitizer, used with supervision, if hands are not visibly soiled or if no water is present

i) Pen/pencil and note pad

j) Petroleum jelly or other lubricant

k) Safety pins in assorted sizes

l) Sanitary pads (individually wrapped) to contain bleeding of injuries

m) Scissors, tweezers, and a needle

n) Thermometer to measure a child's temperature (non-mercury style)

o) Tissues

p) Triangular bandages

q) Water (2 liters of sterile water for cleaning wounds or eyes)

r) Wipes

s) Whistle

t) Zip-lock plastic bags for the disposal of contaminated materials

u) Current first aid book or first aid chart such as the AAP *Pediatric First Aid For Caregivers and Teachers (PedFACTS) Manual*

v) Emergency phone numbers (poison control center, local rescue)

It is important that caregivers always have access to a charged cell phone when away from the center.

Note: In 2003 the American Academy of Pediatrics advised that Syrup of Ipecac should not be used to induce vomiting and should not be included in first aid kits or available at a child care program. This changed a long-standing recommendation.

Figure 10.11
Availability and Contents of First Aid Kits

Sources: Information from "First-Aid Kits: Stock Supplies That Can Save Lives," 2011, retrieved from http://www.majorclinic.com/health/first-aid-kits/FA00067, and *Caring for Our Children: National Health and Safety Performance Standards: Guidelines for out-of-home child care programs* (3rd ed., p. 176), by the American Academy of Pediatrics, the American Public Health Association, and the National Resource Center for Health and Safety in Child Care, 2011, Elk Grove Village, IL and Washington, DC.

Identify a designated meeting place to be certain everyone is accounted for. Conduct regular fire drills to practice these routines and to be certain everyone knows how to respond.

2. Identify where you will go if you must leave the premises and inform families of this evacuation location. Plan how you will notify families if the center needs to be evacuated.

3. Plan how you will protect children and notify families in the case of a natural disaster such as a tornado, flash flood, or earthquake or other emergency such as a chemical spill, terrorist attack, or other violent incident in your vicinity.

Have flashlights, a first aid kit (see Figure 10.11), a cell phone, a battery-operated radio, food and water, blankets, children's books, and paper and crayons readily available nearby. Your local fire marshal and Homeland Security Office can help you make plans for these emergencies. Refer to the websites at the end of this chapter for specific recommendations.

Assessing Risks and Protecting Children: Early childhood professionals must never become complacent about safety. Each staff member must learn to constantly assess current risks by considering what their children are doing, where they are doing it, and how specific children respond to different experiences. Remember, little things can make the difference between a safe environment and a dangerous one. Young children can drown in even a small amount of standing water, strings on jackets can get trapped on slides or climbing equipment and become choking hazards, and an improperly closed door or gate may let children get into traffic or other hazards.

Professionals are expected to ensure children's safety. They need to be vigilant to avoid both acts of omission and acts of commission:

1. Acts of omission: Adults fail to take precautionary measures needed to protect children (e.g., failure to inspect facility for safety, failure to supervise or provide adequate supervision)

2. Acts of commission: Adults' actions or decisions put children at risk (e.g., taking a field trip even though several needed volunteers did not show up to accompany the children)

Directors can protect children and limit the center's liability by carefully writing job descriptions; being certain all staff have appropriate training in all areas of health and safety; maintaining appropriate records, especially accident reports; and securing liability insurance. Although safety management is challenging, creating a culture of acting responsibly can save lives and prevent accidents and injuries. When an accident occurs, you will want to use an injury report form similar to the one in Figure 10.12 to gather the documentation you need.

Teaching Children to Be Safe: Everyday interactions are the best way to teach children how to protect their health and to be safe. Bus safety, for example, is a natural part of riding the bus, and kitchen safety will naturally be integrated into classroom cooking activities. These authentic experiences are more meaningful than educational programs such as "Eddie Eagle" designed to teach gun safety or "Stranger Danger" designed to warn children against talking to strangers (Himle, Miltenberger, Gatheridge, & Flessner, 2004; McBride, n.d.). While these packaged programs have been shown to teach children what to *say,* they have proven to be minimally effective teaching them what to *do* in real-life circumstances. It is important to appreciate that ultimately adults, not children, are responsible for creating safe and healthy environments. Families and teachers should join together in their efforts to create safe environments for their children and their community.

Injury Report Form

Child's Name _____   Birth Date _____

Parents' Contact Information _____

Child's Physician and Contact Information _____

Description of Injury

Date _____   Time _____

Description of injury _____

_____

_____

How did the injury occur? _____

_____

Staff member(s) supervising the child at the time of the injury _____

_____

Other adults who witnessed the injury _____

_____

Child's apparent symptoms and reaction _____

_____

First Aid Administered (if any)

_____

_____

Administered by _____

Assisted by _____

Medical Help Sought (if any)

From whom _____

Time of contact _____

Advice _____

Parent Contact

Attempts _____

Parent advice _____

Recommended Follow-up Care

Description _____

_____

Condition of Child at Time of Release

Description _____

_____
(Signature of person completing form)

Figure 10.12
Sample Injury Report Form

Note: For quick reference and as a time saver, have a form with information above the dotted line completed on each child.

SUMMARY

Children's nutrition, health, and safety are essential ingredients of quality early childhood programs. Nutrition is important for two reasons: (a) Early childhood programs are apt to provide up to 80% of a young child's total nutrition requirements during their formative early years, and (b) children develop lifelong attitudes and habits during early eating experiences. Teachers and caregivers of young children need to be informed about the nutritional requirements of young children, offer children nutritious foods, and create a relaxed and inviting environment at mealtimes and during snacks.

Health affects each area of development. An early childhood program should be proactive by assessing the health status of staff members and children, advocating for preventive health care including a medical home for every child, communicating regularly with families about their child's health, and serving as a resource to help families access the health-related resources they may need.

Child safety includes creating and maintaining a safe environment, preparing for emergencies, protecting children from injury, and promoting safety consciousness and education.

In short, nutrition, health, and safety are components of early care and education that require attention every day. They are ongoing concerns for teachers, caregivers, and those in administrative positions.

Trends and issues related to health, safety, and nutrition include widespread concern about the growing epidemic of childhood obesity caused by overconsumption of foods high in sugar, fat, and salt and the sedentary lifestyle of too many children and families. Legislation has also been passed at the federal level and in many states encouraging and supporting mothers who breast-feed their babies. Federal law now mandates break time for working mothers to express their milk in privacy in a location other than a bathroom, and there is growing support for breast-feeding both in the workplace and in public (National Conference of State Legislatures, 2011).

USEFUL WEBSITES

Interactive Nutrition Websites

Body Mass Index (BMI) Calculator for Children and Teens, sponsored by the Centers for Disease Control and Prevention

apps.nccd.cdc.gov/dnpabmi/

Using a child's birth date, height, and weight, this interactive website calculates a child's BMI and indicates if the child is underweight, a healthy weight, overweight, or obese.

Recommended Dietary Allowance (RDA) calculator, sponsored by *Diet & Fitness Today*, an online health and fitness resource

www.dietandfitnesstoday.com/rda.php

This website calculates the recommended dietary allowances for a wide range of vitamins and minerals based on an individual's age and gender.

Other Nutrition Resources

MyPlate nutritional guidelines, sponsored by the U.S. Department of Agriculture (USDA)

www.choosemyplate.gov/

In 2010, the USDA introduced MyPlate nutritional guidelines to replace the Food Pyramid system it used for many years to describe a balanced diet. This website has comprehensive information on food groups and guidance about how to ensure that children and adults eat a balanced diet.

USDA Healthy Meals Resource System, sponsored by the U.S. Department of Agriculture (USDA)

healthymeals.nal.usda.gov

This comprehensive site has information for child care providers. Topics include nutrition information, recipes, menu planning resources, and food safety guidelines.

Child Care Nutrition Program Resources, sponsored by the National Food Service Management Institute (NFSMI)

www.nfsmi.org/

This organization offers staff training in food service management and posts resources on meal planning and food preparations.

National School Lunch Program, sponsored by the USDA

www.fns.usda.gov/cnd/lunch/

This resource includes information on the operation of the National School Lunch Program and other child nutrition programs. State agency contracts can be found by clicking on "Child and Adult Care Food Program."

Childhood Hunger in America, sponsored by Share our Strength: No Kid Hungry

strength.org/childhood_hunger/

This national nonprofit addresses childhood hunger. It provides statistics documenting childhood hunger and resources to address it.

How to Feed Children, sponsored by Ellyn Satter Associates

www.ellynsatter.com/how-to-feed-i-24.html

Ellyn Satter is the author of *Child of Mine: Feeding with Love and Good Sense*. Her website offers down-to-earth and realistic recommendations about enjoying healthy food with children.

Health and Safety Resources

Caring for Our Children: National Health and Safety Performance Standards: Guidelines for Early Care and Education Programs, 3rd ed. (2011), developed by the National Resource Center for Health and Safety in Child Care and Early Education

nrckids.org/

This website has links to indispensable resources for program administrators, including

- *Child care health and safety guidelines*
- *Obesity prevention*
- *Links to states' child care licensing and regulations websites*
- *Nutrition and physical activity checklists in English and Spanish*

Healthy Child Care America, sponsored by the American Academy of Pediatrics (AAP)

www.healthychildcare.org

This website offers comprehensive health and safety resources for parents and early childhood educators.

Let's Move! America's Move to Raise a Healthier Generation of Kids, sponsored by the White House and others

www.letsmove.gov/

This project is a centerpiece of Michelle Obama's initiative to reduce childhood obesity and to lead children and families toward a healthier lifestyle. There are resources specifically for parents, kids, and schools.

Consumer Product Safety Commission

www.cpsc.gov/

This governmental agency monitors the safety of consumer products. Recalls are posted continuously on its website.

TO REFLECT

1. Some foods are difficult for "little hands" to handle. What can teachers who are eating with young children and even school-age children do to assist them at mealtime? Consider both meals that are provided at the center and lunches or snacks that children bring from home.

2. You have just attended a workshop on nurturing healthy attitudes about food in early childhood programs. The presenter emphasized that providing nutritious meals and snacks is not enough; children have to eat the foods to benefit from them, and children benefit in many ways when they enjoy meals and snacks at school. They learn, for example, about good nutrition, develop their vocabularies, have rich sensory experiences, develop good table manners, and so on. As a novice teacher, you want to regularly prepare snacks and meals with your children. You are convinced they are more likely to eat what they prepare, and that cooking experiences can support their development in many ways. Your director advises that cooking activities can be overwhelming. What does he mean? What kinds of cooking activities would you try first? What rationale would you present to justify your decision to frequently prepare snacks and meals with your children?

3. As a director of a preschool program, you are writing a policy describing when children must be excluded because of illness, and when they can return. What criteria should you use to achieve the balance between a child's need to be cared for by a family member and the family member's need to meet the demands of a job?

CHECK AND APPLY YOUR UNDERSTANDING

1. Identify resources that program directors can use when developing menus for meals and snacks for children from birth to age 5.

2. "Mealtimes feed the spirit as well as the body." Describe some practices that make meals pleasant and relaxed.

3. Identify policies that program directors can put in place to create an environment that helps children and staff stay healthy.

4. What are some of the health-related issues about which you need to inform families? Give an example of something that would require you to contact a family member immediately.

5. What are the characteristics of appropriate rules designed to keep children safe? Identify three rules that meet these criteria.

CHAPTER 11

Assessment: An Essential Component of Effective Early Childhood Programming

NAEYC Administrator Competencies addressed in this chapter:

Management Knowledge and Skills

1. Personal and Professional Self-Awareness
The ability to be a reflective practitioner and apply a repertoire of techniques to improve the level of personal fulfillment and professional job satisfaction.

Early Childhood Knowledge and Skills

3. Child Observation and Assessment
Knowledge and application of developmentally appropriate child observation and assessment methods. Knowledge of the purposes, characteristics, and limitations of different assessment tools and techniques. Ability to use different observation techniques including formal and informal observation, behavior sampling, and developmental checklists. Knowledge of ethical practice as it relates to the use of assessment information. The ability to apply child observation and assessment data to planning and structuring developmentally appropriate instructional strategies.

Learning Outcomes

After studying this chapter, you should be able to:

1. Describe three characteristics of responsible assessment.
2. Discuss the two main purposes for which program directors will use assessment.
3. Compare several methods of documenting children's learning.
4. Identify they types of records programs keep to document children's development and learning.
5. Identify how current national trends in early childhood assessment might affect program decisions at the local level.

Grace's Experience

As an experienced classroom teacher, Grace knows how important it is to have assessment systems in place for both the children and the classroom environment. As a lead teacher, she has much experience in observing children, documenting learning and behavior, and preparing assessment records and portfolios to share with parents. For the past three years as a teacher, she has continually worked to ensure that her classroom met all licensing regulations and program policies. She knows that this takes time and attention to detail.

Since recently becoming the director of the program, Grace feels challenged to ensure that all teachers are following assessment practices and program quality guidelines. In addition, the program's board of directors has expressed concern about center operations, noting that enrollment has decreased and some teacher turnover has occurred with the recent changes in administration. Grace realizes she must now take her classroom experience and translate it into overall program management that aligns with the program's goals. She now must work with her staff to ensure that the center gets back on track and provides the quality early childhood programming that it is known for in the community. Grace has been asked by the board of directors to develop a plan for improvement, and she is hoping this chapter will help her ensure appropriate assessment of children's learning across the classrooms and put an assessment plan in place to ensure overall program quality.

*E*valuation is the process of making judgments about the value or quality of outcomes achieved through the provision of services.

Assessment, an essential component of the evaluation process, is a process through which professionals collect and analyze data to help gain an understanding of children's development and program effectiveness. By using assessment and evaluation information effectively, program directors can enhance program performance and it's success meeting the collective and individual needs of the children and families it serves. When assessment is conducted appropriately, it is linked to program goals. Assessment involves several activities that come together to establish a method for systematically asking and then answering questions regarding individual children's progress and the program's effectiveness in helping all children and families achieve desired outcomes. High-quality, developmentally appropriate programs have an evaluation and assessment plan in place that benefits children and informs instruction. In addition, this plan will put into place an ongoing system to evaluate and improve program effectiveness. Copple and Bredekamp (2009) specifically recommend "an assessment plan that is clearly written, well-organized, complete, comprehensive, and well-understood by directors, teachers, and families" (p. 178). This chapter presents four processes that will help you develop an effective assessment and evaluation plan for an existing center or one that is still in the planning stages. The processes described through this chapter include (a) determining the need for and thus the purposes of assessment; (b) selecting assessment practices and identifying strategies for gathering evidence that are aligned with the program's goals; (c) processing the information collected to evaluate the program's success; and (d) making professional judgments, that is, using assessment results as a tool in the decision-making process.

CALLS FOR "RESPONSIBLE ASSESSMENT"

Professional reactions to high-stakes testing and calls for appropriate assessment began to emerge in the 1990s. The following professional associations have issued position statements supporting appropriate assessment:

American Educational Research Association

National Council of Teachers of Mathematics

American Psychological Association & National Council on Measurement in Education Association of Childhood Education International

Southern Early Childhood Association

National Association for the Education of Young Children & National Association of Early Childhood Specialists in State Departments of Education

National Association of Early Childhood Specialists in State Departments of Education

National Association of School Psychologists

NAEYC (2001) has called assessment that is ethically grounded and supported by sound professional standards *responsible assessment,* which includes the following characteristics:

1. The overall purpose of assessment is to benefit children and families, help teachers in their work, and inform efforts to improve program quality. Copple and Bredekamp (2009) outline four beneficial purposes of assessment:
   a. Planning and adapting curriculum to meet each child's developmental and learning needs
   b. Helping teachers and families monitor children's progress
   c. Evaluating and improving program effectiveness
   d. Screening and identification of children with potential disabilities or special needs.

2. Assessment instruments should be used for specific purposes, must be valid and reliable and the data they generate should be used appropriately.

3. Assessment practices should be collaborative. Teachers and families need to be involved in decision making related to assessment.

4. Assessment of children needs to be "developmentally valid" (Meisels & Atkins-Burnett, 2000), which means it must be
   a. age and stage appropriate in content and data collection methods
   b. culturally and linguistically appropriate
   c. adapted if necessary to meet children's special needs
   d. focused on children's strengths and best performances

5. Assessment must be closely aligned with the program's goals. When used appropriately, assessment practices will be
   a. systematic and ongoing (i.e., there is a plan in place, information is collected on a regular basis)
   b. comprehensive (i.e., covering all domains of development and learning) and performance based (i.e., based on observations and examples of what a child actually does during daily activities); teachers use these data to refine how they plan and implement activities
   c. embedded in classroom activities and consistent with the learning goals of the curriculum
   d. drawn from multiple sources over many points in time (Shepard, Kagan, & Wurtz, 1998b; Child Outcomes Center, 2010)
   e. communicated and shared appropriately (Copple & Bredekamp, 2009)

PURPOSES OF ASSESSMENT AND DOCUMENTATION

The purposes for which you will be using assessment information should inform all aspects of your evaluation plan. Your purposes will inform what is measured, how it is measured, and even the acceptable levels of validity (the degree to which an assessment measures what is intended) and reliability (the accuracy of the assessment tool) (Shepard et al., 1998b). According to the Joint Position Statement of the National Association for the Education of Young Children (NAEYC) and the National Association of Early Childhood Specialists in State Departments of Education (NAECS/SDE) adopted in 2003, assessment of children from birth through the primary grades should be guided by the ethics of the profession; informed by what is known to be age appropriate, culturally and linguistically appropriate; and play a central role in all early childhood programs. The *NAEYC Code of Ethical Conduct* (2011) now includes nine items addressing ethical assessment practices.

Child care directors will use assessment and evaluation within their programs for two main purposes: (a) to promote children's development and learning and (b) to evaluate program effectiveness.

Using Assessment and Evaluation to Promote Children's Development and Learning

Child assessment and evaluation systems designed for the purpose of promoting learning and development include *developmental screening* and *formative assessment*.

Developmental screening is a brief, relatively inexpensive standardized procedure designed to quickly assess a large number of children to identify those who should be referred for further assessment (McAfee, Leong, & Bodrova, 2004). NAEYC recommends that children be screened upon program entry and referred to specialists promptly if further evaluation is needed (Copple & Bredekamp, 2009). According to the Early Childhood Outcomes Center, 2.5% of children between birth and age 3 receive early intervention services. Of this population, 64% are eligible because of a developmental delay (Hebbeler, 2010). The early childhood administrator and the teaching team are in an important position to assist in the identification of developmental differences and to serve as a bridge in connecting parents to available services.

Formative assessment informs teaching and learning. It involves the collection and use of evidence to guide instruction (Dunphy, 2008). Formative assessment (a) determines a child's progress in attaining program goals and objectives, (b) serves as a tool in family-staff communication (e.g., helps families learn about the curriculum, appropriate expectations for children, and their child's performance in the program), and (c) improves the quality of the program by helping teachers determine what is and is not working. Formative assessment procedures require planning, time, and reflection. Program administrators should work to provide teachers with the structural supports necessary to collect and organize assessment information. When time, space, and collaboration supports are in place, teachers are motivated to continually monitor children's development and learning, self-assess and improve their effectiveness and support children's learning and development (Carter, 2008).

Effective assessment requires teachers to understand each child's performance based on their knowledge of child development, cultural and linguistic competencies, and age and grade expectations (i.e., know when a given response is precocious performance, expected performance, or below expected performance; Copple & Bredekamp, 2009). Validity and reliability can be achieved when teachers are well informed regarding the importance of objectivity and accuracy when assessing young children and when they collect assessment data using multiple strategies and appropriate assessment instruments over various points in time (Grisham-Brown, Hemmeter, & Pretti-Frontczak, 2005; Hebbeler, 2010; Shepard et al., 1998b). Developmental validity is also an important concept in early childhood assessment and indicates that the performances being measured are developmentally appropriate for the children being assessed (Epstein, Schweinhart, DeBruin-Parecki, & Robin, 2004). The importance of collecting data to inform caregiver assessment and evaluation leads us to a brief discussion of authentic assessment and ways to document children's performance in the context of the daily lives in child care and education programs.

Authentic Assessment and Documentation Strategies to Determine What Children Know and Are Able to Do: Authentic assessment and documentation methods, also called **performance assessment and documentation**, involve identifying desired results or learning objectives and then observing children to see if they demonstrate these competencies through their daily interactions with adults, other children, and their environment. Authentic approaches to assessment require the teacher to observe and document children's demonstrations of what they know and are able to do. These methods provide teachers with opportunities to apply their knowledge of child development and of particular children within the context of a natural or teacher-created situation (Bergen, 1993/94; Meisels, Dorfman, & Steele, 1995). High-quality authentic assessments of young children share the following characteristics: (a) they are closely aligned with the learning goals identified by the program, (b) they use multiple observation and documentation strategies, and (c) they involve multiple stakeholders (including families and other early childhood professionals; Grisham-Brown, Hallam, & Brookshire, 2006; Grisham-Brown et al., 2005). It is the teacher's responsibility to document children's demonstrations of these behaviors and skills.

Learning objectives that inform our authentic assessment of young children should be guided by state early learning standards (when they exist), program goals, specific curriculum goals, family goals and values, and a general understanding of the typical developmental progression of young children. The next section provides a brief overview of strategies that are commonly used to authentically assess young children in early care and education programs.

Observations.   Observations entail systematically focusing on a child or small group of children to document their behavior, which will support judgments of individual children's competence. This is a popular method of assessing young children's development and learning because it allows a caregiver to see what children are capable of doing as they play and interact with their peers.

These are additional factors that make observation a popular documentation strategy:

1. Teachers or caregivers can position themselves strategically to observe individual children or small groups of children while also monitoring the activities of the whole group.
2. Observations can be conducted by teachers as well as by researchers.
3. Observations can be conducted for long or short intervals of time.
4. Observations can be used in conjunction with any other assessment method.
5. Observations are suitable for use in any type of program because one child or a group of children can be observed and any aspect of development can be assessed.

Disadvantages in using observations for assessment are as follows:

1. The validity of the observation depends on the skill of the observer.
2. The observer's biases are inherent in observations. Teachers often need professional development and practice in learning to record observations objectively.
3. The soundness of observations may depend on the behaviors observed because some aspects of development (e.g., motor skills) are easier to observe than others (e.g., thinking processes).

The purposes of the observations determine the method of observation and the recording system. Several popular methods of observing young children and some of the recording possibilities used by teachers (and researchers) are described in the following subsections. Figure 11.1 illustrates how an anticipatory planning web can be used to plan for assessment and documentation.

Naturalistic observations are observations of a child or small group of children engaged in regular day-to-day activities in their natural setting. These open-ended observations allow the child options that in turn permit the teacher to see the uniqueness of the child more clearly, what Rhodes and Nathenson-Mejia (1992) refer to as a "story of an individual" (p. 503). Observation not only helps teachers know each child, but also can make important contributions toward building positive relationships with children—an important part of quality programming

A key characteristic of authentic assessment is the collection of child created artifacts that demonstrate their knowledge and skills.

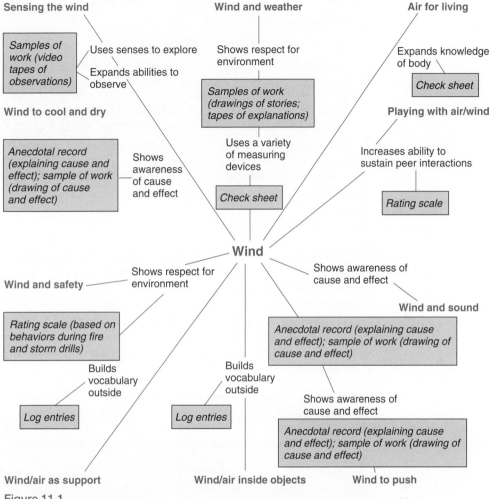

Figure 11.1
Assessment and Documentation Methods Included on Anticipatory Web

and the foundation for children's exploration and learning in the classroom (Jablon, Dombro, & Dichtelmiller, 2007).

Naturalistic observations may be recorded as anecdotal or running records. An **anecdotal record** is a description of an incident in a child's life that occurred during participation in program activities or during a home visit. Characteristics of a good anecdote are as follows:

1. It gives the date, the place, and the situation in which the action occurred. This is called the *setting*.
2. It describes the actions of the child, the reactions of other people involved, and the responses of the child to these reactions.
3. It quotes what the child said and what others said to the child during the action.
4. It supplies "mood cues"—postures, gestures, voice qualities, and facial expressions that give cues as to how the child felt. It does not provide interpretations of the child's feelings but provides only the cues by which a reader may judge what the feelings were.
5. The description is extensive enough to cover the episode. The action or conversation is not left incomplete and unfinished but rather is described until a vignette is created.

Child's name: *Adelae*   **Date:** *2/12/2012*

Setting: *Block center in a child care center: child initiated activity.*

Incident: *Adelae was building a block tower. When the seven-block tower fell, she tried again. This time, she succeeded in getting only six blocks stacked before they fell. She kicked her blocks and walked over to Darius's nine-block tower and knocked it over. When the teacher approached, she cried and shouted "no" when the teacher offered to help her rebuild her tower. (Darius left the center after his tower was knocked over.)*

Comments: *Adelae is showing more patience by rebuilding—a patience not seen last month. However, her crying and destructive responses are not as mature as they should be for a 5-year-old. She needs to be shown ways to cope with common frustrations.*

Figure 11.2
Anecdotal Record of Behavior

Below the narrative account, space should be left for comments. These comments may be interpretive (what the observer believes about the incident) and/or a written professional judgment (what the observer believes should be done to support the child's development). Figure 11.2 is an example of an anecdotal record.

A **running record** is similar to an anecdotal record except that it is more detailed with a total sequence of events. The running record was popularized by Piaget (1952). In a running record, the observer records everything without screening out any information. See the example in Figure 11.3.

Child's name: *Adelae*   **Date:** *5/5/2012*

Setting: *Block center in a child care center: child initiated activity*

	Incident	Comments
9:25	*Adelae watches three or four children play with the blocks.*	*Adelae is interested in the blocks.*
9:30	*She calls to Darius, "What are you doing?" Darius replies, "I'm building a tall, tall building, the biggest one ever." Adelae says, "I can build a big one."*	*She especially likes Darius's tower.* *Adelae is apparently challenged.*
9:31	*Adelae stacks seven blocks. They fall. (She counts the blocks in Darius's tower.) She again starts stacking blocks—with the sixth block, they fall.*	*Adelae knows she almost got the same height tower again.* *Adelae is willing to try again.*
9:35	*She kicks at her blocks three times and then walks over to Darius's tower and strikes it with her hand.*	*Her aggression spreads to Darius.*
9:37	*Ms. Lambert approaches Adelae. Adelae turns her back on Ms. Lambert and cries and shouts "no!" Ms. Lambert kneels and talks to Adelae. Then Ms. Lambert picks up a block, but Adelae runs away.* *(Darius left the center earlier.)*	*She is not yet willing to be comforted or helped.* *Teacher's approach was calming—no more aggression.*

Figure 11.3
Running Record of Behavior

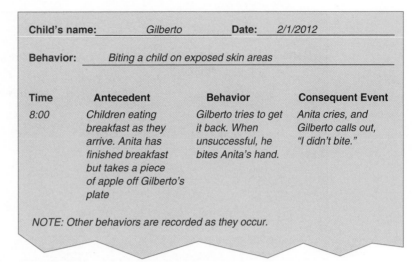

Figure 11.4
Event Sampling Behavior Record

Structured observations are structured in terms of either bringing children into planned environments (e.g., how an infant reacts when a stranger is present and the mother is present and then absent) or identifying a specific defined behavior, observing it in the natural environment, and keeping quantitative records (e.g., Sarah had two biting episodes on Monday and one biting episode on Tuesday). Two types of structured observations are event sampling and time sampling.

Event sampling is a narrative of conditions preceding and following a specified behavior. For these observations, a behavior is preselected (called a *target behavior*), defined very specifically, and then observed (see Figure 11.4).

Time sampling is tallying a specified behavior while it is occurring. A target behavior is preselected, carefully defined, and then observed at specified intervals. Because less writing is required than when using the event sampling method described earlier, the observer can record observations on several children in one session by rotating observations in a predetermined and consistent manner among the children. Using the time periods in the example in Figure 11.5, Child A would be observed during the 1st minute of

Child's name: Carmin			Date: 11/12/2012	
Target Behavior: <u>*Types of interaction in the housekeeping center.*</u>				
Time 1	**Time 2**	**Time 3**	**Time 4**	**Time 5**
<u>9:00</u>	<u>9:05</u>	<u>9:10</u>	<u>9:15</u>	<u>9:20</u>
V+	V+	NV−	V−	0

V = verbal interaction
NV = nonverbal interaction
0 = no interaction
+ = positive
− = negative

Figure 11.5
Time-Sampling Behavior Record

Child's name: Barbara   **Date:** *1/21/2013*

Behavior: <u>Wandering from center to center. (Child stays less than 2 minutes at an activity in one "stretch.")</u>

Days	Time	Subtotal	Total
1	9:04–9:08	4	
	9:12–9:13	1	5
2	9:01–9:04	3	3
3	9:04–9:07	3	
	9:13–9:15	2	5
4	9:01–9:05	4	
	9:12–9:13	1	5
5	9:02–9:07	5	
	9:10–9:11	1	6

Average: 4.8 minutes per day

Figure 11.6
Duration Record of Behavior

each time frame—9:00 to 9:01, 9:05 to 9:06, and so on; Child B would be observed during the 2nd minute of each time frame—9:01 to 9:02, 9:06 to 9:07, and so on; and in a similar way, three other children would be observed.

For non-discrete behaviors (e.g., crying, clinging to adult, wandering around the room), the length of occurrence or duration is often recorded (see the example in Figure 11.6). Both frequency and duration recordings may be summarized in graphs, which give visual representations. Even two complementary behaviors may be plotted on the same graph for a better picture of a child (e.g., daily totals of aggressive and sharing acts). Because some observation techniques such as time sampling require the focused attention of the observer, it is helpful when someone else other than the teacher responsible for the supervision of all children in the group conducts the observation. Directors provide assessment support to teachers when they play a role in conducting these observations.

Interviews.   **Interviews** with families are now used with greater frequency in early childhood programs. The interview method permits a more comprehensive picture of the child's life at home and with peer groups. The *interview method of assessment* generally has the following characteristics:

1. Questions used in an interview are usually developed by teachers and administrators together with the goal of learning important information about each child, such as
   a. how parents see their child
   b. the child's home life, language, and culture
   c. parents' thoughts about their child's strengths, fears, weaknesses, and other insights into how each child fits into his family that will help teachers support his success (Gober, 2002)
2. When possible, interviews are conducted in the child's home language, or a translator is sought for assistance.
3. Parent interview forms help teachers organize information in advance and keep the interview on track. Family interview forms can be given out to families as a questionnaire at the beginning of the year. They help teachers gain insight into the family's background and culture.

Advantages of the interview as an assessment technique are as follows:

1. They can provide valuable information that can be difficult for families to share in writing.
2. Interviews can be used in conjunction with other assessment methods.
3. Interviews are suitable for use in any type of early childhood program.
4. Interviews can help clarify and extend the information found on written forms and can help develop positive and productive relationships.

The interview method also has disadvantages:

1. The information obtained may not be comprehensive or accurate because the questions were unclear or not comprehensive or the interviewee was unable or uncomfortable sharing information.
2. The interviewee's and interviewer's biases are entwined in the information shared and in its interpretation.
3. The interview method is time consuming.

Collecting Samples of Children's Work.   Collecting samples of children's work is a particularly informative strategy to gather data for assessment purposes. Artifacts that illustrate knowledge and skill reveal individual children's unique personality and development as they give clear evidence of what a child knows and can do (McAfee et al., 2004). Samples of children's work serve as an excellent authentic method of assessment if they meet the following criteria:

1. Samples of various types of children's work should be collected:
   • Video or audio recordings of children's dictated accounts of their experiences
   • Children's drawings, paintings, and other two-dimensional art projects; photographs can be used as documentation so that children can take home their artwork
   • Photographs of children's projects (e.g., three-dimensional art projects, block constructions, a completed science experiment)
   • Audio or video recordings of singing, language arts activities, or other classroom events.
2. Samples are collected on a systematic and periodic basis.
3. Samples are dated, with notes describing children's comments and behaviors.
4. A systematic method of organizing children's work is established and aligns with program goals and objectives.

Advantages to using samples of children's work as an assessment technique are as follows:

1. The evidence is a collection of children's real, ongoing activities or products of activities, not a contrived experience for purposes of assessment.
2. Collecting samples is not particularly time consuming.
3. Collecting samples works for all aspects of all programs.
4. Samples can be used as direct evidence of progress.
5. If samples are dated and adequate notes are taken about them, interpretations can be made later by various people.
6. Some samples can be analyzed for feelings in addition to concepts.
7. Samples can be used in conjunction with other assessment methods.

Disadvantages of using samples of children's work are as follows:

1. Samples may not be representative of children's work.
2. Samples of ongoing activities are more difficult to obtain than two-dimensional artwork.
3. Some children do not like to part with their work (but photographs can address these concerns).
4. Adequate storage space for children's work can be a problem (although digital cameras make storage easier).

Tools for Structuring Authentic Assessments: Although authentic assessment resolves the conflict between program goals and what is measured, a gap does exist between an idealized portrayal of authentic assessment and its implementation. Observing, recording, and reporting data are time consuming and can strain even the most generous operating budget. Time constraints in the daily operations of an early childhood program, teacher turnover, and the need for ongoing professional development are challenges with implementation. However, when a clearly defined assessment system is in place, these challenges can be overcome (Oldham & Sprague, 2008). Teachers need a framework that is aligned with program goals for systematically collecting and documenting children's performance. Such a framework ensures that assessments promote children's learning and development and can be understood by family members and policy makers.

Several assessment tools are available to guide teachers in the collection and analysis of authentic assessment information. Because researchers have identified the important constructs of children's learning and development, it is possible to mesh assessment procedures with the educational goals of many quality early childhood programs. The tools described next provide a comprehensive picture of how the child is performing in the program and thus allow teachers to connect assessment results to decision making about curriculum content and teaching strategies. This family of assessment tools is commonly referred to as curriculum-based measures; as such, they focus on demonstrated knowledge and skill achievement:

- **High/Scope Child Observation Record (COR).**   The Infant Toddler Child Observation Record (High/Scope Educational Research Foundation, 2001) and the Revised Preschool Child Observation Record (High/Scope Educational Research Foundation, 2002) are used to assess children age birth to 6. With advances in technology, these assessment instruments are now available in a time-saving CD-ROM and online formats (High/Scope, 2011). Although these were developed specifically to align with the High/Scope curriculum, the developers report that this assessment can be used in most developmentally appropriate early childhood care and education programs. Using notes that describe episodes of a child's behavior in six COR categories (initiative, creative representation, social relations, music and movement, language and literacy, and logic and mathematics) taken over several months, the teacher rates the child's behavior on 28 (Infant and Toddler) and 32 (Preschool) five-level COR items. Teachers score the COR two or three times each year, with the initial ratings given after children have been in the program 6 to 8 weeks.

- **The Work Sampling System.**   The Work Sampling System (WSS) (Meisels et al., 1994) is a performance assessment system designed for children from preschool through grade 5. This approach assesses and documents children's skills, knowledge, behavior, and accomplishments in seven domains (personal/social development, language and literacy, mathematical thinking, scientific thinking, social studies, the arts, and physical development) performed on multiple occasions. The Work Sampling System is made up of developmental guidelines and checklists, portfolios of children's work, and summary reports completed by teachers. Assessment takes place three times a year. The Work Sampling System has been updated with current technology (Meisels et al., 2011), which saves teacher time. Preliminary research on the WSS found that the information collected is reliable and valid as a measurement of children's achievement (FairTest, 2011).

- **Creative Curriculum Developmental Continuum.**   Trister-Dodge, Colker, and Heroman (2003) developed a curriculum-based assessment tool aligned with the goals and intended outcomes of the Creative Curriculum. In 2010, the publishers of the Creative Curriculum developed Teaching Strategies GOLD, a revised version of the original assessment system. This assessment system was developed after an extensive literature review and was narrowed down to 38 standards-based/school-readiness objectives that cover nine areas of development and learning, including objectives for English language learners (Heroman, Burts, Berke, & Bickart, 2010). As designed, the developmental continuum evaluation is completed three times annually, but teachers and caregivers are encouraged to collect artifacts and observation notes to document children's development continually.

- **Assessment, Evaluation, and Programming System for Infants and Children (AEPS) (2nd ed.).**   This assessment system by Bricker and colleagues (2002) is a comprehensive system to link assessment with daily planning to help facilitate children's optimal development. This tool spans from birth to age 6 and covers six developmental domains (fine motor, gross motor, adaptive, cognitive, social-communication, and social). This assessment is in the form of a rating checklist and allows the caregiver to identify the child's level of performance. This tool has been updated with AEPS interactive Web-based technology, which allows for the quick generation of reports that were historically created by hand (Brookes, 2011). This tool is designed to be used either during naturalistic observation of children or, if time is limited, during small group engagements that would allow the caregiver to complete the assessment of several children in a relatively short period of time (over a couple of days).

- **The Early Learning Scale.**   The Early Learning Scale (ELS) developed by Riley-Ayers, Boyd, and Frede (2008) and published by the National Institute for Early Education Research (NIEER) was developed in response to early educators' request for a comphrehensive standards-based assessment system. This assessment is a concise performance-based measure utilizing data collected through observation and work samples. Data is analyzed using a five-point continumn across 10 items that inform instruction and improve student learning across domains. Because the ELS is based on state standards and is not curriculum specific, it can be used in any early childhood classroom (Ayers, Frede, & Jung, 2010).

Standardized Tests: **Standardized tests** are either **criterion referenced**—they compare a child's performance with a preselected or established standard or criterion of performance, or **norm referenced**—they measure a child's performance by comparing it with the performance of others. Standardized tests can be useful when used in conjunction with authentic data collection and analysis; when used in isolation, they are not particularly informative. Standardized tests come with a manual that explains the purposes and uses of the test. The manual describes how the test was constructed; provides specific directions for administering, scoring, and interpreting results; contains tables of norms; and provides a summary of available research data on the test, including measures of its reliability and validity.

Concerns About Standardized Assessment Practices.   Concerns about the use of standardized assessment practices have increased as standardized tests and testing have become more prevalent in programs serving young children. Advocates have become vocal, expressing their concerns about how some assessment practices have the potential for doing harm. The following concerns should be taken seriously by early childhood program directors:

   1. The assessment instrument may not match the program's rationale. One of the greatest dangers is that assessment itself can determine a program's curriculum and its implementation rather than the program determining the how and why of assessment. It is as though the cart were placed before the horse. For example, some program planners take the content of standardized tests and plan activities to teach these items. Teaching to the test narrows the curriculum, putting an inappropriate emphasis on academics (Dahlberg & Asen, 1994; Peel & McCary, 1997). According to Bowman (1990, p. 30), "Curriculum based on tests is narrow and fails to embed knowledge in meaningful contexts, thus making it virtually unusable for the learner." Kohn (2000) stated that when high-stakes testing is employed, instruction becomes less DAP. He explained that important practices and policies (e.g., caring communities, emergent curriculum) are threatened by "a top-down, heavy-handed, corporate-style, standardized version of school reform that is driven by testing" (Kohn, 2001, p. 20). The order should be reversed. A program should be rationally planned and based on current and accurate information about children; tests should be selected to fit the program's goals and objectives.

2. Tests may not meet accepted standards (e.g., acceptable levels of validity and reliability, statistics appropriate to the program's purpose, elimination of inherent cultural and linguistic biases; NRC, 1999b). The psychometric qualities of most standardized measures designed for young children are inadequate (Langhorst, 1989). Scoring errors can also occur (Meisels & Atkins-Burnett, 2000).

3. Testing is likely to be stressful and/or inappropriate for all those involved.

The goal is not to prohibit all standardized testing but for early childhood directors to recognize the following:

1. Assessment instruments should be used only for their intended purposes.
2. Assessment instruments should meet acceptable levels of quality (e.g., validity, reliability, cultural congruence).
3. Placement, retention, and other high-stakes decisions should be made from multiple sources of data.
4. Assessment instruments should be used only if children will benefit and the benefit does not come from reduced group variation. (Schools must be more adaptive to normal variance.)

Shepard (1994) added two principles to the NAEYC's guiding assessment principle— that any assessment practice should benefit children or else it should not be conducted: (a) "The contents of assessments should reflect and model progress toward important learning goals" (p. 208), and (b) the methods of assessment must be developmentally appropriate. To understand how these principles are applied, 30 questions for program administrators to affirm in making assessment decisions were included in the position statement of the National Association for the Education of Young Children and the National Association of Early Childhood Specialists in State Departments of Education (2003).

Shepard et al. (1998b) and the National Research Council (Snow et al., 2008) stated that if standardized testing is mandated, early childhood programs should make efforts to use sampling methods rather than subject all children to testing. For example, the use of *matrix sampling,* a statistical technique whereby each child takes only part of the test, is helpful because the method lessens the testing burden on each child and makes it impossible to use individual scores to make high-stakes decisions: "Before age eight, standardized achievement measures are not sufficiently accurate to be used for high-stakes decisions about individual children and schools" (Snow et al., 2008, p. 53). Epstein et al. (2004) suggested developing systems of analysis so that test scores are only a part of a broader assessment system that includes authentic assessment records. Current thinking does not suggest that standardized measures never be used with young children, but when used, they must be developmentally and culturally appropriate, valid, and reliable for their purpose and are only a part of a child's assessment data.

Identifying Children Needing Intervention Services

The identification of children needing intervention services is a two-stage process. The first stage, usually called **screening**, involves a brief assessment to determine whether referral for more in-depth assessment is needed. The second stage, usually called **diagnostic assessment**, consists of a more complete assessment. If the child is identified as needing intervention, special plans are made.

Developmental screening is the first step in an assessment/intervention process (Nuttall, Romero, & Kalesnik, 1999). Screening is performed individually on large numbers of children and can be done by nonspecialists (general education teachers/caregivers or parents). Since the intent of a screening test is only to determine if further evaluation is warranted, results should be interpreted with care, and neither child placement decisions nor major program decisions should be made based on its results. Screening tests must be valid for the purpose for which they are used and also reliable (Meisels & Atkins-Burnett, 1994; NAEYC, 2011).

According to federal law, diagnostic assessments, administered following screening, must be conducted in a team setting that uses multiple sources of assessment data and must be part of a system of intervention services. Diagnostic assessments should consider the child's developmental trajectory, interactions with others, and cultural and linguistic environment (Greenspan & Weider, 1998). These criteria should be rigorously used to prevent children from being misclassified and receiving interventions that do not meet their needs (Burnette, 1998). Diagnostic assessment data are used to create IFSPs and IEPs, but monitoring the provision and effectiveness of recommended services is a must.

Determining Program Effectiveness and Making Policy Decisions

Assessments designed for the purpose of determining program effectiveness and making policy decisions can be in the form of ongoing formative assesment and/or evaluative **summative assessment** procedures. Formative assessment tells a program how well it is doing in meeting the program's goals. It provides information about where program staff might target their efforts to improve program quality. Summative program assessment is cumulative in nature and is used to determine whether a program has met its goals for both program quality and student learning. More specifically, summative program evaluative processes are used to determine the effectiveness of curriculum and methodology and to provide a judgment about the overall program quality. Program evaluation permits the planning of additions to or revisions of services and even determines changes in program rationale. It is the responsibility of the program administrator to identify a systematic process for continuously evaluating the program's effectiveness. For the purposes of program evaluation, the assessment system should include information from all stakeholders, that is, families, teachers, community members, and children.

The process of program evaluation must also include objective information regarding how successfully a program is meeting its goals. This might include systematically compiling classroom-level assessment information to determine the extent to which all children's learning goals are being achieved. In this way, caregivers' assessment of individual children's learning will be summarized by classroom and reviewed. Through this analysis process, the program director will identify goals that are not consistently being met and then engage in the process of identifying ways to strengthen the program to address these needs.

A Better Way

As a new director, Grace was given the charge to develop a center-wide improvement plan. She realized that assessment of children's learning and the overall program quality were the issues that needed to be addressed in the improvement plan. She held an evening staff meeting at which she divided the teachers into small groups based on the age of the children they taught. She asked them to reflect on the current child assessment practices as well as on the overall quality of the daily operations in their classroom environment. As each group reported back to the larger group, Grace took detailed notes and asked open-ended questions to stimulate discussion and problem solving.

It became apparent that several issues were challenges among all age groups. One was having the time to conduct child assessments; another was that newer staff members needed to be trained in the center's assessment systems. It was also clear that not all teachers knew exactly what child assessment methods were to be in place. The teachers indicated that the development of a clear assessment plan would help ensure that everyone was doing what was required in each classroom. Grace asked for a representative from each age group to help her draft the school-wide assessment plan that would include individual child assessment information as well as program wide assessment practices.

Another result was the need for a systematic checklist that teachers could use to ensure that classrooms met the basic indicators of quality. The teachers said that the development of a "quality assurance checklist" would help all staff know the expectations in the classroom. Several of the lead teachers became enthusiastic at the prospect of a checklist that would help them ensure quality and volunteered to help Grace develop the document.

Since the mid-1990s, there has been a shift toward summative program evaluation. Researchers are looking at child outcomes to measure program quality (Council of Chief State School Officers, 1995; Schorr, 1994). Information about the connection between effective services and desired outcomes for young children and their families can assist in holding decision makers accountable for investing in quality early childhood programs and meeting specified outcomes (Kagan, Rosenkoetter, & Cohen, 1997). Advocates often express their concerns about the practice of testing children to assess individual centers or programs (NRC, 1997, 1999), because of how difficult it is to fairly and accurately assess children from diverse backgrounds and young English language learners (Child Trends, 2010; Copple & Bredekamp, 2009; Espinosa, 2010; NAEYC, 2009b).

For purposes of determining program effectiveness and making policy decisions, children, teachers, and schools are increasingly measured through standardized achievement tests. This is particularly true for publicly funded educational services and in public elementary and secondary schools. One example of a commonly used standardized achievement test for young children is the Yellow Brigance, which covers birth to developmental age 7. However, some states have moved away from using children's standardized test scores as an indicator of program effectiveness. In South Carolina, the Conditions of Learning Assessment Strategy was specifically designed to ensure that programs were ready for children, rather than focusing on children being school ready and has achieved the goal of preventing the state from mandating inappropriate high-stakes testing of young children (Freeman & Brown, 2008).

For overall program quality, assessment must be systematic and ongoing. Program quality should be regularly assessed at both classroom and administrative levels to ensure continual compliance with program goals and quality standards. Overall program quality initiatives such as accreditation; state-initiated Quality Rating and Improvement Systems (QRIS); and the use of published quality assessment instruments such as the Environmental Rating Scales (ECERS and ITERS), the Classroom Assessment Scoring System (CLASS), the High/Scope Program Quality Assessment (PQA), can help program administrators address the quality of their programs from children's learning to organizational and administrative competencies.

RECORD KEEPING

Documentation that is the basis of assessment has always been an important aspect of a staff member's duties; Today, in this climate of increased accountability, documenting children's learning and development is more important and prevalent than ever. Many advantages come from keeping records of children's development and learning, such as the following:

1. Teachers who document children's learning make more productive planning decisions; documentation informs teaching.
2. Systematic documentation of what children know and are able to do can help staff see each child's progress. Staff who work daily with a child may better see progress through a review of this documentation. It can help teachers determine whether skills and concepts are emerging as expected or whether significant lags may call for specialized professional assistance. Records kept over time help specialists determine whether a problem is transient or continuous and can help discover when a problem began and how pervasive its effects are on the child's development. On the basis of the evidence found in the records, specialists can suggest possible solutions to the problem. Good records also permit the independent assessment of a child by more than one person.
3. Documentation communicates to children that their learning is important. Thus, children become more evaluative of their own work. They can see their own progress—especially in collected, dated, and sequenced work samples.
4. Documentation is an important basis for working with families.
5. Records are also beneficial to a child who changes programs frequently. Records of a recently transferred child make it easier for staff to help the child settle into the new setting.
6. Because funding agencies, citizens' groups, boards of directors or school boards, and parents often require evidence of the early childhood program's effectiveness in meeting its goals, the evidence is often best demonstrated by the records that have been kept. The local program's funding agency is also likely to require various records as a basis for subsequent funding.
7. Records also help teachers see the results of new teaching techniques or services.
8. Records and documentation can also be used as data for research and, when used effectively, can drive curriculum and collaboration in early childhood settings (Seitz, 2008).

Possible disadvantages to keeping records of children's learning and development are as follows:

1. A staff member can spend more time keeping records than planning and working with children.
2. A staff member can make a prejudgment based on records and become positively or negatively biased toward a child.
3. Because of the requirements of the Family Educational Rights and Privacy Act (FERPA), staff need special training in developing accurate, appropriate, and relevant records and in developing record protection and handling procedures.
4. Record keeping may become a meaningless activity because the types of data required to be kept may not be congruent with the goals of the local program or because records may be filed and forgotten or may not be used effectively.

Computers are helping programs overcome some of these problems. For example, computers can store information, maintain and generate files, and ensure privacy of records by securing the computer files with passwords so that only authorized individuals have access to certain parts of a child's file. Producers of software have noted teachers' needs for quick, accurate, and secure record keeping.

Types of Records

For purposes of this book, we classify records as background information records, performance records, referral records, and summary records.

Background Information Records: **Background information records** include information gathered from various sources outside the local program. Early childhood professionals are realizing that early experiences in the home and neighborhood and previous early childhood program (or school) experiences provide important "pictures" of a child. Many programs now ask for a considerable amount of information from families. Sometimes, these records are supplemented by additional information obtained by a caseworker or specialist or are volunteered by the family members after admission.

Basic information about a child and the child's family is always part of background information records and includes the child's legal name, home address, and telephone number; birth date, birthplace, number of siblings; and parents' or guardians' legal names, home address and telephone numbers, occupation(s), workplace(s), and workplace telephone number(s).

Medical information is also included in background information records, and completion of medical information records is required before a child is admitted to a program. Finally, records of the child's personal and social history are frequently included as part of background information records. This information may be supplied by a family member or by another adult who knows the child. Family members may record the information on forms, or a staff member may record the information during an interview. The child's personal and social history is likely to include information about birth history (birth weight, problems associated with birth, or birth defects); self-reliance; development, especially affective development and motor skills; previous experiences, such as places the child has visited, and previous group experiences; potential areas of concern such as disabilities, illnesses, fears, and accident proneness; and interests, such as favorite television programs, computer games and activities, books, toys, pets, and games. Occasionally, questions are asked about the family situation, family relationships, and family members' attitudes and may include information about housing; occupations; educational levels; aspirations for their children; and views of child rearing, including guidance methods family members have found to be effective. The NAEYC accreditation system and other accrediting organizations require that teachers gain information about the way families define their own race, religion, language, and home culture. A family interview form that collects backdrop information is one way that this criterion can be met (NAEYC, 2011).

Performance Records: **Children's learning or performance records** include documentation describing children's development and learning that is mandated by funding agencies. The contents of performance records differ according to the local program's goals. In traditional early childhood programs, professionals are likely to assess knowledge, skills, dispositions, and certain affective characteristics in all domains and in many contexts. These programs find that authentic assessment techniques and the documentation required for performance records generated from these techniques are compatible with their beliefs.

Performance records and documentation of children's learning can take several forms. The form depends on the nature of the observation. For example, if a teacher wants to

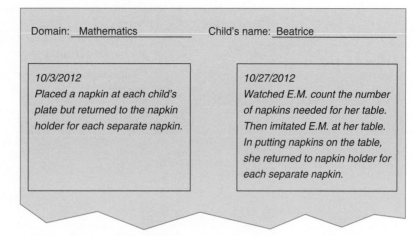

Figure 11.7
Individual Child's Log Entries

assess whether a child can name certain colors, a checklist makes a more appropriate record than a rating scale. Conversely, a social competence, such as "getting along with others," exists on a continuum and thus is better described by using a record that has a continuum format, such as a rating scale. Common forms of performance records include the following:

1. Log entries.   Log entries are short, dated notes. A single entry may not be significant, but multiple entries in one area of development spanning weeks and months often provide useful information. Many teachers find it easier to write logs on several children (and possibly in several domains) on adhesive address labels that can be transferred to an individual child's record to address a specific domain of development (see Figure 11.7). The COR uses these kinds of log entries (High/Scope Educational Foundation, 2002, 2011).

2. Anecdotal notes.   Anecdotes often give more information than logs. Similar to a series of log entries, a series of well-written anecdotes in one domain can reveal patterns of development. As previously discussed, a running record is an even more thorough account of performance. Figure 11.8 is an example of an anecdotal record.

3. Checklists.   A checklist is a prepared list of behaviors based on program goals. The teacher simply indicates if a child exhibits a behavior "consistently," "sometimes," or "not yet." Dating (rather than merely checking) observed behaviors provides more information. Checklists may be completed while actually observing children because information can be recorded quickly, or checklists with more summary types of statements (e.g., "Uses physical one-to-one correspondence") can come from narrative records, such as a

---

Child's name: Connor   **Date:** *11/12/2012*

Sept. 27 Tim and two other boys (Stefan and Mark) were in the sandbox using dump trucks for hauling sand. Stefan remarked that his building needed more sand than the first load they had just delivered. Tim looked and asked, "How much more sand?" "Twice as much," replied Stefan. "Then I'll drive my truck up once and give them a load and come back for one more load of sand," Tim commented.

Figure 11.8
Anecdotal Record

Child's name: _____ *Connor* _____ **Date:** _____ *2/11/2013* _____

Art Concepts

Can recognize these colors: red   _____

                               yellow   _____

                               blue   _____

                               green   _____

                               orange   _____

                               purple   _____

                               black   _____

                               brown   _____

Can arrange four varying grades
of sandpaper from rough to smooth.   _____

Can name the colors and point to
rough and smooth fruit in a
reproduction of Cezanne's painting
Apples and Oranges.   _____

Figure 11.9
Checklist

series of log entries. Sometimes checklists are similar to rating scales because teachers are given the behavioral descriptors and then are asked to check on a continuum (e.g., "no evidence, beginning, developing, or very secure"). An example of a checklist is shown in Figure 11.9.

4. Ratings Ratings assess the quality of an attribute with the judgment indicated on a quality-point scale. Only behaviors that can be described according to the degree to which the competence or trait exists can be recorded on rating scales. Judgments are based on either observations or impressions; thus, the validity of rating scales is based mainly on the adequacy of the observations. Some rating scales rate children's behavior along a continuum from "not yet" to "always"; others use a numerical continuum. (See Figures 11.10 and 11.11 for examples of rating scales.)

Child's name: _____ *Elliot* _____ **Date:** _____ *11/20/13* _____

1. Can put on his or her outdoor clothes

_____
Not   Sometimes   Always
Yet

Figure 11.10
Forced-Choice Rating Scale

Child's name:	Adam		Date:	12/10/12		

1. Motor skills can best be described as:

1 = Not yet seen ← — — — → 5 = Excels in skill

hops		1	2	3	4	5
skips		1	2	3	4	5
climbs steps (ascending)		1	2	3	4	5

Figure 11.11
Numerical Rating Scale

5. Samples of children's work Samples of children's work can take many forms. Common samples are drawings, paintings, and papers showing language and mathematics skills. Less common but very important samples are (a) pictures of three-dimensional art products, block structures, and even two-dimensional materials too large to keep easily; (b) printouts from computer work; (c) audio recordings of oral performances; and (d) video recordings of other performances (e.g., motor skills, interactions with others in the program). Many experts provide advice and examples of strategies for documenting samples of children's work (Helm, Beneke, & Steinheimer, 1998; Ogunnaike-Lafe & Krohn, 2010; Reisman, 2011; Rhodes & Nathenson-Mejia, 1992; Seitz, 2008).

6. Test scores and diagnostic profile information These records are often raw or converted scores or other graphic or descriptive information coming from performance on staff-constructed or standardized instruments.

Referral Records: All early childhood programs that employ specialists to work with children who need special assistance or who may refer children to medical professionals such as psychologists, counselors, speech pathologists, or physical therapists need **referral records**.

Local early childhood programs should develop a separate referral form for each type of referral (different forms for referral to medical specialists, speech pathologists, and so forth). The items on each form differ, but each type should include the signed permission for referral from a parent or legal guardian; the date and the person or agency to which the referral is being made; the name of the staff member referring the child; the specific reasons for the referral; either a digest of or the complete reports from other referrals; the length of time the staff member has been aware of the concern; strategies staff or family members have tried and with what success; and questions or concerns of family members, peers, or the child himself if they are available. Many referral records provide space for the specialist's report after assessment and support services are provided.

Summary Records: **Summary records** summarize and interpret primary data. Background information records and referral records, on the one hand, are kept intact and updated but are rarely summarized. Performance records, on the other hand, written or collected by using various formats and encompassing a length of time, must be reviewed and reduced to a summary format in order to analyze them for either formative or summative purposes.

Summary records are completed several times a year to aid teachers in better understanding each child's progress and interests for the purposes of curriculum planning and communicating with families. Summary records are used to abstract aggregate data (with individual children's identification removed) for aiding program directors in their periodic reports to their funding or sponsoring agencies.

Thus, summary performance records often use broad descriptors of behavior, such as "Likes to write" or "Knows that print is read left to right and top to bottom." These summary statements can be developed from the program's goals for children's development and learning in each domain. In a way, check sheets and report cards given to parents are also summary records. Other summary instruments, designed to assess many domains, are called *developmental assessment systems* (discussed in detail by Cohen, Stern, & Balaban, 1997). The Work Sampling System (Meisels et al., 1994) uses summary records as do many other assessment systems. Commercial curriculum and assessment programs often provide individual child and group summary sheets, which help teachers compile information as a step toward deciding what the information tells them about individual children or the group. Many programs provide software that makes generation of summary records less time consuming (McAfee et al., 2004).

Record Collections

Public school programs have traditionally kept cumulative records on children from entrance to graduation; Head Start and other government-funded programs keep records on children from year to year. Licensed early childhood programs and family child care homes should keep record collections of children served; licensing regulations often require that records be kept available for a specified number of years. The most common type of record collection is the cumulative record. The portfolio has become another recommended method for documentation collection.

Cumulative Records: A **cumulative record**, the summary of a child's entire school career, might be reduced to the size of a file folder. A cumulative record is likely to include the child's name, birth date, parents' or guardians names and addresses; the child's immunization records; each year's attendance record, summary grades, standardized test information; referrals; and information about major events in the child's life, such as the birth of a sibling with a serious chronic condition or a contentious divorce that may impact her behavior or performance.

Portfolios: Danielson and Abrutyn (1997) identified three types of portfolios:

1. **Display portfolios** are photographs and general descriptions of what children do in the classroom, but these portfolios do not focus on an individual child.
2. **Showcase portfolios** show an individual child's best work; however, because the work is only the "best" work, the portfolio may not be an accurate picture of that child.
3. **Working portfolios** show the individual child's process of learning skills and concepts; evidence of typical work illustrating both the child's strengths and weaknesses is included, with all samples clearly connected to program goals.

In this text, the **portfolio**, defined as a method of gathering and organizing evidence of a child's interests, skills, concept development, and dispositions over time with documentation clearly connected to program goals, is a summary record. Thus, the text definition fits Danielson and Abrutyn's definition of a working portfolio. Most programs will use both **process portfolios** (several items collected to document each goal) and **archival portfolios** (final item or items put in the portfolio) for each predetermined sampling date (e.g., September, January, and April).

Constructing a portfolio involves the following steps:

1. Plan with all staff members the types of data that can document specific criteria being used as the learning goals of the local program. Each child's work samples may be different because children can demonstrate their understandings and skills in many ways. A chart could be made of program goals, typical activities, and types of authentic assessment samples that would fit each type of activity. Some excellent samples are described by Dodge, Colker, and Heroman (2002) and Meisels, Dichtelmiller, Jabalon, Dorfman, and Marsden (1997). A general listing of types of contents for working portfolios is given in Figure 11.12. Samples and documentation should come from many sources, including teachers and other professionals, family members, and the children (who should be encouraged to select some of the items).

2. Document each item collected. Collection alone is not enough. The documentation should include the date, whether the child worked independently or with others, and the amount of time and effort required. Gronlund (1998) offered an example of a "Portfolio Documentation Checklist" (p. 6), which saves time documenting each item; more recently, Gronlund and Engle (2011) developed a complete portfolio system structured for teachers so that all areas of development are included.

There is no set prescription for portfolio format and organization. Each portfolio system can be unique and made to fit the program's goals and curriculum (Huffman, 2011). Consistency in portfolio format across a program can contribute to a consistent and comprehensive assessment plan. Portfolios can follow children through their years in a program and a final version can be given to parents upon their children's graduation from the program.

Background information

Health information

Teacher observations

Logs, anecdotal records, running records, etc.

Check sheets

Rating scales

Samples of child's work, such as writing,

    drawing, painting, scissor work,

    audiotapes (storytelling, show and tell, etc.),

    videotapes (projects, gross-motor activities, fine-motor activities, dramatic play, etc.), and photos (artwork—especially 3-D, block-building structures, etc.)

Test scores

Activity chart (shows centers child chose)

Interviews with child

Parent information

Parents' observations

Parent-teacher and parent-teacher-child conference summaries

Parent questionnaires

Parent notes

Figure 11.12
Contents of Working Portfolios

The use of portfolios has expanded into assessment of program quality. The NAEYC revised accreditation system developed between 2006 and 2008 relies heavily on the development of both a program portfolio to show evidence of meeting administrative criteria and a classroom portfolio to show compliance with criteria related to curriculum, teaching, and children's learning experiences.

Family Educational Rights and Privacy Act (FERPA)

Children's records are protected under the Family Educational Rights and Privacy Act (FERPA). This law provides the following:

1. Parents or legal guardians of children who attend a program receiving federal assistance may see information in the program's official files. This information includes test scores, grade averages, class rank, intelligence quotient, health records, psychological reports, notes on behavioral problems, family background items, attendance records, and all other records except personal notes made by a staff member solely for his own use.
2. Records must be made available for review within 45 days of the request.
3. Parents may challenge information irrelevant to education, such as religious preference or unsubstantiated opinions.
4. Contents of records may be challenged in a hearing. If the program refuses to remove material challenged by parents as inaccurate, misleading, or inappropriate, the parent may insert a written rebuttal.
5. With some exceptions (e.g., other officials in the same program, officials in another program to which the student has applied for transfer, some accrediting associations, state educational officials, some financial aid organizations, the courts), written consent of parents is required before program officials may release records. Programs must keep a written record as to who has seen or requested to see the child's records.
6. Parents have the right to know where records are kept and which program officials are responsible for them.
7. Unless a divorced parent is prohibited by law from having any contact with the child, divorced parents have equal access to official records.
8. Most of the foregoing rights pass from parent to child when the child is 18 years of age.
9. Program officials must notify parents (and 18-year-olds) of their rights.

REPORTING

Reporting is becoming a more important aspect of early childhood programs as programs seek to involve family members in their children's development and as programs become more accountable to families, citizens' groups, and funding and regulatory agencies. As is true of all aspects of an early childhood program, reporting practices should be based on program goals. Planning reporting requires administrators to think in terms of four steps in developing a reporting practice: (a) determining the purposes of reporting, (b) facilitating reporting through the collection of assessment data, (c) selecting the methods of reporting, and (d) rethinking reporting practices. Because reporting is so tied to the assessment and recording processes, it is best considered before assessment plans are completed.

Determining the Purposes of Reporting

The first step in developing a reporting practice is to determine the purposes of reporting. For most early childhood programs, a major purpose of reporting is to provide information to family members about their child's progress. Families and staff jointly discuss the child's strengths and needs and plan the next steps in the educative process. Darragh (2009) discussed, specifically, the goal to shift parent relationships to a mutually supportive *co-constructed* relationship and that ongoing assessment is an avenue that builds this relationship with both parties sharing knowledge of the individual child. Another major purpose of reporting is to meet the requirements of funding and regulatory agencies. Although funding and regulatory agencies require reports on many aspects of programs, program success as measured by children's progress is a major component in the reports made to all regulating and sponsoring agencies.

Facilitating Reporting Through Assessment Data

Once the specific purposes of reporting have been determined, the next step is to make a connection between assessment data and these purposes. Several important questions are as follows:

1. *What type of assessment meets the purposes of reporting?* More specifically: (a) What information do family members need about their child's progress? It is likely that much of this information will be the same as teachers need for curriculum decisions. (b) What information does the regulatory or funding agency expect to know about the collective progress of children that in turn will demonstrate the program's value? These data can also be used in rethinking program goals. Information provided to both families and agencies needs to be directly linked to the program's goals. Programs with narrower, academic goals will assess and report children's progress in academic areas; programs with more holistic/developmental goals will gather and report data in many domains of children's development and learning.

2. *In what format will assessment data be recorded?* Generally, standardized tests yield quantitative data—numerical raw scores (e.g., number correct) and numerical converted scores (e.g., percentiles, stanines, developmental ages), and authentic assessment techniques yield qualitative data (e.g., anecdotes, samples of children's work). If one considers assessment data from the standpoint of the ease of reporting only (not in terms of their appropriateness for program goals and the ages of children involved, although these are critical criteria), quantitative data are more difficult to explain to family members, who want to know what the scores mean. Furthermore, composite scores yield no information about the specific strengths and weaknesses in each child's progress; thus, reporting requires a careful interpretation of the sub-score data from which composite scores are determined.

Quantitative data, however, lend themselves to the concise summary data often expected by funding and regulatory agencies; in fact, many standardized achievement tests provide class record/profile data that can be easily incorporated into agency reports. In some cases, however, quantitative scores may not be understood by those reading the agency reports.

Conversely, qualitative data are much easier for families to understand but are more difficult to summarize and definitely do not lend themselves to tables and graphs. If both quantitative and qualitative assessment data have been collected, the teacher must explain each type of data and also show how each type relates to the other.

3. *Against which criterion will assessment outcomes be measured?* For example: Is progress being compared with that of a norming group? Is it measured against specific program goals? Is it being compared with developmental landmarks? This information must be reported.

4. *How will data be assembled?* The ways data are assembled determine the ease of access and the need to summarize before reporting.

Selecting the Methods of Reporting

The third step in planning reporting is to determine the oral and written reporting methods, especially to families. (Agencies usually have their own reporting formats.) Reporting methods are diverse. Most families prefer both written and some oral reports. Common methods include informal reports, report cards, checklists, narrative report letters, and individual conferences.

Informal Reports: Informal reports are perhaps the most common way of reporting—so common that staff may not even be aware that they are communicating information about children's progress. This kind of report may be a casual conversation with a family member in which a staff member mentions, "Lori excels in motor skills," or "Mark is learning the last step in tying his shoes." Family members may note their child's progress while volunteering in the program. Samples of children's work with or without teachers' comments are often sent home. Children, too, report on themselves, such as, "I learned to skip today," or "I shared my boat with everyone at the water table." High-quality programs provide daily reporting to parents such as "What I did Today" forms that document not only nutritional and toileting information (for infants and toddlers), but also information about the child's daily activities.

Narrative Report Letters: Programs using **narrative report letters** usually provide forms on which teachers write a few brief comments about a child's progress under each of several headings, such as psychomotor development, personal and social adjustment,

By posting the work of children this program is able to effectively communicate to families the knowledge and skills their children have demonstrated.

Your Child's Progress

Name_____ Classroom_____

Motor skills:

Jorge can gallop, skip, run, and throw and catch a rubber ball. He enjoys all games that use movement, and his skills indicate that his attainment is high in this area of development.

Personal/social adjustment:

Jorge does not initiate many aggressive acts; however, he still has trouble keeping his hands to himself. He responds to negative overtures from his classmates by hitting.

Language growth:

Jorge appears to enjoy new words. He uses rhyming words and makes up words to fit the rhymes. He is not yet able to express negative feelings toward others with words, however.

General evaluation:

Jorge is progressing nicely. More opportunities to talk with others would help him learn to express himself. He performs well in the room and on the playground as long as he is kept busy and as long as others leave him alone.

Figure 11.13
Narrative Report Letter

cognitive development, language growth, work habits, problem-solving growth, aesthetic growth, self-reliance, and general evaluation. An example of a narrative report letter form is shown in Figure 11.13. Narrative report letters are very appropriate for summarizing authentic assessment records. The advantage of report letters is that teachers can concentrate on a child's specific strengths and needs without giving letter grades or marking "satisfactory/ unsatisfactory" and without noting progress in highly specific areas, such as "knows his address" or "ties her shoes." The two disadvantages to report letters are that (a) they are very time consuming, but computers reduce the time required to prepare them; the computer generates the report template and teachers can easily word process the narrative itself, and (b) unless teachers carefully study their records on each child, they may slip into writing stereotypical comments, especially after writing the first few reports.

Individual Conferences: Many programs schedule **individual conferences** with each child and the child's family members. Conferences permit face-to-face communication among children, families, and teachers.

To effectively discuss children's progress, teachers need to plan the conference by using a written guide sheet that lists the topics and main points to be discussed. The teacher should consult all records on the child and carefully transfer to the guide sheet any information to be shared with family members. A narrative report check sheet, developmental profile, or selected materials from the portfolio given to family members can be used as the guide sheet. Time is provided for family members to ask questions, share observations, and express their concerns as topics listed on the guide sheet are covered. Conferences should end on a positive note, with plans for follow-up for any areas of concern at home or at school. Family members and children can look at the other items in the portfolio at the end of the conference. Many program directors are finding that if teachers give a copy of the guide sheet to each family member a few days before the conference, family members have time to think about the contents and to prepare questions and comments for the conference.

Directors play an important role in supporting teachers during conferences. It can be difficult for teachers to discuss sensitive issues they have observed, such that a child may be significantly behind his peers in a particular domain of development, or that a particular behavior has more intensity, duration, or frequency than considered typical for his age and developmental level. Teachers should not use diagnostic labels or terms they are not qualified to assess. For example, a teacher would not say that a child is hyperactive or has attention deficit disorder but would describe the behavior as observed, such as the child moves quickly from one activity to another. It is important for teachers to use specific, descriptive language and avoid generalizations that characterize and label a child. Directors should be involved in conferences, especially when suggesting additional assessment or screening. Directors can provide an objective perspective to what can be a sensitive and emotional topic for parents and teachers alike. Furthermore, when addressing concerns with parents, consider starting by describing a strength, then addressing the concern, and ending with something positive. Directors play an important role in providing support for both parents and teachers when concerns must be addressed in conferences.

Rethinking Reporting Practices

The final step in developing a reporting practice is to experiment with the reporting plans and revise them if necessary. Reporting practices must not only work for program personnel, but also open dialogue between staff and the recipients of reports, especially families. In short, the only purpose of reporting to families is to establish collaboration on behalf of children.

TRENDS AND ISSUES

As state-funded early childhood systems develop, policy makers are looking carefully at the outcomes reported for children in publicly funded programs (Pew, 2011). Assessment reform is following curriculum reform, and states are moving quickly to develop statewide early childhood systems of accountability that may influence program-level decisions on assessment.

Kagan (2000) challenged early childhood professionals to design assessment systems that capture children's full range of development and learnings (i.e., physical well-being and motor development, social and emotional development, approaches toward learning, communication and language development, and cognitive development) and provide needed safeguards (e.g., avoiding unnecessary assessment, improper techniques, misuse of data).

In 1994, the National Education Goals Panel convened the Goal 1 Early Childhood Assessments Resource Group. The group identified these purposes for assessment in early childhood: (a) to promote children's learning and development; (b) to identify children for health and special learning services; (c) to monitor trends, evaluate programs, and services; and (d) to assess academic achievement and hold individual students, teachers, and schools accountable. Shepard, Kagan, and Wurtz (1998a) outlined how appropriate uses and technical accuracy of assessments for the foregoing purposes change across the early childhood age continuum. Building on the work of the National Education Goals panel, the National Research Council (Snow et al., 2008) at the request of Congress, embarked on a study of developmental outcomes and appropriate assessment of young children. The report, titled *Early Childhood Assessment: Why, What, and How?* (Snow et al., 2008), highlights two key principles: (a) The purpose of assessment should guide assessment decisions and (b) assessment activity should be conducted within a coherent system of medical, educational, and family support systems that promote optimal development for all young children. The remainder of the report provides guidelines in four important areas:

1. Guidelines on purposes of assessment
2. Guidelines on domains and measures of developmental outcomes
3. Guidelines on instrument selection and implementation
4. Guidelines on the development of systems and infrastructure to support early childhood assessment

In 2007, the National Early Childhood Accountability Taskforce, chaired by Sharon Lynn Kagan (Shultz & Kagan, 2008), embarked on developing recommendations to help move our nation toward more coherent and effective early childhood accountability and improvement systems. The report, *Taking Stock: Assessing and Improving Early Childhood Learning and Program Quality,* answered the charge to "develop recommendations for a state accountability system for early education programs for pre-kindergarten children and linking such efforts to standards-based assessment in kindergarten and the primary grades" (p. 4). These national reports continue to influence the development of state wide systems.

Given the characteristics of the early childhood workforce (Schultz & Kagan, 2008) and the time consuming nature of assessment (Carter, 2008; Oldham & Sprague, 2008), assessment systems can be challenging to implement. Many directors and teachers agree with the concept of authentic assessment and believe that it is one of the most appropriate ways to document young children's dynamic learning. Teachers need help in using authentic assessment and will need intense training in purposeful observation, documentation, and analysis of assessment data. Furthermore, many teachers are not familiar with making professional judgments based on broader pictures of children and may even be hesitant in assuming this responsibility. Several authentic assessment systems, such as COR and the Work Sampling System, provide a structure for assessment data and inform teachers of criteria that may be used in making inferences about what children can do. In addition, the systems have the qualities of good standardized tests—that is, strong reliability and predictive validity. These systems can help provide the structure teachers need to implement an appropriate assessment system.

Many professionals are questioning screening practices and the use of the data they generate. Teachers need training in recognizing whether a child's departure from a typical developmental trajectory is a sign of a learning problem or is consistent with cultural and linguistic differences.

Another problem in assessment comes from trying to combine the purposes of assessment and use the data in many ways. Standardized achievement tests are often used for assessment. Although combining purposes saves money and time, such combining often results in the misuse of data, such as using readiness tests for screening or using assessment for determining program effectiveness and also for holding individual children accountable. This is an unethical practice that must be avoided.

With the increasing diversity of the early education population in the United States, another issue is the assessment of English language learners. NAEYC issued a position statement on the appropriate assessment of English language learners and suggested that, as with all assessment of young children, assessment of English language learners should have specific beneficial purposes with appropriate adaptations for children with a home language other than English (NAEYC, 2009a). Finally, a recent educational reform initiative in the field of early childhood care and education is the process termed *recognition and response* (Coleman, Buysee, & Neitzel, 2006). This process is commonly known as *response to intervention* (RtI) and is the process of providing a sound general education curriculum, engaging in the process of systematic and continuous assessment and progress monitoring, and then responding to individual children's needs according to the results of the assessment and evaluation. This approach has gained widespread use in the primary grades, affecting the role of special education practitioners, as more children with special needs are served in the general education setting (Reeves, 2010). RtI is gaining momentum in early childhood education as the basic principles fit with characteristics of quality early childhood programming: ongoing quality instruction, individual intervention, ongoing assessment with progress monitoring, and early identification of developmental differences (Stephens, Pethick, & Flowers, 2010). The Council for Exceptional Children's Division for Early Childhood (DEC), NAEYC, and the National Head Start Association (NHSA) are planning to develop a joint position statement on RtI in early childhood (Goode, 2011). The point to be made here is that assessment is continuing to become even more important to the provision of high-quality early childhood care and education services. To meet this challenge, we must continue to enhance our knowledge and understanding of effective assessment and evaluation.

SUMMARY

Assessing, recording, and reporting are integral parts of an early childhood program. All three practices must be thoughtfully and carefully planned, in keeping with program goals. Providing quality assessment, recording, and reporting assessments is not a simple matter but requires a highly trained staff and leadership by directors.

Similar to the professional concerns about inappropriate curriculum content and teaching strategies, are concerns about assessment. Assessment can support children's development or undermine it. Abuses and misuses have occurred in how assessment methods have been selected and administered (e.g., a disconnect between curriculum/teaching strategies and assessment practices); by the lack of a user-friendly format for young children (e.g., the use of the paper-and-pencil format); by the mis-assessment of young children with disabilities and those from culturally and linguistically diverse families; by the use of single measurements for making high-stakes decisions about children, staff competencies, and program effectiveness; and by the way scores have been interpreted to family members.

Professional associations have called for many changes in assessment, recording, and reporting practices. The major changes recommended include the following:

1. The increased use of ongoing observations of children in actual classroom situations (authentic or performance assessment), and the use of purposeful sampling techniques when standardized tests are mandated to determine program effectiveness.

2. Documentation of authentic performance assessment accomplished by writing logs and anecdotes, checking and rating of certain specified behaviors, and gathering samples of children's work. Other records can include notes taken during interviews and home visits and the summaries of assessments and services provided by specialists.

3. The development of reporting purposes and practices that mirror local program goals and that are verified by authentic performance assessment and appropriate observation records. Usually, the contents of reports are summarized performance records with samples of actual performance used to document the summary data and collected to form a portfolio. The format for reporting may be written, oral, or a combination of the two.

Early childhood professionals are calling for an appropriate assessment system to respond to demands for program accountability while providing safeguards to protect children from inappropriate and potentially harmful assessment practices.

USEFUL WEBSITES

National Association for the Education of Young Children (NAEYC)

www.naeyc.org

This website of the largest professional organization in this area has many position statements related to the assessment of young children and diversity.

National Institute for Early Education Research (NIEER)

nieer.org/

The NIEER website provides the most current research in early education topics, including assessment, and links to other relevant early childhood topics.

Pre[K]Now

preknow.org/

This website is related to the Pew Center Campaign which advocates for state supported pre-K. It includes a daily email update with articles from current newspapers and summaries of research.

Child Trends

www.childtrends.org/

The Child Trends website provides useful links to current research pertaining to state-level early education data and relevant information on current assessment practices.

TO REFLECT

1. It is essential that assessment practices used with vulnerable young children are ethical. Using the *NAEYC Code of Ethical Conduct* (Appendix 2), evaluate the extent to which your center's assessment and evaluation plan might be considered appropriate. If your center does not yet have an evaluation plan, design a sample evaluation plan that would be considered ethical.
2. The director of an early childhood center decided that authentic assessment took too much time and that administering a standardized literacy assessment in the pre-K year would show the quality of her program if the children scored well. What concerns should be shared with this director on the use of one standardized assessment as a reflection of children's learning and her program's overall quality?

CHECK AND APPLY YOUR UNDERSTANDING

1. Review the *NAEYC Code of Ethical Conduct* (Appendix 2) and discuss how this document can help you ensure that your program's assessment plan is responsible and appropriate for young children.
2. Noting the two main purposes for which program directors will use assessment, describe some of the assessment methods discussed in this chapter that apply to each purpose.
3. Discuss some of the different types of documentation of children's learning (performance records) discussed in this chapter. Do you think that one method may be more appropriate than others for young children?
4. Considering the different methods of reporting assessment information, discuss which methods you will include in your program and why.
5. Considering the English language learners in your program, visit the NAEYC website and review *Where We Stand: Screening and Assessment of Young English-Language Learners*. Discuss how your program will work to assess English language learners appropriately.

Working with Families and Communities

Learning Outcomes

After studying this chapter, you should be able to:

1. Compare the strengths and weaknesses of the three approaches to working with families.

2. Develop effective and inclusive plans for communicating with all families on a regular basis.

3. Develop a plan for creating a board of directors with representatives from many sectors of the community.

Grace's Experience

The program that Grace directs has been an important part of the neighborhood for more than 20 years. She knows she is benefiting from the goodwill it has earned over the years. It is respected because of its tradition of quality, outreach projects such as the sing-along the children present at the senior center in the spring are appreciated, and local businesses have always been willing to help out when asked for donations during the center's annual fund-raiser.

Recent years have brought changes to the neighborhood, however. Like many communities, it is more diverse than ever before. Grace now hears unfamiliar languages as she runs errands before and after school, and, for the first time, the center includes several children who are learning English as their second language. Grace is committed to maintaining the center's important role in the community and hopes this chapter will help her learn how to develop and maintain productive relationships with all of the families that enroll their children and the neighborhood where the center makes its home.

Early childhood programs play an important role in the lives of young children and their families. We hope this chapter will help you develop a greater appreciation for the ways families, programs of early care and education, and communities can join forces to improve the quality of life for young children while enhancing their chances for success in school and beyond.

These linkages are essential—neither families nor programs for young children exist in a vacuum. The coordinated interface among home, school, and community creates an essential network of support each child deserves (Bronfenbrenner, 1979). Program administrators, teachers, and care-givers who spend their days with young children have the opportunity to create and nurture relationships with families and begin the process of linking families to their community's educational and social service resources. It is our goal to help you take the lead in strengthening connections between your early childhood program and the families and communities you serve.

EARLY CHILDHOOD EDUCATORS' LONG HISTORY OF PARTNERING WITH FAMILIES

The field's earliest leaders recognized that families were children's first and most influential teachers. Beginning with the pioneering programs of the early 1900s, early childhood educators have embraced their responsibility to support families' efforts to enhance and ensure children's physical, social, and cognitive well-being.

In spite of the fact that families face different challenges today than they did more than a century ago, many of the issues they confront remain the same. Teachers and early childhood professionals continue to work together with one shared goal—to give all children opportunities to pursue their dreams and to achieve success.

Collaboration: A Crucial Element of Quality Programming

Opportunities for programs, families, and communities to work together have long been a crucial component of quality early childhood programming (Larner, 1996; Raab & Dunst, 1997). The theoretical foundation for this three-way collaboration is based on Vygotsky's sociocultural theory (1978) and Bronfenbrenner's ecological systems theory of human development (1979).

Findings reinforced by a growing body of research led the U.S. Congress to identify parental participation as the eighth National Education Goal and called on schools to "promote partnerships that will increase parental involvement in promoting the social, emotional and academic growth of children" (Goals 2000, 1994). The authors of the groundbreaking book *Eager to Learn* also emphasized the importance of schools partnering with families and recommend that "all early childhood programs build alliances with parents to cultivate mutually reinforcing environments for children at home and in early childhood programs" (National Research Council [NRC], 2001, p. 318). The centrality of the relationship linking families with programs for young children is illustrated by these important professional guidelines that include creating partnerships with families as a key component of quality:

- Head Start Performance Standards (Administration for Children and Families, 2007)
- National Association for the Education of Young Children (NAEYC) Early Childhood Program Standards (2005) including the Program Administration Core Competencies that are part of NAEYC Program Accreditation
- *NAEYC Code of Ethical Conduct* (NAEYC, 2011a) and its *Administrator's Supplement* (NAEYC, 2011b)
- Influential position statements, including NAEYC's statements on *Developmentally Appropriate Practice* (NAEYC, 2009), *Linguistic and Cultural Diversity* (NAEYC, 1995), *Violence in the Lives of Children* (NAEYC, 1993) and *Early Childhood Inclusion,* the joint position statement of the Division for Early Childhood (DEC) of the Council for Exceptional Children and NAEYC (DEC/NAEYC, 2009) call for program-family-community collaboration

- *NAEYC's Standards for Early Childhood Professional Preparation Programs* (NAEYC, 2009) that guide the curriculum offered to students enrolled in associate, bachelor's and graduate degree programs
- Environment rating scales (Harms, Clifford, & Cryer, 2005; Harms, Cryer, & Clifford, 2006; Harms, Jacobs, & White, 1995) that are widely used as measures of program quality

---

Application Activity

The *NAEYC Code of Ethical Conduct* (2011) (see Appendix 2) and its *Supplement for Early Childhood Program Administrators* (2011) (see Appendix 3) provide guidance for programs striving to develop and maintain strong collaborative relationships with families and communities. Working in groups, discuss a difficult situation you have encountered while working with families. Identify the core values involved in this situation and the ideals and principles in the NAEYC codes that guide your ethical decision making. Describe a defensible course of action that is true to these ethical principles.

Three Approaches to Working with Families

It will always be true that families are their children's first and most important teachers; however, today's families often rely on outside resources such as early childhood programs and schools to help them care for and educate their young children. Bronfenbrenner's (1979, 2004) ecological systems theory provides a framework for understanding how important it is that families and programs of early care and education develop strong and harmonious partnerships to support children's learning, growth, and development.

Involving families in children's early childhood experiences enhances the program's effectiveness and has long-lasting benefits for children and their families. For example, evidence shows that when families are engaged in their children's early school experiences, children adapt more successfully to school (Tan & Goldberg, 2009) and are more likely to do well academically (Reynolds, Magnuson, & Ou, 2010). Furthermore, when families are engaged during the early childhood years, there is a greater likelihood that they will remain involved during their children's elementary and secondary school years (Henrich & Blackman-Jones, 2006). Efforts to engage families in children's early childhood experiences have become an even higher priority in recent years because of schools' commitment to serving the increasingly diverse populations they are welcoming into their midst (Halgunseth, Peterson, Stark, & Moodie, 2009).

It is interesting to think about how recommended approaches to involving families in their children's education have shifted in recent years. For many years, **parent involvement** programs were seen as the best way for schools to reach out to their students' families. The success of parent involvement efforts is most often measured by how often parents volunteer in their child's classroom or contact their child's teacher or by the number of parents who plan and participate in fund-raising projects, field trips, and class parties (Halgunseth et al., 2009). Parent involvement programs require parents to take the initiative by fitting their involvement into the school's existing programs. This approach is now viewed as taking a deficit perspective because it fails to take into account parents' work schedules, economic constraints, or other barriers that may make direct involvement impractical if not impossible for many families (Souto-Manning & Swick, 2006).

Another popular approach to working with families is one that creates **school/family partnerships** (Halgunseth et al., 2009). This approach focuses on ways that families and schools can work together on projects and initiatives that are meaningful and beneficial to both. These are some of the ways schools reach out to the families and the communities they serve:

- **Parent Education.**   Early childhood programs assist families in their efforts to create healthy homes that support children's physical, emotional, and cognitive development.
- **School-to-Home and Home-to-School Communication.**   Teachers and caregivers use strategies such as newsletters, conferences, phone calls and email to create and maintain lines of communication between school and home.
- **Participation.**   Early childhood programs work to develop effective strategies to recruit and involve families as classroom volunteers and to involve them in school-wide special events.
- **Learning at Home.**   Early childhood programs advise families about how they can create home environments that are conducive to learning and support children's work at school.
- **Decision Making.**   Families are invited to participate in the program's decision making and governance through vehicles such as the center's parent-teacher organization or school advisory council. Some families may become involved in advocacy activities targeting decision-making bodies outside the program itself. They may, for example, attend meetings of the school board or another body that oversees the program's operations.
- **Community Outreach.**   Early childhood programs and parent-teacher groups can engage community members and businesses in the education of young children by soliciting their financial or in-kind support (Epstein et al., 2002).

A third model schools might embrace when working with families is a **family engagement** approach that strives to create an "ongoing, reciprocal, strengths-based partnership between families and their children's early childhood education programs" (Halgunseth et al., 2009, p. 3). This family engagement approach builds on the strengths of children's extended circle of caregivers, which can include parents, grandparents, siblings, aunts and uncles, friends, and neighbors. The family engagement model honors America's increased diversity and integrates the perspectives, strengths, and needs of all children and families, their community, and the programs that serve them. These are the characteristics of the family engagement approach:

- Families advocate for their children as they participate in making decisions related to their education.
- Two-way communication, initiated by both families and program personnel, is ongoing, timely, and consistent. Programs are, to the greatest extent possible, responsive to the linguistic traditions of all families. Families and programs exchange information about children's in-school and out-of-school experiences.
- Both families and program personnel are respected as experts. Family members share their knowledge through volunteering and participating in school events. Teachers and caregivers learn about the homes and communities of the children in their care and use this information to build curriculum and to inform instruction.
- Programs and families recognize opportunities for learning in children's homes and communities and take advantage of ways they can contribute to the program's goals.
- Programs and families create goals for children collaboratively. Families create a home environment that extends learning and helps children achieve those goals.
- Programs ensure that collaborative relationships with families are sustained by providing teachers and administrators with ongoing professional development. They are expected to enhance their knowledge and hone their skills supporting collaboration with families and communities (Halgunseth et al., 2009).

Innovative programs implementing a family engagement approach to working with families "represent a vision of family, school, and community engagement as a shared responsibility and a continuous process that occurs wherever children learn and throughout their development into young adults" (National Family, School, and Community Engagement Working Group, 2010, p. 2). Family engagement projects have successfully reached traditionally hard-to-engage families, supported and reinforced the work of those already engaged, and empowered parent leaders to transform schools. Success stories come from low-performing schools, including those in low-income communities where many families' home language is not English and families' educational attainment is low, in addition to those where professional families are financially comfortable and have, themselves, been successful in school (National Family, School, and Community Engagement Working Group, 2010).

BENEFITS AND CHALLENGES OF WORKING WITH FAMILIES

It is now a generally accepted fact that children benefit when their families are interested and involved in their school experiences. However, in spite of influential position statements; standards for teacher preparation; criteria for accreditation of early childhood programs; and, in some instances, legislation requiring family-school collaboration, the fact remains that early childhood educators are apt to describe working with parents as the most demanding part of their job (Gibbs, 2005). Your responsibility as a program administrator includes creating the expectation that all staff do their best to cultivate positive relationships with families and nurturing a center culture that welcomes and embraces families as partners in your important work.

Threefold Benefits of Family-School Collaboration

Children, families, and programs of early care and education all benefit when the home and child care program work in harmony. When they work together, children and families are supported, benefiting from their shared purpose. If the home and school are at odds, however, viewing each other with suspicion or casting blame, then children's healthy development is in jeopardy. Successful partnerships begin with a desire to work together toward a common goal. But collaboration is not easy and does not come naturally. Adults must work to develop trusting relationships and have patience to overcome the inevitable challenges along the way. When the connections between the home and school are strong, children, families, schools and child care programs, and communities benefit, accomplishing more than any could do if each was acting alone.

Benefits for Children: Whichever approach to working with families described earlier is embraced by your program, you can be assured that children are at a tremendous advantage when program personnel are intentional about partnering with families (Daniel, 2009), when families and teachers agree on what they expect children will learn and be able to do, and when they agree on how to help children achieve those goals (Powell & Gerde, 2006). When operating from these shared understandings, functioning as an extended family, early childhood programs are at their best (Caldwell, 1985). These are some ways children are likely to benefit from these collaborative efforts:

1. Recent demographic changes mean more children than ever before are in out-of home care and the families of many children entering early care and education are immigrants, finding their way in a new culture with an unfamiliar language (Kirmani & Leung,

2008). Furthermore, in some instances, changes in families' economic stability have interrupted and undermined the relationships essential for families' healthy psychological development (Bronfenbrenner & Morris, 1998; Halgunseth et al., 2009; Lee & Burkam, 2002). Children benefit when child care programs, schools, and communities provide support during these kinds of family transitions.

2. Family involvement and engagement in their children's program of early care and education can smooth children's adjustment to school and can reduce anxiety while making school more enjoyable (Tan & Goldberg, 2009).

3. Family involvement and engagement can enhance children's cognitive development, improve behavior, boost academic achievement, and increase language and problem-solving skills. It can also decrease the chances that children will misbehave, be referred into special education classes, be retained, or eventually drop out of school (Henrich & Blackman-Jones, 2006; Pena, 2000; Reynolds et al., 2010).

4. When centers and families collaborate, they are more likely to successfully advocate for the evaluation of children with suspected disabilities and to secure special services when they are needed to enhance children's chances for success (Croft, 2010; Pena, 2000).

5. When children see their families and school personnel work together toward shared goals, they are more likely to develop a positive self-image and a productive orientation to social relationships (Marcon, 1994).

Benefits for Families: Parents[1] benefit when they take advantage of opportunities to participate in their children's early childhood educational experiences. These are some of the benefits family members can enjoy:

1. Participation in early childhood programs can enhance family members' feelings of self-worth and contribute to increased educational and employment opportunities when they have the opportunity to network with other parents in their community (Bermudez & Marquez, 1996; Epstein, 2001).

2. Family members benefit from observing teachers' interactions with young children. Classroom observations can increase their knowledge of child development and give them opportunities to see guidance techniques that are appropriate and effective with young children. Family members who have spent time in their young children's classrooms have been shown to apply this knowledge to interactions with their children in the home (Keyser, 2006; White, 1988).

3. When family members interact with children in an early childhood setting, they are likely to gain confidence in their own ability to nurture and educate their children (Epstein, 2001; Powell, 1989).

4. Families who have a trusting and respectful relationship with their child's teacher can leave their child with confidence. They know they have a caring partner with whom to share the joys and challenges of parenthood and to receive acknowledgement for the important yet often thankless work of being their child's first teacher (Keyser, 2006).

5. Family members involved in targeted programs in their children's schools have been shown to better understand their community schools and the important role they play in their children's education, become motivated to encourage their children to stay in school, and acquire ways to help their children learn both in school and at home (Keyser, 2006; National Family, School, and Community Working Group, 2010).

---

[1]We will use the word *parent* for clarity but appreciate that grandparents, foster parents, and others may be children's primary guardians.

6. When family members participate in their children's programs, they are likely to form friendships and to create support networks. These affiliations often link families of participating children, including children with and without disabilities, enriching the lives of all (Derman-Sparks & Edwards, 2010; Powell, 1989).

Benefits for Programs: Early childhood programs also benefit from family engagement. These are some of the ways:

1. When families help program staff understand their family's makeup and culture, caregivers and teachers are likely to more effectively incorporate aspects of children's home cultures into the classroom. They are likely to become more empathetic and to be better able to work from their understanding of the family's strengths (Derman-Sparks & Edwards, 2010; Gonzalez-Mena, 2008, 2010).

2. Family members who are involved and engaged in the program are more likely to understand its rationale, curriculum, and teaching strategies. Designers of model programs launched in the 1960s found that participating parents had a unique ability to explain the program's services to other parents—they were advocates who helped the program build credibility in their community.

3. Family involvement and engagement can make it possible for the center to comply with program requirements. For example, Head Start Performance Standards mandate that local advisory boards have parent representatives and that parents serve in the classroom as paid employees, volunteers, and observers. In another example, federal guidelines established for programs serving children with disabilities require parents to participate in developing Family Service Plans (FSPs) or their children's Individual Education Plans (IEP). If parents fail to "buy in" to these programs, programs will not be able to meet their legislative mandates.

4. Family members volunteering in the classroom create a smaller adult-child ratio, and more children can benefit from adults' one-on-one attention for activities such as lap reading. The teacher may also be able to plan activities, such as cooking or special crafts, that require an extra pair of adult hands (Gonzalez-Mena, 2010).

5. Family members can serve as classroom resources. Their special talents and interests can make valuable contributions when children are studying particular hobbies, such as playing a musical instrument or gardening. They can also help teachers when children have questions about occupations, such as being a truck driver, a veterinarian, or a mail carrier (Gonzalez-Mena, 2010).

6. Program directors and teachers often view family involvement and engagement as a sign of respect. It enhances staff morale (Epstein, 2001; Souto-Manning, 2010) and can motivate staff to initiate partnerships in return.

7. Involved family members are likely to become the program's biggest boosters. This kind of positive publicity can increase enrollment and help promote the program's reputation and support throughout the community (National Family, School, and Community Working Group, 2010).

8. Family members can serve as program decision makers. This contribution will be discussed later in this chapter.

In spite of evidence that family involvement benefits children, families, and the programs that serve them, the fact remains that not all families are actively involved in their young children's programs of early care and education. One reason might be that programs have not been successful in making all families feel welcome. Is the building accessible and easy to navigate? Are program materials printed in a language families can read? Do program personnel communicate with families in their native language? Does the center and its

Parents, children, and programs benefit when parents are frequent visitors to the classroom.

employees successfully reflect an appreciation and respect for all cultures (Derman-Sparks & Edwards, 2010; Kirmani & Leung, 2008)? Program personnel need to appreciate that families that are in crisis because of illness, homelessness, or another stress-producing situation are sometimes less engaged and less involved because they lack emotional or physical reserves. They may need time and your understanding until their family is again on an even keel and has emotional energy, time, and resources to become involved (Swick & Williams, 2006).

These trends highlight the fact that not all programs are doing a good job of meeting the needs of all families. They should challenge those committed to family engagement and involvement to reach out in innovative ways that are likely to involve these hard-to-reach populations so all children can reap the benefits of robust family involvement.

Application Activity

Describe an activity that will give families an opportunity to become engaged in your center. Identify how children, families, and the center might work together in planning the activity and how each might benefit. Consider if this activity is likely to appeal to traditionally hard-to-reach populations.

Challenges to Family Involvement

Differences Can Create Barriers to Family-School Collaboration: Families and program staff will likely bring different values and beliefs to their interactions with young children. These differences reflect the influences of their culture, family, and personal experiences and can lead to very different expectations about caregiving, children's behavior and development, and the role of families in the center's day-to-day operations (Powell & Gerde, 2006; Souto-Manning, 2010).

Early childhood educators have a responsibility to understand these differences and to eliminate the barriers they create. Some likely sources of difference you may encounter in your work follow in the next sections.

Family Structure.   The children who come to your program are likely to have varied *family structures*. Some family structures have been shown to create stresses that make parental program involvement difficult or put children's physical, social, and emotional development at risk. For example, single mothers and mothers living with partners who are not the child's father are more likely to live in stressful circumstances and are less likely to be involved in their children's early educational experiences (Cooper, 2010). Experienced teachers have been shown to be successful in engaging families living in stress and bringing them into the school community.

Your center may include children with gay or lesbian parents. Teachers often feel uncomfortable including references to gay and lesbian lifestyles in the classroom, but all families should be positively portrayed in classroom discussions and in books and classroom displays. The goal is for children with a mommy and a daddy and children with two mommies or two daddies to get the clear message that their family is a valued and respected part of the school community. Remember to include the perspectives of families headed by gay and lesbian couples in school forms, celebrations, and rituals because if programs make them or their children feel like misfits, they will be reluctant to fully participate in school-sponsored events and activities (Bower & Klecka, 2009; Clay, 2004; Derman-Sparks & Edwards, 2010).

Recent years have seen an increase in the number of grandparents who have become young children's primary guardians, often as a result of a family crisis of one sort or another. These families are likely to have faced unique stresses such as parents' incarceration, substance abuse, child abuse, abandonment, death or mental illness (Pinazo-Hernandis & Tomplins, 2009). Grandparents are also likely to be adjusting to their new role as parents again and may be in the midst of navigating through any number of agencies as they plan for supporting their grandchildren financially, find suitable housing, and care for children's physical and emotional health (Bailey, Letiecq, & Porterfield, 2009; Cox, 2009). They often need particular kinds of outreach if they are to be involved and engaged in their grandchildren's early care and education (Birckmayer, Cohen, Jensen, & Variano, 2005).

These examples illustrate some of the barriers family structures can create that make it difficult for caring adults to participate in their children's educational experiences.

Socioeconomic Status.   Children from affluent families are more likely to enjoy academic success than children living in poverty, and their families are more likely to be involved in their early education (Cooper, 2010). Low-income families face many barriers that can make participating in their children's school difficult. Parents may hesitate to be involved because they are not confident that they are dressed appropriately to come to school, may believe that because their own education was limited they have little to offer, or may even be embarrassed because they are unable to read (Kersey & Masterson, 2009). They may also be unsure that they would be understood if they came to the school, or they may not think their contribution would make a difference. In addition, they may have inflexible work hours or may lack access to reliable transportation. Low-wage workers are also more likely to be at work in the early morning, late at night, and on weekends. These work-related responsibilities may make it impossible for them to participate in events at their child's school and may make scheduling conferences with teachers difficult (Cooper, 2010).

Cultural Diversity.   Culture reflects families' beliefs, values, and ways of interacting. Children are enculturated by their families' day-to-day interactions. They are their family's investment in the future and are being prepared to perpetuate their culture (Christian, 2007; Gonzalez-Mena, 2008). Identifying culturally determined values and ways of interacting helps you understand the families with which you work.

One framework for developing this understanding is to consider the difference between low-context and high-context cultural patterns. In *low-context* cultures, the individual is valued over the group, independence of individuals is a virtue, individuals are encouraged to assert themselves, individual achievement is valued, and communication is verbal and precise. These characteristics usually describe Western Europeans and members of the mainstream, dominant U.S. culture.

By contrast, in *high-context* groups, interdependence, as shown by reliance on the extended family and the community, is valued; achievement within cooperative groups is encouraged and rewarded; contributions to the group are prized; and language is likely to include nonverbal and contextual cues. These characteristics are likely to describe individuals raised in Asian, Southern European, Latino, African American, and Native American traditions (Hall, 1977).

Child-rearing practices, particularly beliefs about "the right way" for children to sleep, eat, toilet, and play reflect culturally determined expectations. In low-context cultures, for example, even very young children sleep alone; they are encouraged to feed themselves at a young age, even if that means Cheerios are thrown on the floor or feeding is a messy affair. Toilet training begins when children are able to get themselves into the bathroom and handle their clothes independently. Solitary play is encouraged by creating settings with enough toys and duplicates of popular options, so that children have access to what they want when they want it.

Children reared in high-context cultures, on the other hand, are likely to sleep in the family bed at least during infancy, and with their parents or siblings throughout the early childhood years; are often fed by adults until they are about age 4 (because this is seen as a way to foster interdependence); may be toilet trained during infancy (in part because their families are likely to believe children should always be held, which gives the caregiver the opportunity to learn the subtle signals indicating they are about to eliminate); and social play may be a necessity because toys are limited and sharing is viewed as a natural way of interacting (Freeman, 1998; Gonzalez-Mena, 2008).

When teachers and caregivers share the culture and language of the families they serve, home values are reinforced and the transition to school is often a smooth one. Significant differences between families and program personnel may create a mismatch between families' expectations and the program's goals, curriculum content, adults' interactional styles, and teaching strategies. This incongruity may mean that children's and families' strengths and competencies go unrecognized. They may feel overwhelmed, isolated, and alienated (García, Coll, & Magnuson, 2000; Keyser, 2006; Kirmani & Leung, 2008; Nagel & Wells, 2009).

Early childhood educators have an important responsibility to bridge these cultural gaps when they occur. Culturally competent programs invest the time and energy needed to develop trusting relationships with the families they serve (Kirmaini & Leung, 2008). They might, for example, invite families to share artifacts and stories from their culture, infuse the cultural values and practices of all participating families into their routines and programming, and include children's home language in the classroom (Nagel & Wells, 2009). Culturally competent programs are able to negotiate cultural differences with families to help all children succeed at home and in out-of-home settings (Gonzalez-Mena, 2008).

Linguistic Diversity.   A child's home language is the language of nurture, emotion, and care. It is a child's link to her extended family, her family's past, and her family traditions. As America becomes more diverse, it is increasingly likely that you will work with families whose home language is not English, and it is more important than ever to find strategies for working with linguistically diverse children and families.

If your center includes families who are English language learners, it is essential to translate program materials so that all participants have access to the information they need. Interpreters are also important so that caregivers and teachers have the opportunity to learn from their children's families, and families can benefit from teachers' and caregivers' insights about their children's learning, growth, and development. One way to reduce the language barrier is identify members of the community who may be able to provide translation services or help out as interpreters. Another option is to use computer software to translate school-home and home-school communications (Kirmani, 2007). When you use translation software, however, you need to be aware of its limitations, such as inaccuracies with verb tense or other grammatical constructions. In addition, the software cannot capture nuances or accurately translate figures of speech.

The most important contribution an early childhood educator can make to families whose home language is not English is to support their use of this language of emotion and nurture while, at the same time, preparing their child for success in the English-speaking settings he will encounter during his school years and beyond (Kirmani, 2007).

Tension between Families and Center Personnel Can Make Collaboration Difficult: Collaborative efforts may also be difficult when home-school relationships are characterized by tension or conflict. Some families may feel inhibited or even inferior around staff members because of their family's structure, cultural, or linguistic differences or because of their own limited or unhappy school experiences (Christian, 2007). When communication with staff members is difficult, these feelings are even more pronounced.

Early childhood educators who lack respect for all families may respond negatively to differences. They may discount what families do for their children. Their attitudes may make it unlikely that the families most in need of help navigating their child's educational setting will get the support they need (Souto-Manning, 2010; Swick & Williams, 2006).

Conflicts may also arise over curriculum content and teaching strategies. Families may expect early childhood experiences to be structured and academic, while best practices include hands-on authentic experiences, an integrated curriculum, and instruction based on teachers' understanding of children's developmental needs. Although both families and teachers want children to achieve, conflicts can emerge about differences of opinion about appropriate academic goals (Gonzalez-Mena, 2008; Kostelnik, Soderman, & Whiren, 2007).

Family members and staff also bring particular perspectives and needs to the parent-teacher relationship. Stress may result if family members expect staff to be sympathetic when they bring a mildly ill child to school because they were not able to arrange alternative backup care, to understand that the bus can be unpredictable and may make them late for afternoon pickup, and to be accommodating when they are not able to pay tuition the first of the month when it comes due (Galinsky, 1988). From their perspective, staff members expect families to appreciate how physically and emotionally exhausting it can be to care for a group of active young children, to respect that they need to leave work on time so they can meet their own family and personal obligations, and to recognize how important it is that tuition payments be made on schedule so the center can meet its payroll and other financial obligations. These conflicting needs and expectations can undermine otherwise healthy and productive relationships.

The attitudes of program staff and families about collaboration itself may also interfere with their working together. The family's right to make decisions about the education of their children may be difficult for some staff members to accept, particularly if cultural differences lead the teacher to believe parents are not caring for their children in the right way (Christian, 2007). What's more, family members' critiquing of the program's curriculum or pedagogy may be seen as meddling, and professionals may resist change based on the opinions of nonprofessionals. These are some reasons why, before the 1960s, working with parents usually took the form of parent education—the school communicated to parents, but parents were not seen as partners and were not involved in programmatic decision making.

Interestingly, teachers' relationships with the families of the children they are working with are apt to change as teachers become more experienced. In the early stages of her professional life, a novice teacher is apt to view families from a deficit perspective. Her approach may be authoritarian or paternalistic, and she may focus on "rescuing" the children she is working with because she thinks their families are not providing for them adequately (Gonzalez-Mena, 2009). With experience, teachers develop an awareness of the importance of working collaboratively with families, and collaboration becomes easier.

Similarly, family members' attitudes and actions can undermine collaboration. Sometimes families constantly call attention to the program's shortcomings or are resistant and unwilling to work with the school. Some families habitually abuse the teacher's time or challenge the teacher's expertise. These behaviors create understandable resistance and resentment on the part of the early childhood professional and can create barriers to effective collaboration (Kraft & Snell, 1980).

These observations point to the important responsibility of the program administrator to lead novice teachers to see families as partners, to mentor experienced teachers who may resist families' involvement or lack the skills to effectively encourage family engagement, and to help families acknowledge teachers' expertise and caring.

Teachers Are Often Not Well Prepared to Work with Families: Beginning teachers often feel ill prepared to work effectively with families (Feeney & Sysko, 1986; Freeman & Knopf, 2007). This remains the case even though standards of professional preparation include the expectation that teachers view families as partners and that they build strong school-home relationships to enhance children's chances for school success.

Preservice teacher preparation programs should work to provide students increased authentic opportunities to work collaboratively with families (Baumgartner & Buchanan, 2010; Freeman & Knopf, 2007), and in-service teachers should have opportunities to participate in professional development designed to enhance their ability to elicit families' engagement in their young children's education (Brown, Knoche, Edwards, & Sheridan, 2009). In-service staff development should be designed to help staff become sensitive to all families' needs and to develop their abilities to communicate effectively across cultures, even when they have to engage in difficult conversations (Croft, 2010; Galinsky, 1987; Powell, 1989).

Meeting the Challenges of Collaboration

Although directors and staff members may experience challenges in working with families, it is likely that these problems can be overcome when family engagement is intentionally embraced. Professionals must develop an understanding of the sources of these differences and show as much acceptance for differing family views as they do for differences in children. These suggestions may help your center achieve these goals:

1. Staff members need to develop positive attitudes about working with families, including families whose structure, culture, language, or ethnicity is different from their own. They also need support in developing skills for working with diverse families and may need coaching and mentoring as they practice translating these skills into practice (Baumgartner & Buchanan, 2010). Many programs are changing their approaches to working with families. Whereas in the past, parents were expected to take the initiative to participate in their children's early education, families and schools are now more apt to work together to identify program needs as well as community resources to meet those needs and contribute to children's success (Halgunseth et al., 2009). See Figure 12.1 for more specific information on the concepts, skills, and attitudes teachers need to bring to their work with families.

2. Program expectations should be realistic (Epstein, 2001). All families will not want, or be able to, participate in every kind of activity. They need opportunities to be

Teachers and Caregivers need to

—know about the families they serve

Many variables influence families' values, strengths, and needs. They have an important influence on how teachers and families communicate and how program personnel can meet their needs. Teachers benefit when they know about

- The family structure and with whom the child lives
- Children's daily routines at home
- The family's first language and cultural background
- The family's beliefs about effective instructional strategies
- The family's approach to child guidance and discipline
- The family's attitude toward play and child-directed activities
- Expectations about age-appropriate self-help skills
- Relationships that are important to children, including those with grandparents and other highly involved members of their extended family
- The family's involvement in the community, for example, if they are active in their church and if they have a broad support network
- Challenges that confront families as a result of poverty, inability to understand or speak English, and the impact of stress-producing circumstances (including homelessness, joblessness, serious illness, death, divorce, single parenting, incarceration, parenting special needs children, etc.; Campbell & Miles, 2008; Gonzalez-Mena, 2008; Powell, 1987, 1991; Swick & Williams, 2006)

—know potential challenges to family engagement

We know that a number of barriers can prevent families' participation in their child's early childhood programs. These include their work or school schedules, access to reliable transportation, the need to care for younger children, or reluctance to come to school because they are uncomfortable with English, feel ill equipped to make meaningful contributions, or cannot forget bad experiences during their own schooling. Barriers such as these may make volunteering in their preschooler's classroom, attending evening meetings that do not include children, or participating in special events difficult or unappealing (Henrich & Blackman-Jones, 2006; Souto-Manning & Swick, 2006).

Families also need to know it is all right to choose *not* to be involved (Sciarra & Dorsey, 1998), although they should be encouraged to suggest ways engagement in their child's educational experiences may be possible for them.

—convey the similarities of goals

Both families and teachers are committed to young children's healthy development and learning. Both want the child to be cared for and educated in a program of early care and education that reflects the values and beliefs of their family, culture, and community (Gonzalez-Mena, 2008; Powell, 1991; Zigler, 1989). That means that teachers and caregivers need to understand the families they serve. When differences emerge, early childhood educators have a responsibility to explore these differences with families. Often mutually agreeable solutions to problems can be found. When that is not possible, programs and families may respectfully agree to disagree—with the understanding that children's health, safety, and well-being will always be foremost in their minds (Gonzalez-Mena, 2008).

—convey the importance of the family

Parents should frequently be reminded that they play *the* most important role in their children's lives. Children's relationships in quality programs of early care and education can last throughout their early years, but the relationships between children and families last a lifetime. Not surprisingly, the quality of these lasting relationships is a stronger predictor of children's development than the quantity and quality of care in early childhood programs (NICHD, 1997). This is why an early childhood educator's role sharing insights about growth, development, and appropriate expectations for children's learning and behaviors with families is so important in both the short and long term.

Figure 12.1
Concepts, Skills, and Attitudes That Characterize Programs Committed to Family Engagement

involved in many ways (Gonzalez-Mena, 2010; Souto-Manning, 2010). The challenge is to be flexible and willing to tailor opportunities to become involved that fit families' available time, expertise, and resources.

3. Involving families can be a developmental process for programs of early care and education (Epstein, 2001). Programs committed to making family engagement an integral part of the program's offerings should develop specific goals and objectives to measure their success (Daniel, 2009; Gonzalez-Mena, 2010; Powell, 1991). The following strategies will help you build collaborative relationships with families:

- Develop a genuine understanding of, and a respect for, diversity.
- Develop strategies that support effective two-way communication with all the families you serve.
- Learn what the families you serve want for their children.
- Learn how local agencies and organizations are involved with families and network with them to meet the needs of the families you serve.
- Evaluate your program's family engagement program to measure its success. (Christian, 2007; Daniel, 2009; Gonzalez-Mena, 2010).

4. Professionals need to learn to work with "difficult" families just as they work with "difficult" children. It is important to remember that all families care deeply about their children. They are likely to feel bewildered, vulnerable, and sensitive about problems their children might be having at school. If you develop a positive relationship with families, you will have a storehouse of good will that will make it easier for them to accept concerns you might have about children's academic progress; physical, emotional, or cognitive development; or behavior (Boutte, Keepler, Tyler, & Terry, 1992). When teachers and caregivers have empathy for what families are feeling, even "difficult" families can become allies working together on children's behalf.

COLLABORATION WITH FAMILIES

Families generally want to be involved in early childhood programs. They rely on program personnel to show them how (Daniel, 1996; Epstein & Sanders, 1998). Families are more likely to be engaged if they believe the invitation for their involvement is sincere. They feel welcome when the program's climate is an inclusive one that shows respect and empathy and an interest in meeting families' particular needs (Bang, 2009).

One way a program shows its commitment to inclusion is by having men and women who represent the diversity of the community on its staff. Other ways are having artifacts and furnishings that reflect the cultural backgrounds, linguistic traditions, and family structures of participating families and inviting families into children's classrooms to share information about their occupations and hobbies, favorite foods and celebrations, and perhaps their traditional dress or treasured artifacts from their homes. Programs also demonstrate a commitment to family engagement by being responsive to families' needs, particularly those of families new to the community. Recent immigrants might benefit, in particular, from English as a Second Language (ESL) programs, help in understanding how classrooms in your center are organized, and explanations of how your communities' public school system operates (Bang, 2009; Gonzalez-Mena, 2010; Kirmani & Leung, 2008; Nagel & Wells, 2009).

Staff-Family Communication

Frequent and effective communication between teachers and caregivers and families is an essential characteristic of quality early care and education. While it can be difficult to keep lines of communication open with all families, the benefits are well worth the investment in time and energy. The following suggestions may help your program communicate effectively with families:

1. Be consistently available. Frequent communication helps program personnel and parents build trust. In fact, frequently communicating teachers and parents are more likely to respect each other than are teachers and parents who communicate infrequently (Kontos & Dunn, 1989).

2. Match your communication style to the family's linguistic, cultural, and educational background. Program personnel should make every effort to communicate in the family's primary language; should carefully avoid educational jargon; and should be conscious of their use of nonverbal communication such as personal space, eye contact, and touching (Gonzalez-Mena, 2008; Seplocha, 2004).

3. Promote positive exchanges. Show interest, respect, and caring for each child and family. Make every effort to begin every interaction with families by sharing something positive about their child—something new he has accomplished or an example of how he has helped or shown consideration for a classmate. If you need to discuss a problem or concern, describe the issue using anecdotes and specifics, listen to the family's perspective, and respond in a professional way that helps develop a partnership with the family (Kersey & Masterson, 2009; Pogoloff, 2004).

4. Support staff members' plans to communicate regularly with all families, using a variety of ways to stay in touch. Morning drop-off and evening pickup times are often perfect for short check-ins to share information about the child's health, eating and sleeping routines, or significant events at home or at school. If children are present, it is important to include them in these conversations. In the morning, you might encourage parents to say something such as, "I'm telling your teacher about the fun you had on the swing at the playground on Sunday" and afternoon pickup might include a conversation such as, "Let's tell your mother how much you enjoyed playing in the mud this morning, and how we changed your clothes when we came in from the playground" (Keyser, 2006).

5. Each classroom should include an area that welcomes families. A bench or small couch is a perfect place for a family member to observe the program in action or to help their child transition between home and school. This is a good place for a bulletin board

Displays in classrooms, foyers, and hallways help families stay informed about center events.

that provides families with information about the daily routine, resources to expand on a recent topic of study, age-specific information about child development, requests for specific kinds of help, invitations for families to become involved, or information about upcoming special events. Families appreciate seeing pictures of their children's days. Inexpensive digital cameras make it possible to regularly show families some of the day's memorable events: a young infant's toothless smile, some of a toddler's joyful first steps, a complex block structure, or the contribution of a special visitor (Reedy & McGrath, 2010). When caring for very young children, daily logs describing the child's experiences and caregiving routines are essential. These logs should include specifics about when the baby's diaper was changed, when and what she ate, when and for how long she slept, and other noteworthy happenings parents would appreciate knowing about. Parents who will not see their baby's primary caregiver at drop-off time should be encouraged to include a short note describing the baby's overnight and early morning routines to help the caregiver meet her particular needs during the day. See Figure 12.2 for an example of a daily log for infants.

Parents of older children appreciate regular updates as well. These can be short notes on a class message board that families can read quickly when they come to the center in the afternoon that tells them about the day's events or reminds them about an upcoming

---

Cuddly Cubs Daily Log

Date _____   **Primary Caregiver** _____

Name _____   **Last Feeding** _____

Arrival Time: _____

Diaper changes: (W = wet, BM = bowel movement, D = dry)

_____ W BM D   _____ W BM D

_____ W BM D   _____ W BM D

_____ W BM D   _____ W BM D

Feedings

Time	Type of Food and Amount/Notes

Naps:

_____ to _____   Notes:_____

_____ to _____   Notes:_____

_____ to _____   Notes:_____

Your child needs:

___ Cereal   ___ Diaper Cream   ____ Wipes

___ Extra clothes   ___ Diapers   _____

Notes:

Figure 12.2
Example of a Daily Log for Infants

NOT OK

Aaron fell off the tricycle and was bleeding all over the place. We applied ice and TLC.

OK

Aaron was riding the trike and lost his balance. He cut his left arm just below the elbow. We stopped the bleeding, washed with soap and water, applied Neosporin and a band-aid. He got a smiley face for his bravery.

NOT OK

Natasha was playing in the sandbox and got some sand in her eye. She screamed for 15 minutes. We flushed with water but she screamed even more. We applied ice and TLC. She said she was OK.

OK

Natasha was building a sand castle when some of the sand flipped up from her shovel into her eye. We flushed with water and applied ice since she was trying to wipe her eye. The cool cloth seemed to calm her down. The whole experience upset her so we tried to comfort her as much as possible. After a few minutes, she was back in the sandbox and enjoying herself again.

_____
(teacher's signature)

Figure 12.3
OK and NOT OK Accident Reports

PTO meeting or a class trip. Sometimes teachers want to share information about a child's special accomplishment or thank families for their recent contribution to the class. Parents are likely to prefer getting this kind of information in writing because it is impossible to predict what will be going on during pickup time and how able the teacher will be to have time for a conversation with a parent about their child (Reedy & McGrath, 2010).

Accident reports are another kind of note you sometimes need to write to parents. Compose these notes carefully. Share facts as needed but take care to neither minimize a minor injury nor alarm parents. Consider the OK and NOT OK examples in Figure 12.3.

Some programs use interactive journals exchanged between teachers and parents on a regular basis to "talk" when they are not able to check in daily. Email may be an appropriate communication tool if the families you serve have easy access to the Internet. In addition to these quick check-ins, regular newsletters let families know about center-wide events and classroom-specific happenings.

As the director, you or individual teachers might also lead special-topics meetings to share information about child development or to address parents' questions about toilet training, appropriate guidance, welcoming a new baby, or other issues they may be facing.

Caregivers should also plan time for in-depth, one-on-one conversations with families to share specific information about their children's growth, development, and learning. As the program director, you will create expectations about how and when teachers communicate with families. When you model effective communication strategies and set high expectations, program personnel are likely to follow your lead.

Family Area: In addition to a family corner in each classroom, the center may have an area designed for families. It should invite relaxed communication among families and between families and professionals. It should be well defined and inviting, with adequate lighting and ventilation, comfortable chairs, and a place to write. If it will be used

Activities sponsored by the center's families can support the program's offerings.

for parent-teacher conferences, plan a private area where sensitive information can be shared confidentially.

Family members appreciate information about child development and about your early childhood program. Consider using bulletin boards and displays to share the following kinds of materials with the families you serve:

1. Information about the program's services, schedule, vacation calendar, names and responsibilities of all staff members, and upcoming special events
2. Materials or websites for parents prepared by organizations focused on young children such as ZERO TO THREE and NAEYC. These materials might help parents prepare for an upcoming parent education event or might follow up on a past session led by program staff
3. Guidelines for helping families choose appropriate books, toys, and media for young children
4. Information about community resources and happenings designed for children and families
5. Directions and recipes for family projects and crafts, such as finger paint, play dough, lunchtime favorites
6. Words to children's favorite songs and finger plays
7. Information on childhood diseases, safety in the home and on the playground, and Consumer Product Safety Commission recalls of products used by children.

Using Social Media: It could be that the families you serve use Facebook and similar social media routinely. If that is the case, it may be appropriate to create Facebook pages for the center or for individual classrooms to keep families informed about both day-to-day happenings and special events. These forums can also help connect families with one another and contribute to the creation of a center and classroom community. Even when you use password-protected invitation-only sites, it is extremely important to protect children's identity and families' privacy. We recommend that you avoid showing children's faces and omit children's names (consider using only their first initial) if you post identifiable pictures to any of these online services.

The Family's Initial Visit: For child care programs with continuous enrollment, a family's first visit is often to tour the center and perhaps to register their child. This is an important time of first impressions for the family and staff alike.

The director should provide (a) an overview of the goals of the program, (b) an explanation of major policies, and (c) application/enrollment forms. This visit might also include an "intake interview" during which the director learns about the child and the family (Hanhan, 2003).

An observant director can use this opportunity to learn about the relationship between the parent and the child, how the child reacts to new situations, how the parent feels about putting the child in the program, the child's personal history, and the parents' opinions of the child's strengths and weaknesses.

If at all possible, the parent and child should be invited to observe in the child's classroom and to meet his teacher(s). It is a good idea to invite the child to become involved in classroom activities, if appropriate. Observation and participation give the parent and child time to become comfortable in the setting and allow the teacher an opportunity to begin to form a relationship with the child and his family.

Spring or Autumn Orientation: Many early childhood programs have an *orientation meeting* in the late spring or early autumn for families that will be enrolling their children for the first time. The purpose of this meeting is to orient families to the program's services and requirements for admission. As director, you will want to use this opportunity to share information about strategies families might use to prepare their children for their transition into your program. This is also an excellent way to begin to establish trusting and cooperative relationships between families and center personnel.

After greeting family members, you might plan to showcase typical classroom activities with a PowerPoint presentation or share a video illustrating the program's hands-on active approach to learning. If children have been invited, you might want to involve them in a read-aloud, songs, or finger plays.

You will also want to use the orientation to review information about food services, transportation, supplies, fees, and other essential policies. You may want to demonstrate how supplies are to be marked and indicate how fees are to be sent to school. This information should also be included in the program's family handbook.

Families want to know how to prepare their child for school success. Discourage them from taking an academic "superbaby" approach. You know that young children are unlikely to benefit from those kinds of skill-and-drill activities, and they may extinguish children's love of learning. You want to stress, however, how important it is for families to be involved in their child's development and learning. You may want to suggest some hands-on activities they can do at home, such as sorting the clean laundry or helping with meal preparations that will help prepare their children for school success. This is also a good time to encourage families to include a story in their child's bedtime routine. You will want to end your presentation with an invitation for general questions, but be sure to remind families to save questions concerning their individual child for a one-on-one conversation.

The meeting should last no longer than an hour. When it is followed by a time for socializing, families have an opportunity to visit with one another and with center personnel. This is a good time to offer a tour of the facility—families always appreciate seeing where their children will spend their days.

Open House or Curriculum Night: An *open house* or *curriculum night* is another way for centers to inform families about their program. Unlike the spring or autumn orientation, the open house or curriculum meeting is held a few weeks after the beginning of the school year. Sometimes these are large group events; in other instances, each classroom hosts the families of its children, and sometimes large-group and classroom-based activities are combined. As the program's director, you will plan and lead these events. The following guidelines should help you be successful:

1. Select a date during the first weeks of school. A meeting after the school year has begun will help you associate children with their families and will strengthen newly formed relationships.

2. Send invitations. If you include an RSVP, you can follow up by telephone or email with families that do not respond. A night meeting is preferable because it is likely to make it possible for more working families to attend. Tuesdays, Wednesdays, and Thursdays are usually the best evenings for meetings, but consider other community events, such as Wednesday night church services, before setting a date. Plan the meeting to last a maximum of 1 hour followed by a time for families to socialize, or plan a simple family supper followed by the meeting for adults. You will want to start early enough to allow children to go to bed at their usual bedtime. Child care services almost always ensure a better turnout. See the Figure 12.4 for a sample open house invitation.

3. Give families time to visit their child's classroom. Ask teachers to arrange their classrooms so families will know how their children spend their days. They should describe the classroom's daily schedule, arrange materials and equipment as they would for children to use them, and display some of the children's work. This will be a good time for them to describe the curriculum and to illustrate what children learn when playing with blocks, at the water or sand table, in the dramatic play center, or when they are using art materials in creative ways.

4. Be prepared to begin on time and prepare an outline of your presentation. For example,

    a. Begin with a warm welcome and your sincere thanks for coming.

    b. Introduce yourself and other staff members.

    c. Briefly describe your background, summarize the program's history, and express confidence and enthusiasm for the coming year.

    d. Indicate that the purpose of this meeting is to share information about your program and the year ahead:

        • Describe the program's goals. A good way to do this is to describe typical activities and explain how they contribute to children's learning, growth, and development. For example, if you tell parents that classrooms for 3- and 4-year-olds provide water play at least once a week, you can explain how this

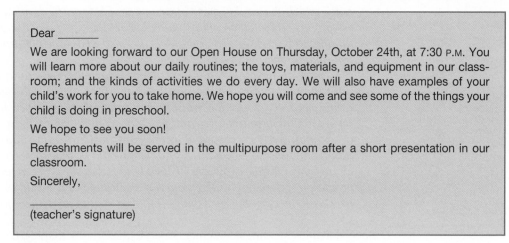

Dear _____

We are looking forward to our Open House on Thursday, October 24th, at 7:30 P.M. You will learn more about our daily routines; the toys, materials, and equipment in our classroom; and the kinds of activities we do every day. We will also have examples of your child's work for you to take home. We hope you will come and see some of the things your child is doing in preschool.

We hope to see you soon!

Refreshments will be served in the multipurpose room after a short presentation in our classroom.

Sincerely,

_____
(teacher's signature)

Figure 12.4
Open House Invitation

activity supports language development, fine-motor skills, and foundational understandings of mathematics and science. A slide show of photographs of children actively engaged in typical classroom activities is an effective way to let families know how their children's days will be structured.

- Describe how your program helps families and teachers communicate regularly.
- Encourage families to call or, if appropriate, email you or their child's teacher any time they have a question about the program or their child.
- Review the program's policies. Point out any that are new or have been changed. It is a good idea to ask families to bring their handbooks for reference—they should have been distributed on or before the first day of the school year.
- Remind families about the calendar, noting days the center will be closed or will dismiss early.
- Describe any new enrichment activities like gymnastics or music classes you will be offering onsite.
- Suggest ways families can help their children get the most out of each day; for example, remind them of the importance of a healthy diet and a regular bedtime.
- Have a short question-and-answer period, but remind families that individual concerns should be discussed one-on-one.
- Invite families to enjoy simple refreshments, to visit with one another, and to look around the facility.
- Thank them again for coming.

A Better Way

Grace's center has always held its beginning-of-the-year orientation at 7:00 P.M. on the Tuesday after Labor Day, and the open house four weeks later, at 7:00 P.M. on a Tuesday in early October. Families are used to this routine. It lets them have dinner with their children, and they can return home by most children's bedtime. This works well for teachers and their families as well. Grace was ready to schedule these meetings at their familiar times. She did not want to change routines too much as she assumed the center's leadership.

As Grace looked over the information sheets families had submitted with their children's applications, she was glad to see many families new to the program. She also noticed that many of these families' names suggested they might be new arrivals in the community. Class lists had, for the first time, Hispanic names such as Garcia, Ortez, and Quiñones as well as Asian names such as Zhāng, Joeng, and Uōng, which she would come to learn were of Mandarin, Cantonese, and Vietnamese origins. These observations made her realize she needed to reach out to these families to be certain they were well informed about the program and had all the information they needed to fit in.

Grace decided she would need to find help in the community to translate essential information for families learning English as their second language, and she would need to arrange for translators at orientation and open house sessions. She set out to find these resources and made the commitment to have translators attend orientation sessions scheduled in the morning, lunchtime, and evening, adding additional times to be certain all families would be able to attend. It was harder to change the schedule of classroom open houses, but she believed that she was making progress by offering several options for orientation and would work toward options for classroom open houses as well—but that might have to wait for next year.

Special-Topics Meetings: As mentioned earlier in this chapter, families often have interests in particular topics, such as how to support children's learning, effective bedtime routines, potty-training strategies that work, helping children prepare for the birth of a sibling, and so on. Articles, brochures, websites, and videos are available from professional associations that provide quick, concise, down-to-earth messages for families on many of these frequently requested topics. They can be valuable resources as you plan for your presentation.

Directors need to determine convenient times for meetings and topics that are of interest to families, and they sometimes compile a list of possible topics and invite families to indicate which they would be interested in and to add additional topics they would like to have addressed. A small committee can help the director plan meetings that meet families' needs at times when interested families can participate.

Special-topics meetings may be for all families, or they can be for small groups of interested family members. The topic for this kind of meeting is predetermined and announced in advance. Sometimes a local expert, perhaps a member of the early childhood faculty from a nearby college or university, might lead the meeting. It is a good idea to plan for a short presentation summarizing the "big ideas"—what families need to know. This overview might be based on resources parents have been provided in advance or distributed at the meeting.

A discussion should follow, giving families the opportunity to apply what they have heard to their own situation and to ask follow-up questions. These meetings should be scheduled for 60 to 75 minutes. Child care services are likely to make it possible for more families to participate, and refreshments always help create a relaxed and collegial atmosphere.

Small-group meetings have several advantages over those involving a large group: (a) They are easier to schedule because fewer families are involved, (b) they make it easier for those who feel uneasy in an individual conference or large-group meeting to become involved, and (c) they meet the particular needs and interests of families and reassure families that others have similar concerns. The major disadvantage is that they put demands on the director and may create work responsibilities in the evening or on weekends. Figure 12.5 is an outline for a special-topics parent education meeting on brain development.

Regularly Scheduled Individual Conferences: Individual family-staff conferences help families understand the program, learn how their child is developing, and appreciate what he is learning. When your center schedules conferences early in the year, family members have an opportunity to help set specific learning goals. These conferences may help avoid problems later because they lay a foundation for teachers and families to work together toward common goals (Neilson & Finkelstein, 1993). Conferences are also important to review progress toward agreed upon learning goals as children prepare to transition from one classroom to the next either during the course of the school year or at the end of the year.

Although the conference setting may be informal, teachers should prepare carefully so they can describe to parents how their children are progressing across developmental domains. Figure 12.6 provides a sample invitation to schedule a conference. Teachers at many centers would benefit from a staff development session designed to help them prepare for individual conferences. Consider sharing the recommendations included in Figure 12.7 as part of this training.

Specially Called Individual Conferences: Unlike regularly scheduled individual conferences, which occur at planned intervals, specially called parent-teacher conferences may be initiated by a parent, teacher or caregiver, or director to address a specific concern. The most common reasons for specially called conferences are problem behaviors such as biting, aggression, uncontrolled anger, and an unwillingness to cooperate. Concerns about other issues may, however, prompt a parent or teacher to schedule a meeting to discuss a child's progress. These specially called conferences should be seen as opportunities for collaborative problem solving. A systematic approach can help families and program personnel work together toward shared goals that will make the child's school experiences more successful and more pleasant for all.

Outline of a Special-Topics Parent Education Meeting
Understanding Brain Development

A resource with much of this content can be found online at http://www.pitc.org/cs/ pitclib/view/pitc_res/118 or by following this path: www.pitc.org -> Library -> Search PITC Resources (search for Brain in the title) -> click on the PowerPoint by Ron Lally

20 minutes—*Opening activity to build community and introduce the topic*

Respond to these questions:

1. What do you want your child to learn? Be specific.
2. What are you doing to help your child learn what you listed in the first question?

15 minutes—*Major concepts of brain development*

- What does the brain look like?
- Weight of infant brain compared to adult brain
  - Bring in a 1-pound melon and a 3-pound melon
- The brain's texture
  - Pass around tofu
- Geography of the brain
  - Distribute diagrams of the brain (see the 1st slide in this PowerPoint: http://www.pitc.org/cs/pitclib/view/pitc_res/118)
  - Direct participants' attention to the
    - **hindbrain**: cerebellum and brainstem
    - **midbrain**: limbic system
    - **forebrain**: cortex

15 minutes—*Application*

Practice identifying which major sections of the brain children might be using when they . . . (prior to the meeting obtain permission from the parents and take pictures of their children when they are sleeping, reading, putting together a puzzle, etc.).

10 minutes—*Mini-lecture*

Identify 10 things parents can do to boost brain power.

20 minutes—*Application and synthesis*

Identify specific actions they could take to support their child's brain development.

Figure 12.5
Special-Topics Parent Education Meeting Outline

Source: Adapted from Deborah Padgett, executive director of Saluda County of South Carolina First Steps. Used with permission.

Teachers often need their director's coaching when addressing problems with families. It may be helpful to guide teachers through the following steps when planning for conference called to address a problem behavior. You may also want to offer to join the conversation to add insights based on your experience and training.

1. Define the behaviors that are causing you concern and provide documentation demonstrating when those behaviors occur. Describe how center personnel have responded to these concerning behaviors.
2. Ask parents if they have observed the same behaviors. Do they know of experiences or conditions that may explain these behaviors? How do they respond to these behaviors at home and other out-of-school settings?

Dear _____

It's hard to believe your child has been in our program for 8 months! It has certainly been a time of growing and learning!

Our center schedules regular family conferences during the month of March. I would like to plan to meet with you for about 30 minutes in the coming weeks.

I am available

- before school from 7:00 A.M.–8:00 A.M.
- during nap time from 12:00 noon–1:30 P.M.
- at the end of the day from 5:00 P.M.–6:00 P.M.

Please suggest some days and times that would work for you, and I will be in touch to confirm a day and time soon.

We will meet in the Parent Resource Center—Room 114. We plan this as a meeting for adult conversation. Please let us know if you will have difficulty arranging care for any younger children.

I look forward to sharing what we have learned about your child's growth and development during the past months, and I hope you do too.

Please return this form by **Tuesday, February 18th.**

I look forward to conferencing with you soon!

Ms. Elaine

- -

Name _____

I am available

Date	Time
_____	_____
_____	_____
_____	_____
_____	_____

What is the best way to contact you? _____

home phone   work phone   cell phone   email

please circle

Figure 12.6
Invitation to Schedule an Individual Conference

3. Agree on behavioral goals and strategies to reinforce desired behaviors.
4. Agree to a follow-up meeting after trying the agreed-upon strategies for a specified time, perhaps 2 or 4 weeks.
5. If parents and teachers are not able to report that they have made progress encouraging the desired behavior, it may be time to seek the advice of a specialist at the local school district, at a nearby college or university, or a practitioner recommended by the family's pediatrician. As the director, you will be responsible for helping the classroom teacher follow through with a referral if needed.

Home Visits: Home visits have a long history in early care and education and are an extremely valuable way for your program's personnel to learn more about the children and families you serve. They provide invaluable insights into the child's community,

1. **Inviting families to make appointments for individual conferences.**   You want to be certain all families know how to schedule conferences and when they can expect those individual conferences to occur. Some programs schedule individual conferences for all children at the same time of the year. If that is the case in your center, remind families when that time is approaching. Other programs, particularly those with year-round admissions, schedule conferences throughout the year, for example, every 6 months on the anniversary of the child's enrollment. In either case, you will want to use your regular newsletter to remind families how important these meetings are, to ask them to come prepared to share insights about their child, and to indicate what teachers hope to accomplish during scheduled conferences.

Intentionally invite both mothers and fathers to parent conferences. All too often, men are unintentionally "disinvited" because they may not be able to participate at the times usually scheduled for conferences or because the school subtly suggests that home-school relationships are "woman's work" (Gonzalez-Mena, 2010). When the child does not live with both parents, include the noncustodial parent in conferences discussing the child's growth, development, and learning.

When a noncustodial parent is involved with his or her child on a regular basis, you will want to communicate with both parents, even if that means sending home two sets of home-school communications or mailing materials to the parent with visitation rights. It is possible that conferences with parents who are separated or divorced will have to be held separately, but the effort is worth the payoff if these meetings will help keep both parents involved in supporting their child's growth and development.

2. **Scheduling conferences.**   Classroom teachers should develop a schedule of conference times and should invite families to choose a time that fits their needs. If possible, schedule only a few conferences each day, perhaps some before the center opens in the morning, some during lunch/nap time, and others in the late afternoon or early evening. Be sensitive to families' individual needs, however, and indicate your willingness to make special accommodations for those who are not able to meet at the suggested times. Be certain to allow at least 30 minutes for each conference and to provide a break between appointments so you have time to jot down notes and prepare for the next family. It is very important to stay on schedule. This shows your respect for family members' time and their other commitments. Be certain to confirm the conference appointment the day before.

3. **The purpose of conferences.**   Conferences enable you to better understand the children and families with whom you are working, to share information about children's progress across developmental domains, and to give family members an opportunity to ask questions or share information related to their child's performance and success. As noted in Chapter 11, conferences are the perfect time to share insights gained when conducting individual assessments, such as the Child Observation Record (COR; High/Scope Educational Research Foundation, 1992) or Work Sampling System (Meisels et al., 1994).

4. **Prepare for conferences carefully.**

    a. In your letter requesting family members to make appointments, explain whether they may bring their enrolled child and other young children to the meeting. If child care is provided or if younger siblings can play quietly during the conference, more families may be able to participate.

    b. Provide an attractive, comfortable, private place for the conference. Consider the nonverbal messages sent by the setting and by your body language. For example, tables and chairs should be adult sized so everyone can be comfortable. The teacher should not sit behind a desk but should create a setting where she can sit next to parents, creating an atmosphere of cooperation and collegiality (Lawrence-Lightfoot, 2003).

Figure 12.7
Staff Development: Guidelines for Effective Parent/Teacher Conferences

c. Provide families who arrive early a comfortable place to wait. It is thoughtful to have simple refreshments and appropriate reading material to make waiting easier.

d. If you have conducted assessments such as the COR or Work Sampling System, have copies of the appropriate reports to give to parents. In addition, you will want to organize the child's portfolio to serve as your outline for the conference. Consider if you want to ask the family any particular questions and have these available so you do not forget to ask.

5. **Conducting a successful conference.**

a. Greet each parent cordially by name.

b. Set a positive tone by asking parents what they are particularly enjoying about their child at this age, and, in return, share a positive anecdote that highlights the child's successes, growth, and development.

c. Describe the child's learning, growth, and development by sharing assessments, if appropriate, and by giving examples of the child's activities in the classroom. You should have developed a portfolio for the child with artifacts illustrating his progress to date. Point out the child's strengths and accomplishments and then note any areas of concern or that need particular attention.

d. Invite the parents to comment, ask questions, and add to the information you have shared.

e. Develop shared goals for the child in the coming months. What does the family and what do you hope he will learn and be able to do by the time of the next scheduled parent-teacher conference? Develop strategies for working toward these goals at home and at school. Following up on these plans should be the basis for the next planned conference and can also help guide informal day-to-day parent-teacher conversations.

f. If the conference has included some difficult conversations, take care not to blame the family, avoid putting them on the defensive, and be careful not to react argumentatively if you encounter a difference of opinion. It is possible the family may blame the teacher or the program if the child is having difficulties or believe their child is simply going through a stage. Family members can be especially unprepared to hear or accept the fact that you recommend screening for a suspected disability.

g. Invite parents to participate in the classroom and explore what kinds of involvement might be most appealing and appropriate.

h. Do not make family members feel rushed; however, in fairness to others who are waiting, it is important to stay on time. If appropriate, invite parents to make another appointment to continue the discussion.

i. Make notes on the conference to include in the child's folder (Seplocha, 2004).

Sometimes older preschoolers and primary-age children are invited to participate in at least part of their family's conference with their teacher. This gives them a meaningful opportunity to develop reflective skills of self-assessment and decision making as they select items to include in their portfolio and explain to their parents why this represents their "best work." Children may also participate in setting goals for the coming weeks and months (Shores & Grace, 1998; Taylor, 1999).

Figure 12.7 (*Continued*)

home, and family and lay a foundation for the creation of positive relationships among children, families, and the program. Visits to children's homes are particularly valuable in settings where the majority of program personnel come from cultural backgrounds and perhaps language traditions that differ from those of the children and families with whom they work. In these instances, home visits have been demonstrated to make teachers more compassionate and empathetic, in short, more successful in working with diverse populations (Lin & Bates, 2010).

Home visits contribute to the creation of a quality program of early care and education in some additional ways:

1. Professionals are seen as caring enough about the child to visit the family.
2. Family members are likely to be more comfortable in their own homes than at the program site. They may provide more information and discuss more of their concerns in this familiar setting.
3. Transitions into care are often easier for children whose teachers visit them in their homes before their first day of school.
4. Home visits can give teachers opportunities to explain the program's goals and to conduct an intake interview and may present opportunities to share information about child development and developmentally appropriate expectations.
5. Family members might become more engaged with their children's learning and with school activities after meeting individually with their child's teacher in their home (Lin & Bates, 2010).

Home visits must always be prearranged so they can be planned for a time that is convenient for the family and the teacher. The teacher should confirm the appointment a day in advance to be certain the previously scheduled time is still convenient. It may be advisable for teachers to make home visits in pairs or for the director to join the classroom teacher, particularly if the families participating in their program live in high-crime neighborhoods or if teachers are unfamiliar with the area. Be sure to make every effort to include a translator if the teacher and family do not speak the same language.

Home visits should last no more than 1 hour. The first 5 to 10 minutes involve greetings and time for teachers, family members, and the child to get acquainted. Then plan a 20- to 30-minute activity to do with the child in the child's room or another quiet place suggested by the family. That leaves 15 to 20 minutes for adult conversation when the teacher can learn more about the family, share information about the program, and answer questions. It is good to have a parting ritual, such as taking a photograph to display in the classroom on the first day of school or offering the child a small gift the child can use in school (Johnston & Mermin, 1994; Keyser, 2006).

Drop-off and pickup are perfect opportunities for teachers and parents to share information.

It is possible that not all families will be comfortable inviting their child's teacher into their home. When this is the case, the teacher might suggest meeting at a nearby park, community center, or family-friendly fast-food restaurant where they can have the same kinds of informal interactions with the child and the family while learning about the child's family and community. Teachers often feel unprepared to visit their students' homes. They are likely to welcome staff development on strategies to ensure successful home visits, for they require careful planning and preparation (Lin & Bates, 2010).

Classroom Visits: Parents are likely to appreciate the opportunity to experience your program firsthand and see their child interacting with peers and adults in their natural setting. Encourage parents to visit, either by appointment or to drop in unannounced, at any time—except when children are settling down for nap or when they are sleeping. It is sometimes helpful to send a personal invitation inviting parents to visit your program or a particular classroom in your center. That extra step might encourage reluctant parents to come and may initiate greater family engagement. See Figure 12.8 for a sample invitation to visit the classroom.

Workdays: Workdays can be popular family involvement events. They can provide an informal setting for families and staff to work together. There are two common types of workdays:

1. In **materials workdays**, adults construct materials and equipment. This may involve making instructional materials and games for the classroom. It might also be an opportunity for families to help build a playground (under the supervision of trained playground installation personnel). As the director, you will be responsible for determining the types of activities families are willing to take part in and providing choices for participants (Dodd & Brock, 1994).
2. **Cleanup/fix-up workdays** may be held in the evening or on the weekend to clean and repair the building, classrooms, the grounds, equipment, or materials.

Newsletters: Newsletters give family members a vehicle for talking with their children about program activities, can provide information about meeting their children's development and learning needs at home, and are a good way for staff and families to communicate.

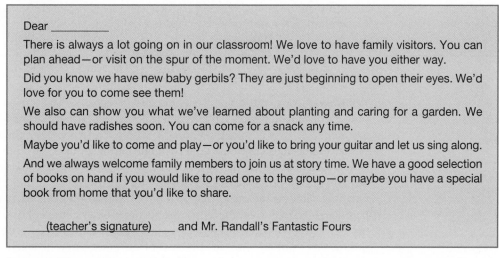

Dear _____

There is always a lot going on in our classroom! We love to have family visitors. You can plan ahead—or visit on the spur of the moment. We'd love to have you either way.

Did you know we have new baby gerbils? They are just beginning to open their eyes. We'd love for you to come see them!

We also can show you what we've learned about planting and caring for a garden. We should have radishes soon. You can come for a snack any time.

Maybe you'd like to come and play—or you'd like to bring your guitar and let us sing along.

And we always welcome family members to join us at story time. We have a good selection of books on hand if you would like to read one to the group—or maybe you have a special book from home that you'd like to share.

____(teacher's signature)____   and Mr. Randall's Fantastic Fours

Figure 12.8
Invitation to Visit the Classroom

These are suggested topics to include in your newsletters:

1. Announcements about the program, including dates for registration, school closings, and other important events and deadlines
2. Information about new books, music, toys, Internet sites and software, and community events for children and families
3. Reprints of articles from local papers, popular magazines, or professional journals of interest to families with young children
4. Ideas for activities the family may enjoy during weekends or during summer or school vacations
5. Recipes from classroom cooking activities
6. Words to favorite songs and finger plays
7. Updates on staff changes and profiles of staff and families
8. Notes of appreciation to family and community volunteers
9. The program's plans for the future

Newsletters should be no more than two pages long. Be careful to avoid professional jargon but make sure they have a polished and professional appearance. Proofread carefully for accuracy and clarity. Like all other written communication, newsletters should take families' reading level into account and should be provided in the primary language of each family, if possible. You can find ideas and resources to help you prepare newsletter articles in the parents' sections of websites for early childhood professional organizations such as NAEYC and ZERO TO THREE. Professional resources such as NAEYC's publication *Teaching Young Children* and the *Exchange* magazine include handouts appropriate to share with families. These resources can make the task of preparing a regular newsletter easier. Newsletters can be copied or possibly emailed to your families. You might even be able to post them on your website or Facebook page. You will need to determine the best strategy for distributing this kind of information to the families you serve.

Application Activity

Identify a topic you think would be of interest to the families of young children. Use an online or print resource to gather information on this topic that will be relevant and helpful to them. Write a newsletter article ¾ to 1 page long on this topic. Take care to have a friendly, but professional tone and to avoid professional jargon. Exchange your article with a classmate. Evaluate each other's work using criteria identified earlier.

Telephone Conversations: Teachers and caregivers should make certain their first telephone conversation with families is a positive one. After that initial call, they should plan to touch base with all families regularly with good news, describing something interesting or successful their child has done. Families are also likely to appreciate a call to inquire how their child is if he has been out of school for a few days or to congratulate them on the arrival of a new baby. This first phone call would be a good time to be certain you have the family's preferred phone number and to find out what time of day is best for parents to talk. For example, for some parents a routine phone call from their child's teacher is appropriate during the workday, and others can accept calls from the center during the workday only in the case of an emergency. If teachers are willing to share their personal phone number with families, this is a good time to indicate when they would be available to talk as well.

Spontaneous telephone conversations can be helpful for sharing information immediately. Parents might call the center to provide teachers insight into a recent event—perhaps their child came home from school worried, was particularly excited about a classroom activity, or is sad because a beloved pet is very sick. Teachers might think a phone call is the best way to alert families to issues they are facing with a child or may find it helpful when a child has had a difficult day. When based on the foundation of a trusting and positive relationship, a telephone call might help prevent a small worry from becoming a major concern.

Even though almost everyone has a telephone, center personnel should be sensitive to the possibility that some families do not have ready access to a telephone. Be alert for signs that this may not be the best way to communicate with some families, particularly those living in poverty. If families do not have a telephone, ask if there is a phone number at which someone could get an urgent message to the family in the case of an emergency, such as an accident or the need to close the center because of a sudden change in the weather.

Other Methods of Communication: Several other methods aid family-staff communication. These are some examples:

1. Informal notes—Notes or short email messages are effective and quick ways to communicate. These are some topics that may prompt you to write a short note or email:

a. Parents will be delighted when you ask them to give their child a "pat on the back" for a job well done. It is always good to be able to pass on a compliment.

b. Families appreciate thanks when they lend a helping hand. Showing your appreciation when families support your program builds loyalty.

c. Families enjoy a photograph of an activity their child particularly enjoyed. Maybe Tyrone built an extra-tall tower in the block center or went down the slide alone for the very first time. His family would appreciate a snapshot with an interpretive note to share these kinds of everyday accomplishments.

d. You might create "Ask Me About" badges to let families know their children have accomplished a goal or reached a milestone. The badges prompt families to ask children about these important events (Stamp & Groves, 1994).

e. It may be appropriate to send a card or note for children's birthdays, but remember that not all cultural or religious traditions celebrate birthdays by focusing attention on the "birthday child."

f. Families are likely to appreciate a note when a family member is ill or is facing another hardship.

2. It could be that Twitter, texting, and similar tools are good ways to quickly communicate short messages to the families you serve. These are particularly helpful ways to get the word out when unexpected situations such as severe weather or a break in a water main make it necessary for you to close the center early.

3. Program Website—A website can identify the program's goals and can include the family handbook, enrollment forms, menus, information about fees, the center's calendar, newsletters, information about parent-teacher organization projects and events, contact information for the director, and other information you want available to the public. While pictures of the facility may be a good addition, avoid posting children's pictures to ensure their privacy. You may want to consider a password-protected section of the website for information for participating families such as each classroom's activities.

4. Program videos—Videos of program activities, including special events, can be shared with families and can also contribute to marketing efforts.

5. Social events—Picnics for the whole family, adult-child breakfasts or going-home snacks, and a recognition event for volunteers help families connect and stimulate good relationships between families and staff. They help build a community within the center.

Family Participation

There is a long tradition of families participating in programs of early care and education. In parent cooperative programs, parents learn about child development and about developmentally appropriate activities by agreeing to lead activities in their children's classrooms. Head Start and other government-sponsored programs create the expectation that parents will be involved as employees and volunteers and will serve on advisory councils. Programs serving children with disabilities also often require families to be involved on a regular basis. The truth is that all children, families, and programs benefit when families are actively involved in their children's education.

Family Members as Volunteers: In effective programs, all families are invited to participate in a variety of ways and are encouraged to suggest unique contributions they might make to the center. Family members are sometimes able to volunteer in classrooms on a regular basis; in other instances, they might be available to help in the classroom just once or twice a year. Some families can contribute to the classroom even though they are not able to visit regularly. They could record favorite books, invite children to visit them in their workplace, or come in periodically to manage the classroom aquarium (Souto-Manning, 2010). Social activities and fund-raising projects are also popular ways for families to be involved. Those kinds of activities are the most likely to involve the greatest numbers of families and may be just the encouragement some families need to become more engaged in their children's early education.

Effective volunteer programs are managed by the program administrator, who helps plan for and organize the volunteers. Once a volunteer program has been launched, volunteers should be able to operate it themselves.

Unfortunately, fathers are often not as likely as mothers to be involved in their children's early childhood programs (Fagan, 1994). Early childhood programs, often inadvertently, may create barriers that make it difficult for fathers to participate or make them feel unwelcome (Gonzalez-Mena, 2010). Activities planned by fathers and specifically designed to appeal to their interests and skills are more likely to engage men in their young children's school experiences (Cunningham, 1994; Fagan, 1994, 1996; Gonzalez-Mena, 2010). It is important to remember to welcome the contributions of fathers. The days of "room mothers" are long gone—many of today's fathers are very involved in their children's early education, so it is important that the language you use to invite them into the center and describe their role is inclusive and encouraging.

Grandparents are another sometimes-overlooked group. We know that grandparents are, increasingly, young children's primary caregivers. They bring particular needs and unique resources to your program. It is worth the effort to reach out to both custodial and noncustodial grandparents—your program will undoubtedly benefit from their contributions and special perspectives (Birckmayer et al., 2005).

Even when rolling out the welcome mat in as many ways as possible, there will always be some families that cannot or choose not to participate (Sciarra & Dorsey, 1998). It is important to respect this decision and to maintain the same kind of positive and productive relationship with all families, regardless of their interest in or ability to participate.

Making a Place for Family Volunteers.   Family members are valuable volunteers because they (a) are likely to know and understand other families' working hours, transportation situation, and community mores; (b) can serve as cultural models for children; (c) help staff members understand children's likes and dislikes, strengths and weaknesses, and home successes and struggles; (d) may be able to serve as interpreters in bilingual and multilingual programs; and (e) can assist staff in program activities, such as storytelling, art, music, and gardening. As volunteers, they may also assist in the positive guidance of children, accompany staff members in home-visiting programs, and serve as ambassadors to the neighborhood.

Specific expectations of volunteers should be determined by the program's needs and the volunteers' abilities. These are some issues to consider:

1. Volunteers should have an orientation to the program's facility and staff, to applicable professional ethics, and to state and local laws regarding personnel qualifications and activities. Orientation could include a broad overview of the program's goals, rules, and regulations; specific tasks and limits of responsibility; classroom management (if involved with children); and a hands-on experience with materials. Volunteers' feedback about the usefulness of the orientation will help you plan future ones.

2. A volunteer's handbook reiterating much of the information given during the orientation program is helpful for staff and volunteers.

3. Teachers and caregivers should be able to decide if they want family volunteers in their classrooms and what they want them to do. They should be coached about appropriate ways to use volunteers' help.

4. In most cases, volunteers are not to be responsible for supervising children alone and cannot be counted in staff-child ratios for licensing. This is important because the program is liable if a volunteer or child under a volunteer's supervision is injured.

5. Teachers and caregivers should have a specific plan for what volunteers are to do during their visits. Avoid giving volunteers only menial jobs or tasks no one else wants to do because they are apt to develop a negative attitude and may lose interest in being involved if they do not feel their talents are being used. Volunteers need guidance if they are to lead a learning activity. They should typically work with individual children or small groups. The teacher should demonstrate what she expects the volunteer to do, provide a brief rationale for the activity, describe what children will learn during this activity, and show the volunteer where she will find the needed materials.

6. Offer a variety of ways for family members to volunteer in the program's support service areas: working in the lunchroom, assisting the school nurse, assisting in the library/media center, helping with the distribution of equipment and materials, working with transportation services, and providing general office support. Be open to families' suggestions as to ways they can help out. They may have a skill or special expertise that would make a great contribution to your program.

7. Volunteers' performance and effectiveness should be assessed by the director, with the teacher if appropriate. Tasks should be tailored to their strengths and interests. That kind of planning makes volunteering a win-win situation.

Occasional Volunteers.   Many family members cannot volunteer on a regular basis but enjoy helping out periodically during the year. One way you might tap into the expertise of family members with diverse perspectives would be to ask them to share information about their culture, language, home country, or family customs. Other families might share information about their careers or their hobbies. They might also be able to contribute by chaperoning field trips, working on fund-raising projects, and helping during special occasions such as the fall open house or class parties. Be sure to encourage fathers, uncles, and grandfathers, in particular. School routines sometimes leave men out—you have an opportunity to make them feel especially welcome.

It is wise to survey family members to learn about their special talents and interests and to encourage them to share them with young children.

Parent Education and Family Resource and Support Programs

The child study movement of the early 1900s made child rearing a science. In the 1960s and 1970s, parent education programs became part of almost all early intervention programs. Parents learned about child development and were encouraged to collaborate with their child's early childhood program or school to help them meet their child's needs. By the 1980s, programs for typically developing children customarily offered family support programs and parent education programs. They continue to be one of the ways programs of early care and education can reach out to the families they serve.

Types of Parent Education and Family Resource and Support Programs: Many types of parent education, family resource, and family support programs are available (Epstein, 2001; National PTA, 2000). Their selection depends on program needs, families' needs and wishes, and program goals. Training techniques may vary as well. Services for families may be either staff directed or family initiated; they may have one focus or be multifaceted; and they may be delivered through direct instruction or indirectly, with family members observing teaching and guidance techniques while visiting in classrooms. Programs may be sponsored by school systems, universities, or community agencies. They might also be cooperatively planned by agencies working together.

Home-Visiting Programs.   Home-visiting programs are most often sponsored by community agencies such as health departments or comprehensive school-readiness initiatives. They are designed to help family members learn how to support their children's early learning and development. They often begin at the birth of a child and demonstrate to families how to talk to and interact with their baby and how to use everyday household materials as educational toys. The exact nature of home-visiting programs depends on the program's objectives, the number of families to be visited, the number and frequency of visits per family, and the program's financial resources.

Family Discussion Groups.   The basic goal of family discussion groups is likely to be to help families learn more about positive parenting practices and child development and learning. Discussion groups can be led by a knowledgeable resource person or by participating parents. Peer support groups are often particularly popular among families of children with disabilities.

Resource Centers.   Parent resource centers provide child-rearing information and may include a toy-lending library that makes quality toys available to participating families. They are typically located in public libraries or another community building and are often sponsored by the state's or the community's comprehensive early childhood program.

Self-Improvement Programs.   Self-improvement programs are designed to empower adult family members to improve their own lives. Services may include instruction in basic adult education including preparation for the General Educational Development (GED) high school equivalency test; English for second-language learners; consumer, nutrition, or health education; information about how to access community resources; how-to classes in home repairs; and other family life topics. This instruction may be formal courses for high school credit or informal workshops. They are usually offered by the public school system for the benefit of all adult residents of a community.

Family Resource and Support Programs.   Family resource and support programs are for all families. To be effective, however, the services must be individualized to support different stages in the family life cycle and to meet other particular needs (e.g., work/ family issues, family crises). Services could include the following:

1. Programs for children, including a home-visiting program, a home-care program, or a center-based program
2. Programs for adults in topics such as family and consumer sciences, child development, adult education, and job counseling
3. Health and nutrition services, including medical services for children and adult family members and classes in child care, safety, and nutrition
4. Social services, such as referrals, recreational activities, and assistance in finding adequate housing and help securing needed food and clothing

EARLY CHILDHOOD EDUCATORS' LONG HISTORY OF PARTNERING WITH THEIR COMMUNITIES

Communities in the United States have traditionally supported families and the educational programs that serve their young children. Demographic and social changes, such as recent waves of immigration, increasingly diverse communities, families' increased mobility, joblessness and economic hardship, and fewer families with young children living near their extended families, have diminished the feeling of community in some locales. Efforts to link families and early childhood programs with their community are particularly important in these rapidly changing and turbulent times (Kirmani & Leung, 2008; NAEYC, 1994).

Because program administrators often work closely with families over an extended period of time and are knowledgeable of and visible within the community, they often have unique opportunities to serve as families' advocates. They can help them access community resources they might need such as Temporary Assistance for Needy Families (TANF), subsidized child care, infant screening programs such as Child Find, child health services such as Medicaid, information about how to access local health clinics' nutrition programs, information about how to access unemployment benefits and job training programs, specialized child care programs such as Head Start, family violence prevention and treatment programs, information about adoption and foster care, and services for those who are homeless.

Business leaders now appreciate the need for employer-supported child care for their employees and for quality early childhood education as the basis for maintaining a competitive workforce for the future (Heckman, 1999; Rolnick & Grunewald, 2003).

Tapping into Family and Community Support Through Advisory Committees and Boards of Directors

Many early childhood programs include representatives from participating families and other members of the community on their program-level *advisory committee,* which addresses issues related to the program's day-to-day operations, and on the agency-level *board of directors,* which is responsible for issues related to finances and legal obligations.

When planning whom to invite to serve on your advisory committee and governing board, look beyond individuals you already know and trust, such as friends or parents of current children. When current parents predominate, the board may act more like a parent-teacher organization than a governing board or may simply become a rubber stamp for the director (Gottlieb, 2005). Board members outside the program are also likely to have a longer view and to be willing to serve your organization for several years.

The first issue to address when establishing a board is to identify the issues it will address. The following tasks are typically assigned to advisory and/or governing boards:

- Creating statements of the organization's purpose, vision, and goals
- Evaluating the program's success meeting expectations identified in the statements of purpose, vision, and goals
- Hiring and evaluating the director
- Setting fees
- Creating salary schedules
- Negotiating fringe benefit packages for employees
- Overseeing the facility, including plans to build, remodel, and perform needed maintenance

The next issue to consider is how many members these governing bodies need. Many states require nonprofit governing boards to have at least 3 members. Experts recommend that effective boards usually have between 7 and 13 members. Group size may vary depending on what needs to be accomplished. A larger group will be needed when the program is being established; facilities are being built or remodeled; and policies, procedures, and handbooks are being created.

Organizations that have a history of running smoothly are likely to need smaller advisory committees and governing boards, whose responsibilities can be characterized as keeping the ship running on course. Small groups are more flexible and members are more likely to have a feeling of unity and purpose. Larger committees and boards, however, bring more expertise to the tasks at hand and there are more people to do the needed work.

The third issue is, "What stakeholders and expertise do you need on your advisory committee and governing board?" Most state licensing laws require that a not-for-profit private early childhood organization operate under a governing board composed, at least in part, of the people it serves. Head Start has specific guidelines about stakeholders' participation on these kinds of governing bodies. Review the list in Figure 12.9 to determine which of these skills and expertise will best serve your organization.

Remember, it is possible that an individual may bring more than one kind of expertise to the table. Refer to Appendix 6 for examples of how you can assess the contribution each potential member may bring to your organization. It is important to learn to identify the leadership potential of even shy and quiet individuals. Can you discover who has vision? Who wants to make something happen? Who can work both independently and interdependently? (Gonzalez-Mena, 2010). When you do, your program will be enriched by the inclusion of many voices. You will want to take demographic factors into account as well, striving for a group of men and women of various ages that reflects the ethnicity, cultures, and socioeconomic status of the community and families you serve.

And finally, create some expectations about how the advisory committee and governing board will operate. See Appendix 7 for an example of a board director position description and statement of commitment.

It is wise to have terms of 2 or 3 years so that these governing bodies will have the benefit of some of the same members' experience each year. Candidates should also be informed of expectations for board membership. Provide a job description that includes the following:

- Purpose of the organization and the role of the advisory committee and board of directors
- Term of office, including term limits
- How members of these governing bodies are expected to support the organization, including responsibilities for participating in events

> **Stakeholders and Those with Specialized Skills and Expertise to Consider as Prospective Members of Your Advisory Committee and Governing Board**
>
> **Stakeholders**
>
> - Parent of child in your program
> - Representative from the licensing agency or another representative from the government
> - Community resident
> - Business owner
>
> **Skills and Expertise**
>
> - Organizational and financial management
> - Community development
> - Administration
> - Academic/education
> - Business/corporate
> - Accounting/banking/investments
> - Fund-raising (both experienced fund-raisers and those who may be able to generate substantial gifts)
> - Laws/regulations
> - Accreditation
> - Knowledge of licensing standards or other regulations
> - Marketing/public relations
> - Personnel
> - Physical plant (architecture, engineer)
> - Strategic or long-range planning
> - Real estate

Figure 12.9
Makeup of Advisory Committee and Governing Board

- Estimate of the time required for this service (About how many hours per month or per year will participating on this committee/board require?)
- Frequency of committee/board meetings (How long are the meetings? Is there a set meeting time, such as noon to 2:00 P.M. on the first Tuesday of the month?)
- List of subcommittees of this committee/board and a description of when they meet
- When an orientation will be provided for members of the committee/board (Gottlieb, 2005)

The director needs to prepare the governing bodies for the work at hand. This training should focus on strategies to help them work together to understand the regulations and accreditation standards (when applicable) within which your program operates; identify problems and generate possible solutions; learn decision-making and consensus-building strategies; and communicate recommendations to all stakeholders, including, when appropriate, parent organizations.

TRENDS AND ISSUES

Early childhood professionals are faced with the responsibility of responding to significant changes in their communities. America is becoming more culturally and linguistically diverse; more mothers of infants and toddlers are entering the workforce than ever before; increased numbers of families are headed by single mothers, including young women with low levels of education; and the economic downturn that began in the late 2000s has created unanticipated hardships as many parents have lost their jobs and sometimes their homes. Increasing numbers of grandparents have become young children's primary guardians, often as a result of a family crisis; and increased life spans mean that many parents of young children face the challenges of being in the "sandwich generation"— responsible for caring for elders while at the same time raising their own families. In addition, continuing military engagements mean you may work with the children of deployed soldiers or veterans who bring home long-term effects from the war.

Many communities remain ill prepared to provide families the safety net they need. As one of the first contacts many families of young children have with the helping professions, early childhood educators have a unique opportunity to support families in their efforts to nurture and care for their young children, preparing them for success in school and beyond.

Early childhood professionals' commitment to children and families can help them access related services. These efforts will, more than ever, make *partnership* and *collaboration* hallmarks of the profession.

SUMMARY

Early childhood educators have a long history of working closely with the families of the children they serve. Parent involvement and parent education have taken many forms from the early 1900s to the present. Today's emphasis is on providing diverse families with needed resources and support programs that serve not only as agents of family change, but also as support systems designed to prevent problems.

Today's early childhood educators strive to form *collaborative partnerships* with parents that emphasize the strengths every family brings to its efforts to nurture and care for their young children. These efforts rely on the creation of respectful relationships that link early care and education professionals with the diverse families they serve. It requires teachers and caregivers of young children to invest the time and effort needed to develop effective strategies to involve all families with their children—for the benefit of children and the communities they will one day lead.

USEFUL WEBSITES

Healthy Children, sponsored by the American Academy of Pediatrics

www.healthychildren.org/English

This is a definitive site with health, child care, and child-rearing advice for parents from the prenatal period through the young adult years.

Child Find

www.childfindidea.org/

Child Find is a public awareness, screening, and evaluation effort designed to locate, identify, and refer young children with disabilities and their families to appropriate services. This multistate effort is an example of resources available to the families of children with disabilities.

National Association for the Education of Young Children, click on "For Families"

www.naeyc.org/families

This collection of resources for families includes advice on selecting quality child care, advocating for quality early care and education, and other topics of interest.

ZERO TO THREE, particularly Parenting Resources

www.zerotothree.org/about-us/funded-projects/parenting-resources/

These science-based resources are designed to help parents nurture their young children's development. This page has links to age-specific handouts, brochures, and guides.

TO REFLECT

1. How can we decide when it is appropriate for families to have "the" say in policy decisions and when the director or board should have it? How might staff members respect the delicate balance of shared family-program responsibilities?
2. Families often bring their own adult concerns (e.g., divorce, stress of being a single parent, financial problems) into formal and informal family-teacher conferences. As a director, how would you advise your teachers to address such concerns?

3. One of the most difficult situations for directors working with families is dealing with family members who do not believe they have the time, abilities, skills, or interests to help their children. When families lack confidence in their child-rearing roles, how does the program build on their strengths? Can all families be empowered? Can cooperation be defined in different ways to accommodate different family-life pressures?

CHECK AND APPLY YOUR UNDERSTANDING

1. Identify the approach to partnering with families that you believe has the greatest potential to engage families in your program and explain why you think it is the best approach for your program.
2. What do you think are the best ways to communicate with the families you serve? Do they respond best to notes sent home with their children, to phone calls, to

email? How can your program use this form of communication to keep families informed and involved in their children's early education?
3. How is your community contributing to your program? How might you reach out to involve the community more effectively?

CHAPTER 13

Contributing to the Profession

NAEYC Administrator Competencies addressed in this chapter:

Management Knowledge and Skills

1. Personal and Professional Self-Awareness
The ability to evaluate ethical and moral dilemmas based on a professional code of ethics

8. Leadership and Advocacy
Knowledge of the legislative process, social issues, and public policy affecting young children and their families
The ability to advocate on behalf of young children, their families and the profession.

Early Childhood Knowledge and Skills

10. Professionalism
Knowledge of different professional organizations, resources, and issues impacting the welfare of early childhood practitioners
Ability to reflect on one's professional growth and development and make goals for personal improvement.

Learning Outcomes

After studying this chapter, you should be able to:

1. Apply the eight criteria of professionalism to the field of early care and education and describe how the field satisfies each.

2. Develop an advocacy plan that indicates which tools would be most effective in addressing an issue the field of early care and education is currently facing at the local, state, or national level.

3. Reflect on your own professional journey. Identify a mentor who has made a significant contribution to your professional development. Describe the most important lesson you have learned about effective mentoring and indicate how you plan to support developing leaders in your center or community.

Grace's Experience

Grace found that working with children came naturally, and she considered herself to be a gifted teacher after only a short time in the classroom. She is now somewhat surprised that she is enjoying the new responsibilities that come with being a program director. She is gaining confidence talking with families, even when faced with a difficult conversation, and her skills as a supervisor and mentor are increasing as well. She is now comfortable as a leader in her own center, and is considering volunteering to serve as an officer in the local early childhood professional organization. Grace is finding that she enjoys the leadership role she has assumed.

Early childhood administrators are leaders. They have a responsibility to ensure the quality of the program they serve. They also have an opportunity to be an advocate. They can work toward ensuring that all families have access to quality early childhood programming by becoming active in their community or in a larger arena. Program administrators also have an opportunity to contribute to the field's efforts to move toward higher standards of practice and increased professionalism.

Some ways program administrators can accomplish these goals are by engaging in informed advocacy; mentoring novices, experienced practitioners, and emerging leaders; making the public aware of the field's reliance on a code of ethics; and, when appropriate, becoming involved in research to increase what we know about the characteristics and lifelong benefits of quality programming for young children.

PROMOTING PROFESSIONALIZATION[1]

Lilian Katz, one of the most influential voices in the field of early care and education, began discussions about the professionalism of the field in the mid-1980s. At that time, she noted that "professionalism" generally denotes praiseworthy work, and she observed that professionals are typically rewarded with high pay and elevated social status (Katz, 1995).

It is now generally agreed that early childhood education is an "emerging" profession (Feeney, 2012). It is neither like the "paradigm professions" of law and medicine, nor are early childhood educators unskilled workers, such as day laborers or short-order cooks, who enter the workplace with little prior training or specialized knowledge and whose employers are likely to consider them to be interchangeable.

To understand where early childhood lies on the professional continuum, consider how it measures up in terms of the following attributes commonly used to determine whether an occupation is or is moving toward becoming a profession (see Figure 13.1 for a depiction of the professional continuum).

1. Professionals *possess specialized knowledge*. They acquire this knowledge and skill and in its application by following a course of *prolonged training*.
2. Professions have rigorous *requirements for entry* into professional training, and training is delivered in *accredited* institutions.
3. Members of a profession have agreed-upon *standards of practice* that guide their efforts to carry out their duties and meet their professional obligations.
4. A profession has a commitment to meet a *significant societal need*.
5. Professionals are *altruistic* and *service oriented* rather than profit oriented. Their primary goal is to meet clients' needs.
6. Professionals provide an *indispensable service* and are recognized as the only group in society that can perform its function.
7. A profession is characterized by *autonomy*—it has control over entry into the field, oversees the quality of the services offered by its members, and regulates itself.
8. A profession has a *code of ethics* that spells out its obligations to society (Feeney, 1995; Katz, 1995).

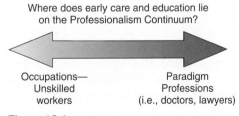

Where does early care and education lie
on the Professionalism Continuum?

Occupations—   Paradigm
Unskilled   Professions
workers   (i.e., doctors, lawyers)

Figure 13.1
A Professional Continuum

[1]Versions of this discussion have been published in "The New Face of Early Childhood Education: Who Are We? Where Are We Going?" by N. K. Freeman and S. Feeney, 2006, *Young Children, 61*(5), pp. 10–16, and also in "Professionalism and Ethics in Early Care and Education," by N. K. Freeman and S. Feeney, 2009, *Continuing Issues in Early Childhood Education* (3rd ed., pp. 196–211), by S. Feeney, A. Galper, and C. Seefeldt (Eds.), Upper Saddle River, NJ: Pearson.

The field of early care and education is making strides in some of these areas, but progress has been slow in others. The following discussion focuses on two particular dimensions of professionalism in which there has been notable progress in recent years. The first is the acquisition of *specialized knowledge* attained through *prolonged training* (number 1 in previous list), and the second is reliance on a *code of ethics* (number 8).

Application Activity

Our discussion focuses on efforts to increase the professionalism of the field by setting higher expectations for professional preparation and by making our reliance on our *Code of Ethical Conduct* explicit. Select one of *the other six* criteria of professionalism in the previous list. Decide where the field of early care and education falls on the professionalism continuum that puts doctors and lawyers at one end and unskilled workers at the other. Provide a rationale for your conclusion.

Moving Toward Professionalism: Professional Preparation and Reliance on the *NAEYC Code of Ethical Conduct*

Professional Preparation: It remains true that many states' licensing regulations are minimal. Some require child care teachers and caregivers to have only a high school diploma or GED and stipulate only that directors and master teachers hold a child development associate (CDA) credential (which is generally considered equivalent to 1 year of postsecondary study; NCCIC/NARA, 2010).

Publically funded programs, however, have begun to raise the bar for entry into the field. The *Improving Head Start Act of 2007* requires 50% of all center-based teachers to hold at least a bachelor's degree in early childhood or a related field by 2013 (Administration for Children and Families, 2007). Publically funded 4K is following suit. Most require teachers to hold at least a bachelor's degree or to be making progress toward attaining a degree (Barnett, Hustedt, Hawkinson, & Robin, 2007).

NAEYC's Program Accreditation Standards also, over time, raise educational requirements across the board. They stipulate that by 2020, 75% of the teachers in an accredited program must have a minimum of a baccalaureate degree in early childhood education or a related field. NAEYC accreditation also requires directors to hold at least a baccalaureate degree and requires them to have specialized coursework in administration, management, and child development and learning or a plan to meet these requirements within 5 years (NAEYC, 2011a).

It is likely that the effects of these policy changes will be felt across the entire field of early care and education, raising expectations for educational attainment in nonprofit and for-profit programs operated under a wide variety of auspices. These developments point to progress the field has made in one criterion of professionalism: requiring early childhood practitioners to have specialized *knowledge gained by following a course of prolonged training*.

Reliance on the *NAEYC Code of Ethical Conduct*:   Reliance on a code of professional ethics is a second criterion of professionalism in which early childhood educators have made strides in recent years. The *NAEYC Code of Ethical Conduct* (2011b) includes statements of the profession's core values and guides practitioners in their efforts to meet their responsibilities to children, families, colleagues, and society. It articulates ideals (how we aspire to behave), and principles (standards of conduct describing what we must and must not do). A Statement of Commitment accompanies the Code. It is not a part of the Code of Conduct but attests to members' resolve to abide by the Code as they work with young children and their families.

NAEYC first adopted its *Code of Ethical Conduct* in 1989 (Feeney & Kipnis, 1989), revised it in 1992, 1997, and 2005, and reaffirmed and updated it in 2011. The field has taken steps to enhance practitioners' reliance on the Code and to make this reliance more apparent to those outside the profession.

One way reliance on the Code has been promoted is by making it an important criterion in NAEYC Accreditation Standards both for programs serving young children and for postsecondary programs preparing teachers for every rung of the professional ladder—from the CDA through doctoral degrees such as Ph.D. and Ed.D. These standards ensure that all practitioners in accredited programs are knowledgeable about the Code, and all who graduate from accredited postsecondary programs have demonstrated their knowledge of and skill applying it in their work.

Two supplements have been designed for use with the original *Code of Ethical Conduct*. They extend the reach of the Code beyond those working directly with young children and their families. The first supplement addresses the particular needs of program administrators (NAEYC, 2011c). It provides guidance as you face situations with ethical dimensions unique to the director, such as filling a much-sought-after opening in the infant room, terminating a teacher because decreased enrollment is forcing you to downsize, and managing relationships with families in a way that lets you keep the needs of children paramount in your decision making.

The second supplement guides adult educators (NAEYC, 2004b). It extends the original Code to meet the needs of those providing training and education, whether in credit-granting institutions such as colleges or universities or in informal professional development activities. As a program director, you are likely to provide professional development designed to meet the particular needs of your staff. This supplement reminds you, for example, to remain true to the approved training plan and helps you have the courage to deny credit to the caregiver who slept through the training activity instead of participating and learning from it.

Several efforts have helped to make the Code widely accessible. The original Code is now reprinted in many introductory textbooks; the Code and both supplements are posted on the NAEYC Website, the original Code in both English and Spanish; and the Code is available from NAEYC in both English and Spanish in an inexpensive brochure format. NAEYC also offers an attractive laminated poster of the Statement of Commitment. Programs that display this poster attest to their pledge to abide by the field's ethical standards.

In addition to making the Code widely available, NAEYC has made efforts to support practitioners' efforts to apply the Code effectively in their work. NAEYC has published two books focusing on professional ethics: *Ethics and the Early Childhood Educator* (Feeney & Freeman, 1999/2005) provides a comprehensive introduction to the Code, describes its development, and offers guidance in applying each of its sections: responsibilities to children, families, colleagues, and the community. This book is often a required text in 2-year and 4-year institutions' early childhood programs. The second book, *Teaching the NAEYC Code of Ethical Conduct* (Feeney, Freeman, & Moravcik, 2000), describes many activities for teaching the Code and includes reproducible materials that help you prepare for effective training sessions.

NAEYC's journal, *Young Children,* includes a regular column that might help you include discussions of ethics in your regular staff meetings. "Focus on Ethics" alternates descriptions of commonly occurring dilemmas with an analysis and resolution of a previously published dilemma. This column is based on NAEYC members' submissions. You might decide to submit a dilemma your center has been grappling with to be considered for publication and analysis. Specifics about how to become involved are included with each article. Other materials to help you teach your staff to apply the Code are identified on the "Teaching the NAEYC Code updates" link from the NAEYC website. This website also includes video clips of an interview with Stephanie Feeney, one of the original Code's authors and a leader in the field's work on professional ethics. Links to those resources are included at the end of this chapter.

You can help make the families you serve and others outside the profession aware of the field's reliance on the *Code of Ethical Conduct*. One way to accomplish this goal is to include the Code (or a link so they can find it online) in your program's family handbook and to put families (and staff) on notice that they can expect your behavior and that of your staff to reflect your commitment to these ethical principles. Another is to prominently display the Statement of Commitment poster attesting to your program's reliance on the Code. You are likely to think of others that will work well in your particular setting.

Other Criteria of Professionalism: Since early care and education is an emerging profession with a rich and unique history, we believe it is more appropriate to satisfy some criteria of professionalism than others. It is unlikely, for example, that early childhood educators would want to abandon our commitment to making a place for novices eager to pursue their education while working in the field. This is why we embrace T.E.A.C.H.® scholarships that support employees' pursuit of their associate's degree while they are working with young children. The field's commitment to the career ladder that has room for beginners as well as experts illustrates why we believe it is appropriate for early care and education to carve out a unique niche on the professionalism continuum that honors our roots while at the same time moving toward greater reliance on standards of practice shown to benefit young children and their families.

As we move toward increased professionalism, it is important that program administrators, as leaders in the field, be active in organizations that support their efforts to remain informed and engaged professionals. Consider the organizations listed in Appendix 8. Participation in organizations that are of particular interest to you can enhance your practice and connect you with the larger community of early childhood educators and advocates.

Application Activity

Rely on the *NAEYC Code of Ethical Conduct* (Appendix 2) and the *Supplement for Early Childhood Program Administrators* (Appendix 3) to resolve one of the following dilemmas. Analyze each dilemma by identifying to whom you have responsibilities. Find guidance in the *NAEYC Code* and *Supplement for Early Childhood Program Administrators* (note item number[s]). Then decide what the "good director" should do in each of these situations.

An enrollment issue: The mother of the next child on your list for admission has told you that she has had her child in five differ-

ent preschools in the past 6 months. She tells you very emotional stories about what she found wrong with each of them.

A personnel issue: Your enrollment is down. You must close a classroom and let a teacher go. Do you choose the last person hired who is an excellent teacher or the long-time employee who has never done a very good job?

A family issue: A parent who has been rude and abusive to staff withdraws her child but then wants to come back to the center.

ENGAGING IN INFORMED ADVOCACY

Advocacy is speaking out for and taking action in support of causes that protect and support vulnerable populations. It is "part of the historical tradition of early childhood education" (Feeney, 2012, p. 71). Advocates sometimes take immediate action such as when they lobby on behalf of specific legislation or build a coalition around a specific issue. In other instances, advocates set goals for what they want to accomplish in the future. They engage in this kind of advocacy when they contribute to political action campaigns or vote for candidates who support their interests.

Early childhood advocates invest their efforts on behalf of young children, their families, and the profession. They can champion a wide variety of causes, all designed to improve the lives of children and families. Our commitment to advocacy is established by the *Statement of Commitment* that accompanies the *NAEYC Code of Ethical Conduct*. It states that early childhood educators agree to "serve as advocate[s] for children, their families, and their teachers in community and society" (NAEYC, 2011b). The Code includes the following ideals that should guide our work, both individually and collectively, on behalf of children, the community, and society:

> *I-1.9—To advocate for and ensure that all children, including those with special needs, have access to the support services needed to be successful.*
>
> *I-4.3—To work through education, research, and advocacy toward an environmentally safe world in which all children receive health care, food, and shelter; are nurtured; and live free from violence in their home and their communities.*
>
> *I-4.4—To work through education, research, and advocacy toward a society in which all young children have access to high-quality early care and education programs.* (NAEYC, 2011b)

Advocacy can involve speaking up in a private or public setting or working on behalf of a particular child or family. Advocacy may also take you into a public arena where you have the opportunity to protect the well-being of children and families in your community, state, or nation.

Your personality, your passion, your available time and energy, and your stage of professional development are all likely to influence the kinds of advocacy that are right for you. When you are a novice in the field, advocacy on behalf of a particular child or family will probably be the best fit for your interests and abilities. As you become more experienced, and particularly when you move into an administrative role, it will be time to reevaluate your strengths and interests. You may be ready to assume a leadership role in your local community, perhaps even on a larger stage. Consider the following list to identify the kinds of advocacy that are right for you:

1. **Individual advocacy** involves professionals in working on behalf of children or families. You engage in **advocacy** when you help a particular child or family gain access to needed services. An example of this kind of personal advocacy is pursuing speech therapy for the child whose poor articulation is making it difficult for him to have positive interactions with his peers.

   Your individual advocacy efforts may also involve sharing your views with individuals or groups to raise their awareness about an issue. This kind of advocacy can be either spontaneous or planned (Robinson & Stark, 2002). Distributing information about the *Campaign for Commercial Free Childhood* to the families of the children in your program and encouraging them to limit the number of commercial messages to which their children are exposed are examples of individual advocacy. You are also engaged in individual advocacy when you write a letter to the editor or submit a guest editorial to your local paper.

2. **Collective advocacy** involves professionals working together on behalf of a group of people, for example, young children, working mothers, or individuals with disabilities. As an early childhood advocate, you are probably focused on securing a "greater societal commitment to improving programs for young children and more support for early childhood educators" (Jacobson & Simpson, 2007, p. 92) and in speaking up "because all is not right for children in our country and the world" (Feeney, 2012, p. 71). Two kinds of collective advocacy target decision makers far removed from the daily lives of young children and their families:

   a. **Public policy advocacy** may involve you in efforts to influence public policies and practices to make them more responsive to the needs of children and families. Public policy advocates challenge those who receive public funds and who develop laws, regulations, and policies to enact policies that support young children and their families (Robinson & Stark, 2002). When a professional organization such as your state NAEYC affiliate communicates its position to the state legislature, the organization's spokespersons are engaged in collective public policy advocacy.

   b. **Private-sector advocacy** includes efforts to make the workplace more family friendly. Successful advocacy efforts have increased the number of corporations that offer employees flexible schedules, job sharing, telecommuting, and part-time employment. Other advocacy efforts have increased the number of corporations that offer onsite employer-supported child care, support breastfeeding mothers, or invest in goods and services for children.

The field of early care and education has a long history of advocacy for children and their families. We hope that you will continue this tradition by seizing opportunities to speak out for those who are most vulnerable and unable to speak out for themselves.

Application Activity

Identify an issue facing your center, your community, or your state. Identify who might help you resolve this issue. Should the target of your advocacy be local policy makers, state-level legislators, or corporate leaders? Identify strategies likely to be most effective to bring attention and eventually action to remedy the problem or resolve the issue.

Becoming an Effective Advocate

Becoming an effective advocate is an important part of becoming a mature professional. But the fact is, many early childhood educators who enjoy their work with children find it difficult to speak with authority to adults, particularly to public-sector or business policy makers. That may be because working directly with children requires a different skill set than leading adults. We know, however, that if we are to attract the public support needed to create a robust and sustainable system of early care and education, we must be effective advocates.

One strategy that helps ensure success is to create coalitions of support and to network with other individuals or groups who share your cause (Ellison & Barbour, 1992; Levine, 1992). That may mean linking with providers of special services such as speech or occupational therapists or working with support groups for mothers such as *Mom's Rising,* a grassroots effort designed to support family-friendly policies and practices. Review Figure 13.2, which identifies characteristics of effective advocates.

Effective Advocates Are

- **Goal oriented.** They know what they want to accomplish and identify the strategies they will use to accomplish their goals.
- **Informed.** They identify decision or policy makers and know the legislative or decision-making timeline so that they contact the right individuals and make good use of their time.
- **Organized.** They present compelling facts and figures accurately and concisely, keeping their audience in mind.
- **Solution oriented.** They help their audience understand the problems and challenges facing children and families and, importantly, provide realistic solutions.
- **Strategic.** They take into account the current political and business climates and budgeting constraints and reach beyond the early childhood care and education community to create coalitions from many stakeholder groups, including parents in influential positions.
- **Flexible.** They are poised to move their issue forward when opportunities present themselves, know how to wait for that strategic moment, and use a variety of advocacy approaches to appeal to multiple audiences when the time is right.

Figure 13.2
Characteristics of Effective Advocates

Sources: Information from "Advocacy Leadership" by H. K. Blank, 1997, *Leadership in Early Care and Education* (pp. 39–45), by S. L. Kagan and B. T. Bowman (Eds.), Washington, DC: National Association for the Education of Young Children; *Advocacy Strategy: The Fundamentals,* by Nonprofit (NP) Action, 2005, Washington, DC: Author, retrieved from www.npaction.org/article/articleview/574/1/229; and *Advocates in Action: Making a Difference for Young Children,* by A. Robinson and D. R. Stark, 2002, Washington, DC: National Association for the Education of Young Children.

An Advocate's Toolbox

Effective advocates are good communicators. They are clear about their message and keep their communications factual, explicit, and direct (Jacobson & Simpson, 2007). They have many tools in their toolbox. Each must be tailored to meet a particular audience's need for information about the problem you have identified and the role members of the audience could play to help you reach the solution you propose.

Position statements are a professional organization's formalized stance on issues related to its mission. NAEYC, the Southern Early Childhood Association (SECA), and the Association for Childhood Education International (ACEI) have developed position statements addressing controversial or critical issues related to early childhood education practice, policy, and professional development. Sometimes two or more professional organizations develop position statements together. For example, *Early Childhood Mathematics: Promoting Good Beginnings* (2010) is a joint position statement of NAEYC and the National Council of Teachers of Mathematics (NCTM). In other instances, allied organizations embrace each other's position statements, as ACEI did when endorsing the *NAEYC Code of Ethical Conduct.*

Position statements typically include extensive reviews of the literature and are a valuable foundation upon which to base your advocacy efforts. They are not usually appropriate, however, for legislators or other decision makers because they are too in-depth and detailed for their purposes. They can be most helpful as you prepare to testify on behalf of legislation or to meet with policy makers in other settings.

A **briefing paper** typically describes one problem, describes the policy you propose, and gives an example of how the policy you propose is working in another locale. Legislators are particularly interested in policies in neighboring states, so provide a close-to-home example whenever possible (Robinson & Stark, 2002).

Talking points are short and to the point. They include "sound bites telling why you support or oppose a particular policy or decision" (Robinson & Stark, 2002, p. 82). Advocates can use talking points when meeting with policy makers or talking to the media.

Key facts handouts are an advocacy tool intended for the public, policy makers, and the media. They are short (one- or two-page) to-the-point summaries of the basic facts surrounding your issue. Any statistics you reference must be accurate and up to date (Robinson & Stark, 2002). See Figure 13.3 for an example of a Key Facts Handout.

Advocating for Changes in South Carolina's Licensing Regulations: Lowering Ratios and Regulating Class Size

Many researchers and professionals consider a low child-adult ratio the *sine qua non* of high-quality child care. (NICHD, 1996, p. 271)

Large-scale research studies show that 88% of infants, 78% of toddlers, and 88% of preschoolers are in programs with *barely adequate* or *inadequate* numbers of adults for the children in their care. (NAEYC, 1993)

When programs lower the number of infants/toddlers/young children each adult cares for:
- Children imitate the language and gestures of others more often and at an earlier age
- Providers have more time for each child
- Children talk and play more often
- Children are less often distressed
- Children are less frequently exposed to danger

When group size is reduced:
- Infections and disease are less likely to spread
- Providers are able to give closer attention to individual children
- Providers spend more time interacting with children and less time "just watching" or disciplining them
- Children have more positive developmental outcomes and, importantly, the benefits persist into the elementary years
- Children are more cooperative and more responsive to adults and other children
- Children are more likely to speak spontaneously
- Children are less likely to wander aimlessly or be uninvolved
- Children score higher on standardized tests

Ratios and Group Sizes in South Carolina and Neighboring States

Age of Children	South Carolina Ratio/Group Size	South Carolina Proposed	North Carolina	Georgia	Mississippi
0–12 months	5:1/Not regulated	5:/10	5:1/10	6:1/12	5:1/10
12–18 months	6:1/Not regulated	5:/10	6:1/12	6:1/12	5:1/10
18–24 months	6:1/Not regulated	6:/12	6:1/12	8:1/16	9:1/10
2 to 3 years	8:1/Not regulated	8:1/16	10:1/20	10:1/20	12:1/14
3 years	12:1/Not regulated	11:/22	15:/25	15:1/30	14:1/14

Figure 13.3
Key Facts Handout

Source: Information from "Research into Action: The Effects of Group Size, Ratios, and Staff Training in Child Care Quality," by NAEYC, 1993, *Young Children, 48*(2), pp. 65–67.

Concrete examples are compelling and often effective ways to demonstrate the importance of the policy or initiative you are recommending. If you are advocating for quality programs for 4-year-olds, for example, you will want to give policy makers a glimpse into a classroom full of authentic hands-on experiences and will need to make it clear to them what children learn when they build with blocks or dress up in the dramatic play center. You can do this by inviting policy makers to your center or by taking the center to them with photos, short videos, and real-life success stories (Jacobson & Simpson, 2007).

Action alerts are tools advocates use to mobilize their support network. They are often emailed to supporters urging them to call their legislators to ask them to vote in support of particular bills under consideration. Action alerts include phone numbers and email addresses of targeted legislators and specific facts advocates can use in their message (Robinson & Stark, 2002).

A number of organizations focused on young children and their families have become more active in the advocacy arena in recent years. It is likely their stepped-up efforts have been prompted by their commitment to retaining public support even in today's bare-bones local, state, and federal budgets. These organizations may be a good place to find resources that support your own local- or state-level advocacy efforts, whether you are concerned with expanding infant/toddler programs, retaining state-supported 4K programs, or increasing services to young children with special needs and their families. Some organizations active in leading advocacy efforts are listed at the end of this chapter. You may know of other advocacy groups that address issues faced in your own community.

NAEYC sponsors an annual *Week of the Young Child* in mid-April. This might be an ideal advocacy opportunity when used as a platform for informing elected officials about issues related to young children and their families, to spotlight a local champion for children, or to grow grassroots advocacy efforts by involving students, programs, and providers in high-profile activities ("Advocates in Action," 2009). By coordinating advocacy efforts in your community, city, or state, you can increase the chances for presenting a unified message that is likely to have a greater impact than would be a single, isolated effort.

Important Reminders!

We hope we have inspired you to become an effective advocate for young children and families on the local, state, or national level. It is important to remember, however, that some agencies or organizations prohibit their employees from taking a public stand on controversial issues. Before you or members of your staff speak out publically, you need to be certain you are following your employer's policies related to advocacy activities. You may not be permitted to participate in rallies or other demonstrations during work hours or may be prohibited from identifying yourself as a public employee in a letter to the editor or a guest editorial in your local paper. It is best to find out about any restrictions that might limit how you can speak out before your community is engaged in heated public debate. That way, you can be assured that the limits are not intended to silence your weighing in on a particular issue but are, instead, related to the agency's established policies.

You also need to be aware of limitations that apply to an NAEYC affiliate (if it is registered as a nonprofit 501(c) (3) organization) and to your program if it has this nonprofit designation. It is not permissible, for example, for nonprofit 501(c) (3) organizations to recognize elected officials who are candidates for reelection with an award during an election year. That means that it would not be possible for your local NAEYC affiliate to honor your local state senator as a *Champion for Children* after she has announced her candidacy for reelection (NAEYC, 2004a).

If the kinds of advocacy efforts described earlier are not permitted by your employer, we encourage you to share information with your friends and family. Maybe you will inspire them to advocate on behalf of children and families.

A Better Way

Grace has become comfortable as a supervisor, mentor, and coach to the teachers in her center, and she is beginning to see herself as a leader in the local early childhood community. She was not willing, however, to talk to the newspaper reporter who recently asked her to comment on proposed changes to the state's child care regulations. She does not consider herself an expert on that issue and did not want to make a misstatement she would later regret.

After studying the guidelines describing tools of effective advocates, Grace decided that she needed to become better informed about how the proposed reduction in adult-child ratios for licensed centers could improve child outcomes. She attended public hearings on the issue and networked with the directors of other high-quality programs in her community. After checking with her board of directors to be certain public advocacy would not violate any established policies, she studied relevant position statements and prepared a key facts handout to summarize the points she wanted to make. She called back the reporter and agreed to be interviewed on the topic. She knew she had done the right thing when the parents of the children in her program thanked her for speaking out publicly on behalf of quality.

INVESTING IN THE PROFESSION'S FUTURE

Supporting Developing Professionals

When you help others find their place in the profession of early care and education, you are engaging in another form of leadership. Some of the ways program administrators can help others find their place in the profession are by

1. Being a resource for those who want to know more about a career in early care and education
2. Welcoming students enrolled in internships or courses that require them to observe or interact with young children or families
3. Mentoring and coaching novices to enhance their skills and knowledge of young children and early childhood education
4. Encouraging emerging leaders to enhance their professional knowledge by enrolling in postsecondary degree programs; pursuing advanced professional development opportunities; and participating in professional organizations, including attending and presenting at local, regional, and national conferences.

Supporting Research

Another way you can contribute to the future of the field is by participating in research projects investigating some topic related to children, families, teaching, or learning. You will first want to be certain proposed projects meet the standards established by the *NAEYC Code of Ethical Conduct's* (2011b) principle addressing research with young children:

P-2.10—Families shall be fully informed of any proposed research projects involving their children and shall have the opportunity to give or withhold consent without penalty. We shall not permit or participate in research that could in any way hinder the education, development, or well-being of children.

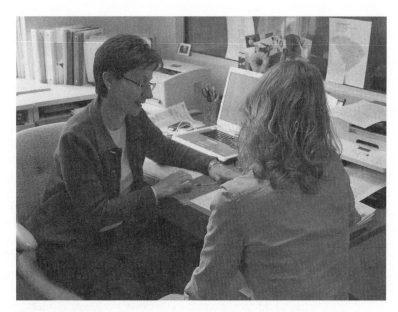

When experienced leaders find time to provide mentoring, they are contributing to the future of the profession.

Then you will want to ask researchers if their project has been approved by the appropriate institutional review board (IRB). This review requires researchers to have a plan to request participants' consent and to have procedures in place to protect the privacy of participating children and adults. Once you are convinced those requirements have been met, we advise you, whenever possible, to grant research requests and invite researchers involved in expanding the field's knowledge base into your program.

Teachers as Researchers

It is important to appreciate that research can be conducted not only by scholars such as university-based researchers, but also by teachers in their own classrooms (Cochran-Smith & Lytle, 1999). Teachers involved in this kind of **action research** (which is sometimes called *teacher research*) explore practical questions within their own world of work "to better understand teaching and learning and to improve practice in specific and concrete ways" (Stremmel, 2007, p. 4). For them, research is an everyday event that informs their practice (Paley, 1981).

As a program administrator, you can create a culture that supports teacher research. This moves teachers away from the view that they transmit knowledge to children and toward the view that they construct knowledge and understandings with the children they teach (Moran, 2007). Action research can take teachers to the cutting edge of best practices and can give them opportunities to collaborate with colleagues, university researchers, and preservice teacher preparation programs (Charlesworth & DeBoer, 2000; Cooney, Buchanan, & Parkinson, 2001; Moran, 2007).

TRENDS AND ISSUES

The field of early childhood care and education is more than 150 years old. While many have made contributions that have shaped our traditions, the field is in a period of rapid change and transition. This book has explored many aspects of leadership and management in early care and education. We hope that you will revisit it often during your professional journey. It has the potential to sustain you on your own journey as a lifelong learner and can help you guide your program as it strives to implement best practices.

Consider the following three linked strategies that can move the field toward our shared goal of providing all children with access to quality experiences in early care and education:

1. Move the field toward greater professionalism. Too often those working with young children see their work as simply a "job." They plan to move on as soon as a better opportunity comes their way. The field needs to continue efforts to equip the entire early care and education workforce with the specialized knowledge and skills they need to enhance young children's learning, growth, and development. At the same time, we need to inform those outside the field: families, policy makers, and the general public, that early childhood educators are uniquely equipped to serve our nation's greatest resource—our young children. Systematic efforts to link increased qualifications with increased compensation will help the field make progress toward enhanced professionalism.

2. Move from "programs" to "systems." Through the years, programs for young children have been developed under a variety of auspices for different purposes. From the early childhood profession's many program models, professionals have learned the elements and principles of quality programming. Most of these are now incorporated into standards adopted by various agencies and professional associations. Professionals now need a commitment to institutionalize these standards while meeting the particular needs of the children, families, and communities they serve.

3. Move from a particular to a universal vision. The diverse nature of our field has, too often, led to a lack of connections among programs, to confusion for policy makers, and to fragmented and inefficient services. *Conceptual* or *visionary leaders* plan for the long term and think in creative ways. They recognize the importance of looking beyond their own programs and circumstances to create linkages with and learn from allied fields, such as psychology, medicine, public health, social work, and anthropology, and to collaborate to meet current and future challenges (Clifford, 1997; Goffin & Washington, 2007; Kagan & Neuman, 1997).

When you become a program administrator, you are taking the first step toward becoming a leader in the field. You will have increased opportunities to contribute to efforts to enhance the quality of programming for young children. We hope you are looking forward to the challenges and opportunities to come.

SUMMARY

Recent years have seen many calls for increased professionalism in early childhood education. Professionalism involves the use of professional knowledge and skills in maintaining, extending, and improving services to children and their families. Professionalism is enhanced when practitioners develop their professional skills and knowledge and commit to abiding by their Code of Ethics. Early childhood educators also affirm their commitment to professionalism by helping novices identify with and become involved in the profession.

Families and children are dependent on professionals who understand their needs and can be effective advocates, both individually and collectively, to help decision makers understand the importance of supporting children and families.

Best practices in our profession are research based. It is important for program administrators to encourage and support researchers and teachers who are working together to increase what we know about young children and how they develop and learn. Researchers benefit from understanding the realities of daily practice, and teachers' work can be informed by researchers' investigations of young children's learning, growth, and development.

The long and diverse history of early childhood care and education has a tradition of impressive individual and collective accomplishments. It has involved professional associations; governmental agencies; private foundations; and religious, civic, and corporate groups in achieving its goals. At the current crossroads, it is important to continue efforts to collaborate at national, state, and local levels so young children and their families can profit from the creation of a shared vision and a sustained effort toward shared goals.

Professionalism is dynamic. Early care and education will continue to evolve as all of us who call ourselves early childhood educators become involved in promoting increased professionalism, helping others find a place in the profession, engaging in informed advocacy, and becoming involved in research. This profession needs administrators who take the leadership role and seize opportunities to make a difference in the lives of young children and their families.

USEFUL WEBSITES

Websites for Professional Ethics Resources

Ethical Codes of the National Association for the Education of Young Children

www.naeyc.org/positionstatements/ethical_conduct

This website includes links to the *Code of Ethical Conduct* and its Supplements:

- *NAEYC Code of Ethical Conduct* (2011)
- *El Código de Conducta Ética y Declaración de Compromiso* (2011)
- *Supplement for Adult Educators* (2004)
- *Supplement for Program Administrators* (2011)

Code of Ethical Conduct Resources, developed by the National Association for the Education of Young Children

www.naeyc.org/ecp/resources

Resources linked from this page include

- *Code of Ethical Conduct PowerPoint Presentation*, based on activities from the NAEYC publication, *Teaching the NAEYC Code of Ethical Conduct*
- *Applying the NAEYC Code*, handout of situations with ethical dimensions for group problem solving
- Interview with Stephanie Feeney on the Code's development and use

Websites for Advocacy Resources

Family and Work Institute

www.familiesandwork.org/

This nonprofit, nonpartisan research organization focuses on the changing workforce, the changing family, and the communities in which they live.

ZERO TO THREE

zerotothree.org/

The mission of this nonprofit organization is to promote the health and development of infants and toddlers through training of professionals, policy makers, and families.

Moms Rising

www.momsrising.org/

This grassroots advocacy organization strives to raise the public's awareness and build support for issues related to children and families. Its goal is to build more family-friendly communities.

NAEYC Affiliate Public Policy Tool Kit

http://www.naeyc.org/policy/advocacy

This comprehensive resource addresses many facets of effective advocacy. It includes helpful information about the legislative process and effective strategies for creating relationships with legislators.

Website for reports of teacher research

Voices of Practitioners

www.naeyc.org/publications/vop/articles

The collection of teacher research reports found by following links from this website demonstrate how teachers conduct inquiry projects in their own classroom to help them understand their children, teaching, and learning. They are inspiring examples that might encourage you to try similar projects in your classroom or center.

TO REFLECT

1. Have you ever noticed that professional conference sessions focused on public policy or systems development are likely to have plenty of empty seats, whereas sessions such as "Music for Monday Mornings" are standing room only? What do you think this says about our profession? How could this situation be changed?

2. A class in administration is discussing collaboration. One student commented, "We always talk about all we can accomplish through collaboration, but doesn't collaboration come with a price tag?" What are the price tags attached to collaboration?

CHECK AND APPLY YOUR UNDERSTANDING

1. Which of the criteria of professionalism does the field of early care and education best satisfy? Provide specifics to support your decision.

2. Identify an issue appropriate for individual advocacy and one that collective advocacy efforts might effectively address.

3. Review the results of a published description of teacher research and summarize how its findings might help a teacher in your program be more effective.

Suppliers of Materials and Equipment for Early Childhood Programs

SUPPLIERS OF CHILDREN'S FURNITURE AND LEARNING MATERIALS

abc School Supply, Inc.
www.abcschoolsupply.com

The Angeles Group
www.angeles-group.com

Becker School Supplies
www.shopbecker.com

Community Playthings
www.communityplaythings.com

Constructive Playthings
www.constructplay.com

Environments, Inc.
www.eichild.com

Jonti-Craft, Inc.
www.jonti-craft.com

Lakeshore Learning Materials
www.lakeshorelearning.com

Nienhuis Montessori Materials
www.nienhuis.com

Nursery Maid Furniture
www.nurserymaid.com

Tout About Toys, Inc.
www.toutabouttoys.com

Tree Blocks
www.treeblocks.com

SUPPLIERS OF PLAYGROUND EQUIPMENT AND DESIGN SERVICES

Child Forms
www.childforms.com

Child Safe Products
www.childsafeproducts.com

GameTime
www.gametime.com

Grounds for Play
www.groundsforplay.com

Kompan
www.Kompan.com

Landscape Structures, Inc.
www.playlsi.com

SUPPLIERS OF CHILDREN'S MUSIC, VIDEOS, AND SOFTWARE

Children's Software Online
www.childrenssoftwareonline.com

The Discovery Channel for Kids
http://kids.discovery.com/

Kimbo Educational
www.kimboed.com

Knowledge Adventure
www.knowledgeadventure.com

Micrograms Software
www.micrograms.com

Music for Little People
www.musicforlittlepeople.com

National Geographic for Kids
http://kids.nationalgeographic.com/kids/

Optimum Resource, Inc.
www.stickybear.com

Rhythm Band Instruments, Inc.
www.rhythmband.com

SUPPLIERS OF SPECIALIZED MATERIALS AND SERVICES

Accu-Cut Systems
www.accucut.com

Insect Lore Products
www.insectlore.com

Puppet Partners
www.puppetpartners.com

SELECTING CHILDREN'S BOOKS

A World of Difference Institute: Recommended Multicultural and Anti-bias Books for Children
www.adl.org/bibliography/

American Library Association/Association for Library Service for Children Lists of Notable Books, Videos, and Recordings
www.ala.org/ala/mgrps/divs/alsc/awards-grants/notalists/index.cfm

The Children's Book Council
www.cbcbooks.org/—see particularly links from the Reading Lists tab

International Reading Association Children's Choices Reading Lists
www.reading.org/Resources/Booklists/ChildrensChoices.aspx

The Horn Book: Teachers and Parents
www.hbook.com/teachersparents/default.asp

University of Calgary Children's Literature Web Guide
people.ucalgary.ca/~dkbrown/index.html

RESOURCES/TOOLS FOR TEACHERS AND PROFESSIONAL DEVELOPMENT

Educational Productions
www.edpro.com

National Association of the Education of Young Children
www.naeyc.org

Program for Infant/Toddler Care
www.pitc.org

Scholastic
www.scholastic.com

ZERO TO THREE
www.zerotothree.org/

BUSINESS MANAGEMENT SOFTWARE

Child Care Office Pro
www.childcareoffice.com

Childcare Manager
www.childcaremanager.com/

Daycare Manager Software
www.daycaresoft.com

EZ Care 2 (SofterWare)
www.softerware.com/ezcare2/

KidKeeper
www.kidkeeper.com

Orgamation Technologies
www.orgamation.com

ProCare Software (Professional Solutions)
www.procaresoftware.com

NAEYC Code of Ethical Conduct and Statement of Commitment

Revised April 2005,
Reaffirmed and Updated May 2011
A position statement of the National Association for the Education of Young Children

Endorsed by the Association for Childhood Education International
Adopted by the National Association for Family Child Care

PREAMBLE

NAEYC recognizes that those who work with young children face many daily decisions that have moral and ethical implications. The **NAEYC Code of Ethical Conduct** offers guidelines for responsible behavior and sets forth a common basis for resolving the principal ethical dilemmas encountered in early childhood care and education. The **Statement of Commitment** is not part of the Code but is a personal acknowledgement of an individual's willingness to embrace the distinctive values and moral obligations of the field of early childhood care and education.

The primary focus of the Code is on daily practice with children and their families in programs for children from birth through 8 years of age, such as infant/toddler programs, preschool and prekindergarten programs, child care centers, hospital and child life settings, family child care homes, kindergartens, and primary classrooms. When the issues involve young children, then these provisions also apply to specialists who do not work directly with children, including program administrators, parent educators, early childhood adult educators, and officials with responsibility for program monitoring and licensing. (Note: See also the "Code of Ethical Conduct: Supplement for Early Childhood Adult Educators," online at www.naeyc.org/about/positions/pdf/ethics04.pdf. and the "Code of Ethical Conduct: Supplement for Early Childhood Program Administrators," online at http://www.naeyc.org/files/naeyc/file/positions/PSETH05_supp.pdf)

CORE VALUES

Standards of ethical behavior in early childhood care and education are based on commitment to the following core values that are deeply rooted in the history of the field of early childhood care and education. We have made a commitment to

- Appreciate childhood as a unique and valuable stage of the human life cycle
- Base our work on knowledge of how children develop and learn
- Appreciate and support the bond between the child and family
- Recognize that children are best understood and supported in the context of family, culture,* community, and society
- Respect the dignity, worth, and uniqueness of each individual (child, family member, and colleague)
- Respect diversity in children, families, and colleagues
- Recognize that children and adults achieve their full potential in the context of relationships that are based on trust and respect

---

* The term *culture* includes ethnicity, racial identity, economic level, family structure, language, and religious and political beliefs, which profoundly influence each child's development and relationship to the world.

CONCEPTUAL FRAMEWORK

The Code sets forth a framework of professional responsibilities in four sections. Each section addresses an area of professional relationships: (1) with children, (2) with families, (3) among colleagues, and (4) with the community and society. Each section includes an introduction to the primary responsibilities of the early childhood practitioner in that context. The introduction is followed by a set of ideals (I) that reflect exemplary professional practice and by a set of principles (P) describing practices that are required, prohibited, or permitted.

The **ideals** reflect the aspirations of practitioners. The **principles** guide conduct and assist practitioners in resolving ethical dilemmas.* Both ideals and principles are intended to direct practitioners to those questions which, when responsibly answered, can provide the basis for conscientious decision making. While the Code provides specific direction for addressing some ethical dilemmas, many others will require the practitioner to combine the guidance of the Code with professional judgment.

The ideals and principles in this Code present a shared framework of professional responsibility that affirms our commitment to the core values of our field. The Code publicly acknowledges the responsibilities that we in the field have assumed, and in so doing supports ethical behavior in our work. Practitioners who face situations with ethical dimensions are urged to seek guidance in the applicable parts of this Code and in the spirit that informs the whole.

Often "the right answer"—the best ethical course of action to take—is not obvious. There may be no readily apparent, positive way to handle a situation. When one important value contradicts another, we face an ethical dilemma. When we face a dilemma, it is our professional responsibility to consult the Code and all relevant parties to find the most ethical resolution.

SECTION I: Ethical Responsibilities to Children

Childhood is a unique and valuable stage in the human life cycle. Our paramount responsibility is to provide care and education in settings that are safe, healthy, nurturing, and responsive for each child. We are committed to supporting children's development and learning; respecting individual differences; and helping children learn to live, play, and work cooperatively. We are also committed to promoting children's self-awareness, competence, self-worth, resiliency, and physical well-being.

Ideals

I-1.1—To be familiar with the knowledge base of early childhood care and education and to stay informed through continuing education and training.

I-1.2—To base program practices upon current knowledge and research in the field of early childhood education, child development, and related disciplines, as well as on particular knowledge of each child.

I-1.3—To recognize and respect the unique qualities, abilities, and potential of each child.

I-1.4—To appreciate the vulnerability of children and their dependence on adults.

I-1.5—To create and maintain safe and healthy settings that foster children's social, emotional, cognitive, and physical development and that respect their dignity and their contributions.

I-1.6—To use assessment instruments and strategies that are appropriate for the children to be assessed, that are used only for the purposes for which they were designed, and that have the potential to benefit children.

I-1.7—To use assessment information to understand and support children's development and learning, to support instruction, and to identify children who may need additional services.

I-1.8—To support the right of each child to play and learn in an inclusive environment that meets the needs of children with and without disabilities.

I-1.9—To advocate for and ensure that all children, including those with special needs, have access to the support services needed to be successful.

I-1.10—To ensure that each child's culture, language, ethnicity, and family structure are recognized and valued in the program.

I-1.11—To provide all children with experiences in a language that they know, as well as support children in maintaining the use of their home language and in learning English.

I-1.12—To work with families to provide a safe and smooth transition as children and families move from one program to the next.

---

* There is not necessarily a corresponding principle for each ideal.

Principles

P-1.1—Above all, we shall not harm children. We shall not participate in practices that are emotionally damaging, physically harmful, disrespectful, degrading, dangerous, exploitative, or intimidating to children. *This principle has precedence over all others in this Code.*

P-1.2—We shall care for and educate children in positive emotional and social environments that are cognitively stimulating and that support each child's culture, language, ethnicity, and family structure.

P-1.3—We shall not participate in practices that discriminate against children by denying benefits, giving special advantages, or excluding them from programs or activities on the basis of their sex, race, national origin, immigration status, preferred home language, religious beliefs, medical condition, disability, or the marital status/family structure, sexual orientation, or religious beliefs or other affiliations of their families. (Aspects of this principle do not apply in programs that have a lawful mandate to provide services to a particular population of children.)

P-1.4—We shall use two-way communications to involve all those with relevant knowledge (including families and staff) in decisions concerning a child, as appropriate, ensuring confidentiality of sensitive information. (See also P-2.4.)

P-1.5—We shall use appropriate assessment systems, which include multiple sources of information, to provide information on children's learning and development.

P-1.6—We shall strive to ensure that decisions such as those related to enrollment, retention, or assignment to special education services, will be based on multiple sources of information and will never be based on a single assessment, such as a test score or a single observation.

P-1.7—We shall strive to build individual relationships with each child; make individualized adaptations in teaching strategies, learning environments, and curricula; and consult with the family so that each child benefits from the program. If after such efforts have been exhausted, the current placement does not meet a child's needs, or the child is seriously jeopardizing the ability of other children to benefit from the program, we shall collaborate with the child's family and appropriate specialists to determine the additional services needed and/or the placement option(s) most likely to ensure the child's success. (Aspects of this principle may not apply in programs that have a lawful mandate to provide services to a particular population of children.)

P-1.8—We shall be familiar with the risk factors for and symptoms of child abuse and neglect, including physical, sexual, verbal, and emotional abuse and physical, emotional, educational, and medical neglect. We shall know and follow state laws and community procedures that protect children against abuse and neglect.

P-1.9—When we have reasonable cause to suspect child abuse or neglect, we shall report it to the appropriate community agency and follow up to ensure that appropriate action has been taken. When appropriate, parents or guardians will be informed that the referral will be or has been made.

P-1.10—When another person tells us of his or her suspicion that a child is being abused or neglected, we shall assist that person in taking appropriate action in order to protect the child.

P-1.11—When we become aware of a practice or situation that endangers the health, safety, or well-being of children, we have an ethical responsibility to protect children or inform parents and/or others who can.

SECTION II: Ethical Responsibilities to Families

Families* are of primary importance in children's development. Because the family and the early childhood practitioner have a common interest in the child's well-being, we acknowledge a primary responsibility to bring about communication, cooperation, and collaboration between the home and early childhood program in ways that enhance the child's development.

Ideals

I-2.1—To be familiar with the knowledge base related to working effectively with families and to stay informed through continuing education and training.

---

* The term *family* may include those adults, besides parents, with the responsibility of being involved in educating, nurturing, and advocating for the child.

I-2.2—To develop relationships of mutual trust and create partnerships with the families we serve.

I-2.3—To welcome all family members and encourage them to participate in the program, including involvement in shared decision making.

I-2.4—To listen to families, acknowledge and build upon their strengths and competencies, and learn from families as we support them in their task of nurturing children.

I-2.5—To respect the dignity and preferences of each family and to make an effort to learn about its structure, culture, language, customs, and beliefs to ensure a culturally consistent environment for all children and families.

I-2.6—To acknowledge families' childrearing values and their right to make decisions for their children.

I-2.7—To share information about each child's education and development with families and to help them understand and appreciate the current knowledge base of the early childhood profession.

I-2.8—To help family members enhance their understanding of their children, as staff are enhancing their understanding of each child through communications with families, and support family members in the continuing development of their skills as parents.

I-2.9—To foster families' efforts to build support networks and, when needed, participate in building networks for families by providing them with opportunities to interact with program staff, other families, community resources, and professional services.

Principles

P-2.1—We shall not deny family members access to their child's classroom or program setting unless access is denied by court order or other legal restriction.

P-2.2—We shall inform families of program philosophy, policies, curriculum, assessment system, cultural practices, and personnel qualifications, and explain why we teach as we do—which should be in accordance with our ethical responsibilities to children (see Section I).

P-2.3—We shall inform families of and, when appropriate, involve them in policy decisions. (See also I-2.3.)

P-2.4—We shall ensure that the family is involved in significant decisions affecting their child. (See also P-1.4.)

P-2.5—We shall make every effort to communicate effectively with all families in a language that they understand. We shall use community resources for translation and interpretation when we do not have sufficient resources in our own programs.

P-2.6—As families share information with us about their children and families, we shall ensure that families' input is an important contribution to the planning and implementation of the program.

P-2.7—We shall inform families about the nature and purpose of the program's child assessments and how data about their child will be used.

P-2.8—We shall treat child assessment information confidentially and share this information only when there is a legitimate need for it.

P-2.9—We shall inform the family of injuries and incidents involving their child, of risks such as exposures to communicable diseases that might result in infection, and of occurrences that might result in emotional stress.

P-2.10—Families shall be fully informed of any proposed research projects involving their children and shall have the opportunity to give or withhold consent without penalty. We shall not permit or participate in research that could in any way hinder the education, development, or well-being of children.

P-2.11—We shall not engage in or support exploitation of families. We shall not use our relationship with a family for private advantage or personal gain, or enter into relationships with family members that might impair our effectiveness working with their children.

P-2.12—We shall develop written policies for the protection of confidentiality and the disclosure of children's records. These policy documents shall be made available to all program personnel and families. Disclosure of children's records beyond family members, program personnel, and consultants having an obligation of confidentiality shall require familial consent (except in cases of abuse or neglect).

P-2.13—We shall maintain confidentiality and shall respect the family's right to privacy, refraining from disclosure of confidential information and intrusion into family life. However, when we have reason to believe that a child's welfare is at risk, it is permissible to share confidential information with agencies, as well as with individuals who have legal responsibility for intervening in the child's interest.

P-2.14—In cases where family members are in conflict with one another, we shall work openly, sharing our observations of the child, to help all parties involved make informed decisions. We shall refrain from becoming an advocate for one party.

P-2.15—We shall be familiar with and appropriately refer families to community resources and professional support services. After a referral has been made, we shall follow up to ensure that services have been appropriately provided.

SECTION III: Ethical Responsibilities to Colleagues

In a caring, cooperative workplace, human dignity is respected, professional satisfaction is promoted, and positive relationships are developed and sustained. Based upon our core values, our primary responsibility to colleagues is to establish and maintain settings and relationships that support productive work and meet professional needs. The same ideals that apply to children also apply as we interact with adults in the workplace. (Note: Section III includes responsibilities to co-workers and to employers. See the "Code of Ethical Conduct: Supplement for Early Childhood Program Administrators" for responsibilities to personnel [*employees* in the original 2005 Code revision], online at http://www.naeyc.org/files/naeyc/file/positions/PSETH05_supp.pdf.)

A—RESPONSIBILITIES TO CO-WORKERS

Ideals

I-3A.1—To establish and maintain relationships of respect, trust, confidentiality, collaboration, and cooperation with co-workers.

I-3A.2—To share resources with co-workers, collaborating to ensure that the best possible early childhood care and education program is provided.

I-3A.3—To support co-workers in meeting their professional needs and in their professional development.

I-3A.4—To accord co-workers due recognition of professional achievement.

Principles

P-3A.1—We shall recognize the contributions of colleagues to our program and not participate in practices that diminish their reputations or impair their effectiveness in working with children and families.

P-3A.2—When we have concerns about the professional behavior of a co-worker, we shall first let that person know of our concern in a way that shows respect for personal dignity and for the diversity to be found among staff members, and then attempt to resolve the matter collegially and in a confidential manner.

P-3A.3—We shall exercise care in expressing views regarding the personal attributes or professional conduct of co-workers. Statements should be based on firsthand knowledge, not hearsay, and relevant to the interests of children and programs.

P-3A.4—We shall not participate in practices that discriminate against a co-worker because of sex, race, national origin, religious beliefs or other affiliations, age, marital status/family structure, disability, or sexual orientation.

B—RESPONSIBILITIES TO EMPLOYERS

Ideals

I-3B.1—To assist the program in providing the highest quality of service.

I-3B.2—To do nothing that diminishes the reputation of the program in which we work unless it is violating laws and regulations designed to protect children or is violating the provisions of this Code.

Principles

P-3B.1—We shall follow all program policies. When we do not agree with program policies, we shall attempt to effect change through constructive action within the organization.

P-3B.2—We shall speak or act on behalf of an organization only when authorized. We shall take care to acknowledge when we are speaking for the organization and when we are expressing a personal judgment.

P-3B.3—We shall not violate laws or regulations designed to protect children and shall take appropriate action consistent with this Code when aware of such violations.

P-3B.4—If we have concerns about a colleague's behavior, and children's well-being is not at risk, we may address the concern with that individual. If children are at risk or the situation does not improve after it has been brought to the colleague's attention, we shall report the colleague's unethical or incompetent behavior to an appropriate authority.

P-3B.5—When we have a concern about circumstances or conditions that impact the quality of care and education within the program, we shall inform the program's administration or, when necessary, other appropriate authorities.

SECTION IV: Ethical Responsibilities to Community and Society

Early childhood programs operate within the context of their immediate community made up of families and other institutions concerned with children's welfare. Our responsibilities to the community are to provide programs that meet the diverse needs of families, to cooperate with agencies and professions that share the responsibility for children, to assist families in gaining access to those agencies and allied professionals, and to assist in the development of community programs that are needed but not currently available.

As individuals, we acknowledge our responsibility to provide the best possible programs of care and education for children and to conduct ourselves with honesty and integrity. Because of our specialized expertise in early childhood development and education and because the larger society shares responsibility for the welfare and protection of young children, we acknowledge a collective obligation to advocate for the best interests of children within early childhood programs and in the larger community and to serve as a voice for young children everywhere.

The ideals and principles in this section are presented to distinguish between those that pertain to the work of the individual early childhood educator and those that more typically are engaged in collectively on behalf of the best interests of children—with the understanding that individual early childhood educators have a shared responsibility for addressing the ideals and principles that are identified as "collective."

Ideal (Individual)

I-4.1—To provide the community with high-quality early childhood care and education programs and services.

Ideals (Collective)

I-4.2—To promote cooperation among professionals and agencies and interdisciplinary collaboration among professions concerned with addressing issues in the health, education, and well-being of young children, their families, and their early childhood educators.

I-4.3—To work through education, research, and advocacy toward an environmentally safe world in which all children receive health care, food, and shelter; are nurtured; and live free from violence in their home and their communities.

I-4.4—To work through education, research, and advocacy toward a society in which all young children have access to high-quality early care and education programs.

I-4.5—To work to ensure that appropriate assessment systems, which include multiple sources of information, are used for purposes that benefit children.

I-4.6—To promote knowledge and understanding of young children and their needs. To work toward greater societal acknowledgment of children's rights and greater social acceptance of responsibility for the well-being of all children.

I-4.7—To support policies and laws that promote the well-being of children and families, and to work to change those that impair their well-being. To participate in developing policies and laws that are needed, and to cooperate with families and other individuals and groups in these efforts.

I-4.8—To further the professional development of the field of early childhood care and education and to strengthen its commitment to realizing its core values as reflected in this Code.

Principles (Individual)

P-4.1—We shall communicate openly and truthfully about the nature and extent of services that we provide.

P-4.2—We shall apply for, accept, and work in positions for which we are personally well-suited and professionally qualified. We shall not offer services that we do not have the competence, qualifications, or resources to provide.

P-4.3—We shall carefully check references and shall not hire or recommend for employment any person whose competence, qualifications, or character makes him or her unsuited for the position.

P-4.4—We shall be objective and accurate in reporting the knowledge upon which we base our program practices.

P-4.5—We shall be knowledgeable about the appropriate use of assessment strategies and instruments and interpret results accurately to families.

P-4.6—We shall be familiar with laws and regulations that serve to protect the children in our programs and be vigilant in ensuring that these laws and regulations are followed.

P-4.7—When we become aware of a practice or situation that endangers the health, safety, or well-being of children, we have an ethical responsibility to protect children or inform parents and/or others who can.

P-4.8—We shall not participate in practices that are in violation of laws and regulations that protect the children in our programs.

P-4.9—When we have evidence that an early childhood program is violating laws or regulations protecting children, we shall report the violation to appropriate authorities who can be expected to remedy the situation.

P-4.10—When a program violates or requires its employees to violate this Code, it is permissible, after fair assessment of the evidence, to disclose the identity of that program.

Principles (Collective)

P-4.11—When policies are enacted for purposes that do not benefit children, we have a collective responsibility to work to change these policies.

P-4.12—When we have evidence that an agency that provides services intended to ensure children's well-being is failing to meet its obligations, we acknowledge a collective ethical responsibility to report the problem to appropriate authorities or to the public. We shall be vigilant in our follow-up until the situation is resolved.

P-4.13—When a child protection agency fails to provide adequate protection for abused or neglected children, we acknowledge a collective ethical responsibility to work toward the improvement of these services.

GLOSSARY OF TERMS RELATED TO ETHICS

Code of Ethics. Defines the core values of the field and provides guidance for what professionals should do when they encounter conflicting obligations or responsibilities in their work.

Values. Qualities or principles that individuals believe to be desirable or worthwhile and that they prize for themselves, for others, and for the world in which they live.

Core Values. Commitments held by a profession that are consciously and knowingly embraced by its practitioners because they make a contribution to society. There is a difference between personal values and the core values of a profession.

Morality. Peoples' views of what is good, right, and proper; their beliefs about their obligations; and their ideas about how they should behave.

Ethics. The study of right and wrong, or duty and obligation, that involves critical reflection on morality and the ability to make choices between values and the examination of the moral dimensions of relationships.

Professional Ethics. The moral commitments of a profession that involve moral reflection that extends and enhances the personal morality practitioners bring to their work, that concern actions of right and wrong in the workplace, and that help individuals resolve moral dilemmas they encounter in their work.

(Continued)

Ethical Responsibilities. Behaviors that one must or must not engage in. Ethical responsibilities are clear-cut and are spelled out in the Code of Ethical Conduct (for example, early childhood educators should never share confidential information about a child or family with a person who has no legitimate need for knowing).

Ethical Dilemma. A moral conflict that involves determining appropriate conduct when an individual faces conflicting professional values and responsibilities.

SOURCES FOR GLOSSARY TERMS AND DEFINITIONS

Feeney, S., & N. Freeman. 2005. *Ethics and the early childhood educator: Using the NAEYC Code.* Washington, DC: NAEYC.

Kidder, R.M. 1995. *How good people make tough choices: Resolving the dilemmas of ethical living.* New York: Fireside.

Kipnis, K. 1987. How to discuss professional ethics. *Young Children* 42 (4): 26–30.

The National Association for the Education of Young Children (NAEYC) is a nonprofit corporation, tax exempt under Section 501(c)(3) of the Internal Revenue Code, dedicated to acting on behalf of the needs and interests of young children. The NAEYC Code of Ethical Conduct (Code) has been developed in furtherance of NAEYC's nonprofit and tax exempt purposes. The information contained in the Code is intended to provide early childhood educators with guidelines for working with children from birth through age 8.

An individual's or program's use, reference to, or review of the Code does not guarantee compliance with NAEYC Early Childhood Program Standards and Accreditation Performance Criteria and program accreditation procedures. It is recommended that the Code be used as guidance in connection with implementation of the NAEYC Program Standards, but such use is not a substitute for diligent review and application of the NAEYC Program Standards.

NAEYC has taken reasonable measures to develop the Code in a fair, reasonable, open, unbiased, and objective manner, based on currently available data. However, further research or developments may change the current state of knowledge. Neither NAEYC nor its officers, directors, members, employees, or agents will be liable for any loss, damage, or claim with respect to any liabilities, including direct, special, indirect, or consequential damages incurred in connection with the Code or reliance on the information presented.

STATEMENT OF COMMITMENT*

As an individual who works with young children, I commit myself to furthering the values of early childhood education as they are reflected in the ideals and principles of the NAEYC Code of Ethical Conduct. To the best of my ability I will

- Never harm children.
- Ensure that programs for young children are based on current knowledge and research of child development and early childhood education.
- Respect and support families in their task of nurturing children.
- Respect colleagues in early childhood care and education and support them in maintaining the NAEYC Code of Ethical Conduct.
- Serve as an advocate for children, their families, and their teachers in community and society.
- Stay informed of and maintain high standards of professional conduct.
- Engage in an ongoing process of self-reflection, realizing that personal characteristics, biases, and beliefs have an impact on children and families.
- Be open to new ideas and be willing to learn from the suggestions of others.
- Continue to learn, grow, and contribute as a professional.
- Honor the ideals and principles of the NAEYC Code of Ethical Conduct.

---

* This Statement of Commitment is not part of the Code but is a personal acknowledgment of the individual's willingness to embrace the distinctive values and moral obligations of the field of early childhood care and education. It is recognition of the moral obligations that lead to an individual becoming part of the profession.

Source: NAEYC. 2011. "Code of Ethical Conduct and Statement of Commitment." Position Statement. Reaffirmation and update of 2005 revision. Washington, DC: Author. www.naeyc.org/files/naeyc/file/positions/PSETH05.pdf. Reprinted with permission from the National Association for the Education of Young Children (NAEYC). www.naeyc.org.

NAEYC Code of Ethical Conduct Supplement for Early Childhood Program Administrators

Adopted July 2006, Reaffirmed and Updated May 2011
A Position Statement Supplement of the National Association for the Education of Young Children

Adopted by the National Association for Family Child Care

Administrators of programs for young children are responsible for overseeing all program operations, serving as leaders in their programs, and representing the field to the community. Early childhood program administrators are called upon to sustain relationships with a wide variety of clients. They interact with and have responsibilities to children, families, program personnel, governing boards and sponsoring agencies, funders, regulatory agencies, their community, and the profession.

Program administrators deal with unique responsibilities and ethical challenges in the course of managing and guiding their programs and assume leadership roles within and beyond their programs. As managers and leaders, they are called upon to share their professional knowledge and expertise with families, personnel, governing boards, and others; demonstrate empathy for the families and children they serve; and communicate respect for the skills, knowledge, and expertise of teaching staff, other personnel, and families. Administrators accept primary responsibility for executing the program's mission as well as developing and carrying out program policies and procedures that support that mission. They also make a commitment to continue their own professional development and the continuing education of the personnel in the program they lead. Administrators also may be advocates for all children being able to gain access to quality programming. Some of the challenges faced by administrators involve balancing their obligations to support and nurture children with their responsibility to address the needs and safeguard the rights of families and personnel and respond to the requirements of their boards and sponsoring agencies.

PURPOSE OF THE SUPPLEMENT

Like those in the field who work directly with young children, program administrators are regularly called upon to make decisions of a moral and ethical nature. The NAEYC Code of Ethical Conduct (revised 2005, reaffirmed and updated 2011) is a foundational document that maps the ethical dimensions of early childhood educators' work in early care and education programs. Program administrators share the ethical obligations assumed by all early childhood educators—obligations that are reflected in the core values, ideals, and principles set forth in the Code. Administrators embrace the central commitment of the early care and education field—and the Code—to ensure the well-being and support the healthy development of young children.

Given the nature of their responsibilities, however, administrators face some additional ethical challenges. Conflicts often surface in the areas of enrollment policies; dealings with personnel; and relationships with families, licensors, governing boards, sponsoring agencies, and others in the community. The existing Code is a valuable resource that addresses many of the ethical issues encountered by administrators. However, it does not provide all of the

Note: This Supplement was reaffirmed by the NAEYC Governing Board in May 2011 and changes were made to Ideals and Principles that regard responsibilities to families to ensure alignment with current family engagement best practices in the field. In addition, references to the Code of Ethical Conduct, Section III, Part C: Responsibilities to Employees were deleted, as Section III, Part C was deleted in the May 2011 update of the Code.

guidance that they need to address the unique ethical issues that arise in their work. This Supplement offers additional core values, ideals, and principles related to the frequently recurring ethical issues encountered by administrators.

CORE VALUES

In addition to the core values spelled out in the NAEYC Code of Ethical Conduct, early childhood program administrators commit themselves to the following additional core values.

We make a commitment to

- Recognize that we have many responsibilities—to children, families, personnel, governing boards, sponsoring agencies, funders, regulatory agencies, the community, and the profession—and that the well-being of the children in our care is our primary responsibility, above our obligations to other constituencies.
- Recognize the importance of and maintain a humane and fulfilling work environment for personnel and volunteers.
- Be committed to the professional development of staff.

CONCEPTUAL FRAMEWORK

This document sets forth a conception of early childhood program administrators' professional responsibilities in five areas, some of which differ from those identified in the NAEYC Code. Each section addresses an area of professional relationships: (1) with children, (2) with families, (3) with personnel, (4) with sponsoring agencies and governing boards, and (5) with the community and society. The items in each section address the unique ethical responsibilities of administrators in early care and education settings.

IDEALS AND PRINCIPLES

This Supplement identifies additional **ideals** that reflect exemplary practice (our aspirations) and **principles** describing practices that are required, prohibited, or permitted. The principles guide conduct and assist practitioners in resolving ethical dilemmas. Together, the ideals and principles are intended to direct practitioners to questions that, when responsibly answered, provide the basis for conscientious decision making. While the Code and this Supplement provide specific direction for addressing some ethical dilemmas, many others will require early childhood program administrators to combine the guidance of the

DEFINITIONS

ADMINISTRATOR

The individual responsible for planning, implementing, and evaluating a child care, preschool, kindergarten, or primary grade program. The administrator's title may vary, depending on the program type or sponsorship of the program. Common titles include director, site manager, administrator, program manager, early childhood coordinator, and principal. (*Note:* The definition of *administrator* and other relevant text in this Supplement are consistent with the Leadership and Management standard of the NAEYC Early Childhood Program Standards and Accreditation Criteria.)

PERSONNEL

Staff members employed, directed, or supervised by an administrator. Here, unless otherwise noted, *personnel* includes all program staff and volunteers providing services to children and/or families. (*Note:* Because program administrators may be supervisors and not employers, we have adopted the terms *personnel* and *staff* in lieu of *employees* for this Supplement to the Code.)

Code and/or this Supplement with their best professional judgment.

The ideals and principles in the Code and this Supplement present a shared framework of professional responsibility that affirms our commitment to the core values of our field. The Code and the Supplement publicly acknowledge the responsibilities that early childhood professionals assume and, in so doing, support ethical behavior in our work. Practitioners who face situations with ethical dimensions are urged to seek guidance in the applicable parts of the Code/Supplement and in the spirit that informs the whole.

The ideals and principles in this Supplement are based on early childhood program administrators' descriptions of ethical dilemmas they have encountered in their work. They are designed to inspire and guide administrators toward actions that reflect the field's current understanding of ethical responsibility.

The Supplement also includes items from the NAEYC Code that directly relate to the work of administrators— some are duplicates of Code ideals or principles, and some are adaptations. Items from the Code that are repeated or adapted for this Supplement are cross-referenced with their corresponding ideals and principles, with the Code references indicated in parentheses. Other items that expand and extend the NAEYC Code were written specifically for this Supplement. (*Note:* There is **not** necessarily a corresponding principle for each ideal.)

1. ETHICAL RESPONSIBILITIES TO CHILDREN

The early childhood program administrator's paramount responsibility is to ensure that programs for children provide settings that are safe, healthy, nurturing, and responsive for each child. Administrators are committed to establishing and maintaining programs that support children's development and learning; promote respect for individual differences; and help children learn to live, play, and work cooperatively. Administrators are also committed to ensuring that the program promotes children's self-awareness, competence, self-worth, resiliency, and physical well-being.

Ideals

I-1.1—To ensure that children's needs are the first priority in administrative decision making, recognizing that a child's well-being cannot be separated from that of his/her family.

I-1.2—To provide a high-quality program based on current knowledge of child development and best practices in early care and education.

Principles

P-1.1—We shall place the welfare and safety of children above other obligations (for example, to families, program personnel, employing agency, community). **This item takes precedence over all others in this Supplement.**

P-1.2—We shall ensure that the programs we administer are safe and developmentally appropriate in accordance with standards of the field, including those developed and endorsed by NAEYC and other professional associations.

P-1.3—We shall have clearly stated policies for the respectful treatment of children and adults in all contacts made by staff, parents, volunteers, student teachers, and other adults. We shall appropriately address incidents that are not consistent with our policies.

P-1.4—We shall support children's well-being by encouraging the development of strong bonds between children and their families and between children and their teachers.

P-1.5—We shall support children's well-being by promoting connections with their culture and collaborating with communities to ensure cultural consistency between the program and families' childrearing practices.

P-1.6—We shall make every effort to provide the necessary resources (staff, consultation, other human resources, equipment, and so on) to ensure that all children, including those with special needs, can benefit from the program.

P-1.7—We shall ensure that there is a plan for appropriate transitions for children when they enter our program, move from one classroom to another within our program, and when they leave.

P-1.8—We shall apply all policies regarding our obligations to children consistently and fairly.

P-1.9—We shall review all program policies set forth by sponsoring agencies and governing bodies to ensure that they are in the best interest of the children.

P-1.10—We shall express our professional concerns about directives from the sponsoring agency or governing body when we believe that a mandated practice is not in the best interest of children.

P-1.11—If we determine that a policy does not benefit children, we shall work to change it. If we determine that a program policy is harmful to children, we shall suspend its implementation while working to honor the intent of the policy in ways that are not harmful to children.

2. ETHICAL RESPONSIBILITIES TO FAMILIES

The administrator sets the tone for the program in establishing and supporting an understanding of the family's role in their children's development. Administrators strive to promote communication, cooperation, and collaboration between the home and the program in ways that enhance each child's development. Because administrators provide the link between the family and direct services for children, they often encounter ethical issues in this area of responsibility.

Ideals

I-2.1—To design programs and policies inclusive of and responsive to diverse families.

I-2.2—To serve as a resource for families by providing information and referrals to services in the larger community.

I-2.3—To advocate for the needs and rights of families in the program and the larger community.

I-2.4—To support families in their role as advocate for their children and themselves.

I-2.5—To create and maintain a climate of trust and candor that fosters two-way communication and enables parents/guardians to speak and act in the best interest of their children.

Principles

P-2.1—We shall work to create a respectful environment for and a working relationship with all families, regardless of family members' sex, race, national origin, immigration status, preferred home language, religious belief or affiliation, age, marital status/family structure, disability, or sexual orientation.

P-2.2—We shall provide families with complete and honest information concerning program philosophy, educational practices, and the services provided.

P-2.3—We shall make every attempt to use two-way communication to convey information in ways that are accessible by every family served.

P-2.4—We shall establish clear operating policies and make them available to families in advance of their child entering the program.

P-2.5—We shall develop enrollment policies that clearly describe admission policies and priorities.

P-2.6—We shall develop policies that clearly state the circumstances under which a child or family may be asked to leave the program. We shall refuse to provide services for children only if the program will not benefit them or if their presence jeopardizes the ability of other children to benefit from the program or prevents personnel from doing their jobs.

P-2.7—We shall assist families in finding appropriate alternatives when we believe their children cannot benefit from the program or when their presence jeopardizes the ability of other children to benefit from the program or prevents personnel from doing their jobs.

P-2.8—We shall apply all policies regarding obligations to families consistently and fairly.

P-2.9—In decisions concerning children and programs, we shall draw upon our relationships with families as well as each family's knowledge of their child. (See also P-3.7 in this Supplement.)

P-2.10—We shall respond to families' requests to the extent that the requests are congruent with program philosophy, standards of good practice, and the resources of the program. We shall not honor any request that puts a child in a situation that would create physical or emotional harm. In such instances, we shall communicate with the family the reason(s) why the request was not honored and work toward an alternative solution.

P-2.11—We shall work to achieve shared understanding between families and staff members. In disagreements, we shall help all parties express their particular needs and perspectives. (*Note:* This is repeated in Section 3 [P-3.16] to emphasize the responsibility to both staff and family members.)

3. ETHICAL RESPONSIBILITIES TO PERSONNEL

Early childhood program administrators are managers with the responsibility for providing oversight for all program operations, as well as serving as leaders in early care and education programs. They are responsible for creating and maintaining a caring, cooperative workplace that respects human dignity, promotes professional satisfaction, and models positive relationships. Administrators must exemplify the highest possible standards of professional practice both within and beyond the program. Ethical responsibilities to personnel include those that are related to working with staff they supervise and/or employ as well as the unions or groups that represent these staff. (*Note:* Administrators' ethical responsibilities to coworkers and employers are included in the Code of Ethical Conduct, Section III, Part A and Part B.)

Ideals

I-3.1—To create and promote policies and working conditions that are physically and emotionally safe and foster mutual respect, cooperation, collaboration, competence, well-being, confidentiality, and self-esteem.

I-3.2—To create and maintain a climate of trust and candor that enables staff to speak and act in the best interest of children, families, and the field of early care and education.

I-3.3—To coach and mentor staff, helping them realize their potential within the field of early care and education.

I-3.4—To strive to secure adequate and equitable compensation (salary and benefits) for those who work with or on behalf of young children.

I-3.5—To encourage and support continual development of staff in becoming more skilled and knowledgeable practitioners.

Principles

P-3.1—We shall provide staff members with safe and supportive working conditions that respect human dignity, honor confidences, and permit them to carry out their responsibilities through performance evaluation, written grievance procedures, constructive feedback, and opportunities for continuing professional development and advancement.

P-3.2—We shall develop and maintain comprehensive written personnel policies that define program standards. These policies shall be given to new staff members and shall be easily accessible and available for review by all staff members.

P-3.3—We shall apply all policies regarding our work with personnel consistently and fairly.

P-3.4—We shall be familiar with and abide by the rules and regulations developed by unions or other groups representing the interests or rights of personnel in our programs.

P-3.5—We shall support and encourage personnel in their efforts to implement programming that enhances the development and learning of the children served.

P-3.6—We shall act immediately to prevent staff from implementing activities or practices that put any child in a situation that creates physical or emotional harm.

P-3.7—In decisions concerning children and programs, we shall draw upon the education, training, experience, and expertise of staff members. (See also P-2.9 in this Supplement.)

P-3.8—We shall work to ensure that ongoing training is available and accessible, represents current understandings of best practice, and is relevant to staff members' responsibilities.

P-3.9—We shall inform staff whose performance does not meet program expectations of areas of concern and, when possible, assist in improving their performance.

P-3.10—We shall provide guidance, additional professional development, and coaching for staff whose practices are not appropriate. In instances in which a staff member cannot satisfy reasonable expectations for practice, we shall counsel the staff member to pursue a more appropriate position.

P-3.11—We shall conduct personnel dismissals, when necessary, in accordance with all applicable laws and regulations. We shall inform staff who are dismissed of the reasons for termination. When a dismissal is for cause, justification must be based on evidence of inadequate or inappropriate behavior that is accurately documented, current, and available for the staff member to review.

P-3.12—In making personnel evaluations and recommendations, we shall make judgments based on fact and relevant to the interests of children and programs.

P-3.13—We shall make hiring, retention, termination, and promotion decisions based solely on a person's competence, record of accomplishment, ability to carry out the responsibilities of the position, and professional preparation specific to the developmental levels of children in his/her care.

P-3.14—We shall not make hiring, retention, termination, and promotion decisions based on an individual's sex, race, national origin, religious beliefs or other affiliations, age, marital status/family structure, disability, or sexual orientation. We shall be familiar with and observe laws and regulations that pertain to employment discrimination. (Aspects of this principle do not apply to programs that have a lawful mandate to determine eligibility based on one or more of the criteria identified above.)

P-3.15—We shall maintain confidentiality in dealing with issues related to an employee's job performance and shall respect an employee's right to privacy regarding personal issues.

P-3.16—We shall work to achieve shared understandings between families and staff members. In disagreements, we shall help all parties express their particular needs and perspectives. (*Note:* This is repeated from Section 2 [P-2.11] to emphasize the responsibility to both staff and family members.)

4. ETHICAL RESPONSIBILITIES TO SPONSORING AGENCIES AND GOVERNING BODIES

Programs providing early care and education operate under a variety of public and private auspices with diverse governing structures and missions. All early childhood program administrators are responsible to their governing and funding bodies. Administrators ensure the program's stability and reputation by recruiting, selecting, orienting, and supervising personnel; following sound fiscal practices; and securing and maintaining licensure and accreditation. Administrators are also responsible for overseeing day-to-day program operations and fostering positive relationships among children, families, staff, and the community.

Administrators' responsibilities to sponsoring agencies and governing bodies are optimally met in a collaborative manner. Administrators establish and maintain partnerships with sponsoring agency representatives, board members, and other stakeholders to design and improve services for children and their families.

Ideals

I-4.1—To ensure to the best of our ability that the program pursues its stated mission.

I-4.2—To provide program leadership that reflects best practices in early care and education and program administration.

I-4.3—To plan and institute ongoing program improvements.

I-4.4—To be ambassadors within the community, creating goodwill for program sponsors as well as for the program itself.

I-4.5—To advocate on behalf of children and families in interactions with sponsoring agency staff and governing body members for high-quality early care and education programs and services for children.

Principles

P-4.1—We shall ensure compliance with all relevant regulations and standards.

P-4.2—We shall do our jobs conscientiously, attending to all areas that fall within the scope of our responsibility.

P-4.3—We shall manage resources responsibly and accurately account for their use.

P-4.4—To ensure that the program's sponsoring agency and governing body are prepared to make wise decisions, we shall thoroughly and honestly communicate necessary information.

P-4.5—We shall evaluate our programs using agreed-upon standards and report our findings to the appropriate authority.

P-4.6—In presenting information to governing bodies we shall make every effort to preserve confidentiality regarding children, families, and staff unless there is a compelling reason for divulging the information.

5. ETHICAL RESPONSIBILITIES TO COMMUNITY, SOCIETY, AND THE FIELD OF EARLY CHILDHOOD EDUCATION

Like those of all early childhood educators, administrators' responsibilities to the community include cooperating with agencies and professionals that share the responsibility for children, supporting families in gaining access to services provided by those agencies and professionals, and assisting in the development of community programs and services.

Early childhood program administrators often have the knowledge, expertise, and education to assume leadership roles. For this reason, they are responsible to the community, society, and the field of early childhood education for promoting the education and well-being of young children and their families.

Ideals

I-5.1—To provide the community with high-quality early care and education programs and services. (I-4.1)

I-5.2—To serve as a community resource, spokesperson, and advocate for quality programming for young children. To serve as a conduit between the community and programs by coordinating and collaborating with key community representatives.

I-5.3—To uphold the spirit as well as the specific provisions of applicable regulations and standards.

I-5.4—To increase the awareness of the public and policy makers about the importance of the early years and the positive impact of high-quality early care and education programs on society.

I-5.5—To advocate on behalf of children and families for high-quality programs and services for children and for professional development for the early childhood workforce.

I-5.6—To join with other early childhood educators in speaking with a clear and unified voice for the values of our profession on behalf of children, families, and early childhood educators.

I-5.7—To be an involved and supportive member of the early childhood profession.

I-5.8—To further the professional development of the field of early childhood education and to strengthen its commitment to realizing its core values as reflected in NAEYC's Code of Ethical Conduct and this Supplement. (I-4.8)

I-5.9—To ensure that adequate resources are provided so that all provisions of the Code of Ethical Conduct and this Supplement can be implemented.

Principles

P-5.1—We shall communicate openly and truthfully about the nature and extent of services that we provide. (P-4.1)

P-5.2—We shall apply for, accept, and work in positions for which we are personally well-suited and professionally qualified. We shall not offer services that we do not have the competence, qualifications, or resources to provide. (P-4.2)

P-5.3—We shall carefully check references and not hire or recommend for employment any person whose competence, qualifications, or character makes him or her unsuited for the position. (P-4.3)

P-5.4—When we make a personnel recommendation or serve as a reference, we shall be accurate and truthful.

P-5.5—We shall be objective and accurate in reporting the knowledge upon which we base our program practices. (P-4.4)

P-5.6—We shall be knowledgeable about the appropriate use of assessment strategies and instruments and interpret results accurately to families. (P-4.5)

P-5.7—We shall be familiar with laws and regulations that serve to protect the children in our programs and be vigilant in ensuring that these laws and regulations are followed. (P-4.6)

P-5.8—We shall hold program staff accountable for knowing and following all relevant standards and regulations.

P-5.9—When we become aware of a practice or situation that endangers the health, safety, or well-being of children, we have an ethical responsibility to protect children or inform parents and/or others who can. (P-4.7)

P-5.10—We shall not participate in practices in violation of laws and regulations that protect the children in our programs. (P-4.8)

P-5.11—When we have evidence that an early childhood program is violating laws or regulations protecting children, we shall report the violation to appropriate authorities who can be expected to remedy the situation. (P-4.9)

P-5.12—We shall be honest and forthright in communications with the public and with agencies responsible for regulation and accreditation.

P-5.13—When a program violates or requires its employees to violate NAEYC's Code of Ethical Conduct, it is permissible, after fair assessment of the evidence, to disclose the identity of that program. (P-4.10)

P-5.14—When asked to provide an informed opinion on issues, practices, products, or programs, we shall base our opinions on relevant experience, knowledge of child development, and standards of best practice.

The core NAEYC Code of Ethical Conduct is online at **www.naeyc.org/files/naeyc/file/positions/PSETH05_supp.pdf**

Source: NAEYC. 2011. "Code of Ethical Conduct Supplement for Early Childhood Program Administrators." Position statement supplement. Reaffirmation and update of 2006 version. Washington, DC: Author. www.naeyc.org/positionstatements/ethical_conduct. Reprinted with permission from the National Association for the Education of Young Children (NAEYC). www.naeyc.org.

Recommended Furniture, Furnishings, and Materials

PART 1: INFANT/TODDLER MATERIALS GUIDE

The infant/toddler classroom inventory is an excerpt from larger guidance documents developed to support a grant program initiated by the South Carolina Department of Social Services to provide child care programs with guidance in selecting materials to enhance the quality of services offered to young children and their families. The specific materials and quantities recommended through these guides align with the South Carolina ABC Quality Child Care Program Standards and the Infant Toddler Environmental Rating Scale–Revised Edition (Infant/Toddler Inventory). For access to the complete document please direct your internet browser to Infant/Toddler Materials Guide:

scpitc.org/pdf/Infant_Toddler%20Materials% 20Guide

Parent Communication

	Young Infants	Mobile Infants	Older Infants
Message center (bulletin board, binder, folders, etc.)		1	

General Storage

	Young Infants	Mobile Infants	Older Infants
Cubbies or individual storage bins/baskets		1 per child	
Lockable cabinet or closet for teacher personal belongings		As needed	
Closed storage for materials not in use		As needed	
Lockable storage cabinet for hazardous materials (knives, sanitizer)		1	

Diapering Area

	Young Infants	Mobile Infants	Older Infants
Heavy duty diapering table w/6-in. high edge for safety		1	
Waterproof & washable table pad without seams on top		1	

	Young Infants	Mobile Infants	Older Infants
Wall storage unit for diapering supplies		1	
Heavy duty trash can w/lid & foot-operated opener		1	
Steps to diapering surface (mobile infants & older infants)		1	

Eating Area

	Young Infants	Mobile Infants	Older Infants
Glider rockers or other adult seating for feeding infants		1 or 2	
Bottle warmer		1	
Low chairs		1 per child	
Low tables		1–2	
Food service thermometer		1	
Bibs		2 per infant	
Small cups		2 per infant	
Plates		2 per infant	
Bowls		2 per infant	
Baby forks and spoons		2 per infant	
Serving utensils		2 sets	
Serving plates		4	
Serving bowls		4	

Sleeping Area

	Young Infants	Mobile Infants	Older Infants
Cribs	1 per infant	N/A	N/A
Crib sheets	2 per infant	N/A	N/A
Evacuation cribs	1 per 5 infants	N/A	N/A
Mats or cots	N/A		1 per infant
Mat or cot sheets	N/A		2 per infant
Blankets	N/A		1 per infant
Optional Sleeping Accessories			
Cot carrier (dolly)	N/A		1 per classroom

Cozy/Book Area

	Young Infants	Mobile Infants	Older Infants
Thick mat (2 mats placed side by side are hazardous because infants can get wedged into the crack)		1 or 2 as space allows	
Pillows (used with close supervision to prevent danger of suffocation)		Boppies for young infants	2–3

	Young Infants	Mobile Infants	Older Infants
Book holders—wall-hanging type and/or book display shelf and/or basket	1 or 2		
Puppets, stuffed animals and/or soft dolls	4	6	8
Assorted books (board, vinyl, cloth)	At least 2 per child	At least 2 per child	At least 2 per child

Manipulatives Area

	Young Infants	Mobile Infants	Older Infants
Containers	Based on the materials present		
Shelves (24-in. high)	Based on the materials present		
Cause-and-effect toys (pop-up toys, jack-in-the box, etc.)	Variety of these providing at least 2 per child, including 4 sets of exact duplicates	Variety of these providing at least 3 per child	
Grasping toys (rattles, rings, squeeze toys)			
Stacking/nesting toys			
Shape sorters			
Lacing toys (lacing beads, lacing cards, etc.)	N/A		
Peg board set	N/A		
Simple puzzles with knobs (4–6 pieces)	N/A		
Peg board set	N/A		
Interlocking toys (beads, blocks, rings, etc.)	N/A		
Puzzles with knobs (6–10 pieces)	N/A		
Puzzles without knobs, including framed and floor puzzles	N/A		
Hammering toys	N/A		

Dramatic Play Area

	Young Infants	Mobile Infants	Older Infants
Low storage shelves	Select as needed		
Storage bins	Select as needed		
Mirror	Select 3–5 items	1	
Cloth dolls (varying skin tones)		2	
Stuffed animals		2	
Plastic dolls		2	
Phones		2	
Toy cooking utensils (pots, pans, spatulas, large spoons)		1 set	
Toy flatware (forks, spoons, knives)		1 set	
Toy dishes (plates, bowls)		1 set	

	Young Infants	Mobile Infants	Older Infants
Bags, (purses, briefcases, toolbag)	N/A	2–3	
Toy food	N/A	1 set	
Dress-up clothing (community helpers, fantasy, etc.)	N/A	4 articles of clothing	
Toy kitchen (stove, oven, refrigerator, etc.)	N/A	2 pieces	
Small table and 2 chairs	N/A	1 set	

Blocks Area

	Young Infants	Mobile Infants	Older Infants
Low storage shelves	Select as needed		
Storage bins	Select as needed		
Soft blocks	10 blocks		
Large cardboard blocks	N/A	10 blocks	
Wooden unit blocks	N/A	25	75
Cars or trucks	N/A	4	
Toy animals	N/A	1 set (6–12 figures)	
Road signs	N/A	1 set	
Community figures	N/A	1 set (6–12 figures)	

Art Area

	Young Infants	Mobile Infants	Older Infants
Low storage shelves	Art activities using tools are not recommended for children under 9 months	Select as needed	
Storage bins		Select as needed	
Easel		1	
Paint brushes		6–8	
Child-safe scissors		6–8	
Smocks		6–8	
Play-doh tools (cookie cutters, rollers, etc.)		1 set	

Sensory/Science Area

	Young Infants	Mobile Infants	Older Infants
Low storage shelves	Select as needed		
Storage bins	Select as needed		
Teething toys	10		
Aquarium	1		
Tracking tube (mounted on an incline)	1		
Sensory table	N/A	1	
Sensory table accessories (shovels, cups, funnels, sifters, etc.)	N/A	10 items	

	Young Infants	Mobile Infants	Older Infants
Items that float and sink (separate items)	N/A	10 items	
Live plants	N/A	2	
Light table	N/A	1	
Classroom pet/supplies	N/A	1	
Magnets (large enough that children cannot swallow)	N/A	1 set	

Music Area

	Young Infants	Mobile Infants	Older Infants
Low storage shelves	Select as needed		
Storage bins	Select as needed		
Rattles, squeaking toys	10 items		
CDs (variety of genres)	3 genres		
Musical instruments	1 per child		
Scarves, ribbons	6		
Music player (CD, MP3, etc.)	1		

Indoor/Active Play Area

	Young Infants	Mobile Infants	Older Infants
Low storage shelves	Select as needed		
Storage bins	Select as needed		
Assorted balls	6–8		
Large vinyl covered climbing structure	1		
Thick mat	1		
Tunnel	N/A	1	
Push toys	N/A	4	
Pull toys	N/A	4	
Rocking boat/stairs	N/A	1	
Loft (toddler size)	N/A	1	
Bean bags with bucket	N/A	1 set	

Outdoor Play/Active Area

	Young Infants	Mobile Infants	Older Infants
Parachute	1		
Multiple-child stroller	1		
Outdoor mats/blanket	1 to 2		
Balls	10		
Baskets to carry materials outside	As needed		
Tricycles	N/A	3–5	
Push toys	N/A	3	

	Young Infants	Mobile Infants	Older Infants
Pull toys	N/A	3	
Scooters—no pedals	N/A	3	
Foot-propelled vehicles	N/A	2	
Sandbox	N/A	1	
Sand toys	N/A	10 items	
Toddler size climbing structure	N/A	1	

PART 2: PRESCHOOL MATERIALS GUIDE

The preschool classroom inventory is an excerpt from a larger document developed to support a grant program initiated by the South Carolina Department of Social Services to provide child care programs with guidance in selecting materials to enhance the quality of services offered to young children and their families. The specific materials and quantities recommended through these guides align with the South Carolina ABC Quality Child Care Program Standards and the Early Childhood Environmental Rating Scale–Revised Edition (Preschool Inventory). For access to the complete documents please direct your Internet browser to Preschool Materials Guide:

scpitc.org/pdf/Preschool%20Materials%20Guide

General Use Furniture

Furniture and Storage	
Child-sized tables (so that seated children's elbows reach the tabletop)	At least 2
Child-sized chairs (so that seated children's feet touch the floor)	20
Cubbies	20
Mats or cots	20
Adult chair	1
Lockable storage (for hazardous/toxic cleaning supplies, materials not in current use, and teachers' possessions)	1

Block Center

Furniture and Storage	
Storage shelf	As needed
Containers for materials	As needed
Carpet—solid color and tight weave	1

Materials to Support Learning	
Unit blocks (hardwood)	1 set (200–300 blocks of various shapes and sizes)
Family figures (multiethnic) (6–8 figures)	1 set
Community workers or career people (multiethnic) (6–8 figures)	1 set
People with physical impairments (6–8 figures)	1 set
Cars (4–6 cars)	1 set
Trucks (4–6 trucks)	1 set
Specialized blocks (tabletop blocks, door and window blocks, colored blocks, etc.)	2 sets
Animals (jungle, forest, domesticated, farm, aquatic): large and/or small	3 or 4 sets
Community vehicles (4–6 vehicles)	1 set
Traffic signs	1 set
Dinosaurs (4–10)	1 set
Wooden train & track	1 set
Specialized blocks (large hollow blocks, see-through blocks)	1 set

Dramatic Play Center

Furniture and Storage	
Kitchen set—either four separate pieces, which will also set off the area, or a one-piece unit	1
Small table and chairs (table & 2–4 chairs)	1
Wooden rocking chair (child size)	1
Storage shelves	As needed
Containers to keep materials organized	As needed
Child-size sofa and/or chair(s)	1–2
Materials to Support Learning	
Multiethnic dolls (w/removable clothing or diapers, bibs, and bottles as appropriate)	2 each gender
Doll bed & bedding (at least 1 blanket)	1
Dishes (1 place setting for each child allowed in the center)	1 set
Plastic flatware (1 place setting for each child allowed in the center)	1 set
Pots and pans (one large pot, one small pot, one frying pan)	1 set
Cooking utensils (4–5 pieces)	1 set
Mirror (unbreakable)	1
Pretend food	1 set
Dress-up items	5
Phones	1–2
Containers to keep materials organized	As needed
Pretend iron & ironing board (child size)	1
Doll high chair	1
Child-size sofa and/or chair(s)	1
House-cleaning tools (e.g., broom, dust pan, brush, vacuum, mop, duster)	1 set

Materials to Support Learning (Continued)	
Prop boxes developed around scenarios: grocery store, office, hospital, pet store/veterinarian, firefighter, post office/mail carrier, etc.	Several
Newspapers & magazines	3–5

Art Center

Furniture and Storage	
Storage shelf	1
Small table and chairs (table & 4–6 chairs) (count toward room essentials)	1
Double easel w/clips to hold paper	1
Materials to Support Learning	
12-in. paint brushes (six 1-in. wide bristles, six ½-in. wide bristles, six ¼-in. wide bristles)	1 ½ doz.
Blunt point scissors (metal, not plastic)	1 doz.
Large scissors (adult use)	1
Paint cover-ups (can be old shirts provided by donation)	6
Paint drying rack	1
Paint cups with lids	1 doz.
Play-Doh tools (i.e., rolling pins & cookie cutters; at least 1 tool per child)	1 set
Lap chalkboards or whiteboards w/erasers	4
Trays for finger painting (1 per child)	1 set
Paper punches	4–6
Alternative painting utensils	1 doz.
Stampers & stamp pads	1 set
Staplers & staples	2

Manipulatives Center

Furniture and Storage	
Storage shelf	1
Small table and chairs (table & 4–6 chairs) (count toward room essentials)	1
Open storage containers (one for each set of materials)	As needed
Materials to Support Learning	
Lego or Duplo blocks (larger size for younger children)	1 set
Counting cubes	1 set
Unifix cubes	1 set
Tower building set	1
Snap blocks	1 set
Magna-tiles	1 set
Bristle blocks	1 set
Ring construction set	1

Materials to Support Learning (Continued)	
Tall stacker pegs	1 set
Jumbo connecting disks	1 set
Pipes to connect	1 set
Gears	1 set
Tinkertoys	1 set
Manipulatives	
Assorted math manipulatives (bears, dinosaurs, vehicles, etc.)	1 set
Sorting trays	2
25-hole peg boards	4
Large round pegs—100	1 box
Beads (various shapes/colors) and laces (larger size for younger children)	1 set
Plastic/wood nuts & bolts	1 set
Sewing cards w/strings	1 set
Soft counters	1 set
Small peg boards & pegs	2
Lacing shapes	1 set
Locks & latches	1 set
Nesting toys	1 set
Puzzles & Games	
Pattern blocks w/picture cards	1 set
Shape puzzle	1
Wooden puzzles (assorted) varying difficulty (6–26 pieces) including knob puzzles	6
Number puzzles	1 set
Dominoes	1 set
Lotto, memory, or bingo games	2
Floor puzzles	1 or 2
Additional game	1
Giant pattern blocks	1 set
Sound boxes	1 set
Smelling bottles	1 set
Feely box	1

Literacy/Book/Library Center

Furniture and Storage	
Book display shelf	1
Storage shelf	As needed
Pillows & cushions	2
Mat or carpeting	1
Materials to Support Learning	
Assorted books	25
Flannel board	1
Flannel board story sets	2–3

Materials to Support Learning (Continued)	
Additional books	25
Book & CD	2–3 sets
Big books	2–3
Assorted puppets (family, animals, community helpers, etc.)	4–6

Science/Discovery Center

Furniture and Storage	
Storage/display shelf	1
Small table & chairs (table & 4 chairs; may count toward room essentials)	1
Open storage containers	1 for each set of materials
Materials to Support Learning	
Color paddles	1 set
Sink & float items (2–3 items that float & 2–3 items that sink)	1 set
Magnifiers	1 set
Living things to take care of (plants, animals, outdoor garden)	3–5
Magnets	1 set
Collections of natural objects	3–5
Trays to hold collections for examination	3–5
Balance scale	1
Prisms	2
Kaleidoscopes	2
Bug house	1
Mirror trays	1 set
Realistic plastic animals	1 set
Science games	2
Science books	2–3

Music and Movement Center

Furniture and Storage	
Storage shelf	1
Open storage containers	1 for each set of materials
Materials to Support Learning	
CD player (equipped for use with headphones)	1
Headphones w/adapter plug to use both at the same time	2 sets
Rhythm instruments (1 instrument per child)	1 set
Drums	2
CDs—assorted styles of music: classical, multicultural, folk, and children's music.	6–12
Digital voice recorder	1
Xylophone	1
Additional rhythm sticks, bells, shakers, or drums	5–10
Dance & movement props (ribbons, scarves, streamers)	1 per child

Sand and Water Center

Furniture and Storage	
Storage shelf	As needed
Storage containers	As needed
Sand/water table w/lid	1
Materials to Support Learning	
Waterproof smocks	4–6
Large spoons, scoops, and/or shovels (at least 2 items per child in the center)	1 set
Sieves or strainers	2
Boats	1 set
Sand/water wheels	1 set
Water pump	1
Basters	2
Funnels (1 per child in center)	1 set
Molds (2 per child in center)	1 set
Vehicles for sand play (1 per child in center)	1 set
Bubble wands (1 per child in center)	1 set

Computer Center

Furniture and Storage	
Computer desk—child sized	2
Chairs—child sized, or bench seating for two with one additional chair	2
Materials to Support Learning	
Computer, monitor, keyboard, mouse, mouse pad	1
Earphones	2
Age-appropriate software programs	2–3
Printer	1
Additional software programs	2–3

Outdoors

Furniture and Storage	
Storage containers	As needed
Materials to Support Learning	
Wagon	1
Tricycles, or riding toys without pedals	2
Balls	4–5
Plastic hand shovels	4–5
Sand sifters	4–5
Large trucks	1 set
Parachute	1
Jump ropes	2–3
Hoops	2–3

Materials to Support Learning (Continued)	
Riding toys (additional tricycles, scooters, wagon)	1–2
Large traffic signs, traffic cones	1 set
Balance beam	1
Water table	1
Gigantic building materials	1 set
Rocking boat	1
Air pump	1
Buckets and wide paint brushes (at least 2 in., for "painting" w/water)	4–5

PART 3: SCHOOL-AGE MATERIALS GUIDE

The School-Age Materials Inventory presented in this text is (at the time of this printing) still in development and was funded by the American Recovery and Reinvestment Act through the South Carolina Department of Social Services. The specific items and quantities listed have been intentionally aligned with the School-Age Environmental Rating Scale and the South Carolina ABC Quality Child Care Program.

Classroom Essentials

Child-sized tables (so that seated children's elbows reach the tabletop)	At least 2
Child-sized chairs (so that seated children's feet rest on the floor)	1 per child
Cubbies	1 per child
Mats or cots	1 per child
Adult chair	
Lockable storage (for hazardous/toxic cleaning supplies, materials not in current use, teachers' possessions)	

Blocks/Building

Furniture and Storage	
Storage shelves	As needed
Containers for storage	As needed
Materials to Support Learning	
Blocks (large hollow wooden)	1 set (18–20 pcs per set)
Blocks (unit building blocks) intermediate set	1 set (118–200 pcs per set)
Carpet square/rug	1
Cars	1 set (at least 10 pcs)
Trucks	1 set (at least 10 pcs)
Traffic signs	1 set (at least 10 pcs)
Lincoln Logs	1 set
Large sheets or canvas for creating caves or tents	
Specialized blocks (tabletop blocks, door & window blocks, colored blocks, etc.)	2 sets

Blocks/Building (Continued)

Family figures (multiethnic)	1 set
Community workers or career people (multiethnic)	1 set
Animals (jungle, forest, domesticated, farm, or wild): large and/or small	3–4 sets
Dinosaurs	1 set
Wooden train & track	1set
Specialized blocks (large hollow blocks, see-through blocks)	1 set

Dramatic Play

Furniture and Storage	
Containers to keep materials in	As needed
Costumes/dress-up clothes	6
Mirror	1
Prop boxes such as beauty parlor, restaurant, doctor, grocery store, office, hospital, pet store/veterinarian, firefighter, post office/mail carrier, etc.	4 or more
Materials to Support Learning	
Tables & chairs	Seating for 4
Dishes & flatware	1 place setting for each child allowed in the center
Pots & pans	1 set
Toy food	1 set
Cooking utensils	1 set of 4–5 pieces
Kitchen set	4 separate pieces
Phones	1–3
Multiethnic dolls (w/removable clothing or diapers, bibs, & bottles as appropriate)	2 each gender
Doll bed & bedding	At least 1
Doll high chair	1
Wooden rocking chair (child size)	1
Toy iron & ironing board (child size)	1
Child-size sofa and/or chair(s)	1
House-cleaning tools (e.g., broom, dust pan, brush, vacuum, mop, duster)	1 set
Newspaper & magazines	3–5

Art and Crafts Creative Construction

Furniture and Storage	
Storage shelves	As needed
Containers for storage	As needed
Table (counts toward room essentials)	1
Materials to Support Learning	
Chairs (counts toward room essentials)	4–6
Double easel w/clips to hold paper	1
Paint (assorted colors)	6 (different colors)
12-in. paint brushes (six 1-in. wide bristles, six ½-in. wide bristles, six ¼-in. wide bristles)	1-1/2 doz.

Art and Crafts Creative Construction (Continued)

Paint cups with lids	1 doz.
Paint cover-ups (can be old shirts provided by donation)	6
Paint drying rack	1
Blunt-point scissors (metal, not plastic)	1 doz.
Large scissors (adult use)	1
White paper for painting	3 pks
Construction paper (assorted colors)	3 pks
Markers	3 boxes
Crayons	3 boxes
Stamper pad	1 set (approx 9)
Stamps (assorted)	1 set (approx 20)
Glue	6
Tape & dispenser	2
Stapler & staples	2
Hole puncher	2
Magazines	Variety
Play-Doh	Assorted colors
Play-Doh tools (i.e., rolling pins & cookie cutters)	At least 1 tool per child
Craft items (such as pom-poms, textured collage shapes, fun foam sheets, pipe stems, etc.)	Variety (6 items)
Lap chalkboards or whiteboards with erasers	4
Trays for finger painting (1 per child)	1 set
Paper punches	4–6
Alternative painting utensils	1 doz.
Scissors (crinkle-cut/craft)	12
Modeling clay	
Paper cutter with fixed blade	1
Glitter	6 assorted colors
Needles, thread, yarn, velcro, fabric	Variety
Camera & film or digital camera with memory	1

Math/Manipulatives/Puzzles/Games

Furniture and Storage	
Storage shelves	As needed
Table	1
Chairs	4–6
Containers for storage	1 for each set of materials
Small Building Toys	
Lego or Duplo blocks (larger size for younger children)	1 set
Counting cubes	1 set
Unifix cubes	1 set
Tower-building set	1
Snap blocks	1 set
Tinkertoys or K'Nex	1 set

Small Building Toys	
Magna-tiles	1 set
Thistle blocks	1 set
Ring construction set	1
Tall stacker pegs	1 set
Jumbo connecting disks	1 set
Pipes to connect	1 set
Manipulatives	
Assorted math counters (bears, dinosaurs, vehicles, etc.)	1 set
Sorting trays	2 or more
Beads and buttons (various shapes/colors) and laces (larger size for younger children)	1 set
Plastic/wood nuts and bolts	1 set
Gears	1 set
Weaving frame	2
Soft counters	1 set
Locks and latches	1 set
Triolo workshop	1
Spirograph	2
Puzzles & Games	
Shape puzzles (assorted) varying difficulty	1 set
Jigsaw puzzles (assorted) varying difficulty	6
Number puzzles (assorted) varying difficulty	1 set
Games (e.g., memory, checkers, dominos)	1 set each
Math-related tools: calculators, abacas, protractors, compasses	2 of each type
Tools for measuring: cups, spoons, containers, scales, rulers, tape measurers, yardsticks, etc.	A variety of these items
Time-awareness materials: clocks, kitchen timers, sand timers, timelines, etc.	A variety of these items
Floor puzzles (assorted) varying difficulty	2 or more
Toy money	2 sets
Cash register	1
Patterning materials: pattern blocks w/picture cards, pegs and pegboards, cut-out shapes, geoboards	A variety of these items
Board games of varying levels of difficulty, such as Candy Land, Chutes and Ladders, Sorry, Connect Four, Monopoly, Scrabble, Jenga, Checkers, Pick Up Sticks, jacks, marbles, etc.	8
Playing cards (standard deck and specialized games such as Uno, Concentration, Guess Who, Old Maid, Go Fish, Crazy Eights, etc.)	3 or more

Science/Discovery

Furniture and Storage	
Storage/display shelf	As needed
Table (may count toward room essentials)	1
Chairs (may count toward room essentials)	2–4

Science/Discovery (Continued)

Open storage containers	1 for each set of materials
Trays to hold collections for examination	2–3
Materials to Support Learning	
Mirror trays	1 set
Kaleidoscopes	2
Color paddles	1 set
Living things to take care of—plants, small animals, garden	3–5
Microscope & magnifiers	1
Collections of natural objects	3–5
Magnets	2
Thermometer (alcohol only)	1
Aquarium &/or terrarium	1
Ant farm	1
Balancing scale	1
Butterfly nets	2
Sink and float items	6
Outdoor thermometer	1
Classroom safe science specimens	1 set (4)
Greenhouse kit	1
Prisms	3
Gardening tools	2 sets
Rain gauge	1
Eye droppers, tweezers, sifters, funnels	2 or more of each
Weather chart	1
Maps & globe	1 or more of each
Books, magazines, field guides about nature/science	Variety

Library/Cozy Area/Home Like Area

Furniture and Storage	
Book display shelf	1
Storage shelves	As needed
Soft items such as bean bag, big cushions, etc.	2
Materials to Support Learning	
Carpet square/rug	1
Assorted books (for age 5 and up) in the following categories: fantasy, factual, stories about people, animals and nature/science, differing cultures & abilities	At least 1 book for every child; at least 1 book from each category
Puppets	4
Magnetic write & wipe board with markers	1
Word magnets	1
Magazines (age appropriate for children such as Stone Soup: The Magazine for Children, Highlights for Children, National Geographic, Children's Digest, Kreative Kids. Age appropriate for teens, such as Young Miss, Boys Life, Girls Life, Teen, etc.)	3 or more
Flannel board	1
Flannel board story sets	2–3

Library/Cozy Area/Home Like Area

Book and CD	2–3 sets
Big books	2–3
Assorted puppets (family, animals, community helpers, etc.)	4–6
Couch or loveseat or rocking chairs	1–2

Music and Movement

Furniture and Storage	
Storage shelf	As needed
Open storage containers	1 for each set of materials
Materials to Support Learning	
CD player (equipped with head phones)	1
CDs (assorted styles of music: classical, multicultural, folk, and children's music)	6 or more
Headphones w/adapter plug to use both at the same time	2
Digital voice recorder	1
Movement & activity CDs for children	3
Dance items such as scarves, ribbons, streamers	At least 1 for each child
Rhythm instruments (sticks, bells, shakers, drums, etc.)	At least 1 for each child
Xylophone	1

Sand and Water Center

Furniture and Storage	
Sand/water table w/lid	1
Storage containers	1 for each set of materials
Materials to Support Learning	
Waterproof smocks	4–6
Large spoons, scoops, shovels, cups, pitchers	At least 1 for each child
Sieves, strainers, funnels	2 of each
Boats	1 set
Sand/water wheels	1 set
Water pump	1
Basters, eye droppers, squeeze bottles	2 of each
Molds	1 per child
Vehicles for sand play	1 per child
Bubble wands	1 per child

Homework Area

Computer desk—child sized	4–6
Chairs—child sized, or bench seating for two with one additional chair	At least 1 for each child
Furniture and Storage	
Paper & pencils	Variety
Dictionary	1
Thesaurus	1

Homework Area (Continued)

Computer, monitor, keyboard, mouse, mouse pad	1
Earphones	1 for each computer
Software programs	Variety
Printer	1

Outdoor Area

Storage	As needed
Wagon	1
Tricycles, or riding toys without pedals	2
Balls	4–6
Plastic hand shovels	2–3
Parachute	1
Jump ropes	2–3
Hoops	2–3
Riding toys (additional tricycles, scooters, wagon)	1–2
Large traffic signs, traffic cones	1 set
Balance beam	1
Water table	1
Gigantic building materials	1 set
Rocking boat	1
Air pump	1

Sources: Parts 1 and 2, *Infant/Toddler Materials Guide* and *Preschool Materials Guide* were developed by Herman T. Knopf and Kerrie L. Welsh, University of South Carolina. Used by permission of the University of South Carolina. Part 3, *School Age Materials Guide*, was prepared by the USC Child Development Research Center. Used by permission of the University of South Carolina.

Poisonous Plants

This is a list of common plants that might be in your environment that have been involved in plant poisonings. It is not exhaustive but identifies some of the most commonly occurring plants that can be dangerous to children.

COMMON PLANTS THAT CAN CAUSE SKIN IRRITATION OR DERMATITIS

Do not let children touch these plants:

Bull nettle (*Cnidoscolus stimulosus*)
Spotted spurge (*Euphorbia maculata*)
Trumpet creeper (*Campsis radicans*)
Poison oak (*Toxicodendron pubescens*)
Poison ivy (*Toxicodendron radicans*)
Wood nettle (*Laportea canadensis*)

COMMON PLANTS THAT CAN BE POISONOUS IF EATEN

Indoor Plants

Aroids (*Dieffenbachia, Monstera, Philodendron, Spathiphyllum*)	Leaves
Mistletoe (*Phoradendron serotinum*)	Berries
Poinsettia (*Euphorbia pulcherrima*)	Milky sap

Source: Adapted from *Poisonous Plant Resource Sheet for Child Care Providers.* (n.d.). Alexander Krings, Herbarium, Department of Plant Biology, NC State University, Raleigh, NC 27695-7612. Used with permission. Available online at www.cals.ncsu.edu/plantbiology/ncsc/Poisonplants/resourcesheet.pdf

Outdoor Plants

Trees

Black cherry (*Prunus serotina*)	All parts, except ripe fruit flesh
Black locust (*Robinia pseudoacacia*)	Inner bark, twigs, young leaves, seeds
Mulberry (*Morus* spp.)	Unripe fruits and milky sap

Shrubs and bedding plants

Azalea (*Rhododendron* spp.)	All parts
Boxwood (*Buxus* spp.)	Leaves
Caladium (*Caladium* spp.)	All parts
Cardinal flower (*Lobelia cardinalis*)	All parts
Castor-bean (*Ricinus communis*)	Seeds
Heavenly-bamboo (*Nandina domestica*)	Berries (potentially)
Hollies (*Ilex* spp.)	Berries, when eaten in quantity
Hydrangea (*Hydrangea* spp.)	Bark, leaves, flower buds
Jimsonweed (*Datura stramonium*)	All parts
Lantana (*Lantana camara*)	Unripe fruits
Lobelia (*Lobelia* spp.)	All parts
Madagascar periwinkle (*Catharanthus roseus*)	All parts
Mountain-laurel (*Kalmia latifolia*)	All parts
Oleander (*Nerium oleander*)	All parts
Pokeweed (*Phytolacca americana*)	All mature parts

Rhododendron (*Rhododendron* spp.)	All parts
Sheep-laurel, Lamb-kill (*Kalmia* spp.)	All parts
Tomato (*Lycopersicon esculentum*)	Stems and leaves

Vines

English ivy (*Hedera helix*)	All parts
Hyacinth bean (*Dolichos lablab*)	Pods and seeds
Peppervine (*Ampelopsis arborea*)	Unknown, caution with berries
Porcelain berry (*Ampelopsis brevipedunculata*)	Unknown, caution with berries
Sweet Pea (*Lathyrus* spp.)	Seeds
Vetchling (*Lathyrus* spp.)	Seeds
Virginia creeper (*Parthenocissus quinquefolia*)	Berries
Yellow Allamanda (*Allamanda cathartica*)	All parts
Yellow kessamine (*Gelsemium sempervirens*)	All parts
Wisteria (*Wisteria* spp.)	Seeds

How to Avoid Plant Poisoning

These steps will help you keep the children in your care safe:

1. Learn to recognize and name the dangerous plants around your facility.
2. Keep plants and plant parts away from infants and young children.
3. Teach children to keep unknown plants and plant parts out of their mouths.
4. Teach children to recognize poison ivy and other dermatitis-causing plants.
5. Do not allow children to make "tea" from leaves or suck nectar from flowers.
6. Do not rely on pets, birds, squirrels, or other animals to indicate nonpoisonous plants.
7. Label garden seeds and bulbs and store out of reach of children.
8. Be proactive. If unsure of whether or not a plant around your facility is poisonous, ask an expert.

In Case of Emergencies

Call a physician or your local poison control center immediately! Be prepared to provide the following information:

1. Name of the plant, if known
2. What parts and how much were eaten
3. How long ago it was eaten
4. Age of individual
5. Symptoms observed
6. A good description of the plant; save the specimen for identification by an expert

Governing Board Profile Worksheets

Governing Board Profile Worksheet—Sample 1

Current Board Directors	Term ending 2009			Term ending 2010			Term ending 2011		
	Alex T.	Jane R.	Tom F.	Lisa S.	Tina C.	Art P.	Stan B.	Maria S.	Albert B.
GENDER:									
• Female		X		X	X			X	
• Male	X		X			X	X		X
AGE:									
• 20–35		X				X			X
• 36–55	X			X			X	X	
• 56+			X		X				
RACE/ETHNICITY:									
• African American	X			X	X				X
• Caucasian		X	X			X			
• Native American								X	
• Hispanic							X		
• Asian American									
• Other:									
RESIDES IN THE:									
• City		X		X		X		X	
• Suburbs	X		X				X		X
• Rural Areas					X				
CONSTITUENCY:									
• Parent	X			X			X		
• Civic/Business			X			X			X
• Educator		X						X	
• Community					X				X
• Other:									
SKILLS:									
• Fund-Raising			X	X	X				X
• Public Relations		X						X	
• Strategic Planning	X						X		X
• Financial	X		X						
• Personnel							X		
• Laws/Regulations/Accreditation	X			X		X	X	X **Certified Teacher**	
• Education Expertise									
OTHER:									

Governing Board Profile Worksheet—Sample 2

Categories to Consider	Mike M.	Leo J.	Jane G.	Allen S.	Doris G.
Area of expertise/professional skills:					
• Organizational and financial management				X	X
• Community development		X	X	X	X
• Administration				X	X
• Academic/education					
• Business/corporate					
• Accounting/banking/investments					
• Fund-raising (both experienced fund-raisers and those with leverage in getting funds)					
• Laws/regulations		X	X		
• Accreditation					
• Governmental agency representative		X	X		
• Marketing		X	X		
• Personnel					
• Physical plant (architecture, engineer)					
• Strategic or long-range planning					
• Public relations					
• Real estate	X		X	X	
• Community resident		X	X	X	X
• Parent of child in school		X		X	
• Business owner					
Demographics:					
• Under age 35	X				
• Age 35–50		X	X	X	X
• Age 51–65					
• Age 65+					
• Female			X		X
• Male	X	X		X	
• Physically disabled					
• Race/ethnic background					
• Asian		X			
• African American				X	X
• Hispanic					
• Native American					
• Caucasian	X		X		
• Geographic location					
• City dweller	X		X	X	X
• Suburbanite		X			

Categories to Consider	Mike M.	Leo J.	Jane G.	Allen S.	Doris G.
• Financial position					
• Salaried	X		X		
• Hourly employee					
• Enrolled in college					
• Philanthropic reputation		X			
• Children are eligible for free/reduced-price lunch	X			X	X

Source: From *Creating an Effective Charter School Governing Board Guidebook,* by F. Martinelli, 2000, St. Paul, MN: Charter Friends National Network. Used with permission of The Annie E. Casey Foundation. Available online at www.charterschoolcenter.org/

Governing Board Job Description and Agreement

SAMPLE BOARD DIRECTOR POSITION DESCRIPTION AND STATEMENT OF COMMITMENT

1. Attend regular meetings of the board, which are scheduled to last two hours. The board meets at least six (6) times per year. Be accessible for personal contact in between board meetings.
2. Provide leadership to board committees. Each board member is expected to serve as an active member of at least one committee. Committee work may require additional meetings and the completion of assigned tasks. At present, the board's committees are program handbooks and policies, resource development/fund-raising, strategic planning, board development, personnel, finance, and executive.
3. Commit to supporting fund-raising and resource development activities.
4. Responsibly review and act upon committee recommendations brought to the board for action.
5. Prepare in advance for board meetings; take responsibility for becoming informed about upcoming issues.
6. Tap into personal and professional skills, relationships, and knowledge for the advancement of the program.

I am aware that this board position description is an expression of good faith and provides a common ground from which board members can operate. Additional information describing the program's mission, the services it offers, its key policies and procedures, and board responsibilities is contained in the board orientation materials and bylaws, which I have read.

_____   _____

Board Member's Signature   Date

Source: Adapted from *Creating an Effective Charter School Governing Board Guidebook,* by F. Martinelli, 2000, St. Paul, MN: Charter Friends National Network. Used with permission of The Annie E. Casey Foundation. Available online at www.charterschoolcenter.org/

APPENDIX 8

Professional Organizations of Interest to Early Childhood Educators

Alliance for Early Childhood Finance
www.earlychildhoodfinance.org

American Academy of Pediatrics
www.aap.org

American Montessori Society
www.amshq.org

The Association of Christian Schools International
www.acsi.org/

Association Montessori International/USA
www.montessori-ami.org

Campaign for Commercial Free Childhood
www.commercialfreechildhood.org

The Center for the Child Care Workforce
www.ccw.org

The Center for Early Childhood Leadership
www.nl.edu/cecl

Child Care Action Campaign
www.childcareaction.org

Child Care Law Center
www.childcarelaw.org

Child Welfare League of America
www.cwla.org

Children's Defense Fund
www.childrensdefense.org

Council of Chief State School Officers
www.ccsso.org

Council for Exceptional Children
www.cec.sped.org

Council for Professional Recognition
www.cdacouncil.org

Division for Early Childhood of the Council for Exceptional Children
www.dec-sped.org

Early Head Start National Resource Center
www.ehsnrc.org/

Families and Work Institute
www.familiesandwork.org

US Department of Agriculture Food and Nutrition Information Center
www.nal.usda.gov/fnic

Foundation for Child Development
www.fcd-us.org/

High/Scope Educational Research Foundation
www.highscope.org

International Reading Association
www.reading.org

National After School Association
www.naaweb.org

National Association of Child Care Professionals
www.naccp.org

National Association for Bilingual Education
www.nabe.org

National Association for Child Care Resource and Referral Agencies
www.naccrra.org

National Association of Early Childhood Specialists in State Departments of Education
www.naecs-sde.org

National Association for the Education of Young Children
www.naeyc.org

National Association for Family Child Care
www.nafcc.org

National Association for Sick Child Daycare
www.nascd.com

National Association of State Boards of Education
www.nasbe.org

National Association of State Directors of Special Education
www.nasdse.org

National Black Child Development Institute
www.nbcdi.org

National Center for Children in Poverty
www.nccp.org

National Coalition for Campus Children's Centers
www.campuschildren.org

National Head Start Association
www.nhsa.org

The National Institute for Early Education Research
http://nieer.org

National Latino Children's Institute
www.nlci.org

National PTA
www.pta.org

National Women's Law Center
www.nwlc.org

Society for Research in Child Development
www.srcd.org

Southern Early Childhood Association
southernearlychildhood.org

Special Education Resources for General Educators
serge.ccsso.org

The Urban Institute
www.urban.org

ZERO TO THREE: National Center for Infants, Toddlers, and Families
www.zerotothree.org

References

Chapter 1

AAA. (n.d.). *AAA Newsroom: Diamond rating system*. Retrieved from newsroom.aaa.com/diamond-ratings/

Administration for Children and Families (ACF). (2007). *Head Start Act*. Retrieved from eclkc.ohs.acf.hhs.gov/hslc/Program%20 Design%20and%20Management/Head%20Start%20Requirements/ Head%20Start%20Act/headstartact.html

Annie E. Casey Foundation. (2009). *Kids Count Data Center*. Retrieved from datacenter.kidscount.org/data/acrossstates/Rankings. aspx?ind=44

Association for Supportive Child Care. (2011). *The child care connection*. Tempe, AZ: Author. Retrieved from asccaz.org/kithandkin. html

Barnett, W. S. (1995). Long-term effects of early childhood programs on cognitive and school outcomes. *Future of Children, 5*(3), 25–50.

Barnett, W. S., Epstein, D. J., Carolan, M. E., Fitzgerald, J., Ackerman, D. J., & Friedman, A. H. (2010). *The state of preschool 2010*. New Brunswick, NJ: National Institute for Early Education Research (NIEER). Retrieved from nieer.org/yearbook/

Barnett, W. S., Hustedt, J. T., Hawkinson, L. E., & Robin, K. B. (2006). *The state of preschool 2006*. New Brunswick, NJ: The National Institute for Early Education Research.

Brown-Lyons, M., Robertson, A., & Layzer, J. (2001). *Kith and kin— Informal child care: Highlights from recent research*. New York: National Center for Children in Poverty. Retrieved from www. nccp.org/publications/pdf/text_377.pdf

Burchinal, M. R., Roberts, J. E., Nabors, L. A., & Bryant, D. M. (1996). Quality of center child care and infant cognitive and language development. *Child Development, 67,* 606–620.

Carnegie Corporation of New York. (1994). Starting points: Executive summary of the report of the Carnegie Corporation of New York Task Force on Meeting the Needs of Young Children. *Young Children, 49*(5), 58–61.

Center on the Developing Child at Harvard University. (2007). *A science-based framework for early childhood policy: Using evidence to improve outcomes in learning, behavior, and health for vulnerable children*. Retrieved from http://developingchild.harvard.edu/ resources/reports_and_working_papers/policy_framework/

Children's Defense Fund. (2006). *Improving children's health: Understanding children's health disparities and promising approaches to address them*. Washington, DC: Author. Retrieved from www.childrensdefense.org/site/DocServer/CDF_Improving_ Children_s_Health_FINAL.pdf?docID=1781

Committee for Economic Development, Research, and Policy. (1987). *Children in need: Investment strategies for the educationally disadvantaged: Executive summary*. New York: Author.

Committee for Economic Development, Research, and Policy. (1991). *The unfinished agenda: A new vision for child development and education*. New York: Author.

Committee for Economic Development, Research, and Policy. (1993). *Why child care matters: Preparing young children for a more productive America*. New York: Author.

Cost, Quality, and Child Outcomes Study Team. (1995). *Cost, quality, and child outcomes in child care centers, public report* (2nd ed.). Denver: University of Colorado–Denver, Economics Department.

Cranley Gallagher, K. (2005). Brain research and early childhood development—A primer for developmentally appropriate practice. *Young Children, 60*(4), 12–20.

Dulewicz, V., & Higgs, M. (2005). Assessing leadership styles and organizational context. *Journal of Managerial Psychology, 20*(2), 105–123.

Garbarino, J., & Ganzel, B. (2000). The human ecology of early risk. In J. P. Shonkoff & S. J. Meisels (Eds.), *Handbook of early childhood intervention* (2nd ed., pp. 76–93). New York: Cambridge University Press.

Helburn, S. W., & Culkin, M. L. (1995a). *Cost, quality, and child outcomes in child care centers: Executive summary*. Denver: University of Colorado–Denver.

Helburn, S. W., & Culkin, M. L. (1995b). Cost, quality, and child outcomes in child care centers: Key findings and recommendations. *Young Children, 50*(4), 40–44.

Lerman, R. I., & Schmidt, S. R. (1999). *Overview of economic, social, and demographic trends affecting the U.S. Labor Market*. Washington, DC: The Urban Institute. Retrieved from www.urban.org/url. cfm?ID=409203

Meisels, S. J., & Shonkoff, J. P. (2000). Early childhood intervention. In J. P. Shonkoff & S. J. Meisels (Eds.), *Handbook of early childhood intervention* (2nd ed., pp. 3–34). New York: Cambridge University Press.

National Association for the Education of Young Children (NAEYC). (2009). Developmentally appropriate practice in early childhood programs serving children from birth through age 8. Washington, DC: Author. Retrieved from www.naeyc.org/files/naeyc/file/positions/ PSDAP.pdf

National Association for the Education of Young Children Academy for Early Childhood Program Accreditation. (2007). *NAEYC Early Childhood Program Standards*. Washington, DC: Author.

National Association of Child Care Professionals (NACCP). (n.d.). National Accreditation Commission for Early Care and Education Programs. Retrieved from http://naccp.org/displaycommon. cfm?an=1&subarticlenbr=237

National Association for Regulatory Administration and National Child Care Information and Technical Assistance Center. (2006). *The 2005 child care licensing study: Final report*. Conyers, GA: National Association for Regulatory Administration.

National Child Care Information and Technical Assistance Center, National Association for Regulatory Administration (NARA). (2010). *The 2008 child care licensing study: Final report*. Lexington, KY: NARA. Retrieved from www.naralicensing.org/Licensing_Study

National Infant & Toddler Child Care Initiative and ZERO TO THREE Policy Center. (2010). Infant/ toddler early learning guidelines implementation toolkit. Washington, DC: Author. Retrieved from http:// www.zerotothree.org/public-policy/webinars-conference-calls/ it-elg-implementation-toolkit-introduction-508-compliant.pdf

National Institute of Child Health and Human Development (NICHD) Early Child Care Research Network. (1998). Early child care and self-control, compliance, and problem behavior at twenty-four and thirty-six months. *Child Development, 69,* 1145–1170.

Olson, L. (2002). Starting early. Quality counts 2002: Building blocks for success. *Education Week, 21*(17), 10–12, 14, 16, 18–22.

Paulsell, D., Mekos, D., Del Grosso, P., Rowand, C., & Banghart, P. (2006). *Strategies for supporting quality in kith and kin child care: Findings from the Early Head Start enhanced home visiting pilot evaluation.* Princeton, NJ: Mathematica Policy Research. Retrieved from www.mathematica-mpr.com/publications/PDFs/kithkinquality.pdf

Petersen, S., Jones, L. & McGinley, K. A. (2008). *Early Learning Guidelines for Infants and Toddlers: Recommendations to states.* Washington, DC: ZERO TO THREE.

Ramey, C. T., & Ramey, S. L. (1998). Early intervention and early experience. *American Psychologist, 58,* 109–120.

Rolnick, A., & Grunewald, R. (2003, March). Early childhood development: Economic development with a high public return. *Fedgazette,* Federal Reserve Bank of Minneapolis. Retrieved from http://minneapolisfed.org/pubs/fedgaz/03-03/earlychild.cfm

Sameroff, A. J., & Fiese, B. H. (2000). Transactional regulation: The development ecology of early intervention. In J. P. Shonkoff & S. J. Meisels (Eds.), *Handbook of early childhood intervention* (2nd ed., pp. 135–159). New York: Cambridge University Press.

Schweinhart, L. J., Montie, J., Xiang, Z., Barnett, W. S., Belfield, C. R., & Nores, M. (2005). *Lifetime effects: The High/Scope Perry Preschool Study through age 40* (Monographs of the High/Scope Educational Research Foundation, 14). Ypsilanti, MI: High/Scope Press.

Shonkoff, J. P., & Phillips, D. A. (Eds.). (2000). *From neurons to neighborhoods: The science of early childhood development.* Washington, DC: National Academy Press.

Shore, R., & Shore, B. (2009). KIDS COUNT Indicator Brief: Reducing the child poverty rate. Baltimore, MD: Annie E. Casey Foundation. Retrieved from http://www.aecf.org/~/media/pubs/initiatives/kids%20count/K/kidscountindicatorbriefREducingthechildpovert/reducingchildpoverty.pdf

U.S. Department of Education, Office of Special Education and Rehabilitative Services, Office of Special Education Programs. (2007). *27th annual (2005) report to Congress on the implementation of the Individuals with Disabilities Education Act* (Vol. 1). Washington, DC: Author.

U.S. Department of Labor, Bureau of Labor Statistics. (2011). *Families with own children: Employment status of parents by age of youngest child and family type, 2009–10 annual averages.* Retrieved from http://www.bls.gov/news.release/famee.t04.htm

Urban Institute. (2004). *Primary child care arrangements for children under age 5 with employed mothers.* Washington, DC: Author.

ZERO TO THREE. (2007). *The infant-toddler set-aside of the child care and development block grant: Improving quality child care for infants and toddlers.* Washington, DC: Author. Retrieved from www.zerotothree.org/site/DocServer/Jan_07_Child_Care_Fact_Sheet.pdf?docID=2621

Zinzeleta, E., & Little, N. K. (1997). How do parents really choose early childhood programs? *Young Children, 52*(7), 8–11.

Chapter 2

Barnett, W. S. (1986). Methodological issues in economic evaluation of early intervention programs. *Early Childhood Research Quarterly, 1,* 249–268.

Barnett, W. S., Frede, E. C., Mobasher, H., & Mohr, P. (1987). The efficacy of public preschool programs and the relationship of program quality to program efficacy. *Educational Evaluation and Policy Analysis, 10*(1), 37–39.

Bloom, P. J. (2010). *Measuring work attitudes in the early childhood setting* (2nd ed.). Lake Forest, IL: New Horizons.

Bredekamp, S. (Ed.). (1987). *Developmentally appropriate practice in early childhood programs serving children from birth through age 8* (Exp. ed.). Washington, DC: National Association for the Education of Young Children.

Bronfenbrenner, U. (1979). *The ecology of human development: Experiments by nature and design.* Cambridge, MA: Harvard University Press.

Bronfenbrenner, U. (1986). Ecology of the family as a context for human development: Research perspectives. *Developmental Psychology, 22,* 723–742.

Bronfenbrenner, U. (1989). Ecological systems theory. In R. Vasta (Ed.), *Six theories of child development: Revised formulations and current issues. Annals of child development: A research annual* (Vol. 6, pp. 187–249). Greenwich, CT: JAI.

Bryant, D. M., Clifford, R. M., & Peisner, E. S. (1991). Best practices for beginners: Developmental appropriateness in kindergarten. *American Educational Research Journal, 28,* 783–803.

Charlesworth, R., Hart, C. H., Burts, D. C., Thomasson, R. H., Mosley, J., & Fleege, P. O. (1993). Measuring the developmental appropriateness of kindergarten teachers' beliefs and practices. *Early Childhood Research Quarterly, 8,* 255–276.

Clark, C. M., & Peterson, P. L. (1986). Teachers' thought processes. In M. C. Wittrock (Ed.), *Handbook of research on teaching* (3rd ed., pp. 255–296). New York: Macmillan.

Copple, C., & Bredekamp, S. (Eds.). (2009). *Developmentally appropriate practice in early childhood programs serving children from birth through age 8* (3rd ed.). Washington, DC: National Association for the Education of Young Children.

Dewey, J. (1897). My pedagogic creed. *School Journal, 54,* 77–80.

Dewey, J. (1916). *Democracy and education: An introduction to the philosophy of education.* New York: Macmillan.

Dopyera, J. E., & Lay-Dopyera, M. (1990). Evaluation and science in early childhood education: Some critical issues. In C. Seefeldt (Ed.), *Continuing issues in early childhood education* (pp. 285–299). New York: Merrill/Macmillan.

Edwards, P. A., Gandini, L., & Forman, G. (Eds.). (1998). *The hundred languages of children: The Reggio approach–advanced reflections* (2nd ed.). Greenwich, CT: Ablex.

Egan, K. (1983). *Education and psychology: Plato, Piaget, and scientific psychology.* New York: Teachers College Press.

Erikson, E. H. (1950). *Childhood and society.* New York: Norton.

Frede, E. C. (1998). Preschool program quality in programs for children in poverty. In W. S. Barnett & S. S. Boocock (Eds.), *Early care and education of children in poverty: Promises, programs and long-term outcomes* (pp. 77–98). Buffalo: State University of New York Press.

Frost, J. L. (1992). *Play and playscapes.* Albany, NY: Delmar.

Gardner, H. (1983). *Frames of mind: Theory of multiple intelligences.* New York: Basic Books.

Gardner, H. (1999). *The disciplined mind: What all students should understand.* New York: Simon & Schuster.

Gesell, A. (1931). Maturation and patterning of behavior. In C. Murchinson (Ed.), *A handbook of child psychology* (pp. 209–235). Worchester, MA: Clark University Press.

Goncu, A. (Ed.). (1999). *Children's engagement in the world: Sociocultural perspectives.* London: Cambridge University Press.

Guralnick, M. J. (1988). Efficacy research in early childhood intervention programs. In S. L. Odom & M. B. Karnes (Eds.), *Early intervention for infants and children with handicaps: An empirical base* (pp. 75–88). Baltimore, MD: Brookes.

Harms, T., Clifford, R. M. & Cryer, D. (2005). *Early Childhood Environment Rating Scale–Revised.* New York: Teachers College Press.

Harms, T., Cryer, D., & Clifford, R. M. (2006). *Infant/Toddler Environment Rating Scale–Revised.* New York: Teachers College Press.

Harms, T., Cryer, D., & Clifford, R. M. (2007). *Family Child Care Environment Rating Scale–Revised.* New York: Teachers College Press.

Harms, T., Jacobs, E. V., & White, D. R. (1995). *School-Age Care Environment Rating Scale.* New York: Teachers College Press.

Haskins, R. (1989). Beyond metaphors: The efficacy of early childhood education. *American Psychologist, 44,* 247–282.

Hauser-Cram, P. (1990). Designing meaningful evaluations of early childhood services. In S. Meisels & J. Shonkoff (Eds.), *Handbook of early childhood intervention* (pp. 583–602). New York: Cambridge University Press.

Hemmeter, M. L., Maxwell, K. L., Ault, M. J., & Schuster, J. W. (2001). *Assessment of practices in early elementary classrooms.* New York: Teachers College Press.

High/Scope Educational Research Foundation. (1998). *High/Scope Program Quality Assessment.* Ypsilanti, MI: High/Scope Press.

Hitz, M. C., & Wright, D. (1988). Kindergarten issues: A practitioners' survey. *Principal, 67*(5), 28–30.

Horowitz, F. D., & O'Brien, M. (1989). In the interest of the nation: A reflective essay on the state of our knowledge and the challenges before us. *American Psychologist, 44,* 441–445.

Hunt, J. M. (1961). *Intelligence and experience.* New York: Ronald Press.

Jacobs, F. (1988). The five-tiered approach to evaluation: Context and implementation. In H. B. Weiss & F. H. Jacobs (Eds.), *Evaluating family programs* (pp. 37–68). New York: Aldine DeGruyter.

Jersild, A. T. (1946). *Child development and the curriculum.* New York: Teachers College Press.

Kagan, S. L. (1991). Excellence in early childhood education: Defining characteristics and next decade strategies. In S. L. Kagan (Ed.), *The care and education of America's young children: Obstacles and opportunities* (pp. 237–258). Chicago, IL: University of Chicago Press.

Katz, L. G. (1984). The professional preschool teacher. In L. G. Katz (Ed.), *More talks with teachers* (pp. 27–42). Urbana, IL: ERIC Clearinghouse on Elementary and Early Childhood Education.

Katz, L. G. (1991). Pedagogical issues in early childhood education. In S. L. Kagan (Ed.), *The care and education of America's young children: Obstacles and opportunities* (pp. 50–68). Chicago, IL: University of Chicago Press.

Katz, L. G. (1999, March). *Multiple perspectives on the quality of programs for young children.* Keynote address at the International Conference of the World Organization for Early Childhood Education, Hong Kong. (ERIC Document Reproduction Service No. ED428868)

Kohlberg, L., & Mayer, R. (1972). Development as the aim of education. *Harvard Educational Review, 42,* 449–496.

Kostelnik, M. J. (1992). Myths associated with developmentally appropriate programs. *Young Children, 47*(4), 17–23.

Ladson-Billings, G. (2009). *The dreamkeepers: Successful teachers of African American children* (2nd ed.). San Francisco, CA: Jossey-Bass.

Meisels, S. J. (1985). The efficacy of early intervention: Why are we still asking these questions? *Topics in Early Childhood Special Education, 5,* 1–12.

Meshanko, R. (1996). *What should our mission statement say?* Retrieved from www.npgoodpractice.org/what-should-our-mission-statement-say

Miller, L. B., Bugbee, M. R., & Hyberton, D. W. (1985). Dimensions of preschool: The effects of individual experience. In I. E. Sigel (Ed.),

Advances in applied developmental psychology (Vol. 1, pp. 25–90). Norwood, NJ: Ablex.

National Association for the Education of Young Children. (1997). NAEYC position statement. Developmentally appropriate practice in early childhood programs serving children from birth through age 8. In S. Bredekamp & C. Copple (Eds.), *Developmentally appropriate practice in early childhood programs* (rev. ed., pp. 3–30). Washington, DC: Author.

National Association for the Education of Young Children & the National Association of Early Childhood Specialists in State Departments of Education. (1991). Guidelines for appropriate curriculum content and assessment in programs serving children ages 3 through 8: A position statement. *Young Children, 46*(3), 21–38.

Nilsen, B. A. (2000). *Week by week: Plans for observing and recording young children.* Albany, NY: Delmar.

Oakes, P. B., & Caruso, D. A. (1990). Kindergarten teachers' use of developmentally appropriate practices and attitudes about authority. *Early Education and Development, 1,* 445–457.

Parent evaluation of child care program. (1989, June). *Child Care Information Exchange,* no. 67, 25–26.

Plomin, R. (1997). *Behavioral genetics.* New York: Freeman.

Pogrow, S. (1996, September 25). On scripting the classroom. *Education Week,* pp. 20, 52.

Powell, D. R. (1987a). Comparing preschool curricula and practices: The state of research. In S. L. Kagan & E. F. Zigler (Eds.), *Early schooling: The national debate* (pp. 190–211). New Haven, CT: Yale University Press.

Powell, D. R. (1987b). Methodological and conceptual issues in research. In S. L. Kagan, D. R. Powell, B. Weissbourd, & E. F. Zigler (Eds.), *America's family support system* (pp. 311–328). New Haven, CT: Yale University Press.

Rogoff, B., & Chavajay, P. (1995). What's become of research on the cultural basis of cognitive development? *American Psychologist, 50,* 859–877.

Sigel, I. E. (1990). Psychoeducational intervention: Future directions. *Merrill-Palmer Quarterly, 36,* 159–172.

Skinner, B. F. (1938). *The behavior of organisms: An experimental analysis.* Englewood Cliffs, NJ: Prentice Hall.

Smith, B. S. (1997). Communication as a curriculum guide: Moving beyond ideology to democracy in education. *Childhood Education, 73,* 232–233.

Sommerville, C. J. (1982). *The rise and fall of childhood.* Beverly Hills, CA: Sage.

Spodek, B. (1987). Thought processes underlying preschool teachers' classroom decisions. *Early Child Care and Development, 28,* 197–208.

Spodek, B. (1991). Early childhood curriculum and cultural definitions of knowledge. In B. Spodek & O. N. Saracho (Eds.), *Yearbook in early childhood education,* Vol. 2: *Issues in early education* (pp. 1–20). New York: Teachers College Press.

Stott, E., & Bowman, B. (1996). Child development knowledge: A slippery base for practice. *Early Childhood Research Quarterly, 11,* 169–183.

Swadener, B. B., & Kessler, S. (Eds.). (1991). Reconceptualizing early childhood education [Special issue]. *Early Education and Development, 2*(2).

Vygotsky, L. S. (1978). *Mind in society* (M. Cole, S. Schribner, V. John-Steiner, & E. Souberman, Trans.). Cambridge, MA: Harvard University Press.

Weikart, D. P. (1981). Effects of different curricula in early childhood intervention. *Educational Evaluation and Policy Analysis, 3,* 25–35.

Weikart, D. P. (1983). A longitudinal view of preschool research effort. In M. Perlmutter (Ed.), *Development and policy concerning children with special needs. The Minnesota Symposia on Child Psychology* (Vol. 16, pp. 175–196). Hillsdale, NJ: Erlbaum.

Wood, D. J., Bruner, J., & Ross, G. (1976). The role of tutoring in problem solving. *Journal of Child Psychology and Psychiatry, 17,* 89–100.

Wolery, R. A., & Odom, S. L. (2000). An administrator's guide to preschool inclusion. Chapel Hill: University of North Carolina, FPG Child Development Center, Early Childhood Research Institute on Inclusion.

Chapter 3

ACF (Administration for Children and Families). (2007). Head Start Act as amended. Retrieved from eclkc.ohs.acf.hhs.gov/hslc/Head%20Start%20Program/Program%20Design%20and%20Management/Head%20Start%20Requirements/Head%20Start%20Act/

American Academy of Pediatrics, American Public Health Association, and National Resource Center for Health and Safety in Child Care (AAP/APHA/NRCHSCC). (2011). *Caring for our children: National health and safety performance standards: Guidelines for out-of-home child care programs* (3rd ed.). Elk Grove Village, IL: American Academy of Pediatrics and Washington, DC: American Public Health Association. Retrieved from http://nrckids.org/CFOC3/index.html

Bloom, P. J. (1989). *The Illinois directors' study: A report to the Illinois Department of Children and Family Services.* Evanston, IL: National College of Education, Early Childhood Professional Development Project.

Caruso, J. J. (1991). Supervisors in early childhood programs: An emerging profile. *Young Children, 46*(6), 20–26.

Charlesworth, R., Hart, C. H., Burts, D. C., & DeWolf, M. (1993). The LSU studies: Building a research base for developmentally appropriate practice. In S. Reifel (Ed.), *Advances in early education and day care: Perspectives in developmentally appropriate practice* (Vol. 5, pp. 3–28). Greenwich, CT: JAI.

Cost, Quality, and Child Outcomes Study Team. (1995). *Cost, quality, and child outcomes in child care centers, public report.* Denver: Economics Department, University of Colorado-Denver.

Council for Professional Recognition. (n.d.). *CDA Competency Standards.* Washington, DC: Author. Retrieved from www.cdacouncil.org/the-cda-credential/how-to-earn-a-cda/preschool/step-1-explore

Early, D. M., Bryant, D. M., Pianta, R. C., Clifford, R. M., Burchinal, M. R., Ritchie, S . . . . Barbarin, O. (2006). Are teachers' education, major, and credentials related to classroom quality and children's academic gains in pre-kindergarten? *Early Childhood Research Quarterly, 21*(2), 174–195.

Education Commission of the States. (2002). State-funded pre-kindergarten programs: Curriculum, accreditation, and parental involvement standards. Retrieved from www.ecs.org/dbsearches/Search_Info/EarlyLearningReports.asp?tbl=table8

Fields, M., & Mitchell, A. (2007, June). *ECE/Elementary Licensure Survey.* Paper presented at the midyear conference of the National Association for Early Childhood Teacher Educators, Pittsburgh, PA.

Freeman, N. K., & Feeney, S. (2006). The new face of early care and education: Who are we? Where are we going? *Young Children, 61*(5), 10–16.

Goldstein, L. S. (1997). Between a rock and a hard place in the primary grades: The challenge of providing developmentally appropriate early childhood education in an elementary school setting. *Early Childhood Research Quarterly, 12,* 3–27.

Harms, T., Clifford, R., & Cryer, D. (2005). *Early childhood environment rating scale* (Rev.). New York: Teachers College Press.

Herr, J., Johnson, R. D., & Zimmerman, K. (1993). Benefits of accreditation: A study of directors' perceptions. *Young Children, 48*(4), 32–35.

Jones, R. C., Martin, S., & Crandall, M. (2009). *Early childhood public school teacher licensure for the fifty states and Washington, DC: An inquiry to ascertain student age ranges for public school licensure.* Fayetteville: University of Arkansas.

Kontos, S., Howes, C., & Galinsky, E. (1997). Does training make a difference to quality in family child care? *Early Childhood Research Quarterly, 12,* 351–372.

Mancke, J. B. (1972). Liability of school districts for the negligent acts of their employees. *Journal of Law and Education, 1,* 109–127.

Mead, S. (2011). *PreK-3rd: Principals as crucial instructional leaders.* New York: Foundation for Child Development. Retrieved from fcd-us.org/resources/prek-3rd-principals-crucial-instructional- leaders

Mims, S. R., Scott-Little, C., Lower, J. K., Cassidy, D., & Hestenes, L. L. (2008). Education level and stability as it relates to early childhood classroom quality: A survey of early childhood program directors and teachers. *Journal of Research in Childhood Education, 23*(2), 227–237.

Mitchell, A. (2000). The case for credentialing directors now and considerations for the future. In M. L. Culkin (Ed.), *Managing quality in young children's programs: The leader's role* (pp. 152–169). New York: Teachers College Press.

Mitchell, A. W. (2005). *Stair steps to quality: A guide for states and communities developing quality rating systems for early care and education.* Alexandria, VA: United Way Success by 6™. Retrieved from www.earlychildhoodfinance.org/downloads/2005/MitchStairSteps_2005.pdf

Morgan, G. G. (1996). Licensing and accreditation: How much quality is "quality"? In S. Bredekamp & B. A. Wilier (Eds.), *NAEYC accreditation: A decade of learning and the years ahead* (pp. 129–138). Washington, DC: National Association for the Education of Young Children.

Morgan, G. G. (2000). The director as a key to quality. In M. L. Culkin (Ed.), *Managing quality in young children's programs: The leader's role* (pp. 40–58). New York: Teachers College Press.

National Association of Child Care Resource and Referral Agencies (NACCRRA). (2011). *2011 Update: We can do better: NACCRRA's ranking of state child care center standards and oversight.* Retrieved from www.naccrra.org/publications/naccrra-publications/publications/chapters1to5.pdf

National Association of Elementary School Principals (NAESP) Foundation Task Force on Early Learning. (2011). *Building & supporting an aligned system: A vision for transforming education across the pre-K–grade three years.* Washington, DC: Author. Retrieved from www.naesp.org/resources/1/NAESP_Prek-3_C_pages.pdf

National Association for the Education of Young Children. (2011). NAEYC *Accreditation: All criteria document.* Washington, DC: Author. Retrieved from www.naeyc.org/academy/primary/viewstandards

National Association for the Education of Young Children. (2007). *NAEYC accreditation: Program administrator definition and competencies.* Washington, DC: Author. Accessed from www.naeyc.org/files/academy/file/Program%20Admin%20Def%20and%20Competencies.pdf

National Association for Regulatory Administration & Technical Assistance Center. (2006). *The 2005 child care licensing study: Final report*. Conyers, GA: Author. Retrieved from nara.affiniscape.com/associations/4734/files/2005%20Licensing%20Study%20Final%20Report_Web.pdf

National Association of Elementary School Principals. (2005). *Leading early childhood learning communities: What principals should know and be able to do*. Alexandria, VA: Author. Retrieved from web.naesp.org/misc/ECLC_ExecSum.pdf

National Child Care Information Center (NCCIC). (2011). *QRIS definition and statewide systems*. Retrieved from nccic.acf.hhs.gov/resource/qris-definition-and-statewide-systems

National Child Care Information Center & National Association for Regulatory Administration (NCCIC/NARA). (2010). *The 2008 child care licensing study*. Lexington, KY: National Association for Regulatory Administration. Retrieved from www.naralicensing.org/Licensing_Study

Rohacek, M., Adams, G. C., & Kisker, E. E. (2010). *Understanding quality in context: Child care centers, communities, markets, and public policy*. Washington, DC: The Urban Institute. Retrieved from www.urban.org/url.cfm?ID=412191

Scott, L. C. (1983). Injury in the classroom: Are teachers liable? *Young Children, 38*(6), 10–18.

Snider, M. H., & Fu, V. R. (1990). The effects of specialized education and job experience on early childhood teachers' knowledge of developmentally appropriate practice. *Early Childhood Research Quarterly, 5*, 68–78.

Surr, J. (1992). Early childhood programs and the Americans with Disabilities Act (ADA). *Young Children, 47*(2), 18–21.

Talley, K. (1997). National accreditation: Why do some programs stall in self-study? *Young Children, 52*(3), 31–37.

U.S. Department of Health and Human Services. (2006). *Promoting quality in afterschool programs through state child care regulations*. Accessed from www.nccic.acf.hhs.gov/afterschool/childcareregs.pdf

Vu, J. A., Jeon, H., & Howes, C. (2008) Formal education, credential, or both: Early childhood program classroom practices. *Early Education & Development, 19*(3), 479–504.

West, L. S. (2001, April). *The influence of principals on the institutionalization of developmentally appropriate practices: A multiple case study*. (ERIC Document Reproduction Service No. ED456543). Paper presented at the annual meeting of the American Educational Research Association, Seattle, WA.

Chapter 4

American Academy of Pediatrics, American Public Health Association, and National Resource Center for Health and Safety in Child Care (AAP/APHA/NRCHSCC). (2011). *Caring for our children: National health and safety performance standards: Guidelines for out-of-home child care programs* (3rd ed.). Elk Grove Village, IL: American Academy of Pediatrics and Washington, DC: American Public Health Association. Retrieved from nrckids.org/CFOC3/PDFVersion/list.html

Aronson, S. S. (Ed.). (2002). *Healthy young children: A manual for programs* (4th ed.). Washington, DC: National Association for the Education of Young Children.

Child Care Partnership Project: T.E.A.C.H. Early Childhood® Project. (n.d.). Retrieved from www.childcareservices.org/ps/teach.html

National Association of Child Care Resource & Referral Agencies (NACCRRA) & Save the Children. (2010). *Protecting children in child care during emergencies*. Retrieved from doh.state.fl.us/demo/ems/emsc/ProtectChildrenInChildCareDuringEmergencies.pdf

National Association for the Education of Young Children. (2011a). Code of Ethical Conduct and Statement of Commitment. Retrieved from www.naeyc.org/files/naeyc/file/positions/Ethics%20Position%20Statement2011.pdf

National Association for the Education of Young Children. (2011b). NAEYC *Accreditation: All criteria document*. Washington, DC: Author. Retrieved from nrckids.org/CFOC3/PDFVersion/list.html

National Association for the Education of Young Children. (2011c). *NAEYC Code of Ethical Conduct Supplement for Early Childhood Program Administrators*. Retrieved from www.naeyc.org/files/naeyc/file/positions/Supplement%20PS2011.pdf

National Child Care Information Center & National Association for Regulatory Administration (NCCIC/NARA). (2010). *The 2008 child care licensing study*. Lexington, KY: National Association for Regulatory Administration. Retrieved from www.naralicensing.drivehq.com/2008_Licensing_Study/1005_2008_Child%20Care%20Licensing%20Study_Full_Report.pdf

Chapter 5

Abbott-Shim, M. S. (1990). In-service training: A means to quality care. *Young Children, 45*(2), 14–18.

Alexander, N. P. (2000). *Workshops that work!: The essential guide to successful training and workshops*. Lewisville, NC: Gryphon House.

Ashton-Warner, S. (1963). *Teacher*. New York: Simon & Schuster.

Balaban, N. (1992). The role of the child care professional in caring for infants, toddlers, and their families. *Young Children, 47*(5), 66–71.

Bandura, A. (1982). Self-efficacy mechanisms in human agency. *American Psychologists, 37*, 122–147.

Barker, L., Wahlers, K., Watson, K., & Kibler, R. (1987). *Groups in process*. Upper Saddle River, NJ: Prentice Hall.

Barnett, W. S. (2003). Low wages = low quality: Solving the real preschool teacher crisis. Retrieved from nieer.org/resources/policybriefs/3.pdf

Baumgartner, J. J., Carson, R. L., Apavaloaie, L., & Tsouloupas, C. (2009). Uncovering common stressful factors and coping strategies among childcare providers. *Child Youth Care Forum, 38*, 239–251.

Bellm, D., Whitebook, M., & Hnatiuk, P. (1997). *The early childhood mentoring curriculum: A handbook for mentors*. Washington, DC: Center for the Child Care Workforce.

Bloom, P. J. (1995). Shared decision making: The centerpiece of participatory management. *Young Children, 50*(4), 55–60.

Bloom, P. J. (1997). Navigating the rapids: Directors reflect on their careers and professional development. *Young Children, 52*(7), 32–38.

Bloom, P. J. (2000a). *Circle of influence: Implementing shared decision making and participative management*. Lake Forest, IL: New Horizons.

Bloom, P. J. (2000b). Images from the field: How directors view their organizations, their roles, and their jobs. In M. L. Culkin (Ed.), *Managing quality in young children's programs: The leader's role* (pp. 59–77). New York: Teachers College Press.

Bloom, P. J. (2000c). *Workshop essentials: Planning and presenting dynamic workshops*. Lake Forest, IL: New Horizons.

Bloom, P. J., Sheerer, M., & Britz, J. (1991). *Blueprint for action: Achieving center-based change through staff development*. Mt. Rainer, MD: Gryphon.

Bredekamp, S. (1990). *Regulating child care quality: Evidence from NAEYC's accreditation system*. Washington, DC: National Association for the Education of Young Children.

Brown, N. H., & Manning, J. P. (2000). Core knowledge for directors. In M. L. Culkin (Ed.), *Managing quality in young children's programs: The leader's role* (pp. 78–96). New York: Teachers College Press.

Bureau of Labor Statistics, U.S. Department of Labor. (2010). *Career guide to industries, 2010–11 edition: Child day care services.* Retrieved from www.bls.gov/oco/dg/dgs032.htm.

Carnegie Corporation of New York. (1994). Starting points: Meeting the needs of young children. *Young Children, 49*(5), 58–61.

Carroll, M., Smith, M., & Oliver, G. (2008). Recruitment and retention in front-line services: The case of childcare. *Human Resource Management Journal, 19*(1), 59–74.

Carter, M. (1992). Honoring diversity: Problems and possibilities for staff and organization. In B. Neugebauer (Ed.), *Alike and different: Exploring our humanity with children* (rev. ed., pp. 70–81). Washington, DC: National Association for the Education of Young Children.

Carter, M. (1993). Developing a cultural disposition in teachers. *Child Care Information Exchange, 90,* 52–55.

Carter, M., & Curtis, D. (1998). *The visionary director: A handbook for dreaming, organizing, and improvising in your center.* St. Paul, MN: Redleaf.

Caruso, J. J., & Fawcett, M. T. (1999). *Supervision in early childhood education: A developmental perspective* (2nd ed.). New York: Teachers College Press.

Center for Career Development in Early Care and Education at Wheelock College. (2000). *The power of mentoring.* Boston, MA: Wheelock College, Institute for Leadership and Career Initiatives.

Center for Child Care Workforce. (2004). Current data on the salaries and benefits of the U.S. early childhood education workforce. Washington, DC: Center for the Child Care Workforce.

Child Care Services Association. (n.d.). *The T.E.A.C.H. Early Childhood® National Technical Assistance & Quality Assurance Center.* Chapel Hill, NC: Author. Retrieved from www.childcareservices.org/ps/teach_ta_qac.html#3

Cinnamond, J., & Zimpher, N. (1990). Reflectivity as a function of community. In R. Clift, W. Houston, & M. Pugach (Eds.), *Encouraging reflective practice in education* (pp. 57–72). New York: Teachers College Press.

Clarke-Stewart, A., & Gruber, C. (1984). Day care forms and features. In R. C. Ainslie (Ed.), *Quality variations in day care* (pp. 35–62). New York: Praeger.

Clyde, M., & Rodd, J. (1989). Professional ethics: There's more to it than meets the eye. *Early Child Development and Care, 53,* 1–12.

Collins, J. E., & Porras, J. I. (1994). *Built to last: Successful habits of visionary companies.* New York: Harper Business.

Cost, Quality, and Child Outcomes Study Team. (1995). *Cost, quality, and child outcomes in child care centers, public report* (2nd ed.). Denver: Economics Department, University of Colorado–Denver.

Council for Early Childhood Professional Recognition. (1996). *The Child Development Associate system and competency standards: Pre-school caregivers in center-based programs.* Washington, DC: Author.

Cryer, D., Wagner-Moore, L., Burchinal, M., Yazejiana, N., Hurwitza, S., & Wolery, M. (2005). Effects of transitions to new child care classes on infant/toddler distress and behavior. *Early Childhood Research Quarterly, 20*(1), 37–56.

Cuffaro, H. (1995). *Experimenting with the world: John Dewey and the early childhood classroom.* New York: Teachers College Press.

Curbow, B., Spratt, K., Ungaretti, A., McDonnell, K., & Breckler, S. (2001). Development of the child care worker job stress inventory. *Early Childhood Research Quarterly, 15*(4), 515–535.

Drucker, P. (1990). *Managing the nonprofit organization: Principles and practices.* New York: HarperCollins.

Duff, R. E., Brown, M. H., & Van Scoy, I. J. (1995). Reflection and self-evaluation: Keys to professional development. *Young Children, 50*(4), 81–88.

Early, D. M., Bryant, D. M., Pianta, R. C., Clifford, R.M., Burchinal, M. R., Ristchie, S., . . . Barbarin, O. (2006). Are teachers' education, major, and credentials related to classroom quality and children's academic gains in pre-kindergarten? *Early Childhood Research Quarterly, 21*(2), 174–195.

Elicker, J., & Fortner-Wood, C. (1995). Adult-child relationships in early childhood programs. *Young Children, 51*(1), 69–78.

Feeney, S., & Freeman, N. K. (1999/2005). *Ethics and the early childhood educator: Using the NAEYC Code.* Washington, DC: National Association for the Education of Young Children.

Feeney, S., Moravcik, E., Nolte, S., & Christensen, D. (2010). *Who am I in the lives of children? An introduction to early childhood education* (8th ed.). Upper Saddle River, NJ: Pearson.

Freeman, N. K., & Brown, M. H. (2000). Evaluating the child care director: The collaborative professional assessment process. *Young Children, 55*(5), 20–28.

Galinsky, E., Howes, C., Kontos, S., & Shinn, M. (1994). The study of children in family child care and relative care: Key findings and policy recommendations. *Young Children, 50*(1), 58–61.

Griffin, G. A. (Ed.). (1999). *The education of teachers: Ninety-eighth yearbook of the National Society for the Study of Education.* Chicago, IL: University of Chicago Press.

Hale-Jinks, C. M., Knopf, H., & Kemple, K. M. (2006). Tackling teacher turnover in childcare: Understanding causes and consequences, identifying solutions. *Childhood Education, 82,* 219–226.

Hayden, J. (1996). *Management of early childhood services: An Australian perspective.* Wadsworth Falls, NSW: Social Science Press.

Hebbeler, K. (1995). *Shortages in professions working with young children with disabilities and their families.* Chapel Hill, NC: National Early Childhood Technical Assistance System.

Hennig, M., & Jardin, A. (1976). *The managerial woman.* New York: Pocket Books.

Hewes, D. W. (2000). Looking back: How the role of the director has been understood, studied, and utilized in ECE programs, policy, and practice. In M. L. Culkin (Ed.), *Managing quality in young children's programs: The leader's role* (pp. 23–39). New York: Teachers College Press.

Honig, A. S. (1993). Mental health for babies: What do theory and research teach us? *Young Children, 48*(3), 69–76.

Hoy, W., & Miskel, C. (1987). *Educational administration.* New York: Random House.

Hurst, B., Wilson, C., & Cramer, G. (1998). Professional teaching portfolios: Tools for reflection, growth, and advancement. *Phi Delta Kappan, 79,* 578–582.

Jones, E. (1986). *Teaching adults: An active learning approach.* Washington, DC: National Association for the Education of Young Children.

Jones, E., & Nimmo, J. (1994). *Emergent curriculum.* Washington, DC: National Association for the Education of Young Children.

Jorde-Bloom, P. (1995). Shared decision making: The centerpiece of participatory management. *Young Children, 50*(4), 55–60.

Jorde-Bloom, P. (1997). Leadership: Defining the elusive. *Leadership Quest, 1*(1), 12–15.

Kagan, S. L. (1994). Leadership: Rethinking it—Making it happen. *Young Children, 49*(5), 50–54.

Kagan, S. L., & Bowman, B. T. (1997). Leadership in early care and education: Issues and challenges. In S. L. Kagan & B. T. Bowman (Eds.), *Leadership in early care and education* (pp. 3–8). Washington, DC: National Association for the Education of Young Children.

Kagan, S. L., Rivera, A. M., Brigham, N., & Rosenblum, S. (1992). *Collaboration: Cornerstones of an early childhood system.* New Haven, CT: Yale University, Bush Center in Child Development and Social Policy.

Katz, L. G., (1995). *Talks with teachers of young children: A collection.* Norwood, NJ: Ablex.

Kelley, R. (1991). *The power of followership: How to create leaders who people want to follow and followers who lead themselves.* New York: Doubleday.

Kisker, E. E., Hofferth, S. L., Phillips, D. A., & Farquhar, E. (1991). *A profile of child care settings: Early education and child care in 1990.* Washington, DC: U.S. Department of Education.

Kremer-Hazon, L., & Ben-Peretz, M. (1996). Becoming a teacher: The transition from teacher's college to classroom life. *International Review of Education, 32*(4), 413–422.

Lawler, E. E., Mohrman, S. A., & Ledford, G. E., Jr. (1992). *Employee involvement and total quality management.* San Francisco: Jossey-Bass.

Leithwood, K., & Jantzi, D. (2008). Linking leadership to student learning: The contributions of leader efficacy. *Educational Administration Quarterly, 44*(4), 496–528.

Likert, R. (1967). *The human organization.* New York: McGraw-Hill.

Machado, A. S. (2008). Teachers wanted: No experience necessary. *Childhood Education, 84*(5), 311–314.

Marshall, N., Creps, C., Burstein, N., Glantz, E., Roberson, W. W., & Barnett, S. (2001). *The cost and quality of full day, year-round early care and education in Massachusetts: Preschool classrooms.* (ERIC Document Reproduction Service No. ED475638)

Mitchell, A. (1996). Licensing: Lessons from other occupations. In S. L. Kagan & N. E. Cohen (Eds.), *Reinventing early care and education: A vision for a quality system* (pp. 101–123). San Francisco: Jossey-Bass.

Morgan, G. G. (2000). The director as a key to quality. In M. L. Culkin (Ed.), *Managing quality in young children's programs: The leader's role* (pp. 40–58). New York: Teachers College Press.

Morrison, A. M. (1992). *The new leaders: Guidelines on leadership diversity in America.* San Francisco: Jossey-Bass.

National Association for the Education of Young Children. (1988). Early childhood teacher education. Traditions and trends: An executive summary of colloquium proceedings. *Young Children, 44*(1), 53–57.

National Association for the Education of Young Children. (2005). *Accreditation criteria and procedures of the National Academy of Early Childhood Programs.* Washington, DC: Author.

National Association for the Education of Young Children. (2009). *NAEYC Standards for early childhood professional preparation programs.* Washington, DC: Author. Retrieved from www.naeyc.org/files/naeyc/file/positions/ProfPrepStandards09.pdf

National Child Care Information Center (NCCIC). (n.d.). *Early childhood professional development systems toolkit–Qualifications, credentials, and pathways.* Washington, DC: U.S. Department of Health & Human Services. Retrieved from nccic.acf.hhs.gov/pubs/goodstart/pd_section6.html

National Child Care Information Center & National Association for Regulatory Administration (NCCIC/NARA). (2010). *The 2008 child care licensing study.* Lexington, KY: National Association for Regulatory Administration. Retrieved from www.naralicensing.org/Licensing_Study

National Early Childhood Accountability Task Force. (2007). *Taking stock: Assessing and improving early childhood learning and program quality.* Philadelphia, PA: Foundation for Child Development, Pew Charitable Trust, Joyce Foundation.

National Research Council and Institute of Medicine. (2000). *Early childhood intervention: Views from the field. Report of a workshop.* Washington, DC: National Academy Press.

Neugebauer, R. (2000). What is management ability? In M. L. Culkin (Ed.), *Managing quality in young children's programs: The leader's role* (pp. 97–111). New York: Teachers College Press.

Newman, M., Rutter, R. A., & Smith, M. S. (1989). Organizational factors that affect school sense of efficacy, community, and expectations. *Sociology of Education, 62,* 221–238.

Newman, S. B., Vander Ven, K., & Ward, C. R. (1992). *Guidelines for the productive employment of older adults in child care.* Pittsburgh, PA: Generations Together.

Olson, L. (2002). Starting early. Quality Counts 2002: Building blocks for success. *Education Week, 21*(17), 10–12, 14, 16, 18–22.

Pew Research Center. (2010). The decline of marriage and the rise of new families. Philadelphia, PA: Author. Retrieved from www.pewsocialtrends.org/files/2010/11/pew-social-trends-2010-families.pdf

Phillips, D., Mekos, D., Scarr, S., McCartney, K., & Abbott-Shim, M. (2000). Within and beyond the classroom door: Assessing quality in child care centers. *Early Childhood Research Quarterly, 15*(4), 475–496.

Piscitelli, B. (2000). Practicing what we preach: Active learning in the development of early childhood professionals. In N. J. Yelland (Ed.), *Promoting meaningful learning: Innovations in educating early childhood professionals* (pp. 37–46). Washington, DC: National Association for the Education of Young Children.

Pratt, C. (1948). *I learn from children.* New York: Simon & Schuster.

Quality, Compensation, and Affordability. (1998). The updated staffing study: A valuable resource for advocates. *Young Children, 53*(5), 42–43.

Rand, M. K. (2000). *Giving it some thought: Cases for early childhood practice.* Washington, DC: National Association for the Education of Young Children.

Rodd, J. (1998). *Leadership in early childhood: The pathway to professionalism* (2nd ed.). New York: Teachers College Press.

Rosenholtz, S. J., Bassler, D., & Hoover-Dempsey, K. (1986). Organizational conditions of teacher learning. *Teaching and Teacher Education, 2*(2), 91–104.

Ryan, S., Whitebook, M., Kipnis, F., & Sakai, L. (2011). Professional development needs of directors leading in a mixed service delivery preschool system. *Early Childhood Research to Practice, 13*(1), 1–14. Retrieved from ecrp.uiuc.edu/v13n1/ryan.html

Schiller, P., & Dyke, P. C. (2001). *The practical guide to quality child care.* Beltsville, MD: Gryphon.

Schneider, A. M. (1991, November). *Mentoring women and minorities into positions of educational leadership: Gender differences and implications for mentoring.* Paper presented at the annual conference of the National Council of States on Inservice Education, Houston, TX. (ERIC Document Reproduction Service No. ED344843)

Sciarra, D. J., & Dorsey, A. G. (1998). *Developing and administering child care centers* (4th ed.). Albany, NY: Delmar.

Shoemaker, C. J. (2000). *Leadership and management of programs for young children* (2nd ed.). Upper Saddle River, NJ: Pearson.

Smylie, M. (1992). Teacher participation in school decision making: Assessing willingness to participate. *Educational Evaluation and Policy Analysis, 14*(1), 53–67.

Stott, E., & Bowman, B. (1996). Child development knowledge: A slippery base for practice. *Early Childhood Research Quarterly, 11,* 169–183.

Taking the Lead Initiative. (1999). *The many faces of leadership.* Boston, MA: Wheelock College, Center for Career Development in Early Care and Education.

Taking the Lead Initiative. (2000). *The power of mentoring.* Boston, MA: Wheelock College, Center for Career Development in Early Care and Education.

Talan, T. N., & Bloom, P. J. (2004). *Program administration scale: Measuring early childhood leadership and management.* New York: Teachers College.

Tertell, E. A., Klein, S. M., & Jewett, J. L. (Eds.). (1998). *When teachers reflect: Journeys toward effective, inclusive practice.* Washington, DC: National Association for the Education of Young Children.

Title 5, Section 552a, U.S. Code 2011, Edition in force on January 7, 2011. Retrieved from uscode.house.gov/uscode-cgi/fastweb.exe? getdoc+uscview+t05t08+27+0++%28%29%20%20AND%20 %28%285%29%20ADJ%20USC%29%3ACITE%20AND%20 %28USC%20w%2F10%20%28552a%29%29%3ACITE%20%20% 20%20%20%20%20%20%20

Trawick-Smith, J., & Lambert, L. (1995). The unique challenges of the family child care provider: Implications for professional development. *Young Children, 50*(3), 25–32.

United States Census Bureau (2010). Retrieved from 2010.census. gov/2010census/data/

Wesley, P. W. (2002). Early intervention consultants in the classroom: Simple steps for building strong collaboration. *Young Children, 57*(4), 30–35.

Whitebook, M. (2010). Working for worthy wages: The child care movement, 1970–2001. Retrieved from www.ccw.org/storage/ ccworkforce/documents/publications/worthywages.pdf

Whitebook, M., & Sakai, L. (2003). Turnover begets turnover: An examination of job and occupational instability among child care center staff. *Early Childhood Research Quarterly, 18,* 273–293.

Whitebook, M., Hnatiuk, P., & Bellm, D. (1994). *Mentoring in early care and education: Refining an emerging career path.* Washington, DC: Center for the Child Care Workforce.

Whitebook, M., Sakai, L., Gerber, E., & Howes, C. (2001). Then & now: Changes in child care staffing, 1994–2000 (Technical Report). Washington, DC: Center for the Child Care Workforce.

Willer, B. (Ed.). (1994). A conceptual framework for early childhood professional development: NAEYC position statement, adopted November 1993. In J. Johnson & J. B. McCracken (Eds.), *The early childhood career lattice: Perspectives on professional development* (pp. 4–21). Washington, DC: National Association for the Education of Young Children.

Chapter 6

American Academy of Pediatrics, American Public Health Association, and National Resource Center for Health and Safety in Child Care, (2011). *Caring for our children: National health and safety performance standards: Guidelines for out-of-home child care programs,* (3rd ed.). Elk Grove Village, IL: American Academy of Pediatrics and Washington, DC: American Public Health Association. Retrieved nrckids.org/CFOC3/PDFVersion/list.html

Americans with Disabilities Act. Retrieved from www.usdoj.gov/crt/ ada/adahom1.htm

Baker, K. R. (1968). Extending the indoors outside. In S. Sunderlin & N. Gray (Eds.), *Housing for early childhood education* (pp. 59–70). Olney, MD: Association for Childhood Education International.

Beaty, J. J. (1996). *Preschool appropriate practices* (2nd ed.). Orlando, FL: Harcourt, Brace.

Bergen, D., Reid, R., & Torelli, L. (2001). *Educating and caring for very young children. The infant/toddler curriculum.* New York: Teachers College Press.

Berry, P. (1993). Young children's use of fixed playground equipment. *International Play Journal, 1,* 115–131.

Bodrova, E., & Leong, D. J. (2003). Do play and foundational skills need to compete for the teacher's attention in an early childhood classroom? *Young Children, 58*(3), 10–17.

Boutte, G., Van Scoy, I., & Hendley, S. G. (1996). Multicultural and nonsexist prop boxes. *Young Children, 52*(1), 34–39.

Bredekamp, S., & Copple, C. (Eds.). (1997). *Developmentally appropriate practice in early childhood programs: Revised.* Washington, DC: National Association for the Education of Young Children.

Bullard, J. (2010). *Creating environments for learning.* Upper Saddle River, NJ: Pearson.

Caples, S. E. (1996). Some guidelines for preschool design. *Young Children, 51*(4), 14–21.

Cavallaro, C. C., Haney, M., & Cabello, B. (1993). Developmentally appropriate strategies for promoting full participation in early childhood settings. *Topics in Early Childhood Special Education, 13,* 293–307.

Cradock, A. L., O'Donnell, E. M., Benjamin, S. E., Walker, E., & Slining, M. (2010.) A review of state regulations to promote physical activity and safety on playgrounds in child care centers and family child care homes. *Journal of Physical Activity & Health* 7(Supplement 1), 108–119.

Cryer, D., Harms, T., & Riley, C. (2003). *All about the ECERS-R: A detailed guide in words and pictures to be used with the ECERS-R.* Lewisville, NC: Pact House Publishing.

Curtis, D., & Carter, M. (2003). *Designs for living and learning: Transforming early childhood environments.* St. Paul, MN: Redleaf Press.

DeBord, K., Hestenes, L. L., Moore, R. C., Cosco, N., & McGinnis, J. R. (2002). Paying attention to the outdoor environment is as important as preparing the indoor environment. *Young Children, 57*(3), 32–35.

Edwards, L., & Torcellini, P. (2002). *A literature review of the effects of natural light on building occupants.* Golden, CO: National Renewable Energy Laboratory. Retrieved from www.nrel.gov/ docs/fy02osti/30769.pdf

Energy Independence and Security Act (originally named the Clean Energy Act) of 2007. Public Law 110-140, 110th Congress (2007) (enacted). Retrieved from frwebgate.access.gpo.gov/cgi-bin/get-doc.cgi?dbname=110_cong_public_laws&docid=f:publ140.110. pdf

Frost, J. L. (1992). *Play and playscapes.* Albany, NY: Delmar.

Frost, J. L. (2001). *Children and injuries.* Tuscon, AZ: Lawyers & Judges Publishing Company, Inc.

Frost, J. L., Wortham, S., & Reifel, S. (2012). *Play and child development* (4th ed.). Upper Saddle River, NJ: Pearson.

Gonzalez-Mena, J. & Eyer, D. W. (2009). *Infants, toddlers, and caregivers* (7th ed.). Boston, MA: McGraw Hill.

Greenman, J. T. (2005). *Caring spaces, learning places: Children's environments that work* (rev. ed.). Redmond, WA: Exchange Press.

Greenman, J. T., & Stonehouse, A. (1996). *Prime times: A handbook for excellence in infant and toddler programs.* St. Paul, MN: Redleaf.

Guddemi, M., & Eriksen, H. (1992). Designing outdoor learning environments for and with children. *Dimensions of Early Childhood, 20*(4), 15–24, 40.

Harms, T., Clifford, R. M., & Cryer, D. (2005). *Early Childhood Environment Rating Scale–Revised.* New York: Teachers College Press.

Harms, T., Cryer, D., & Clifford, R. M. (2006). *Infant/Toddler Environment Rating Scale–Revised* New York: Teachers College Press.

Harms, T., Jacobs, E. V., & White, D. R. (1995). *School-Age Care Environment Rating Scale*. New York: Teachers College Press.

Henniger, M. L. (1993). Enriching the outdoor play experience. *Childhood Education, 70,* 87–90.

Henniger, M. L. (1994). Planning for outdoor play. *Young Children, 49*(4), 10–15.

Hirsh, E. S. (Ed.). (1996). *The block book* (3rd ed.). Washington, DC: NAEYC.

Howes, C. (1983). Caregiver behavior in center and family day care. *Journal of Applied Developmental Psychology, 4,* 99–107.

Hurd, F. (2009). Carpet aids learning in high performance schools. *Educational Facility Planner, 43*(4), 19–22.

Hyson, M. C. (1994). *The emotional development of young children: Building an emotion-centered curriculum*. New York: Teachers College Press.

Jensen, B. J., & Bullard, J. A. (2002). The mud center: Recapturing childhood. *Young Children, 57*(3), 16–19.

Johnson, H. S., & Maki, J. A. (2009). Color sense. *American School & University, 81*(13), 143–145.

Johnson, J. E., Christie, J. F., & Yawkey, T. D. (1999). *Play and early childhood development* (2nd ed.). Upper Saddle River, NJ: Allyn & Bacon/Longman/Pearson Education.

Katz, L. G., & Chard, S. C. (2000). *Engaging children's minds: The project approach* (2nd ed.). Norwood, NJ: Ablex.

Klein, T. P., Wirth, D., & Linas, K. (2003). Play: Children's context for development. *Young Children, 58*(3), 38–45.

Knopf, H. T., & Welsh, K. (2010). Infant/toddler materials guide. Columbia, SC: SCPITC.

Koralek, D. (2002). Let's go outside! Outdoor settings for play and learning. *Young Children, 57*(3), 8–9.

Kostelnik, M. J., Soderman, A. K., & Whiren, A. P. (2007). *Developmentally appropriate curriculum: Best practices in early childhood education* (4th ed.). Upper Saddle River, NJ: Pearson.

Lally, J. R., Griffin, A., Fenichel, E., Segal, M. M., Szanton, E. S., & Weissbourd, B. (1995). *Caring for infants and toddlers in groups: Developmentally appropriate practice*. Arlington, VA: ZERO TO THREE.

Lally, J. R., Provence, S., Szanton, E., & Weissbourd, B. (1986). Developmentally appropriate care for children from birth to age 3. In S. Bredekamp (Ed.), *Developmentally appropriate practice in early childhood programs serving children from birth through age 8* (exp. ed., pp. 17–33). Washington, DC: National Association for the Education of Young Children.

Lally, J. R., & Stewart, J. (1990). *Infant/toddler caregiving: A guide to setting up environments*. Sacramento, CA: Far West Laboratory for Educational Development and California Department of Education Press.

Maxwell, L. E. (2007). Competency in child care settings: The role of the physical environment. *Environment and Behavior, 39,* 229–245.

Meltz, B. F. (1990, December 4). A little privacy: Children need a space to call their own. *Tallahassee Democrat,* p. D1.

Myhre, S. M. (1993). Enhancing your dramatic-play area through the use of prop boxes. *Young Children, 48*(5), 6–11.

National Association for the Education of Young Children. (1998). *Accreditation criteria and procedures of the National Association for the Education of Young Children*. Washington, DC: Author.

National Association for the Education of Young Children Academy for Early Childhood Program Accreditation. (2005). *NAEYC Early Childhood Program Standards*. Washington, DC: Author. Retrieved from www.naeyc.org/academy/primary/viewstandards

O'Donnell, J., & Koch, W. (2011, February 8). Some consumers resist "green" light bulbs. *USA Today*. Retrieved from www.usatoday.com/tech/science/environment/2011-02-07-lightbulbs_N.htm

Olds, A. R. (2001). *Child care design guide*. New York: McGraw-Hill.

Olsen, H., Hudson, S. D., & Thompson, D. (2010). Strategies for playground injury prevention: An overview of a playground project. *American Journal of Health Education, 41*(3),187–192.

Osmon, F. (1971). *Patterns for designing children's centers*. New York: Educational Facilities Laboratories.

Perry, J. P. (2003). Making sense of outdoor pretend play. *Young Children, 58*(3), 26–30.

Poest, C. A., Williams, J. R., Witt, D. D., & Atwood, M. E. (1990). Challenge me to move: Large muscle development in young children. *Young Children, 45*(5), 4–10.

Prescott, E. (1987). The environment as organizer of intent in child-care. In C. S. Weinstein & T. G. David (Eds.), *Spaces for children: The built environment and child development* (pp. 73–86). New York: Plenum.

Read, M. A. (2007). Sense of place in early childhood environments. *Early Childhood Education Journal, 34*(6), 387–392.

Read, M. A., & Upington, D. (2009). Young children's color preferences in the interior environment. *Early Childhood Education Journal, 36,* 491–496.

Rivkin, M. S. (1995). *The great outdoors: Restoring children's right to play outside*. Washington, DC: National Association for the Education of Young Children.

Shade, D. D. (1996). Software evaluation. *Young Children, 51*(6), 17–21.

Sosna, D. (2000). More about woodworking with young children. *Young Children, 55*(2), 38–39.

Stewart, W. (2009). The components of good acoustics in a high performing school. *Educational Facility Planner, 43*(4), 28–30.

Talbot, J., & Frost, J. L. (1989). Magical playscapes. *Childhood Education, 66,* 11–19.

Tarr, P. (2004). Consider the walls. *Young Children 59*(3), 88–92.

Thompson, D., & Hudson, S. (2003). The inside information about safety surfacing. *Young Children, 58*(2), 108–111.

Tinsworth, D., & McDonald, J. (2001). *Special study: Injuries and deaths associated with children's playground equipment*. Washington, DC: U.S. Consumer Product Safety Commission.

Torelli, L., & Durrett, C. (n.d.). *Landscapes for learning: The impact of classroom design on infants and toddlers*. Retrieved from www.spacesforchildren.com/impact.html

Trawick-Smith, J. (1992). How the classroom environment affects play and development: Review of the research. *Dimensions of Early Childhood, 20*(2), 27–30.

U.S. Consumer Project Safety Commission (USCPSC). (2008). *Public playground safety handbook*. Retrieved from http://www.cpsc.gov/cpscpub/pubs/325.pdf

Wallach, F., & Edelstein, S. (1991). *Analysis of state regulations for elementary schools focused on playgrounds and supervision*. New York: Total Recreation Management Services.

West, S., & Cox, A. (2001). *Sand and water play: Simple, creative activities for young children*. Beltsville, MD: Gryphon.

Winter, S. M., Bell, M. J., & Dempsey, J. D. (1994). Creating play environments for children with special needs. *Childhood Education, 71,* 28–32.

Chapter 7

Adams, G., & Poersch, N. O. (1997). Who cares? State commitment to child care and early education. *Young Children, 52*(4), 66–69.

Barbett, S., & Korb, R. A. (1999). *Current funds, revenues, and expenditures of degree-granting institutions: Fiscal year 1996*.

Washington, DC: U.S. Department of Education, Office of Educational Research and Improvement.

Barnett, W. S., Epstein, D. J., Carolan, M. E., Fitzgerald, J., Ackerman, D. J., &. Friedman, A. H. (2010). *The state of preschool 2010*. New Brunswick, NJ: National Institute for Early Education Research (NIEER). Retrieved from nieer.org/yearbook/

Bellm, D., Breuning, G. S., Lombardi, J., & Whitebook, M. (1992). On the horizon: New policy initiatives to enhance child care staff compensation. *Young Children, 47*(5), 39–42.

Brandon, R. N., Kagan, S. L., & Joesch, J. M. (2000). *Design choices: Universal financing for early care and education*. Seattle: University of Washington.

Bureau of Labor Statistics, U.S. Department of Labor. (2009). *Occupational outlook handbook, 2010–11 edition: Child care workers*. Retrieved from www.bls.gov/oco/ocos170.htm

Carnegie Corporation of New York. (1996). *Years of promise: A comprehensive learning strategy for America's children*. New York: Author.

Center for the Child Care Workforce. (2000). *Current data on child care salaries and benefits in the United States*. Washington, DC: Author.

Child Care and Development Fund Report for State and Territory Plans. (2011). Retrieved from http://nccic.acf.hhs.gov/files/resources/sp1011full-report.pdf

Cost, Quality, and Child Outcomes Study Team. (1995). *Cost, quality, and child outcomes in child care centers, Public report* (2nd ed.). Denver: University of Colorado–Denver, Economics Department.

Education Week. (2000, January). *Special report: Quality Counts 2000: Who should teach?* Washington, DC: Editorial Projects in Education, Inc.

Einbinder, S. D., & Bond, J. T. (1992). *Five million children: 1992 update*. New York: National Center for Children in Poverty.

Hayes, C. D., Palmer, J. L., & Zaslow, M. (1990). *Who cares for America's children: Child care policy for the 1990s*. Washington, DC: National Academy Press.

Howes, C., Smith, E., & Galinsky, E. (1998). *The Florida child care quality improvement study: 1996 report*. New York: Families and Work Institute.

Kagan, S. L. (2000). Financing the field: From mistakes to high stakes. *Young Children, 55*(3), 4–5.

Mitchell, A., & Morgan, G. G. (2001). *New perspectives on compensation strategies*. Boston, MA: Wheelock College, Institute for Leadership and Career Initiatives.

Morgan, G. G. (1999). *The bottom line for children's programs: What you need to know to manage the money*. Watertown, MA: Steam Press.

National Association of Child Care Resource & Referral Agencies. (2010). *State budget cuts: America's kids pay the price*. Arlington, VA: Author. Retrieved from www.naccrra.org/policy/economic-stimulus-briefing-room/docs/January6FinalNACECMVOI.pdf

National Association of Child Care Resource and Referral Agencies. (2011). *Research and data*. Retrieved from www.naccrra.org/randd/

National Association for the Education of Young Children Policy Brief. (2001). Financing the early childhood education system. *Young Children, 56*(4), 54–57.

National Center for Education Statistics. (1997). *The condition of education 1997*. Washington, DC: U.S. Department of Education.

National Institute for Early Education Research. (2011). *Latest research*. Retrieved from http://nieer.org/docs/index.php?DocID=120

National Research Council. (2001). *Eager to learn: Educating our preschoolers*. B T. Bowman, S. Donovan, & M. S. Burns (Eds.). Washington, DC: National Academy Press.

National Women's Law Center. (2009). *Campaign aims to inform families about tax credits*. Retrieved from www.nwlc.org/press-release/campaign-aims-inform-families-about-tax-credits-0

Neugebauer, R. (1993a). Employer interest in child care growing and diversifying. *Child Care Information Exchange, 94*, 66–72.

Neugebauer, R. (1993b). State-of-the-art thinking on parent fee policies. *Child Care Information Exchange, 94*, 4–12.

Odom, S. L., Wolery, R. A., Lieber, J., & Horn, E. (2002). Social policy and preschool inclusion. In S. L. Odom (Ed.), *Widening the circle: Including children with disabilities in preschool programs* (pp. 120–136). New York: Teachers College Press.

Olenick, M. (1986). *The relationship between day-care quality and selected social policy variables*. Unpublished doctoral dissertation, University of California, Los Angeles.

Powell, I., Eisenberg, D. R., Moy, L., & Vogel, J. (1994). Costs and characteristics of high-quality early childhood education programs. *Child and Youth Care Forum, 23*, 103–118.

Queralt, M., & Witte, A. D. (1998). Influences on neighborhood supply of child care in Massachusetts. *Social Service Review, 17*, 17–47.

Rohacek, M. H., & Russell, S. D. (1998). Public policy report. Child care subsidy yields returns. *Young Children, 53*(2), 68–71.

Sandham, J. L. (2002). Adequate financing. Quality Counts 2002: Building blocks for success. *Education Week, 21*(17), 43–46.

Schulman, K., & Adams, G. (1998). *The high cost of child care puts quality care out of reach for many families*. Washington, DC: Children's Defense Fund.

Schulman, K., & Blank, H. (2002). State child care assistance policies. *Young Children, 57*(1), 66–69.

Schulman, K., Blank, H., & Ewen, D. (2001). *A fragile foundation: State child care assistance policies*. Washington, DC: Children's Defense Fund.

SELF-HELP North Carolina Community Facilities Fund. (2002). *The business side of child care: A reference manual for child care advocates and lenders*. Durham, NC. Retrieved from www.self-help.org/business-and-nonprofit-loans/business-and-nonprofit-files/business-nonprofit-technical-assistance-resources/Business.Side.of.Child.Care.Manual.pdf

Sosinsky, L. S., Lord, H., & Zigler, E. (2007). For-profit/nonprofit differences in center-based child care quality: Results from the National Institute of Child Health and Human Development Study of Early Care and Youth Development. *Journal of Applied Developmental Psychology, 28*(5–6), 390–410.

Stephens, K. (1991). *Confronting your bottom line: Financial guide for child care centers*. Redmond, WA: Exchange Press.

Stoney, L. (1999). Looking into new mirrors: Lessons for early childhood finance and system building. *Young Children, 54*(3), 54–57.

Stoney, L., & Greenberg, M. (1996). The financing of child care: Current and emerging trends. Special issue on financing child care. *Future of Children, 6*(2), 83–102.

U.S. Bureau of Labor Statistics. (2008). *Occupational employment statistics (OES) program survey*. Washington, DC: U.S. Department of Labor.

U.S. Bureau of the Census. (1997). *Who's minding our preschoolers?* Washington, DC: U.S. Department of Commerce.

U.S. Department of Health and Human Services. (1999). *Access to child care for low-income working families*. Washington, DC: Author.

Vandell, D. L., & Wolfe, B. (2000). *Child care quality: Does it matter and does it need to be improved?* Washington, DC: Department of Health and Human Services.

Whitebook, M., & Eichberg, A. (2002). Finding a better way: Defining policies to improve child care workforce compensation. *Young Children, 57*(3), 66–72.

Whitebook, M. (2002). *Working for worthy wages. The child care compensation movement, 1970–2001.* New York: Foundation for Child Development.

Willer, B. (1990). Estimating the full cost of quality. In B. Willer (Ed.), *Reaching the full cost of quality in early childhood programs* (pp. 1–8). Washington, DC: National Association for the Education of Young Children.

Willer, B. (1992). An overview of the demand and supply of child care in 1990. *Young Children, 47*(2), 19–22.

Chapter 8

American Marketing Association. (2011). *Marketing definitions.* Retrieved from www.marketingpower.com/AboutAMA/Pages/DefinitionofMarketing.aspx

Godin, S. (2002). *Purple cow.* New York: Portfolio.

Hiam, A. (2004). *Marketing for dummies* (2nd ed.). Indianapolis, IN: Wiley Publishing.

Lamb, C. W., Hair, J. F., & McDaniel, C. (2006). *Essentials of marketing* (6th ed.). Winfield, KS: Southwestern College Press.

McNamara, C. (2007). *All about marketing.* Retrieved from www.managementhelp.org/mrktng/mrktng.htm

Chapter 9

Barnett, W. S. (2008). *Preschool education and its lasting effects: Research and policy implications.* Boulder, CO, and Tempe, AZ: Education and the Public Interest Center & Education Policy Research Unit.

Baumel, J. (2010, February). *Understanding special education laws and rights: A parent's guide to the many layers of special education law.* Retrieved from www.greatschools.org/special-education/legal-rights/524-understanding-special-education-laws-and-rights.gs?page=all

Behrmann, M. M., & Lahm, E. A. (1994). Computer applications in early childhood special education. In J. L. Wright & D. D. Shade (Eds.), *Young children: Active learners in a technological age* (pp. 105–120). Washington, DC: National Association for the Education of Young Children.

Belfield, C. R., Nores, M., Barnett, S., & Schweinhart, L. (2006). *The High/Scope Perry Preschool Program: Cost-benefit analysis using data from the age-40 follow-up study.* Center for Cost-Benefit Studies of Education Teachers College, Columbia University. Retrieved from www.cbcse.org/media/download_gallery/High%20Scope%20Perry%20Preschool.pdf

Bergen, D. (1994). Teaching strategies: Developing the art and science of team teaching. *Childhood Education, 70,* 300–301.

Bergen, D., & Coscia, J. (2001). *Brain research and childhood education: Implications for educators.* Olney, MD: Association for Childhood Education International.

Betz, C. (1994). Beyond time-out: Tips from a teacher. *Young Children, 49*(3), 10–14.

Birckmayer, J., Kennedy, A., & Stonehouse, A. (2008). *From lullabies to literature: Stories in the lives of infants and toddlers.* Washington, DC: National Association for the Education of Young Children.

Bontá, P., & Silverman, B. (1993). Making learning entertaining. In N. Estes & M. Thomas (Eds.), *Rethinking the roles of technology in education* (pp. 1150–1152). Cambridge: Massachusetts Institute of Technology.

Bransford, J., Brown, A. L., & Cocking, R. R. (Eds). (1999). *How people learn: Brain, mind, experience and school.* Washington, DC: National Research Council.

Bredekamp, S., & Rosegrant, T. (1995). Reaching potentials through national standards: Panacea or pipe dream? In S. Bredekamp & T. Rosegrant (Eds.), *Reaching potentials: Transforming early childhood curriculum and assessment* (Vol. 2, pp. 5–14). Washington, DC: National Association for the Education of Young Children.

Brenneman, K., Stevenson-Boyd, J., & Frede, E. C. (2010). *Math and science in preschool: Policies and practice* [policy brief]. National Institute Early Education Research, Graduate School of Education, Rutgers. Retrieved from nieer.org/resources/policybriefs/20.pdf

Bronfenbrenner, U. (1989). Ecological systems theory. *Annals of Child Development, 6,* 187–224.

Caldwell, B. M. (1991). Continuity in the early years: Transitions between grades and systems. In S. L. Kagan (Ed.), *The care and education of America's young children: Obstacles and opportunities* (pp. 69–90). Chicago, IL: University of Chicago Press.

Cardelle-Elawar, M., & Wetzel, K. (1995). Students and computers as partners in developing students' problem-solving skills. *Journal of Research on Computing in Education, 27,* 378–401.

Carlisle, A. (2001). Using multiple intelligences theory to assess early childhood curricula. *Young Children, 56*(6), 77–83.

Carter, M. (2010). Helping teachers think about technology. *Exchange, 32*(1), 30–33.

Chaille, C., & Britain, L. (1991). *The young child as scientist: A constructivist approach to early childhood education.* New York: HarperCollins.

Chaille, C., & Britain, L. (1997). *The young child as scientist: A constructivist approach to early childhood science education.* New York: Longman.

Chipman, M. (1997). Valuing cultural diversity in the early years: Social imperatives and pedagogical insights. In J. P. Isenberg & M. R. Jalongo (Eds.), *Major trends and issues in early childhood education* (pp. 43–55). New York: Teachers College Press.

Clements, D. H., & Nastasi, B. K. (1992). Computers and early childhood education. In M. Gettinger, S. N. Elliott, & T. R. Kratochwill (Eds.), *Preschool and early childhood treatment directions* (pp. 187–246). Hillsdale, NJ: Erlbaum.

Clements, D. H., Sarama, J., & DiBiase, A.-M. (Eds.). (2003). *Engaging young children in mathematics: Findings of the 2000 National Conference on Standards for Preschool and Kindergarten Mathematics Education.* Mahwah, NJ: Erlbaum.

Clewett, A. S. (1988). Guidance and discipline: Teaching young children appropriate behavior. *Young Children, 43*(4), 25–36.

Copple, C., & Bredekamp, S. (Eds.). (2009). *Developmentally appropriate practice in early childhood programs* (3rd ed). Washington, DC: National Association for the Education of Young Children.

Couse, L. J., & Chen, D. W. (2010). A tablet computer for young children? Exploring its viability for early childhood education. *Journal of Research on Technology in Education, 43*(1), 75–98.

Daily, S., Burkhauser, M., & Halle, T. (2010). A review of school readiness practices in the states: Early learning guidelines and assessments. *Early Childhood Highlights, 1*(3). Retrieved from http://www.childtrends.org/Files/Child_Trends-2010_06_18_ECH_SchoolReadiness.pdf

Day, C. B. (2006) Leveraging diversity to benefit children's social-emotional development and school readiness. In B. Bowman &

E. K. Moore (Eds.), *School readiness and social-emotional development: Perspectives on cultural diversity* (pp. 23–32). Washington, DC: National Black Child Development Institute, Inc.

Denning, R., & Smith, P. (1997). Cooperative learning and technology. *Journal of Computers in Mathematics and Science Teaching, 16,* 177–200.

Derman-Sparks, L., & A.B.C. Task Force. (1989). *Anti-bias curriculum: Tools for empowering young children.* Washington, DC: National Association for the Education of Young Children.

Derman-Sparks, L., & Edwards, J. O. (2010). *Anti-bias education for young children and ourselves.* Washington, DC: National Association for the Education of Young Children.

Desouza, J. M., & Staley, L. M. (2002). The Reggio Emilia philosophy inspires scientific inquiry: A professional development model. *Dimensions of Early Childhood,* (winter), 3–8.

Devereux Early Childhood Initiative. (Ed.). (2011). *Prevalence of preschool protective factors as perceived by parents and teachers* (Rep. No. 2). Retrieved from www.devereux.org/site/DocServer/Bulletin-2.pdf?docID=3564

DeVries, R., Reese-Learned, H., & Morgan, P. (1991). Socio-moral development in direct-instruction, eclectic, and constructivist kindergartens: A study of children's enacted interpersonal understanding. *Early Childhood Research Quarterly, 6,* 473–517.

Dewey, J. (1916). *Democracy and education: An introduction to the philosophy of education.* New York: Macmillan.

Diener, P. L. (2009). *Inclusive early childhood education: Development, resource and practice.* Belmont, CA: Wadsworth Cengage Learning.

Dodge, D. T., Jablon, J., & Bickart, T. S. (1994). *Constructing curriculum for the primary grades.* Washington, DC: Teaching Strategies.

Dogget, L., & Wat, A. (2010). Why preK for all. *Phi Delta Kappan, 92*(3), 8–11. Retrieved from www.kappanmagazine.org/content/92/3/8.abstract

Dozier, M. K., Stovall, K. C., & Albus, K. E. (1999). Attachment and psychopathology in adulthood. In J. Cassidy & P. R. Shaver (Eds.), *Handbook of attachment: Theory, research and clinical applications* (pp. 671–687). New York: Guilford Press.

Drew, W. F., Christie, J., Johnson, J. E., Meckley, A.M., & Nell, M.L. (2008). Constructive play: A value-added strategy for meeting early learning standards. *Young Children, 63*(4), 38–44.

Dunn, T. D. (2009). Strategies for building classroom community. *Teaching Young Children, 3*(2), 28–29.

Elkind, D. (1998). Computers for infants and young children. *Child Care Information Exchange, 123,* 44–46.

Elkind, D. (2006). The values of outdoor play. *Exchange, 171,* 6–8.

Epstein, A. S. (2009). *Me, you, us: Social-emotional learning in preschool.* Ypsilanti, MI, & Washington, DC: High/Scope Press & The National Association for the Education of Young Children.

Espinosa, L. (2010). *Getting it right for young children from diverse backgrounds: Applying research to improve practice.* Upper Saddle River, NJ & Washington, DC: Pearson Learning Solutions & the National Association for the Education of Young Children.

Essa, E. L., Favre, K., Thweatt, G., & Waugh, S. (1999). Continuity of care for infants and toddlers. *Early Child Development and Care, 148,* 11–19.

Every Child Ready to Read. (2011). *Read. Learn. Grow.* American Library Association. Retrieved from www.everychildreadytoread.org/

Fedor v. Mauwehu Council of Boy Scouts, 143 A.2d 466 (Conn. 1958).

Fox, S. (2003, July/August). A puzzling learning tool: Understanding technology as a learning tool. *Child Care Information Exchange, 152,* 40–74.

Freeman, N. K., & Somerindyke, J. (2001). Social play at the computer: Preschoolers scaffold and support peers' computer competence. *Information Technology in Childhood Education Annual, 2001*(1), 203–213.

Friedman, S. L., & Haywood, H. C. (Eds.). (1994). *Developmental follow-up: Concepts, domains, and methods.* San Diego: Academic Press.

Fromberg, D. P. (2002). *Play and meaning in early childhood education.* Boston, MA: Allyn & Bacon.

Frost, J. L., Wortham, S. C., & Reifel, S. (2012). *Play and child development* (4th ed.). Upper Saddle River, NJ: Pearson.

Gallagher, K. C., & Mayer, K. (2008). Enhancing development and learning through teacher-child relationships. *Young Children, 63*(6), 80–87.

Gardner, H. (1993). *Multiple intelligences: The theory in practice.* New York: Basic/HarperCollins.

Gartin, B. C., & Murdick, N. L. (2005). Idea 2004: The IEP. *Remedial and Special Education, 26*(6), 327–331. doi:10.1177/07419325050260060301

Gartrell, D. J. (1995). Misbehavior or mistaken behavior? *Young Children, 50*(5), 27–34.

Gartrell, D. J. (1998). *A guidance approach for the encouraging classroom.* Albany, NY: Delmar.

Gartrell, D. J. (2000). *What the kids said today.* St. Paul, MN: Redleaf.

Gilliam, W. S. (2005). Prekindergarteners left behind: Expulsion rates in state prekindergarten systems. New America Foundation. Retrieved from www.newamerica.net/blog/topics/pre-k?page=20

Gonzalez-Mena, J. (2008). *Diversity in early care and education: Honoring differences* (5th ed.). Boston, MA: McGraw-Hill.

Gonzalez-Mena, J., & Eyer, D. W. (2011). *Infants, toddlers, and caregivers* (9th ed.). Boston, MA: McGraw-Hill.

Greenman, J. T. (2001). *What happened to the world? Helping children cope in turbulent times.* South Watertown, MA: Bright Horizons Family Solutions.

Gronlund, G. (2008). Creative and thoughtful strategies for implementing learning standards: Standards, standards everywhere. *Young Children, 63*(4) 10–13.

Hart, C. H., Burts, D. C., & Charlesworth, R. (Eds.). (1997). *Integrated curriculum and developmentally appropriate practice—Birth to age eight.* Albany: State University of New York Press.

Hatch, J. A. (2002). Accountability showdown: Resisting the standards movement in early education. *Phi Delta Kappan, 83,* 457–462.

Haugen, K. (1998). Using technology to enhance early learning experiences. *Child Care Information Exchange, 123,* 47–50.

Haugland, S. W. (1992). Effects of computer software on preschool children's developmental gains. *Journal of Computing in Childhood Education, 3*(1), 15–30.

Haugland, S. W. (1999). What role should technology play in young children's learning? *Young Children, 54*(6), 26–31.

Haugland, S. W., & Wright, J. L. (1997). *Young children and technology: A world of discovery.* Boston, MA: Allyn & Bacon.

Head Start Office in Administration for Children and Families. (2007). *Head Start reauthorization P.L. 110–134.* Retrieved from www.acf.hhs.gov/programs/ohs/policy/im2008/acfimhs_08_01_a1.html

Head Start Office in Administration for Children and Families (2010). *Head Start child development and learning framework: Promoting positive outcomes in early childhood programs serving children 3–5 years old.* Washington, DC: U.S. Department of Health and Human Services, Administrator for Children and Families. Retrieved from http://eclkc.ohs.acf.hhs.gov/hslc/tta-system/teaching/eecd/Assessment/Child%20Outcomes/HS_Revised_Child_Outcomes_Framework(rev-Sept2011).pdf

Heidemann, S., & Hewitt, D. (2010). Play: The pathway from theory to practice (rev. ed.). St. Paul, MN: Redleaf Press.

Helburn, S. W. (Ed.). (1995). *Cost, quality, and child outcomes in child care centers* (Technical report). Denver: University of Colorado–Denver, Department of Economics, Center for Research in Economics and Social Policy.

Helm, J. H. (2008). Got standards: Don't give up on engaged learning!, *Young Children 63*(4), 14–20.

Helm, J. H., & Katz, L. G. (2010). *Young investigators: The project approach in the early years* (2nd ed.). New York: Teachers College Press.

Helping young children in frightening times. (2001). *Young Children, 56*(6), 6–7.

Hemmeter, M. L., & Grisham-Brown, J. (1997). Developing children's language skills in inclusive early childhood classrooms. *Dimensions of Early Childhood, 25*(3), 6–13.

Hitz, R., & Driscoll, A. (1988). Praise or encouragement? *Young Children, 43*(5), 6–13.

Hohmann, M., & Weikart, D. P. (1995). *Educating young children: Active learning practices for preschool and child care programs.* Ypsilanti, MI: High/Scope Press.

Hohmann, M., & Weikart, D. P. (2002). *Educating young children* (2nd ed.). Ypsilanti, MI: High/Scope Press.

Honig, A. S. (1995). Singing with infants and toddlers. *Young Children, 50*(5), 72–78.

Honig, A. S. (2002). *Secure relationships: Nurturing infant/toddler attachment in early care settings.* Washington, DC: National Association for the Education of Young Children.

Horn, E., Lieber, J., Li, S., Sandall, S., & Schwartz, L. (2000, Winter). Supporting young children's IEP goals in inclusive settings through embedded learning opportunities. *Topics in Early Childhood Special Education, 20*(4), 208–223. doi:10.1177/027112140002000402

Howes, C. (1997). Children's experiences in center-based child care as a function of teacher background and adult-child ratio. *Merrill-Palmer Quarterly, 43,* 404–425.

Howes, C., Hamilton, C. E., & Matheson, C. (1994). Children's relationships with peers: Differential associations with aspects of the teacher-child relationship. *Child Development, 65,* 253–256.

Howes, C., Phillips, D., & Whitebook, M. (1992). Thresholds of quality: Implications for the social development of children in center-based child care. *Child Development, 63,* 449–460.

Hyman, I. (1997). *The case against spanking.* San Francisco: Jossey-Bass.

International Reading Association & National Association for the Education of Young Children. (1998). *A joint position statement. Learning to read and write: Developmentally appropriate practices for young children.* Washington, DC: National Association for the Education of Young Children. Retrieved from www.naeyc.org/files/naeyc/file/positions/PSREAD98.PDF

Isenberg, J. P., & Jalongo, M. R. (2000). *Creative expression and play in early childhood* (3rd ed.). Upper Saddle River, NJ: Pearson.

Isenberg, J. P., & Quisenberry, N. (2002). A position paper of the Association for Childhood Education International. Play: Essential for all children. *Childhood Education, 79,* 33–39.

Jablon, J. R., Dombro, A. L., & Dichtelmiller, M. L. (2007). *The power of observation for birth through eight* (2nd ed.). Washington, DC: Teaching Strategies and the National Association for the Education of Young Children.

Jacobs, G., & Crowley, K. (2010). *Reaching standards and beyond in kindergarten: Nurturing children's sense of wonder and joy in learning.* Thousand Oaks, CA, & Washington, DC: Corwin & the National Association for the Education of Young Children.

Jacobson, L. (2002). Defining quality. Quality Counts 2002: Building blocks for success. *Education Week, 21*(17), 24–28, 30–31.

Jones, B., Valdez, G., Norakowski, J., & Rasmussen, C. (1994). *Designing learning and technology for educational reform.* Oakbrook, IL: North Central Regional Educational Laboratory.

Jones, E., & Nimmo, J. (1994). *Emergent curriculum.* Washington, DC: National Association for the Education of Young Children.

Jones, N. P. (2008). 2, 4, or 6: Grouping children to promote social and emotional development. *Young Children, 63*(3), 34–39.

Kagan, S. L., & Neuman, M. J. (1997). Highlights of the Quality 2000 initiative: Not by chance. *Young Children, 52*(6), 54–62.

Katz, L. G. (1991). *Readiness: Children and schools.* Urbana, IL: ERIC Clearinghouse on Elementary and Early Childhood Education. (ERIC Document Reproduction Service No. ED330495)

Katz, L. G. (1995a). A developmental approach to the education of young children: Basic principles. *International School Journal, 14*(2), 49–60.

Katz, L. G. (1995b). *Talks with teachers of young children: A collection.* Norwood, NJ: Ablex.

Katz, L. G., & Chard, S. C. (2000). *Engaging children's minds: The project approach* (2nd ed.). Norwood, NJ: Ablex.

Katz, L. G., & McClellan, D. E. (1997). *Fostering children's social competence: The teacher's role.* Washington, DC: National Association for the Education of Young Children.

Kilpatrick, W. H. (1918). The project method. *Teachers College Record, 19,* 319–335.

King, E. W., Chipman, M., & Cruz-Jansen, M. (1994). *Educating young children in a diverse society.* Boston, MA: Allyn & Bacon.

Kirkwood, D. (2011). 50 things to do instead of time-out. *Early Years: The Journal of the Texas Association for the Education of Young Children, 32*(1), 9–10.

Knapp, M. S. (Ed.). (1995). *Teaching for meaning in high-poverty classrooms.* New York: Teachers College Press.

Kohn, A. (1991). Don't spoil the promise of cooperative learning. *Educational Leadership, 48* (5), 93–94.

Kohn, A. (2001). Five reasons to stop saying "Good Job!" *Young Children, 56*(5), 24–28.

Kontos, S., Howes, C., & Galinsky, E. (1997). Does training make a difference to quality in family child care? *Early Childhood Research Quarterly, 12,* 351–372.

Kontos, S., Howes, C., Shinn, M., & Galinsky, E. (1995). *Quality in family child care and relative care.* New York: Teachers College Press.

Koralek, D. (2008). Integrating curriculum in the early years and beyond. *Young Children, 63*(2), 10–11.

Kromhout, O. M., & Butzin, S. M. (1993). Integrating computers into the elementary school curriculum: An evaluation of nine Project CHILD model schools. *Journal of Research on Computing in Education, 26*(1), 55–69.

Krueger, A. (1999). Experimental estimates of education production functions. *Quarterly Journal of Economics, 114,* 497–532.

Lally, J. R. (1995). The impact of child care policies and practices on infant/toddler identity formation. *Young Children, 51*(1), 58–67.

Lamb, M. E. (1998). Non-parental child care: Context, quality, correlates. In W. Damon, I. E. Sigel, & K. A. Renninger (Eds.), *Handbook of child psychology.* Vol. 4: *Child psychology in practice* (5th ed., pp. 73–134). New York: Wiley.

Lee Pesky Learning Center. (2010). *10 things you should know about the Idaho Early Literacy Project.* Retrieved from www.lplearningcenter.org/LinkClick.aspx?fileticket=F_ap8zazd2A%3D&tabid=5461

Levine, J. (2008). A classroom community: Where everybody knows your name. *Child Care Information Exchange, 30*(5), 49–52.

Lynch, E. W., & Hanson, M. J. (Eds.). (1998). *Developing cross-cultural competence: A guide for working with children and their families* (2nd ed.). Baltimore: Brookes.

Lyons, R. (2011). *Reading disabilities: Why do some children have difficulty learning to read? What can be done about it?* Retrieved from www.dys-add.com/R.Lyon.WhyCantRead.pdf

Macrina, M., Hoover, D., & Becker, C. (2009). The challenge of working with dual language learners: Three perspectives: Supervisor, mentor and teacher. Young *Children 64*(2), 27–34.

Mallory, B. L. (1998). Education of young children with developmental differences: Principles of inclusive practices. In C. Seefeldt & A. Galper (Eds.), *Continuing issues in early childhood education* (2nd ed., pp. 213–237). Upper Saddle River, NJ: Pearson.

Marcon, R. A. (1992). Differential effects of three preschool models on inner-city 4-year-olds. *Early Childhood Research Quarterly, 7,* 517–530.

Marion, M. (1999). *Guidance of young children.* Upper Saddle River, NJ: Pearson.

Marshall, H. H. (1995). Beyond "I like the way . . ." *Young Children, 50*(2), 26–28.

McCormick, L., & Feeney, S. (1995). Modifying and expanding activities for children with disabilities. *Young Children, 50*(4), 10–17.

Meece, D., & Soderman, A.K. (2010). Positive verbal environments: Setting the stage for young children's social development. *Young Children, 65*(5), 81–86.

Miller, L. G., & Albrecht, K. M. (2000). *Innovations: The comprehensive infant curriculum.* Beltsville, MD: Gryphon.

Minnesota early literacy project. (2011). Retrieved May, 2011, from University of Minnesota, Center for Early Education & Development website: http://www.cehd.umn.edu/ceed/projects/earlyliteracyproject/default.html

Mitchell, A., & David, J. (Eds.). (1992). *Explorations with young children: A curriculum guide for the Bank Street College of Education.* Mt. Rainer, MD: Gryphon.

Mosteller, F. (1995). The Tennessee study of class size in the early school grades. *Future of Children, 5,* 113–127.

Nastasi, B. K., & Clements, D. H. (1994). Effectance motivation, perceived scholastic competence, and higher-order thinking in two cooperative computer environments. *Journal of Educational Computing Research, 10,* 241–267.

National Association for the Education of Young Children. (1995). *Position statement: Responding to linguistic and cultural diversity: Recommendations for effective early childhood education.* Washington, DC: Author.

National Association for the Education of Young Children. (1996). *Guidelines for preparation of early childhood professionals.* Washington, DC: Author.

National Association for the Education of Young Children. (2005). *Accreditation criteria and procedures of the National Academy of Early Childhood programs.* Washington, DC: Author.

National Association for the Education of Young Children. (2009). *Position statement: Developmentally appropriate practice in early childhood programs serving children from birth through age 8.* Washington, DC: Author. Retrieved from www.naeyc.org/files/naeyc/file/positions/position%20statement%20Web.pdf

National Association for the Education of Young Children. (2011b). *Recommended adult-child ratios within group size.* NAEYC Torch Resource Library database. Washington, DC: NAEYC.

National Association for the Education of Young Children & the Division for Early Childhood Education. (2007). *A joint position statement. Promoting positive outcomes for children with disabilities: Recommendations for curriculum, assessment, and program evaluation.* Washington, DC, & Missoula, MT: Authors. Retrieved from www.naeyc.org/files/naeyc/file/positions/PrmtgPositiveOutcomes.pdf

National Association for the Education of Young Children and the Fred Rogers Center for Early Learning and Children's Media. (2011a). *Technology in early childhood programs serving children from birth through 8 Draft.* Washington, DC, & Latrobe, PA: Authors.

National Association for the Education of Young Children & the National Association of Early Childhood Specialists in State Departments of Education. (2002). *A joint position statement. Early learning standards: Creating the conditions for success.* Washington, DC, & Alexandria, VA: Authors. Retrieved from www.naeyc.org/files/naeyc/file/positions/position_statement.pdf

National Association for the Education of Young Children & the National Association of Early Childhood Specialists in State Departments of Education. (2003). *A joint position statement. Early childhood curriculum, assessment, and program evaluation: Building an effective, accountable system in programs for children birth through age 8.* Washington, DC, & Alexandria, VA: Authors. Retrieved from www.naeyc.org/files/naeyc/file/positions/pscape.pdf

National Center for Education Statistics. (2000). *The kindergarten year: Findings from the Early Childhood Longitudinal Study, Kindergarten Class of 1998–99, Fall 1998.* Washington, DC: U.S. Department of Education. Retrieved from nces.ed.gov/pubs2001/2001023.pdf

National Council of Teachers of Mathematics. (2000). *Principles and standards for school mathematics.* Reston, VA: Author. Retrieved from standards.nctm.org/document/index.htm

National Council of Teachers of Mathematics. (2006). *Curriculum focal points for pre-kindergarten through grade 8 mathematics.* Retrieved from /www.nctm.org/standards/content.aspx?id=270

National Council of Teachers of Mathematics & National Association for the Education of Young Children. (2010). *Early childhood mathematics: Promoting good beginnings.* Washington, DC: National Association for the Education of Young Children. Retrieved from www.naeyc.org/positionstatements/mathematics

National Education Reform, 20 USC C.F.R. § Chapter 68 (2010). Retrieved from uscode.house.gov/download/pls/20C68.txt

National Research Council. (1999). *How people learn: Brain, mind, experience, and school.* Washington, DC: National Academy Press.

National Research Council. (2001). *Eager to learn: Educating our preschoolers.* B T. Bowman, S. Donovan, & M. S. Burns (Eds.). Washington, DC: National Academy Press.

Nemeth, K. (2009). Meeting the home language mandate: Practical strategies for all classrooms. *Young Children, 64*(2), 36–42.

Neuman, S. B., Copple, C., & Bredekamp, S. (2000). *Learning to read and write: Developmentally appropriate practices for young children.* Washington, DC: National Association for the Education of Young Children.

NICHD Early Child Care Research Network. (1996). Characteristics of infant care: Factors contributing to positive caregiving. *Early Childhood Research Quarterly, 11,* 269–306.

NICHD Early Child Care Research Network. (1998). Early child care and self-control, compliance, and problem behavior at twenty-four and thirty-six months. *Child Development, 69,* 1145–1170.

NICHD Early Child Care Research Network. (2000). The relation of child care to cognitive and language development. *Child Development, 71,* 958–978.

National Institute of Early Education Research. (2008). *Connecting neurons, concepts and people: Brain development and its implications*. Retrieved from nieer.org/resources/policybriefs/17.pdf

Nores, M., & Barnett, S. (2009). *Benefits of early childhood interventions across the world: (Under) Investing in the very young*. National Institute of Early Education Research. Retrieved from nieer.org/docs/?DocID=277

Novick, R. (1998). The comfort corner: Fostering resiliency and emotional intelligence. *Childhood Education, 74,* 200–204.

O'Dell, S. M., Vilardo, B. A., Kern, L., Kokina, A., Ash, A. N., Seymour, K. J., . . . Kollar, R. B. (2011, April). JPBI ten years later: Trends in research studies. *Journal of Positive Behavioral Interventions, 13*(2), 78–86. Abstract retrieved from pbi.sagepub.com/

Office of Special Education and Rehabilitative Services. (2007). *Overview and technical assistance and dissemination to improve services and results for children with disabilities: Federal register*. Office of Special Education & Rehabilitative Services. Retrieved from www.gpo.gov/fdsys/pkg/FR-2011-08-09/html/2011-20184.htm

Parette, H. P., Quesenberry, A. G., & Blum, C. (2009). Missing the boat with technology usage in early childhood settings: A 21st century view of developmentally appropriate practice. *Early Childhood Education Journal, 37*(5), 335–343.

Peth-Pierce, R. (2001). *A good beginning: Sending America's children to school with the social and emotional competence they need to succeed*. Monograph based on two papers commissioned by the Child Mental Health Foundations and Agencies Network (FAN). Chapel Hill: University of North Carolina.

Phillips, C. B. (1994a). The challenge of training and credentialing early childhood educators. *Phi Delta Kappan, 76,* 214–217.

Phillips, C. B. (1994b). The movement of African-American children through sociocultural contexts: A case of conflict resolution. In B. L. Mallory & R. S. New (Eds.), *Diversity and developmentally appropriate practices: Challenges for early childhood education* (pp. 137–154). New York: Teachers College Press.

Phillips, D. A., & Crowell, N. A. (Eds.). (1994). *Cultural diversity in early education: Results of a workshop*. Washington, DC: National Academy Press.

Phipps, P. A. (1999). Is your program brain compatible? *Child Care Information Exchange, 126,* 53–57.

Piaget, J. (1959). *Language and thought of the child* (3rd ed.). London: Routledge & Kegan Paul.

Pre[K]Now. (2011, May 4). The republican budget war on children [Electronic mailing list message]. Retrieved from www.businessweek.com/investor/content/may2011/pi2011053_671120.htm

Raikes, H. (1996). A secure base for babies: Applying attachment concepts to the infant care setting. *Young Children, 51*(5), 59–67.

Raikes, H. H., & Edwards, C. P. (2009). *Extending the dance in infant & toddler caregiving: Enhancing attachment & relationships*. Baltimore, MD, & Washington, DC: Brookes Publishing & The National Association for the Education of Young Children.

Raver, C. (2002). Emotions matter: Making the case for the role of young children's emotional development for early school readiness. *SRCD Social Policy Report, 16*(3). Ann Arbor, MI: Society for Research in Child Development.

Ray, A., Bowman, B., & Brownell, J. O. (2006). Teacher-child relationships, social-emotional development, and school achievement. In B. Bowman & E. K. More (Eds.), *School readiness and social emotional development: Perspectives on cultural diversity* (pp. 7–22). Washington, DC: National Black Child Development Institute, Inc.

Ray, J. A., Pewitt-Kinder, J., & George, S. (2009). Partnering with families of children with special needs. *Young Children, 64*(5), 16–22.

Riley, D., San Juan, R. R., Klinkner, J., & Ramminger, A. (2008). *Social & emotional development: Connecting science and practice in early childhood settings*. St. Paul, MN, & Washington, DC: Redleaf Press and The National Association for the Education of Young Children.

Rinde, M. (2011, January 11). Black, Hispanic students continue to fail state tests in higher numbers. *The Trenton Times*. Retrieved from www.nj.com/mercer/index.ssf/2011/01/black_hispanic_students_contin.html

Roberts, S. K., & Crawford, P. A. (2008). Real life calls for real books: Literature to help children cope with family stressors. *Young Children, 63*(5), 12–17.

Rofrano, F. (2002). "I care for you": A reflection on caring as infant curriculum. *Young Children, 57*(1), 49–51.

Rosegrant, T., & Bredekamp, S. (1992). Planning and implementing transformational curriculum. In S. Bredekamp & T. Rosegrant (Eds.), *Reaching potentials: Appropriate curriculum and assessment for young children* (Vol. 1, pp. 66–73). Washington, DC: National Association for the Education of Young Children.

Rushton, S., & Larkin, L. (2001). Shaping the learning environment: Connecting brain research to developmentally appropriate practices. *Early Childhood Education Journal, 29*(1), 25–33.

Russell-Fox, J. (1997). Together is better: Specific tips on how to include children with various types of disabilities. *Young Children, 52*(4) 81–83.

Salovey, P., & Sluyter, D. (Eds.). (1997). *Emotional development and emotional intelligence: Educational implications*. New York: Basic.

Santrock, J. (2010). *Children* (11th ed.). Boston, MA: McGraw-Hill.

Schickedanz, J. A. (2008). *Increasing the power of instruction: Integration of language, literacy and math across the preschool day*. Washington, DC: National Association for the Education of Young Children.

Schiller, P. (2010). Early brain development review and update. *Exchange, 32*(6), 26–32.

Schiller, P. (2009). Program practices that support intentionality in teaching. *Child Care Information Exchange, 31*(1), 57–60.

Schiller, P., & Willis, C. A. (2008). Using brain-based teaching strategies to create supportive early childhood environments that address learning standards. *Young Children, 63*(4), 52–55.

Scott-Little, C., Kagan, S. L., Frelow, V. S., & Reid, J. (2008, February). *Inside the content of infant-toddler early learning guidelines: Results from analysis, issues to consider and recommendations*. National Center for Children and Families. Retrieved from ccf.tc.columbia.edu/pdf/Inside%20the%20Content%20of%20Infant-Toddler%20ELGs-Brief.pdf

Shepard, L. A., Kagan, S. L., & Wurtz, E. (1998). Goal One: Early Childhood Assessments Resource Group recommendations. *Young Children, 53*(3), 52–54.

Shiller, V. M., & O'Flynn, J. C. (2008). Using rewards in the early childhood classroom: A reexamination of the issues. *Young Children, 63*(6), 88, 90–93.

Shonkoff, J. P., & Phillips, D. A. (Eds.). (2000). *From neurons to neighborhoods: The science of early childhood development*. Washington, DC: National Academy Press.

Small, M. (1998). *Our babies, ourselves: How biology and culture shape the way we parent*. New York: Anchor Books.

Sousa, D. (2006). *How the brain learns* (3rd ed.). Thousand Oaks, CA: Corwin.

Stephens, K. (1999). Primed for learning: The young child's mind. *Child Care Information Exchange, 126,* 44–48.

Sullivan, A. K., & Strang, H. R. (2002/03). Bibliotherapy in the classrooms: Using literature to promote the development of emotional intelligence. *Childhood Education, 79,* 74–80.

Swick, K., Van Scoy, I., & Boutte, G. (1994). Multicultural learning through family involvement. *Dimensions of Early Childhood, 22*(4), 17–21.

Taylor, B. J. (1999). *A child goes forth: A curriculum guide for preschool children.* Upper Saddle River, NJ: Pearson.

Theilheimer, R. (2006). Molding to the children: Primary caregiving and continuity of care. *Zero to Three Bulletin, 26*(3), 50–54.

Thomas, W., & Collier, V. (2002). *A national study of school effectiveness for language minority students' long-term academic achievement.* Santa Cruz, CA: Center for Research on Education, Diversity & Excellence.

Thompson, P. W. (1992). Notations, conventions, and constraints: Contributions to effective use of concrete materials in elementary mathematics. *Journal of Research in Mathematics Education, 23,* 123–147.

Thompson, R. A. (1997). Early sociopersonality development. In W. Damon (Series Ed.) & N. Eisenberg (Vol. Ed.), *Handbook of child psychology.* Vol. 3: *Social, emotional, and personality development* (5th ed., pp. 25–104). New York: Wiley.

Thompson, R. A. (2008). *Connecting neurons, concepts and people: Brain development and its implications* (Rep. No. 17). National Institute of Early Education Research. Retrieved from nieer.org/resources/policybriefs/17.pdf

U.S. Department of Education. (2011). *Building the legacy: Idea 2004.* Retrieved from http://idea.ed.gov/

Vance, E., & Weaver, P. J. (2002). *Class meetings: Young children solving problems together.* Washington, DC: National Association for the Education of Young Children.

Vygotsky, L. S. (1978). *Mind in society* (M. Cole, S. Schribner, V. John-Steiner, & E. Souberman, Trans.). Cambridge, MA: Harvard University Press.

Wagenblast v. Odessa School Dist., 758 P. 2d 968 (Wash. 1988).

Wardle, F. (1999). In praise of developmentally appropriate practice. *Young Children, 54*(6), 4–12.

Wasik, B. (2008). When fewer is more: Small group in early childhood classrooms. *Early Childhood Education Journal, 35,* 515–521. doi 10.1007/s10643-008-0245-4.

Watson, A., & McCathren, R. (2009). Including children with special needs: Are you and your early childhood program ready? *Young Children, 64*(2), 20–26.

Wien, C. A. (1996). Time, work, and developmentally appropriate practice. *Early Childhood Research Quarterly, 11,* 377–403.

Wien, C. A. (Ed.). (2008). *Emergent curriculum in the primary classroom: Interpreting the Reggio Emilia approach in schools.* New York & Washington, DC: Teachers College Press & the National Association for the Education of Young Children.

Williams, K. C. (1997). "What do you wonder?" Involving children in curriculum planning. *Young Children, 52*(6), 78–81.

Winter, S. (1999). *Early childhood inclusion model: A program for all children.* Olney, MD: Association for Childhood Education International.

Wolfe, J., & Brandt, R. (1998). What we know from brain research. *Educational Leadership, 56*(3), 8–14.

Wurm, J. P. (2005). *Working the Reggio way: A beginner's guide for American teachers.* St. Paul, MN, & Washington, DC: Redleaf Press & the National Association for the Education of Young Children.

Chapter 10

Alkon, A., Bernzweig, J., To, K., Wolff, M., & Mackie, J. F. (2009). Child care health consultation improves health and safety policies and practices. *Academic Pediatrics, 9*(5), 366–370.

Ambinder, M. (2010). Beating obesity. *The Atlantic, 305*(4), 72–80, 82–83.

American Academy of Family Physicians, American Academy of Pediatrics, American College of Physicians, & American Osteopathic Association. (2007). *Consensus statement: Joint Principles of the Patient-Centered Medical Home.* Retrieved from http://www.aafp.org/online/etc/medialib/aafp_org/documents/policy/fed/jointprinciplespcmh0207.Par.0001.File.dat/022107medicalhome.pdf

American Academy of Pediatrics, American Public Health Association, & National Resource Center for Health and Safety in Child Care (AAP/APHA/NRCHSCC). (2010). Preventing childhood obesity in early care and education programs: Selected standards from *Caring for our children: National health and safety performance standards; guidelines for early care and education programs* (3rd ed.). Elk Grove Village, IL: American Academy of Pediatrics and Washington, DC: American Public Health Association. Retrieved from nrckids.org/CFOC3/PREVENTING_OBESITY

American Academy of Pediatrics, American Public Health Association, & National Resource Center for Health and Safety in Child Care (AAP/APHA/NRCHSCC). (2011). *Caring for our children: National health and safety performance standards: Guidelines for out-of-home child care programs* (3rd ed.). Elk Grove Village, IL: American Academy of Pediatrics and Washington, DC: American Public Health Association. Retrieved from nrckids.org/CFOC3/PDFVersion/list.html

Anderson, P. M., & Butcher, K. F. (2006). Childhood obesity: Trends and potential causes. In C. Paxson, E. Donahue, C. T. Orleans, & J. A. Grisso (Eds.), *Childhood obesity. The future of children, 16*(1), 19–45. Princeton, NJ: The Woodrow Wilson School of Public and International Affairs and the Bookings Institution. Retrieved from http://futureofchildren.org/publications/journals/journal_details/index.xml?journalid=36

Austin, J. S. (2000). When a child discloses sexual abuse: Immediate and appropriate teacher responses. *Childhood Education, 77,* 2–5.

Austin, L. J. E., Whitebook, M., Connors, M., & Darrah, R. (2011). *Staff preparation, reward, and support: Are quality rating and improvement systems addressing all of the key ingredients necessary for change?* Berkeley, CA: Center for the Study of Child Care Employment, University of California at Berkeley. Retrieved from www.irle.berkeley.edu/cscce/wp-content/uploads/2011/06/CSCCE_QRISPolicyReport2011.pdf

Bar-Or, O. (2000). Juvenile obesity, physical activity, and lifestyle changes. *The Physician and Sports Medicine, 28*(11), 51–58.

Berk, L. (2008). *Infants and children: Prenatal through middle childhood* (6th ed.). Boston, MA: Pearson/Allyn & Bacon.

Bhattacharya, J., & Currie, J. (2001). Youths and nutrition risk: Malnourished or misnourished? In J. Gruber (Ed.), *Risky behavior among youths: An economic analysis* (pp. 483–521). Chicago, IL: University of Chicago Press.

Birch, L. L., Johnson, S. L., & Fisher, J. A. (1995). Children's eating: The development of food acceptance patterns. *Young Children, 50*(2), 71–78.

Brennan, P., Mednick, S., & Kandal, E. (1991). Congenital determinants of violence and property offending. In D. J. Pepler & K. H. Rubin (Eds.), *The development and treatment of childhood aggression* (pp. 87–90). Hillsdale, NJ: Erlbaum.

Brown, M. Z., & Gerberich, S. G. (1993). Disabling injuries to child-care workers in Minnesota, 1985 to 1990: An analysis of potential risk factors. *Journal of Occupational Medicine, 35*(12), 1236–1243.

Child Welfare League of America. (1945). *Day-care: A partnership of three professions.* Washington, DC: Author.

Coleman, M., Willinga, C., & Bales, D. (2010). Engaging families in the fight against the overweight epidemic among children. *Childhood Education, 86*(3), 150–156.

Colker, L., (2005). *The cooking book: Fostering young children's learning and delight.* Washington, DC: National Association for the Education of Young Children.

Cost, Quality, and Child Outcomes Study Team. (1995). *Cost, quality, and child outcomes in child care centers, Public report* (2nd ed.). Denver: University of Colorado-Denver, Economics Department.

Cryer, D., Harms, T., & Riley, C. (2003). *All about the ECERS-R: A detailed guide in words and pictures to be used with the ECERS-R.* Lewisville, NC: Pact House Publishing.

Dehghan, M., Akhtar-Danesh, N., & Merchant, A. T. (2005). Childhood obesity, prevalence and prevention. *Nutrition Journal 4*(24). Retrieved from www.nutritionj.com/content/4/1/24/

Division of Early Childhood of the Council for Exceptional Children. (2007). *Position statement: Identification of and intervention with challenging behavior.* Missoula, MT: Author. Retrieved from www.dec-sped.org/uploads/docs/about_dec/position_concept_papers/PositionStatement_Chal_Behav_updated_jan2009.pdf

Dooling, M. V., & Ulione, M. S. (2000). Health consultation in child care: A partnership that works. *Young Children, 55*(2), 23–26.

Drake, M. M. (1992). Menu evaluation, nutrient intake of young children, and nutrition knowledge of menu planners in child care centers in Missouri. *Journal of Nutrition Education, 24,* 145–148.

Federal Interagency Forum on Child and Family Statistics. (2002). *America's children: Key national indicators of well-being 2002.* Washington, DC: U.S. Government Printing Office.

Gilliam, W. (2005). *Prekindergartener's left behind: Expulsion rates in state prekindergarten systems.* New Haven, CT: Yale University, Child Study Center.

Goals 2000: Educate America Act. (1994). Washington, DC: 103rd Congress. Retrieved from www2.ed.gov/legislation/GOALS2000/TheAct/index.html

Grabert, J. C. (2009). Integrating early childhood mental health into early intervention services. *Zero to Three, 29*(6), 13–17.

Harms, T. O. (1992). Designing settings to support high-quality care. In B. Spodek & O. N. Saracho (Eds.), *Yearbook in early childhood education.* Vol. 3: *Issues in child care* (pp. 169–186). New York: Teachers College Press.

Harris, J. L., Pomeranz, J. L., Lobstein, T., & Brownell, K. D. (2009). A crisis in the marketplace: How food marketing contributes to childhood obesity and what can be done. *Annual Review of Public Health 30,* 211–225.

Hassink, S. G. (2006). *A parent's guide to childhood obesity: A road map to health.* Elk Grove Village, IL: American Academy of Pediatrics.

Himle, M. B., Miltenberger, R. G., Gatheridge, B. J., & Flessner, C. A. (2004). An evaluation of two procedures for training skills to prevent gun play in children. *Pediatrics 113*(1), 70–77. Retrieved from pediatrics.aappublications.org/cgi/reprint/113/1/70

Holland, M. (2004). "That food makes me SICK": Managing food allergies and intolerances in early childhood settings. *Young Children 59*(2), 42–46.

Huettig, C. I., Sanborn, C. F., MiMarco, N., Popejoy, A., & Rich, S. (2004). The O generation: Our youngest children are at risk for obesity. *Young Children, 59*(2), 50–55.

Javernick, E. (1988). Johnny's not jumping: Can we help obese children? *Young Children, 43*(2), 18–23.

Kalich, K. A., Bauer, D., & McPartlin, D. (2009). "Early Sprouts" establishing healthy food choices for young children. *Young Children 64*(4), 49–55.

Kaphingst, K. M., & Story, M. (2009). Child care as an untapped setting for obesity prevention: State child care licensing regulations related to nutrition, physical activity, and media use of preschool-aged children in the United States. *Preventing Chronic Disease, 6*(1), 1–14.

Kaplan, P. (1998). *The human odyssey.* Pacific Grove, CA: Brooks/Cole.

Kordas, K. (2010). Iron, lead, and children's behavior and cognition. *Annual Review of Nutrition, 30,* 123–148.

Lanphear, B. (2001). Blood lead levels below "acceptable" value linked with IQ deficits, according to new study. *LEAD Action News, 8*(3). Retrieved from www.lead.org.au/lanv8n3/lanv8n3-3.html

Lee, J. M., Zoellner, J., Sandretto, A. M., & Ismail, A. I. (2010). Don't children grow out of their obesity?: Weight transitions in early childhood. *Clinical Pediatrics 49*(5), 466–469.

Levin, D. E. (2003). *Teaching young children in violent times: Building a peaceable classroom.* Cambridge, MA: Educators for Social Responsibility and National Association for the Education of Young Children.

Linn, S. (2004). *Consuming kids: The hostile takeover of childhood.* New York: The New Press.

Lozoff, B., Jimenez, E., Hagen, J., Mollen, E., & Wolf, A. W. (2000). Poorer behavior and developmental outcome more than 10 years after treatment for iron deficiency in infancy. *Pediatrics, 105*(4), E51.

Mayo Clinic. (2007). *Hand-washing: Do's and don'ts.* Retrieved from www.mayoclinic.com/health/hand-washing/HQ00407

McBride, N. (n.d.) *Child safety is more than a slogan: "Stranger Danger" warnings not effective at keeping kids safer.* National Center for Missing and Exploited Children. Retrieved from www.missingkids.com/missingkids/servlet/NewsEventServlet?LanguageCountry=en_US&PageId=2034

Mikkelsen, E. J. (1997). Responding to allegations of sexual abuse in child care and early childhood education programs. *Young Children, 52*(3), 47–51.

Morgan, B., & Gibson, R. K. (1991). Nutritional and environmental interactions in brain development. In R. K. Gibson & A. C. Petersen (Eds.), *Brain maturation and cognitive development: Comparative cross-cultural perspectives* (pp. 91–106). New York: Aldine De Gruyter.

Murray, C. G. (2000). Learning about children's social and emotional needs at snack time—Nourishing the body, mind, and spirit of each child. *Young Children, 55*(2), 43–52.

National Association for the Education of Young Children. (1997). Prevention of child abuse in early childhood programs and the responsibilities of early childhood professionals to prevent child abuse. Washington, DC: Author. Retrieved from www.naeyc.org/files/naeyc/file/positions/PSCHAB98.PDF

National Association for the Education of Young Children Academy for Early Childhood Program Accreditation. (2007). *NAEYC early childhood program standards.* Washington, DC: Author.

National Child Care Information Center & National Association for Regulatory Administration (NCCIC/NARA). (2010). *The 2008 child care licensing study.* Lexington, KY: National Association for Regulatory Administration. Retrieved from www.naralicensing.org/Licensing_Study

National Conference of State Legislatures. (2011). *Breastfeeding Laws.* Retrieved www.ncsl.org/IssuesResearch/Health/BreastfeedingLaws/tabid/14389/Default.aspx

National Food Service Management Institute. (2009). *Child Care Fact Sheet: Introducing solid foods to infants.* The University of Mississippi: Author. Retrieved from www.nfsmi.org/documentlibraryfiles/PDF/20090210032350.pdf

Nord, M., Andrews, M., & Carlson, S. (2008). *Household food security in the United States, 2007*. Washington, DC: United States Department of Agriculture. Retrieved www.ers.usda.gov/Publications/ERR66/ERR66.pdf

Ostrosky, M. M., & Meadan, H. (2010). Helping children play and learn together. *Young Children, 65*(1), 104–110.

Perry, P. (2001). Sick kids. *American Way, 4,* 64–65.

Powell, L. M., Szczypka, G., Chaloupka, F. J., & Braunschweig, F. J. (2007). Nutritional content of TV food advertisements seen by children and adolescents in the US. *Pediatrics, 120*(3), 576–583.

Prevent Child Abuse New York. (2008). *2008 child abuse and neglect fact sheet*, Albany, NY: Author. Retrieved from www.preventchildabuseny.org/files/1413/0392/1135/2008CANFactSheet.pdf

Rideout, V., & Hamel, E. (2006). *The media family: Electronic media in the lives of infants, toddlers, preschoolers and their parents*. Menlo Park, CA: Henry J. Kaiser Family Foundation

Romaine, N., Mann, L., Kienapple, K., & Conrad, B. (2007). Menu planning for childcare centres: Practices and needs. *Canadian Journal of Dietetic Practice and Research 68*(1), 7–13.

Satter, E. (2000). *Child of mine: Feeding with love and good sense* (3rd ed.). Boulder, CO: Bull Publishing.

Senate Committee on Health, Education, Labor and Pensions. (2008). *Confronting childhood obesity: Creating a roadmap to healthier futures*. Washington, DC: U.S. Government Printing Office.

Shore, R. (1997). *Rethinking the brain: New insights into early development*. New York: Families and Work Institute.

Shoup, J. A., Gattshall, M., Dandamundi, P., & Estabrooks, P. (2008). Physical activity, quality of life, and weight status in overweight children. *Quality of Life Research, 17*(3), 407–412.

Simmons, B. J., Stalsworth, K., & Wentzel, H. (1999). Television violence and its effects on young children. *Early Childhood Education Journal, 26*(3), 149–153.

Slaby, R. G., Roedell, W. C., Arezzo, D., & Hendrix, K. (1995). *Early violence prevention: Tools for teachers of young children*. Washington, DC: National Association for the Education of Young Children.

Stanford, B. H., & Yamamoto, K. (Eds.). (2001). *Children and stress: Understanding and helping*. Olney, MD: Association for Childhood Education International.

Stoneham, L. (2001). Diabetes on a rampage. *Texas Medicine, 97*(11), 42–48.

Strupp, B. J., & Levitsky, D. A. (1995). Enduring cognitive effects of early maturation: A theoretical reappraisal. *Journal of Nutrition, 125,* 2221S–2232S.

Sweitzer, S. J., Briley, M. E., Roberts-Gray, C., Hoelscher, D. M., Harrist, R. B., Staskel, D. M., & Almansour, F. D. (2010). Lunch is in the bag: Increasing fruits, vegetables, and whole grains in sack lunches of preschool-aged children. *Journal of the American Dietetic Association, 110*(7), 1058–1064.

Twells, L., & Newhook, L. A. (2010). Can exclusive breastfeeding reduce the likelihood of childhood obesity in some regions of Canada? *Canadian Journal of Public Health, 101*(1), 36–39.

United States Breastfeeding Committee. (2002). *Breastfeeding and child care* (issue paper). Raleigh, NC: United States Breastfeeding Committee. Retrieved from www.usbreastfeeding.org/

U.S. Department of Agriculture. (2005). *Dietary guidelines for Americans*. Washington, DC: Author. Retrieved from www.health.gov/dietaryguidelines/dga2005/document/default.htm

U.S. Department of Agriculture. (2009). *Access to affordable and nutritious food: Measuring and understanding food deserts and their consequences*. Washington, DC: Author. Retrieved from www.ers.usda.gov/Publications/AP/AP036/AP036.pdf

U.S. Department of Education. (2001). *Twenty-third annual report to Congress on the implementation of the Individuals with Disabilities Education Act*. Washington, DC: Author.

Upshur, C., Wenz-Gross, M., & Reed, G. (2009). A pilot study of early childhood mental health consultation for children with behavioral problems in preschool. *Early Childhood Research Quarterly, 24*(1), 29–45.

Vermeer, H. J., & van IJzendoorn, M. H. (2006). Children's elevated cortisol levels at daycare: A review and meta-analysis. *Early Childhood Research Quarterly, 21*(3), 390–401.

Wardle, F. (1990). Bunny ears and cupcakes for all: Are parties developmentally appropriate? *Child Care Information Exchange, 74,* 39–42.

Whitaker, R. C., Wright, J. A., Pepe, M. S., Seidel, K. D., & Dietz, W. H. (1997). Predicting obesity in young adulthood from childhood and parental obesity. *New England Journal of Medicine, 337*(13), 869–873.

Whitebook, M., Howes, C., & Phillips, D. A. (1998). *Who cares? Child care teachers and the quality of child care in America* (Final report, National Child Care Staffing Study). Washington, DC: Center for the Child Care Workforce.

Chapter 11

AEPS interactive. (2011). Brookes Publishing Co. Retrieved from www.brookespublishing.com/store/books/bricker-aeps/aepsi.htm

American Educational Research Association. (2000). *Position statement on high stakes testing*. Washington, DC: Author.

American Educational Research Association, American Psychological Association, & National Council on Measurement in Education. (1999). *Standards for educational and psychological testing*. Washington, DC: American Educational Research Association.

Association of Childhood Education International. (1991). On standardized testing. *Childhood Education, 67,* 132–142.

Bergen, D. (1993/94). Authentic performance assessments. *Childhood Education, 70,* 99, 102.

Bowman, B. T. (1990). Child care: Challenges for the 90's. *Dimensions, 18*(4), 27, 29–31.

Bricker, D., Pretti-Frontczak, K., Johnson, J., Straka, E., Capt, B., Slentz, K., & Waddell, M. (2002). *Administration guide: Assessment, evaluation, and programming system for infants and children*. Baltimore, MD: Brookes Publishing.

Burnette, J. (1998). *Reducing the disproportionate representation of minority students in special education* (ERIC/OSEP Digest #E566). Reston, VA: ERIC Clearinghouse on Disabilities and Gifted Education. (ERIC Document Reproduction Service No. ED417501)

Carter, M. (2008). What are we doing? Where are we going? *Exchange, 30*(6), 32–36.

Child Outcome Center. (2010). *Outcomes measurement system framework and self assessment*. Retrieved from www.fpg.unc.edu/~eco/pages/frame_dev.cfm

Child Trends. (2010). *Early school readiness*. Child Trends Data Bank. Retrieved from www.childtrendsdatabank.org/?q=node/104

Cohen, D. H., Stern, V., & Balaban, N. (1997). *Observing and recording the behavior of young children* (4th ed.). New York: Teachers College Press.

Coleman, M. R., Buysse, V., & Neitzel, J. (2006). *Recognition and response: An early intervening system for young children at risk for learning disabilities. Full Report.* Chapel Hill: The University of North Carolina at Chapel Hill, FPG Child Development Institute.

Copple, C., & Bredekamp, S. (Eds.). (2009). *Developmentally appropriate practice in early childhood programs* (3rd ed.). Washington, DC: National Association for the Education of Young Children.

Council of Chief State School Officers. (1995). *Moving toward accountability for results: A look at ten states' efforts.* Washington, DC: Author.

Dahlberg, G., & Asen, G. (1994). Evaluation and regulation: A question of empowerment. In P. Moss & A. Pence (Eds.), *Valuing quality in early childhood services* (pp. 157–171). New York: Teachers College Press.

Danielson, C., & Abrutyn, L. (1997). *An introduction to using portfolios in the classroom.* Alexandria, VA: Association for Supervision and Curriculum Development.

Darragh, J. (2009, May/June). Informal assessment as a tool for supporting parent partnerships. *Child Care Information Exchange,* 91–93. Retrieved from secure.ccie.com/resources/view_article.php?article_id=5018791&action=view

Dodge, D. T., Colker, L. J., & Heroman, C. (2002). *The creative curriculum.* Washington, DC: Teaching Strategies, Inc.

Dunphy, E. (2008). *Supporting early learning and development through formative assessment.* Dublin, Ireland: National Council for Curriculum and Assessment.

Epstein, A. S., Schweinhart, L. J., DeBruin-Parecki, A., & Robin, K. B. (2004). Preschool assessment: A guide to developing a balanced approach. *Preschool Policy Matters, 7,* 1–11. Retrieved from nieer.org/resources/policybriefs/7.pdf

Espinosa, L. (2010). *Getting it right for young children from diverse backgrounds: Applying research to improve practice.* Boston, MA & Washington, DC: Pearson Learning Solutions & the National Association for the Education of Young Children.

FairTest. (2011). *Work sampling system.* Rebus Planning Associates, Inc. Retrieved from fairtest.org/work-sampling-system

Freeman, N., & Brown, M. (2008). An authentic approach to assessing pre-kindergarten programs: Redefining readiness. *Childhood Education, 84*(5), 267–272.

Gober, S. Y. (2002). *Six simple ways to assess young children.* Albany, NY: Delmar Thompson Learning.

Goode, S. (2011). *Response to intervention (RTI) in early childhood.* National Early Childhood Technical Assistance Center. Retrieved from www.nectac.org/topics/RTI/RTI.asp

Greenspan, S. I., & Weider, S. (1998). *The child with special needs: Encouraging intellectual and emotional growth.* Reading, MA: Perseus Books.

Grisham-Brown, J. L., Hallam, R., & Brookshire, R. (2006). Using authentic assessment to evidence children's progress towards early learning standards. *Early Childhood Education Journal, 34*(1), 47–53.

Grisham-Brown, J. L., Hemmeter, M. L., & Pretti-Frontczak, K. L. (2005*). Blended practices for teaching young children in inclusive settings.* Baltimore, MD: Brookes.

Gronlund, G. (1998). Portfolios as an assessment tool: Is collection of work enough? *Young Children, 53*(3), 4–10.

Gronlund, G., & Engle, B. (2011). *Focused portfolios: A complete assessment for the young child.* Retrieved from www.focusedportfolios.com/

Hebbler, K. (2010, May 11). *Toward a unified vision of assessment for young children.* PowerPoint presentation at Listening and Learning about Early Learning Tour, Chicago, IL.

Helm, J. H., Beneke, S., & Steinheimer, K. (1998). *Windows on learning: Documenting young children's work.* New York: Teachers College Press.

Heroman, C., Burts, D., Kerke, K., & Bickart, T. (2010). *Teaching strategies GOLD birth through kindergarten.* Washington, DC: Teaching Strategies, Inc.

High/Scope Educational Research Foundation. (2001). *Preschool child observation record.* Ypsilanti, MI: High/Scope Press.

High/Scope Educational Research Foundation (2002). *The child observation record for infants and toddlers.* Ypsilanti, MI: High/Scope Press.

High/Scope Educational Research Foundation. (2011). *Etools for online assessment.* Retrieved from highscope.org/Content.asp?ContentId=5

Huffamn, P. (2011). *Look what I did: Why portfolio-based assessment works.* Early Childhood News. Retrieved from www.earlychildhoodnews.com/earlychildhood/article_view.aspx?ArticleID=495

Jablon, J. R., Dombro, A. L., & Dichtelmiller, M. L. (2007). *The power of observation for birth through eight* (2nd ed.). Washington, DC: Teaching Strategies, Inc.

Kagan, S. L., Rosenkoetter, S., & Cohen, N. E. (Eds.). (1997). *Considering child-based outcomes for young children: Definitions, desirability, feasibility, and next steps.* New Haven, CT: Yale University, Bush Center in Child Development and Social Policy.

Kohn, A. (2000). *The case against standardized testing: Raising the scores, running the schools.* Portsmouth, NH: Heinemann.

Kohn, A. (2001). Fighting the tests: Turning frustration into action. *Young Children, 56*(2), 19–24.

Langhorst, B. H. (1989). *Assessment in early childhood: A consumer's guide.* Portland, OR: Northwest Regional Educational Laboratory.

McAfee, O., Leong, D. J., & Bodrova, E. (2004). *Basics of assessment: A primer for early childhood educators* (B. Pollack, Ed.). Washington, DC: National Association for the Education of Young Children.

Meisels, S. J., & Atkins-Burnett, S. (1994). *Developmental screening in early childhood: A guide* (4th ed.). Washington, DC: National Association for the Education of Young Children.

Meisels, S. J., & Atkins-Burnett, S. (2000). The elements of early childhood assessment. In J. P. Shonkoff & S. J. Meisels (Eds.), *Handbook of early childhood intervention* (2nd ed., pp. 231–257). New York: Cambridge University Press.

Meisels, S., Dichtelmiller, M., Jablon, J., Dorfman, A., & Marsden, D. (1997). *Work sampling in the classroom: A teacher's manual. The Work Sampling System.* Ann Arbor, MI: Rebus.

Meisels, S. J., Dorfman, A., & Steele, D. (1995). Equity and excellence in group-administered and performance-based assessments. In M. T. Nettles & A. L. Nettles (Eds.), *Equity in educational assessment and testing* (pp. 196–211). Boston: Kluwer Academic Publishers.

Meisels, S. J., Jablon, J. R., Marsden, D. B., Dichtelmiller, M. L., Dorfman, A. B., & Steele, D. M. (1994). *An overview: The Work Sampling System.* Ann Arbor, MI: Rebus.

Meisels, S. J., Marsden, D. B., Jablon, J. R., Dorfman, A. B., & Dichtelmiller, M. K. (2011). *The Work Sampling System.* Retrieved from www.pearsonassessments.com/HAIWEB/Cultures/en-us/Productdetail.htm?Pid=PAworksampl

National Association for the Education of Young Children. (2009a). *Where we stand on assessing young English language learners.* Retrieved from www.naeyc.org/files/naeyc/file/positions/WWSEnglishLanguageLearnersWeb.pdf

National Association for the Education of Young Children. (2009b). *Position statement: Developmentally appropriate practice in early childhood programs serving children from birth through age 8*. Washington, DC: Author. Retrieved from www.naeyc.org/files/naeyc/file/positions/PSDAP.pdf

National Association for the Education of Young Children. (2011). *Torch Resource Library*. Retrieved from National Association for the Education of Young Children website: http://www.naeyc.org/academy/primary/torch

National Association for the Education of Young Children & the National Association of Early Childhood Specialists in State Departments of Education. (2003). *Position statement: Early childhood curriculum, assessment, and program evaluation: Building an effective, accountable system in programs for children birth through age 8*. Washington, DC: National Association for the Education of Young Children.

National Association of Early Childhood Specialists in State Departments of Education. (2001). *Still unacceptable trends in kindergarten entry and placement*. Denver, CO: Author.

National Association of School Psychologists. (1999). *Position statement on early childhood assessment*. Bethesda, MD: Author.

National Research Council. (1997). *Educating one and all: Students with disabilities and standards-based reform*. Washington, DC: National Academy Press.

National Research Council. (1999). *High stakes testing for tracking, promotion, and graduation*. Washington, DC: National Academy Press.

Nuttall, E. V., Romero, I., & Kalesnik, J. (Eds.). (1999). *Assessing and screening preschoolers: Psychological and educational dimensions* (2nd ed.). Boston: Allyn & Bacon.

Ogunnaike-Lafe, Y., & Krohn, J. (2010). Using document panels to record, reflect and relate learning experiences. *Exchange, 32*(3), 92–96.

Oldham, E., & Sprague, P. (2008). Riding the assessment tide. *Exchange, 180*, 63–69.

Peel, J., & McCary, C. E. (1997). Visioning the "little red schoolhouse" for the 21st century. *Phi Delta Kappan, 78*, 698–705.

Pew Charitable Trust. (2011). *Pre-K as a school turnaround strategy*. Retrieved from www.preknow.org/

Piaget, J. (1952). *The origins of intelligence in children*. New York: Norton.

Reeves, S. (2010, Summer). Response to intervention (Rti) and tier systems: Questions remain as educators make challenging decisions. *Delta Kappa Gamma Bulletin, 76*(4), 30. Retrieved from www.dkg.org/atf/cf/%7B70E631E4-44B9-4D36-AE7D-D12E4520FAB3%7D/LPB-BulletinSummer2010.pdf

Reisman, M. (2011). Learning stories: Assessment through play. *Exchange, 32*(2), 90–94.

Riley-Ayers, S., Boyd, J. S., & Frede, E. (2008). Improving teaching through systematic assessment: Early learning scale. New Brunswick, NJ: NIEER.

Riley-Ayers, S., Frede, E. C., & Jung, K. (2010). *Early Learning Scale: Technical Report*. National Institute for Early Education Research. Retrieved from http://nieer.org/pdf/Early_learning_scale_tech_report_Sept_2010.pdf

Roskos, K. A., & Neuman, S. B. (1994). Of scribbles, schemas, and storybooks: Using literacy albums to document young children's literacy growth. *Young Children, 49*(2), 78–85.

Schorr, L. B. (1994). The case for shifting to results-based accountability. In N. Young, S. Gardner, L. Coley, L. Schorr, & C. Bruner (Eds.), *Making a difference: Moving to outcome-based accountability for comprehensive service reforms* (pp. 13–28). Falls Church, VA: National Center for Service Integration.

Schultz, T., & Kagan, S. L. (Eds.). (2008). *Taking stock: Assessing and improving early childhood learning and program quality*. National Early Childhood Accountability Task Force. Retrieved from http://ccf.tc.columbia.edu/pdf/Task_Force_Report.pdf

Seitz, H. (2008). The power of documentation. *Young Children, 63*(2), 88–93.

Shepard, L. A. (1994). The challenges of assessing young children appropriately. *Phi Delta Kappan, 76*, 206–212.

Shepard, L. A., Kagan, S. L., & Wurtz, E. (1998a). Goal One Early Childhood Assessments Resource Group recommendations. *Young Children, 53*(3), 52–54.

Shepard, L. A., Kagan, S. L., & Wurtz, E. (Eds.). (1998b). *Principles and recommendations for early childhood assessments*. Washington, DC: National Education Goals Panel.

Snow, C. E., & VanHemel, S. B. (Eds.). (2008). *Early childhood assessment: Why, what and how?* Report of the National Research Council of the National Academies. Retrieved from http://www.acf.hhs.gov/programs/opre/hs/national_academy/reports/early_child_assess/early_child_assess.pdf

Southern Early Childhood Association. (1990/1996/2000). *Assessing development and learning in young children*. Retrieved from http://www.southernearlychildhood.org/upload/pdf/Assessing_Development.pdf

Stephens, T. L., Pethick, L., & Flowers, A. (2010). Response-to-intervention: Utilizing effective assessment practices in early childhood. *Early Years: The Journal of the Texas Association for the Education of Young Children, 31*(3), 19–24.

Trister-Dodge, D., Colker, L. J., & Heroman, C. (2003). *Creative Curriculum Developmental Continuum Assessment Toolkit for Ages 3–5*. Washington, DC: Teaching Strategies, Inc.

Chapter 12

ACF (Administration for Children and Families). (2007). Head Start Act. Retrieved from http://eclkc.ohs.acf.hhs.gov/hslc/Head%20Start%20Program/Program%20Design%20and%20Management/Head%20Start%20Requirements/Head%20Start%20Act

Bailey, S. J., Letiecq, B. L., & Porterfield, F. (2009). *Journal of Intergenerational Relationships, 7*(2–3), 144–158.

Bang, Y. (2009). Helping all families participate in school life. *Young Children, 64*(6), 97–99.

Baumgartner, J. J., & Buchanan, T. K. (2010). "I have HUGE stereotypes"; Using eco-maps to understand children and families. *Journal of Early Childhood Teacher Education, 31*(2), 173–184.

Bermudez, A., & Marquez, J. (1996). An examination of a four-way collaborative to increase parental involvement in the schools. *The Journal of Educational Issues of Language Minority Students, 16*, 1–16.

Birckmayer, J., Cohen, J., Jensen, I. J., & Variano, D. A. (2005). Kyle lives with his Granny—Where are his Mommy and Daddy? *Young Children 60*(3), 100–104.

Boutte, G. S., Keepler, D. L., Tyler, V. S., & Terry, B. Z. (1992). Effective techniques for involving "difficult" parents. *Young Children, 47*(3), 19–22.

Bower, L., & Klecka, C. (2009). (Re)considering normal: Queering social norms for parents and teachers. *Teaching Education, 20*(4), 357–373.

Bronfenbrenner, U. (1979). *The ecology of human development: Experiments by nature and design*. Cambridge, MA: Harvard University Press.

Bronfenbrenner, U. (2004). *Making human beings human: Bioecological perspectives on human development*. Thousand Oaks, CA: Sage Publications.

Bronfenbrenner, U., & Morris, P. A. (1998). The ecology of developmental process. In W. Damon (Series Ed.) & R. M. Lerner (Vol. Ed.), *Handbook of child psychology*. Vol. 1: *Theoretical models of human development* (pp. 993–1028). New York: Wiley.

Brown, J. R., Knoche, L. L., Edwards, C. P., & Sheridan, S. M. (2009). Professional development to support parent engagement: A case study of early childhood practitioners. *Early Education and Development, 20*(3), 482–506.

Caldwell, B. M. (1985). What is quality child care? In B. M. Caldwell & A. Hillard (Eds.), *What is quality child care?* (pp. 1–16). Washington, DC: National Association for the Education of Young Children.

Campbell, L., & Miles, M. S. (2008). Implementing parenting programs for custodial grandparents. In B. Hayslip & P. Kaminski (Eds.), *Parenting the custodial grandchild: Implications for clinical practice.* (pp. 115–130). New York: Springer.

Christian, L. G. (2006). Understanding families: Applying family systems theory to early childhood practice. *Young Children, 61*(1), 12–20.

Clay, J. W. (2004). Creating safe, just places to learn for children of lesbian and gay parents: The NAEYC Code of Ethics in action. *Young Children, 59*(6), 34–38.

Coleman, M., & Wallinga, C. (2000). Teacher training in family involvement: An interpersonal approach. *Childhood Education, 76,* 76–81.

Cooper, C. E. (2010). Family poverty, school-based parental involvement, and policy-focused protective factors in kindergarten. *Early Childhood Research Quarterly, 25*(4), 480–492.

Cox, C. (2009). Custodial grandparents: Policies affecting care. *Journal of Intergenerational Relationships, 7*(2–3), 177–190.

Croft, C. (2010). Talking to families of infants and toddlers about developmental delays. *Young Children, 65*(1), 44–46.

Cunningham, B. (1994). Portraying fathers and other men in the curriculum. *Young Children, 49*(6), 4–13.

Daniel, J. (1996). Family-centered work and child care. *Young Children, 51*(6), 2.

Daniel, J. (2009). Intentionally thoughtful family engagement in early childhood education. *Young Children, 64*(5), 10–14.

DEC/NAEYC. (2009). *Early childhood inclusion: A joint position statement of the Division for Early Childhood (DEC) and the National Association for the Education of Young Children (NAEYC).* Chapel Hill: The University of North Carolina, FPG Child Development Institute. Retrieved from www.naeyc.org/files/naeyc/file/positions/DEC_NAEYC_EC_updatedKS.pdf

Derman-Sparks, L., & Edwards, J. O. (2010). *Anti-bias education for young children and ourselves.* Washington, DC: NAEYC.

Division for Early Childhood Task Force on Recommended Practices. (1993). *DEC recommended practices: Indicators of quality in programs for infants and young children with special needs and their families.* Reston, VA: Council for Exceptional Children.

Dodd, E. L., & Brock, D. R. (1994). Building partnerships with families through home-learning activities. *Dimensions of Early Childhood, 22*(2), 37–39, 46.

Epstein, J. L. (1991). Paths to partnerships: What we can learn from federal, state, district, and school initiatives. *Phi Delta Kappan, 72,* 344–349.

Epstein, J. L. (2001). *School, family, and community partnerships: Preparing educators and improving schools.* Boulder, CO: Westview.

Epstein, J. L., & Sanders, M. (1998). What we learn from international studies of school-family-community partnerships. *Childhood Education, 74,* 392–394.

Epstein, J. L., Sanders, M. G., Simon, B. S., Salinas, K. C., Jansorn, N. R., & Van Voorhis, F. L. (2002). *School, family, and community partnerships: Your handbook for action* (2nd ed.). Thousand Oaks, CA: Corwin.

Fagan, J. (1994). Mother and father involvement in day care centers serving infants and young toddlers. *Early Child Development and Care, 103,* 95–101.

Fagan, J. (1996). Principles for developing male involvement programs in early childhood settings: A personal experience. *Young Children, 51*(4), 64–71.

Feeney, S., & Sysko, L. (1986). Professional ethics in early childhood education: Survey results. *Young Children, 42*(1), 15–20.

Freeman, N. K. (1998). Look to the east to gain a new perspective, understand cultural differences, and appreciate cultural diversity. *Early Childhood Education Journal, 26* (2), 79–82.

Freeman, N. K., & Knopf, H. T. (2007). Learning to speak with a professional voice: Initiating preservice teachers into being a resource for parents. *Journal of Early Childhood Teacher Education, 28*(2), 141–152.

Galinsky, E. (1987). *The six stages of parenthood.* Reading, MA: Addison-Wesley.

Galinsky, E. (1988). Parents and teacher-caregivers: Sources of tension, sources of support. *Young Children, 43*(3), 4–12.

García Coll, C., & Magnuson, K. (2000). Cultural differences as sources of developmental vulnerabilities and resources. In J. P. Shonkoff & S. J. Meisels (Eds.), *Handbook of early childhood intervention* (2nd ed., pp. 94–114). New York: Cambridge University Press.

Gibbs, N. (2005, February 21). Parents behaving badly: Inside the new classroom power struggle: What teachers say about pushy moms and dads who drive them crazy. *Time,* 40–48.

Goals 2000: Educate America Act. (1994). Washington, DC: 103rd Congress. Retrieved from www.ed.gov/legislation/GOALS2000/TheAct/index.html

Gonzalez-Mena, J. (2008). *Diversity in early care and education: Honoring differences* (5th ed.). New York: McGraw-Hill.

Gonzalez-Mena, J. (2009). Family centered early care and education. In S. Feeney, A. Galper, & C. Seefeldt (Eds.), *Continuing issues in early childhood education* (3rd ed., pp. 369–386). Upper Saddle River, NJ: Pearson.

Gonzalez-Mena, J. (2010). *50 early childhood strategies for working and communicating with diverse families* (2nd ed.). Upper Saddle River, NJ: Pearson.

Gottlieb, H. (2005). *Board diversity: A bigger issue than you think.* Help 4 NonProfits: Community Driven Institute. Retrieved from www.help4nonprofits.com/NP_Bd_Diversity_Art.htm

Halgunseth, L. C., Peterson, A., Stark, D. R., & Moodie, S. (2009). *Family engagement, diverse families, and early childhood education programs: An integrated review of the literature.* Washington, DC: National Association for the Education of Young Children, The Pew Charitable Trusts. Retrieved from www.naeyc.org/files/naeyc/file/research/FamEngage.pdf

Hall, E. T. (1977). *Beyond culture.* Garden City, NY: Anchor Press/Doubleday.

Hanhan, S. F. (2003). Parent-teacher communication: Who's talking? In G. Olsen & M. L. Fuller (Eds.), *Home-school relations: Working successfully with parents and families* (2nd ed., pp. 111–133). Boston: Allyn & Bacon.

Harms, T., Clifford, R. M., & Cryer, D. (2005). *Early Childhood Environment Rating Scale–Revised.* New York: Teachers College Press.

Harms, T., Cryer, D., & Clifford, R. M. (2006). *Infant/Toddler Environment Rating Scale–Revised.* New York: Teachers College Press.

Harms, T., Jacobs, E. V., & White, D. R. (1995). *School-Age Care Environment Rating Scale.* New York: Teachers College Press.

Heckman, J. J. (1999). *Policies to foster human capital.* Berkely: University of California at Berkeley, Aaron Wildavsky Forum, Richard and Rhoda Goldman School of Public Policy. Retrieved from www.ounceofprevention.org/includes/tiny_mce/plugins/filemanager/files/Fostering%20Human%20Capital.pdf

Henrich, C. C., & Blackman-Jones, R. (2006). Parent involvement in preschool. In E. Zigler, W. S. Gilliam, & S. M. Jones (Eds.), *A vision for universal preschool education* (pp. 149–168). New York: Cambridge University Press.

High/Scope Educational Research Foundation. (1992). *High/Scope child observation record.* Ypsilanti, MI: High/Scope Press.

Johnston, L., & Mermin, J. (1994). Easing children's entry to school: Home visits help. *Young Children, 49*(5), 62–68.

Kersey, K. C., & Masterson, M. L. (2009). Teachers connecting with families in the best interest of children. *Young Children, 64*(5), 34–38.

Keyser, J. (2006). *From parents to partners: Building a family-centered early childhood program.* St. Paul, MN: Redleaf Press.

Kirmani, M. H. (2007). Empowering culturally and linguistically diverse children and families. *Young Children, 62*(6), 94–98.

Kirmani, R., & Leung, V. (2008) *Breaking down barriers; Immigrant families and early childhood education in New York.* New York: The Coalition for Asian American Children and Families. Retrieved from http://www.cacf.org/resources_publications.html#breakingthebarriers

Kontos, S., & Dunn, L. (1989). Attitudes of caregivers, maternal experiences with day care, and children's development. *Journal of Applied Developmental Psychology, 10,* 37–51.

Kostelnik, M. J., Soderman, A. K., & Whiren, A. P. (2007). *Developmentally appropriate curriculum: Best practices in early childhood education* (4th ed.). Upper Saddle River, NJ: Pearson.

Kraft, S., & Snell, M. (1980). Parent-teacher conflict: Coping with parental stress. *Pointer, 24,* 29–37.

Larner, M. (1996). Parents' perspectives on quality in early care and education. In S. Kagan & N. Cohen (Eds.), *Reinventing early care and education: A vision for quality systems* (pp. 21–42). San Francisco: Jossey-Bass.

Lawrence-Lightfoot, S. (2003). *The essential conversation: What parents and teachers can learn from each other.* New York: Ballentine Books.

Lee, V. E., & Burkam, D. T. (2002). *Inequality at the starting gate: Social background differences in achievement as children begin school.* Washington, DC: Economic Policy Institute.

Lin, M., & Bates, A. B. (2010). Home visits: How do they affect teachers' beliefs about teaching and diversity? *Early Childhood Education Journal, 38,* 179–185.

Marcon, R. A. (1994). Doing the right thing for children: Linking research and policy reform in the District of Columbia Public Schools. *Young Children, 50*(1), 8–11.

Meisels, S. J., Jablon, J. R., Marsden, D. B., Dichtelmiller, M. L., Dorfman, A. B., & Steele, D. M. (1994). *An overview: The Work Sampling System.* Ann Arbor, MI: Rebus.

Nagel, N. G., & Wells, J. G. (2009). Honoring family and culture: Learning from New Zealand. *Young Children, 65*(4), 40–44.

National Association for the Education of Young Children. (1993). *Violence in the lives of children.* Washington, DC: Author. Retrieved from oldweb.naeyc.org/about/ positions/psviol98.PDF

National Association for the Education of Young Children. (1994). *Principles to link by: Integrated service systems that are community-based and school-linked.* Washington, DC: Author.

National Association for the Education of Young Children. (1995). *Responding to linguistic and cultural diversity: Recommendations for effective early childhood education.* Washington, DC: Author. Retrieved from www.naeyc.org/files/naeyc/file/positions/PSDIV98.PDF

National Association for the Education of Young Children. (2009). *NAEYC standards for early childhood professional preparation programs.* Washington, DC: Author. Retrieved from www.naeyc.org/files/naeyc/file/positions/ProfPrepStandards09.pdf

National Association for the Education of Young Children. (2011a). *Code of Ethical Conduct and Statement of Commitment.* Washington, DC: Author.

National Association for the Education of Young Children. (2011b). *Code of Ethical Conduct: Supplement for Early Childhood Program Administrators.* Washington, DC: Author.

National Association for the Education of Young Children Academy for Early Childhood Program Accreditation. (2005). *NAEYC early childhood program standards.* Washington, DC: Author.

National Family, School, and Community Engagement Working Group. (2010). *Taking leadership, innovating change: Profiles in family, school and community engagement.* Cambridge, MA: Harvard Family Research Project. Retrieved from www.hfrp.org/publications-resources/browse-our-publications/taking-leadership-innovating-change-profiles-in-family-school-and-community-engagement

National PTA. (2000). *Building successful partnerships: A guide for developing parent and family involvement programs.* Indianapolis, IN: National Educational Service.

National Research Council. (2001). *Eager to learn: Educating our preschoolers.* B. Bowman, M. S. Donovan, & M. S. Burns (Eds.). Washington, DC: National Academy Press.

Neilsen, L. E., & Finkelstein, J. M. (1993). A new approach to parent conferences. *Teaching K–8, 24*(1), 90–92.

NICHD Early Child Care Research Network. (1997). Child care in the first year of life. *Merrill-Palmer Quarterly, 43,* 340–360.

Pena, D. (2000). Parent involvement: Influencing factors and implications. *Journal of Educational Research, 94,* 42–54.

Pinazo-Hernandis, S., & Tompkins, C. J. (2009). Custodial grandparents: The state of the art and the many faces of this contribution. *Journal of Intergenerational Relationships, 7*(2–3), 137–143.

Pogoloff, S. M. (2004). Facilitate positive relationships between parents and professionals. *Intervention in School & Clinic, 40*(2), 116–120.

Powell, D. R. (1987). Day care as a family support system. In S. L. Kagan, D. R. Powell, B. Weissbourd, & E. F. Zigler (Eds.), *America's family support programs: Perspectives and prospects* (pp. 115–132). New Haven, CT: Yale University Press.

Powell, D. R. (1989). *Families and early childhood programs.* Washington, DC: National Association for the Education of Young Children.

Powell, D. R. (1991). How schools support families: Critical policy tensions. *Elementary School Journal, 91,* 307–319.

Powell, D. R., & Gerde, H. K. (2006). Considering kindergarten families. In D. F. Gullo (Ed.), *K today: Teaching and learning in the kindergarten year* (pp. 26–34). Washington, DC: National Association for the Education of Young Children.

Raab, M., & Dunst, D. J. (1997). Early childhood program assessment scales and family support practices. In S. Reifel (Series Ed.) & C. J. Dunst & M. Wolery (Vol, Eds.), *Advances in early education and day care.* Vol. 8: *Family policy and practice in early education and child care programs* (pp. 105–131). Greenwich, CT: JAI.

Reedy, C. K., & McGrath, W. H. (2010). Can you hear me now? Staff-parent communication in child care centers. *Early Child Development and Care, 180*(3), 347–357.

Reynolds, A. J., Magnuson, K. A., & Ou, S. (2010). Preschool-to-third grade programs and practices: A review of research. *Children and Youth Services Review, 32*(8), 1121–1131.

Rolnick, A., & Grunewald, R. (2003, March). Early childhood development: Economic development with a high public return. *Fedgazette*, Federal Reserve Bank of Minneapolis. Retrieved from minneapolisfed.org/pubs/fedgaz/03-03/earlychild.cfm

Sciarra, D. J., & Dorsey, A. G. (1998). *Developing and administering child care centers* (4th ed.). Albany, NY: Delmar.

Seplocha, H. (2004). Partnerships for learning: Conferencing with families. *Young Children, 59*(5), 96–98.

Shores, E. F., & Grace, C. (1998). *The portfolio book: A step-by-step guide for teachers*. Beltsville, MD: Gryphon.

Souto-Manning, M. (2010). Challenges to consider, strengths to build on. *Young Children, 65*(2), 82–88.

Souto-Manning, M., & Swick, K. J. (2006). Teachers' beliefs about parent and family involvement: Rethinking our family involvement paradigm. *Early Childhood Education Journal, 34*(2), 187–193.

Stamp, L. N., & Groves, M. M. (1994). Strengthening the ethic of care: Planning and supporting family involvement. *Dimensions of Early Childhood, 22*(2), 5–9.

Stewart, I. S. (1982). The real world of teaching two-year-old children. *Young Children, 37*(5), 3–13.

Swick, K. J., & Williams, R. D. (2006). An analysis of Bronfenbrenner's bio-ecological perspective for early childhood educators: Implications for working with families experiencing stress. *Early Childhood Education Journal, 33*(5), 371–378.

Tan, E. T., & Goldberg, W. A. (2009). Parental school involvement in relation to children's grades and adaptation to school. *Journal of Applied Developmental Psychology, 30*, 442–453.

Taylor, B. J. (1999). *A child goes forth: A curriculum guide for preschool children*. Upper Saddle River: Pearson.

Vygotsky, L. S. (1978). *Mind in society* (M. Cole, S. Schribner, V. John-Steiner, & E. Souberman, Trans.). Cambridge, MA: Harvard University Press.

White, B. (1988). *Educating infants and toddlers*. Lexington, MA: Lexington Books.

Zigler, E. F. (1989). Addressing the nation's child care crisis: The school of the twenty-first century. *American Journal of Orthopsychiatry, 59*, 484–491.

Chapter 13

ACF (Administration for Children and Families). (2007). Head Start Act. Retrieved July 15, 2011, from http://eclkc.ohs.acf.hhs.gov/hslc/Head%20Start%20Program/Program%20Design%20and%20Management/Head%20Start%20Requirements/Head%20Start%20Act

Advocates in Action: Using the Week of the Young Child as an advocacy event. (2009). *Young Children, 62*(2), 72–73.

Barnett, W. S., Hustedt, J. T., Hawkinson, L. E., & Robin, K. B. (2007). *The state of preschool in 2006*. New Brunswick, NJ: National Institute for Early Education Research.

Blank, H. K. (1997). Advocacy leadership. In S. L. Kagan & B. T. Bowman (Eds.), *Leadership in early care and education* (pp. 39–45). Washington, DC: National Association for the Education of Young Children.

Charlesworth, R., & DeBoer, B. B. (2000). An early childhood teacher moves from DIP to DAP: Self-study as a useful research method for teacher researcher and university professor collaboration. *Journal of Early Childhood Teacher Education, 21*(2), 149–154.

Clifford, R. M. (1997). Partnerships with other professionals. *Young Children, 52*(5), 2–3.

Cochran-Smith, M., & Lytle, S. L. (1999). The teacher research movement: A decade later. *Educational Researcher, 28*(7), 15–25.

Cooney, M. H., Buchanan, M., & Parkinson, D. (2001). Teachers as researchers: Classroom inquiry initiatives at undergraduate and graduate levels in early childhood education. *Journal of Early Childhood Teacher Education, 22*(3), 151–159.

Ellison, C., & Barbour, N. (1992). Changing child care systems through collaborative efforts: Challenges for the 1990s. *Child and Youth Care Forum, 21*, 299–316.

Feeney, S. (1995). Professionalism in early childhood teacher education: Focus on ethics. *Journal of Early Childhood Teacher Education, 16*(3), 13–15.

Feeney, S. (2012). *Professionalism in early childhood education: Doing our best for young children*. Upper Saddle River, NJ: Pearson.

Feeney, S., & Freeman, N. K. (1999/2005). *Ethics and the early childhood educator: Using the NAEYC Code*. Washington, DC: National Association for the Education of Young Children.

Feeney, S., Freeman, N. K., & Moravcik, E. (2000). *Teaching the NAEYC Code of Ethical Conduct: Activity Sourcebook*. Washington, DC: National Association for the Education of Young Children.

Feeney, S., & Kipnis, K. (1989). *Code of Ethical Conduct and Statement of Commitment*. Washington, DC: National Association for the Education of Young Children.

Goffin, S. G., & Washington, V. (2007). *Ready or not: Leadership choices in early care and education*. New York: Teachers College Press.

Jacobson, L., & Simpson, A. (2007). Communicating about early childhood education: Lessons from working with the news media. *Young Children, 62*(3), 89–93.

Kagan, S. L., & Neuman, M. J. (1997). Conceptual leadership. In S. L. Kagan & B. T. Bowman (Eds.), *Leadership in early care and education* (pp. 59–64). Washington, DC: National Association for the Education of Young Children.

Katz, L. (1995). The nature of professions: Where is early childhood education? In L. Katz (Ed.), *Talks with teachers of young children: A collection* (pp. 219–235). Norwood, NJ: Ablex.

Levine, M. (1992). Observations on the early childhood profession. *Young Children, 47*(2), 50–51.

Moran, M. J. (2007). Collaborative action research and project work: Promising practices for developing collaborative inquiry among early childhood preservice teachers. *Teaching and Teacher Education, 23*(4), 418–431.

National Association for the Education of Young Children. (2004a). *NAEYC advocacy toolkit*. Washington, DC: Author. Retrieved from www.naeyc.org/files/naeyc/file/policy/toolkit.pdf

National Association for the Education of Young Children. (2004b). *Code of Ethical Conduct and Statement of Commitment: Supplement for Early Childhood Adult Educators*. Washington, DC: Author. Retrieved from www.naeyc.org/files/naeyc/file/positions/ethics04.pdf

National Association for the Education of Young Children. (2011a). *NAEYC accreditation: All criteria document*. Washington, DC: Author. Retrieved from www.naeyc.org/files/academy/file/AllCriteriaDocument.pdf

National Association for the Education of Young Children. (2011b). *Code of Ethical Conduct and Statement of Commitment*. Washington, DC: Author. Retrieved from naeyc.org/about/positions/PSETH11.asp

National Association for the Education of Young Children. (2011c). *Code of Ethical Conduct and Statement of Commitment: Supplement for Early Childhood Program Administrators*. Washington, DC: Author. Retrieved July 11, 2011, from http://www.naeyc.org/files/naeyc/file/positions/Supplement%20PS2011.pdf

National Association for the Education of Young Children & the National Council of Teachers of Mathematics. (2010). *Early childhood mathematics: Promoting good beginnings*. Retrieved from www.naeyc.org/files/naeyc/file/positions/psmath.pdf

National Child Care Information Center & National Association for Regulatory Administration (NCCIC/NARA). (2010). *The 2008 child care licensing study*. Lexington, KY: National Association for Regulatory Administration. Retrieved from www.naralicensing.org/Licensing_Study

Nonprofit (NP) Action. (2005). *Advocacy strategy: The fundamentals*. Washington, DC: Author. Retrieved from www.npaction.org/article/articleview/574/1/229

Paley, V. G. (1981). *Wally's stories*. Cambridge, MA: Harvard University Press.

Robinson, A., & Stark, D. R. (2002). *Advocates in action: Making a difference for young children*. Washington, DC: National Association for the Education of Young Children.

Stremmel, A. J. (2007). *Voices of practitioners: The value of teacher research: Nurturing professional and personal growth through inquiry*. Washington, DC: NAEYC. Retrieved from www.naeyc.org/files/naeyc/file/vop/Voices-Stremmel.pdf

Name Index

Subject Index